Colombia

Jens Porup

Kevin Raub, Robert Reid, César G Soriano

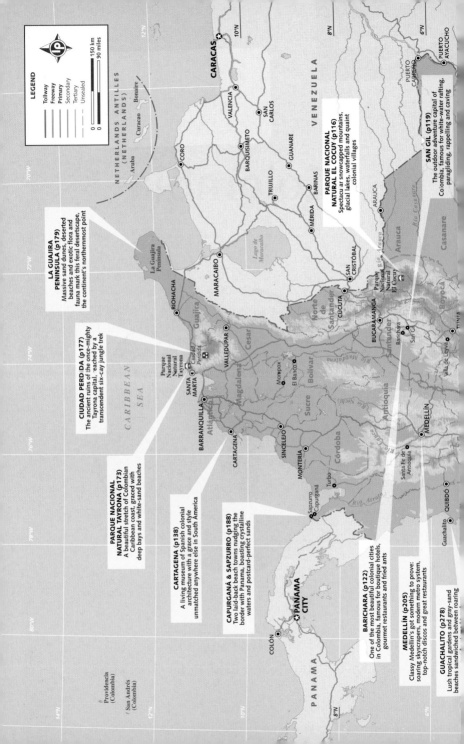

LEGEND

Tollway
Freeway
Primary
Secondary
Tertiary
Unsealed

0 —— 150 km
0 —— 90 miles

NETHERLANDS ANTILLES (NETHERLANDS)
Aruba   Curaçao   Bonaire

CARACAS

VENEZUELA

Providencia (Colombia)

San Andrés (Colombia)

PANAMA

PANAMA CITY

COLÓN

CARIBBEAN SEA

LA GUAJIRA PENINSULA (p179)
Massive sand dunes, deserted beaches and exotic flora and fauna mark this feral desertscape, the continent's northernmost point

CIUDAD PERD DA (p177)
The ancient ruins of the once-mighty Tayrona capital, reached by a transcendent six-cay jungle trek

PARQUE NACIONAL NATURAL TAYRONA (p173)
A beautiful stretch of Colombian Caribbean coast, graced with deep bays and white-sand beaches

CARTAGENA (p138)
A living museum of Spanish colonial architecture with a grace and style unmatched anywhere else in South America

CAPURGANÁ & SAPZURRO (p188)
Two laid-back beach towns nudging the border with Panama, boasting crystalline waters and postcard-perfect sands

BARICHARA (p122)
One of the most beautiful colonial cities in Colombia, famous for boutique hotels, gourmet restaurants and fried ants

MEDELLÍN (p205)
Classy Medellín's got something to prove: soaring skyscrapers, modern metro system, top-notch discos and great restaurants

GUACHALITO (p278)
Lush tropical gardens and gray-sand beaches sandwiched between roaring

PARQUE NACIONAL NATURAL EL COCUY (p116)
Spectacu ar snowcapped mountains, glacial lakes, waterfalls and quaint colonial villages

SAN GIL (p119)
The outdoor adventure capital of Colombia, famous for white-water rafting, paragliding, rappelling and caving

RIOHACHA
SANTA MARTA
BARRANQUILLA
CARTAGENA
SINCELEJO
MONTERÍA
Turbo
Sapzurro
Capurganá
QUIBDÓ
Guachalito
MARACAIBO
VALLEDUPAR
Mompox
El Banco
CÚCUTA
SAN CRISTÓBAL
BUCARAMANGA
Barichara
San Gil
Villa de Leyva
Santa Fe de Antioquia
MEDELLÍN
CORO
VALENCIA
SAN CARLOS
BARQUISIMETO
TRUJILLO
GUANARE
BARINAS
MÉRIDA
ARAUCA
PUERTO CARREÑO
PUERTO AYACUCHO

La Guajira Peninsula
Lago de Maracaibo
Parque Nacional Natural Tayrona
Ciudad Perdida
Parque Nacional Natural El Cocuy

Guajira
Cesar
Magdalena
Atlántico
Bolívar
Sucre
Córdoba
Antioquia
Norte de Santander
Santander
Boyacá
Casanare
Arauca

Río Magdalena
Río Atrato
Río Cauca
Río Arauca
Río Casanare

VALLE DE COCORA (p237)
This spectacular day walk outside Salento takes you through wax palm cloud forest

LAGO CALIMA (p248)
Perfect winds year-round make this a mecca for windsurfers and kitesurfers

LAGUNA DE LA COCHA (p264)
An island in a lake, clad in cloud forest and shrouded in mist

BOGOTÁ (p62)
Colombia's booming capital, with a colonial heart, student-filled bars and a ritzy north boasting chic eateries and nightclubs

PUERTO NARIÑO (p293)
A model of sustainable living surrounded by canopied jungles and wildlife including the Amazon's famous pink dolphins

ELEVATION

3200m
2400m
1800m
1200m
600m
0

PACIFIC OCEAN

BRAZIL

PERU

ECUADOR

Equator

QUITO

On the Road

JENS PORUP Coordinating Author
Here I am in war paint. The glare's ferocious on Nevado del Ruiz, and I still managed to get sunburned. The rangers wouldn't let us proceed any higher up the mountain because of heavy snowfall. Soaking in the thermal spa afterward went a long way toward curing our cracking headaches.

ROBERT REID OK, I'm a total softie. With all those Andes nearby, bike trails and late-night life-is-for-joy *salsatecas*, or half-a-hundred interesting museums to check out, Bogotá is at its best for me just sitting with a hot mug of *canelazo* tea in La Candelaria.

KEVIN RAUB Everyone is a little hesitant upon arrival at Volcán de Lodo El Totumo. Once you're in, though, it's quite an experience. It feels like a mud orgy as everyone frolics around under the mud – picture hopping in a hot tub with seven strangers but with silky, lukewarm gunk instead of water. It was the most action I got on my trip!

CÉSAR G SORIANO Strapped into a harness with the pilot, I have nowhere to go but up. We run off the cliff into oblivion, the wind catches our sail and soon we're soaring over verdant valleys and canyons. For anyone who's ever dreamed of flying, paragliding is the only way to see Colombia.

For full author biographies see p337.

Colombia Highlights

Few countries can compete with Colombia for sheer diversity of landscapes. A twitch in altitude takes you from the baking sands of the Caribbean to the emerald-green hills of the coffee region. Continue to climb and there's bustling Bogotá, Colombia's Gotham. Keep climbing – further still! – and you'll find snowy mountains and monster glaciers, and the eerie, unique vegetation of the *páramo* (high-mountain plains). From the jungles of the Amazon to the throbbing discos of the cities, from the volcanoes of the southern mountains to the Darién Gap, Colombia is so chock full of things to do and see, you may find it hard to pick favorites. Here are just a few of ours.

RICHARD CUMMINS

1 CARTAGENA

I was amazed at the history and cultural heritage of the walled city of Cartagena (p138). I highly recommend staying within the old city, having lunch in the Plaza de Santo Domingo and cocktails at the Café del Mar. The colonial architecture in this city is amazing and, surprisingly, has been maintained utilizing traditional construction methods (labor-intensive handcraftsmanship). This is not to say that some places aren't a bit run down – there are some blemishes – but my impression is that it is a very beautiful place.

David McAlister, Traveler, USA

ALEXANDER GARCÍA VIVAS

SKY HIGH IN SAN GIL

For adrenaline junkies, there is no better destination than San Gil (p119) – the outdoor capital of Colombia. Visitors can choose from a variety of death-defying extreme sports, from white-water rafting down Class 4-5 rapids to rappelling down waterfalls. But for anyone who has ever dreamt of flying, nothing compares to the sensation of paragliding, as you float peacefully over San Gil and take in views of the Río Chicamocha canyon. This place is for the birds!

**César G Soriano,
Lonely Planet Author**

2

FERIA DE CALI

If it's a party that drives you or you want to show off your salsa moves, don't miss this carnival (p18), which is full of life, color, food and lots of music. This weeklong event, held in Cali in December and January, celebrates regional cultural diversity with a colorful parade of salsa dancing schools and traditional ethnic groups.

Carlos Solarte, Lonely Planet Staff

3

CÉSAR G SO

4

SAN AGUSTÍN

I went to San Agustín (p255) to see the famous stone statues and monuments. While the statues were every bit as impressive as I'd expected, it was the jaw-dropping scenery that really stuck in my mind – wave after wave of rolling green hills and fields of coffee, sugarcane and maize. All in all, it was worth every minute of the bone-shaking bus ride to get there.

Danny Heap, Lonely Planet Staff

JANE SWE

CROSSING THE PUENTE DE OCCIDENTE IN AN INDIAN AUTORICKSHAW

The Puente de Occidente (p219) – the bridge of the west – is a 5km excursion from Santa Fe de Antioquia and worth the trip, the book recommends, if you don't mind the one-hour walk in the midday heat or you can reach a deal with a local taxi. But what's this lined up beside the cathedral in the main square? It's an assembly of bright red Indian Bajaj autorickshaws, their pilots all dressed in Hawaiian shirts. One of them takes me on a tour to the bridge and back, while his little daughter, chatting away with me in the backseat, improves my Spanish on the way.

Tony Wheeler, Lonely Planet Founder, Australia

TONY WHEELER

PICTURE-PERFECT BARICHARA

My perfect day in Barichara (p122) begins with a strong cup of *tinto* (black coffee) at one of the cute cafes on the palm-lined plaza. We spend the day exploring and photographing the cobbled streets, adobe red-roofed buildings and boutique shops of Barichara – Colombia's most beautiful colonial village. For lunch, I splurge on the filet mignon topped with fried ants at Color de Hormiga.

**César G Soriano,
Lonely Planet Author**

KRZYSZTOF DYDYNSKI

ROBERTO ORRU / ALAMY

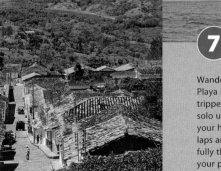

LAZING ON PLAYA BLANCA

Wander the salt-white sands of Playa Blanca (p153) until the day-trippers ship out, then snorkel solo until it's time to curl up in your hammock as the Caribbean laps and lulls you to sleep. Hopefully the few travelers who share your paradise don't snore.

**Emily Wolman,
Lonely Planet Staff**

EXPLORING THE VALLE DE COCORA

Salento and nearby Valle de Cocora (p237) are two of my favorite places in Colombia. The town itself has amazing views in every direction. Riding the overloaded jeep (18 people!) to the trailhead is a hoot, and the slender wax palms play hide-and-seek with the fog in these moss-green mountains.

**Jens Porup,
Lonely Planet Author**

8

ALUMBRADO NAVIDEÑO

Anyone traveling to Colombia around Christmastime should not miss *los alumbrados* of Alumbrado Navideño (p18) – the magnificent display of Christmas lights along the Río Medellín (millions of light bulbs are used!). Various stalls are set up along the river at night, so a stroll to check out the lights is also a great opportunity to taste the local food and buy a few souvenirs.

Jasna Bratic, Lonely Planet Staff

9

10

THE ROAD TO THE TOP OF THE CONTINENT

Traveling in Colombia can be an intimidating journey for the uninitiated – military checkpoints are frequent and not without a small amount of firepower. They are harmless for the most part (I was checked and searched nine times), but not quite as innocuous as the faux checkpoints manned by Wayuu children along the coastal road to Cabo de la Vela and Punta Gallinas (p183). Nothing can prepare you for the sheer hilarity of tiny children forcing your car to stop and extorting candy or other yummy treats from you before allowing you to pass. It's sweet, beautiful and not without a small dose of irony – these kids could very well grow up to work on the real thing for the Colombian military.

Kevin Raub, Lonely Planet Author

Contents

Regional Map Contents

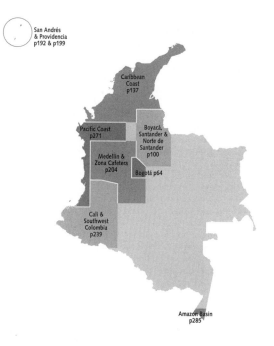

Destination Colombia

Colombia's back.

After decades of civil conflict, Colombia is now safe to visit and travelers are discovering what they've been missing. The diversity of the country may astonish you. Modern cities with skyscrapers and discos? Check. Gorgeous Caribbean beaches? Check. Jungle walks and Amazon safaris? Check. Colonial cities, archaeological ruins, high-mountain trekking, whale-watching, coffee plantations, scuba diving, surfing, the list goes on.

No wonder the 'magic realism' style of Colombian author Gabriel García Márquez emerged from here – there is a dreamlike quality to Colombia. Here at the equator, with the sun forever overhead, the fecund earth beneath your feet, heart-stopping vistas in every direction and the warmth of the locals putting you at ease – you may find it difficult to leave.

Although international news reports seldom show it, Colombia is one of the most well-developed countries in Latin America. Universities here produce legions of finely educated, ambitious professionals and the country boasts a reliable legal system with low levels of corruption. World-class health care and hospitals round out its enviable social infrastructure. Its optimistic middle class believes hard work will be rewarded – and it is.

Colombian culture, like the country's weather, varies by altitude. The essence of Colombia resides in the mountains in the alpine cities of Bogotá, Medellín and Cali, and the smaller cities of the Zona Cafetera. This is the industrial heartland of the country. Geographical isolation has kept the accent relatively unaffected by outside influence; Spanish here is precise and easy to understand. The infrastructure in the mountain region is good, the water drinkable, the roads well maintained. In the heat of the Caribbean coast, life is slower, and the culture more laid-back. The accent is the unhurried drawl of the Caribbean basin, and the infrastructure, unfortunately, is still in need of some attention.

Colombia's role in the drug trade continues to play out in the background. The improved security situation is due in large part to funding from Washington. This has made little dent in the cocaine business, however, which continues to operate in the deep jungle and the remote mountains. The great richness of Colombia's tropical soil is both its blessing and its curse – huge varieties of tropical fruit grow here, and Colombia is a major agricultural exporter. It is also the world's largest producer of cocaine, and this is unlikely to change anytime soon.

'Plan Colombia' has successfully driven the violence from the cities and the main tourist routes, and brought peace to most of Colombia. While President Álvaro Uribe deserves great credit for this (Colombians call him their first saint), many are deeply worried by the election of US President Barack Obama. Without continued US foreign aid, the widespread fear is that the country will fall back into chaos.

In darker days people used to say, 'if only it weren't for the violence and drugs, Colombia would be paradise.' Well the drugs may still be here but the violence is gone, at least for now, and it is, indeed, paradise. It is an easy country to fall in love with, and many travelers do. It may well become your favorite country in South America.

FAST FACTS

Population: 46 million (estimated)

GDP growth (2008): 5.2%

Principal legal exports: petroleum, coffee, coal, gold, bananas, cut flowers, chemicals, emeralds, cotton products, sugar, livestock

Percentage of exports that go to the US: 34.6%

US foreign aid to Colombia (2008): US$544 million

Unemployment rate: 11.1%

Percentage of vote President Uribe won in the 2006 election: 62.35%

Life expectancy: 69 years (men), 77 years (women)

Internet country code: .co

Number of 'u's in the country's name: zero

Getting Started

Off the tourist radar for so long, Colombia is only just getting used to receiving tourists again.

On the one hand, this means Colombia is relatively uncrowded and still good value. On the other hand, few people speak English. You'll enjoy your holiday a great deal more if you speak some Spanish. If nothing else, bring a phrasebook, a smile and some courage – Colombians will forgive bad grammar if you make an effort.

The majority of foreign travelers in Colombia are backpackers, and there is a growing network of foreign-owned hostels. The budget traveler will find the country pleasantly easy on the wallet. There are plenty of dorm beds on offer, buses are cheap and efficient, and budget meals are never more than a short walk away.

The midrange and top-end traveler looking for greater creature comforts and good service will find them, although there may be fewer options. While all the major cities boast four-star hotels, and the Caribbean and Pacific coasts are home to quality, all-inclusive resorts, the midrange category is almost nonexistent in Colombia. That said, Colombia's best hotels and resorts are significantly cheaper than rivals in more touristy destinations, making Colombia a bargain no matter how you look at it.

WHEN TO GO

Colombia has no high and low season, per se. The peak seasons are Semana Santa (Holy Week), December and January, and all *puentes* (three-day weekends), when bus transport can be crowded and some hotels full. Mid-June to mid-July are also crowded during school holidays.

See Climate Charts (p298) for more information.

Situated right at the equator, the weather in Colombia fluctuates very little, meaning that anytime is a good time to visit the country. There are two pronounced rainy seasons between December and March and in July and August, but it can (and does) rain at any time of the year.

December through to January is a period of almost nonstop partying in Colombia and is a good time to visit if you want to attend the maximum number of festivals on offer (see p17).

IS IT SAFE?

Short answer: yes.

Fine print: anything can happen. Just as anything can happen in your home country, so too it can happen in Colombia.

Compared with neighboring countries, in particular Venezuela and Ecuador, Colombia is much safer. The average traveler visiting the destinations included in this book will run little risk. The principal concern should be safety in the cities. A street-savvy traveler who keeps their wits about them is unlikely to be mugged, and if they are, coughing up what small amount of cash is on hand (try to head out with no more than COP$50,000 in your wallet) should avoid any further confrontation.

The risk of kidnapping or guerrilla-inspired violence is negligible. Are you a celebrity, diplomat or uniformed member of the US Armed Forces? If so, perhaps you should reconsider your trip. Remote pockets of the country, especially the high mountains and the deep jungle, continue to be controlled by the Fuerzas Armadas Revolucionarias de Colombia (FARC) and/or paramilitaries. These regions include the Chocó, parts of Nariño, Putumayo, and the jungle area east of the Andes (except for Los Llanos and the area around Leticia). The Pacific coast remains borderline, but is well patrolled by the Colombian marines.

Conditions in Colombia could, at least in theory, change rapidly. If you are concerned, check conditions online before going. A good place to start is Lonely Planet's Thorn Tree forum (thorntree.lonelyplanet.com).

COSTS & MONEY

By Latin American standards, Colombia is cheap. A backpacker can expect to spend an average of COP$50,000 to COP$100,000 per day, more if you plan on doing a lot of clubbing. If you want a more comfy trip, with midrange hotels, some better restaurants and a flight from time to time, you'll average somewhere between COP$200,000 and COP$300,000 per day. Some resort areas, especially along the Caribbean and Pacific coasts, have all-inclusive resort packages that cost COP$200,000 to COP$300,000 per person, which is pretty good value anywhere.

Remember that bus ticket prices are always negotiable. Start with a polite, *'Hay discuenta?'* (Is there a discount?) then move on down the line. Prices will immediately drop at least 30%. This doesn't work during holiday periods when buses are full.

HOW MUCH?

Set meal COP$3000-7000

Internet cafe (per hr)
COP$1200-2000

Dorm bed COP$15,000-22,000

Six-pack of beer
COP$9000

Postage for a letter to the US COP$10,000

TRAVEL LITERATURE

Most recent literature on Colombia consists of journalists' accounts of the so-called 'war on drugs,' and US involvement in the country. A highly recommended personal account is *More Terrible Than Death: Violence, Drugs, and America's War in Colombia* (2003) by Robin Kirk. A similar book, *Killing Peace: Colombia's Conflict and the Failure of US Intervention* (2002), by Garry Leech, offers a condensed analysis of the United States' involvement in Colombia.

Another controversial book on the subject is *America's Other War: Terrorizing Colombia* (2005) by Doug Stokes, a critical account of US policy in Colombia that gets its message across by using declassified documents. The reading is a little dry and academic, but the tone is unmistakably critical of US involvement. For more left-wing reading, check out Mario Murillo's *Colombia and the United States: War, Terrorism, and Destabilization* (2003).

For a history of Colombia's recent troubles through the eyes of those affected, read *The Heart of the War in Colombia* (2002) by Constanza Ardila Galvis. *Colombia: A Brutal History* (2004) by Geoff Simons is also worth a read.

COCAINE HOLIDAY? CONSIDER THE CONSEQUENCES

Lots of travelers head to Colombia to take drugs. Cocaine is cheap, so why not?

What may appear a harmless diversion directly contributes to the violence and mayhem that play out in the Colombian countryside every day. People fight and die for control of the cocaine trade. Purchasing and consuming cocaine helps finance that conflict. It's estimated that FARC alone collects between US$200 and $300 million per year from cocaine production.

Worse still, the by-products from the production of cocaine are extremely damaging to the environment (see p51). The production process requires toxic chemicals such as kerosene, sulfuric acid, acetone and carbide, which are simply dumped afterward on the ground or into streams and rivers. Further it's estimated that between 50,000 and 300,000 hectares of virgin rainforest are cut down every year for coca production.

Colombia is one of the most beautiful countries in the world. The people, the music, the dancing, the food – there is already enough stimulation to overwhelm the senses. It is best enjoyed with an ice-cold *cerveza michelada* (beer with rock salt and lime juice), not with cocaine.

TOP **PICKS**

•Bogotá
COLOMBIA
PACIFIC
OCEAN

TOP ECOLODGES

The Pacific coast has lots of great ecolodges, perfect for whale-watching, scuba diving, surfing monster waves or just plain relaxing. For more intense jungle time, try the Amazon; for a Caribbean beach, go for Tayrona. There are also two fine thermal spas in the Zona Cafetera.

- **El Cantil** (p279) One of the Pacific coast's most famous ecolodges, it also sponsors an annual pro-am surfing competition.
- **El Almejal** (p276) This fine ecolodge near the town of El Valle runs a turtle-hatching program in season.
- **Ecohabs** (p175) These pricey digs offer top-end accommodations right in the middle of a national park.
- **Reserva Natural Palmarí** (p294) Technically in Brazil, this ecolodge is a short boat ride down-river from Leticia.
- **Termales de Santa Rosa** (p230) Set next to a stunning series of waterfalls. Hot thermal springs bubble up next to a quality hotel.

BEST BEACHES

Colombia has world-class beaches. Its Caribbean beaches are picture-postcard perfect with white sand. The Pacific coast beaches, meanwhile, are something different entirely – black-sand beaches sandwiched between wild jungle and pounding surf.

- **Jonny Cay** (p193) Colombia's holiday islands offer classic Caribbean sun, sand and sea.
- **La Miel** (p188) Technically inside Panama, just a short walk from the border town of Sapzurro.
- **Taroa Beach** (p184) Isolated beach at the tip of the continent.
- **Tayrona** (p173) Jaw-dropping national park.
- **Guachalito** (p278) The most beautiful beach on the Pacific coast, with an abundance of fabulous tropical gardens.
- **Ladrilleros** (p280) A budget taste of the Pacific coast.

UNMISSABLE HIKES

Colombia's varied terrain has some of the world's most stunning hikes. You'll find jungle, mountain, snowcapped peaks, and everything in between.

- **Ciudad Perdida** (p177) This sweaty six-day trek takes you to the ruins of the extinct Tayrona civilization.
- **El Cocuy** (p116) A high-mountain trek that rarely drops below 4000m and crosses several glaciers. Not for the faint of heart (or short of breath).
- **Los Nevados** (p225) A classic one-day excursion takes you above 5000m to the snowline of Nevado del Ruiz. Longer treks and mountaineering opportunities are on offer for those with the time and the muscle power.
- **Valle de Cocora** (p237) This fabulous one-day walk in the heart of the coffee country takes you through forests of wax palm – the tallest palm in the world, and Colombia's national tree.
- **Tierradentro** (p258) This four-to-six hour hike follows a circular ridgeline with views of the surrounding hills, and takes in all the tombs of this pre-Columbian culture.
- **Barichara** (p123) Walk the ancient stone trail of the Guane people on this two-hour stroll.

DON'T LEAVE HOME WITHOUT...

■ your passport, and a visa if you need one
■ scanning your passport photo page to keep in your email account
■ up-to-date vaccinations
■ a hat and sunscreen
■ a sweater and rain jacket – it gets cold in the mountains
■ a small flashlight (torch)
■ toilet paper (just in case)
■ insecticide-treated mosquito net if you're going to malarial zones
■ some English-language reading material
■ some nice shoes to go out salsa dancing
■ this guidebook
■ a smile
■ a healthy sense of patience

Between Legitimacy and Violence: A History of Colombia, 1875–2002 (2006) by Marco Palacios offers the broad storyline of Colombia, covering the main social and economic trends in the country's modern history.

Colombia has very little racial tension, but it wasn't always that way. Nancy Appelbaum offers a critical look at the *paísa* myth of Antioquia and the history of race in Colombia in her 2003 book, *Muddied Waters: Race, Region, and Local History in Colombia, 1846–1948*.

Finally, no traveler will want to miss Charles Nicholl's book *The Fruit Palace* (1994), a hilarious diary of his wanderings through the country in the 1980s. Think Hunter S Thompson meets Colombian drug barons. (Spoiler: he survives to tell the tale.)

INTERNET RESOURCES

BBC News (news.bbc.co.uk) The Beeb has excellent South American coverage.

El Tiempo (eltiempo.com.co) Spanish-language readers will want to browse the website of Colombia's leading newspaper.

Lonely Planet (www.lonelyplanet.com) Lonely Planet's website includes a dedicated Colombia page with photos, travel tips and the ever-useful Thorn Tree online forum.

Parques Nacionales Naturales de Colombia (www.parquesnacionales.gov.co) The national parks office has detailed information (in Spanish) on all 54 national parks.

Poor But Happy (www.poorbuthappy.com/colombia) An online forum used mostly by expats living in Colombia, the site is a good place to go for practical information.

Turismo Colombia (www.turismocolombia.com) The government's official tourism website has good tourist information in Spanish and English.

Events Calendar

Colombians love a party, and when they let their hair down – whoa, you're in for a treat. Almost every small town, it seems, has an annual bash, with beauty pageants, parades, live music, bullfights, and lots and lots of drinking. Many of Colombia's biggest events happen around Christmas and run into the new year. Semana Santa (Holy Week), during Easter, is also cause for much celebration with pomp and ceremony in many smaller colonial towns, attracting tourists and worshippers from around the world.

CARNAVAL DE BLANCOS Y NEGROS   Jan 5-6
Pasto's annual post-Christmas bash, the Carnaval de Blancos y Negros (see boxed text, p262), originated during Spanish rule, when slaves were allowed to celebrate on January 5 and their masters joined in the festivities by painting their faces black. On the following day, the slaves painted their faces white. These days, pretty much everyone gets roaring drunk and throws talcum powder in everyone else's faces until you're coughing up powdery mucus. Great fun.

FERIA DE MANIZALES
The highlight of Manizales' annual festival (p221) is the bullfighting – the feria (fair) attracts some of the world's best bullfighters and Colombia's feistiest bulls. There's also the usual assortment of parades and craft fairs and, of course, a beauty pageant.

FEBRUARY

FIESTA DE NUESTRA SEÑORA DE LA CANDELARIA   Feb 2
A solemn procession is held in Cartagena (p146) to honor the town's patron saint at the Convento de la Popa, during which the faithful carry lit candles. Celebrations begin nine days earlier, the so-called Novenas, when pilgrims flock to the convent.

FEBRUARY & MARCH

CARNAVAL DE BARRANQUILLA
Forty days before Easter is Mardi Gras, or Carnaval as it's known in Colombia. Barranquilla's Carnaval

(see boxed text, p162) is the second biggest in South America after Rio de Janeiro's in Brazil. This otherwise grim port city goes crazy with four days of drinking and dancing. There are parades, costumes and a marathon concert of Colombian musical groups. It concludes on Fat Tuesday (the day before Ash Wednesday) with the symbolic burial of 'festival icon' Joselito Carnaval.

MARCH & APRIL

SEMANA SANTA IN POPAYÁN
The most famous Semana Santa (Holy Week) celebration is held in Popayán (p252), with nighttime processions on Maundy Thursday and Good Friday. Thousands of believers and tourists come to take part in this religious ceremony and the accompanying festival of religious music.

SEMANA SANTA IN MOMPOX
Colombia's second-most important Semana Santa (Holy Week) celebration is in the sleepy river town of Mompox (p158), near the Caribbean coast.

FESTIVAL IBEROAMERICANO DE TEATRO
Held during Semana Santa (Holy Week), this biennial festival of Latin American theater (p80) takes place every even-numbered year, and ends with a fireworks spectacular in Bogotá's football stadium.

AUGUST

FESTIVAL DE MÚSICA DEL PACIFICO PETRONIO ÁLVAREZ
This Cali festival (p243) celebrates the music of the nearby Pacific coast.

FERIA DE LAS FLORES   early Aug
This weeklong feria is Medellín's most spectacular event. The highlight is the Desfile de Silleteros (p208), when up to 400 campesinos (peasants) come down from the mountains and parade along the streets carrying flowers on their backs.

SEPTEMBER

FESTIVAL MUNDIAL DE SALSA
Don't miss this classic Cali festival (p243). It's not really a worldwide festival, but you'll still see some

amazing dancers, and there are often free shows at the outdoor Los Cristales amphitheater.

CONGRESO NACIONAL GASTRONÓMICO
Every year top chefs from different countries are invited to come and cook up a storm in tiny colonial Popayán (p252).

FESTIVAL INTERNACIONAL DE JAZZ
Many North American bands come for this Medellín festival (p209). There are usually a couple of free concerts.

FESTIVAL INTERNACIONAL DE TEATRO
Held since 1968, Manizales' theater festival (p222) is the country's second most important theater festival (after Bogotá's Festival Iberoamericano de Teatro). It lasts for about a week and features free shows in Plaza de Bolívar.

OCTOBER

FESTIVAL DE CINE DE BOGOTÁ
With a 20-year history, the city's film festival (p80) attracts films from all around the world, including a usually strong Latin American selection.

ROCK AL PARQUE   late Oct
Three days of rock/metal/pop/funk/reggae bands rocking out at Parque Simón Bolívar in Bogotá (p80). It's free, and swarming with fans.

NOVEMBER

REINADO NACIONAL DE BELLEZA   Nov 11
This event, also known as the Carnaval de Cartagena or Fiestas del 11 de Noviembre, is the city's most important annual bash. The national beauty pageant celebrates Cartagena's independence day (p146). Miss Colombia, the beauty queen, is announced on November 11, the high point of the event. The fiesta, which includes street dancing, music and fancy-dress parades, strikes up several days before the pageant and the city goes wild.

DECEMBER & JANUARY

ALUMBRADO NAVIDEÑO   Dec 7 to Jan 7
Every Christmas, Colombian cities compete to see who can put up the most elaborate lighting display along their respective rivers – Medellín often wins. The Festival of Lights in Villa de Leyva in early December is also a major national event that attracts Colombians from Bogotá and afar.

FERIA DE CALI   Christmas to Jan 7
During Cali's annual bash (p243), commerce pretty much grinds to a halt and the parties spill into the streets. Food and beer pavilions magically appear, and spontaneous dancing in the streets is not unknown. The Río Cali is illuminated by lights all along the river. The bullfights are also renowned.

Itineraries
CLASSIC ROUTES

CARIBBEAN BEACHES
(WITH A TWIST)   Four Weeks / Venezuela to Panama

Colombia has world-class Caribbean beaches, plus a few coastal surprises (ruins, rainforest, mountains). The start and finish points are rather remote here; you may want to use Santa Marta or Cartagena as your base.

Start at **Cabo de la Vela** (p181), a stunning setting of desert and sea. Enjoy the peace; you won't find too many other tourists here.

Head southwest to **Taganga** (p170), just outside **Santa Marta** (p164). From here, do the sweaty, six-day trek to **Ciudad Perdida** (p177) or walk into **Parque Nacional Natural (PNN) Tayrona** (p173), lingering on its otherworldly beaches. If all-inclusive resorts are more your thing, check out **El Rodadero** (p165) for some luxury. Then head west to **Barranquilla** (p159), and its raucous Carnaval.

Head to **Cartagena** (p138) and spend time exploring its glorious backstreets and nearby, the **Islas del Rosario** (p152).

If you're not in a hurry, spend a few days visiting **Playa Blanca** (p153) and the Caribbean islands of **San Andrés** (p191) and **Providencia** (p198).

From Cartagena head southwest, visiting **Tolú** (p184), then to **Turbo** (p186) and across to **Capurganá** (p188) on the Panamanian border. Linger here on the beach, snorkeling the reefs.

Adventurous beach bums, this one's for you. There are classic white-sand beaches, sure – but also a few surprises.

THE SEE-(ALMOST)-EVERYTHING ROUTE
Two Months / Bogotá to Bogotá

From Bogotá, head north to **Villa de Leyva** (p105). Explore its cobbled streets and enjoy its colonial charm for a couple of days, then visit **San Gil** (p119) for hiking and rafting, making time on the way for historic **Barichara** (p122). Passing through **Girón** (p129) and **Bucaramanga** (p125), continue on to check out quaint **Mompox** (p155). Next stop: **Cartagena** (p138), the jewel of the Caribbean. You'll need a week to explore this exquisite colonial city, along with **Santa Marta** (p164) and other attractions on the Caribbean coast. Time permitting, Cartagena is also the jumping-off point for a jaunt to the islands of **San Andrés** (p191) and **Providencia** (p198).

From the Caribbean, bus your way south to **Medellín** (p205), with a quick detour to colonial **Santa Fe de Antioquia** (p217). Next head south to the Zona Cafetera and enjoy some time in the nature reserves around **Manizales** (p220) and the Valle de Cocora outside **Salento** (p236).

Further south is **Cali** (p239) and the city's sweaty, hopping salsa joints. Travel down through **Popayán** (p249) to the archaeological ruins at **Tierradentro** (p258) and **San Agustín** (p255). Return to Bogotá via the **Desierto de la Tatacoa** (p267), or continue south to Quito in Ecuador.

Plenty of time? This loop takes you through all the main tourist regions in Colombia. Numerous side trips are possible along this route. Careful, though – you could easily end up spending six months on this route instead of two!

ROADS LESS TRAVELED

NOOKS & CRANNIES   One Month / Cabo de la Vela to Santuario de Las Lajas
Follow this route to encounter the tucked away delights from Colombia's
northernmost tip to its southern border with Ecuador.

Start out east of Santa Marta at **Cabo de la Vela** (p181), at the northern tip
of South America, a striking landscape where the desert meets the sea. Head
west to explore **Cartagena** (p138), then southwest to tiny **Capurganá** (p188),
a cute beachside town some are calling the 'next Taganga,' set right on the
border with Panama. Indulge in diving, beaching and jungle walks galore.

From here fly via Medellín to Bahía Solano on the **Pacific coast** (p269), great
during whale-watching season, and spend a few days on the spectacular rainy,
gray beaches along this coastline, sandwiched between jungle and sea. There
are fine, midrange ecolodges where you can surf and go diving near **Bahía
Solano** (p270), **El Valle** (p275) and **Guachalito** (p278), near **Nuquí** (p277).

From Nuquí fly to often-overlooked **Pereira** (p227) and party in the city's
thumping *discotecas*. Head east then south to the **Desierto de la Tatacoa** (p267), a
tiny desert between the mountains and river. The star-gazing is awesome.

Head south from here, past Cali and Popayán to **Pasto** (p261), a pleasant
town on the border with Ecuador. Be sure to visit nearby **Laguna de la Cocha**
(p264), and if **Volcán Galeras** (p264) ever stops grumbling, hike to the top of
the volcano for views all the way to the Pacific Ocean. Finish off your trip
with a visit to **Santuario de Las Lajas** (p266), a striking cathedral built in the
middle of a gorge near Ipiales, on the border with Ecuador.

Want to poke your
nose where no one
else goes, and still
stay safe? Want to
explore a little bit
deeper your second
time through?
Consider the
following sites.

PACIFIC COAST
Two to Three Weeks / Bahía Solano to Cali

Long off-limits due to La Violencia, the exotic Pacific coast is reopening as a tourist destination. It boasts tropical jungle, diving, whale-watching, world-class sportfishing and high surf. Black-sand beaches and heavy rainfall make for an unusual beach vacation.

Start your trip in **Bahía Solano** (p270). Numerous nearby beach resorts can organize activities, including walks into the adjacent jungle. From Bahía Solano, head south to **El Valle** (p275). During turtle season you can spot turtles laying eggs on the beach, and pay a visit to a biological research station. Hike south to the northern end of **Ensenada de Utría** (p276) and take a boat across to the national park's visitors center, where you can spend the night. During whale season you can watch the whales as they enter the narrow bay and play a few hundred meters offshore. Take a boat to **Nuquí** (p277) and visit nearby **Guachalito** (p278), a beautiful beach with well-tended tropical gardens. Walk along its long, clean, black-sand beach, as tiny crabs scuttle away. Return to Nuquí and hang out for an overnight cargo boat heading south to **Buenaventura** (p279).

Take a water taxi from Buenaventura to the beach town of **Ladrilleros** (p280), a budget destination popular with *caleños* (Cali residents). You'll find surf, sand and occasional sun here. Finally, organize a weekend dive cruise to **Isla Gorgona** (p284), and spend two days visiting this former prison island and diving the coral reefs. Advanced divers can dive with a school of hundreds of hammerhead sharks on remote **Isla Malpelo** (p283), but give yourself an extra week. From Buenaventura return to Cali via **San Cipriano** (p281), deep in the tropical forest and only accessible by a unique hand-propelled rail cart.

Colombia's Pacific coast is the ultimate off-the-beaten-path destination. It isn't cheap – all transport is by small plane and boat – but the rewards are definitely worth it.

TAILORED TRIPS

DIVING COLOMBIA

Colombia has enough fabulous dive sites to satisfy everyone from the beginner to the Jacques Cousteau wannabe. If you're after a PADI card, or a Divemaster certification, spend some time hanging out in hippie haven **Taganga** (p170) on the Caribbean coast, which offers some of the cheapest accreditation courses in the world.

For crystal-clear Caribbean waters, the reef diving off **San Andrés** (p191) and **Providencia** (p198) is world class. The more adventurous will want to visit **Capurganá** (p188), which has superior diving to Taganga, and is just a short walk to the Panamanian border.

Divers looking for a challenge should not miss **Isla Malpelo** (p283), where you can dive with schools of sharks numbering in the thousands. It's a minimum eight-day live-aboard dive cruise; be sure to book this one well in advance.

For a less challenging taste of the Pacific coast's diving, take a weekend dive cruise to **Isla Gorgona** (p284), and visit the ruins of the island's former penal colony.

NATIONAL PARKS & PROTECTED AREAS

Colombia has 54 national parks spread across the country, some easily accessible and others so remote that their number of yearly visitors can be counted on two hands.

One of the most frequently visited parks, **Parque Nacional Natural (PNN) Tayrona** (p173), is popular among aspiring beach bums. Also well known on the Caribbean coast is the **PNN Corales del Rosario y San Bernardo** (p152), just off the coast of Cartagena. Most visitors base themselves at Playa Blanca and take boat trips out to the cays and islets.

Travelers seeking fresh alpine air and glacier-wrapped peaks should head for **PNN El Cocuy** (p116). Considered off-limits for security reasons a few years ago, the park has been safe for a while and is now well set up for trekkers. Closer to Bogotá, the **Santuario de Flora y Fauna de Iguaque** (p110) is lower in elevation, but still offers some fine hikes to a group of alpine lakes. The beautiful **Laguna de Guatavita** (p97) can be reached from the capital in a day trip and has spiritual significance.

Budding vulcanologists will want to visit the **PNN Los Nevados** (p225), located southeast of Manizales. It contains several volcanic cones, some of them active. If the jungle is more your thing, it's hard to beat the **PNN Amacayacu** (p292) in Colombia's Amazon Basin.

History

A cynic might redraw the Colombian blue, yellow and red flag as gold, brown and white – representing the three local products that, for better or worse, the country has been most associated with over the years: gold, coffee and (processed) cocaine. In reality, Colombia's past and present is far more complex: a rare Latin American nation with little history of military dictators, but where conversations of ongoing subjects like guerrilla groups, paramilitaries, Liberals, Conservatives, Hugo Chávez, US free-trade agreements, Caribbean-influenced music and hot chocolate invariably link back to the days when the first Spaniards rowed ashore in 1500.

One of the best books on Colombia's history is David Bushnell's *The Making of Modern Colombia: A Nation in Spite of Itself* (1993), which follows colonization, partisan conflicts throughout independence, and the emergence of cocaine politics in the 1980s.

PRE-COLUMBUS COLOMBIA

Set at the point where South America meets Central America, present-day Colombia saw the continent's first inhabitants arrive between 12,500 and 70,000 years ago, having migrated from the north. Most – such as the ancestors of the Inca – just passed through. Little is known of the groups who did stick around (eg the Calima, Muisca, Nariño, Quimbaya, Tayrona, Tolima and Tumaco). By the time the Spaniards arrived, the first inhabitants were living in small, scattered communities, subsisting on agriculture or trade. They hardly rivaled the bigger civilizations flourishing in Mexico and Peru.

The area's biggest pre-Columbian sites (San Agustín, p255; the Tierradentro, p258; and Ciudad Perdida, p177) were already long abandoned when the Spaniards arrived. Ciudad Perdida, the Tayrona jungle city, was built in the 11th century with hundreds of stone terraces linked with stairways.

The Muisca, one of the country's larger indigenous groups, occupied present-day Boyacá and Cundinamarca, near Bogotá (itself named from a Muisca word), and numbered 600,000 when the Spanish arrived.

The official site of the US Colombian embassy is www.colombiaemb.org. It has good up-to-date information on the country.

SPANISH CONQUEST

Colombia is named after Christopher Columbus, even though he never set foot on Colombian soil. Alonso de Ojeda, one of Columbus' companions on his second voyage, was the first European to set foot here in 1500. He briefly explored the Sierra Nevada de Santa Marta and was astonished by the wealth of the local indigenous people. Attracted by the presumed riches of the locals, the shores of present-day Colombia became the target of numerous expeditions by the Spaniards. Several short-lived settlements were founded along the coast, but it was not until 1525 that Rodrigo de Bastidas laid the first stones of Santa Marta, which is today the earliest surviving town. In 1533 Pedro de Heredia founded Cartagena; with a better harbor it quickly became the principal center of trade.

TIMELINE

10,000 BC	5500 BC	11th century AD
Some early arrivals create little stone chips at the site of El Abra in modern-day Bogotá – the earliest known evidence of human habitation in modern-day Colombia.	Early groups of pre-Muisca begin moving to present-day Colombia, where they eventually become the biggest indigenous group between the Inca and Maya by the time of Columbus.	The Tayrona begin building their largest city, the legendary Ciudad Perdida (or Lost City), in lush rainforest, which would be 'discovered' only in 1975.

> ### GOLD!
>
> From day one of their arrival, tales of gold overwhelmed the conquistador mind-set. Eventually glimpses of gold artifacts, and stories of much more inland, gave birth to the myth of El Dorado, a mysterious jungle kingdom abundant in gold and, in some versions, surrounded by mountains of gold and emeralds. Long into the colonial period, the struggling Nueva Granada viceroyalty was based on a one-export economy: gold.
>
> Eventually the legend became linked with the Muiscas and their famous Laguna de Guatavita (p97), which has suffered endless efforts to dig up enough wealth to change the world. Not much was ever found, alas.
>
> Read more in John Hemming's fascinating book, *The Search for El Dorado* (2001).

In 1536 an advance toward the interior began independently from three directions: under Gonzalo Jiménez de Quesada (from Santa Marta), Sebastián de Belalcázar (aka Benalcázar; from present-day Ecuador) and Nikolaus Federmann (from Venezuela). All three managed to conquer much of the colony and establish a series of towns, before meeting in the Muisca territory in 1539.

Of the three, Quesada got there first, crossing the Valle del Magdalena and Cordillera Oriental in 1537. At the time, the Muiscas were divided into two rival clans – one ruled by the Zipa from Bacatá (present-day Bogotá), the other by Zaque in Hunza (present-day Tunja) – whose rivalry helped Quesada conquer both clans with only 200 men.

Belalcázar, a deserter of Francisco Pizarro's Inca-conquering army, subdued the southern part of Colombia, founding Popayán and Cali. After crossing Los Llanos and the Andes, Federmann arrived in Bogotá shortly after Belalcázar. The three groups squabbled for supremacy until King Carlos V of Spain, finally, in 1550, established a court of justice in Bogotá and brought the colony under the control of the viceroyalty of Peru.

The Explorers of South America (1972), by Edward J Goodman, brings to life some of the more incredible explorations of the continent, from those of Columbus to Humboldt, some of which refer to Colombia.

COLONIAL DAYS

In 1564 the Crown established a new authority, the Real Audiencia del Nuevo Reino de Granada, which had dual military and civil power and greater autonomy. The authority was run by a governor, appointed by the King of Spain. The Nuevo Reino at that time comprised present-day Panama, Venezuela (other than Caracas) and all of Colombia, except what is today Nariño, Cauca and Valle del Cauca, which were under the jurisdiction of the Presidencia de Quito (present-day Ecuador).

The population of the colony, initially consisting of indigenous communities and the Spanish invaders, diversified with the arrival of African slaves to Cartagena, South America's principal slave-trading port. During the 16th and 17th centuries the Spaniards shipped in so many Africans that they

The largest indigenous group between the Maya and Inca at the time of the Spanish Conquest, the Muiscas inspired El Dorado myths with their gold *tujos* (offerings), while their *chicha* (fermented-corn beer) still intoxicates Colombians today.

1400	1500	1537–38
The San Agustín culture – the northernmost extension of the Inca, some believe – perhaps foresee shiny-hatted explorers from the east, and leave behind hundreds of stone figures.	On his second journey to the New World, Alonso de Ojeda lands at Cabo de la Vela – and a scientist onboard surprises the crew by discovering the place isn't actually Asia.	Disobedient conquistador Gonzalo Jiménez de Quesada twice founds a new settlement, Santa Fe de Bogotá. First, without permission from the Crown, in 1537 – then, after asking if it's OK, in 1538.

eventually surpassed the indigenous population in number. The emergence of *criollos* (locally born whites) added to the mix.

With the growth of the Spanish empire in the New World, a new territorial division was created in 1717, and Bogotá became the capital of its own viceroyalty, the Virreinato de la Nueva Granada. It comprised the territories of what are today Colombia, Panama, Ecuador and Venezuela.

As Spaniards ran the show in Colombia throughout the colonial period, the local demographic picture became increasingly complex, as the country's three racial groups – mestizos (people of European-indigenous blood), *mulatos* (people with European-African ancestry) and *zambos* (African-indigenous people) – mixed.

INDEPENDENCE WARS

As Spanish domination of the continent increased, so too did the discontent of the inhabitants – particularly over monopolies of commerce and new taxes. The first open rebellion against colonial rule was the Revolución Comunera in Socorro in 1781, which broke out against tax rises levied by the Crown. It began taking on more pro-independence overtones (and nearly taking over Bogotá) before its leaders were caught and executed. When Napoleon Bonaparte put his own brother on the Spanish throne in 1808, the colonies refused to recognize the new monarch. One by one, Colombian towns declared their independence.

In 1812 Simón Bolívar, who was to become the hero of the independence struggle, appeared on the scene. He won six battles against Spanish troops, but was defeated the following year. Spain recovered its throne from Napoleon and then set about reconquering the colonies, finally succeeding in 1817.

Meanwhile, in 1815 Bolívar had retreated to Jamaica and taken up arms again. He went back to Venezuela, but Spanish forces were too strong in Caracas, so Bolívar headed south, with an army, and marched over the Andes into Colombia, claiming victory after victory.

The most decisive battle took place at Boyacá on August 7, 1819. Three days later Bolívar arrived triumphantly in Bogotá. Though some lesser battles were yet to come (including a victory at Cartagena in 1821), a congress met shortly after the Boyacá battle and pronounced the independent Republic of Colombia – comprising today's Venezuela, Colombia and Panama.

Although the conquistador Sebastián de Belalcázar was rewarded for killing thousands of indigenous people, the Spanish Crown sentenced him to death for ordering the assassination of rival conquistador Jorge Robledo in 1846.

AFTER INDEPENDENCE

With Colombia independent, a revolutionary congress was held in Angostura (modern-day Ciudad Bolívar, in Venezuela) in 1819. Still euphoric with victory, the delegates proclaimed the Gran Colombia, a new state uniting Venezuela, Colombia, Panama and Ecuador (although Ecuador and parts of Venezuela were still technically under Spanish rule).

The Angostura congress was followed by another one, held in Villa del Rosario, near Cúcuta, in 1821. It was there that the two opposing tendencies, centralist and federalist, first came to the fore. The two currents persisted throughout Bolívar's administration, which lasted to 1830. What followed after Bolívar's departure was a new (but not the last) inglorious page of Colombia's history. The split was formalized in 1849 when two political par-

1564	1717	1808
The Spanish Crown establishes the Real Audiencia del Nuevo Reino de Granada in Bogotá, subject to the viceroyalty of Peru in Lima.	Bogotá becomes capital of the viceroyalty of Nueva Granada, an area that encompasses present-day Colombia, Ecuador, Venezuela and Panama.	Napoleon defeats Spanish King Ferdinand VII and installs his brother on the Spanish throne, sending a glimmer of possibility for independence-minded thinkers across South America.

THE FALL OF SIMÓN BOLÍVAR

Known as 'El Libertador,' Simón Bolívar led armies to battle the Spanish across northern South America, won the Colombian presidency, and ranks as one of the nation's great heroes. It's therefore surprising how it ended for him: humiliated, jobless, penniless and alone. He said, shortly before his death from tuberculosis in 1830, 'There have been three great fools in history: Jesus, Don Quixote and I.'

How did it happen? A proponent of a centralized republic, Bolívar was absent – off fighting back the Spanish in Peru and Bolivia – during much of his administration, leaving the running of the government to his vice president, and rival, the young federalist Francisco de Paula Santander, who smeared Bolívar's ideas of being a lifetime president with the 'm' word: monarchistic.

In 1828 Bolívar finally assumed dictatorship to a republic out of control, and restored a (hugely unpopular) colonial sales tax. Soon after, he narrowly escaped an assassination attempt (some believe Santander planned it) and a long-feisty Venezuela finally split from the republic. By 1830 Bolívar had had enough, abandoning the presidency – and then his savings, through gambling. He died a few months later.

ties were established: the Conservatives (with centralist tendencies) and the Liberals (with federalist leanings). Fierce rivalry between these two forces resulted in a sequence of insurrections and civil wars, and throughout the 19th century Colombia experienced no fewer than eight civil wars. Between 1863 and 1885 alone there were more than 50 antigovernment insurrections.

In 1899 a Liberal revolt turned into the Thousand Days War, which resulted in a Conservative victory and left 100,000 dead. In 1903 the US took advantage of the country's internal strife and fomented a secessionist movement in Panama, then a Colombian province. By creating an independent republic there, the US was able to build and control a canal across the Central American isthmus. It wasn't until 1921 that Colombia eventually recognized the sovereignty of Panama and settled its dispute with the US.

LA VIOLENCIA

The turn of the 20th century saw the unwelcome loss of Panama, but a welcome period of peace, as the economy started to boom (particularly due to coffee) and the country's infrastructure expanded under the defused partisan politics of leader General Rafael Reyes. The brief lapse into a gentler world didn't last long, however. Labor tensions rose (following a 1928 banana strike), and the struggle between Liberals and Conservatives finally exploded in 1946 with La Violencia, the most destructive of Colombia's many civil wars to that point (with a death toll of some 200,000). Following the assassination of Jorge Eliécer Gaitán, a charismatic, self-made populist Liberal leader, more widespread riots broke out around the country (which came to be known as El Bogotazo in Bogotá – where Gaitán was killed – and

Colombia's red, yellow and blue tricolor flag was adopted in 1861. Yellow represents the land, blue symbolizes the ocean and red is the blood spilled by patriots.

1819	**1830**	**1886**
Simón Bolívar – crossing Los Llanos with an army of Venezuelans and Nueva Granadans from present-day Colombia – defeats the Spanish army at Boyacá and the Republic of Gran Colombia is founded.	After a rocky start, Gran Colombia splits into Colombia (including modern-day Panama), Ecuador and Venezuela; Bolívar sends himself into exile, then dies in Santa Marta.	Colombia elects Dr Rafael Núñez, who helps ease tension between state and church with new 'regeneration' policies outlined in a constitution that will stay in place for over a century.

COLOMBIAN COFFEE

Colombia's coffee boom began in the early 20th century, and found its exclamation point when the mustached Juan Valdéz, and his mule, became the Colombian Coffee Federation's icon in 1959 (voted the world's top ad icon as recently as 2005). In 2004 Juan Valdéz went after Starbucks, opening more than 60 cafes in Colombia, the US and Spain – helping locals shift from a cup of weak coffee to espresso.

Despite competition from low-cost, lower-quality beans from Vietnam, Colombia's high-quality arabica-bean industry still employs 570,000 and brings the country US$1.6 billion annually.

El Nueve de Abril elsewhere). Liberals soon took up arms throughout the country, supposedly even playing soccer in Puerto Tejada with decapitated heads of Conservative leaders.

The incomprehensible brutality stemmed from generations of Colombians being raised as either Liberals or Conservatives and imbued with a deep mistrust of the opposition. From 1946 to 1957, these 'hereditary hatreds' were the cause of countless atrocities, rapes and murders, particularly in rural areas.

The 1953 coup of General Gustavo Rojas Pinilla was the only military intervention the country experienced in the 20th century, but it was not to last. In 1957 the leaders of the two parties signed a pact to share power for the next 16 years. The agreement, later approved by plebiscite (in which women were allowed to vote for the first time), became known as the Frente Nacional (National Front). During the life of the accord, the two parties alternated in the presidency every four years. In effect, despite the enormous loss of lives, the same people were returned to power. Importantly, the agreement also disallowed political parties beyond the Liberals and the Conservatives, forcing any opposition outside of the normal political system and sowing the seeds for guerrilla insurrection.

Gabriel García Márquez depicts the back-and-forth brutality of Liberal and Conservative rivalries and vendettas in ongoing conflicts from 1885 to 1902 from the fictional village of Macondo in his magic realism novel One Hundred Years of Solitude.

GUERRILLAS & PARAMILITARIES

While the new National Front helped ease partisan tensions between Conservatives and Liberals, new conflicts were widening between wealthy landowners and the rural mestizo and indigenous underclass, two-thirds of whom lived in poverty by the end of La Violencia. Splinter leftist groups began emerging, calling for land reform. Colombian politics hasn't been the same since. Much of what happened has been documented by international human rights groups such as Human Rights Watch.

New communist enclaves in the Sumapáz area, south of Bogotá, worried the Colombian government so much that the CIA-trained and funded military bombed the area in May 1964. The bombing emboldened some leftist groups, including one – under the leadership of Pedro Marín (or

1899	**1903**	**1948**
The three-year Thousand Days War between Liberals and Conservatives erupts around the country, providing a key backdrop for Gabriel García Márquez' *One Hundred Years of Solitude*.	Long cut off from the rest of Colombia, Panama secedes from the country – with a lot of sneaky meddling from a canal-focused US to aid the process.	Likely Liberal presidential candidate, populist leader Jorge Eliécer Gaitán, is murdered leaving his office, setting off Bogotá and the country into bloody riots – the culprits are never identified.

Manuel Marulanda, aka Sureshot) and the more military mind-set of Jacobo Arenas – called the Fuerzas Armadas Revolucionarias de Colombia (FARC; Revolutionary Armed Forces of Colombia), which became increasingly organized, and started fighting back.

Other armed guerrilla groups included a fellow Marxist rival, the Ejército de Liberación Nacional (ELN; National Liberation Army), which built its popularity from a radical priest, Father Camilo Torres, who joined up (and was killed in his first combat experience). The urban-based M-19 (Movimiento 19 de Abril, named for the contested 1970 presidential election) favored dramatic statements, such as the robbery of a Simón Bolívar sword and seizing the Palace of Justice in Bogotá in 1985. When the military's recapture of the court led to 115 deaths, the group gradually disintegrated.

FARC's fortunes continued to rise, though, particularly when President Belisario Betancur negotiated peace with the rebels in the 1980s. This, along with the M-19 siege, so irritated defense secretary general Fernando Landazábal that he created a major *autodefensa* (paramilitary) funded by land-owners. The roots of these groups – all generally offshoots of the military – began in the 1960s, but grew in the '80s. For example, Landazábal's XIV Brigade would soon kill hundreds of suspected FARC collaborators in the Magdalena Valley. Paramilitaries also targeted members of FARC's political party, the Unión Patriótica (UP; Patriotic Union), which gained over 300,000 votes in the 1986 presidential election; their increased exposure, however, led to more than 300 murders of UP politicians in just six months.

As communism collapsed around the globe, the political landscape for the guerrillas shifted increasingly to drugs and kidnapping (kidnapping alone, by one account, brought FARC some US$200 million annually), and paramilitary groups were given license to be involved with drug cartels as long as they kept after the guerrillas – even if it occasionally meant killing off young people in villages supportive of the FARC or ELN.

After 9/11, 'terrorism' became the new buzz word applied to guerrillas, and even some paramilitaries. One group that made the US list of international terrorists, and which had notoriously been paid US$1.7 million by Chiquita fruit company, was the infamous and brutal Autodefensas Unidas de Colombia (AUC; United Self-Defense Forces of Colombia). Linked with cocaine since 1997, it was inspired by paramilitary groups previously under the watch of the slain Medellín cartel leader Rodríguez Gacha. The AUC was later run by brothers Fidel and Carlos Castaño, who set out to avenge their father who was slain by guerrillas. AUC, with a force of up to 10,000 troops, were as well known for terrorizing the countryside as the guerrillas. When the Uribe administration (p31) offered lenient sentences for paramilitaries or guerrillas who demobilized, AUC handed over their guns in 2006.

But the violence is not over. In 2008 the number of deaths of union leaders rose, paramilitary groups formed under new names (eg Black Eagles)

For accounts from FARC and paramilitary leaders, Steven Dudley's engaging *Walking Ghosts: Murder & Guerrilla Politics in Colombia* (2004) follows the rise and fall of FARC's Unión Patriótica party. Mario A Murillo's *Colombia & the United States: War, Unrest & Destabilization* (2004) is another left-leaning take.

Guardabosques, a 2008 UN/Colombia social program, began offering coca planters US$100 monthly to switch from coca to coffee or honey, or even ecotourism. Most were used to earning over 300% more growing coca than crops such as bananas.

1964	1974	1981
Funded by the US, the Colombian military drops napalm on a guerrilla-held area, giving rise to the Fuerzas Armadas Revolucionarias de Colombia (FARC); the Ejército de Liberación Nacional (ELN) and M-19 follow.	The National Front ends, and newly elected president Alfonso López Michelsen taxes the rich, and launches the first major counterinsurgency against all three main guerrilla groups.	Pablo Escobar's Medellín Cartel battles M-19 and the cartel's hitmen join with other paramilitary groups; meanwhile homosexuality is declared legal by the government in Bogotá.

THE DISPLACED

Caught in the crossfire between paramilitaries and guerrilla forces, and sometimes outright targets in what the UN says is a 'strategy of war,' one in 20 Colombians (about 3 million) have become *desterrados* (dispossessed, or displaced) since the 1980s, making Colombia home to more displaced persons than any country except Sudan.

The situation is ugly. About 860 additional people become displaced daily, forced out of their homes at gunpoint – usually stolen for the land, livestock or its location on drug transport routes – sometimes not until after a loved one is murdered. Most of the dispossessed are left to fend for themselves, living in tarp-covered huts outside the main cities. The lucky ones who are able to obtain new land frequently find it in areas with no infrastructure, schools or hospitals. Often, displaced children fall into a world of drugs and crime.

But there has been some improvement of late. For instance, in March 2008 the UN World Food Program began a three-year, US$157 million program to assist 550,000 people. Yet some locals feel they have waited long enough. In September 2008 several dozen displaced Colombians briefly occupied Bogotá's Parque 93, in the ritzy north of the city, in protest about the lack of government aid.

Read personalized tales of the poverty the displaced face in Alfred Molano's *The Dispossessed: Chronicles of the Desterrados of Colombia* (2005).

---

and FARC continued the bloodbath by planting land mines that killed 180 civilians in 2007. In all, paramilitaries and guerrillas each killed about 300 civilians in 2007 according to Amnesty International, who also said in a 2008 report, 'The Colombian authorities are in absolute denial, even refusing to admit there's an armed conflict in their country.'

Killing Pablo: The Hunt for the World's Greatest Outlaw (2002), by Mark Bowden, is an in-depth exploration of the life and times of Pablo Escobar and the operation that brought him down. While the book has some small inaccuracies, it is a fun crime read.

COCAINE POLITICS

Colombia is the world's biggest supplier of cocaine, despite exhaustive efforts to track down cartel leaders, drop devegetation chemicals on coca farms, and step up military efforts. All for that little *erythroxylum coca* leaf – which you can buy in its unprocessed form in some Colombia markets. When the first Europeans arrived, they at first shook their heads over locals chewing coca leaves, but when (forced) work output started to decline, they allowed its usage. Eventually the Europeans (and the world) joined in, and in the centuries to follow, Andean cocaine eventually found its way worldwide for medicinal uses and disco parties.

Cartel Days

The cocaine industry boomed in the early 1980s, when the Medellín Cartel, led by former car thief (and future politician) Pablo Escobar, became the principal mafia. Its bosses eventually founded their own political party, established two newspapers and financed massive public works and public

1982	1983	1985
Pablo Escobar is elected to the Colombian Congress; President Belisario Betancur grants amnesty to guerrilla groups and frees hundreds of prisoners; Colombia drops out of the contest to hold the World Cup.	Justice Minister Rodrigo Lara Bonilla is assassinated for supporting an extradition treaty with the US.	Superior Court Judge Tulio Manuel Castro Gil, who indicted Escobar for Lara Bonilla's assassination, is murdered; the M-19 guerrilla group lays siege to Bogotá's Palace of Justice.

housing projects. At one point, Escobar even stirred up secession sentiments for the Medellín region. By 1983 Escobar's personal wealth was estimated to be over US$20 billion, making him one of the world's richest people (number seven according to *Forbes* magazine).

When the government launched a campaign against the drug trade, cartel bosses disappeared from public life and even proposed an unusual 'peace treaty' to President Belisario Betancur. For immunity from both prosecution and extradition, they offered to invest their capital in national development programs and pay off Colombia's entire foreign debt (some US$13 billion!). The government said 'no' to the drug lords, and the violence escalated.

The cartel–government conflict heated up in August 1989, when Liberal presidential candidate Luis Carlos Galán was gunned down by drug lords. The government's response was to confiscate nearly 1000 cartel-owned properties and sign a new extradition treaty with the US, which led to a cartel-led campaign of terror resulting in bombed banks, homes, newspaper offices, and in November 1989, an Avianca flight from Bogotá to Cali, which killed all 107 onboard.

After the 1990 election of Liberal César Gaviria as president, things calmed briefly, when extradition laws were sliced and Escobar led a surrender of many cartel bosses. However, Escobar soon escaped from his luxurious house arrest and it took an elite, US-funded 1500-man special unit 499 days to track him down, shooting him dead atop a Medellín rooftop in 1993.

Amid the violence, the drug trade never slowed. New cartels have learned to forsake the limelight; by the mid-1990s, guerrillas and paramilitaries chipped in to help Colombia keep pace with the world's rising demand.

URIBE & THE US

Fed up with violence, kidnappings and highways deemed too dangerous to use, the nation turned to right-wing hardliner Álvaro Uribe – a politician from Medellín who had studied at Oxford and Harvard, and whose father had been killed by FARC. Uribe ran on a full-on antiguerrilla ticket during the testy 2002 presidential election. While his predecessor Andrés Pastrana had tried negotiating with FARC and ELN, Uribe didn't bother, quickly unleashing two simultaneous programs: a military push back of groups such as FARC, and a demobilization offer for both paramilitaries and guerrillas, who were promised lenient sentences in exchange for weapons and information. In the post-9/11 era, his branding of guerrillas as 'terrorists' helped garner even more US support, which runs between US$500 and US$600 million annually.

A rare Latin American ally with the US, Uribe is wildly popular in his country – even his harshest critics acknowledge much overdue progress made under his watch. From 2002 to 2008, notably, murder rates fell 40% overall, highways cleared of FARC roadblocks became safe to use, and

Many midlevel drug traffickers, getting their first taste of wealth, become obsessed with Mexican mariachi gear. Most of it is kept out of public, but if you see a mariachi, you might not want to ask him to show you what's in his guitar case.

As Álvaro Uribe was being sworn into office in 2002, guerrilla units camped at Bogotá's outskirts sent rockets aimed at the Casa de Nariño. Instead the rockets landed in a working-class barrio, killing 19 people.

Under Álvaro Uribe's watch (amid the US-funded Plan Patriot program that bumped up the size of the Colombian security forces by 33%), the number of FARC troops fell from 17,000 in 2002 to 11,000 in 2008.

1989	1991	1993
The M-19 demilitarizes; the cartels declare war on the government and the extradition treaty, and a government building near the Paloquemao market in Bogotá is destroyed by a bomb.	George Bush Snr signs the Andean Trade Preference Act, which he says will 'expand economic alternatives…to help halt the production…of illegal drugs.' It doesn't.	One-time Congress member – and a more famous cocaine warlord – Pablo Escobar is killed a day after his 44th birthday on a Medellín rooftop by Colombian police aided by the US.

PLAN COLOMBIA

In 2000 the US entered the war against the drug cartels, with the controversial 'Plan Colombia,' concocted by the Clinton and Pastrana administrations to curb coca cultivation by 50% within five years. As the decade closed, and with US$5 billion spent, even the normally rah-rah US International Trade Commission called the program's effectiveness 'small and mostly direct.' The worldwide street price for Colombian cocaine hadn't changed – indicating no lack of supply – and, after a few years of dipping coca cultivation, by 2007, a UN report concluded that cocaine production rose by 27% in 2007 alone, rebounding to its 1998 level.

Originally the money was supposedly to be split half-and-half between efforts to equip/train the Colombian military, and developmental projects to offer campesinos (peasants) attractive alternatives to coca farming. It didn't turn out that way. Nearly 80% of the money ended up with the military (as well as helicopter-drop devegetation chemicals that infamously killed food crops, along with elusive coca crops). In 2007 a Pentagon official told *Rolling Stone* that Plan Colombia ended up being less about 'counternarcotics' than 'political stabilization,' in particular the ongoing fight with FARC.

Emerging in the first decade of the century, new harder-to-track *cartelitos* (smaller sized mafia groups) replaced the extinguished mega cartels (capped with the 2008 extradition to the US of Medellín narco king Don Berna). The *cartelitos* run from dropped devegetation chemicals and relocate to harder-to-reach valleys (particularly near the Pacific coast). Many are linked to FARC, who tax coca farmers (earning FARC between US$200 to US$300 million annually, according to the *New York Times*). Other *cartelitos*, however, are linked with paramilitary groups, who sometimes benefit from government money.

As a result, Colombia still supplies about 90% of the USA's cocaine – often getting there overland via Mexican cartels. With Barack Obama in office, it's unclear how or if Plan Colombia will continue.

For more, see *Plan Colombia* (2003), an hour-long documentary by Gerard Ungerman that unveils how narcotraffickers are cashing in from the steady flow of US aid.

Uribe's go-ahead for a successful Rambo-style rescue in 2008 of high-profile kidnap victims from FARC (including French-Colombian politician Ingrid Betancourt) did a lot to keep the president's approval ratings regularly near the 80% mark.

In March 2008, Uribe approved a tricky bombing mission across Ecuador's border, resulting in the successful killing of FARC leader Raúl Reyes and the retrieval of computer files that indicated that FARC were trying to acquire uranium for bombs (the files were later authenticated by Interpol). In May 2008, the *Economist* predicted defeat of the guerrillas was 'only a matter of time.'

The bombing mission, however, nearly set the region into broader conflict, with Venezuelan president Hugo Chávez immediately getting into the action and moving tanks to the Colombian border, but things soon settled – particularly

While Colombia's international reputation as a dangerous country of kidnappings and cocaine continues to soften, the national tourist board got into the act with a new campaign in 2008 ('the only risk is wanting to stay') to attract visitors.

1994	1998	2000
Colombia's World Cup team is eliminated from the World Cup when defender Andrés Escobar taps in an own goal versus the US team; 10 days later he's murdered outside a bar in Medellín.	President Andrés Pastrana pulls troops from a New Jersey–sized area during cease-fire negotiations with FARC, claiming in a PBS interview that both sides are 'looking forward to achieving a peace process in the next four years.'	Colombia and the US agree on the expansive Plan Colombia to cut coca cultivation by 2005; the US eventually spends over US$5 billion with no drop in cocaine production over its first decade.

after the contents of seized computer files from the raid embarrassingly showed Chávez had contributed up to $300 million to FARC. Meanwhile, back in Colombia, Uribe's popularity hit 90% approval levels.

Not all news for Uribe has been so cheery, however. Scandals followed him throughout his first term, and – after a controversial amendment to the constitution (allowing him consecutive terms) – his second. By 2008, following his public feuds with the Colombian Supreme Court, 60 congressmen had been arrested or questioned for alleged 'parapolitics' links with paramilitaries (Uribe's cousin was also implicated, and even fled to the Costa Rican embassy for protection, though the charges were later dropped).

Even more embarrassing were widely published reports of *falso positivos* (false 'positives'), the local moniker referring to killed civilians who were posthumously dressed in guerrilla uniforms. Implications of the controversy spread through the military, and Uribe fired 27 officers in November 2008, the same time leading commander General Mario Montoya resigned. Amnesty International estimates that nearly half of these deaths were by local military groups financed by the US.

LOOKING AHEAD

Colombia faces an interesting transitional period over the coming years. A 2009 referendum will be held to allow Uribe to run for a third presidential term, prompting some criticism that Uribe may be emerging as yet another authoritarian strongman in a region with no shortage of such leaders.

Much of Colombia's economic plans hinge on the upcoming US-Colombia free-trade agreement (*tratado de libre comercio*, or TLC). Since 1991 the US has had a confusing overlap of various trade agreements with the Andean countries (Colombia, Ecuador, Peru and Bolivia) beginning with the Andean Trade Preference Act (ATPA) in 1991 and expanded significantly under George W Bush's watch with the Andean Trade Promotion and Drug Eradication Act (ATPDEA). Under such programs, Colombia's exports to the US have steadily risen (including a 50% increase from 2003 to 2007, with a notable rise in flower exports).

Throughout 2007 and 2008, however, the US Congress fought over the policy's renewal (which expired at the end of 2008) that proposes new provisions to allow 80% of US exports to Colombia to go tariff-free. Opponents, chiefly the Democratic party (along with the USA's new president Barack Obama), pointed to a recent bump in the numbers of killed union leaders, while mostly Republican backers found some surprising endorsements from newspapers such as the *New York Times* and *Washington Post*, whose editorial boards noted overall progress in human rights, and how eased trade restrictions could benefit US workers following the economic crisis of 2008. As this book goes to press, it seems more likely than not that some free-trade agreement will be passed.

In November 2008 more than 20,000 indigenous Colombians (part of Organización Nacional Indígena de Colombia, or ONIC) blocked traffic in a march along the highway outside Cali to protest slow-moving land reform.

Despite a rocky start to 2008 with Colombian-Venezuelan relations (Chávez sending tanks to the border and news he assisted FARC), by summer the leaders patched things up, meeting to discuss ongoing trade between the countries, which amounts to as much as $6 billion a year.

The CIA World Factbook website (www.cia.gov) has a breakdown of Colombian government, economy and population issues to keep you in the know.

2006	2008	2009
Colombia agrees to a free-trade deal with the US after two years of talks, while opponents vow to fight the agreement; pop singer Shakira's *Hips Don't Lie* breaks the 10-million mark in global sales.	Colombian military undertake an operation across the border in Ecuador – killing a FARC leader and setting the region into a near conflict; 20,000 indigenous people march for property rights near Cali.	A specially held referendum decides whether President Uribe can run for a third-straight term.

The Culture

Most travelers we know have the same reaction to Colombia: 'People in Colombia are so nice!'

And it's true! You'll find Colombians to be some of the warmest, most genuinely friendly and honest people you'll encounter in South America. Despite ongoing threats of civil war, despite whatever personal hardships they may bear, their good humor and amiable nature abounds. Even travelers with limited Spanish are rarely taken advantage of (which unfortunately can't be said about all South American countries).

THE NATIONAL PSYCHE

The geography of Colombia – mountains and sea – has influenced the national psyche. Colombia is principally an Andean nation, and the majority of the population live in the mountains in Bogotá, Medellín and Cali. The way of life here is industrious and hardworking, and the Spanish dialect clear, precise and easy to understand. Infrastructure is excellent, the roads are good and the water generally safe to drink (a source of local pride). Long isolated from the rest of the continent, this is the center of Colombian culture.

The Caribbean coast, on the other hand, has been in constant contact with the rest of the Caribbean basin for centuries, and the culture here has more in common with neighboring Venezuela, Cuba and the Dominican Republic. The way of life is slow and languorous, doubtless a by-product of the oppressive heat. *Costeños* (people from the coast) have a reputation for their laid-back demeanor, and speak the thick Caribbean Spanish spoken throughout the West Indies, which may be difficult for the student of Spanish to understand. The staples on the coast are fish and plantain, rather than rice and meat, and unlike the mountain cities, the roads are poorly maintained and the water never safe to drink.

For all their differences, the rivalry between the two regions is friendly, and over a bottle of aguardiente in a nightclub, the salsa and reggaetón blotting out any real conversation, you would be hard pressed to tell the difference.

Because most Colombians tend to live at home until they are married, 'love motels' are a part of most Colombians' sex lives – you can't really take the boyfriend home when your parents are in the next room, now can you?

LIFESTYLE

Although it's becoming an increasingly urbanized nation, Colombians continue to value and live by their traditions. The purpose of life is not to get rich, but to live. The Colombian is bound by strong family ties, not just to immediate blood relatives but to his extended family as well. There is nothing more important than family. While notionally a Catholic nation, only a small percentage of the country regularly attend mass, yet Colombians remain a deeply spiritual people.

Colombians live by *tiempo colombiano* (Colombian time). On the surface, *tiempo colombiano* refers to the Colombian's lack of punctuality, but it is also deeply indicative of the country's state of mind. If someone is late to meet you, don't take it personally; rather it's a recognition that there are few things worth rushing for, and things will sort themselves out one way or another.

The greatest cultural divide in Colombia is the divide between the central mountains and the Caribbean coast; the second greatest divide, and perhaps more fundamental, is the divide between the city and the country. Nowhere is this more apparent than in the war against cocaine production. It is a war led by city politicians, who have little sympathy for the farmers who grow coca leaf for no other reason than that they are poor, and the reality for the farmers is that the crop is profitable, well-suited to the region and much in demand. It is a war the city politicians are winning, and in the process farmers caught up in this conflict (both innocent and guilty) are being driven from their land. Some move to the city; many have crossed the border in to Ecuador as refugees. According to the UNHCR, up to half a million Colombian refugees live in neighboring countries. An untold number have been killed by land mines, paramilitary death squads, or the Colombian military itself; the US State Department catalogs these numerous tragedies in report after report on their website. The UNHCR estimates that more than 2.5 million Colombians have been displaced at some point in the last 15 years.

The minimum wage per month in Colombia is COP$481,500 (US$207), and fluctuates annually. The Colombian earning COP$800,000 to COP$1 million (US$345 to US$430) per month has arrived in the middle class; COP$5 million (US$2150) a month and you are definitely upper crust. The cost of living varies between the regions; Bogotá is the most expensive. A family of four can live well on COP$1 million a month pretty much anywhere.

Despite Colombia's infamy as a drug exporter, Colombians as a rule do not use drugs. Cocaine production has funded the ongoing civil war for decades, and although La Violencia may have ebbed, consuming cocaine is perceived as supporting that conflict.

ECONOMY

In Colombia security and economy are one. Since President Uribe took power in 2002 (see p31), the dramatically improved security situation has given both local businesses and foreign investors confidence to invest in Colombia. As a result, the economy has grown at an annual rate of 5% under Uribe; the average Colombian is much better off now.

In fact, Colombia boasts one of the largest middle-class populations in Latin America. Where many of its neighbors suffer great disparity in wealth, with virtually nothing between the very rich and very poor, Colombia's well-educated, substantial middle class gives poorer Colombians hope that they can go to school, get a degree and maybe one day own their own home, with a car, a washing machine and the lot. The country's free-market policies and relatively low level of corruption have helped the middle class to flourish.

The biggest thing on a lot of Colombians' minds these days, however, is trade with the US. The US gobbles up more than a third of Colombia's exports, many of which – such as bananas, coffee, chocolate, clothing and fresh-cut flowers – are currently tariff-free under the Andean Trade Promotion and Drug Eradication Act (ATPDEA). Since its signing in the late '90s, Colombian business has boomed (stimulated by lowered US tariffs) and good jobs (by Colombian standards) have been created in those industries.

ATPDEA was never meant to be permanent, and has been extended several times while the Tratado de Libre Comercio (TLC, a free-trade agreement with the US) is being negotiated. Ratification of the TLC was stalled in the US Senate at the time of writing, where Democratic lawmakers have questioned the high rate of violence against union leaders in Colombia. Meanwhile, ATPDEA is due to expire at the end of 2008. Failing a further extension, or the ratification of the TLC, Colombia will no longer be able to compete against other Latin American countries such as Brazil, Chile and Peru, which do have a free trade agreement with the US, and many Colombian workers may lose their jobs as a result.

Whether the TLC is signed or not, Colombian workers are still likely to lose out. Some economists call it a 'damned if you do, damned if you don't'

For some dry and dusty statistics, check out the Departmento Administrativo Nacional de Estadística (the national statistics bureau) – www.dane.gov.co (in Spanish).

situation. If Colombia ratifies the TLC, it will throw open the doors to US taxpayer-subsidized genetically modified corn, wheat and cotton. Colombian farmers won't be able to compete, and will go out of business. On the other hand, if the TLC isn't ratified and ATPDEA expires, the rebound in US import tariffs will put a serious damper on Colombian clothing manufacturers, banana producers and coffee growers, among others.

For better or worse, Colombia's fate is tied to that of the United States. Millions of expat Colombians in Miami and New York send home monthly remittances to their families; this alone accounts for a significant portion of Colombian GDP.

POPULATION

Colombia is urbanizing rapidly. Efforts to reduce coca cultivation have pushed many subsistence farmers off their land, resulting in their relocation to inner-city slums.

While Colombians could generally be said to be a mixed race people, certain ethnic groups still dominate different parts of the country. Many European immigrants populated Medellín, while much of the population of Cali is descended from former slaves. Bogotá and surrounds are dominated by a large indigenous population. Both the Caribbean and Pacific coasts have a high proportion of Afro-Colombians. The border region with Ecuador is dominated by the same Andean people that populate the mountain regions of Ecuador. Many immigrants from the Middle East have settled on the Caribbean coast (among whom the singer Shakira, who has a Lebanese background, is the most famous offspring).

For complete coverage of Colombian football, see www.futbolred.com/mustang.

The Colombian national population currently hovers around 46 million, making it the third most populous country in Latin America after Brazil and Mexico. It is now slightly larger than its former colonizer, Spain.

SPORTS
Soccer

Colombians love *fútbol* (soccer). The national league has 18 teams across the country, and attracts rowdy and boisterous crowds during the two seasons (February to June and August to December). While many second-string players from Brazil and Argentina play in the league, the standard of play is by no means world-class, making for entertaining, error-prone matches.

Colombian clubs participate in the South American Champions League (Confederación Sudamericana de Fútbol), and it was a great source of Colombian pride when the outmanned Cúcuta club advanced to the 2006 South American finals against Boca Juniors of Buenos Aires (Cúcuta lost).

Kings of the Mountains: How Colombia's Cycling Heroes Changed Their Nation's History (2003) by Matt Rendell is a great introduction to cycling culture in Colombia.

It will be many years yet before the most infamous moment in Colombian soccer is forgotten. In the 1994 World Cup, defender Andrés Escobar scored an own goal, eliminating the Colombian team from the tournament in the first round. Upon returning to Colombia, he was shot dead in the street by a man who reportedly shouted 'goal!' each of the 12 times he pulled the trigger.

Cycling

Another popular pastime is cycling. On Sunday, large sections of Bogotá are closed to traffic so the locals can take their exercise (see p79). Ciclovia, as this Sunday tradition is called, is also catching on in other Colombian cities, including Cali and Medellín. It should come as no surprise that such a mountainous country has produced many world-class cyclists, and Colombians regularly take part in the Tour de France.

TEJO

This uniquely Colombian game originates from Boyacá, north of Bogotá. It consists of throwing a heavy metal disc at a clay board studded with a circle of tiny paper pouches of gunpowder. You score points for landing the disc inside the circle and for hitting one of the pouches of gunpowder, which lets off a satisfying bang. The game is generally accompanied by large quantities of beer, and is great fun.

Baseball
After soccer, baseball is the second-most popular team sport in Colombia. It is especially popular on the Caribbean coast. Major League Baseball player Edgar Rentería of Barranquilla had the winning hit in the seventh game of the 1997 World Series for the Florida Marlins.

Car Racing
While car racing is not especially popular in this country, Colombian Juan Pablo Montoya won numerous races as a Formula One driver, and now competes on the US Nascar circuit.

Bullfighting
Colombia ranks third worldwide, after Spain and Mexico, in the popularity of bullfighting. The season peaks during the holiday period between mid-December and mid-January, and attracts some of the world's best matadors. The January Feria de Manizales is of great appeal to aficionados.

MULTICULTURALISM
Because of the many decades of violence in Colombia, the last 60 years or so has seen little in the way of immigration, meaning the country is more or less monocultural.

Visitors may notice how little racism exists in Colombia. Slavery was abolished in 1821, and the country has the largest black population in South America after Brazil. The last four centuries have seen plenty of interbreeding meaning most Colombians are mixed race.

What little discrimination that exists in Colombia is based more on a divide between modern and indigenous ways of life. Small pockets of indigenous people continue to live their traditional lifestyles, especially the indigenous population in the southern mountains near Ecuador, the Kogi in the Sierra Nevada de Santa Marta and the indigenous people of the Amazon region. These people are perceived by some as out of touch and backward given their cultural difference, and sometimes suffer discrimination as a result.

MEDIA
There is very little censorship in Colombia, and the media says what it likes without government interference. While the major media networks (RCN, Caracol etc) generally endorse government and big business, independent television station Canal Uno constantly questions the actions of the government, and has won many awards for its investigative reporting.

Notably absent in Colombia are attack ads and smear campaigns. Advertisements, both television and print, may not name a competing product or opposition candidate. Advertising may only be used to promote your own product or candidacy, not to tear down a competitor. The motive behind this is to prevent slander and libel. Those accustomed to political mud slinging may find the idea rather refreshing.

RELIGION

Colombia is a Catholic nation, although few people these days regularly attend mass. Before 1991 the Constitution only recognized the Catholic Church; marriages conducted by non-Catholic ministers, for example, were not considered valid under the law. The 1991 Constitution acknowledges all other faiths, although non-Catholics remain a small minority.

On San Andrés and Providencia, which were originally settled by the English, a majority of the islanders remain Protestant.

As in other Latin American countries, Colombia has Mormons and evangelical Christian missionaries, but their overtures fall largely on deaf ears.

WOMEN IN COLOMBIA

If you asked a Colombian what the most important thing in life was, most would answer 'family.' For those travelers accustomed to the radical individualism of much of the developed world, it can be difficult to fully grasp what this means for Colombians, and for women specifically.

Women are the heart of a Colombian household. Machismo may be alive and well outside the home, where men are unquestionably in charge, but inside the Colombian home, women rule the roost. Some might argue this is a healthy balance between male and female power, with clearly delineated roles within the everyday environment, somehow equal in its own way. Feminists will doubtless argue it limits opportunities for economic advancement for women. Both are right.

In the countryside, women generally do not attend university, and tend to marry young; in the city, middle- and upper-class women make up a high percentage of university students, although many ultimately choose not to pursue careers in order to start a family.

Women make up a significant number of the country's high-ranking politicians and diplomats, including cabinet ministers and ambassadors. In fact, a quota law passed in 2000 requires that at least 30% of appointed positions in the executive branch be filled by females. There is certainly a cultural shift underway – even if mostly a legislated one.

Women, single or married, prefer the title *señora*, not s*eñorita*.

Bogotá is Colombia's cultural capital. For a taste of what's on, check out www.cultura recreacionydeporte .gov.co.

ARTS

Colombian culture expresses itself most truly in its music, its dance (as danced in nightclubs and bars) and in the ever popular *telenovelas* (soap operas) that rule the airwaves.

The arts in Colombia – in terms of literature, painting, sculpture and theater – are a fringe interest. Still, artsy travelers interested in discovering what their Colombian brethren are up to may find a few things of interest. Bogotá is the artistic capital of Colombia.

Music

Colombia is famous for its music. We don't mean Shakira (who, despite being a Colombian, isn't particularly popular in her own country), or the multiple Grammy-winner singer Juanes (who is). Vallenato and cumbia both were born on Colombia's fertile soil, and the country has borrowed the Caribbean's salsa and made it its own. Merengue and reggaetón are popular as well.

Vallenato, born a century ago on the Caribbean coast, is based on the German accordion. Carlos Vives, one of the best-known modern Latin musical artists, transformed vallenato into a vibrant pop beat and spread it across the country.

Cumbia, a lively 4/4 style with guitars, accordion, bass, drums and the occasional horn, is the most popular of the Colombian musical styles over-

THE RHYTHM OF COLOMBIA

Here are 10 songs to get you into Colombia's groove.

- 'Bonita,' Cabas
- 'Cuatro Rosas,' Jorge Seledon
- 'El Carpintero del Amor,' Andrés Cepeda
- 'Hijo de Tuta,' Lisandro Meza
- 'La Camisa Negra,' Juanes
- 'La Canoa Ranchá,' Grupo Niche
- 'La Vamo a Tumbar,' Grupo Saboneo
- 'Somos Pacifico,' Choquibtown
- 'Te Mando Flores,' Fonseca
- 'Vivo en Limbo,' Kaleth Morales

seas and has had the most influence on international music, from Mexico to Argentina and New York.

Salsa spread throughout the Caribbean and hit Colombia in the late 1960s. Cali and Barranquilla have since become Colombia's bastions of salsa music, but it's heard all across the country and is the most popular club music in Bogotá. Today, Colombia has innumerable salsa bands and plenty of excellent *salseros* (salsa singers). Considered among the best are Joe Arroyo from the Caribbean coast and Grupo Niche from Cali.

Joropo, the music of Los Llanos, is usually accompanied by a harp, *cuatro* (a type of four-string guitar) and maracas. It has much in common with the music of the Venezuelan Llanos.

Colombia has also generated many unique rhythms from the fusion of Afro-Caribbean and Spanish influences, including *porro, currulao, merecumbe, mapalé* and *gaita.*

Colombian Andean music is strongly influenced by Spanish rhythms and instruments, and differs noticeably from the indigenous music of the Peruvian and Bolivian highlands. Among typical old genres are the *bambuco, pasillo* and *torbellino,* instrumental styles featuring predominantly string instruments.

In the cities, especially Bogotá and Medellín, many discos play techno and house; big-name international DJs sometimes play both cities.

Literature

Think of Colombian literature and Nobel Laureate Gabriel García Márquez springs to mind. Colombia has a long (if modest) literary tradition, however, which began to form shortly after independence from Spain in 1819 and gravitated into the sphere of European romanticism. Rafael Pombo (1833–1912) is generally acclaimed as the father of Colombian romantic poetry and Jorge Isaacs (1837–95), another notable author of the period, is particularly remembered for his romantic novel *María,* which can still be spotted in cafes and classrooms around the country.

José Asunción Silva (1865–96), one of Colombia's most remarkable poets, is considered the precursor of modernism in Latin America. He planted the seeds that were later developed by Nicaraguan poet Rubén Darío. Another literary talent, Porfirio Barba Jacob (1883–1942), known as 'the poet of death,' introduced the ideas of irrationalism and the language of the avant-garde.

Talented contemporaries of García Márquez include poet, novelist and painter Héctor Rojas Herazo, and Álvaro Mutis, a close friend. Of the younger

Efraim Medina Reyes is making a name for himself as the author of quirky titles *Masturbation Techniques between Batman and Robin* (2003) and *Sexuality of the Pink Panther* (2004).

GABRIEL GARCÍA MÁRQUEZ – COLOMBIA'S NOBEL LAUREATE

Gabriel García Márquez, or 'Gabo' as he is affectionately known, is the key figure of Colombian literature. Born March 6, 1928 in the town of Aracataca in the department of Magdalena, he has written primarily about Colombia, but lived most of his adult life in Mexico and Europe.

García Márquez began writing as a journalist in the 1950s and worked as a foreign correspondent, from where he criticized the Colombian government and basically forced himself into exile. He gained fame through his novels, particularly *One Hundred Years of Solitude,* published in 1967. It mixed myths, dreams and reality, and tantalized readers with a new form of expression dubbed *realismo mágico* (magic realism) – now so popular that it is invariably the first genre that you will learn about in any introduction to Latin American literature course.

In 1982 García Márquez won the Nobel Prize for Literature. Since then, he has created a wealth of fascinating work that extends well beyond magic realism. *Love in the Time of Cholera* (1985) is a story based loosely on the courtship of his parents. *The General in his Labyrinth* (1989) is a historical novel that recounts the tragic final months of Simón Bolívar's life. *Strange Pilgrims* (1992) is a collection of 12 stories written by the author over the previous 18 years. *Of Love and Other Demons* (1994) is the story of a young girl raised by her parents' slaves, set amid the backdrop of Cartagena's inquisition. In 1996 García Márquez returned to his journalistic roots with the literary nonfiction novel *News of a Kidnapping*. The book relates a series of kidnappings ordered by Medellín cartel boss, Pablo Escobar.

García Márquez seemed to be tying up his career when he published the first volume of his memoirs, *Living to Tell the Tale,* in 2002, but didn't fail to surprise when he came back in 2004, at the age of 76, with yet another novel *Memories of My Melancholy Whores,* the story of a dying old man who falls in love with an adolescent girl who sells her virginity to support her family.

In May 2008 he announced that he had finished a new novel, a 'novel of love.' The title had not been announced as we went to press.

generation, seek out the works of Fernando Vallejo, a highly respected iconoclast who has claimed that García Márquez lacks originality and is a poor writer; popular young expat Santiago Gamboa; and Mario Mendoza and Laura Restrepo, prolific writers who have each cranked out five major works in recent years.

Television

The *telenovela*, incomprehensible to many English-speakers, with its over-the-top acting and convoluted soap-opera–style plots, dominates the airwaves in Colombia. Sitcoms and hour-long dramas are sometimes introduced, but they inevitably wind up turning into *telenovelas*, or disappearing. *Telenovelas* tend to only run a year or two. Channels Caracol and RCN battle it out for the top *telenovelas* in the country.

The Colombian media enjoy a high level of freedom of the press, and hard-hitting news shows and exposés are popular. The longest-running shows are *El Mundo Según Pirry, Septima Día* and *La Noche.*

Colombians, as a rule, have little interest in television shows from the United States, either dubbed or subtitled; your joking reference to *Friends* or *Seinfeld* is likely to get no more than a blank stare. Local versions of syndicated reality shows are popular though, including *Factor X,* the Colombian version of *American Idol,* and *Cambio Extremo,* the local incarnation of *Extreme Makeover,* the plastic surgery extravaganza.

Cinema

Colombian cinema is preoccupied with the country's dark side – the on-going civil war that continues to rage in the jungle, and the ever-present temptations of easy money in the drug business.

The most internationally famous of recent Colombian films, *Maria, Llena Eres de Gracia* (Maria Full of Grace, 2004), a Colombian-US coproduction, is about a pregnant 17-year-old flower-industry employee who leaves her small-town existence to smuggle heroin into the US as a mule. Catalina Sandino Moreno was nominated for an Academy Award for Best Actress for her role in the film.

Soñar No Cuesta Nada (Dreaming Costs Nothing, 2006) tells the story of a group of soldiers who discover a cache of millions of dollars hidden by the FARC in the jungle. Based on a true story, it chronicles their attempt to keep the money and their ultimate capture.

Colombia's most filmed city is Cartagena. The English-language adaptation of Márquez's *Love in the Time of Cholera* (2007) is the most recent movie filmed in this highly photogenic city.

Architecture

Colombia has some lovely colonial architecture. Cartagena is the real highlight here – the old walled city (p140) boasts tiled roofs, pleasantly worn balconies and flower-filled courtyards along twisting, narrow streets. Villa de Leyva (p105) and Popayán (p249) are also famous for their old-world charm.

Bogotá is home to a few well-preserved examples of 17th-century mannerist-baroque structures known as *arquitectura santafereña,* including the Capilla del Sagrario (p69) and the Casa del Marqués de San Jorge (p76).

The Spanish Empire left a legacy of many colonial churches and convents. In the early days these were generally small and modest, but later tended to reach monumental dimensions. Unlike in Mexico or Peru, colonial churches in Colombia have rather austere exteriors, but their interiors are usually richly decorated. Cali's Iglesia de la Ermita (p242) is a good example of this style.

Modern urban architecture tends toward the functional rather than inspirational, and there is little of note. Bogotá and Medellín, in particular, have impressive skylines of glass, cement and steel.

> In the late 1990s, *Yo Soy Betty la Fea* (I'm Ugly Betty) turned *telenovelas* on their head with a rarely seen unattractive (and decidedly comical) protagonist. It was a hit across Latin America and was remade into the hit US show, *Ugly Betty*.

Painting & Sculpture

Fernando Botero is to Colombian painting what García Márquéz is to the country's literature – the name that overshadows all others. Both achieved their success as expatriates, which in itself says something about the arts climate in Colombia.

Two other famous Colombian painters, often overlooked, are Omar Rayo (1928–), known for his geometric drawings, and Alejandro Obregón (1920–1992), a Cartagena painter famous for his abstract paintings.

Colombia is also home to a good deal of colonial religious art. Gregorio Vásquez de Arce y Ceballos (1638–1711) was the most remarkable painter of the colonial era. He lived and worked in Bogotá and left behind a collection

---

FAT BEFORE HIS TIME – THE HUGE SUCCESS OF BOTERO

Fernando Botero (b 1932) is the most widely recognized Colombian painter and sculptor. Born in Medellín, he had his first individual painting exhibition in Bogotá at the age of 19 and gradually developed his easily recognizable style – characterized by the abnormal fatness of his figures. In 1972 he settled in Paris and began experimenting with sculpture, which resulted in a collection of *gordas* and *gordos*, as Colombians call these creations. Today, his paintings dot the walls of world-class museums and his monumental public sculptures adorn squares and parks in cities around the globe, including Paris, Madrid, Lisbon, Florence and New York.

of more than 500 works, now distributed among churches and museums across the country.

Since the end of World War II, the most distinguished painters are Pedro Nel Gómez, known for his murals, watercolors, oils and sculptures; Luis Alberto Acuña, a painter and sculptor who used motifs from pre-Columbian art; Guillermo Wiedemann, a German painter who spent most of his creative period in Colombia and drew inspiration from local themes, though he later turned to abstract art; Edgar Negret, an abstract sculptor; Eduardo Ramírez Villamizar, who expressed himself mostly in geometric forms; and Rodrigo Arenas Betancur, Colombia's most famous monument-maker.

These masters were followed by a slightly younger generation, born mainly in the 1930s, including artists such as Armando Villegas, a Peruvian living in Colombia, whose influences ranged from pre-Columbian motifs to surrealism; Leonel Góngora, noted for his erotic drawings; and the most internationally renowned Colombian artist, Fernando Botero (see p41).

The recent period has been characterized by a proliferation of schools, trends and techniques. Artists to watch out for include Bernardo Salcedo (conceptual sculpture and photography), Miguel Ángel Rojas (painting and installations), Lorenzo Jaramillo (expressionist painting), María de la Paz Jaramillo (painting), María Fernanda Cardozo (installations), Catalina Mejía (abstract painting) and the talented Doris Salcedo (sculpture and installations).

Theater & Dance

There are a number of large theaters in Bogotá that present classics, and the usual assortment of amateur, avant-garde theaters; the latter often boast more performers than audience members, as they're not of much interest to the average Colombian.

In Colombia, dance is something you do, not something you watch – and Colombians love to dance (see p38).

Bogotá (p88) and Medellín (p213) have the liveliest theater scenes. Of greater interest to aficionados are the biennial international theater festivals in Bogotá (p80) and Manizales (p208), which attract top-flight theaters from all over the Spanish-speaking world. The Bogotá festival culminates in a free fireworks spectacular at the football stadium.

Food & Drink

Colombians are blessed with a fertile country – fish and plantain on the coast; an eye-popping array of tropical fruit, coffee, chocolate and dairy in the mountains; and cheap, fresh vegetables and meat on all corners. The preferred cuisine is unseasoned, unspiced food, prepared simply and ungarnished. Simplicity is key here. This is not Mexico – put a drop of hot sauce in a vat of stew and no Colombian will touch it. This is not Argentina – the steak here is good, but not the *pampas*-fed delicacy of that southern country. Nor is it Spain, the colonial master whose political (and gastronomic) influence was never as strong here as it was elsewhere. Rice, beans, some meat or fish, a salad, fresh tropical fruit juice, and your average Colombian is content.

Or perhaps Colombians prefer simple food so they can taste the natural ingredients. The quality of food here is high (as is the high standard of hygiene in its preparation), meaning even those with the most jaded taste buds will find something unique to tempt their palate.

For 199 exceptional photographs and 133 regional recipes try the extraordinary *Taste of Colombia* (1997) by Benjamin Villegas and Antonio Montana.

STAPLES & SPECIALTIES

Colombian cuisine is referred to as *comida criolla* (Creole food). There are two distinct regional variations of *comida criolla* – the mountain highlands, where most of the population lives, and the Caribbean and Pacific coasts. They differ primarily in availability of ingredients (more fish and plantain on the coast, for example).

Breakfast in Colombia, regardless of region, is eggs. A popular Colombian variation is *huevos pericos* (eggs scrambled with tomato and onion). On the coast this is accompanied with *patacones* (mashed, fried plantain) and in the mountains, *arepa* (a thick corn tortilla), although some people prefer *almojábanas*, *pan de bono* (see Quick Eats, p46) or *buñuelos* (deep-fried curd-cheese-and-flour balls) instead. This is washed down with a small cup of *tinto* (black coffee) or hot chocolate made with milk. A less popular breakfast alternative is *caldo de costilla* (beef-rib broth).

For a sobering look at the food production industry in Colombia and its effect on the country, check out *Bananas and Business: The United Fruit Company in Colombia, 1899-2000* (2005) by Marcelo Bucheli.

The midday meal is *almuerzo*, and the typical plate, eaten everywhere, is *comida corriente* (literally, 'fast food'), often ironically called the *almuerzo ejecutivo* (executive lunch). It is a two-course meal which consists of soup followed by the *seco* (literally, the 'dry,' nonsoup portion of the meal) – rice, beans, choice of meat, a token salad, and a glass juice. On the coasts you're likely to see *patacones* instead of rice, and fish instead of chicken or beef. The meal tends to be heavy on the carbohydrates and light on the protein and fat.

Colombians prefer to eat dinner – which consists of the same basic staples as lunch – at home. For this reason many restaurants are open for lunch and closed for dinner.

The website www.onlinereceptenboek.nl has recipes for some of Colombia's most famous dishes.

Colombia boasts many regional specialties above and beyond rice and beans. *Sancocho* is a thick stew of meat, vegetables, yucca and corn; Colombians will argue passionately over which region makes the best *sancocho*. *Sancocho de gallina del campo* (farm-style chicken stew) is not to be missed. *Bandeja paisa* (the 'paísa platter') is a gut-busting mound of sausage, beans, rice, egg and *arepa*. Originally from Antioquia, the dish can be found across the country, and, indeed, the world – some New Yorkers swear by it as a hangover cure.

DRINKS
Nonalcoholic Drinks

Coffee is Colombia's number-one drink, and its biggest (legal) export. Vendors amble the streets with thermoses of coffee and milk and for a few

---

ALL HAIL THE MIGHTY LULO

No trip to Colombia is complete without sampling the country's astonishing variety of tropical fruit. All the usual suspects are present here, including *piña* (pineapple), mango and papaya, and three kinds of passion fruit – the tart yellow *maracuyá*, sweet orange *granadilla*, and tiny, mouth-puckering *curuba*. Some may recognize the feijoa and the tamarillo (and its paler cousin, *tomate de árbol*); those who've been to Cuba will recognize the *mamey sapote*, principally on Colombia's Caribbean coast. *Guayaba* (guava) is cheap, and even the poorest of the poor still send their children off to school with glass jars of homemade guava juice.

There are many other fruits seen almost nowhere else in the world. The *uchuva* (physalis, or ground cherry) has been spotted in North American supermarkets, exported from Colombia; the size of a grape, they are sweet and tart; pop them whole into your mouth. The *guanabana* (soursop) you're less likely to see overseas, as it travels poorly, but it makes divine juice, especially when made with milk. The Chocó boasts the *borojó*, rumored to be an aphrodisiac. Street vendors often sell the *mamoncillo*, similar to lychee or rambutan, but with a smooth, green skin.

A highlight is the *lulo*. It is indigenous to Colombia; aside from the border regions with Ecuador and Venezuela, it is grown nowhere else. It resembles a persimmon, and is orange, with a thin, inedible skin covered in microscopic spines that prick the fingertips. If they bother you, run your fingers through your hair – the oil will remove the tiny spines. A *lulo* is not ripe and ready to eat until very soft. Your thumb should make an indentation and not spring back. Before then it is unpleasantly tart.

The *lulo*, like most fruit in Colombia, is consumed in the form of juice. It also forms the base for *champús* and *luladas*, both delightful concoctions of Cali and Popayán. Astonish the locals by eating *lulo* straight, with a spoon. Or, for a mouth-watering light breakfast, try a bowl of quality granola, sugar-free yogurt and a fresh, super-ripe *lulo* scooped on top. Grate fresh nutmeg over the lot. It's not the Colombian way – but it is divine!

---

coins will pour you a small plastic cup of *tinto* (black coffee, called *perico* in Bogotá), *pintado* ('painted' with a little milk), or *cafe con leche* (with more milk).

Those planning a pilgrimage to the land of Juan Valdéz may be in for something of a disappointment, however. In contrast to neighboring Venezuela, Colombia exports all of its very best beans, leaving a mediocre brew for its own citizens. You can also visit coffee plantations in the Zona Cafetera – well worth doing at harvest time – and purchase coffee directly from the growers.

Less known is that Colombia also produces tea. The lush, green tropical hills mimic those of Darjeeling, although they produce a far less sought-after product. Most tea sold in Colombia is grown domestically, and while it's drinkable it's not the proper cuppa you may be accustomed to. Loose leaf is difficult to find.

Coffee in Colombia, 1850-1970: An Economic, Social and Political History (1980) by Marco Palacios is an academic look at how coffee changed the Colombian economy and played a role in developing the nation.

More popular than black tea in Colombia is herbal tea *(tisanes)*. Popular varieties include *cidrón* (citrus leaves), *yerbabuena* (mint) and *manzanilla* (chamomile). Those looking to doze off before a long bus ride should try *valeriana* (valerian), which will knock you right out.

Other popular hot drinks include *aguapanela* – raw, unrefined cane sugar *(panela)* cooked in boiling water with a squeeze of lemon juice – and *chocolate santafereño*, which is hot chocolate served with freshly curded cheese at the bottom of your mug.

Colombians produce and consume vast quantities of soft drink *(gaseosa)*. In addition to the usual suspects, Postobón produces sickly sweet fruit-flavored *gaseosas* in flavors like grape and apple. Less popular is the sweet cola Colombiana, for hard-core sugar freaks only.

Those wanting a quick thirst-quencher in Colombia's often toasty climate should look first at the water faucet – Colombian tap water is good to drink. No, really. The tap water in Bogotá, Medellín, Cali, most of the Zona Cafetera, and in many of the small mountain towns may be consumed without a second thought. The only important exception to this rule is the Caribbean coast, where the infrastructure is poor and the water toxic. Colombians are proud of their tap water. If you're in a smaller town and you're not sure, ask.

Alcoholic Drinks

Colombians like to drink. They don't tend to drink with meals and when they do go out drinking, many Colombians drink to get drunk. The preferred beverages for this purpose are beer, rum and aguardiente.

Colombian beer is of the thin, pilsner variety popular in Latin America. This is understandable; in the tropical heat, you want something refreshing, not microbrewery finesse. There is no competition in the Colombian beer market – every bottle of domestic beer is produced by Bavaria, a subsidiary of SABMiller of South Africa. Club Colombia is the best of the lot. Other beers include Águila (popular on the Caribbean coast), Poker (seen more in the south), Pilsner (of Medellín), Brava (a sweet, high-alcohol brew), and the ubiquitous Costeña, whose main virtue is being cheap.

Whichever beer you imbibe, be sure to ask for it *michelada*. Seen nowhere else in South America, *cerveza michelada* is beer served in a glass rimmed with rock salt with a shot of lime juice in the bottom. It is refreshing on a hot day, and available countrywide.

Colombian rum is excellent. It is amber-colored; white rum and Jamaican-style black rum are not popular and are hard to find. Colombian rum is smooth, goes down easy and is good value for the price. Two main brands dominate the market: Ron de Caldas and Ron Medellín. Many travelers say they prefer Ron de Caldas. Supermarkets carry aged versions of the same brands, which have exceptional flavor if you don't mind paying a bit extra. In Bogotá you may also find the white rum, Tres Esquinas.

Aguardiente is an aniseed-flavored white liquor popular in Colombia and sometimes seen in Venezuela. It is sickly sweet and at 27% alcohol, packs a punch. Colombians prefer it to rum because it is cheaper. Most travelers don't like it, but it's worth trying at least once. Brands tend to be regional. Blanco de Valle is from Cali, Antioqueña from Medellín, and Cristal and Nectar from Bogotá. Supermarkets carry a sugar-free version that claims to offer a less-severe hangover.

In nightclubs it is typical to purchase a whole bottle of rum or aguardiente (or both) to share among the group. Both are generally consumed straight-up in small plastic cups. The cocktail is undeveloped in Colombia and, in many places, unknown.

Colombia has a few vineyards producing mediocre wine that are mainly good for novelty value. Quality imported Chilean and Argentine wines are widely available.

In rural areas you may come across *guarapo* or *chicha* (the latter not to be confused with the nonalcoholic beverage from Peru of the same name). They are homemade alcoholic beverages made by fermenting maize and *panela* and sometimes fruit. The strength of this homebrew can vary a lot, so sip wisely.

CELEBRATIONS

Drinking and dancing are essential parts to any Colombian celebration. Colombians attending gringo parties in Colombia are always baffled by the English speaker's desire to sit down. What's the point of a party if you can't dance?

> The main bar zone in a city is called the *zona rosa*. This is where you'll find the city's most happening nightlife.

> For anything that you might want to learn about Colombia's coffee industry (the government version of the story, anyway), go to www .juanvaldez.com.

> Slang for a hangover in Colombia is *guayabo* (wa-ya-bo); literal translation: 'guava tree.'

For this reason bars and pubs as such do not really exist in Colombia. Music tends to be loud and the dance floor a central point of the architecture. Those wanting a quiet drink earlier in the evening may like to find an *estanco*, a small, streetside bar, often with no interior seating, that sells cheap beer to go or to drink at the small huddle of plastic chairs and tables.

As far as food goes, because of Colombia's location at the equator, farmers harvest all year round, so there is little variation in ingredients throughout the year; there is no seasonal produce. That said, Colombians are fond of turkey at Christmas time, and *natilla*, a kind of sweet milk pudding, is the typical Christmas dessert. *Buñuelos*, although eaten throughout the year, are also a typical Christmas treat. They are made of small, white, curd cheese and rolled with flour into doughy balls, then deep-fried until golden brown.

During Semana Santa (Holy Week), it is customary to celebrate an abbreviated form of Lent by eating only fish during that week; but even this rule is honored more in the breach than the observance. (*No hay nada mas larga que una semana sin carne*, goes the Colombian proverb – there's nothing longer than a week without meat.)

Regardless of the celebration or occasion – baby shower or birthday, Christmas or Easter – in Colombia the host provides all the food and drink. The guests need bring only their appetites.

WHERE TO EAT & DRINK

Travelers happy to eat a typical set meal will have no trouble finding a filling lunch, from COP$3000 to COP$8000. *Restaurantes* serving *comida corriente* are ubiquitious throughout the country, although many open for lunch only.

Breakfast and dinner can be more problematic. Fewer restaurants are open in the early morning and evening hours as Colombians generally eat these meals at home. You can usually find a *panadería* (bakery) serving hot rolls and coffee in the morning, and a few restaurants will usually be open serving a typical egg-based breakfast, priced from COP$3000 to COP$5000.

Those interested in finer dining should plan on venturing out in the evening. The major cities all have restaurant districts where you can browse a dozen or so spots and inspect the menus before deciding. You'll pay from COP$15,000 to COP$30,000 a main in the better restaurants.

Colombians enjoy a good burger and roasted chicken as much as anyone, and a quick (if not inspiring) meal can be had from COP$5000 to COP$10,000, including french fries.

Upscale supermarkets in Colombia often have a handful of independent restaurants selling wraps, sushi, pastries etc inside the store, and are usually good value. In any event a visit to the supermarket is heartily recommended, to marvel at the wide array of fruit and to stock up on Colombia's fabulous (and fabulously cheap) dark chocolate.

Quick Eats

Colombia has plenty of street vendors and as a general rule they are cheap and the food preparation hygienic.

In big cities, Colombians with the munchies head to their nearest *panadería*. The Colombian *almojábana* is a small, bun-shaped bread with a distinct tart flavor and is best eaten fresh from the baker's oven. It's made from yucca starch, maize flour and cheese.

In Cali and in the Valle de Cauca (around Cali) *almojábanas* are called *pan de bono* and are bagel-shaped instead of bun-shaped. Although *buñuelos* are technically Christmas fare they are eaten all year round, and are best enjoyed very fresh.

Secrets of Colombian Cooking (2004) by Patricia McCausland-Gallo is lacking on quality photographs, but has stellar recipes to show you how to make authentic Colombian food with black-belt precision.

Many of Colombia's best restaurants offer a 30% discount on Tuesdays (from March to November) to diners paying with a Visa card. See www .visa.com.co for details.

BIG-ASS ANTS

If you are out for a culinary adventure, try a *hormiga culona* (giant fried ant – or literally, 'ant with a big ass') or go ahead and get a kilo of the crispy critters. They are unique to Santander and aren't picked at on plates, but purchased by weight in shops. Make sure to go during the prime ant-eating season from March to May.

Empanadas (meat and/or cheese pastries) are ubiquitous and often served with a mildly piquant green sauce; quality can vary from the mind-blowing homemade variety to the microwaveable frozen kind in some bars.

In some of the smaller mountain towns you can expect to see women selling homemade *arepas* grilled over impromptu oil-drum barbecues. Made principally with white corn, they are served with butter and salt; for a gooey treat go for *arepa con queso* (*arepa* stuffed with cheese). A Venezuelan-style *arepa*, which is a thicker version, is popular on the Caribbean coast; you may also spot them here and there in the cities. *Arepa con huevo* is a popular, greasy snack. It's prepared by taking the Venezuelan-style *arepa*, cutting it down the middle, cracking a whole raw egg into the center and then deep-frying the lot.

Brits, Aussies and Kiwis will be delighted to find Colombians make awesome meat pies. Called *pasteles de hojaldre* (pastry pies), they are hearty and packed with meat. You'll find these in upscale *panaderías* and in supermarket bakeries.

Fresh fruit is a popular snack in Colombia; expect to see street vendors at most major intersections. *Mango viche* (crunchy green mango served with lime juice and salt) is popular. In Cali and parts of the Pacific and Caribbean coasts, you'll see women on street corners selling *chontaduro*, a typical mid-afternoon snack. If you come across a street vendor with what looks like a fish tank of red liquid, you're about to enjoy *salpicón*, a watermelon-based fruit salad. Slices of pineapple and papaya are also very popular, and are sold in plastic bags so your fingers don't get sticky.

When ordering a steak, ask for rare (*jugoso*), medium-rare (*medio-jugoso*), medium-well (*tres-quatro*), or well-done (*bien cocinado*).

VEGETARIANS & VEGANS

Vegetarianism is not particularly popular in Colombia. There are a handful of vegetarian restaurants in the major cities, most of which serve lunch only. Vegetarians may like to ask for a set lunch (*comida corriente*) without the meat, but be aware that the beans are often cooked with traces of lard or bacon fat.

Supermarkets are probably your best bet if you want control over what goes into your mouth. Colombian supermarkets offer a full range of fresh vegetables and fruit at prices that would make a North American or European jealous.

HABITS & CUSTOMS

When a Colombian invites you out to eat it is expected that they will pay (*te invito*). Likewise, if you invite someone out to eat it is expected that you will pay. The exception to this rule is if you are on a date, in which case the man is expected to pay.

Midrange and top-end restaurants may add a 10% service charge to the bill. In midrange establishments it is acceptable to politely decline to pay this charge (*sin servicio, por favor*); unless you give it to your waiter directly, tips rarely make it into their hands and will usually end up in the manager's till. In top-end places you should pay the service charge unless you feel the service was in some way substandard.

TOP EATS IN COLOMBIA

Colombia is not generally known for its culinary delights. Picky eaters might be disappointed. The following offer the best options for a Colombian dining experience:

- Color de Hormiga, Barichara (p124)
- Andrés Carne de Res, Chía, Bogotá (p85)
- Antique, Villa de Leyva (p109)
- El Maná, San Gil (p121)
- Quinua y Amaranto, La Candelaria, Bogotá (p84)
- Anderson's, La Candelaria, Bogotá (p84)
- Donde Chucho, Santa Marta (p169)
- Restaurante La Regatta, San Andrés Town (p197)
- El Cantil, Guachalito (p279)
- El Solar, Cali (p245)
- Cali Viejo, Cali (p244)

EAT YOUR WORDS

The following is a list of words and phrases you may find useful, along with their pronunciations and English translations. See the Language chapter (p327) for more information on Colombian Spanish and its pronunciation.

Useful Phrases

I want..., please.
kee·*yeh* ro... por·fa·*vor* — Quiero..., por favor.

I'd like the set meal, please.
kee·*yeh* ro ra·la ko·*mee*·da ko·*ryen*·te·por·fa·*vor* — Quiero la comida corriente, por favor.

What is today's special?
kwal·es·el·*pla*·to·del·*dee*·a — ¿Cuál es el plato del día?

What do you recommend?
ke·me·re·ko·*myen*·da — ¿Qué me recomienda?

I'm a vegetarian.
soy·ve·khe·ta·*rya*·no/a — Soy vegetariano/a (m/f).

Is service included in the bill?
la·*kwen*·ta·een·*kloo*·ye·el·ser·*vee*·syo — ¿La cuenta incluye el servicio?

The menu/bill, please.
la·*kar*·ta/*kwen*·ta·por·fa·vor — La carta/cuenta, por favor.

Thank you, that was delicious.
moo·chas *gra*·syas es·*ta*·ba *moo* ee *ree* koh — Muchas gracias, estaba muy rico.

Food Glossary

agua (con/sin gas)	ah·gwa (kon/seen gas)	water (carbonated/noncarbonated)
agua de llave	ah·gwa day *jaw*·bay	tap water
agua potable	ah·gwa po·*ta*·ble	drinking water
aguacate	ah·gwa·*ka*·tay	avocado
ají	ah·*hee*	chili
ajiaco	a·hee·*a*·ko	similar to *sancocho*, a stew typical of the Bogotá region
ajo	a·*ho*	garlic
almojábana	ahl·mo·*hah*·ba·na	bun-shaped bread made from yucca starch, maize flour and cheese

arepa	a·*reh*·pa	thick corn tortilla
arequipe	a·ray·*kee*·pay	super sweet dessert of milk and sugar
arroz	a·*ros*	rice
avena	a·*bay*·nuh	oats; oat milk
azúcar	a·*soo*·kar	sugar
bandeja paísa	ban·*de*·kha pay·*ees*·a	platter with sausage, beans, rice, egg and *arepa*
borojó	bo·ro·*ho*	fruit from the Chocó; reputed aphrodisiac
buñuelos	boon·*way*·los	deep-fried curd-cheese-and-flour balls
cabro, cabrito	ka·bro, ka·*bree*·to	goat
calamar	ka·la·*mar*	squid
camarón	ka·ma·*ron*	shrimp
cangrejo	kan·*gre*·kho	crab
carne	*kar*·ne	meat
cerdo, chancho	*ser*·do, *chan*·cho	pork
cerveza	ser·*ve*·sa	beer
cerveza michelada	ser·*ve*·sa mee·chay·*la*·da	beer with lime and salt
ceviche	se·*vee*·che	raw seafood marinated in lime juice
ceviche guapense	se·*vee*·che gwa·*payn*·se	ceviche specialty of Guapi, served with mayonnaise and ketchup
champús	cham·*poos*	sweet drink made of *lulo* and corn
chicharrón	chee·cha·*ron*	fried chunk of pork or pork skins
chocolatina	cho·ko·la·*tee*·na	chocolate bar
choclo	*cho*·klo	sweet corn
chuleta	choo·*lay*·tah	breaded, fried meat
chuzo	*choo*·so	shish kebab
(la) comida corriente	(la) ko·*mee*·da ko·*ryen*·te	set menu or fast food
cordero	kor·*de*·ro	mutton, lamb
domicilio	do·mo·*see*·lee·o	home delivery
empanada	em·pa·*na*·da	meat and/or cheese pastry
ensalada	en·sa·*la*·da	salad
estofado	es·to·*fa*·do	stew
fruta	*froo*·ta	fruit
girafa	hee·*rah*·fah	giraffe; tall, thin three-liter jug of beer
helado	e·*la*·do	ice cream
hogao	o·*gow*	Medellín slang for *huevos pericos*
huevos fritos/revueltos	we·vos *free*·tos/re·*vwel*·tos	fried/scrambled eggs
huevos pericos	we·vos *pay*·ree·kos	eggs scrambled with tomato and onion
jamón	kha·*mon*	ham
jugo	*hoo*·go	juice
langosta	lan·*gos*·ta	lobster
langostina	lan·gos·*tee*·na	king prawn
leche	*le*·che	milk
lechona	le·*cho*·na	stuffed pig
lomo	*lo*·mo	beefsteak
lulada	loo·*lah*·dah	drink made from the juice and pulp of *lulo*
mantequilla	man·tay·*kee*·ya	butter
maracuyá	ma·ra·*koo*·ya	passion fruit

mariscos	ma·*rees*·kos	seafood
mondongo	mon·*don*·go	tripe
mora	*mo*·ra	blackberry
naranja	na·*ran*·ha	orange
oblea	o·*blay*·a	large wafer and *arequipe* 'sandwich'
pan	pan	bread
papas fritas	*pa*·pas *free*·tas	french fries
parrillada	pa·ree·*ya*·da	grilled meat
torta	*tor*·ta	cake
pasteles de hojaldre	pa·*stehl*·es day oh·*hal*·dray	pastry pies
pavo	*paw*·bo	turkey
pescado	pes·*ka*·do	fish
pollo, gallina	*poi*·yo, ga·*yee*·na	chicken
postre	*pos*·tre	dessert
queso	*kay*·so	cheese
sancocho	san·*koh*·cho	typical Colombian stew
sandía	san·*dee*·a	watermelon
sopa	*so*·pa	soup
tallarines	ta·ya·*ree*·nes	noodles
tinto	*tin*·toh	black coffee
tisane	tee·*sahn*	herbal tea
torta	*tor*·ta	cake
trucha	*troo*·cha	trout
verduras	ver·*doo*·ras	vegetables

Environment

One of Colombia's most appealing attractions is the diversity of its environment. From snowcapped, craggy Andean mountains and the flat plains of Los Llanos, to the lush tropical forests of the Amazon basin and rolling green valleys throughout – it's a total eye-candy experience. Nature lovers will be enamored with the abundance of flora and fauna. Despite its modest size, Colombia is the second most biodiverse country on earth.

THE LAND

Colombia may not be the biggest country in the world, but it's no lightweight. After you head south through the chain of Central American minicountries, it is the first South American behemoth. Colombia covers 1,141,748 sq km, roughly equivalent to the combined area of California and Texas (or France, Spain and Portugal). It is the 26th largest country in the world, and the fourth-largest in South America, after Brazil, Argentina and Peru.

While most people assume that Colombia is just a tropical land, the country's physical geography is amazingly varied. The country's environment is generally divided into five habitat categories: wet tropical forests, dry tropical forests, tropical grasslands, mountain grasslands, and deserts and scrublands.

The western part, almost half of the total territory, is mountainous, with three Andean chains – Cordillera Occidental, Cordillera Central and Cordillera Oriental – running roughly parallel north–south across most of the country. A number of the peaks are over 5000m, making them higher than anything in the United States. Two valleys, the Valle del Cauca and Valle del Magdalena, are sandwiched between the three cordilleras. Both valleys have their own eponymous rivers, which flow north, unite and eventually empty into the Caribbean near Barranquilla.

Apart from the three Andean chains, Colombia features an independent and relatively small range, the Sierra Nevada de Santa Marta, which rises from the Caribbean coastline to soaring, snowcapped peaks. It is the world's highest coastal mountain range, and its twin summits of Simón Bolívar and Cristóbal Colón (both 5775m) are the country's highest.

More than half of the territory east of the Andes is vast lowland, which is generally divided into two regions: Los Llanos to the north and the Amazon River basin to the south. Los Llanos, roughly 250,000 sq km in area, is a huge open swath of grassland that constitutes the Orinoco River basin. The Amazon, stretching over some 400,000 sq km, occupies Colombia's entire southeast and lies in the Amazon basin. Most of this land is covered by a thick rainforest crisscrossed by rivers.

Colombia also has a number of islands. The major ones are the archipelago of San Andrés and Providencia (in the Caribbean Sea, 750km northwest of mainland Colombia), the Islas del Rosario and San Bernardo (near the Caribbean coast), and Gorgona and Malpelo (along the Pacific coast).

WILDLIFE

Colombia claims to have more plant and animal species per square kilometer than any other country in the world. Its variety of flora and fauna is second only to Brazil's, even though Colombia is seven times smaller than its neighbor. Colombia's abundance of wildlife is the result of the country's varied climate zones and microclimates, which have spawned diverse ecosystems and allowed wildlife to evolve independently.

The famous German geographer and botanist Alexander von Humboldt explored and studied regions of Colombia and described it all in amazing detail in *Personal Narrative of Travels to the Equinoctial Regions of America, During the Year 1799-1804.*

Colombia is the only South American nation to have coastlines on both the Pacific Ocean and Caribbean Sea.

Animals

From pink dolphins to colorful parrots, tiny cats to giant rats, Colombia has some of the most diverse animal life on the planet. It has nearly 1700 recorded species of birds – 74 of which are native to the country – representing about 19% of all the birds on the planet. Colombia also has about 450 species of mammal (including 15% of the world's primates), 600 species of amphibian, 500 species of reptile and 3200 species of fish.

Some of the most interesting mammals include sleek cats such as the jaguar and the ocelot, red howler monkeys, spider monkeys, the three-toed sloth, giant anteaters, the goofy piglike peccary and tapir, and the hideous-looking capybara, or *chiguiro*, the world's largest living rodent that can grow to 48cm tall and weigh 55kg.

The waters of Colombia's Amazon are home to the famous rose-colored *boto* (Amazon River dolphin), the Amazonian manatee, and one of the most feared snakes, the anaconda *(Eunectes murinus)*. Contrary to the Jennifer Lopez movie, anacondas are rarely longer than 6.1m (20ft). Still, that's a big-ass snake.

Colombia's famous aviary includes 132 species of hummingbirds, 24 species of toucans, 57 types of colorful parrots and macaws, plus kingfishers, trogons, warblers and six of the world's seven vultures, including the Andean Condor – a national symbol of Colombia.

There is also abundant marine life in the country's extensive river systems and along its two coastlines. The islands of San Andrés and Providencia boast some of the largest and most productive coral reefs in the Americas. In 2000 Unesco declared this area the Seaflower Biosphere Reserve in order to protect the ecosystem. The reefs are considered among the most intact in the Caribbean and play an important ecological role in the health of the sea. They provide feeding and nesting grounds for four species of endangered sea turtles and numerous types of fish and lobster. It has been determined that the health of certain fish stocks in the Florida Keys hinges directly on their ability to spawn in the Colombian reefs.

ENDANGERED SPECIES

The vast savannah of Los Llanos is home to some of the most endangered species in Colombia. Among them is the Orinoco crocodile, which can reach 7m in length. According to The Nature Conservancy, only 1800 of these crocs remain in the wild, making it one of the most critically endangered reptiles in the world. Other endangered creatures from Los Llanos include the Orinoco turtle, giant armadillo, giant otter and black-and-chestnut eagle.

The cottontop tamarin, a tiny monkey weighing just 500g, and its larger cousin, the brown spider monkey, are two of the most critically endangered primates in the world, according to the 2008 International Union for Conservation of Nature (IUCN) Red List of Threatened Species. Other critically endangered or endangered animals on the IUCN list include Handley's slender mouse opossum, mountain grackle and the mountain tapir.

Two of the Amazon River's most famous residents, the pink river dolphin and the Amazonian manatee are considered vulnerable.

Plants

Colombia's flora is equally as impressive as its fauna and includes more than 130,000 types of plant, a third of which are endemic species. This richness does not convey the whole picture: large areas of the country, such as the inaccessible parts of the Amazon, have undiscovered species. It is estimated that, at a minimum, 2000 plant species have yet to be identified and an even greater number have yet to be analyzed for potential medicinal purposes.

Bird-watching enthusiasts should pick up *A Guide to the Birds of Colombia* (1986) by Stephen L Hilty and William L Brown. Two great online resources for bird-watchers are www.colombiabirding.com and www.proaves.org.

Colombia is the world's second-largest exporter of cut flowers, after the Netherlands. About US$1 billion worth of flowers are exported every year, mostly to the US. Americans buy 300 million Colombian roses on Valentine's Day.

Colombia is the world's third-largest exporter of coffee (after Brazil and Vietnam). Between December 2007 and November 2008, Colombia exported nearly 700 million kg of coffee beans. For more info on Colombia's coffee, visit www.juanvaldez.com (no joke!).

Fans of orchids will be bloomin' excited to learn that Colombia has some 3500 species of orchids, more than any other country. Many of them are unique to the country, including *Cattleya trianae*, the national flower of Colombia. Orchids grow in virtually all regions and climate zones of country, but are mostly found in altitudes between 1000m and 2000m, particularly in the northwest department of Antioquia.

Further up into the clouds you will find the frailejón, a unique, yellow-flowering, perennial shrub that only grows at altitudes above 3000m. There are some 88 species of frailejón, most native to Colombia. You'll find them in places like Sierra Nevada de Santa Marta, Sierra Nevada del Cocuy and Santuario de Iguaque.

NATIONAL PARKS & RESERVES

Colombia has some of the most splendid, pristine nature in the Americas. The country has 55 national parks, flora and fauna sanctuaries and other natural reserve areas, all administered by the government's **Parques Nacionales Naturales (PNN) de Colombia** (www.parquesnacionales.gov.co).

Unfortunately, simply declaring an area a national park has not stopped the guerrilla activity, drug cultivation, illegal ranching, logging, mining or poaching. About a dozen national parks are located in guerrilla strongholds and are not safe for foreigners. This includes, sadly, the beautiful Sierra de la Macarena. Most parks in the Amazon Basin (except Amacayacu) and along the Ecuadorian border should also be considered off-limits. Other parks, such as Los Katios, a Unesco World Heritage Site near Darién Gap, are open but remain dodgy and access is limited; check the current security situation before proceeding.

On the bright side, many parks that were off-limits just a few years ago are now open for tourists, including most of El Cocuy and a good chunk of Sierra Nevada de Santa Marta. With the recent growth in tourism and ecotourism, the government is finally pumping pesos into its long-underfunded national parks system. New parks have recently opened and more are in the planning

For information on Colombia's national parks, visit the official government website at parquesnacionales.gov.co, or the park tourism site at www.colparques.net.

GREEN FEVER

Colombia produces the largest percentage of the world's emeralds (50%; compared to Zambia's 20% and Brazil's 15%). Some estimate that the mines inside Colombia may actually contain up to 90% of the world's emerald deposits. This is good news for emerald prospectors but may not bode so well for the local environment – and perhaps Colombia as a whole. The fighting and destruction related to the production of these glamorous gems has had an impact on the country not so different from cocaine and heroin.

The main emerald mining areas in Colombia include Muzo, Coscuez, La Pita and Chivor, all in the Boyacá department. Although the Muisca people mined emeralds in pre-Columbian times, the Spanish colonialists went crazy for the green stones and greatly expanded the operations. They enslaved the indigenous locals to mine the gems and eventually replaced those workers with slave labor from Africa. Many of today's miners are the direct descendants of those slaves and live in only slightly better conditions.

The areas' rich deposits have led to several environmental and social problems. Rampant digging has torn up the countryside and, in an attempt to find new digging sites or to improve their squalid living conditions, miners have continuously pushed further into the forest. Fierce battles have repeatedly been fought between rival gangs of miners, claiming lives and ravaging the mines. Between 1984 and 1990 alone, in one of the bloodiest 'emerald wars' in recent history, 3500 people were killed in Muzo. Yet 'green fever' continues to burn among fortune hunters and adventurers from the four corners of the country and it surely won't stop until the last bewitching green gem is mined.

stages. Established parks are finally getting much-needed visitor amenities such as lodging and dining facilities, a rarity in Colombia.

This has not necessarily been a good thing. In a controversial move, PNN has begun contracting with private companies to develop and operate tourist facilities inside some parks. Amacayacú on the Amazon River is now run by the luxury hotel chain Decameron. Sure, the park looks terrific now, with five-star cabins and a gourmet restaurant, but budget travelers and locals can no longer afford to visit this amazing place.

Colombia's most popular parks are situated along the country's pristine beaches. Parque Nacional Natural Tayrona is by far Colombia's most popular national park, followed by Parque Nacional Natural Corales del Rosario y San Bernardo and Parque Nacional Natural Isla Gorgona.

Gaviotas: A Village to Reinvent the World (1998), by Alan Weisman, tells the story of Colombian villagers who transformed their barren hamlet in Los Llanos into a global model for a sustainable community.

Many other national parks offer just simple accommodations including basic cabins, dorms or camping. Travelers wishing to stay overnight must book ahead with the PNN central office in Bogotá (p68). There are also PNN regional offices in most large cities and at the parks. Most parks have an admission fee, payable at the visitors center or regional PNN office.

It is always a good idea to check ahead of time with tour agencies and the parks department for up-to-date security and weather conditions of any park before visiting.

Private Parks

Perhaps the biggest news in the Colombian park scene has been the large growth of privately owned and operated nature reserves. These are run by individual proprietors, rural communities, foundations and nongovernmental organizations. Many are just small, family reserves, sometimes offering accommodations and food. About 230 of these private parks are affiliated with the **Asociación Red Colombiana de Reservas Naturales de la Sociedad Civil** (http://resnatur.org.co).

Yet another new player in the park scene is the corporation. Future parks might look a lot more like the new **Parque Nacional del Chicamocha** (www.parque nacionaldelchicamocha.com), near Bucaramanga. This for-profit, corporate-run resort opened in December 2006, at a reported cost of US$20 million. In

---

SNORTING THE RAINFOREST, ONE LINE AT A TIME

In 2006 Colombian vice president Francisco Santos Calderón launched a controversial marketing campaign linking casual drug use to the disappearance of the Amazon rainforest. The Shared Responsibility Initiative aims to dispel the myth that cocaine use is a victimless crime. The victim, in this case, is the Amazon ecosystem.

Calderón went a step further in November 2008, traveling abroad to plead his case directly to Europeans, who are the fastest-growing consumers of cocaine. According to Calderón, four sq meters of rainforest are destroyed for every gram of cocaine snorted. Drug money also helps fund the terrorist activities of Fuerzas Armadas Revolucionarias de Colombia (FARC) and other guerrilla groups, he argued. 'For somebody who drives a hybrid, who recycles, who is worried about global warming – to tell them that a night of partying will destroy 4 sq meters of rainforest might lead them to make another decision,' said Calderón.

Calderón admits he is fighting an uphill battle. The so-called 'war on drugs' has done little to curb the world's insatiable appetite for the white stuff. Since 2000, the US has given Colombia US$4.9 billion toward eradicating the cocaine trade. From a strategic perspective, this 'war on drugs' has been a complete and utter failure. An October 2008 report by the US government found that coca cultivation in Colombia has actually grown by 15% since 2000. Global street prices for cocaine are at record lows. Demand is up. The Amazon is down. Advocates for drug legalization argue that prohibition and unjust drug policies are the real culprits. The debate continues.

NATIONAL PARKS & PRIVATE RESERVES

Protected Area	Features	Activities	Best time to visit
Parque Nacional Natural Amacayacu (p292)	accessible to Amazon, reptiles, monkeys, fish, birds	canoeing, trekking, kayaking, wildlife spotting	August-April
Parque Nacional del Chicamocha (private; p125)	spectacular canyon and river, reptiles, birds	walking, bird-watching, paragliding, canopying, horseback-riding	year-round
Parque Natural Chicaque (private; p98)	cloud forest near Bogotá, birds	walking, bird-watching, horseback-riding	year-round
Parque Nacional Natural El Cocuy (p116)	spectacular alpine peaks, lakes and valleys	walking, trekking, horseback-riding	January-March
Parque Nacional Natural Corales del Rosario y San Bernardo (p152)	coral islands archipelago, fish, sea life	diving, snorkeling, swimming, kayaking	December-March
Parque Nacional Natural Farallones de Cali (p247)	tropical forests, mountains, cloud forests, waterfalls, monkeys	hiking, bird-watching, swimming, camping	year-round
Santuario de Flora y Fauna de Iguaque (p110)	mountain lakes, cultural history, historical sites	walking, hiking	January & February, July & August
Laguna de la Cocha (p264)	cloud-forest–covered island in a lake	walking, hiking, bird-watching, fishing	year-round
Parque Nacional Natural Isla Gorgona (p284)	tropical jungles and coral islands, humpback whales, monkeys	whale-watching, bird and wildlife spotting, swimming, hiking	February & March, September-December
Santuario de Flora y Fauna Los Flamencos (p180)	coastal lagoons and marshes, pink flamingos	bird-watching, canoeing	March-June, September-November
Santuario de Flora y Fauna Malpelo (p283)	tropical island and coral reefs, sharks, sea life	diving, snorkeling, beach-bumming	December-March
Parque Nacional Natural Old Providence (also known as McBean Lagoon; p198)	coastline and islets, mangroves, crabs, sea life	walking, snorkeling, diving, kayaking	year-round
Parque Nacional Natural Los Nevados (p225)	snowcapped Andean volcanoes and cloud forest	hiking, mountaineering	December-March, July & August
Parque Nacional Natural Tayrona (p173)	coastal rainforest and beaches, monkeys, corals	walking, trekking, swimming, snorkeling, diving, nude sunbathing	year-round
Parque Nacional Natural Puracé (p254)	volcano, Andean forests, waterfalls, hot springs	hiking, walking, bird-watching, fishing	year-round

addition to hiking and trekking opportunities, this commercial theme park features dozens of restaurants, cafes, thrill rides, a zoo, cable cars and, coming soon, a luxury hotel complex.

ENVIRONMENTAL ISSUES

Deforestation, soil erosion, poor water quality or quantity, and air pollution are all major issues affecting Colombia's environment, flora and fauna.

The issues behind Colombia's environmental problems run deep. Poverty and unequal land distribution, which have their roots back in the colonial era, are much to blame for the human encroachment into virgin forests. Each year settlers cut down nearly 405,000 hectares of forest, converting the land to fields. Nowhere is this impact more visible than from the air. Flying into Leticia's airport, peer out the window and you'll notice plumes of smoke rising as far as the eye can see. The Amazon rainforest is literally going up in smoke.

Like other countries, the rapid push to develop a market-based economy and compete globally has put pressure on Colombia to build on its land and exploit its natural resources. While similar environmental destruction occurred in North America and Europe many generations ago, the same thing is only just now happening in Colombia – before our eyes and video cameras.

Between 600,000 and 900,000 hectares of forest are lost every year to human encroachment, farming, legal and illegal logging, and mining and oil exploration. Such deforestation has increased the rate of extinction for many plant and animal species and destabilized soils, leading to the silting of rivers and devastation of marine species.

Even more troubling is the environmental impact of the illegal drug trade (see boxed text, p54). Estimates vary widely, but between 50,000 and 300,000 hectares are cleared every year to grow coca plants, the main ingredient in cocaine. Other illegal cash crops include marijuana and opium poppies. Attempts to stop farmers cultivating coca simply cause the producers to relocate. They move higher up the slopes and to the more remote, virgin forests of the Andes (aided by an increase in opium cultivation, which favors higher altitudes) and deeper into parks and the Amazon basin. Nearly two-thirds of the Colombian Andes, an area that is vital to the conservation of Colombia's water supply, has been deforested as a result of both migration and drug cultivation.

Cocaine processors certainly couldn't care less about following environmental regulations or about limiting their ecological footprint on the rainforest. Processing coca plants into cocaine is a hazardous job, requiring toxic chemicals including kerosene, sulfuric acid, acetone and carbide. These toxins are simply dumped on the ground or into delicate streams and rivers. In addition, armed guerrillas and drug runners operating in these forest areas have little respect for their impact on local wildlife.

Anti-drug efforts by the Colombian government (and, in large part, funded by the United States' war on drugs) have also taken their toll on the environment, though to a lesser extent. The most common method of eradication has been aerial fumigation of coca fields; these hazardous herbicides destroy not just the coca plants, but surrounding vegetation as well, and no doubt seep into the watershed.

Conservación Internacional is one of Colombia's most influential environmental advocacy groups. To learn more about their positive work, check out http://conservation.org.co

Conservation Efforts

After decades of ignoring the issue, Colombia is finally making major efforts to save its precariously sensitive environment. Colombia is a signatory of the Kyoto Protocol and other international environmental agreements. Environmental activism is a growing movement among young Colombians, and many environmental NGOs have launched in recent years including groups such as Conservación Internacional and ProAves.

International governments have also lent a helping hand. One major success story is the unprecedented 'debt for nature' Tropical Forest Conversation Act of 2004. Under the 12-year agreement, the US government's USAID organization and NGOs World Wildlife Fund, The Nature Conservancy and Conservación Internacional will contribute $10 million toward canceling part of Colombia's debt to the US. In return, Colombia will invest $10 million to protect tropical forests in key areas of the Andes, the Caribbean coast and Los Llanos plains in the Orinoco River basin.

Environmentalists now wield more clout in government policy. In 2006 Colombian president Álvaro Uribe signed the controversial General Forestry Law that opened up the country's forests to logging. Colombian and international environmental groups sued the government – and won. The Colombia Constitutional Court in 2008 ruled that the Forestry Law was unconstitutional because indigenous communities were never consulted. Score one for the greens.

Colombia Outdoors

Colombia is one of the most beautiful countries in the world. Exploring the dramatic variety of landscapes is a highlight of any visit – from the *páramo* (high-mountain plains) to the jungles of the Pacific coast, the stunning green lushness of the Zona Cafetera to the dry, Hades-like heat of the Caribbean coast, both the outdoor dabbler and the hard-core trekking guru will find something to fascinate them.

There's high-mountain trekking and mountaineering in Parque Nacional Natural (PNN) El Cocuy and Parque Nacional Natural (PNN) Los Nevados, white-water rafting and paragliding in San Gil, kitesurfing and windsurfing at Lago Calima and the Caribbean coast, world-class scuba diving near San Andrés, Capurganá and Isla Malpelo, whale-watching up and down the Pacific coast, sportfishing for marlin and sailfish on the coast of the Chocó, and bird-watching pretty much everywhere.

The most comprehensive guide to kitesurfing in Colombia can be found at www.colombiakite.com.

For decades the countryside held great danger, and Colombians were trapped in their cities. No longer. Now that peace has come to Colombia, locals and foreigners alike are taking advantage of the chance to get out and see what this amazing country has to offer.

KITESURFING & WINDSURFING

Colombia is one of the cheapest places in the world to go kitesurfing and windsurfing. The star spot is not where you might think. Lago Calima (1800m, p248), a man-made reservoir 86km north of Cali, boasts year-round 18 to 25 knot winds, and attracts world champions to its competitions held every August and September. There's no beach here; it's a man-made reservoir, after all, and access to the water is via the grassy slopes along the lake.

There's good kitesurfing on the Caribbean coast, where the winds are best from January to April. Good spots include La Boquilla (p155) just outside Cartagena, Cabo de la Vela (p181), Tolú (p184) and San Andrés (p191).

The casual traveler will find the learning curve for windsurfing much shorter than for kitesurfing; it's also a fair bit cheaper. Prices vary considerably. Expect to pay roughly COP$40,000 per hour for windsurfing instruction and COP$50,000 to COP$80,000 per hour for kitesurf instruction. Rentals go for around COP$40,000 to COP$50,000 per hour. If you've got your own gear, you'll pay COP$20,000 to COP$30,000 for each water entrance.

Brazil is famous for its jungle, Chile for the Andes, Venezuela for Los Llanos, Mexico for the Caribbean coast, Costa Rica for its surfing – Colombia has them all.

PARAGLIDING

Colombia's varied mountain terrain means there are lots of great thermals to ride if you want to go paragliding *(parapente)*. The country's paragliding capital is arguably Bucaramanga (p126), which attracts paragliders from around the world. Tandem flights are cheap – a mere COP$50,000 – which elsewhere in the country go for up to COP$80,000. You can also enroll in a 10-day paragliding course for COP$1 million and become an internationally accredited paragliding pilot.

Other popular spots for paragliding include nearby San Gil (p120) and Parque Nacional del Chicamocha (p125); urban paragliders can test their wings on the outskirts of Medellín (p208), where a number of schools offer tandem flights and instruction.

DIVING & SNORKELING

Colombia's Caribbean coast offers scuba diving at budget prices. San Andrés (p193) and Providencia (p200) offer classic Caribbean diving, with excellent

WHALE-WATCHING

Every year whales living near Chile's Antarctica waters make the 8000km journey to Colombia's Pacific coast to give birth and raise their young. These are humpback whales (*yubartas*, sometimes called *jorobadas*), and more than 800 have been recorded off the Colombian coast. They grow to 18m long and weigh up to 25 tons; there are few things cuter than spotting a *ballenato* (baby whale) already the size of a small truck, nosing its way through the surface.

The best whale-watching is from June through to November. Whales can be seen all along the Pacific coast, and there are comfortable resorts where you can relax before and after a boat tour. Sometimes whales come so close to shore they can be seen from the beach, or lookouts in the hills.

Popular spots to go whale-watching include Bahía Solano (p270), El Valle (p275), Nuquí (p277), Guachalito (p278), and Parque Nacional Natural (PNN) Ensenada de Utría (p276) in the Chocó. Buenaventura (p279) and Ladrilleros (p280) are also great whale-watching spots, and at nearby Isla Gorgona (p284) it's also possible to go scuba diving with the whales. Most whale-watching tours last 1½ to two hours and cost around COP$30,000 to COP$40,000 per person (although these prices can vary widely depending on the operator). Here we've detailed a few top spots to take a tour.

El Cantil The most luxurious hotel in Guachalito, near Nuquí, El Cantil has six duplex cabins, and is surrounded by papaya plants and coconut palms. A small hydroelectric plant produces power for the restaurant and bar; the cabins are entirely without electricity. Candles are provided, or bring your flashlight. The restaurant (which is famous for its food) sits a short walk up the hill, giving you a great spot from which to spot whales in season. It can organize whale-watching and diving expeditions, and has surfing guides who can show you where the best spots are. It runs the 'Surfing the Jungle' (www.nuquilatinprocolombia.com) surfing competition in November.

- Nearest town: Nuquí (see p277)
- Whale-watching package tour: COP$700,000 to COP$1 million
- Information: ☎ 57 4 252 0707; www.elcantil.com

visibility, fine coral reefs and a variety of marine life. There are even two sunken ships you can visit.

On the coast itself, Taganga (p172) offers some of the cheapest diving courses on the planet. Here you can get your PADI or NAUI certification for around COP$550,000 for a four-day course. The diving itself is second-rate, but at these prices, who cares?

Cartagena also boasts good diving nearby (see p145). The Islas de Rosario (p152) in particular is famous for its diving, although warm-water currents have damaged the reef somewhat, and the diving is no longer as good as it once was. Better still are the Islas de San Bernardo (p186) near Tolú.

Selva Humeda de Colombia by Richard Evans Schultes, et al, has some great photos of wildlife and the jungle in Colombia, and makes a great coffee-table book.

The Caribbean coast's real jewels for diving are the small towns of Capurganá and Sapzurro (p188), just minutes from the Panamanian border. Once too dangerous to visit, they are now slowly attracting adventurous travelers seeking the best beaches and reefs. The tricky bit is getting here – you'll either need to endure a long boat journey from Turbo, or fly from Medellín.

Colombia's Pacific coast, on the other hand, offers a completely different diving experience. There is slightly less visibility, but the quantity and size of the marine life is jaw-dropping. Isla Malpelo (p283), a small Colombian island 500km west of the continent, boasts schools of more than a thousand sharks. It can only be reached by joining a minimum eight-day live-aboard dive cruise from Buenaventura on Colombia's Pacific coast, Puntarenas in Costa Rica, or Puerto David, Panama.

El Almejal The most luxurious and expensive resort in the Bahía Solano area, El Almejal also has the most ingenious cabin design – the opposite walls of the sitting-room area open completely, allowing the sea breeze to pass right through. A small creek spills into a man-made swimming hole near the back of the cabins; select a nearby cabin for the soothing sound of flowing water to gently lull you to sleep. A turtle-breeding facility collects and hatches turtle eggs before returning them to the sea (September to December). Concrete stairs behind the hotel lead uphill to a lookout point – in whale-watching season you can sometimes spot whales playing in the waters just off the coast. Nonguests are also allowed to use the spot; just swing by reception first to ask permission.

- Nearest town: El Valle (see p275)
- Whale-watching package tour: COP$700,000 to COP$1 million
- Information: ☎ 57 4 230 6060; www.almejal.com.co

Parque Nacional Natural (PNN) Ensenada de Utría This narrow inlet of water is one of the best places to see whales close-up while staying on dry land. During the calving season the whales enter the *ensenada* (narrow bay) and play just a few hundred meters from shore. Long closed due to security concerns, the visitors center on the eastern shore of the *ensenada* was reopening at time of research, including newly refurbished cabins designed to accommodate up to 30 people.

- Nearest town: between Nuquí and El Valle (see p276)
- Whale watching: COP$300,000 to COP$400,000 per boat, plus accommodations and park entrance
- Information: contact tour agency Mano Cambiada in Nuquí; ☎ 314 618 8900, 311 872 7887; www.nuquipacifico.com

Isla Gorgona (p284), a larger island near the coast, also offers fine diving, and in whale-watching season you can observe them from below the waves. There are also some diving opportunities near Playa Huína, (p274) outside Bahía Solano, where a warship that survived Pearl Harbor has been sunk to create an artificial reef.

Colombia has numerous hyperbaric chambers, should you find yourself with a case of 'the bends.' On the Caribbean coast, there's the **Naval Hospital** (☎ 5 665 3987) on Isla del Rosario. On San Andrés, **Hospital Timothy Britton** (☎ 8 512 7444) has a decompression chamber. The only chamber on the Pacific coast is outside Buenaventura at **Base Naval Bahía Malaga Hospital** (☎ 2 246 0649, emergency 2 246 0871).

BIRD-WATCHING

Colombia has some of the greatest biodiversity of birds in the world, and easily rivals Venezuela next door. More than 1700 bird species have been recorded here. Even the casual observer will find plenty to delight – the Andean mountains are full of hummingbirds (more than 132 species), the Amazonian jungle is full of toucans, parrots and macaws, and Parque Nacional Natural (PNN) Puracé, outside Popayán, is home to three condors, which the wardens will tempt down with food so you can see them up close. The Pacific coast boasts swarms of pelicans, herons and other water birds.

Some 70% of the country's birds live in the Andean cloud forest, one of the most endangered ecosystems in the world. Good bird-watching spots

Birds of Northern South America (2007) by Robin Restall is the essential bird-watcher's field guide to Colombian birds, with full-color plates for every bird you're likely to see here.

include Río Blanco (p224) near Manizales, and Km18 (p243) near Cali. The Amazon basin near Leticia (p286) is also an excellent spot for jungle birds; as is the Chocó (p270). Colombia also boasts the western third of the Los Llanos (p134) region, shared by Venezuela, a fine spot to see the birds that region attracts.

For a countrywide overview of the Important Bird Areas (IBAs), an invaluable resource is http://aicas.humboldt.org.co, which breaks the country down by department. The Red Nacional de Observadores de Aves (Colombian Bird Watchers Network, RNOA, www.rnoa.org) is also a good place to start. For Andean bird-watching, you may be able to find a guide through www.mapalina.com.

Finding bird-watching guides in Colombia can be difficult. In many remote areas, locals can take you where they know birds are, but it'll be up to you to find them. One reputable bird-watching tour company is Colombia Birding (www.colombiabirding.com). Run by a bilingual Colombian, its network of local guides can show you around many of the country's most popular bird-watching areas. It charges US$100 per day plus expenses. Its website has information on birds by region in Colombia.

A Guide to the Birds of Colombia (1986), by Steven L Hilty and William L Brown, is a must for Amazon bird viewers, and this guide to Colombia's 1700 species of birds has no rival for its coverage of birds of the Amazon basin.

CANOPYING

Sometimes called 'zip lines' in North America, this sport involves strapping yourself into a harness and zipping around the forest canopy on cables. You use a heavy leather glove on top of the cable to brake.

The last several years have seen an explosion in popularity of this sport in Colombia, particularly in the mountain regions. One of the best is in Río Claro, halfway between Medellín and Bogotá, where a series of canopy lines zigzags across the river. It's a hoot in its own right, and it also provides a great vantage point from which to spot the local birds.

Other spots where you can go canopying include Los Yarumos (p224) outside Manizales, Las Ardillas (p251) near Popayán, the shores of Embalse Guatapé (p215), outside Medellín, and Termales San Vicente (p231) outside Pereira. There are also several canopy lines near Villa de Leyva (p105) and San Gil (p119).

HIKING & TREKKING

Colombia has some of South America's best hiking opportunities. The country is most famous for two long treks in particular. One, Ciudad Perdida (p177) on the Caribbean coast, can only be reached by a sweaty, six-day trek through the jungle and across waist-high rivers. At the end you arrive at the long-forgotten ruins of the Tayrona civilization. The other, El Cocuy (p112), is a high-mountain trek that rarely drops below 4000m and crosses glaciers along the way. The scenery is among Colombia's best, and those with the lungs for it should not miss it.

For comprehensive information on bird-watching in Colombia, see www.proaves.org.

The casual hiker looking for good one-day walks has many options to choose from. The country's best one-day hike is the Valle de Cocora (p237), outside Salento. This walk takes you up into the national park amid wax palms – the largest palm in the world, and Colombia's national tree. Manizales (p220) has numerous walks nearby. The one-day trip to the slopes of Nevado del Ruiz in Parque Nacional Natural (PNN) Los Nevados (p225) is popular. Short walks in Recinto del Pensamiento (p223), Río Blanco (p224) and Los Yarumos (p224) are also worth the trip.

Those wanting a taste of the jungle have several options on the Pacific coast, including a recommended walk from El Valle (p275) to Lachunga at the northern end of the Ensenada de Utría (p276), where you can visit and stay the night in the national park. In Capurganá (p188) you can walk across the frontier to visit beautiful La Miel, a beach just north of the Panamanian border.

In the south of the country, Tierradentro (p258) boasts a spectacular one-day walk that traverses a triangular ridgeline and visits all of the nearby tombs. Weather permitting, Volcán Puracé (p254) near Popayán can be summited in one day, and the Farallones de Cali (p247) outside that city have several day walks, and longer walks.

MOUNTAIN BIKING

There's something about mountains that makes bicyclists want to conquer them. Bicycling is very popular in Colombia, although most of it is road cycling. Mountain biking per se is most popular in San Gil (p119) and Villa de Leyva (p105) where several bike rental shops can facilitate your adrenaline fix. A local group in Bogotá also organizes mountain-biking trips in the outskirts of the city (p79). Prices for bike rental vary from region to region, depending on the quality of the bike – expect to pay anywhere from COP$10,000 to COP$50,000 per half-day bike rental.

For a longer, more challenging mountain-bike ride, Kumanday Expeditions in Manizales (p221) offers four-day bike trips through the high-mountain *páramo* of Parque Nacional Natural (PNN) Los Nevados. Because of the remoteness and altitude (over 4000m), a guide and support vehicle are mandatory. This tour doesn't run often, and isn't cheap. You'll need to contact Kumanday for its latest prices, which will also vary depending on the size of your group.

WHITE-WATER RAFTING, CANOEING & KAYAKING

The rafting capital of Colombia is San Gil (p119). The rapids are spectacular Class IV and V; you're in for some serious thrills (and spills). San Agustín (p255) is a close second. Here you can go white-water rafting on the Río Magdalena, one of Colombia's most important rivers. There are easy Class II and III trips, and longer, more difficult trips for the experienced rafter. For a quiet paddle through the jungle, Río Claro (p219), roughly halfway between Medellín and Bogotá, offers smooth Class I trips along the nearby river. It's a fine spot to admire the flora and fauna instead of obsessing about falling out of the raft.

Canoeing and kayaking aren't especially popular in Colombia, but you can rent kayaks in both San Gil and San Agustín. You can also rent sea kayaks in Ladrilleros (p280) for a paddle around Bahía Malaga.

To encourage adventure tourism, the Colombian government has deployed the army to many of the most popular outdoor spots to make them safe for foreign tourists.

Bogotá

Cradled by cool Andean peaks and named after a nearby ancient site, Colombia's engaging capital is a city of 1000 neighborhoods – each adding a different take on a lively metropolis. On one hand, Bogotá is still slowly recovering from an enduring perception as a dangerous hot bed of drugs and street crime; at the same time it's a surprising leader in forward-thinking progressive projects. On Sundays 122km of roads are closed to cars and left for more than a million locals to enjoy on bikes, while the recently built TransMilenio bus system purposely connects posh 'fantasy land' neighborhoods in the north with working-class ones in the south.

Most visitors here gravitate to the cobbled historic center – La Candelaria – where senators lunch at restaurants housed in 300-year-old homes that reinvent themselves as drinks-only venues after hours for the lively (lefty) student scene. Most traditional attractions are here – radiating out from Plaza de Bolívar – and gorgeous Cerro de Monserrate is just east.

It's a very different scene up north, where you'll find boutique hotels, safe strolls after dark, and well-heeled locals piling into chic districts like Zona Rosa. The flip side of the city, of course, is the grittier south and southwest. These barrios get a bad rap, and some aren't altogether safe to visit, but areas like the cheerful Cuadra Picha club zone welcome all.

Then at night Bogotá's steady flow of drinks will make you light-footed. Try a hot mug of *canelazo* (aguardiente, sugarcane, cinnamon and lime), which comes sugar-coated and filled with the local spirit. Or indulge in the city's one great unifier and dunk a chunk of white cheese right into your hot chocolate. Hey, it's the one thing every *bogotano* seems to agree on.

HIGHLIGHTS

- Ogle evidence of the country's El Dorado myths with the glittering displays in the **Museo del Oro** (p77)
- Add cheese to your hot chocolate – a Bogotá tradition – in a La Candelaria cafe, such as **La Puerta Falsa** (p83)
- Take a Sunday trek, among the pilgrims, up the towering **Cerro de Monserrate** (p76) for a sweeping view of the capital
- Ponder all things plump at the (free!) **Museo Botero** (p72)
- Hit Bogotá's club scene – there's one for everyone: camp drag shows at **Vinacure** (p88), live coastal-style vallenato shows at **Gaira Café** (p87) or a working-class club ghetto at **Cuadra Picha** (p88)

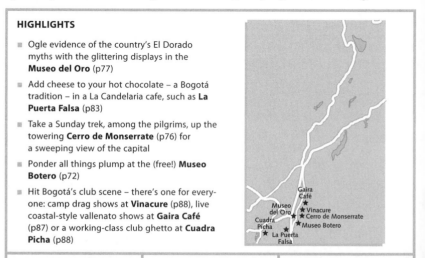

■ TELEPHONE CODE: 01   ■ POPULATION: 8 MILLION   ■ ELEVATION: 2574M

HISTORY

Long before the Spanish Conquest, the Sabana de Bogotá, a fertile highland basin which today has been almost entirely taken over by the city, was inhabited by one of the most advanced pre-Columbian Indian groups, the Muisca. The Spanish era began when Gonzalo Jiménez de Quesada and his expedition arrived at the Sabana, founding the town on August 6, 1538 near the Muisca capital, Bacatá.'

The town was named Santa Fe de Bogotá, a combination of the traditional name, Bacatá, and Quesada's hometown in Spain, Santa Fe. Nonetheless, throughout the colonial period the town was simply referred to as Santa Fe.

At the time of its foundation Santa Fe consisted of 12 huts and a chapel where a mass was held to celebrate the town's birth. The Muisca religious sites were destroyed and replaced by churches.

During the early years Santa Fe was governed from Santo Domingo (on the island of Hispaniola, the present-day Dominican Republic), but in 1550 it fell under the rule of Lima, the capital of the Viceroyalty of Peru and the seat of Spain's power for the conquered territories of South America. In 1717 Santa Fe was made the capital of the Virreynato de la Nueva Granada, the newly created viceroyalty comprising the territories of present-day Colombia, Panama, Venezuela and Ecuador.

Despite the town's political importance, its development was hindered by the area's earthquakes, and also by the smallpox and typhoid epidemics that plagued the region throughout the 17th and 18th centuries.

After independence the Congress of Cúcuta in 1821 shortened the town's name to Bogotá and decreed it the capital of Gran Colombia. The town developed steadily and by the middle of the 19th century it had 30,000 inhabitants and 30 churches. In 1884 the first tramway began to operate in the city and, soon after, railway lines were constructed to La Dorada and Girardot, giving Bogotá access to the ports on the Río Magdalena.

Rapid progress came only in the 1940s with industrialization and the consequent peasant migrations from the countryside. On April 9, 1948 the popular leader Jorge Eliécer Gaitán was assassinated, sparking the uprising known as El Bogotazo. The city was partially destroyed; 136 buildings were burnt to the ground and 2500 people died.

Tranquil life in Bogotá was rocked again on November 6, 1985 when guerrillas of the M-19 revolutionary movement invaded the Palace of Justice in Bogotá and made hostages of the 300-plus civilians in the building. By the next day, 115 people were dead, including 11 supreme court judges.

In the past decade or so, Bogotá has made many surprising advances – murder rates are down by a reported 70%, and a host of progressive projects under successive mayors (eg the 300km of CicloRuta bike lanes).

CLIMATE

Bogotá is the third-highest capital in South America, after La Paz and Quito. It sits at an altitude of about 2600m; at this height altitude sickness can occur. You may feel a bit dizzy when you arrive. Take it easy for a day or two – it should soon go away. See p325 for more information.

The main dry season lasts from December to March, and there is also a second, less dry period with only light rainfall from July to August. The wettest months are April and October. The mean annual rainfall is about 1020mm.

The city's average temperature is 14°C year-round. The temperature drops to about 9°C at night and rises to around 18°C (higher on sunny days) during the day. In the rainy season there is less difference between daytime and nighttime temperatures.

ORIENTATION

Sprawling Bogotá stretches mostly north–south (and west in recent years) with the towering peaks of Monserrate and Guadalupe providing an easterly wall.

Locating an address in the city is generally a breeze. Calles run east–west, rising in number as you go north, while Carreras go north–south, increasing in number as they go west (away from the mountains). Handily, any street address also indicates the nearest cross streets; Calle 15 No 4-56, for example, is on 15th Street between Carreras 4 and 5.

The bulk of visitors stick with two major areas of Bogotá – Central Bogotá and Northern Bogotá.

Central Bogotá has four main parts: the partially preserved colonial sector La Candelaria (south of Av Jiménez and between Carreras 1

BOGOTÁ

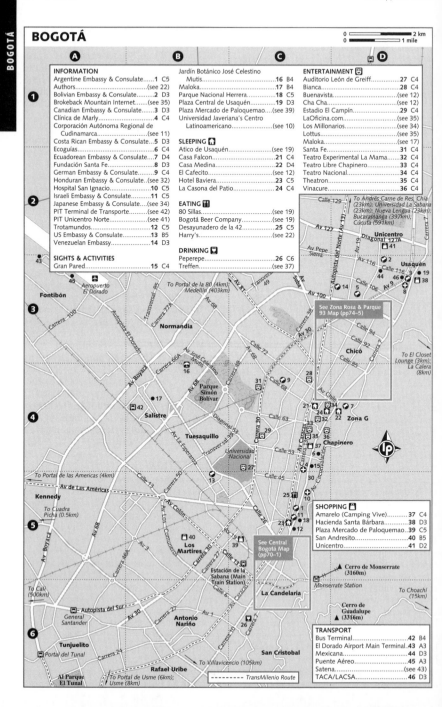

0 —————— 2 km
0 —————— 1 mile

INFORMATION
Argentine Embassy & Consulate......**1** C5
Authors...(see 22)
Bolivian Embassy & Consulate........**2** D3
Brokeback Mountain Internet.......(see 35)
Canadian Embassy & Consulate......**3** D3
Clínica de Marly..............................**4** C4
Corporación Autónoma Regional de
  Cudinamarca..............................(see 11)
Costa Rican Embassy & Consulate...**5** D3
Ecoguías...**6** C4
Ecuadorean Embassy & Consulate...**7** D4
Fundación Santa Fe........................**8** D3
German Embassy & Consulate........**9** C4
Honduran Embassy & Consulate..(see 32)
Hospital San Ignacio.....................**10** C5
Israeli Embassy & Consulate..........**11** C5
Japanese Embassy & Consulate...(see 34)
PIT Terminal de Transporte.........(see 42)
PIT Unicentro Norte....................(see 41)
Trotamundos................................**12** C5
US Embassy & Consulate...............**13** B5
Venezuelan Embassy.....................**14** D3

SIGHTS & ACTIVITIES
Gran Pared...................................**15** C4

Jardín Botánico José Celestino
  Mutis..**16** B4
Maloka...**17** B4
Parque Nacional Herrera...............**18** C5
Plaza Central de Usaquén.............**19** D3
Plaza Mercado de Paloquemao....(see 39)
Universidad Javeriana's Centro
  Latinoamericano......................(see 10)

SLEEPING
Atico de Usaquén........................(see 19)
Casa Falcon.................................**21** C4
Casa Medina................................**22** D4
El Cafecito..................................(see 12)
Hotel Baviera...............................**23** C5
La Casona del Patio.....................**24** C4

EATING
80 Sillas......................................(see 19)
Bogotá Beer Company.................(see 19)
Desayunadero de la 42................**25** C5
Harry's...(see 22)

DRINKING
Peperepe....................................**26** C6
Treffen..(see 37)

ENTERTAINMENT
Auditorio León de Greiff.............**27** C4
Bianca...**28** C4
Buenavista...................................(see 12)
Cha Cha......................................(see 12)
Estadio El Campín........................**29** C4
LaOficina.com.............................(see 35)
Los Millonarios...........................(see 34)
Lottus..(see 35)
Maloka..(see 17)
Santa Fe......................................**31** C4
Teatro Experimental La Mama......**32** C4
Teatro Libre Chapinero................**33** C4
Teatro Nacional..........................**34** C4
Theatron......................................**35** C4
Vinacure......................................**36** C4

SHOPPING
Amarelo (Camping Vive)...........**37** C4
Hacienda Santa Bárbara............**38** D3
Plaza Mercado de Paloquemao...**39** C5
San Andresito............................**40** B5
Unicentro..................................**41** D2

TRANSPORT
Bus Terminal.............................**42** B4
El Dorado Airport Main Terminal.**43** A3
Mexicana...................................**44** D3
Puente Aéreo.............................**45** A3
Satena..(see 43)
TACA/LACSA...............................**46** D3

and 10), with lots of students, bars and hostels; the aged business district 'city center' (focused on Carrera 7 and Calle 19, between Av Jiménez and Calle 26); the highrise-central of Centro Internacional (based on Carreras 7, 10 and 13, roughly between Calles 26 and 30); and, just east toward the hills, the bohemian eatery district Macarena.

Northern Bogotá is known as the wealthiest part of the city. The north, more or less, begins 2km north of Centro Internacional. A scene of theaters, antique shops and many gay bars, the sprawling Chapinero (roughly between Carrera 7 and Av Caracas, from Calle 40 to Calle 72 or so) is scruffier than areas further north, beginning with Zona G, a pint-sized strip of high-end eateries (east of Carrera 7 and Calle 80). Ten blocks north, lively Zona Rosa (or Zona T; stemming from the 'T-shaped' pedestrian mall between Carreras 12 and 13, at Calle 82A) is a zone of clubs, malls and hotels. A more sedate version – with many restaurants – rims the ritzier Parque 93 (Calle 93 between Carreras 11A & 13), part of the Chicó neighborhood, and the one-time pueblo plaza at Usaquén (corner Carrera 6 and Calle 119). The rather unappealing modern buildings of the so-called 'financial district' line Calle 100 between Av 7 and Carrera 11.

The most popular links between the center and north are Carrera Séptima (Carrera 7) and Carrera Décima (Carrera 10), crowded with many *busetas* (small buses). Another, Av Caracas (which follows Carrera 14, then Av 13 north of Calle 63) is the major north–south route for the TransMilenio bus system. Calle 26 (or Av El Dorado) leads west to the airport.

The working-class barrios of Bogotá looming far south and west from La Candelaria have (occasionally well-deserved) dodgier reputations.

Maps

Maps are a problem in Colombia. Most aren't much good. For Bogotá you're best off with the freebies available from the tourist information centers. And if you're traveling about the country using your own wheels, get the German Reise *Kolumbien* (1:1,400,000) before arriving. See www.reise-know-how.de for info.

INFORMATION
Bookstores

There are plenty of bookstores both in the center and in the northern part of the city. Most of the books are in Spanish.

Authors (Map p64; ☎ 217 7788; Calle 70 No 5-23; ⏱ 10am-8pm Mon-Sat, noon-6pm Sun) An all-English bookstore fills two floors with a huge collection of novels, plus Lonely Planet guidebooks.

BOGOTÁ IN

Two Days
Start in La Candelaria, with a snack at **La Puerta Falsa** (p83), a look at **Plaza de Bolívar** (p69) then see sculptures of chubby bodies at the **Museo Botero** (p72). Lunch at **Quinua y Amaranto** (p84) then walk over to take in Colombia's golden past at **Museo del Oro** (p77), and grab dinner in **Macarena** (p84).

For a second day, you'll want to ride up **Monserrate** (p76) for massive capital views, then taxi or bus north to a few neighborhoods good for walking between – Zona G, Zona Rosa and Parque 93, where you can shop, eat and salsa.

Four Days
Follow the two-day itinerary, then take a day trip to the salt cathedral at **Zipaquirá** (p95) – easily reached by public transport – or sacred lake of **Guatavita** (p97). You can fit in both if you splurge on a taxi, stopping off at **Andrés Carne de Res** (p85) in Chía for a surreal dinner/dance night to top it off.

On the last day, check out Sunday flea markets. **Usaquén** (p90) has a nice one in a pueblo-style setting, while the City Center's **Mercado de San Alejo** (p90) has coca leaves and is near **Mirador Torre Colpatria** (p77) with open-air views. Afterward grab a hot cup of *canelazo* (made with aguardiente, sugarcane, cinnamon and lime) in a cafe in **La Candelaria** (p85), and stay up late at the low-key tango bar **El Viejo Almacén** (p86).

Librería Lerner (Map pp70-1; ☎ 334 7826; Av Jiménez 4-35; ⏱ 9am-7pm Mon-Fri, 9am-2pm Sat) A great bookstore in the center that stocks many Spanish-language guidebooks on Colombia, as well as the full gamut of maps, including the AutoGuía Turística de Colombia (a color, spiral-bound map/guide; COP$19,900), and the 12-map series of national routes Mapas de Ruta (sold individually for COP$1200, or as a packet for COP$13,000).

Cultural Centers
All the listed centers have their own libraries and host various events.
Alianza Colombo Francesa (Map pp70-1; ☎ 341 1348; www.alianzafrancesa.org.co, in Spanish; Carrera 3 No 18-45)
British Council (Map pp74-5; ☎ 325 9090; www.british council.org/colombia; Carrera 9 No 76-49, piso 5)
Centro Colombo Americano (Map pp70-1; ☎ 334 7640; www.colombobogota.edu.co; Calle 19 No 2-49; ⏱ 7:30am-7pm Mon-Fri, 8:30am-2pm Sat & Sun) Often has free films.
Centro Cultural Gabriel García Márquez (Map pp70-1; ☎ 283 2200; www.fce.com.co; Calle 11 No 5-60) Opened in 2008 and a modern addition to La Candelaria, this expansive new complex pays homage to Colombia's most famous author in name, but its events span the cultural spectrum way past literature. There's also a giant bookstore (with a few English titles), a hamburger restaurant and cafe.

Emergency
Don't expect English – if you're not savvy with the *español* have someone else call.

Ambulance ☎ 125
Fire ☎ 123
Police ☎ 123
Tourist police ☎ 337 4413

Internet Access
It's not difficult finding internet access. Nearly all accommodations listed have wi-fi access and/or computers to use. There are also many many cafes, most of which have telephone booths for making long-distance or international calls. PIT tourist information centers offer visitors 15 minutes' free internet. The wi-fi revolution is in full swing, available at many cafes, bars and restaurants, many of which flaunt 'wi-fi zone' decals.

A few convenient choices, most with telephone service, include the following:
AC&C Internet (Map pp74-5; Carrera 15 No 94-80; ⏱ 8am-8pm Mon-Fri, 8am-4pm Sat)
Brokeback Mountain Internet (Map p64; Calle 60 No 9-60; per hr COP$1500; ⏱ 11am-10pm Mon-Sat) Internet access with playful name in Chapinero.
El Tibet (Map pp70-1; Carrera 4 No 12-26; per hr COP$1500; ⏱ 9am-9pm Mon-Fri, 9am-8pm Sat, 9am-6pm Sun)
ETB (Map pp70-1; Carrera 7 No 19-65; per hr COP$1100; ⏱ 8am-7pm Mon-Fri, 9am-4pm Sat, 10am-4pm Sun)

Laundry
Most hotels provide this service for their guests. Guesthouses charge about COP$3000 per kilogram, whereas upmarket establish-

ments will probably offer dry cleaning only and will charge per item.

Lavarapido (Map pp70-1; Calle 15 No 4-14; per kg COP\$3500; 🕑 8:30am-7pm Mon-Sat, 8:30am-1pm Sun) Drop-off laundry in La Candelaria.

Libraries

Biblioteca Luis Ángel Arango (Map pp70-1; ☎ 343 1212; www.lablaa.org; Calle 11 No 4-14; 🕑 8am-8pm Mon-Sat, 8am-4pm Sun) This library bills itself 'busiest in the world,' hosts art exhibits and stages concerts. Its simple top-floor cafe has Monserrate views.

Biblioteca Nacional (Map pp70-1; ☎ 243 5969; www .bibliotecanacional.gov.co; Calle 24 No 5-60; 🕑 8am-6pm Mon-Fri) You will need a library card to visit.

Medical Services

It's preferable to use private clinics rather than government-owned institutions, which are cheaper but may not be as well equipped.

Clínica de Marly (Map p64; ☎ 343 6600; Calle 50 No 9-67) A recommended clinic with doctors covering most specialties; sometimes handles vaccinations.

Dr Paul Vaillancourt (Map pp74-5; ☎ 635 6312; Carrera 11 No 94A-25, oficina 401; 🕑 8am-noon & 2-5pm Mon-Fri) A recommended English-speaking, half-Canadian doctor, who charges COP\$100,000 per consultation (no medical insurance accepted).

Fundación Santa Fe (Map p64; ☎ 215 2852; Av 9 No 116-20, oficina 209; 🕑 9am-1pm & 2-6pm Mon-Fri) If you're heading to Brazil (or any area requiring immunization against yellow fever), this is the best place to get your vaccination (COP\$46,000). Note that the vaccination must be 10 days old before arriving in Brazil.

Hospital San Ignacio (Map p64; ☎ 288 8188; Carrera 7 No 40-62) A university hospital with a high level of medical expertise, but long queues.

Money

Banks in Bogotá tend to work 9am to 3pm or 3:30pm Monday to Friday. The banks below also change cash, but check the *casas de cambio* (currency exchanges) beforehand, which may offer the same rates and do things much more quickly. Money changers at the airport have slightly worse exchange rates – and require a thumb print to cash in your pesos!

All banks shown below give cash advances on Visa and/or MasterCard. Most banks have ATMs.

American Express (Map pp74-5; ☎ 313 1146; Calle 85 No 20-32)

Bancolombia (Map pp70-1; ☎ 342 1309; Carrera 8 No 13-17) Changes traveler's checks. There is another branch on Carrera 3 No 18-19.

Citibank (Map pp74-5; cnr Carrera 12A & Av 82, Zona Rosa)

Edificio Emerald Trade Center (Map pp70-1; ☎ 236 6181; Av Jiménez No 5-43; 🕑 7:30am-7pm Mon-Fri, 8am-4:30pm Sat) There are several exchange offices here.

Titán Intercontinental (Map pp70-1; ☎ 336 0549; Carrera 7 No 18-42) A *casa de cambio*; can also receive money from overseas.

Western Union (Map pp70-1; ☎ 287 1265, 635 3560; Calle 28 No 13-22, local 28; 🕑 9am-5pm Mon-Fri, 9am-1pm Sat) Can wire money.

Post

Avianca City Center (Map pp70-1; ☎ 342 7513; Carrera 7 No 16-36; 🕑 8am-6:30pm Mon-Fri, 9am-2pm Sat); Centro Internacional (Map pp70-1; ☎ 342 6077; Carrera 10 No 26-53; 🕑 8am-6:30pm Mon-Fri, 9am-2pm Sat)

FedEx (Map pp70-1; ☎ 291 0100; Carrera 7 No 16-50; 🕑 9am-7pm Mon-Fri, 9am-2pm Sat)

Post office (Map pp70-1; Carrera 7 No 27-54; 🕑 9am-7pm Mon-Fri, 9am-1:15pm Sat) Branch of Adpostal. The main office in La Candelaria (cnr Carrera 7 & Calle 13) was under renovation at last pass.

Telephone & Fax

All over Bogotá, you'll see locals holding up *llamadas* (calls) signs; they allow calls on their cell phones for around COP\$250 per minute nationally. Otherwise, most internet cafes and numerous telephone centers offer national calls for the same rate, or from COP\$300 to COP\$600 per minute for international calls.

Telecom (Map pp70-1; ☎ 561 1111; Calle 23 No 13-49; 🕑 7am-7pm) The main office is in the city center, but you can make long-distance calls and send faxes from branch offices throughout the city, including one in La Candelaria (cnr Carrera 8 & Calle 12).

Tourist Information

Colombia's energetic **Instituto Distrital de Turismo** (www.bogotaturismo.gov.co) is making visitors feel very welcome, with a series of **PITs** (Puntos de Información Turística) opening at key locations around Bogotá. Very friendly English-speaking staff at these centers give out excellent city maps, find hotels, double as guides, point you to Spanish instructors or call for bus times. A couple of PIT locations offer free walking tours (scheduled separately in English or Spanish). New PIT locations should appear in both airport terminals by the time you arrive.

Parques Nacionales Naturales de Colombia (Ecoturismo; Map pp70-1; ☎ 353 2400, ext 138; www .parquesnacionales.gov.co, in Spanish; Carrera 10 No 20-34; 🕑 8am-4pm Mon-Fri) This central office has information on Colombia's national parks and can help arrange accommodations at some. Also see p53.

PIT Centro Histórico (Map pp70-1; ☎ 283 7115; cnr Carrera 8 & Calle 10; ⏰ 8am-6pm Mon-Sat, 10am-4pm Sun) Facing Plaza de Bolívar, this location has frequent walking tours.

PIT Terminal de Transporte (Map p64; ☎ 295 4460; La Terminal, Transversal 66 No 35-11, módulo 5; ⏰ 7am-7pm Mon-Sat, 10am-4pm Sun) At the arrival hall of the main bus station.

PIT Unicentro Norte (Map p64; ☎ 612 1967; Avenida 15 No 123-30, piso 1; ⏰ noon-7pm Mon-Sat, 10am-4pm Sun)

Travel Agencies

Aviatur (Map pp70-1; ☎ 282 5662; www.aviatur.com; Calle 19 No 4-62; ⏰ 8am-6:30pm Mon-Fri, 8am-6pm Sat) Run by a French guy, the posh, well-organized Aviatur has fancily dressed staff who book tours to various destinations around the country, including some of the national parks that Aviatur leases from the government.

Destino Bogotá (Map pp74-5; ☎ 753 4887; www .destinobogota.com; Av Chile No 12-65, oficina 405; ⏰ 7:30am-6pm Mon-Fri) Offers many playful city and area tours. Haunted Bogotá? Party-bus club-hopping? Salsa lesson and club debut? Check. Plus more standard fare like a worthy Guatavita/Zipaquirá day trip. Most trips require minimum of two or four people; city tours start at COP$40,000 per person, day trips start at COP$110,000. English-speaking staff (and guides) sometimes lower rates.

Ecoguías (Map p64; ☎ 347 5736, 212 1423; www .ecoguias.com; Carrera 3 No 55-10; ⏰ 9am-5:30pm Mon-Fri) This well-run adventure-travel company run by a Brit who's lived in Colombia for over a decade focuses on ecotourism trips to various regions of the country, like Ciudad Perdida, the coffee region and ecolodges at Nuquí on the Pacific coast (three-night tours run about US$260 per person not including flight). They're less about drop-by visitors, than trip pre-planners, but can organize good Bogotá day trips or loops to Villa de Leyva and Zipaquirá, or book mansion stays in off-the-radar Honda.

Sal Si Puedes (Map pp70-1; ☎ 283 3765; www.sal sipuedes.org, in Spanish; Carrera 7 No 17-01, oficina 640; ⏰ 8am-5pm Mon-Thu, 8am-2pm Fri) This is an associa- tion of outdoor-minded people who organize weekend walks in the countryside (COP$30,000 per person, including transport and Spanish-speaking guides). Most last nine or 10 hours. Drop by for a schedule.

Trotamundos Centro Internacional (Map p64; ☎ 599 6413; www.trotamundos.com.co; Diagonal 35 No 5-73; ⏰ 9am-5pm Mon-Fri, 10am-12:30pm Sat); La Candelaria (Map pp70-1; ☎ 566 4892; Calle 19 No 1-85; ⏰ 8:30am- 5pm Mon-Fri, 10am-12:30pm Sat) Colombia's STA Travel rep can help get discounted international airfares or AeroRepública's 15% discount on domestic fares for those under 25.

Visa Information

DAS (Map pp74-5; ☎ 601 7200; Calle 100 No 11B-27; ⏰ 7:30am-4pm Mon-Thu, 7:30am-3pm Fri) A 30-day visa extension can be obtained here. Your passport, two photocopies of your passport (picture page and arrival stamp) and two passport-sized photos are required, and you'll need to show an air ticket out of the country in most cases. Show up first to fill out forms, then they'll direct you to a nearby Bancafe to pay the COP$60,600 fee. You get the extension on the spot.

DANGERS & ANNOYANCES

Things have become safer here in recent years, but, as in most cities, safety in Bogotá depends on both where you are and what time it is. Of the most visited places, La Candelaria (near some poorer areas like Egipto, just southeast) is generally safe, but has a more questionable reputation after 9pm or so. (We've had no problems in several weeks spent in the area, but visitors occasionally do.) At its north end, Parque de los Periodistas (Av Jiménez and Carrera 4) has seen muggings after dark – as well as some drug sales. La Perseverancia barrio, just north of Macarena, has a dodgy rep too.

One notorious areas for knife-point mug- gings is along the seemingly innocent walk up to Monserrate – either on the mountainside trails, or the short walk between the cable-car station and Quinta de Bolívar just below. At the time of research, we met a 70-year-old German traveler who was *bitten* by two thieves after he tried to fight back; the same area on busy weekends is generally quite safe.

The north is, on the whole, a different story. Many locals walk well after dark between, say, Zona Rosa and Parque 93's club/restaurant scene. That said, the area has seen a few iso- lated bombings, including a couple in October 2008 that led to injuries. And we met a local who had resisted a purse-snatching while in her car and got her hand sliced up badly.

The lesson here is to not fight back if you've been targeted – hand over your money and move on. Meanwhile, avoid deserted streets and take taxis after hours.

SIGHTS

Most attractions are in historic La Candelaria, where Bogotá was born, and you'll prob- ably want more than a day to look around the area.

If you're thinking of going to a museum on a Sunday, think twice – Bogotá has half-a-hundred options, and most get crammed with locals, particularly on free day (the last Sunday of the month); we've seen 45-minute lines outside a modest museum or two not even listed here! It's quieter during the week.

When walking about, pop into random churches too. Most are beauties, often dating from the 17th and 18th centuries – often with more elaborate decoration than the exterior would suggest. Some show off a distinctive Spanish-Moorish style called Mudejar (mainly noticeable in the ceiling ornamentation) as well as paintings of Colombia's best-known colonial-era artist, Gregorio Vásquez de Arce y Ceballos.

La Candelaria

Blissfully alive and chock full of key things to see, La Candelaria is Bogotá's colonial barrio, with a mix of carefully restored 300-year-old houses, some rather dilapidated ones, and still more marking more modern eras. It's best to avoid walking alone here after 9pm.

The following sections are grouped, more or less, in relation to the barrio's center, Plaza de Bolívar.

PLAZA DE BOLÍVAR

The usual place to start discovering Bogotá is Plaza de Bolívar (Map pp70–1), marked by a bronze statue of Simón Bolívar (cast in 1846 by Italian artist, Pietro Tenerani). It was the first public monument in the city.

The square has changed considerably over the centuries and is no longer lined by colonial buildings; only the Capilla del Sagrario (see right) dates from the Spanish era. Other buildings are more recent and flaunt different architectural styles.

The main plaza's dominating building, facing from the northeast corner, is the neoclassical **Catedral Primada** (Map pp70–1; ☎ 341 1954; Plaza de Bolívar; ♥ 9am-1pm & 4-6pm Tue-Fri, 9am-6pm Sat & Sun), which stands on the site where the first mass *may* have been celebrated after Bogotá had been founded in 1538 (some historians argue it happened Plazoleta del Chorro de Quevedo, just east). Either way, it's Bogotá's largest. The original simple thatched chapel was replaced by a more substantial building in 1556–65, which later collapsed due to poor foundations. In 1572 the third church went up, but the earthquake of 1785 reduced it to ruins. Only in 1807 was the massive building – that stands to this day – initiated and it was

GREEN PEOPLE WATCHING FROM ABOVE

While walking around La Candelaria, try keeping one eye down for fresh dog feces and missing pot-hole covers, *and* another one up for a unique art project peering down from rooftops, window ledges and balconies. Made in the past decade, the art works – green figures made from recycled materials representing local *comuneros* (common folks you find on the street) – come from local artist Jorge Olavé.

Note the guy watching over Plaza de Bolívar from atop the **Casa de Comuneros** (Map pp70–1) at the southwest corner – best seat in town.

successfully completed by 1823. It was partially damaged during the Bogotazo riots in 1948. Unlike many Bogotá churches, the spacious interiors have relatively little ornamentation. The tomb of Jiménez de Quesada, the founder of Bogotá, is in the largest chapel off the right-hand aisle. There's a shop if you need a Catedral T-shirt.

Next door, the baroque **Capilla del Sagrario** (Sagrario Chapel; Map pp70–1; ☎ 341 1954; Plaza de Bolívar, Carrera 7 No 10-40; ♥ 7:30am-noon & 1-5:30pm Mon-Fri, 3-5:30pm Sun) has more to see, including six large paintings by Gregorio Vásquez.

On the northern side of the square is the **Palacio de Justicia** (Map pp70–1; closed to the public), a massive, rather styleless edifice serving as the seat of the Supreme Court. It's seen its troubles. The first court building, erected in 1921 on the corner of Calle 11 and Carrera 6, was burnt down by a mob during the Bogotazo. A modern building was then constructed here, but in 1985 it was taken by M-19 guerrillas and gutted by fire in a fierce 28-hour offensive by the army in an attempt to reclaim it. The new building was designed in a completely different style.

The western side of the plaza is taken over by the French-style **Edificio Liévano** (Map pp70–1; closed to the public), which is now home to the *alcaldía* (mayor's office). The building was erected between 1902 and 1905.

On the southern side of the plaza stands the neoclassical **Capitolio Nacional** (Map pp70–1; closed to the public), the seat of Congress. It was begun in 1847 (its square-facing facade was built by English architect Thomas Reed),

BOGOTÁ

CENTRAL BOGOTÁ

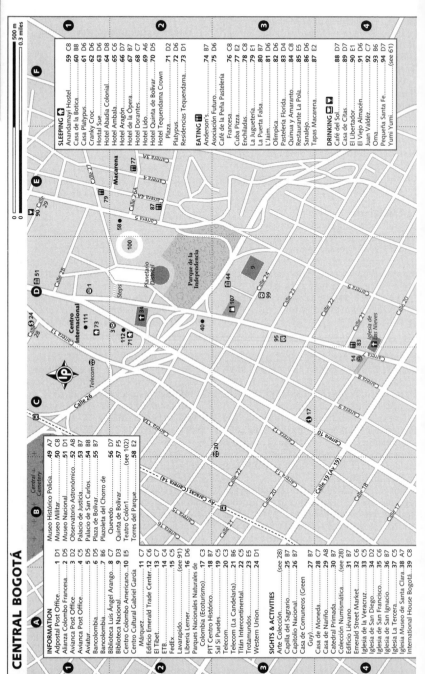

500 m
0.3 miles

Macarena

Parque de la Independencia

Planetario Distrital

Centro Internacional

Iglesia de las Nieves

Central Cemetery

Telecom

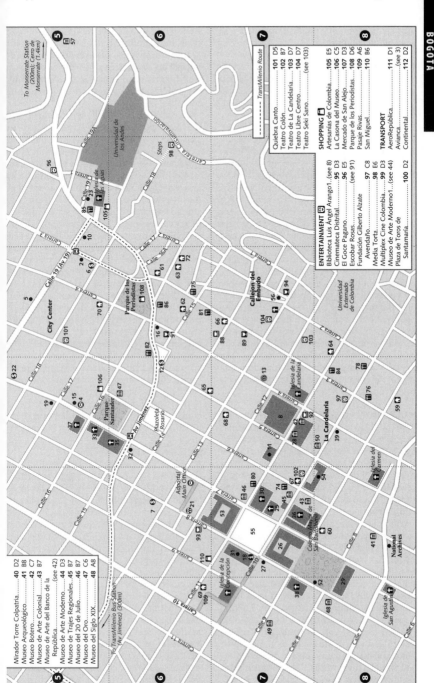

but due to numerous political uprisings was not completed until 1926.

EAST ON CALLE 11

Some of La Candelaria's most popular sights, as well as the new Centro Cultural Gabriel García Márquez (p66), are within a couple of blocks east of the plaza.

The late-16th-century home that houses the **Museo del 20 de Julio** (Casa del Florero; Map pp70-1; ☎ 282 6647; www.mincultura.gov.co, in Spanish; Calle 11 No 6-94; adult/student COP$3000/2000; ☑ 9am-5pm Tue-Fri, 10am-4pm Sat & Sun) marks the spot where a 'broken vase was heard around the world.' Apparently. Just after Napoleon overcame Spain in 1810, a local Creole Antonio Morales came here, according to the story, and demanded an ornate vase from its Spanish owner José González Llorentes, which led to a fistfight on the street (plus one shattered vase, and some hurt feelings) – eventually spurring a rebellion.

Some staff smirk at the story ('probably broke on purpose later to defend the story' one staff member glibly guessed). But in these hallowed halls you can see the broken vase in question. One exhibit dares to ask 'what would we be without the vase?' Ponder the chilling concept while looking through the upstairs period-piece rooms with fun paintings of the era plus a small exhibit on women's role in the struggle for independence.

MUSEO BOTERO & CASA DE MONEDA

This slightly confusing web of **museums** (Map pp70-1; admission free; ☑ 9am-7pm Mon & Wed-Sat, ☑ 10am-5pm Sun), run by the Banco de la Republicano, is easily one of Bogotá's top attractions. Filling most of the block, you'll find several overlapping collections, including the superb Museo Botero, a coin collection and two art collections.

Past a fountain-filled courtyard and small store of Botero-themed wares you'll find the location's highlight, the **Museo Botero** (Map pp70-1; ☎ 343 1331; www.lablaa.org/museobotero.htm; Calle 11 No 4-41). Set over two floors at the front of the building here are several halls dedicated to all things chubby: hands, oranges, women, mustached men, children, birds, violins, Fuerzas Armadas Revolucionarias de Colombia (FARC) leaders – all, of course, the robust paintings and sculptures of Colombia's most famous artist, Fernando Botero. (Botero himself donated these works.) The collection also includes several works by Picasso, Chagall,

Renoir, Monet, Pissarro and Miró, and hilarious sculptures by Dalí and Max Ernst.

Just behind is the **Museo de Arte del Banco de la República** (www.lablaa.org/museodearte.htm), past a wall-fountain and wine bar. It shows changing exhibits, and its auditorium hosts many free events.

At the west end of the block, you'll find the historic **Casa de Moneda** (Mint; Map pp70-1; www.lablaa.org; Calle 11 No 4-93), which now houses the Colección Numismática in most of its front two floors. The exhibits (with a bit of English) start with pre-Columbian exchanges of pots and lead chronologically to misshapen coins, the introduction of a centralized bank in 1880 and how the cute tree art on the current 500-peso coin was made in the late 1990s.

Behind the coins are the 10 halls of the **Arte Colección**, reached by overly elaborate ramps. Most of it sticks with modern splashes of oils by Colombian artists; the best, perhaps, are the giant figurative paintings by Luis Caballero (1943–95) on the first floor. A bit at odds with the rest are the two first-floor halls towards the east, focusing on 17th- and 18th-century religious objects, including two extraordinary *custodias* (monstrances). The largest was made of 4902g of pure gold encrusted with 1485 emeralds, one sapphire, 13 rubies, 26 diamonds, 168 amethysts, one topaz and 62 pearls. But who's counting?

If art overload has left you in need of a coffee fix, there's a Juan Valdéz cafe (Map pp70-1) next door to the Museo Botero.

EAST ON CALLE 10

Up from the southeast corner of Plaza de Bolívar is a host of historical sights. Starting on the south side of Calle 10, the **Iglesia de San Ignacio** (Map pp70-1; Calle 10 No 6-35) was begun by the Jesuits in 1610 and, although opened for worship in 1635, it was not completed until their expulsion in 1767. It was the largest church during colonial times and perhaps the most magnificent. It's undergoing a long-winded renovation. Hopefully when it reopens visitors should be able to see one of the city's most richly decorated churches.

Across the street, and filling the gorgeous one-time home of Simón Bolívar's mistress Manuelita Sáenz, the simple **Museo de Trajes Regionales** (Museum of Regional Clothing; Map pp70-1; ☎ 282 6531; www.uamerica.edu.co/museo/museo.html, in Spanish; Calle 10 No 6-18; adult/student COP$2000/1500; ☑ 10am-4:30pm Mon-Fri, 10am-4pm Sat) displays colorful Spanish and pre-Columbian fashions neatly tagged with photos of models playfully posing in them. The museum also hosts some interesting courses; at last pass, courses to learn to make plastic figurines met 2pm to 5pm Thursday (one month course, COP$20,000).

Around the corner at Carrera 6, the **Museo de Arte Colonial** (Museum of Colonial Art; Map pp70-1; ☎ 341 6017; Carrera 6 No 9-77; adult/student COP$2000/1500; ☼ 9am-5pm Tue-Fri, 10am-4pm Sat & Sun) occupies a one-time Jesuit college and does a nice job of tracing the evolution of how religious and portrait art pieces are made, particularly by Colombia's favorite Baroque artist Gregorio Vásquez de Arce y Ceballos (1638–1711). Its upstairs exhibits begin with a messy gallery space (eg trial sketches on walls) and lead into a hall with sketch pieces and a couple of dozen (finished) Vásquez works from the museum's collection of nearly 200 by the artist. Downstairs exhibits focus on religious artifacts.

Another block north, on the south side of the street, you'll see the massive edifice of **Palacio de San Carlos** (Map pp70-1; Calle 10 No 5-51), which has seen a few lives, notably as the presidential HQ of Simón Bolívar, who narrowly escaped an assassination attempt here in 1828 when his friend-with-privileges Manuelita Sáenz tipped him off and became known in Bogotá circles as 'the liberator of the liberator.' A (dramatically worded) sign in Latin under his window (to the right) retells it.

Across the street, admire the facade of the Italian-style **Teatro Colón** (p88), which has had various names since its birth in 1792. This latest version you see opened as Teatro Nacional in 1892 and was designed by Italian architect Pietro Cantini. Its lavish interiors are undergoing a long renovation that – apparently – will be done sometime in 2010 (though some staff we talked to doubt it). Normally, concerts, opera and ballet are performed here, and day-time tours are on offer.

Another block east, the two-floor **Museo Militar** (Military Museum; Map pp70-1; ☎ 281 2548; Calle 10 No 4-92; admission free; ☼ 9am-4:30pm Tue-Sun) is run by military guys in fatigues, and may be interesting to some for its playful models sporting the history of military uniforms (note the 'anti-terrorist' outfit), a delirious 'Conquest of Space' exhibit of floating gods and Wright Brothers'-type contraptions in a sea of stars, and courtyard of artillery and aircraft including a presidential helicopter.

SOUTH OF PLAZA DE BOLÍVAR

Beyond the **Capitolio Nacional**, reached via Carreras 8 or 7, on the south side of Plaza de Bolívar, is Colombia's presidential building, the neoclassical **Casa de Nariño** (Map pp70–1), erected at the beginning of the 20th century. President Uribe lives and works here. It's named for Antonio Nariño, a colonial figure with ideas of independence and who secretly translated France's human rights laws into Spanish – and went to jail for it, a couple of times. In 1948 the building was damaged during the Bogotazo riots and only restored in 1979. It's theoretically possible to visit if you plan a week ahead. Ask a PIT information office for help.

You don't need permission to watch the **changing of the presidential guard** – best seen from the east side – which is held at 4pm on Wednesday, Friday and Sunday.

Facing the palace from the west (on Carrera 8) is one of Bogotá's most richly decorated churches, the **Iglesia Museo de Santa Clara** (Map pp70-1; ☎ 337 6762; www.museoscolombianos.gov.co; Carrera 8 No 8-91; adult/student COP$2000/1500; ☼ 9am-5pm Tue-Fri, 10am-4pm Sat & Sun), now run by the government as a museum. Considering all the other same-era churches that can be seen for free, many visitors pass on this one, but it is a stunner. Built between 1629 and 1674, the single-nave construction features a barrel vault coated in golden floral motifs looking down over walls entirely covered in paintings (98 not including the closed-off loft, by our count) and statues of saints.

A block south, you'll pass the white **Observatorio Astronómico** (Map pp70–1). Conceptualized by celebrated Colombian botanist José Celestino Mutis, the 1803 tower is reputedly the first astronomical observatory built on the continent. It's possible to visit on the third Thursday of each month, but you must reserve a week ahead. Email your name, nationality and passport number to museos@ unal.edu.co to reserve a spot.

Nearby, the fun **Museo del Siglo XIX** (Museum of the 19th Century; Map pp70-1; ☎ 281 9948; Carrera 8 No 7-93; admission incl guide COP$2300; ☼ 8:30am-4:30pm Mon-Fri, 9am-1pm Sat) offers a look inside something *other* than Spanish colonial Bogotá. The museum fills a former Repúblicano-style home built intentionally in English and French styles in two swoops (in 1850 and 1880). A visit takes in a sample of 19th-century capital life, with a refashioned pharmacy, corsets galore, and

BOGOTÁ

ZONA ROSA & PARQUE 93

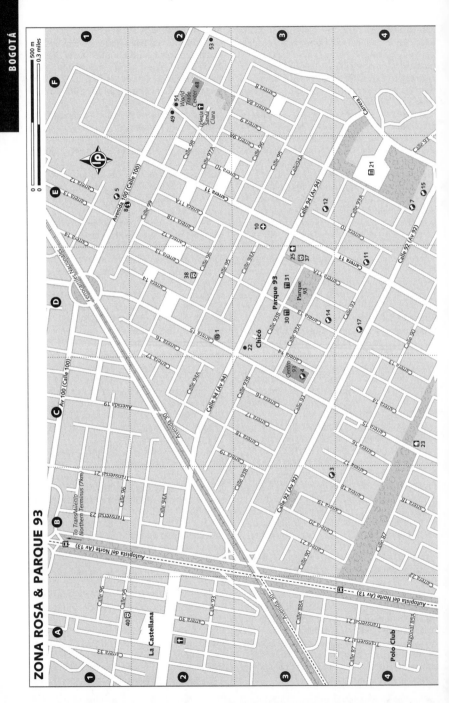

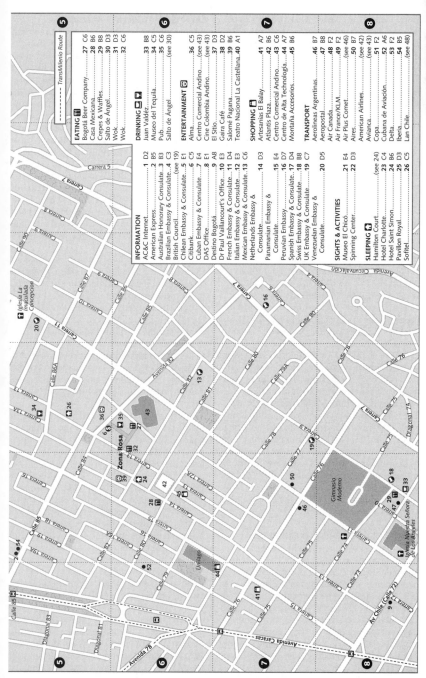

an all-decked-out parlor with a secret chamber and porcelain spit jars. Don't miss the 3000-piece toy doll collection, the culmination of six decades of collection by a couple local *señoras*.

A couple of blocks east, the **Museo Arqueológico** (Archeological Museum; MUSA; Map pp70-1; ☎ 243 1048; Carrera 6 No 7-43; adult/student COP$3000/2000; ☼ 8:30am-5pm Tue-Fri, 9:30am-5pm Sat, 10am-4pm Sun) is a quirky, not quite fully realized survey of pre-Columbian groups through pottery pieces from around the country. Perhaps best is the building, a lovely 17th-century townhouse that seems almost surprised with its latest incarnation. Signs are subtitled in English, and a timeline charts back from 1492, including early groups like Ilama (from 700BC).

Note: Guards around the president's palace stand at barriers on Carreras 7 and 8. It's OK to pass them, just show the contents of your bag and stay clear of the fence-side sidewalks.

WEST OF PLAZA DE BOLÍVAR
The surprisingly worthwhile **Museo Histórico Policia** (Museum of Police History; Map pp70-1; ☎ 233 5911; Calle 9 No 9-27; admission free; ☼ 8am-5pm Tue-Sun) not only gets you inside the lovely ex-HQ (built in 1923) of Bogotá's police force, but gives you 45 minutes or so of contact time with 18-year-old, English-speaking local guides who are serving a one-year compulsory service with the police (interesting tales to be heard). The best parts otherwise follow cocaine-kingpin Pablo Escobar's demise in 1993 – with a model dummy of his bullet-ridden corpse – or the surreal juxtaposition of a Neanderthal-fight mural before cases and cases of more modern means of killing each other (pistols and rifles).

While you're in the area, take a look at the crafts for sale at **Pasaje Rivas** (p90).

PLAZOLETA DEL CHORRO QUEVEDO
No one agrees exactly where Bogotá was originally founded – some say by the Catedral Primada on the Plaza de Bolívar, others say here, in this wee **plaza** (Map pp70-1; cnr Carrera 2 & Calle 13) lined with cafes, a small white church and many boho street vendors (or hacky-sack players). It's a cute spot any time of day, but particularly as dark comes – and students pour onto the scene – in the narrow funnel-like alley leading past pocket-sized bars just north.

Cerro de Monserrate & Around
Bogotá's proud symbol – and convenient point of reference – is this white-church-topped 3152m **Monserrate peak** (Map p64) flanking the city's east, about 1.5km from La Candelaria and visible from most parts across Sabana de Bogotá (Bogotá savannah, sometimes called the valley). The top has gorgeous views of the 1700-sq-km capital sprawl. On a clear day you can even spot the symmetrical cone of Nevado del Tolima, part of Los Nevados volcanic range in the Cordillera Central, 135km west.

The **church** up top is a major mecca for pilgrims, due to the church's altar statue of the Señor Caído (Fallen Christ), dating from the 1650s, to which many miracles have been attributed. The church was erected after the original chapel was destroyed by an earthquake in 1917.

On Saturday or Sunday morning, consider following the hordes up a steep **1500-step hike** – past snack stands – to the top (60 to 90 minutes up); on other days, it can be dangerous, as thefts occur, so take the regular *teleférico* (cable car) or funicular which alternate schedules up the mountain from the **Monserrate station** (☎ 284 5700; www.cerromonserrate.com; return before/after 5:30pm COP$13,400/17,000, on Sunday COP$8000; ☼ 7:45am-midnight Mon-Sat, 5:30am-6pm Sun). Generally the funicular goes before noon (3pm on Saturday), the cable car after.

A couple of over-priced restaurants in historic homes overlook the mountainside nearby. **Casa Santa Clara** (☎ 281 9309) is open for a COP$12,000 tamale and hot chocolate breakfast on Sundays.

About 250m downhill to the west, the lovely **Quinta de Bolívar** (Map pp70-1; ☎ 336 6419; www.quintadebolivar.gov.co; Calle 20 No 2-91 Este; adult/student COP$3000/2000; ☼ 9am-5pm Tue-Fri, 10am-4pm Sat & Sun) is set in a garden at the foot of the Cerro de Monserrate. The mansion was built in 1800 and donated to Simón Bolívar in 1820 in gratitude for his liberating services. Bolívar spent 423 days here over nine years. Its rooms are filled with period pieces, including Bolívar's sword. Less is said about its later days as a mental institution.

Perhaps best is walking through the gorgeous garden grounds around – follow the paths to the left (north) to reach the covered bath where Bolívar preferred cleaning himself in cold water. There's an English-language brochure available for COP$2500, or a Spanish-language audio-guide for COP$1000.

The funicular is a 20-minute walk up from the Iglesia de las Aguas (along the brick walkways with the fountains – up past the Universidad de los Andes), at the northeast edge of La Candelaria – but you're best off now doing it on weekends, particularly in the mornings, when many pilgrims are about. During the week, the trail and the short walk between Quinta de Bolívar and Monserrate occasionally see robberies. You're best off taking a taxi or the bus that reads 'Funicular' up to the station.

City Center

Not a heart-breaker, Bogotá's scrappy business center – busiest along Calle 19 and Carrera 7 – is easiest to deal with on Sunday, when Ciclovia shuts down Carrera 7, and the Mercado de San Alejo flea market (p90) is in force. Some of its most-visited parts (notably the Museo del Oro) cluster near La Candelaria by Av Jiménez.

MUSEO DEL ORO

Bogotá's most famous museum, the recently renovated **Gold Museum** (Map pp70-1; ☎ 343 2222; www.banrep.gov.co/museo; Calle 16 No 5-41; admission free Sun, other days COP$2800, audio guide COP$6000; ☯ 9am-6pm Tue-Sat, 10am-4pm Sun) contains more than 55,000 pieces of gold and other materials from all the major pre-Hispanic cultures in Colombia. All is laid out in logical, thematic rooms over three floors – with descriptions in Spanish and English.

Second-floor exhibits break down findings by region, with descriptions of how pieces were used. There are lots of mixed animals in gold (eg jaguar/frog, man/eagle); and note how women figurines indicate how women of the Zenú in the pre-Columbian north surprisingly played more important roles in worship.

The third-floor 'Offering' room exhibits explain how gold was used in rituals, such as ornate *tunjos* (gold offerings) thrown into the Laguna de Guatavita (p97); the most famous one, actually found near the town of Pasca in 1969, is the unlabeled gold boat, called the Balsa Muisca. It's uncertain how old it is, as generally only gold pieces that include other materials that can be carbon-dated.

There's more to understanding the stories than the descriptions tell, so try taking a free one-hour tour (in Spanish: 9am, 11am, 3pm, 4pm; in English: 11am, 3pm, 4pm), which varies the part of the museum to be highlighted. Audio guides are available in Spanish, English and French.

IGLESIA DE SAN FRANCISCO & OTHER CHURCHES

Built between 1557 and 1621, the **Church of San Francisco** (Map pp70-1; ☎ 341 2357; cnr Av Jiménez & Carrera 7; ☯ 7am-7:30pm Mon-Fri, 7am-1:30pm & 5:15-7:30pm Sat & Sun), just west of the Gold Museum, is Bogotá's oldest surviving church. Of particular interest is the extraordinary 17th-century gilded main altarpiece, which is Bogotá's largest and most elaborate piece of art of its kind. It's hard to get a close look, as masses run nearly hourly all day. It's less intrusive to look up at the green-and-gold Mudejar ornamentation of the ceiling under the organ loft.

Just north along Carrera 7 are a couple other interesting churches. The **Iglesia de la Veracruz** (Map pp70-1; Calle 16 No 7-19; ☯ mass 8am, noon & 6pm) is known as the National Pantheon because many of the heroes of the struggle for independence have been buried here.

Next door is the **Iglesia La Tercera** (Map pp70-1; Calle 16 No 7-54; ☯ 8am-noon & 2-5pm), with a fine stone facade and lovely wood-carved altars in walnut and cedar set on white walls below a wood-carved ceiling.

MUSEO DE ARTE MODERNO

Opened in the mid-1980s in a spacious hall designed by revered local architect Rogelio Salmona, the **Museum of Modern Art** (MAMBO; Map pp70-1; ☎ 286 0466; www.mambogota.com, in Spanish; Calle 24 No 6-00; adult/student COP$4000/2000; ☯ 10am-6pm Tue-Sat, noon-5pm Sun) focuses on various forms of visual arts (painting, sculpture, photography, video) from the beginning of the 20th century to the present. Exhibits change frequently, often highlighting Latin America artists. The cinema here screens about four films daily.

MIRADOR TORRE COLPATRIA

Monserrate offers superb views, but only from the 46th-floor outside deck of the **Colpatria Tower** (Map pp70-1; ☎ 283 6697; Carrera 7 No 24-89; admission COP$3000; ☯ 11am-5pm Sat, Sun & holidays) can you catch a superb view of the bullring, backed by office buildings and the mountains – there are also fine 360° vistas across the city. The 162m-high skyscraper – Colombia's tallest – was finished in 1979.

SALMONA TOWN

If you're lucky enough to go on a city walk with a *bogotano*, the conversation will invariably lead, at some point, to some red-brick modern building – like the new Centro Cultural Gabriel García Márquez, parts of the Universidad Nacional, or the National Archives. When you hear 'This building was built by…,' stop them right there, and take a guess by whom: Rogelio Salmona?

Colombia's most famous architect, Salmona helped reshape the cityscape of contemporary Bogotá with red-brick towering buildings with geometric curves and, often, big views. His works are many – including the Museo de Arte Moderno and the **Torres del Parque** (Map pp70–1), the residential towers overlooking the bullring in Centro Internacional, where the architect lived till his death, aged 78, in 2007. He also designed García Márquez' studio in Cartagena.

Salmona – born to French and Spanish parents in Paris – lived and studied in Bogotá most of his life, though he left during the aftermath of the 1948 riots when he helped design the conceptual city Chandigarh, in India, with Le Corbusier.

He told *El Tiempo* shortly before his death from cancer, 'Good architecture becomes ruins. Bad architecture disappears.' His looks to stand a good while longer.

Speaking of bulls, they seem to like it too. A few locals *swear* that a loose bull recently ran down Carrera 7 from the ring, into the tower, and knocked over someone stepping off an elevator. Look before exiting.

Centro Internacional

Business offices look over the Carrera 7 in this busy pocket of the city, where you'll find a few attractions and lots of business meetings. In January and February, the Plaza de Toros de Santamaria (p89) gets crammed with bullfighting fans. It's just north of the green Parque de la Independencia.

The area's principal attraction, the **Museo Nacional** (National Museum; Map pp70–1; ☎ 334 8366; www .museonacional.gov.co, in Spanish; Carrera 7 No 28-66; adult/student COP$3000/2000; ☷ 10am-6pm Tue-Sat, 10am-5pm Sun) is housed in the expansive, Greek cross–shaped building called El Panóptico, designed as a prison by English architect Thomas Reed in 1874. Walking through the (more or less) chronological display of Colombia's past, you pass iron-bar doors into white-walled halls.

The ground floor looks at pre-Columbian history, with rather oblique references to past groups and some gripping Muisca mummies that may date as far back as 1500 years. Things pick up on the second floor, where in room 9 (surrounded, oddly enough, by Spanish co-lonial art) you can see an English-language video of how a recently built road disrupted life in a Caribbean town.

On the third floor, room 16 gives the best sense of old prison life – with old cells now done up in various exhibits. The first on the right regards Jorge Gaitán, the populist leader

whose 1948 assassination set off the Bogotazo violence – and coincidentally delayed the opening of this museum! There's also a hall devoted to playful modern art by local artists Botero, Obregón and Weiderman. Curiously the La Violencia period of the 20th century and guerrilla groups are scarcely covered.

Afterwards, the lovely gardens have a nice glass cafe, and there are many good eating options on nearby Calle 29.

Northern Bogotá

For shoppers, high-class foodies, or the boutique-hotel and club crowd, Bogotá's north offers endless options. For traditional travelers – looking for quirky museums, street fairs and hot chocolate – the north trails La Candelaria.

The three main areas are **Zona G** (roughly between Calles 69 and 70, east of Carrera 7), most popular for eating; a 15-minute walk north **Zona Rosa** overflows with commercial action, centered at its T-shaped pedestrian heart 'Zona T' (at Av 82A between Carreras 12 and 13).

A 10-minute walk north leads to the slightly more polite **Parque 93**, with a tidy patch of green lined with nice (and chain) restaurants.

A few blocks east, **Museo El Chicó** (Map pp74-5; ☎ 623 1066; www.museodelchico.com, in Spanish; Mercedes Sierra de Pérez, Carrera 7A No 93-01; adult/student COP$2500/1500; ☷ 10am-5pm Mon-Fri, 8am-noon Sat) is housed in a fine 18th-century *casona* (large, rambling house) surrounded by what was once a vast hacienda, now little more than a garden. It features a collection of historic objects of decorative art, mostly from Europe, plus a kids' park.

The **World Trade Center** (Map pp74-5; cnr Calle 100 & Carrera 8A) is the heart of Calle 100's 'financial district,' with business offices and a couple of hotels.

Once a pueblo outside Bogotá, and now enveloped in the metropolis, the atmospheric neighborhood of **Usaquén** (Map p64), about 30 blocks northeast of Parque 93, still lives like a village – albeit one with upper-class locals and a quaint central plaza surrounded by stylish antique shops, chic bars and fusion-style eateries. The roughly 10-square-block area is centered by the quaint **Plaza Central de Usaquén** (Map p64; btwn Carreras 6 & 6A & Calles 118 & 119). It's best coming on Sunday for its flea market.

Western Bogotá

Many travelers limit their western forays to trips to the bus station or airport, but there are a few here-and-there attractions. At 360 hectares, **Parque Simón Bolívar** (Map p64) is slightly larger than New York's Central Park, something that more than a few of the weekend draw of 200,000 local park go-ers like to point out. It's a nice spot, with lakes, bike paths and walkways, public libraries, stadiums and many events including the beloved Rock al Parque in October or November. The 'Simón Bolívar' stop on TransMilenio's E line reaches the east end of the park (at Av Ciudad de Quito and Calle 64).

West of the park (reachable by foot via a pedestrian bridge over busy Av 68, then past the El Salitre sports complex), the **Jardín Botánico José Celestino Mutis** (Map p64; ☎ 437 7060; www.jbb .gov.co, in Spanish; Calle 63 No 68-95; ☿ 8am-5pm Mon-Fri, 9am-5pm Sat & Sun) has a variety of national flora

HIGHLIGHTS OF SOUTHERN & WESTERN BOGOTÁ

It's a sad state of affairs, but the bulk of Bogotá – pretty much anything outside La Candelaria, Centro Internacional or the north – is still smeared with a reputation for being dangerous. It's partly true, but there are many places you can visit. Here's our top five:

Peperepe tejo hall (p90)
Cuadra Picha (p88)
Parque Simón Bolívar (above)
Plaza de Mercado de Paloquemao (right)
Maloka (right)

from different climatic zones, some in gardens and others in greenhouses. Airport-bound buses along Autopista El Dorado pass by near the gardens.

A kilometer south, and a short walk from the bus station in the planned neighborhood of La Salistre, **Maloka** (Map p64; ☎ 427 2707; www .maloka.org, in Spanish; Carrera 68D No 51; museum/ cinema/both COP$8000/10,000/17,000; ☿ 8am-5pm Mon-Fri, 10am-7pm Sat, 11am-7pm Sun) is a kid-oriented interactive center of science and technology. Lots of kids in uniform amble about the eight rooms – using physics to lift a car, or playing in the life-sized toy-block park. There's also a high-tech Cine Domo cinema, which plays 40-minute films on a huge dome-ceiling.

A bit closer to the center, **Plaza de Mercado de Paloquemao** (Map p64; cnr Av 19 & Carrera 25; ☿ roughly 8am-1pm) is a real-deal, messy Colombian market.

ACTIVITIES

If you're looking for a place to kick around a football or go for a jog, try the Parque Simón Bolívar (left), or just go for a climb up Monserrate (p76) on weekend mornings.

Bogotá rock-climbers head off to nearby Suesca (p95), but if you want to hone your skills in town, there is a towering climbing wall at **Gran Pared** (Map p64; ☎ 285 0903; www.gran pared.com, in Spanish; Carrera 7 No 50-02; per hr with equipment & instructor COP$16,000, without instructor COP$12,000; ☿ 10am-9:45pm Mon-Sat, 10am-5:45pm Sun).

Higher-priced hotels frequently have gyms. One popular exercise spot for locals into the exercise-bike regime is **Spinning Center** (Map pp74-5; ☎ 636 0590; Calle 94 No 14-47; day/10-day ticket COP$20,000/100,000; ☿ 5am-10pm Mon-Thu, 5am-9pm Fri, 7am-5pm Sat, 7am-3pm Sun).

For real biking, nothing beats Bogotá's incredible 300km network of **CicloRuta** – separate bike lanes that cross the city. Or **Ciclovia**, when 122km of roads open for bikes and pedestrians only on Sundays and holidays from 7am to 2pm. Even if you're on foot, there's a big open **jazzercise session** at the **Parque Nacional Herrera** (Map p64; cnr Carrera 7 & Calle 39) on Sunday mornings too.

Sadly, there are presently no rental bikes available in Bogotá. You can buy a cheapie for about COP$100,000 at shops on Calle 13 between Carreras 17 and 20.

If you don't want to buy a bike, there there are a few agencies that run tours. **Cyclota** (www .cyclota.com, tomascastrillon@unionelementl.com) is a new outfit run by a young English-speaking biker who leads personalized mountain rides or Ciclovia rides, as well as a 'Ruta Verde' ride from Parque Nacional Herrera to Jardín Botánico José Celestino Mutis. City rides cost US$65/55 per person for a group of two/three, including bike, helmet, hotel pick-up and a snack. Cyclota also helped organize a new bike race **Cordillera** (www.cordillera-colombia.com), a 300km ride scheduled for November 2009.

COURSES

Spanish in Colombia comes with a clearer pronunciation than some Latin American destinations. Ask at a hostel or drop by a PIT location (p67) to find out about Spanish-language tutors. A few schools with organized classes follow:

International House Bogotá (Map pp70-1; ☎ 336 4747; www.ihbogota.com; Calle 10 No 4-09; ☷ 8am-6pm Mon-Fri, 8am-1pm Sat) Offers group Spanish-language courses in La Candelaria (US$200 per week for five four-hour mornings) or private tutors (US$29 per hour).

Nueva Lengua (☎ 861 5555; www.nuevalengua .com/spanish; Universidad La Sabana, Km21 Autopista del Norte, edificio G, oficina 109) This language school offers a number of study programs – also at its branches in Medellín and Cartagena. A 25-hour week with a private teacher costs US$460, a 20-hour week in a small class is US$180, and a four-week (minimum) study-and-volunteer program, including work at an orphanage or hospital, is US$460.

Universidad Javeriana's Centro Latinoamericano (Map p64; ☎ 320 8320, ext 4620; www.javeriana .edu.co; Transversal 4 No 42-00, piso 4) Bogotá's best-known school of the Spanish language, which offers private lessons (COP$91,000 per hour) or 120-hour courses (COP$2,350,000 per person).

The other potential big gap in knowledge is dancing. Everyone in Bogotá, pretty much, can salsa like a demon. If you're looking for a dance instructor, a local's advice is 'find yourself a girlfriend or boyfriend and have them teach you.' PITs and some hostels know local tutors.

BOGOTÁ FOR CHILDREN

Some Bogotá attractions are particularly oriented to kids. Maloka (p79) is a children-oriented science museum with a dome cinema, and Museo El Chicó (p78) has a kid's park and library. In the Museo Nacional (p78) you can see mummies and old jail cells. Vendors sell bird seed for the (many) pigeons in Plaza de Bolívar (p69). And you can marvel at the funny hats of the changing of the presidential guard nearby (p73).

Media Torta (p89) is a free kid-oriented concert on Sunday afternoons.

TOURS

Destino Bogotá offers a host of unusual city tour and small-scale day trips, while Sal Si Puedes runs weekend walking trips around the Bogotá area. See p68. Also some of the PIT information centers offer free walking tours daily; see p67.

See p79 for biking tours of Bogotá's network of bike lanes.

FESTIVALS & EVENTS

A mix of local and national festivals takes place constantly throughout the year. The following is a selection of the best. Also ask around as smaller festivals are held each month.

Feria Taurina (Jan & Feb) Bogotá has its bullfighting season when the major corridas take place, with bullfights held on most Sundays. Famous international matadors are invited, mostly from Spain and Mexico.

Festival Iberoamericano de Teatro (Mar & Apr) A theater festival featuring groups from all of Latin America and beyond takes place in every evenly numbered year.

May Day Parade (May 1) Don't tell mom if you're attending this one. Lefty *bogotanos* of various stripes cram into Plaza de Bolívar and along Carrera 7. It's often a scene to avoid. Some participants are known to throw *petos* (paint-filled 'bombs' that are very loud) at police.

Festival de Jazz (Sep) Organized by the Teatro Libre, this festival features local and national Latin jazz artists, plus an occasional US or European star.

Festival de Cine de Bogotá (Oct) With a 20-year history, the city's film festival attracts films from all around the world, including a usually strong Latin American selection.

Hip Hop al Parque (Oct) Two days of hip-hop taking over Parque Simón Bolívar.

Rock al Parque (Oct & Nov; www.rockalparque.gov.co) Three days of (mostly South American) rock/metal/pop/funk/reggae bands at Parque Simón Bolívar. It's free and swarming with fans.

Expoartesanías (Dec) This crafts fair gathers together artisans and their products from all around the country. Crafts are for sale and it's an excellent place to buy them.

SLEEPING

Bogotá is seeing a hotel boom, with new big business-oriented chains (Hilton, Marriott) coming in during the life of this book – particularly along Av El Dorado in (remote) Salitre, a few kilometers east of the airport. Many other high-end choices loom way way north. It's fine to be up there if you want more security for 10pm walks, or to be near malls and dress-up bars. If travel's your game and time's short, La Candelaria is where most of Bogotá's attractions are.

Central Bogotá
LA CANDELARIA
In the past couple of years, the historic suburb of La Candelaria has seen an explosion in hostels – including at least a handful not included here. Generally hostels' private rooms are better than cheapie rooms in the several dated, grubby hotels around here. Higher-end travelers have a couple fine locales with more colonial spirit than you'll find anywhere else in the capital.

Budget
Hostal Sue (Map pp70–1; ☎ 334 8894; www.hostalsue .com; Calle 16 No 2-55; dm/s/d COP$15,000/30,000/45,000; 🖳) Next to Platypus, and frankly a bit of a step down in quality, the friendly Sue (and its two satellite locales) has a fine string of rooms in a cool colonial-style layout. Only the lone double room gets a private bathroom.

Cranky Croc (Map pp70–1; ☎ 314 427 5299; www .crankycroc.com; Calle 15 No 3-46; dm COP$17,000-19,000, s/d with shared bathroom COP$30,000/42,000, with private bathroom COP$40,000/50,000; 🖳) Opened in 2008, this Australian-run hostel has five dorms and five rooms around several communal areas, including a staff-run kitchen with made-to-order breakfasts and a computer room.

our pick **Platypus** (Map pp70–1; ☎ 341 2874, 341 3104; www.platypusbogota.com; Calle 16 No 2-43; dm COP$17,000, s/d with shared bathroom COP$30,000/40,000, with private bathroom COP$40,000/45,000; 🖳) Run by a Bogotá legend, Germán Escobar, a friendly world-traveler who opened a hostel in La Candelaria when no one dared. The hostel fills three homes with simple, clean rooms. There's a cozy kitchen area, and friendly staff (including Germán) offer great travel info. Reserve ahead.

Hotel Aragón (Map pp70–1; ☎ 284 8325; fax 342 6387; Carrera 3 No 14-13; s/d with shared bathroom COP$20,000/35,000) A bit cheaper than hostels' private rooms, and sporting a style seen nowhere else (less grooveburg and more woodsy art deco), the 24-room Aragón has classic dark-wood floor rooms with an antique or two. Shared kitchen, but no internet.

Anandamayi Hostel (Map pp70–1; ☎ 341 7208; www .amandamayihostel.com; Calle 9 No 2-81; dm/s/d COP$ 23,000/70,000/80,000; 🖳) South of most of the hostel zone, this lovely whitewashed colonial home has gorgeous rooms with wood-beam ceilings and plenty of wool blankets. Some serve as dorms, others as private rooms with desks overlooking the central courtyard with hammocks.

Hotel Dorantes (Map pp70–1; ☎ 334 6640, 341 5365; www.hoteldorantes.com; Calle 13 No 5-07; s/d COP$40,000/60,000; 🖳) For a little stately grandeur – albeit faded – the Dorantes has ornate rooms with worn-out floors and makeshift bathrooms put in the corner.

Midrange & Top End
Hotel Ambala (Map pp70–1; ☎ 342 6384; www .hotelambala.net; Carrera 5 No 13-46; s/d/tr incl breakfast COP$65,000/98,000; 🖳) Something like a Bogotá 'capsule hotel,' this friendly 22-room hotel has a trace of colonial style in its closet-sized rooms with tile floors, a single framed print, TV and telephone.

Hotel Quinta de Bolívar (Map pp70–1; ☎ 337 6500; www.hotelquintadebolivar.com; Carrera 4 No 17-59; s/d incl breakfast COP$68,000/110,000; 🖳) This new, bright 20-room makeover of a house gets points for trying to revitalize a slightly dodgy street in nearby City Center. The small rooms are colorful and clean, with telephone, TV and Botero prints on the walls.

Hotel Lido (Map pp70–1; ☎ 341 2582; www.hotellido plaza.com; Calle 11 No 9-45; s/d COP$70,000/120,000; 🖳) On a block of tailors, a block-and-a-half south of the main square, this neat 20-room job has compact carpeted rooms, with TV, telephone and private bathrooms.

Casa Platypus (Map pp70–1; ☎ 281 1801; www .platypusbogota.com; Carrera 3 No 16-28; s/d incl breakfast COP$100,000/130,000; 🖳) Still unfinished when we dropped by, this new 'boutique' branch to the Platypus hostel nearby goes for the private-bathroom crowd, with small, rather simple, wood-floor rooms, plus a wee observation deck and a wonderful all-wood TV room overlooking nearby Av Jiménez.

Hotel Abadia Colonial (Map pp70–1; ☎ 341 1884; www.abadiacolonial.com; Calle 11 No 2-32; s/d incl breakfast COP$120,000/180,000; 🖳) More intimate than other higher-priced hotels in La Candelaria, this pleasant 12-room hotel has tidy white-walled rooms with colorful blankets, wall safes and a sense of colonial style, while adding floor heaters and TV. Breakfast is served in one of the pleasant courtyard seating areas.

Casa de la Botica (Map pp70–1; ☎ 281 0811; www.hotel casadelabotica.com; Calle 9 No 6-45; s/d COP$300,000/336,000, s/d incl breakfast COP$355,000/391,000; 🖳) Near Congress commuters on a central lane dominated by the Colegio Mayor de San Bartolomé, this 10-room wonder pairs colonial style with a modern feel in its carpeted rooms. Opt up for the bigger suite – with fireplace and full windows overlooking a tiny rock garden. There's wi-fi throughout and an upstairs restaurant.

ourpick Hotel de la Ópera (Map pp70-1; ☎ 336 2066; www.hotelopera.com.co; Calle 10 No 5-72; r incl breakfast COP$297,000-371,000; ste incl breakfast COP$434,000; 🖳 🐾) La Candelaria's poshest hotel – named for the leotard shows at Teatro Colón next door – features gracefully restored rooms of two historic Spanish-colonial townhouses enveloping two courtyards (it's 'totally colonial!' to quote insistent staff). Higher-priced rooms get small balconies; the suites are sprawling with ornate details. Surprises include a tucked-away spa and swimming pool, and the superb top-floor Mirador restaurant. The hotel plans to add 15 more rooms by the time this book's published.

CENTRO INTERNACIONAL

The center's grubby loud blocks have several hotels – some pleasant enough – but we've focused on the nicer areas to the north in the Centro Internacional.

El Cafecito (Map p64; ☎ 285 8308; www.cafecito.net; Carrera 6 No 34-70; dm/s/d COP$20,000/30,000/50,000; 🖳) Bogotá's lone hostel outside La Candelaria is set up in a quaint neighborhood of redbrick English-style townhouses, nice but rather removed. The six dorms, a lone double and lone single have wood floors – all have shared bathrooms. There's a nice 1st-floor restaurant too.

Hotel Baviera (Map p64; ☎ 320 3564; www.hotelbaviera.com.co; Calle 32 No 13-32; s/d incl breakfast COP$148,000/187,000; 🖳) In a tower amid more towers, the friendly Baviera has 40 spacious apartments, with slightly dated furnishings, each comprised of a step-in kitchen, sitting area with balcony and small bedroom. There's a communal gym and sauna for guests to use.

Residencias Tequendama (Map pp70-1; ☎ 381 3700; Carrera 10 No 27-51; old/renovated apt incl breakfast COP$290,000/385,000; 🖳) Peso-per-quality-point, the towering Residencias' apartment-style rooms get our nod over its more famous cousin Tequendama next door, despite a bit of a hodgepodge vibe that may stem

from its owners: the military. Only go with renovated rooms.

Hotel Tequendama Crown Plaza (Map pp70-1; ☎ 382 0300; bogha@interconti.com; Carrera 10 No 26-20; s/d from COP$445,000/890,000; 🅿 ✗ 🖳) Bogotá is in love with this historic, overpriced hotel, with 578 rooms. We're less smitten, but it's fine.

Northern Bogotá

If you understand 'per diem' without blinking – ie are here on business – or are used to the high life, you may be best served by the hotels scattered north of Calle 65, many of which are within walking distance of the lively scene of Zona G, Zona Rosa or Parque 93. There are many more not listed here, on and north of Calle 100 (aka 'the financial district') as well as the swank chain Hoteles Royal (www.hotelesroyal.com).

ZONA G

Casa Falcon (Map p64; ☎ 211 0941; jcartagena64@gmail.com; Calle 69 No 11A-64; s/d incl breakfast COP$72,000/103,000; 🖳) Steps from the TransMilenio 'Flores' stop – and a rare cheapie up north – the OK 12-room Falcon is a bit like the dated budget hotels of La Candelaria.

ourpick La Casona del Patio (Map p64; ☎ 212 8805; www.lacasonadelpatio.net; Carrera 8 No 69-24; s/d incl breakfast COP$95,000/127,000; 🖳) This lovely guesthouse has eight rooms with a TV/computer room overlooking the cute namesake 'yellow patio.' Rooms are pleasant with wood floors and picture-themed for area attractions. Avoid 'Monserrate' though – it's above the neighboring restaurant, which gets loud on weekend nights (no sleep till 2am!). No laundry service.

ourpick Casa Medina (Map p64; ☎ 217 0288; www.hoteles-charleston.com, in Spanish; Carrera 7A No 69A-22; r incl breakfast COP$600,000-660,000, ste COP$700,000-840,000; 🖳) Set up in a richly colonial style building – only built in 1945 (with a slightly less-atmospheric '90s annex in back) – Casa Medina's mix of 58 rooms make it easily one of Bogotá's finest hotels, with a chic tweak to colonial gems like ornate wood-carved wall panels and ceiling beams. Try for suites with fireplaces.

ZONA ROSA & PARQUE 93

Hotel Charlotte (Map pp74-5; ☎ 218 1625; Carrera 15 No 87-94; s/d incl breakfast COP$207,000/256,000; 🖳) Between Zona Rosa and Parque 93, this recently spruced up 50-room mod-styled hotel overlooks a leafy CicloRuta path and has three cozy cafes on the ground floor.

Hotel Saint Simon (Map pp74-5; ☎ 621 8188; www .saintsimonbogota.com; Carrera 14 No 81-34; s/d incl breakfast COP$178,000/254,000; 🖳) This friendly midranger in Zona Rosa has nice staff, but the grandeur fades after you leave the nice lobby – rather dated furnishings and flowery wallpaper give rooms no points for style.

Hamilton Court (Map pp74-5; ☎ 621 5455; www .ghlhoteles.com; Carrera 14 No 81-20; s/d incl breakfast COP$301,000/370,000; ⊠ 🖳) Next to the Saint Simon, this standard business hotel's 'suites' are carpeted, with a separate sleeping area and seating area with sofa. Not particularly inspired, but clean and fresh.

Sofitel (Map pp74-5; ☎ 621 2666; www.sofitel.com; Carrera 13 No 85-80; r from COP$350,000; ⊠ 🖳) One of Zona Rosa's best-run hotels, the Sofitel is on a relatively quiet block a couple minutes' walk from the malls, restaurants and clubs. The sea-of-marble lobby leads up to nice, L-shaped rooms. There's also a gym and Mediterranean restaurant.

Pavillon Royal (Map pp74-5; ☎ 650 2555; www .hotelesroyal.com; Calle 94 No 11-45; s/d incl breakfast from COP$450,000/525,000; 🖳) The poshest of the Royal chain, the 30-room Pavillon is a block from Parque 93, filling two stately, red-orange towers with a sleek, modern lobby and stylish rooms.

USAQUÉN

ⓞⓤⓡⓟⓘⓒⓚ Atico de Usaquén (Map p64; ☎ 657 8910; www .hotelesroyal.com; Calle 117 No 5-10; s/d/ste incl breakfast COP$290,000/340,000/380,000; 🖳) One of Bogotá's most intimate boutique hotels, this new eight-room modern spot is a couple blocks from Usaquén's quaint plaza and area shops, bars and eateries. Each rooms have shaggy carpets, chic design and big looks at mountains from windows – particularly from the lone suite's wrap-around balcony.

EATING

Fusion is the word these days for many restaurateurs in Bogotá who are running Mediterranean, Italian, Californian or pan-Asian influences through many typical Colombian dishes. The latest dinner destinations include Zona G's chic eateries and Macarena's slightly boho scene, just north of La Candelaria, where many restaurants close up the kitchen and continue on into the night with drinks (only) for the lively student scene.

Central Bogotá
LA CANDELARIA

Café de la Peña Pastelería Francesa (Map pp70-1; ☎ 336 7488; croissants COP$1500; Carrera 3 No 9-66; ⏰ 8am-8pm Mon-Sat, 9am-6pm Sun) This simple French-run bakery, with local art adorning the walls of a couple seating areas, makes some of the nicest sweets and *pan de chocolate* around the center.

La Puerta Falsa (Map pp70-1; Calle 11 No 6-50; candies COP$1000, meals COP$4000; ⏰ 7am-11pm Mon-Sat) This is Bogotá's most famous snack shop – with displayed multicolored candies beckoning you into the tiny spot that's been in business since 1816. Grab a sticky *breva* candy, eggs or tamales for breakfast, or sit with *chocolate completo* (hot chocolate with cheese, buttered bread and a biscuit; COP$4000).

Asociación Futuro (Map pp70-1; Calle 15 No 2-21; set meals from COP$4200; ⏰ 7am-8pm Mon-Fri, 7am-7pm Sat, 8am-1pm Sun) Splitting its breakfast trade evenly between locals and backpackers from nearby hostels, this cute corner pad churns out great set breakfasts and Colombian dishes later on. The community-run spot employs staff from a poor area.

L' Jaim (Map pp70-1; ☎ 281 8635; Carrera 3 No 14-79; set meal COP$6200; ⏰ 11am-5pm Sun-Fri) This little bit of Israel transported to Bogotá serves great *shawarma* (chopped meat and veggies

---

LATE-NIGHT SNACKING FOR THE DRUNK

ⓞⓤⓡⓟⓘⓒⓚ Desayunadero de la 42 (Map p64; cnr Calle 42 & Av Caracas; dishes from COP$8000; ⏰ 24hr) For decades, bleary-eyed, ultradrunk *bogotanos* have staggered in to this modest eatery for a bit of wholesome revival. It's a big space but can get packed at 3am some nights – most drinkers opting for eye-opening (but pricey) plates of *calentado* (literally 'reheated leftovers,' a mix of rice, meat, yucca, plantains and beans) or a *caldo con carne* (soup with sliced potatoes and giant chunks of fatty beef) – both about COP$15,000.

Selfless research methods attest that the waiters are *very* patient with various late-night antics, like smuggled-in half-full glasses of aguardiente.

served with pita and hummus) plus felafel and baklava.

ourpick **Quinua y Amaranto** (Map pp70-1; ☎ 565 9982; Calle 11 No 2-95; set lunch COP$9000; 8am-8pm Mon-Fri, 8am-4pm Sat) This sweet spot – run by ladies in the open-front kitchen – goes all vegetarian, with tasty quinoa-based lunches and empanadas, salads and coffee later on.

Enchiladas (Map pp70-1; ☎ 286 0312; Calle 10 No 2-12; dishes COP$9000-22,000; noon-5pm Sun-Tue, noon-9pm Wed-Sat) For great Mexican meals (veggie and meat), try this lovely spot with Mayan reliefs, a toasty fireplace and old Mexican film photos on the walls. The giant, tasty meat-filled platter of enchiladas and chilaquilas 'General Lee' is named for a gringo regular (not a US Civil War general; COP$22,000). Skip the tacos.

Sanalejo (Map pp70-1; ☎ 334 6171; Av Jiménez No 3-73; mains COP$8000-30,000; noon-10pm Mon-Wed, noon-midnight Thu-Sat) A romantic candle-lit series of rooms in this orange-and-green home off Jiménez cooks up pastas, but is better for its meats (like the 'Baby Beef' – a chunky serve of steak with fries for COP$22,000). Best of all, it's open for dinner.

Anderson's (Map pp70-1; Carrera 6 No 10-19; mains COP$20,000-28,000; noon-3pm Mon-Sat, 6-10pm Fri) Run by a Nebraskan, this seven-table eatery – filled with bohos, judges and Congressmen – is a cozy wood-floor spot with an open kitchen and excellent dishes, like a stacked filet mignon atop hash browns and a super banana foster for dessert.

CITY CENTER
Olimpica (Map pp70-1; Av Jiménez No 4-70; 7am-9pm Mon-Sat, 9am-4pm Sun) Supermarket, about a five-minute walk from most hostels.

Pastelería Florida (Map pp70-1; ☎ 341 0340; Carrera 7 No 21-46; snacks from COP$1000, chocolate completo COP$4000; 6am-10pm Mon-Sat, 6:30am-8pm Sun) Those needing a bit of pomp or history with their *chocolate santafereño* should make the hike to this classic snack shop/restaurant (a legendary spot for hot chocolate since 1936), with uniformed waiters serving up a variety of cakes.

Restaurante La Pola (Map pp70-1; ☎ 566 5654; Calle 19 No 1-85; set lunch COP$8000; 11am-5pm Mon-Sat) A classic spot, La Pola – on the road to Monserrate – has a mix of old-style rooms and a small courtyard, and offers an excellent lunch deal of meats (the *carne a la criolla*, a dish of yummy beefsteak with onion and tomato sauce, is superb), along with juice

and some of the city's best *ajiaco* (soup with chicken, corn, potato, cream and capers).

MACARENA
A dozen blocks north of La Candelaria (or a couple uphill from Centro Internacional), Macarena is an up-and-coming dining district – with a stream of excellent, stylish choices – holding true to its local roots, with passersby likely to pop in and chat with diners.

There are also many worthy choices on Calle 29, just northeast of the Museo Nacional, in Centro Internacional.

Cuba Pizza (Map pp70-1; ☎ 352 1835; Calle 26A No 3A-26; pizzas COP$5000; 12:30-11pm Mon-Sat) This cramped basement space is run by a born-again dough maker who credits 'a lot of love' for why her incredibly underpriced pizzas, topped with interesting ingredients such as octopus, are of the best in town.

La Juguetería (Map pp70-1; ☎ 341 1188; Calle 27 No 4A-03; dishes COP$15,000-28,000; noon-3:30pm & 7pm-midnight Mon-Sat, 1-4:30pm Sun) Freaky toy-house in Macarena that serves steaks. Glass-top tables feature xylophones and demonic dolls, while merry-go-round horses watch over from the walls. Hard to walk away unfazed.

Tapas Macarena (Map pp70-1; ☎ 243 9004; Carrera 4A No 26-01; tapas COP$8000-20,000; noon-3pm, 6:30-11pm Tue-Sat) Run by a Dutch/Colombian couple, this cool corner spot is tiny with a play on the usual tapas, including sautéed beef with Indonesian peanut sauce, and Dutch cheese plates. Plenty of Belgian beers too.

Northern Bogotá
ZONA G
Bogotá's primo dining area fills a couple blocks of converted brick houses into a mix of excellent eateries (Argentine steaks, Italian, French), about 10 blocks south of Zona Rosa.

Harry's (Map p64; ☎ 321 3940; www.harrysasson.com; Calle 70 No 5-57; burgers COP$25,000, steaks from COP$40,000; noon-midnight Mon-Sat, noon-5pm Sun) The busiest of the dressed-up spots, Harry's has a massive covered patio, sidewalk seats and slick bar area – popular for an afternoon beer or glass of wine, and more substantial Argentine steaks and seafood dishes later on. There's a nice bakery too, offering salads, sandwiches and sweets.

ZONA ROSA & PARQUE 93
Sometimes called 'Zona T' for its T-shaped pedestrian zone filled with bars, restaurants and

---

BOGOTÁ CHAINS

We're not accustomed to touting chains, but Bogotá has some surprisingly worthy ones you'll find in most neighborhoods, particularly in the north.

Bogotá Beer Company (Map p64; ☎ 802 6784; www.bogotabeercompany.com; Carrera 6 No 119-24; burgers COP$15,000; ⏱ noon-1am or 2am) These pubby-style beer joints revolve a few seasonal brews and make excellent burgers. This Usaquén locale is a bit more laid-back than the other half-a-dozen, like the busy one in **Zona Rosa** (Map pp74-5; Carrera 12 No 83-33).

Crepes & Waffles (Map pp74-5; ☎ 211 2530; Carrera 9 No 73-33; crepes COP$8900-27,000; ⏱ 11:45am-10:30pm Mon-Sat, 11:45am-9pm Sun) Of the many locations of this ever-busy chain – which employs women in need – we like this one best: a two-story brick home with sidewalk seats between Zona G and Zona Rosa. Like the others, it serves up veggie, meat and seafood crepes, plus irresistible ice-cream-topped waffles (COP$5000).

Wok (Map pp74-5; ☎ 236 4939; Calle 93B No 12-28; noodles COP$13,000-16,000; ⏱ noon-11pm Mon-Sat, noon-9pm Sun) The cool chain does a good version of Chinese, Japanese, Indonesian and Cambodian noodles that attracts locals at all hours. Another convenient location is in Zona Rosa (Map pp74-5; Carrera 13 No 82-74).

---

a few chains, the area of Zona Rosa also has oodles more options on surrounding blocks. If you need a peso break, nearby Carrera 15 is lined with places selling COP$700 empanadas and COP$3900 pizza-and-soda deals. Ten blocks north, the more-sedate Parque 93 and Calle 94 have even classier spots.

Casa Mexicana (Map pp74-5; ☎ 257 3407; Calle 80 No 14-08; dishes COP$20,000-29,000; ⏱ noon-9:30pm Mon-Sat) A block from Zona Rosa's main action, this happy corner spot has Zapata pics on the walls, colorful sundresses on the waitresses and yummy Mexican specialties on the plate.

Salto de Ángel (Map pp74-5; ☎ 236 3139; Carrera 13 No 93A-45; dishes COP$17,000-25,000; ⏱ noon-midnight Mon-Sat, noon-5pm Sun) Parque 93's best location – a raised restaurant with cavernous rooms topped with bamboo poles and huge windows overlooking the park – the 'Angel Falls' is often full. It's probably just as good for its setting and drinks (or an excellent slushy cantaloupe juice, COP$4000) as it is for its typical fare: steaks, salads, sandwiches, fajitas.

USAQUÉN

Once a village to the north, Usaquén has been overtaken by Bogotá – but still lives at its own quiet pace. You'll find snazzy Chinese, Mediterranean or burger joints within a block of the main plaza.

80 Sillas (Map p64; ☎ 619 2471; Calle 118 No 7-09; dishes COP$12,000-15,000; ⏱ noon-11pm Mon-Sat, noon-5pm Sun) Usaquén's busiest spot is all about putting a modern spin on traditional ceviche, set in a redone colonial farmhouse on the southwestern corner of the plaza. You can pick from a host of ceviche styles (such as

ginger or a hearty *criollo* with bacon, potato, lemon and cheese). Yes, careful reader, there are 80 seats.

FURTHER NORTH

Andrés Carne de Res (☎ 863 7880; www.andrescarnederes.com, in Spanish; Calle 3 No 11A-56, Chía; meals from COP$35,000; ⏱ noon-3am Fri-Sun) Hang onto your hats. This legendary steakhouse blows everyone away – even repeat visitors – for its all-out-fun atmosphere with decent steaks and all sorts of surreal decor and designed gimmicks such as menus retracting from the rafters. For most, it's more than a meal – but a leave-the-watch-at-home expanse of late-night rumba. Staff will get you on the floor if you resist joining in. The catch is that it's out of town – in Chía, 23km north towards Zipaquirá. A taxi from Bogotá costs about COP$25,000 to COP$40,000.

DRINKING

Some of the city's most atmospheric bars – that is, if you're into 300-year-old homes with corner fireplaces and old tile floors – are in La Candelaria, a great spot to try a hot mug of *canelazo* (a drink made with aguardiente, sugarcane, cinnamon and lime), while watering holes get more Euro-styled and upscale around Zona Rosa or Parque 93.

Central Bogotá

LA CANDELARIA

Considering the student scene in the area, La Candelaria cafes focus on drinks alone after hours. You can find plenty of life around the corner of Calle 15 and Carrera 4 – with reggae, rock and tango bars – or along Calle 11 by

---

COFFEE

Coffee's huge in Bogotá – supposedly nine in 10 households brew a pot daily – but much of it isn't very good. That's a pity considering the quality of the bean Colombia produces. The two big chains here – Juan Valdéz and Oma – are Starbucks-styled, but do as reliable a job with a *tinto* (black coffee) or cappuccino or *cafe americano* as anyone in town. You'll find them all over town (particularly the mustached icon of Juan Valdéz); the north has the most, so here are a couple central locales:

Oma (Map pp70-1; cnr Carrera 8 & Calle 12; ◷ 7:30am-8pm Mon-Fri, 9am-6pm Sat) Also carries sandwiches.

Juan Valdéz (Map pp70-1; Museo Botero, Calle 11 No 4-41; ◷ 7am-11pm Mon-Sat, 10am-7pm Sun) Another nice locale is between Zona G and Zona Rosa at Calle 73 & Carrera 9.

For good independent cafe options, try one of the cafes on Calle 14 between Carreras 3 and 4, such as the cozy **Café del Sol** (Map pp70–1; Calle 14 No 3-60; ◷ 8am-8pm), filled with lots of happy couples when we visited, and tempting sandwiches made to order.

Universidad de la Salle (cnr Calle 11 & Carrera 2), but our favorite is Callejón del Embudo (or 'funnel') – the tiny alley north of Plazoleta de Chorro de Quevedo, lined with sit-and-chat cafes and bars selling *chicha* (an indigenous corn beer). Be warned: one bartender swore 'too much *chicha* is really bad for the brain!'

El Viejo Almacén (Map pp70-1; ☎ 284 2364; Calle 15 No 4-18; ◷ 7pm-3am Tue-Sat) One of half a dozen bars/clubs on the block, the Viejo Almacén is a classic tango dive. Soft lit space with oodles of Carlos Gardel pics, a wall of 5000 dusty tango LPs, and couples taking a step or two as some of the vinyl spins. Beer is COP$1500.

Yumi Yumi (Map pp70-1; Carrera 3 No 16-40; ◷ 11am-midnight Mon-Sat) Right off Av Jiménez, this pocket-sized lounge/restaurant – run by a bleach-haired Brit bloke and mustached local chef – fills with student passersby and hostel guests for excellent, experimental two-for-one cocktails (try the sour *lucita*, with tequila and *lulo* fruit) for COP$14,000. The Thai curry special on Monday and Tuesday (COP$9000) is the best touch of Bangkok in Bogotá.

Pequeña Santa Fe (Map pp70-1; ☎ 281 5587; Carrera 2 No 13-14; ◷ noon-10pm Sun-Wed, noon-1am Thu-Sat) A cozy, historic two-story home with a fireplace by the bar and soft-lit lot upstairs sits next to the evocative Plazoleta del Chorro de Quevedo. It's one of a few great spots here to sample a hot mug of '*canelazo* Santa Fe' (a yerba-buena tea with aguardiente), or a beer.

Casa de Citas (Map pp70-1; ☎ 282 6368; Carrera 3 No 13-35; ◷ noon-10pm Mon-Tue, noon-3am Wed-Sat) Named for an earlier incarnation – when prostitutes advertised themselves from the balcony above – the saloon-styled Citas is now an atmospheric

cafe, adorned with Castro photos, that hosts live rumba, jazz or salsa shows Thursday through to Saturday. Great COP$7500 set lunch during the day too.

CENTRO INTERNACIONAL

The business district tends to clear out after dark. You can find a few bars up the hill in Macarena.

El Libertador (Map pp70-1; ☎ 245 1220; Calle 29 No 5-90; ◷ 6pm-3am Tue-Sat) Busy with 20-something cool kids, this posh cocktail bar, above a restaurant on a boutique-eats strip near Museo Nacional, has soft-light rooms with lounge seats, a mounted deer head and pricey malt whiskeys (from COP$16,000).

CHAPINERO

This sprawling bohemian district with many gay bars and theaters sits south of the high-end eateries of the more polite northern neighbor Zona G. Start on Calle 60, between Carreras 8 and 9, and head south on Carrera 9. Further south, Calle 51 between Carrera 7 and 8 is something of a 'student street' with half a dozen flirt-all-day, glassed-in bars and a couple dance clubs.

A quirky option in Chapinero is **Treffen** (Map p64; ☎ 249 5058; Carrera 7 No 56-17; ◷ 3pm-3am Mon-Sat), which means 'encounter' in German, but no words describe the bar's cartoon nightmare mood, with nooks and crannies filled with stuffed animals, colorful tables and games menus.

Northern Bogotá

Though the area's more famous for its clubs (and malls!), you'll have no problem finding a place for a cocktail, beer or coffee around Zona Rosa or Parque 93. In the former, start in the pedestrian mall (Zona T), where you can find several bars, including the enduringly popular Irish-style **Pub** (Map pp74-5; ☎ 691 8711; Carrera 12A No 83-48; ☯ noon-late) with Murphy's on tap and fish and chips.

A couple blocks northwest, the raucous **Museo del Tequila** (Map pp74-5; ☎ 256 6614; Carrera 13A No 86A-18; ☯ noon-1am Tue-Sat, noon-6pm Sun) serves excellent Mexican food, but is more proud of showing off (and pouring from) the 1585 bottles of tequila that grace its walls.

Up in Parque 93, **Salto de Ángel** (Map pp74-5; ☎ 236 3139; Carrera 13 No 93A-45; ☯ noon-midnight Mon-Sat, noon-5pm Sun) is the go-to for late-night drinks.

ENTERTAINMENT

Bogotá has far more cultural activities than any other city in Colombia. Check out the Friday edition of local paper *El Tiempo,* which carries a what's-on section, *Eskep,* listing coming events and short reviews. Other listings you'll find around town include **Plan B** (www.planb.com .co) and the slightly edgier **Go** (www.goguiadelocio .com, COP$3000), available at newsstands and at Zona G bookstore Authors (see p65). *Cartel Urbano* is a free alternative monthly available in some hipper bars and restaurants. There are more listings at www.terra.com.co.

For schedules and tickets to many events (theater, rock concerts, football games), check **Tu Boleta** (www.tuboleta.com).

Nightclubs

That Colombia was deemed the 'third happiest country' in the world in 2008 may be solely due to the joy found on dance floors nationwide, and notably so across the capital. There's all sort of ambience and musical rhythm on offer – from rock, techno and metal to salsa, vallenato and samba. If you don't know how to dance, be prepared to prove it. Strangers frequently ask each other to dance and everyone seems to know the words to every song played.

The relatively laid-back club scene of La Candelaria caters to local students, who don't always care what they're wearing. Up north, particularly the chic scene around the sparkling, vibrant (if pretentious) *salsatecas* and clubs of Zona Rosa and Parque 93, you may be turned away for not being dressed up to the part (or, in uglier situations, minority visitors may find some clubs eternally 'full').

Cover charges vary from free to COP$10,000 or COP$25,000, depending on the scheduled event or day of the week.

CENTRAL BOGOTÁ

Escobar Rosas (Map pp70-1; ☎ 341 7903; Calle 15 No 4-02; cover incl 3 drinks COP$12,000-15,000; ☯ 8pm-late Thu-Sat) An unsigned sad little corner building opens into one of La Candelaria's most popular dance places – a gritty, cramped, two-level place with electronic, funk and rock music for arty youth. *Carpe diem!*

Quiebra Canto (Map pp70-1; ☎ 243 1630; Carrera 5 No 17-76; cover on weekends about COP$7000; ☯ 6:30pm-2:30am Wed-Sat) Name-dropped first – for years now – by salsa-seekers across town, the Canto is a double-level disco a short walk from La Candelaria. Wednesday is big with expats for electronica DJs, but weekends go for live salsa.

El Goce Pagano (Map pp70-1; ☎ 243 2546; Carrera 1 No 20-04; cover COP$20,000; ☯ 7pm-3am Fri-Sat) Nearing 40, the divey salsa/reggae bar near Los Andes university is a smoky place with DJs and sweat-soaked bodies.

Buenavista (Map p64; ☎ 245 4427; Carrera 6A No 35-37; cover COP$10,000-15,000; ☯ 6pm-3am Thu-Sat) Totally unpretentious salsa club located in a brick house, a short taxi ride north of La Candelaria, with about 20 tables and live Cuban bands on weekends.

Cha Cha (Map p64; ☎ 311 257 1972; www.elchacha .com; Carrera 7 No 32-36, piso 41; cover COP$25,000-50,000; ☯ 10pm-4am Thu-Sun) Atop the old Hotel Hilton in Chapinero (with sweeping city views), the glitzy Louis XVI–meets-art-deco club brings in fairly casual locals for a mix of DJs spinning various rhythms *del noche* – rumba, salsa, electronica. And Sunday night is 'Sungay' night.

NORTHERN BOGOTÁ

Salomé Pagana (Map pp74-5; ☎ 218 4076; Carrera 14A No 82-16; cover free to COP$15,000; ☯ 6pm-3am) For Zona Rosa, it's a surprisingly divey, red-walled *salsateca,* run by the gray-haired collector César Pagano, who hits the black-and-white checkered dance floor most weekend nights. A mix of locals come for salsa and *son cubano* wearing whatever: tennis shoes or high heels.

Gaira Café (Map pp74-5; ☎ 636 2696; Carrera 13 No 96-11; cover after 8pm COP$20,000; ☯ 9am-10pm Mon-Wed, 9am-3am Thu-Sat, 9am-6pm Sun) Vallenato legend Carlos Vives' ultrafun dancehall/restaurant for live vallenato – or modern takes on it. Locals

GAY & LESBIAN BOGOTÁ

Bogotá has a large, frequently changing gay scene, mostly centered in Chapinero. Browse www
.guiagaycolombia.com/bogota, in Spanish, for more details on dozens of varied clubs and bars,
or check online listings from **Colombia Diversa** (www.colombiadiversa.org), a not-for-profit organization promoting gay and lesbian rights in Colombia.

On a small road (between Carreras 9 and 13) in the heart of Chapinero, **Theatron** (Map
p64; ☎ 249 2092; www.theatrondepelicula.com, in Spanish; Calle 58 No 10-32; cover free to
COP$250,000; ☒ 9pm-late Thu-Sat) is made from a huge converted film house, with three dance
floors (and themes) and various parties. It's men only at Theatron's slick annex here **Lottus**.
Outside you'll see Turkish baths and a *'hostal.'*

There are dozens of bars in the area. **LaOficina.com** (Map p64; ☎ 249 4948; Calle 59 No
13-22) is a low-key kick-starter bar for late night parties, with no cover and crowds dispersing
after midnight. **Bianca** (Map p64; ☎ 314 5187; Calle 72 No 20-90; ☒ 7pm-late Mon-Sat) is a
women-only rumba bar.

Meanwhile, **Cha Cha** (p87) hosts a full-on 'Sungay night' that benefits Bogotá's Colombia
Diversa organization (cover COP$15,000).

pack in for food and rum drinks, and dance in
the tight spaces around tables to an 11-piece
band. Cocktails are about COP$15,000, sand-
wiches and salads from COP$11,000.

Vinacure (Map p64; ☎ 255 8355; Av Caracas No 63-52;
cover COP$20,000; ☒ Wed-Sat) An unreal makeover
of a historic theatre, this camp electronica
disco has a giant flesh-to-flesh dance floor for
fun-seeking *bogotanos* of all persuasions; all
eyes equally fasten onto the red-curtain stage
for wild drag queen karaoke shows later on.

Alma (Map pp74-5; ☎ 622 8289; Calle 85 No 12-81;
cover COP$20,000; ☒ Wed-Sat) Bogotá's beautiful,
snobby, ritzy crowd elbows its way into this
new Zona Rosa three-floor club that varies its
musical styles – salsa, rock, electronic, funk.
Don't be surprised to be turned away.

El Sitio (Map pp74-5; ☎ 616 7372; www.elsitiobar.com;
Carrera 11A No 93B-12; cover from COP$20,000; ☒ noon-1am
Mon-Tue, noon-3am Wed-Sat) This ultratrendy bar/
restaurant off Parque 93 has a large interior
and frequent rumba bands.

WESTERN BOGOTÁ
One place in way west Bogotá (about 6km
west of La Candelaria) that's starting to get
local attention is the so-called Cuadra Picha
(or 'Rotten Block'; Calle 6 Sur & Carrera 71,
near Av 1 de Mayo), a block-plus full of loud,
welcoming open-front bars geared for many
working-class partiers that's attracting some
Zona Rosa folks. It's safe, well lit, and you can
stroll from one venue to the other as there is
no cover charge. Clubs indicate their styles
(vallenato, rumba, electronica, Iron Maiden) –
not that you won't hear the blasting music.

It's busiest on weekends, but is open nightly
to 5am or 6am.

Cinemas
Bogotá has dozens of cinemas offering the
usual Hollywood fare. Major universities
have *cineclubes* (film clubs) showing films
on campus or using commercial cinemas
or the auditoriums of other institutions –
accessible to all. Tickets run up to COP$9000
after 3pm, COP$6000 before 3pm.

Cine Colombia Andino (Map pp74-5; ☎ 404 2463;
Centro Comercial Andino, Carrera 12 No 82-01, piso 3)
Multiplex cinema in Zona Rosa's Andino mall.

Cinemateca Distrital (Map pp70-1; ☎ 284 8076;
www.cinematecadistrital.gov.co, in Spanish; Carrera 7 No
22-79) Art cinema hosts frequent film festivals.

Maloka (Map p64; ☎ 427 2707; www.maloka.org,
in Spanish; Carrera 68D No 51; museum/cinema/both
COP$8000/10,000/17,000; ☒ 8am-5pm Mon-Fri, 10am-
7pm Sat, 11am-7pm Sun)) Its CineDomo screens giant
kid-friendly educational films on its massive dome ceiling.

Multiplex Cine Colombia (Map pp70-1; ☎ 404 2463;
Calle 24 No 6-01) A six-screen multiplex in the city center.

Museo de Arte Moderno (Map pp70-1; ☎ 286 0466)
Screens various art-house films daily except Monday.

Theater
Bogotá is big on theater with more than a
dozen options. Many lefty, politicized troupes
dominate La Candelaria, while more mainstream options linger 'uptown' in the north.

TRADITIONAL
Teatro Colón (Map pp70-1; ☎ 284 7420; www.bogota
-dc.com/eventos/teatro/colon.html, in Spanish; Calle 10 No

5-32) La Candelaria's most famous – and the city's loveliest – stage is undergoing a long renovation until 2010. When it reopens, it'll resume its repertoire of large-scale opera and the occasional drama for a dress-up, high-end crowd.

Teatro Nacional (Map p64; ☎ 217 4577; Calle 71 No 10-25) Similar in its programming to Teatro Colón.

Teatro Nacional La Castellana (Map pp74-5; ☎ 256 1399; Calle 95 No 30-13) An offshoot of Teatro Nacional.

ALTERNATIVE

Teatro de La Candelaria (Map pp70-1; ☎ 281 4814; Calle 12 No 2-59; tickets adult/student COP$15,000/8000) One of the edgiest theaters in the center, with a mix of political shows (often lefty, sometimes covering women's-rights issues) that always know when to put in a joke to diffuse any tension.

Teatro Seki Sano (Map pp70-1; ☎ 284 8687; Calle 12 No 2-65) Another alternative-theater option, next door to Teatro de La Candelaria.

Fundación Gilberto Alzate Avendaño (Map pp70-1; ☎ 282 9491; www.fgaa.gov.co; Calle 10 No 3-16) This cultural institute in La Candelaria hosts many events (including dance and theater, and also some concerts). In 2008 a Goya painting was stolen during an art exhibit here.

Teatro Experimental La Mama (Map p64; ☎ 211 2709; www.teatrolamama.com; Calle 63 No 9-60) Now in its fifth decade, this alternative, 'experimental' theater in Chapinero stages various performances by amateur groups not shy to provoke.

Teatro Libre Centro (Map pp70-1; ☎ 281 4834; www.teatrolibre.com; Calle 13 No 2-44) This is another venue for small theater, although most of its productions are now presented in the theater group's new branch, **Teatro Libre Chapinero** (Map p64; ☎ 217 1988; Calle 62 No 10-65; tickets COP$20,000-80,000).

Live Music

Clubs across town stage live music nightly across Bogotá (see p87), and outdoor events like Rock al Parque (p80) are huge festivals that attract fans from across the continent. Posters around town tout big-name acts, who play at Estadio El Campín, Parque Simón Bolívar or Parque Jaime Duque (on the way to Zipaquirá, north of the city). Check for listings in Go (www.goguiadelocio.com).

Biblioteca Luis Ángel Arango (Map pp70-1; ☎ 343 1212; www.lablaa.org; Calle 11 No 4-14) This huge La Candelaria library hosts a healthy selection of instrumental and vocal concerts;

regular Wednesday events are more expensive (from COP$15,000) than other days (about COP$5000).

Auditorio León de Greiff (Map p64; ☎ 316 5000; Universidad Nacional, cnr Carrera 30 & Calle 45) Despite the uni's rad students, this stage goes with traditional philharmonics and orchestras – many concerts are held on Saturday.

Media Torta (Map pp70-1; ☎ 281 7704; www.mediatorta .gov.co; cnr Calle 18 & Carretera Circunvalación; ☼ noon-4pm Sun) Live kid-oriented concerts are staged for free at noon on Sundays at a band stage above La Candelaria. Take the steps up from the end of Calle 18.

Sports

Many outsiders equate Colombia's national sport – football (soccer) – with the shooting of Andrés Escobar after his own goal eliminated Colombia from the 1994 World Cup, but seeing games here is generally a calm affair (perhaps wearing neutral colors isn't a bad idea though). The two big rivals here are the (blue-and-white) **Los Millonarios** (Map p64; ☎ 347 7080; www.millonarios.com.co; Carrera 9 No 7-09) and (red-and-white) **Santa Fe** (Map p64; ☎ 544 6670; Calle 64A No 38-08).

The principal venue is the **Estadio El Campín** (Map p64; ☎ 315 8726; Carrera 30 No 57-60). Games are played on Wednesday night and Sunday afternoon. Tickets can be bought at the stadium before the matches (from COP$6000).

For international matches, check with **Federación Colombiana de Fútbol** (www.colfutbol.org, in Spanish) for locations that sell tickets.

Bullfighting is invariably popular, with fights held at the **Plaza de Toros de Santamaría** (Map pp70-1; cnr Carrera 6 & Calle 27) on most Sundays in January and February. Tickets are available from the bullring's box office (from COP$20,000). The events bring the area to a standstill, while the bullring itself (a 1931 red-brick ring) often fills to capacity (14,500), or beyond.

Also consider a round of *tejo* (p90).

SHOPPING

Locals are in love with the malls, but Sunday flea markets and the crusty Plaza de Mercado de Paloquemao are more inviting attractions. Also, look along Carrera 9, south of Calle 60, for Chapinero's antique shops.

Crafts & Souvenirs

Artesanías de Colombia (Map pp70-1; ☎ 286 1766; www.artesaniasdecolombia.com.co; Carrera 3A No 18A-60;

TEJO!

Gunpowder, lead weights, alcohol? That's a dream mix anywhere, and in Colombia, it's perfectly legal. The rural tradition of *tejo* (a loud pre-Columbian game where 2kg weights are tossed to a clay pit to hit and explode gunpowder-filled triangular pieces of wax paper called *mechas*) goes indoors in Bogotá, particularly found in working-class districts of the south.

One classic *tejo* hall is **Peperepe** (Map p64; ☎ 289 1541; Calle 7 No 8-20; ☽ 11am-midnight Thu-Sat). A couple kilometers south of La Candelaria, this relatively cheerful place has four long lanes you use for free if you buy (minimum) one 'box of beer' (24 Poker beers, for COP$43,000). The open-view urinal allows those using the facilities (many of whom are tipsy gray-haired gents in suits) to keep watching the game, never mind the passing ladies (and gals do play).

The streets around the hall get dark and empty at night. Considering the lack of direct public transport, you're best off taking a taxi.

☽ 9am-6pm Mon-Fri, 10am-2pm Sat) In a hacienda next to the Iglesia de las Aguas, this classy shop has higher-end crafts (lots of home accessories, plus purses, toys, hammocks and some clothing).

Artesanías El Balay (Map pp74-5; Carrera 15 No 75-63; ☽ 9am-7:45pm Mon-Sat, 11am-7:45pm Sun) Up north, this is one of many Carrera 15 choices near Zona Rosa, with a huge room of handicrafts, plus a Colombia flag football (COP$27,000).

La Casona del Museo (Map pp70-1; Calle 16 No 5-22/24; ☽ 10am-7pm Mon-Sat, 10am-5pm Sun) By the Gold Museum, this old building houses a convenient, cheerful collection of nice souvenir stands (the best for handicrafts being Colombia es Bella on the second floor) and a nice cafe.

Pasaje Rivas (Map pp70-1; cnr Carrera 10 & Calle 10) A couple of blocks west of Plaza de Bolívar, this nontouristy craft market is a good spot for cheap buys, including lots of straw hats, T-shirts, toy figurines, baskets and ruanas (Colombian ponchos). The entrance next to Iglesia de la Concepción reads 'Pasaje Paul.'

San Miguel (Map pp70-1; ☎ 243 6273; Calle 11 No 8-88; ☽ 9am-6pm Mon-Sat, 10am-2pm Sun) Open for 70 years, and with many old-timers milling over new options, this classic hat maker is the best of the bunch on the block. Mostly felt fedoras or cowboy hats pressed before your eyes.

Flea Markets

Sunday flea markets are great fun for old posters, souvenirs and various handicrafts. Most are held on holidays too.

Mercado de San Alejo (Map pp70-1; Carrera 7 btwn Calles 24 & 26; ☽ 9am-5pm Sun) This City Center classic fills a parking lot, with coca leaves and coca tea available, and a host of yesteryear items (posters, books, knickknacks) that are fun to sift through.

Parque de los Periodistas (Map pp70-1; cnr Av Jiménez & Carrera 3; ☽ 9am-5pm Sun) Facing La Candelaria's north end, this market is really about junk – old radios, electronics, videotapes, tools and whatnot.

Plaza Central de Usaquén (aka Los Toldos de San Pelayo; Map p64; Carrera 6A btwn Calles 119 & 119A; ☽ 9am-5pm Sun) Just north of the main square in the villagelike Usaquén, you'll find food, colorful purses, assorted handicrafts and bamboo saxophones – there's a satellite area a couple of blocks east too.

Shopping Centers & Malls

One of Bogotá's biggest shopping areas is **San Andresito** (Map p64; Carrera 38 btwn Calles 8 & 9; ☽ 9am-6pm), which spreads over several city blocks. It's packed with a couple of thousand stalls that have almost everything that can be bought in Colombia. It is one of the cheapest places to buy video, hi-fi and TV equipment, computers, film and photographic gear, watches, cassettes and CDs, and clothing and footwear. Urban buses and *busetas* go there from the center – you can catch them on Calle 19.

An attraction in itself, the **Plaza de Mercado de Paloquemao** (Map p64; cnr Calle 19 & Carrera 25; ☽ 4am-noon or so) is a real-deal local wholesale market, with livestock, handicrafts and produce. Watch out for animal killings if that's not your thing; otherwise it's at its loveliest on Friday and Sunday mornings when it's filled with flowers (try to get here by 4am or 5am), brought in to stock Bogotá shops.

Other more traditional malls – packed with shops, fast-food outlets, *casas de cambio*, internet cafes and movie theaters – include the following:

Atlantis Plaza (Map pp74-5; Calle 81 No 13-05; ☽ 10am-8pm Mon-Wed, 10am-9pm Thu-Sat, noon-

BOGOTÁ

7pm Sun) Modern mall with ATMs, Hard Rock Café and a multiplex cinema.

Centro Comercial Andino (Map pp74-5; ☎ 621 3111; Carrera 11 No 82-71; ☷ 8am-10pm Mon-Sat, 10am-10pm Sun) Most popular Zona Rosa mall.

Hacienda Santa Bárbara (Map p64; ☎ 612 0388; Carrera 7 No 115-60; ☷ 10am-11pm Mon-Sat, 10am-8:30pm Sun) Built around a colonial *casona* (large, old house; 1847), making the place a fine combination of historic and modern architecture, and is quieter than the Zona Rosa scene.

Unicentro (Map p64; Av 15 No 123-30) Shop like it's 1976! The city's first big mall is still a busy scene of daily shopping.

Electronics

If you're not finding the electronic accessory you need at a mall, the **Centro de Alta Technología** (Map pp74-5; Carrera 15 No 77-05; ☷ 9am-7pm Mon-Fri, 10am-7pm Sat), or the adjoining Unilago Mall, is packed with digital camera and computer stands.

Gold & Emeralds

Mines from around Bogotá bring in plenty of precious stones, such as the gold items sold in *joyerías* (jewelry shops) on Carrera 6 between Calles 12 and 13.

Mined chiefly from the Muzo area, emeralds, meanwhile, are sold in the flourishing emerald street market at the southwestern corner of Av Jiménez and Carrera 7 and nearby Plaza Rosario, where dozens of *negociantes* (traders) buy and sell stones – sometimes on the sidewalks.

In years past, the beauty of Colombia's emeralds had been overshadowed by the dangerous conditions in which they were mined. Some locals compared Colombia's emerald market with the diamond industry in Africa. In 2005, in an effort to clean up the industry and its questionable labor practices and criminal activity, the government abolished tariffs and taxes associated with mining, effectively ending the power of the black market and associated elements. Travelers can now buy emeralds in good conscience, but should still be cautious about paying too much. Haggle hard.

Camping & Outdoor Equipment

While imported camping and trekking gear is increasingly available, it can be expensive. Locally produced gear is cheaper and often of reasonable quality.

Amarelo (aka Camping Vive; Map p64; ☎ 211 8082; Calle 57 No 9-29, local 301; ☷ 9am-5pm Mon-Fri, 9am-noon Sat) This small shop sells and rents all the camp-

ing gear you'll need (eg a tent is COP$8000 per day) and takes bookings for rooms in its bungalow at Suesca. Sells boots too.

Montaña Accesorios (Map pp74-5; ☎ 530 6103; www .montanaaccesorios.com; Carrera 13A No 79-46; ☷ 9am-6pm Mon-Fri, 10am-5pm Sat) Small Colombia-based outfitter selling its own fleece jackets, backpacks and jackets.

For information on bikes, see p79.

GETTING THERE & AWAY
Air

Bogotá's airport, **Aeropuerto El Dorado** (Map p64; ☎ 425 1000, 413 9053; www.elnuevodorado.com; Av El Dorado), which handles all domestic and international flights, is 13km northwest of the center and has two terminals. The principal one (El Dorado) is a kilometer west of **Puente Aéreo** (☎ 413 9511; Av El Dorado), principally used for some of Avianca's international and domestic flights.

At El Dorado, you'll find money-exchange services at the arrivals gate; when entering the departures hall, head to the left end to reach arrivals. Rates are generally a bit worse than at banks in the city center. ATMs and internet access points are only found upstairs in the departures hall – up the stairs from the check-in counter (accessible to all).

Most airline offices in Bogotá are in the north; some have more than one office. Here are some locations:

Air Canada (Map pp74-5; ☎ 296 6353; World Trade Center, Calle 100 No 8A-49, torre B, piso 8)
Air France/KLM (Map pp74-5; ☎ 650 6000, 326 6030; Carrera 9A No 99-07, torre 1, piso 5)
Aires (Map pp74-5; ☎ 321 3649; www.aires.com.co, in Spanish; Carrera 11 No 76-11, local 103)
Aerolineas Argentinas (Map pp74-5; ☎ 313 2854; Calle 76 No 11-17, piso 5)
Aeropostal (Map pp74-5; ☎ 342 6077; www.aeropostal .com; Calle 73 No 9-42, piso 1)
AeroRepública (Map pp70-1; ☎ 342 7221, 320 9090;

AIR DEPARTURE TAX

Everyone leaving Colombia by air must pay a departure tax – US$33 if you stayed under 30 days, US$65 if over 30 days. It's sometimes included in your ticket. Either way, you'll need to get (and hold onto) a receipt at the separate counter in the departures hall before checking in at the airport. It's payable in US dollars or Colombian pesos.

Centro Internacional, Carrera 10 No 27-51, local 165) One of many offices.

Air Plus Comet (Map pp74–5; ☎ 319 0860; www .aircomet.com; Calle 76 No 11-17, piso 5)

American Airlines (Map pp74–5; ☎ 439 7777; Atlantis Plaza, Carrera 81 No 13-05)

Avianca (Map pp70–1; ☎ 342 6077; Carrera 10 No 26-53)

Avianca (Map pp74–5; ☎ 256 5810; www.avianca.com; Centro Comercial Andino, Carrera 11, No 81-17)

Continental (Map pp70–1; ☎ 800 944 02 19; Hotel Tequendama International, Carrera 10A No 26-35)

Copa (Map pp74–5; ☎ 650 2622; Citibank Bldg, Carrera 9A No 99-02, local 108)

Cubana de Aviación (Map pp74–5; ☎ 610 5800; www .solysonviajes.com; Carrera 18 No 79A-30)

Delta (Map pp74–5; ☎ 547 5964, 376 0033; www.delta .com; Carrera 7 No 99-11)

Iberia (Map pp74–5; ☎ 610 5066; Carrera 19A No 85-11)

Lan Chile (Map pp74–5; ☎ 651 3970; www.lan.com; World Trade Center, Calle 100 No 8A-49, torre B)

Mexicana (Map p64; ☎ 215 2626; www.mexicana .com; Carrera 15 No 112-36, oficina 108)

Satena (Map p64; ☎ 423 8530; www.satena.com; Aeropuerto El Dorado)

TACA/LACSA (Map p64; ☎ 414 8560; Calle 113 No 7-21, local 123)

There are also plenty of domestic flights to destinations all over the country. Some of the major routes are given on p315.

Bus

The **bus terminal** (La Terminal; Map p64; ☎ 423 3600; www.terminaldetransporte.gov.co; Diagonal 23 No 69-60, off Av de La Constitución), about 5km west of the city center in the squeaky-clean planned neighborhood of La Salitre, is housed in a huge, arched red-brick building divided into five *módulos* (units). South-bound buses leave at the west end from No 1 (color-coded yellow), west-bound from No 2 (blue), north/east-bound from No 3 (red). *Colectivo* vans leave for some nearby towns like Villavicencio from No 4, while all arrivals come into No 5 (at the station's eastern end).

There are plenty of food options, ATMs, left luggage rooms, (clean) bathrooms and even showers (COP\$6000), and a PIT information center in *módulo* No 5, which will help you track down bus times or call for accommodations.

Each *módulo* has a number of side-by-side ticket vendors from various companies, sometimes trying to hassle you for their buses. For some long-distance destinations – particularly to the Caribbean coast – you can haggle. The

usual type of bus is the *climatizado*, which is air-conditioned.

DOMESTIC BUSES

For all domestic destinations in the Domestic Bus Routes table (opposite) there are frequent departures during the day (for destinations like Medellín, Cali or Bucaramanga usually half hourly) by a few different companies (at least). Shop around for prices and departure times.

Direct buses to Villa de Leyva (from COP\$15,000, three to four hours) are less frequent. At time of research, **Flota Valle de Tenza** (☎ 428 1008) had one bus daily departing at 6am (COP\$16,000, three to four hours), **Libertadores** (☎ 428 1053) had services at 4:50am and 2:30pm daily, and **Alianza** (☎ 295 1864) had departures at 9am and 4pm on Saturday and Sunday only. All these buses go from *módulo* No 3.

If you have time to kill, the kid-oriented Maloka (p79) is nearby.

INTERNATIONAL BUSES

Buses for cities around South America depart from *módulo* 2 (blue) in the bus terminal. **Expreso Ormeño** (☎ 410 7522) sells tickets for most destinations. The following departures go twice daily on days listed:

Destination	Price (COP\$)	Duration	Departure
Buenos Aires	805,000	7 days	Tue & Sun
Caracas	138,000	28 hours	Tue, Thu & Sun
Guayaquil	253,000	44 hours	Tue & Sun
Lima	391,000	3 days	Tue & Sun
Mendoza	782,000	6½ days	Tue & Sun
Quito	207,000	32 hours	Tue & Sun
Santiago	644,000	5¼ days	Tue & Sun

GETTING AROUND

Rush hour in the morning and afternoon can really clog roads – and space on the buses.

To/From the Airport

Both El Dorado and Puente Aéreo terminals are accessible from the center by *busetas* and *colectivos* marked 'Aeropuerto.' In the center you catch them on Calle 19 or Carrera 10. At the airport they park next to the El Dorado terminal. They all pass by Puente Aéreo en route. Urban transport to the airport stops at about 8pm.

If going by taxi (about COP\$15,000), you pay a *sobrecargo* (surcharge) of COP\$3100.

DOMESTIC BUS ROUTES

Destination	Distance (km)	Price (COP$)	Duration (hr)	Módulo (No)
Armenia	316	35,000-40,000	7	yellow (1)
Barranquilla	985	100,000-130,000	17-20	blue (2) & red (3)
Bucaramanga	393	64,000-75,000	8-9	red (3)
Cali	511	45,000-55,000	8-10	yellow (1) & blue (2)
Cartagena	1090	138,000-140,000	7-8	red (3)
Cúcuta	584	77,000-95,000	15-16	red (3)
Ipiales	948	84,000	22	red (3)
Manizales	278	35,000-40,000	8-9	blue (2)
Medellín	399	35,000-60,000	9	yellow (1) & blue
Neiva	325	25,000-35,000	5-6	yellow (1)
Pasto	921	74,000-76,000	18-20	yellow (1)
Pereira	360	39,000-43,000	7-9	yellow (1)
Popayán	646	65,000-70,000	12	yellow (1)
Ráquira	125	16,000-17,000	3-4	red (3)
San Agustín	529	42,000-52,000	9-10	yellow (1)
San Gil	290	35,000-54,000	6-7	red (3)
Santa Marta	952	100,000-120,000	16-17	red (3) & blue (2)
Tunja	120	12,000-16,000	3	red (3)
Villavicencio	132	19,000-21,000	2-3	red (3)
Zipaquirá	50	3,000	2-3	red (3)

El Dorado terminal has a special taxi service aimed at protecting passengers from overcharging by taxi drivers. At the exit from the baggage-claim area there's a taxi booth where you get a computer printout indicating the expected fare to your destination. You then take the taxi, which waits at the door, and show the printout to the driver. The fare is paid upon arrival at your destination.

To/From the Bus Terminal

There are both buses and *colectivos* running between the bus terminal and the city center, but the service stops around 9pm. During rush hour the bus trip between the terminal and the city center may take up to an hour.

Take a northbound *colectivo* marked 'Terminal' from Carrera 10 anywhere between Calles 17 and 26. You can also take a bus or *colectivo* from Calle 13 west of Av Caracas.

The best and fastest way is a taxi (COP$8000 to COP$12,000). The same applies if you are going from the terminal to the city center; you can take a bus or *colectivo*, but it's best to go by taxi.

The bus terminal has an organized taxi service like the one at the airport.

Bicycle

Bogotá has one of the world's most extensive bike-route networks, with over 300km of separated, clearly marked bike paths called CicloRuta. Free Bogotá maps from tourist information centers show the CicloRuta paths.

In addition, on Sunday and holidays, about 120km of city roads are closed to traffic from 7am to 2pm for a citywide Ciclovia, a well-run event to get Bogotá out on two wheels. Fruit juice vendors and bike repair stands line the cross-town event. The catch is that no one – and we tried hard to find someone – rents bikes currently. Consider going on a bike tour or buying a cheapie (see p79). Ciclovia runs along Carrera 7 all the way from La Candelaria to Usaquén – it's worth witnessing even if on foot.

Bus & Buseta

Apart from TransMilenio (see p94), Bogotá's public transport is operated by buses and *buseta* (small buses). They all run the length and breadth of the city, usually at full speed if traffic allows.

Except on a few streets, there are no bus stops – just wave down the bus or *buseta*. Board via the front door and pay the driver or the assistant; you won't get a ticket. In buses you get off through the back door, where there's a bell to ring to let the driver know to stop. In *busetas* there's usually only a front door through which all passengers get on and off.

When you want to get off tell the driver *'por acá, por favor'* (here, please).

Each bus and *buseta* displays a board on the windscreen indicating the route and number. For locals they are easily recognizable from a distance, but for newcomers it can be difficult to decipher the route description quickly enough to wave down the right bus.

Flat fares, regardless of distance traveled, are posted, and range from COP$1000 to COP$1200. It's sometimes slightly higher at night (after 8pm) and on Sunday and holidays.

There are also minibuses called *colectivos,* which operate on major routes. They are faster and cost about COP$1200.

Taxi

Bogotá's impressive fleet of Korean-made yellow cabs are a safe, reliable and relatively inexpensive way of getting around. They all have meters and drivers almost always use them. When you enter a cab, the meter should read '25' – which relates to a coded pricing scheme (a laminated card should be hanging on the front passenger seat to see). Taxi trips on Sundays and holidays, or after dark, include a COP$1500 surcharge; trips to the airport have a COP$3100 surcharge.

A 10km ride (eg from Plaza de Bolívar to Calle 100 in northern Bogotá) shouldn't cost more than COP$15,000. If you are going to make a couple of trips to distant places, it may be cheaper to hire a taxi by the hour for about COP$14,000 per hour.

You can either wave down a taxi on the street or request one by phone from numerous companies that provide radio service; try **Taxis Libres** (☎ 311 1111), **Taxi Express** (☎ 411 1111), **Radio Taxi** (☎ 288 8888) or **Taxi Real** (☎ 333 3333).

Naturally don't ride with a taxi that refuses to use a meter. Most drivers are honest, but it's worth confirming the final fare with the price card. Some drivers, particularly in late hours, will round fares up a bit. Drivers don't often get tips.

TransMilenio

The ambitiously named **TransMilenio** (www.tran milenio.gov.co) has revolutionized Bogotá's public transport. After numerous plans and studies drawn up over 30 years to build a metro, the project was eventually buried and a decision to introduce a fast urban bus service called TransMilenio was taken instead.

It is, in essence, a bus system masquerading as a subway. Covering 84km with a fleet of 1100 buses, TransMilenio has 114 of its own self-contained stations (keeping things orderly and safe). Buses run have their own lanes, which keeps them free from auto traffic. The service is cheap (COP$1500), frequent and operates from 5am to 11pm Monday to Saturday, 6am to 10pm Sunday. Tickets are bought at the entrance of any TransMilenio station. TransMilenio serves up to one million people daily, so buses get *very* crowded at rush hour; transfers at Av Jiménez resemble punk-rock mosh pits.

On posted maps in stations, routes are color coded, with different numbered buses corresponding to various stops. The main TransMilenio line runs along Av Caracas from the north to south of town. There are also lines on Carrera 30, Av 81, Av de Las Americas and a short spur on Av Jiménez to Carrera 3. There are plans to build more lines, including one to the airport. There are three terminuses, but the only one of real use to travelers is the **northern terminus** (Portal del Norte; Calle 170).

It takes practice to understand which bus to take. 'Ruta Facil' routes, for example, stop at every station on a line, while others zip along some sort of express route – leapfrogging, in confusing patterns, several stations at a time.

You can also preplan your routes online at www.surumbo.com; click on your departure and destination station for options. Most key north–central routes change in Calle 22, while Av Jiménez has many more transfers (sometimes meaning an underground walk between neighboring stations).

Key routes:

La Candelaria to Zona G From 'Las Aguas' or 'Museo del Oro' stations, take D70 to Calle 22, switch to B13 to 'Flores.'

La Candelaria to Zona Rosa From 'Las Aguas' or 'Museo del Oro,' take D70 to Calle 22, switch to B13 to Calle 85.

La Candelaria to Portal del Norte (for Zipaquirá buses) Take B74 direct to 'Portal del Norte' (last stop).

Portal del Norte to La Candelaria Take J72 from 'Portal del Norte' direct to 'Museo del Oro' or 'Las Aguas.'

Zona G to La Candelaria From 'Flores' take H13 to 'Calle 22,' switch to J24 to 'Museo del Oro' or 'Las Aguas.'

Zona G to Zona Rosa From 'Flores' take B1 or B13 to 'Calle 85.'

Zona Rosa to La Candelaria From 'Calle 85' take H13 to Calle 22, switch to J24 to 'Museo del Oro' or 'Las Aguas.'

The free maps available from tourist informa-tion centers show all TransMilenio stations.

AROUND BOGOTÁ

Most *bogotanos* looking for a break from the city also look for warmth. Some towns within a couple of hours – like the trashy club town of Melgar – rest way below Bogotá's eleva-tion, with rising temperatures. There are also significant changes in landscape outside the capital, where you can find lakes, waterfalls, cloud forests, mountains and a maze of small towns and villages, many of them holding onto their colonial fabric. The most popular overnight destination is Villa de Leyva (p105), covered in the Boyacá, Santander & Norte de Santander chapter.

NORTH OF BOGOTÁ

Many day-trippers out of the capital head this way. It's possible to combine a trip to Zipaquirá and Guatavita in a day – a taxi to both, with a couple hours at each, runs about COP$150,000 depending on your negotiation skills. Ecoguías (p68) offers all-inclusive three-day tours to Villa de Leyva that stop in Zipaquirá and Guatavita for about COP$800,000 per person. Agencies like Destino Bogotá (p68) offer combo day trips to Zipaquirá and Guatavita.

Zipaquirá
☎ 1 / pop 101,000 / elev 2650m

The most popular day trip from Bogotá, 50km north, Zipaquirá is a cute historic town noted for its salt mines, particularly the one fash-ioned as a surreal walk following Jesus' last steps and finishing in a three-part cavern-ous cathedral 190m below the ground. Salt was a major resource in this area before the Spanish showed up in those metal hats, and local mines still churn out 40% of Colombia's salt resources.

Zipaquirá's main plaza is lined with cafes and ATMs and has a lovely church to peek into. For further info see www.zipaquira .gov.co.

In the mountains about 500m southwest are two underground cathedrals carved out of salt. The first opened in 1954, then was closed in 1992 for safety reasons. You can visit its stunning replacement **salt cathedral** (☎ 852 4035, 852 9890; www.catedraldesal.gov.co; admis-sion COP$14,000, on Wed COP$8000; ⏰ 9am-4:40pm). It was built between 1991 and 1995 (a total of 250,000 tons of salt were removed).

All visitors must join regularly departing groups on hour-long tours – you can leave them once you're inside if you want. The walk leads past 13 stages of Jesus' fateful day, with hollowed-out crosses symbolizing nakedness or death (sadly the view of No 11 – of the crucifixion – is now somewhat marred by the unfortunate placement of the souvenir shop just behind). The tradition of mixing religion with salt has logical roots: work in the mines was dangerous so altars were made. Eventually it grew to this. The 75m long mine can ac-commodate 8400 people and holds service on (very busy) Sundays.

About 15km northeast, the town of **Nemocón** is home to another huge (and less touristy) salt mine that can be visited daily. This one has been in use for 400 years, once serving as the town hall.

Few spend the night in Zipaquirá, but **Hotel Colonial** (☎ 852 2690, 852 1793; Calle 3 No 6-57/43; s/d COP$25,000/40,000) is a cute hacienda-style hotel with 50 simple clean rooms a block-and-a-half southwest of the main square.

GETTING THERE & AWAY
One way to Zipaquirá is hopping on one of the frequent buses from the Portal del Norte TransMilenio station at Calle 170, about a 45-minute ride from the center. From here, buses to Zipaquirá (COP$2600, 1½ to 2½ hours) are marked and go every 15 minutes or so. From Zipaquirá it's possible to catch a few daily buses on to Villa de Leyva.

The alternative is to take the **Turistren** (www .turistren.com.co, in Spanish), which runs Saturday and Sunday from Bogotá to Zipaquirá (re-turn COP$30,000). The train departs Bogotá's **Sabana Station** (☎ 375 0556-8; Calle 13 No 18-24) at 8:30am, stops briefly at **Usaquén Station** (☎ 629 7407; Calle 100 & Carrera 9A) at 9:20am and reaches Zipaquirá at 11:30am. (At research time, curiously, it returned from nearby Cajicá, 15km south!)

A return taxi from Bogotá should run about COP$75,000 including time to see the mine.

Suesca
☎ 1 / pop 14,000 / elev 2584m

One of Colombia's most popular rock-climbing destinations lurks just south of this colonial town, 65km north of Bogotá. Arriving

BOGOTÁ

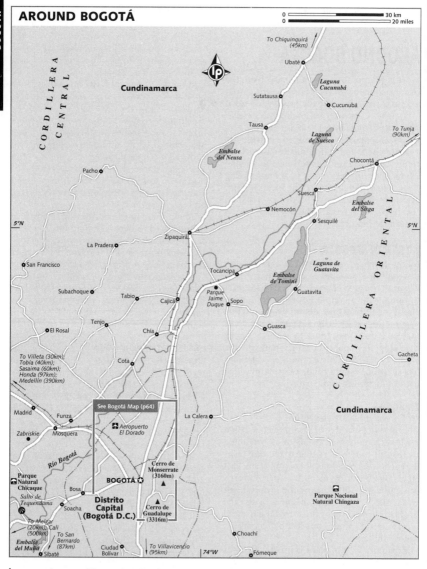

AROUND BOGOTÁ

0 ——— 30 km
0 ——— 20 miles

To Chiquinquirá (45km)

CORDILLERA CENTRAL

Cundinamarca

Ubaté

Laguna Cucunubá

Sutatausa

Cucunubá

Tausa

To Tunja (90km)

Laguna de Suesca

Pacho

Embalse del Neusa

Chocontá

Suesca

5°N   5°N

Nemocón

Embalse del Sisga

Zipaquirá

Sesquilé

La Pradera

CORDILLERA ORIENTAL

San Francisco

Tocancipá

Laguna de Guatavita

Subachoque

Tabio

Cajicá

Parque Jaime Duque

Embalse de Tominé

Guatavita

Tenjo

Sopo

El Rosal

Chía

Guasca

To Villeta (30km); Tobía (40km); Sasaima (60km); Honda (97km); Medellín (390km)

Cota

Gacheta

See Bogotá Map (p64)

Madrid   Funza

La Calera

Cundinamarca

Zabriskie   Mosquera

Aeropuerto El Dorado

Río Bogotá

Parque Natural Chicaque

Bosa

Cerro de Monserrate (3160m)

Salto de Tequendama

BOGOTÁ

Distrito Capital (Bogotá D.C.)

Soacha

Cerro de Guadalupe (3316m)

Parque Nacional Natural Chingaza

To Melgar (20km); Cali (500km)   To San Bernardo (87km)

Choachí

Embalse del Muña

Sibaté

Ciudad Bolívar

To Villavicencio (95km)

74°W

Fómeque

by car or bus, you'll pass the 2km long sandstone Guadalupe formations standing up to 370m high along the Río Bogotá, and home to 400 (and counting) routes.

Many visitors come for day trips from Bogotá, particularly on weekends, when the half a dozen (or so) outfitters open their doors to greet a couple of hundred climbers daily.

There are also rafting options, but the water is much warmer in Tobía (p98).

A Spanish-language guide for Suesca climbs (COP$18,000) can be found at Gran Pared in Bogotá (p79).

English-speaking guide **Hugo Rocha** (☎ 315 826 2051, 314 276 6485; hugoirocha@hotmail.com) has been here for over a decade, offering day/

overnight trips and lessons. Hugo also works with **Campo Base** (deaventuraporcolombia@yahoo.com), a climbing school, which offers a five-day course for COP$400,000, a day climb (including equipment) for COP$100,000, and two rooms offering B&B accommodations for COP$20,000.

El Vivac Hostel (☎ 311 284 5313; tent/dm/r COP$20,000/ 20,000/55,000) is a farm-turned-hostel run by a local woman climber pioneer who arranges climbs and rents bikes (COP$10,000).

There are also many camping options, or you can rent a full cabaña from **Amarelo** (☎ in Bogotá 1 217 8082) for COP$45,000 per person.

To get to Suesca, take the TransMilenio to its northern terminus at Portal del Norte, and catch a frequent direct 'Alianza' bus (COP$5000, 40 minutes).

Laguna de Guatavita
elev 3000m

Many hopes of finding El Dorado, it was once believed, converged on this small, circular lake about 50km northeast of Bogotá. Rimmed by mountains, lovely Guatavita was the sacred lake and ritual center of the Muisca people, where – half a millennium ago – the gold-dust-coated Zipa, the Muisca *cacique*, would throw precious offerings into the lake from his ceremonial raft and then plunge into the waters to obtain godlike power.

These days, you can't follow the Zipa's lead (no swimming), but there are several lookouts on a trail above the water. The area is higher up than Bogotá – and you'll feel the difference on the 15-minute hike up to the lakeside hilltops from the **site entrance** (Colombian/foreigner COP$8000/12,000; ☺ 9am-4pm Tue-Sun).

During the week, the trails are far less crowded than on the busy weekends. Previously permits were required to visit the site – that's no longer necessary. For additional details, contact the **Corporación Autónoma Regional de Cudinamarca** (☎ in Bogotá 1 320 9000; www.car.gov.co, in Spanish; Carrera 7A No 36-45, Bogotá).

The town of **Guatavita**, 18km southwest, is the chief gateway. On weekends, you're likely to find transport to the lake, but it's not guaranteed. The town was created in the mid-1960s – for locals displaced by the nearby reservoir Embalse de Tominé – and does a fine job of re-creating the white-washed Spanish colonial template, with a cute bullring, a pedestrian mall center with souvenir shops, restaurants, a museum and a hotel or two. It's dead quiet during the week.

SLEEPING

Most travelers day trip here only. Some locals who weekend this way prefer staying at the nearby town of Guasca, about 15km south. A worthy option is the horse ranch **Hacienda**

LAKE OF (FOOLS') GOLD

Traditionally, the Muisca felt that Laguna de Guatavita – once set in a perfectly round crater rimmed by green mountains – was created by a crashing meteor that transported a golden god who resided in the lake's floor. (Turns out, it's now believed, boring ol' volcanoes may be more likely the lake's creator.) The Muisca paid tribute to the the god by crafting elaborate *tunjos* (ornate gold pendants and idols), inscribed with wishes, and tossing them to into the lake. (You can see many such pieces at Bogotá's Museo del Oro; see p77.)

This led to a frenzy for gold for the Spaniards, and many other outsiders, who naturally felt they reached a watery El Dorado. Over the years many painstaking, fruitless efforts were made to uncover the treasures lurking below.

In the 1560s, a wealthy merchant Antonio de Sepúlveda cut a gap on one side – still visible today – to drain the lake, yielding a mere 232 pesos of gold. Sepúlveda died bankrupt.

By the late 19th century an English company managed to drain the lagoon, finding only 20-odd objects – not nearly enough to pay off the £40,000 or eight years invested in the project.

In the 1940s, US divers with metal detectors searched out treasures, and the Colombian authorities – finally – banned such activities in 1965. Not to say that all treasure seekers obeyed. In the '90s access to the lake required a permit to keep track of visitors (illegally coming with scuba gear to search out fortunes).

Despite its fame, Guatavita never yielded much gold. Colombia's best-known piece – the Balsa Muisca (also at the Museo del Oro) – was actually found in a cave near the village of Pasca.

The golden god must be getting a chuckle over all this.

Betania (☎ 091 850 4987; www.hotelhaciendabetania.com; Vereda Trinidad sector; r from COP$65,000), which offers two-hour rides for COP$30,000.

GETTING THERE & AWAY

Laguna de Guatavita is not convenient to reach by public transport. Buses go from the TransMilenio northern terminus (Portal del Norte) in northern Bogotá to the town of Guatavita, via Sesquilé. About 11km north of town, the bus passes the 7km uphill road to the lake – no public transport. Ask to get out, and walk or hitch (follow the signs to the right near the Escuela Tierra Negra), or go on to Guatavita, where on Sundays, *colectivos* leave from the central plaza to the lake directly. Taxis are scarce here.

A return taxi from Bogotá costs about COP$110,000.

WEST OF BOGOTÁ

Those heading to the beach, Medellín or coffee country head west from Bogotá. Many don't stop, but there are a few places that qualify as destinations. If you're heading that way by your own means, note that two highways head out of Bogotá – take the northerly route via La Vega (west on Calle 80), a nicer drive than the southern route via Facatavita, which hooks up with the La Vega route (after many suburbs and truck jams) at Villeta, about 65km west.

Cloud forest *(bosque de niebla)* hikes await only 20km west of Bogotá in the gorgeous privately owned **Parque Natural Chicaque** (☎ in Bogotá 1 368 3118; www.chicaque.com, in Spanish; admission Colombians/foreigners COP$8000/20,000; ⏱ 8am-4pm). The 3-sq-km area features half a dozen walks (about 8km altogether), which are among the nation's best marked. During rainy season, walks lead to waterfalls. On weekends you can hire a horse to ride back up the steep hill paths.

You arrive above the trails, and below – a steep hike down – you'll find various **accommodations** (campsite/dm/bungalow incl all meals COP$37,000/68,000/208,000) including a nice bungalow for two. You can also camp up at the entrance for COP$8500 (no meals).

The reserve is a few kilometers off the Soacha–La Mesa road. To get there from Bogotá's center, take a bus or *colectivo* along Carrera 10 to the busy, unpleasant town of Soacha, and negotiate a *colectivo* (about COP$10,000 to COP$15,000).

Many white-water rafting, rappelling and kayaking trips from Bogotá go to **Tobía**, a rising center for adventure sports about 20km north of Villeta and 75km from Bogotá. On weekends it's possible to show up and arrange rafting trips here with one of the half dozen companies and find accommodations; it's very quiet during the week. Most visitors take day trips with Bogotá travel agencies (p68). Also check with **Los Tobianos** (☎ 312 576 7278; www.lostobianos .com) about many of the activities available.

Colombia is only starting to pick up on the spa craze. Near Sasaima (60km west of the city) is **El Refugio** (☎ 1 243 3564; www.elrefugiohotelspa .com; r from COP$279,000, cabañas COP$1,116,000; 🏊), a lovely 12-room hotel. Rooms are gorgeous, wood-floor deals with bright colors and nice wood furnishings. There's a pool and several spa packages.

About 132km west of Bogotá – and at the cross roads for Medellín, Cartagena and Cali – hot **Honda** is a historic town that looks just awful from buses and cars zipping through. In the center, though, there are a number of atmospheric historic buildings that are starting to get some love. Ecoguías (p68) in Bogotá can arrange overnight stays in **colonial mansions** (d weekday/weekend COP$250,000/500,000) here, as well as boat trips on the Río Magdalena and trips to nearby Río Claro (p219).

SOUTH OF BOGOTÁ

The unique climate conditions of the Andean highlands been conducive to the preservation of mummies across parts of Colombia – some of which have been relocated as far away as the British Museum in London. One place you can see some is the 'mummy town' of **San Bernardo**, about 87km southeast of Bogotá. A century ago, several dozen bodies were un-earthed from the cemetery after interment fees were not paid and diggers, surprisingly, found mummies – a product of the unique soil and the local diet of *guatila* fruit. Some are on view in glass cases in the cemetery crypt in town. You're best off having your own transport to get here.

About 60km southwest, **Melgar** is some-thing of 'Colombia's Blackpool,' a cheesy resort town with water parks (not the sea), and a number of nightclubs that serve many weekend *bogotano* trippers coming for warm weather and trashy fun. There are regular buses servicing the area.

Boyacá, Santander & Norte de Santander

This is Colombia's heartland, a region of deep gorges, fast-flowing rivers and soaring, snow-capped mountains. It was one of the first areas settled by Spanish conquistadores, and a number of their colonial towns still stand today. It's here that the seeds of revolution were sowed, culminating in victory at Puente de Boyacá that ultimately led to Colombia's independence.

The departments of Boyacá, Santander and Norte de Santander are often overlooked by tourists rushing to the Caribbean coast or coming from Venezuela. But the region is a destination in and of itself. There's much to see and do, from 450-year-old colonial villages to spectacular national parks.

Outdoor lovers can choose between white-water rafting and paragliding in San Gil, mountain biking and horseback riding in Villa de Leyva, or trekking through the glacial peaks of Parque Nacional Natural (PNN) El Cocuy. For less-extreme options, dine alfresco at a trendy restaurant in Barichara, shop for pottery in Ráquira or hit the fashionable clubs of Bucaramanga. The perfectly preserved town of Barichara, with its cobbled streets, stone churches and excellent dining and lodging options might be the highlight of your trip to Colombia.

HIGHLIGHTS

- Go on a bicycle or horseback tour through the lovely countryside surrounding the charming colonial village of **Villa de Leyva** (p105)
- Rappel, paddle, paraglide or spelunk your way around the ecotourist sites of **San Gil** (p119)
- Get lost on the cobblestone roads and alleys of the beautiful colonial village of **Barichara** (p122)
- Take a hike along an ancient, fossil-strewn road from Barichara to the tiny hamlet of **Guane** (p125)
- Trek amid the spectacular alpine scenery of **Parque Nacional Natural El Cocuy** (p116)

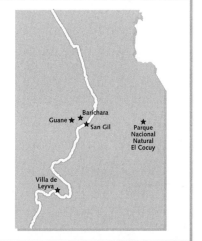

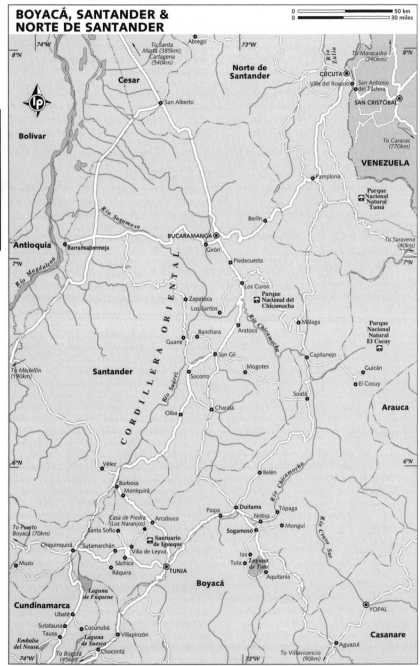

BOYACÁ, SANTANDER & NORTE DE SANTANDER

History

The Muiscas (Boyacá) and the Guane people (Santander) once occupied the regions north of what is now Bogotá. Highly developed in agriculture and mining, the Muisca traded with their neighbors and came into frequent contact with Spanish conquistadores. It was their stories of gold and emeralds that helped fuel the myth of El Dorado. The conquistadores' search for the famed city also sparked settlements and the Spanish founded several cities, including Tunja in 1539.

Several generations later, Colombian nationalists first stood up to Spanish rule in Socorro (Santander), stoking the flames of independence for other towns and regions. It was also here that Simón Bolívar and his upstart army took on Spanish infantry, winning decisive battles at Pantano de Vargas and Puente de Boyacá. Colombia's first constitution was drawn up soon after in Villa del Rosario, between the Venezuelan border and Cúcuta.

Climate

Climate varies with the changing altitude. With an elevation of 2960m and an average temperature of 12°C, Güicán is one of the highest and coldest towns in this region; the other extreme is Cúcuta, where hot, muggy weather is the norm and temperatures hover around 27°C. The mountain towns of Tunja and Pamplona are cooler than lower-lying Bucaramanga. Barichara has a perfect year-round average temperature of 22°C.

Getting There & Around

The region is easily accessible by public transportation. Most of its cities are located along the safe and modern highway that stretches from Bogotá in the south to the Caribbean coast. Buses are frequent, comfortable and economical. There are regular buses along the main highway from Bogotá to Bucaramanga and beyond. Cúcuta is a major entry point for travelers coming from Venezuela.

Within the region, intercity buses and minivans depart frequently, so you never have to wait long. But in smaller towns, buses may only run once or twice a day. Taxis are plentiful but can be pricey. In Villa de Leyva, a bike or horse might be a more suitable and fun way to explore the countryside.

By plane, many cities, including Bucaramanga and Cúcuta, are increasingly served by low-cost airlines.

BOYACÁ

The department of Boyacá evokes a sense of patriotism among Colombians; it was here that Colombian troops won their independence from Spain at the Battle of Boyacá. The department is dotted with quaint colonial towns; you could easily spend a few days bouncing between them. Boyacá's crown jewel is the spectacular PNN El Cocuy, located 249km northeast of the department capital, Tunja.

TUNJA

☎ 8 / pop 150,000 / elev 2820m

Often overlooked by travelers rushing on to Villa de Leyva, Tunja, the capital of Boyacá and a bustling student center, has plenty to offer the discerning tourist, with fine colonial architecture, an imposing central square and elegant mansions adorned with some of South America's most unique artwork.

Tunja was founded by Gonzalo Suárez Rendón in 1539 on the site of Hunza, the pre-Hispanic Muisca settlement. Almost nothing is left of the indigenous legacy, but much colonial architecture remains. Tunja is particularly noted for its colonial churches; several imposing examples dating from the 16th century stand almost untouched by time. With nearly a dozen universities, Tunja is also a center of learning. One in five residents is a student, giving the city a youthful vibrancy.

Tunja is the highest and coldest departmental capital in Colombia. Its mountain climate can be windy or wet any time of the year. If you've forgotten your winter woollies, there are plenty of shops north of the main square.

Information

Banco BBVA (Carrera 11) Has an ATM.
Bancolombia (Carrera 10 No 22-43) Has an ATM and changes traveler's checks and currency.
Virtual Net (☎ 743 6056; Carrera 10 No 19-83; per hr COP$1000; ☼ 9am-7pm)
Internet Orbitel (☎ 743 0955; Calle 20 No 10-26; per hr COP$1400; ☼ 8am-9pm) Internet and international phone calls.
Tourist office (☎ 742 3272; Carrera 9 No 19-68; ☼ 8am-noon & 2-6pm) Secretaría de Educación, Cultura y Turismo, inside the Casa del Fundador Suárez Rendón.

Sights

Tunja is a trove of colonial-era churches noted for their Mudejar art, an Islamic-influenced style, developed in Christian Spain between

BOYACÁ, SANTANDER & NORTE DE SANTANDER

BOYACÁ, SANTANDER &
NORTE DE SANTANDER

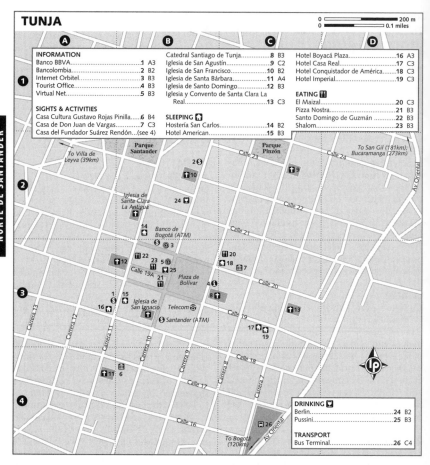

TUNJA

INFORMATION
Banco BBVA.................................**1** A3
Bancolombia...............................**2** B2
Internet Orbitel...........................**3** B3
Tourist Office..............................**4** B3
Virtual Net.................................**5** B3

SIGHTS & ACTIVITIES
Casa Cultura Gustavo Rojas Pinilla.....**6** B4
Casa de Don Juan de Vargas............**7** C3
Casa del Fundador Suárez Rendón...(see 4)

Catedral Santiago de Tunja..............**8** B3
Iglesia de San Agustín....................**9** C2
Iglesia de San Francisco.................**10** B2
Iglesia de Santa Bárbara................**11** A4
Iglesia de Santo Domingo...............**12** B3
Iglesia y Convento de Santa Clara La
Real.....................................**13** C3

SLEEPING
Hostería San Carlos......................**14** B2
Hotel American...........................**15** B3

Hotel Boyacá Plaza.......................**16** A3
Hotel Casa Real...........................**17** C3
Hotel Conquistador de América.......**18** C3
Hotel Imperial............................**19** C3

EATING
El Maizal...................................**20** C3
Pizza Nostra...............................**21** B3
Santo Domingo de Guzmán **22** B3
Shalom....................................**23** B3

DRINKING
Berlin......................................**24** B2
Pussini.....................................**25** B3

TRANSPORT
Bus Terminal..............................**26** C4

the 12th and 16th centuries. It's particularly visible in the ornamented coffered vaults. As well as its churches, some of Tunja's best sights are its historic mansions that have been opened as museums.

CASA DEL FUNDADOR SUÁREZ RENDÓN

One of the finest historic mansions in town is the **Casa del Fundador Suárez Rendón** (☎ 742 3272, 742 3441; Carrera 9 No 19-68; admission COP$1500; ⏰ 8am-6pm), the original home of the founder of Tunja. Built in the mid-16th century on the eastern side of Plaza de Bolívar, it's a fine example of a magnificent aristocratic residence from the times of the Spanish Conquest. Its most interesting feature is the ceiling, covered with intriguing scenes (see the boxed text,

opposite) that were only recently discovered when a ceiling collapsed. There's also a good bookstore and artisan workshops.

CASA DE DON JUAN DE VARGAS

Once home to scribe Juan de Vargas, **Casa de Don Juan de Vargas** (☎ 742 6611; Calle 20 No 8-52; admission COP$2000; ⏰ 9am-noon & 2-5pm Tue-Fri, 10am-4pm Sat & Sun) is another splendid 16th-century residence. It also has been converted into a museum and has a collection of colonial artworks on display. Here again, the most captivating features are the ceilings, covered with eclectic paintings.

CASA CULTURAL GUSTAVO ROJAS PINILLA

This small but lovely colonial home was the **birthplace of Gustavo Rojas Pinilla** (☎ 742 6814, 742

2511; Calle 17 No 10-64; admission free; ⏰ 8am-noon & 2-6pm Mon-Fri), who became president of Colombia in a 1953 military coup with promises of reform. Instead, his tenure was marked by corruption and brutality until he too was overthrown three years later. The ground floor contains an art gallery with regular exhibits by local art students. Upstairs, a small museum explores Pinilla's life through photographs, documents and personal belongings.

IGLESIA DE SANTO DOMINGO
The nondescript exterior of the mid-16th-century **Iglesia de Santo Domingo** (Carrera 11 No 19-55) hides one of the most richly decorated interiors in Colombia. To the left as you enter is the large Capilla del Rosario, dubbed La Capilla Sixtina del Arte Neogranadino (Sistine Chapel of New Granada's Art). Decorated by Fray Pedro Bedón from Quito, the chapel is exuberantly rich in wonderful, gilded wood carving – a magnificent example of Hispano-American baroque art. The statue of the Virgen del Rosario in the altar niche is encrusted in mother-of-pearl and clad with mirrors.

IGLESIA Y CONVENTO DE SANTA CLARA LA REAL
Founded in 1571, the **Iglesia y Convento de Santa Clara La Real** (☎ 742 5659; Carrera 7 No 19-58; admission COP$2000; ⏰ 8am-noon & 2-6pm) is thought to be the first convent in Nueva Granada. In 1863 the nuns were expelled and the convent was used for various purposes, including serving as a hospital. The church, however, continued to provide religious services. The single-naved church interior shelters a wealth of colonial artwork on its walls, most of which comes from the 16th to 18th centuries. Note

the golden sun on the ceiling, a Spanish trick to help the *indígenas* convert to Catholicism (the sun was the principal god of the Muisca people). Next to the choir is the cell where Madre Francisca Josefa, a mystic nun looked upon as Colombia's St Teresa, lived for 53 years (1689–1742).

OTHER CHURCHES
Catedral Santiago de Tunja (Carrera 9 No 19-28) on Plaza de Bolívar is Tunja's largest church and stylistically the most complex, dating to 1554. **Iglesia de Santa Bárbara** (Carrera 11 No 16-62) was completed in 1599; its Capilla de la Epístola has an outstanding Mudejar ceiling. **Iglesia de San Agustín** (☎ 742 2312; cnr Carrera 8 & Calle 23), now a library, faces Parque Pinzón on a site believed to be the heart of Hunza, the Musica capital. **Iglesia de San Francisco** (Carrera 10 No 22-23), built from 1550 to 1572, boasts a splendid main retable framed into an elaborate gilded arch at the entrance to the presbytery. Note the impressively realistic sculpture of Christ (carved in 1816), *Cristo de los Mártires*.

Festivals & Events
Semana Santa (Easter Week) Boyacá is one of the most traditional departments, so religious celebrations in the countryside and Tunja itself are observed with due solemnity. Processions circle the city streets on Maundy Thursday and Good Friday.
Festival Internacional de la Cultura (Sep) A cultural event that includes theater performances, concerts and art exhibitions.
Aguinaldo Boyacense (Dec) A religious feast that runs for a week before Christmas with parades and dances.

Sleeping
Hotel American (☎ 742 2471; Calle 11 No 18-70; s/d with shared bath COP$12,000/22,000, with private bath

TUNJA'S ENIGMATIC CEILING PAINTINGS
Several colonial mansions in Tunja, including the Casa del Fundador Suárez Rendón and the Casa de Don Juan de Vargas, have their ceilings adorned with unusual paintings featuring a strange mishmash of motifs taken from very different traditions. They include mythological scenes, human figures, animals and plants, coats of arms and architectural details. You can spot Zeus and Jesus amid tropical plants or an elephant under a Renaissance arcade – you probably haven't seen anything like that before. In fact, there's nothing similar anywhere in Latin America.

The source of these bizarre decorations seems to be Juan de Vargas himself. He was a scribe and had a large library with books on European art and architecture, ancient Greece and Rome, religion and natural history. It seems that the illustrations in the books were the source of motifs for the anonymous painters who worked on these ceilings. Since the original illustrations were in black and white, the color schemes are by the design of these unknown artisans.

COP$25,000/35,000) This basic but clean hotel is the cheapest option downtown. All rooms have lukewarm water and TV. The hotel also has a popular, cheap restaurant.

Hotel Imperial (☎ 314 206-1326; Calle 19 No 7-43; s/d COP$20,000/25,000) Bathed in color and light, Hotel Imperial has 17 clean, comfy rooms and friendly staff. Check the rooms first; some are tiny closets with hobbit-sized doors.

Hotel Conquistador de América (☎ 742 3534; Calle 20 No 8-92; s/d COP$25,000/40,000; ✗) A colonial building at the corner of Plaza de Bolívar has 20 ample rooms, with private bathrooms, hot showers and TVs. Some rooms are dim and boxy while the larger rooms facing the street can be noisy, so pick your poison.

our pick Hostería San Carlos (☎ 742 3716; Carrera 11 No 20-12; s/d/tr COP$30,000/50,000/70,000) Located in an old colonial home and run by a friendly granny, the San Carlos is the best downtown budget option. This character-filled hotel has 11 comfy rooms with period furnishings, including a five-bed room for big groups.

Hotel Casa Real (☎ 310 852 1636; hotelcasareal@yahoo .es; Calle 19 No 7-65; s/d/tr COP$40,000/50,000/60,000; ✗) This relatively new hotel, located between the bus station and the main plaza, is sparsely furnished but painted in colorful pastel designs. All 11 rooms come with private bathroom and hot water.

Hotel Boyacá Plaza (☎ 740 1116; hotelboyaca plaza@hotmail.com; Calle 18 No 11-22; s/d with break-fast COP$104,140/140,080; P ✗ ▣) This small, business-style hotel, with attentive service and smart rooms, is located two blocks from the Plaza de Bolívar.

Eating

Shalom (☎ 740 5494; Calle 19A No 10-64, Pasaje de Vargas; breakfast COP$4000-6000; ⌚ 7am-4:30pm) There are many coffee shops along Pasaje de Vargas, but this is one of the few that actually serves a full breakfast including *huevos pericos* (scrambled eggs with tomato and onion) and warm *arepas* (corn pancakes).

Pizza Nostra (☎ 740 2040; Calle 19 No 10-36; pizzas COP$5600-9500; ⌚ noon-11pm) Located in the pedestrian zone just off Plaza de Bolívar, this popular fast-food joint has a huge selection of yummy pizzas.

El Maizal (Carrera 9 No 20-30; mains COP$10,000-13,000; ⌚ breakfast, lunch & dinner) This restaurant doesn't look very elegant, but has long been popular with the locals for its tasty regional dishes, huge portions and daily set meal specials.

Santo Domingo de Guzmán (☎ 742 2619; Carrera 11 No 19-66; mains COP$5000-18,000; ⌚ 7am-8pm) One of downtown Tunja's most popular eateries, this family-run restaurant serves traditional dishes in a homey atmosphere. There's also a bakery and fruit stand on-site.

Drinking

Pussini (☎ 743 2047; Carrera 10 No 19-53; coffee COP$2500, beer COP$6000; ⌚ 8:30am-10pm) Cafe by day, pub by night, Pussini is the pulse of Plaza de Bolívar. The two levels of the bar are covered in wood, right up to the bamboo ceilings. For non-coffee or beer drinkers, there's also a fully stocked bar. Drink up!

Berlin (☎ 743 3999; Carrera 10 No 21-49; drinks COP$2000-13,000; ⌚ noon-midnight) This swanky rooftop bar has a sleek interior bathed in neon and thumping Spanish and English rock. The highlight is its heated terrace overlooking the city. Berlin is hidden on the 5th floor of the San Francisco Plaza office building.

Getting There & Away

The bus terminal is on Av Oriental, a short hilly walk southeast of Plaza de Bolívar. Buses to Bogotá (COP$18,000, 2½ to three hours) depart every 10 to 15 minutes. Northbound buses to San Gil (COP$20,000, 4½ hours), Bucaramanga (COP$35,000, seven hours) and beyond run at least every hour.

Minibuses to Villa de Leyva (COP$5000, 45 minutes) depart regularly until about 6pm.

PUENTE DE BOYACÁ

Puente de Boyacá is one of the most important battlefields of Colombia's modern history. On August 7, 1819 and against all odds, the armies of Simón Bolívar defeated Spanish troops led by General José María Barreiro, sealing Colombia's independence.

Several monuments have been erected on the battlefield. The centerpiece is the **Monumento a Bolívar**, an 18-meter-high sculpture topped by the statue of Colombia's hero and accompanied by five angels symbolizing the so-called **países bolivarianos**, the countries liberated by Bolívar – Venezuela, Colombia, Ecuador, Peru and Bolivia. An eternal flame for Bolívar burns nearby.

The **Puente de Boyacá**, the bridge which gives its name to the battlefield and over which Bolívar's troops crossed to fight the Spaniards, is just a small, simple bridge reconstructed in 1939.

The battlefield is on the main Tunja–Bogotá road, 15km south of Tunja. Any bus passing along this road will drop you off.

VILLA DE LEYVA

☎ 8 / pop 8000 / elev 2140m

One of the most beautiful colonial villages in Colombia, Villa de Leyva is a city frozen in time. Declared a national monument in 1954, photogenic Villa de Leyva has been preserved in its entirety with cobblestone roads and whitewashed buildings.

The city's physical beauty and mild, dry climate have long attracted outsiders. The town was founded in 1572 by Hernán Suárez de Villalobos, who named it for his boss, Andres Díaz Venero de Leyva, the first president of the New Kingdom of Granada. It was originally a retreat for military officers, clergy and nobility.

In recent years, an influx of wealthy visitors and expats has slowly transformed this once-hidden gem. Boutique hotels, gourmet restaurants and tacky tourist shops are replacing many of the old family *hosterías* and cafes. The 2007 *telenovela* (soap opera) *Zorro: La Espada y la Rosa* was filmed here, bringing further publicity to the city. On weekends, the narrow alleys can get downright crammed with day-trippers from Bogotá. But thankfully on weekdays, the city reverts to a peaceful, bucolic village.

Despite its changing face, Villa de Leyva remains an alluring destination. It is still very much a traditional city, where locals greet strangers with *'Buenos días'* or *'Buenas tardes.'* It is one of the loveliest places in Colombia, filled with history, museums, festivals and sightseeing opportunities. Don't miss it.

Information

Take a virtual tour of Villa de Leyva at www .expovilla.com or www.villadeleyva.net.

ATMs (Plaza Mayor, Calle 12) Several ATMs on the south side of the square.

Police (☎ 732 0236, 732 1412; Carrera 10 No 11-10)

Quinternet I & II (Carrera 9 No 11-77 and Carrera 9 No 11-96; per hr COP$1600; ☺ 10am-1pm & 3-9pm) Internet cafes.

Telecom (☎ 732 1040; Plaza Mayor, Carrera 9 No 12-36; ☺ 7am-10pm)

Tourist office (Oficina de Turismo; ☎ 732 0232; cnr Carrera 9 & Calle 13; ☺ 8am-1pm & 3-6pm Mon-Sat, 9am-1pm & 3-6pm Sun) Provides free maps, brochures and can book activities and tours. The Tourist Police has a small information kiosk outside the bus terminal.

Sights

Villa de Leyva is a leisurely place made for wandering around charming cobblestone streets, listening to the sound of church bells and enjoying the lazy rhythm of days gone by. Small as it is, the town has six museums, most of which are in old colonial buildings. Villa de Leyva is also famous for its abundance of fossils from the Cretaceous and Mesozoic periods, when this area was underwater. Look closely and you'll notice that fossils have been used as construction materials in floors, walls and pavements. For a marvelous bird's-eye view of the town, hike up one of the many hills surrounding the village (see p107). And when you're ready for a break, stroll into a local cafe for a *tinto* (black coffee) and sample the local treat, *besos de novia* (girlfriend's kisses).

PLAZA MAYOR

At 120m by 120m, **Plaza Mayor** is one of the largest town squares in the Americas. It's paved with massive cobblestones and surrounded by magnificent colonial structures and a charmingly simple parish church. The vast plaza is interrupted only by a small Mudejar fountain in its middle, which provided water to the village inhabitants for almost four centuries. Unlike most Colombian cities where the main squares have been named after historic heroes, the one in Villa de Leyva is traditionally and firmly called Plaza Mayor.

As you stroll about, pop into the **Casa de Juan de Castellanos** (Carrera 9 No 13-15), **Casona La Guaca** (Carrera 9 No 13-57) and **Casa Quintero** (cnr Carrera 9 & Calle 12), three meticulously restored colonial mansions just off the plaza that now house quaint cafes, restaurants and shops.

CASA MUSEO DE LUIS ALBERTO ACUÑA

Featuring works by the painter, sculptor, writer and historian who was inspired by influences ranging from Muisca mythology to contemporary art, **Casa Museo de Luis Alberto Acuña** (Plaza Mayor; admission COP$3000; ☺ 9am-6pm) has been set up in the mansion where Acuña (1904–93) lived for the last 15 years of his life.

CASA MUSEO DE ANTONIO NARIÑO

Antonio Nariño was known as the forefather of Colombia's independence and **Casa Museo de Antonio Nariño** (☎ 732 0342; Carrera 9 No 10-25; admission COP$3000; ☺ 8am-noon & 2-5pm Thu-Tue) is the

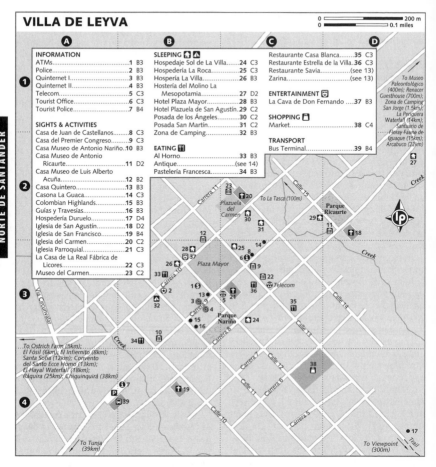

VILLA DE LEYVA

0 — 200 m
0 — 0.1 miles

INFORMATION
ATMs...1 B3
Police..2 B3
Quinternet I...................................3 B3
Quinternet II..................................4 B3
Telecom...5 C3
Tourist Office................................6 C3
Tourist Police................................7 B4

SIGHTS & ACTIVITIES
Casa de Juan de Castellanos........8 C3
Casa del Premier Congreso..........9 C3
Casa Museo de Antonio Nariño.10 B3
Casa Museo de Antonio
  Ricaurte...................................11 D2
Casa Museo de Luis Alberto
  Acuña.......................................12 B2
Casa Quintero..............................13 B3
Casona La Guaca..........................14 C3
Colombian Highlands...................15 B3
Guías y Travesías.........................16 B3
Hospedería Duruelo......................17 D4
Iglesia de San Agustín..................18 D2
Iglesia de San Francisco...............19 B4
Iglesia del Carmen.......................20 C2
Iglesia Parroquial.........................21 C3
La Casa de La Real Fábrica de
  Licores.....................................22 C3
Museo del Carmen.......................23 C2

SLEEPING
Hospedaje Sol de La Villa.........24 C3
Hospedería La Roca.................25 C3
Hospería La Villa....................26 B3
Hostería del Molino La
  Mesopotamia...........................27 D2
Hotel Plaza Mayor.................28 B3
Hotel Plazuela de San Agustín.29 C2
Posada de los Ángeles............30 C2
Posada San Martín...................31 C2
Zona de Camping.....................32 B3

EATING
Al Horno..............................33 B3
Antique..........................(see 14)
Pastelería Francesca..............34 B3

Restaurante Casa Blanca........35 C3
Restaurante Estrella de la Villa.36 C3
Restaurante Savia...............(see 13)
Zarina............................(see 13)

ENTERTAINMENT
La Cava de Don Fernando 37 B3

SHOPPING
Market..............................38 C4

TRANSPORT
Bus Terminal......................39 B4

To Museo
Paleontológico
(400m); Renacer
Guesthouse (700m);
Zona de Camping
San Jorge (1.5km);
La Periquera
Waterfall (14km);
Santuario de
Floray Fauna de
Iguaque (15km);
Arcabuco (22km)

Carrera 11
Calle 15
To La Tasca (100m)
Plazuela del Carmen
Parque Ricaurte
Creek
To La Tasca (100m)
Plaza Mayor
Telecom
Creek
Carrera 10
Parque Nariño
Calle 14
Calle 13
Via Circunvalar
To Ostrich Farm (5km);
El Fósil (6km); El Infiernito (8km);
Santa Sofía (12km); Convento
del Santo Ecce Homo (13km);
El Hayal Waterfall (18km);
Ráquira (25km); Chiquinquirá (38km)
Carrera 8
Calle 12
Carrera 6
Calle 11
Carrera 5
Calle 10
To Tunja (39km)
To Viewpoint (300m)
Trail

house where he lived until his death in 1823. Nariño was a fierce defender of human rights and is also revered for translating Thomas Paine's *Rights of Man* into Spanish. The house has been converted into a museum containing colonial objects and memorabilia related to this great man.

CASA MUSEO DE ANTONIO RICAURTE
Antonio Ricaurte fought under Bolívar and is remembered for his act of self-sacrifice in the battle of San Mateo (near Caracas in Venezuela) in 1814. Defending an armory and closely encircled by the Spaniards, he let them in, then set fire to the gunpowder kegs and blew up everyone, including himself. The battle was won. **Casa Museo de Antonio Ricaurte**

(Calle 15 No 8-16, Parque Ricaurte; admission COP$3000; 9am-6pm) is the house where Ricaurte was born in 1786. It's now a museum, which displays period furniture and weapons as well as some related documents.

CASA DEL PRIMER CONGRESO DE LAS PROVINCIAS UNIDAS
On October 4, 1812, legislators met here to install the First Congress of the short-lived United Provinces of New Granada and elect its first president, Camilo Torres Tenorio. The 2nd floor of the **Casa del Primer Congreso** (cnr Carrera 9 & Calle 13; admission free; 10am-1pm & 2-5pm Mon-Sat) houses a small museum that contains the congressional desk, documents and other artifacts.

LA CASA DE LA REAL FÁBRICA DE LICORES

This huge colonial factory once supplied the entire region with its boozy needs. Today, the **Fábrica de Licores** (Calle 13 s/n btwn Carreras 8 & 9; admission free; 🕑 10am-noon & 2-6pm Mon-Fri & Sun, 2-8pm Sat) is a museum with rotating exhibits by artists such as renowned Colombian painter Duván López.

MUSEO DEL CARMEN

One of the best museums of religious art in the country, **Museo del Carmen** (Plazuela del Carmen; admission COP$3000; 🕑 10am-1pm & 2-5pm Sat, Sun & holidays) is housed in the convent of the same name. It contains valuable paintings, carvings, altarpieces and other religious objects dating from the 16th century onward.

MUSEO PALEONTOLÓGICO

About 1km northeast of town, **Museo Paleontológico** (☎ 732 0466; Via Arcabuco; admission COP$3000; 🕑 9am-noon & 2-5pm Tue-Sun) has a collection of locally found fossils dating from the period when the area was a sea bed (100 to 150 million years ago).

CHURCHES

Villa de Leyva has four churches, all dating back to the town's early years. The **Iglesia Parroquial** (Plaza Mayor; 🕑 7-8am & 6:30-8pm Mon-Sat, 7-8am, 10-11am, noon-1pm & 6:30-8pm Sun), the parish church facing the main square, was built in 1608 and has hardly changed since that time. It boasts a marvelous baroque main retable. The only other church currently in religious service, the **Iglesia del Carmen** (Calle 14 No 10-04; 🕑 6:30-8am Mon-Sat, 6:30-8am & 11am-noon Sun), has interesting paintings in the chancel and the wooden structure supporting the roof. **Iglesia de San Francisco** (cnr Carrera 8 & Calle 10) and **Iglesia de San Agustín** (Parque Ricaurte) no longer serve a religious purpose and are not open to the public.

Activities

There are many **hiking** possibilities all around Villa de Leyva, as well as some longer treks in the Santuario de Iguaque (p110). In town, there's a great hike that begins directly behind Renacer Guesthouse (p108), passing two waterfalls to reach a spectacular bird's-eye view of the village; the round-trip hike takes less than two hours. For a shorter trip but a less dramatic view, walk southeast of the market and climb the hill behind the Hospedería Duruelo.

The alternative to foot power is **cycling** or **horseback riding**; both can be booked at the tourist office or directly from one of the tour operators following. Bikes cost about COP$3000 per hour and COP$10,000 for a half-day; horses are COP$5000 per hour.

Swimming holes can be found beneath many of the nearby waterfalls. The two most spectacular falls in the area are La Periquera and El Hayal. In town, you can take the plunge at the freshwater swimming pool at Hostería del Molino La Mesopotamia (p109). More extreme sporting options in the area include **rappelling**, **canyoning** and **caving**. These activities can be arranged through the following tour companies.

LOCAL VOICE: OSCAR GILÈDE

Age: 40
Occupation: Biologist; owner of Renacer Guesthouse
Residence: Villa de Leyva

'I first came to Villa de Leyva as a biologist to conduct scientific research on ecological disturbances. Now I am devoted to environmental education, scientific tourism and ecotourism.

'Villa de Leyva is one of the oldest and best-preserved colonial cities in Colombia, characterized by its architectural beauty, museums, history and surroundings. Don't miss **El Infiernito** (p110), the Stonehenge of Colombia, or **El Fósil** (p110), a 120-million-year-old kronosaurus that's an excellent example of fossils found in this region. Don't leave without visiting **Santuario de Flora y Fauna de Iguaque** (p110), the Muisca cradle of civilization and best place in the area to observe birds and the great diversity of Colombian Andes flora.

'Colombia is more than just drugs or coffee. It is a major destination for ecotourism. It has a wealth of natural and cultural diversity and friendly people ready to assist you at a moment's notice.'

Tours

Taxis at the bus terminal offer return trips to the surrounding sights. The standard routes include El Fósil, El Infiernito and Convento del Santo Ecce Homo (COP$60,000), and Ráquira and La Candelaria (COP$80,000). Prices are per taxi for up to four people and include stops at the sights.

Colombian Highlands (☎ 732 1379, 310 552 9079; www.colombianhighlands.com; colombianhighlands@ hotmail.com; Carrera 9 No 11-02; ☒ 9am-noon & 1-8pm) Run by biologist and Renacer Guesthouse owner Oscar Gilède, this agency has a variety of off-beat tours including ecotours, nocturnal hikes, bird-watching, rappelling/abseiling, canyoning, caving and hiking and rents bikes and horses. English is spoken.

Guías y Travesías (☎ 732 0742, 311 461 1298; guia devilladeleyva@yahoo.com; Calle 11 No 8A-30) This agency rents out bicycles and can provide maps and recommended cycling routes. Regional hikes and tours are also available.

Festivals & Events

Ferias y Fiestas Patronales de la Virgen Del Carmen (mid-July) This festival and fair honors the patron saint of Villa de Leyva.

Festival de las Cometas (Aug) Locals and some foreign kite fans compete in this colorful kite festival.

Festival Gastronómico (Sep) A festival for foodies celebrating the region's tasty culinary traditions.

Festival Nacional del Árbol (mid-Oct) A green celebration aimed at increasing awareness of the environment and conservationism

Festival de Luces (Dec) This fireworks festival is usually on the first or second weekend of December.

Sleeping

Villa de Leyva has a large selection of hotels in all price ranges. Note that prices rise on weekends when it may be hard to find a room. During high seasons including Semana Santa and December 20 to January 15, prices can more than double. Plan ahead.

BUDGET

Zona de Camping (☎ 311 550 7687, 314 381 4108; cnr Carrera 10 & Calle 11; campsite per person high/low season COP$8000/6000) This walled, grassy field has sites and a simple bathhouse, but not much else. Pitch your tent upon arrival and the caretaker will find you later; if the gate is locked, call for the key.

Zona de Camping San Jorge (☎ 732 0328, 311 213 1125; campingsanjorge@gmail.com; Vereda Roble; campsite per person high/low season COP$8000/6000) Located about 2km northeast of town, this huge grassy field

has space for 120 tents with lovely views of the surrounding mountains. Amenities include a small restaurant and shop, spotless bathrooms with hot water and a huge shared kitchen. It's a 25-minute walk from the plaza: walk north on Carrera 9, passing Museo Paleontológico. At the T-intersection, turn right, then make an immediate left down the well-signed gravel road to the campground.

ourpick Renacer Guesthouse (☎ 732 1201, 311 308 3739; www.colombianhighlands.com; 1.2km northeast of plaza; campsite per person COP$6000, dm/s/d/ste COP$14,000/20,000/38,000/60,000; ☐ Ⓟ ☒) This delightful 'boutique hostel' is the creation of biologist and tour guide extraordinaire Oscar Gilède of Colombian Highlands (left). Everything about this place feels like home – hammocks surrounding an immaculate garden; a communal, open-air kitchen with brick oven; spotless dorms, rooms and a luxury suite. It's a bit tricky to find, but Oscar will pay for guests' first taxi ride from the bus station. Or stop by Colombian Highlands for directions.

Hospedería La Villa (☎ 732 0848; hospederialavilla@ hotmail.com; Calle 12 No 10-11; s/d COP$15,000/25,000) Located just off the plaza, this is one of the cheapest places in town with clean, albeit sparse rooms.

Hospedería La Roca (☎ 732 0331; Plaza Mayor; r per person COP$35,000; ☒) Located directly on the main square, the charming La Roca was recently renovated top-to-bottom. The 23 pleasant rooms surround a gorgeous, plant-filled courtyard. All rooms have high ceilings, TV and modern en-suite bathrooms with hot water.

Posada de los Ángeles (☎ 732 0562; Carrera 10 No 13-94; r per person incl breakfast COP$40,000; ☒) A pastel-colored affair with modern bathrooms, tile floors and mosquito nets. The historic house overlooks Iglesia del Carmen and serves up a great breakfast.

MIDRANGE & TOP END

Hospedaje Sol de La Villa (☎ 732 0224; Carrera 8A No 12-28; s/d COP$30,000/60,000; ☒) Located on a quiet side street, this sunny hotel is painted in cheerful, bright colors. All rooms are clean and comfy and have TV and private bathroom with hot water.

Posada San Martín (☎ 732 0428; Calle 14 No 9-43; s/d/tr incl breakfast COP$30,000/50,000/80,000; ☒) Hidden behind a high wall in a beautiful old home, this quiet and welcoming guesthouse has five rooms, all with private bathroom.

Hotel Plaza Mayor (☎ 732 0425, 313 387 2258; www.hotelplazamayor.com.co; Carrera 10 No 12-31; s/d from COP$110,000/193,000; ☒) The grand dame of Villa de Leyva. Its 31 rooms are all furnished to high standards and customer service is unsurpassed. The rooftop patio restaurant overlooks the main square and features traditional food and live music.

Hostería del Molino La Mesopotamia (☎ 732 0235; Carrera 8 No 15A-265; s/d/tr incl breakfast COP$110,000/ 150,000/190,000; ☒☒☒) Built in 1568, this old flour mill is one of the oldest and most beautiful buildings in town. Unfortunately, its age is showing and we've received several complaints. Still, it's worth a visit to check out the colonial architecture, furnishings and artwork. Nonguests can swim in the spring-fed, fossil-walled swimming pool for COP$5000.

Hotel Plazuela de San Agustín (☎ 732 1607, 310 299 6221; www.hotelplazuela.com; Calle 15 s/n; s/d/ste COP$200,000/ 220,000/240,000) This posh, boutique hotel appropriately calls itself a house-museum. The path leading into the colonial hotel is paved with fossils. Inside, the 20 rooms feature period furnishings and exposed wood beams, all overlooking lovely courtyards.

Eating

Restaurante Casa Blanca (☎ 732 0821; Calle 13 No 7-16; mains COP$6000-18,000; ☒ 10am-5pm) One of the better budget restaurants in town, Casa Blanca offers a choice of tasty à la carte sandwiches, mains and set meals.

Pastelería Francesa (Calle 10 No 9-41; No 7-16; mains COP$1500-5000; ☒ breakfast & lunch Thu-Mon) Ooh la la! An authentic French bakery with croissants, baguettes, tarts, quiches, coffees and hot chocolate.

Restaurante Estrella de la Villa (Calle 13 No 8-85; set meals COP$5000; ☒ 8am-8pm) A good alternative to the Casa Blanca, this one has reasonable food and prices. It also serves breakfast.

Al Horno (☎ 732 1996; Carrera 10 No 11-23; mains COP$7000-14,000; ☒ 10am-10pm) This colorful and atmospheric bistro has a menu with 12 different types of pizza, plus spaghetti, fettuccine, burgers, sandwiches, crepes and desserts.

Zarina (☎ 732 0735; Casa Quintero; mains COP$13,000-18,000; ☒ lunch & dinner) In-the-know locals vote this Lebanese joint the best eatery in town. There's no *shawarma*, but you can enjoy a genuine felafel with tahini.

ourpick Antique (☎ 732 0208; Casona La Guaca, Carrera 9 No 13-55; mains COP$12,000-26,000; ☒ lunch & dinner) The place to impress your sweetie,

this romantic rooftop restaurant is bathed in candlelight and Spanish love songs. The daring and delicious Nuevo-Colombian menu features amazing dishes such as trout with mango, coconut and prawn sauce, plus an extensive wine list.

Restaurante Savia (Casa Quintero; mains COP$12,000-28,000; ☒ 4-10pm Fri, 10am-10pm Sat & Sun) The delightful Savia (previously Xirrus and Don D'Bill) specializes in inventive vegetarian, vegan and organic fare. Carnivores will love the fresh seafood and poultry dishes such as chicken in mango sauce. A plaque outside commemorates the last concert performed by former Elvis Presley drummer Bill Lynn before he died in Villa de Leyva in 2006.

Entertainment

La Cava de Don Fernando (☎ 732 0073; Carrera 10 No 12-03; beers COP$2500; ☒ 2pm-2am) If you just want to drink, this small bar on the corner of the plaza has blaring music and freely flowing alcohol.

La Tasca (☎ 732 0877; Calle 15 No 12A-25; cover charge varies; ☒ 8pm-late Fri & Sat) The only *discoteca* in town, La Tasca features live music, drinking, dancing and late-night dining.

Shopping

Check out the colorful market held every Saturday on the square three blocks southeast of Plaza Mayor. It's best and busiest early in the morning.

Villa de Leyva has a quite a number of handicraft shops noted for fine basketry and good-quality woven items such as sweaters and ruanas (ponchos). There are some artisan shops on Plaza Mayor and more in the side streets, particularly on Carrera 9. A number of weavers have settled in town; their work is of excellent quality and their prices are reasonable. Most craft shops open only on weekends.

Getting There & Away

The bus terminal is three blocks southwest of the Plaza Mayor, on the road to Tunja. Minibuses run between Tunja and Villa de Leyva every 15 minutes from 5am to 6pm (COP$5000, 45 minutes, 39km). There are only two direct buses daily to Bogotá (COP$14,000, four hours); your best bet is to go to Tunja and change.

AROUND VILLA DE LEYVA

Don't leave Villa de Leyva without exploring some of the many nearby attractions, including archeological relics, colonial monuments, petroglyphs, caves, lakes and waterfalls.

The area is completely safe. You can walk to some of the nearest sights, or go by bicycle or on horseback (see p107). You can also use local buses, go by taxi or arrange a tour with Villa de Leyva's tour operators (p108). If you choose to go by taxi, make sure you confirm with the driver all the sights you want to see and agree on a price before setting off.

Ostrich Farm

About 5km southwest of Villa de Leyva, in the direction of El Fósil, is a slightly incongruous **Ostrich Farm** (☎ 315 854 9406; adult/child COP$4000/3000; 🕑 9am-4:30pm Tue-Sun), home to more than 120 ostriches and a handful of llamas, horses and sheep. There's a small shop that sells ostrich leather shoes and enormous ostrich eggs. There's also a restaurant where you can sample ostrich meat, but it's only open on weekends.

El Fósil

This impressive 120-million-year-old baby **kronosaurus fossil** (☎ 311 269 4067; admission COP$5000; 🕑 8am-6pm) is the world's most complete specimen of this prehistoric marine reptile. The fossil is 7m long; the creature was about 12m in size but the tail did not survive. The fossil remains in place exactly where it was found in 1977.

The fossil is off the road to Santa Sofía, 6km west of Villa de Leyva. You can walk there in a bit more than an hour, or take the Santa Sofía bus, which will drop you off 80m from the fossil.

Estación Astronómica Muisca (El Infiernito)

The **Muisca observatory** (admission COP$3000; 🕑 9am-noon & 2-5pm Tue-Sun) dates from the early centuries AD and was used by the Muiscas to determine the seasons.

This Stonehenge-like site contains 30-odd cylindrical stone monoliths sunk vertically into the ground about 1m from each other in two parallel lines 9m apart. By measuring the length of shadows cast by the stones, the *indígenas* were able to identify the planting seasons.

The observatory was also a ritual site, a fact that thwarted Spanish plans to Christianize the Muiscas. So the Spanish renamed it El Infiernito (The Little Hell) and promoted its association with the devil to keep the Muisca people away.

The site is 2km north of El Fósil. There's no public transport, but you can walk there from the fossil in 25 minutes. Bicycle, horse and taxi are other means of transport.

Convento del Santo Ecce Homo

Founded by the Dominican fathers in 1620, the **convent** (admission COP$2500; 🕑 9am-5pm) is a large stone-and-adobe construction with a lovely courtyard. The floors are paved with stones quarried in the region, so they contain ammonites and fossils, including petrified corn and flowers. There are also fossils in the base of a statue in the chapel.

The chapel boasts a magnificent gilded main retable with a small image of Ecce Homo and the original wooden ceiling. Look out for the drawing of Christ in the west cloister – from different angles it appears that the eyes open and close.

Part of the convent has been turned into an ethnography museum, with displays of agricultural tools and traditional dress worn by the Muiscas and the convent members.

The convent is 13km from Villa de Leyva. The morning bus to Santa Sofía will drop you off from where it's a 15-minute walk to the convent.

A return taxi trip (for up to four people) from Villa de Leyva to El Fósil, El Infiernito and Ecce Homo will cost about COP$35,000, including waiting time allowing for visiting the three sights.

SANTUARIO DE IGUAQUE

High above the surrounding valley and shrouded in mist is a pristine wilderness that Muiscas consider to be the birthplace of mankind. According to Muisca legend, the beautiful goddess Bachué emerged from Laguna de Iguaque with a baby boy in her arms. When the boy became an adult they married, bore children and populated the earth. In old age, the pair transformed into serpents and dove back into the sacred lake.

Today, this Muisca Garden of Eden is a 67.5-sq-km national park called **Santuario de Flora y Fauna de Iguaque** (admission Colombians/foreigners COP$8000/25,000). There are eight small mountain lakes in the northern reserve including Laguna de Iguaque, all sitting at an altitude of between 3550m and 3700m. This unique *páramo* (high-mountain plains), neotropical ecosystem contains hundreds of species of flora and fauna but is most noted for the frailejón, a shrub typical of the highlands.

It can get pretty cold here, with temperatures ranging between 4°C and 13°C. It's also very wet, receiving an average of 1648mm of rain per year. The best months to visit are January, February, July and August. Come prepared.

The **visitors center** (dm/campsite per person COP$18,000/5000) has a restaurant and offers simple accommodations in a grubby-looking dorm, or you can pitch a tent outside. Lodging reservations are required and can be made at Bogotá's Parques Nacionales Naturales de Colombia office (p67).

To get to the park from Villa de Leyva, take the Arcabuco-bound bus (departs 6am, 7am, 8am and 10am and returns 1pm, 2pm and 4pm) and tell the driver to drop you off at Casa de Piedra (also known as Los Naranjos) at Km12. From here, walk up the rough road to the visitors center (3km). The hike from the visitors center to Laguna de Iguaque takes about three hours. A leisurely return trip takes five to six hours, or longer if you plan to visit some of the other lakes.

RÁQUIRA
☎ 8 / pop 1600 / elev 2150m

Brightly painted facades, a jumble of craft shops and stacks of freshly fired mud and clay pots make a welcoming sight along the main street of this one-horse town. Ráquira, 25km southwest of Villa de Leyva, is the pottery capital of Colombia where you'll find everything from ceramic bowls, jars and plates to toys and Christmas decorations. There are many workshops in and around the village where you can watch pottery being made. There are also dozens of craft shops around the main square, all selling pretty much the same stuff including pottery, hammocks, baskets, bags, ponchos, jewelry and woodcarvings. Ráquira is a pleasant place to spend an afternoon shopping, but unless you're really into handicrafts, you'll probably get bored very quickly.

Sleeping & Eating
If you must stay overnight, there are a few simple hotels in town. Restaurants are even more rare, and the few that exist are basic at best. Pack a picnic, or head to nearby market town of Sutamarchán where you'll find many good roadside restaurants.

Hostería Nemqueteba (☎ 735 7083; r COP$30,000; ✗ ✍) Bright rooms with high ceilings come with desk, TV and a clean bathroom. There's a nice patio and a decent restaurant, but avoid the swimming pool, which looks like a habitat for a kronosaurus.

Hotel Suaya (☎ 735 7029; r per person COP$20,000; ✗) A block off the main plaza, Hotel Suaya is set in an old wooden house. Rooms are clean, have hot water and some have views of the main street.

Getting There & Away
Ráquira is 5km off the Tunja–Chiquinquirá road, down a side road branching off at Tres Esquinas. Four minibuses run daily between Villa de Leyva and Ráquira (COP$3000, 45 minutes). A taxi from Villa de Leyva will set you back about COP$25,000. A handful of buses from Bogotá also call here daily.

LA CANDELARIA
☎ 8 / pop 300 / elev 2255m

This tiny hamlet set amid arid hills, 7km beyond Ráquira, is noted for the **Monasterio de La Candelaria** (☼ 9am-5pm). The monastery was founded in 1597 by Augustine monks and completed about 1660. Part of it is open to the public. Monks show you through the chapel (note the 16th-century painting of the Virgen de la Candelaria over the altar), a small museum, the library, and the courtyard flanked by the cloister with a collection of 17th-century canvases hanging on its walls. Some of these artworks were allegedly painted by Gregorio Vásquez de Arce y Ceballos and the Figueroa brothers.

Only two buses a day call at La Candelaria, both of which come from Bogotá. Another option is to walk along the path from Ráquira (one hour). The path begins in Ráquira's main plaza, winds up a hill to a small shrine at the top and then drops down and joins the road to La Candelaria.

A return taxi from Villa de Leyva to Ráquira and La Candelaria can be arranged for around COP$60,000 (up to four people), allowing some time in both villages.

CHIQUINQUIRÁ
☎ 8 / pop 60,000 / elev 2590m

Chiquinquirá is the religious capital of Colombia, attracting flocks of devoted Catholic pilgrims due to a 16th-century miracle involving a painting of the Virgin Mary.

The *Virgin of the Rosary* was painted around 1555 by Spanish artist Alonso de Narváez in Tunja. It depicts Mary cradling baby Jesus and flanked by Saint Anthony of Padua and Saint Andrew the Apostle. Soon after it was completed, the image began to fade, the result of shoddy materials and a leaky chapel roof. In 1577 the painting was moved to Chiquinquirá, put into storage and forgotten.

A few years later, Maria Ramos, a pious woman from Seville, rediscovered the painting. Though it was in terrible shape, Ramos loved to sit and pray to the image. On December 26, 1586 before her eyes and prayers, the once faded and torn painting was miraculously restored to its original splendor. From then on its fame swiftly grew and the miracles attributed to the Virgin multiplied.

In 1829 Pope Pius VII declared the Virgen of Chiquinquirá patroness of Colombia. Dubbed 'La Chinita' by locals, the image was canonically crowned in 1919, and in 1927 her sanctuary declared a basilica. Pope John Paul II visited the city in 1986.

Sights

Dominating the Plaza de Bolívar, the **Basílica de la Virgen de Chiquinquirá** houses the **Sacred Image**. Construction of the huge neoclassical church began in 1796 and was completed in 1812. The spacious three-naved interior boasts 17 chapels and an elaborate high altar where the painting is displayed. The painting measures 113cm by 126cm and is the oldest documented Colombian painting. Overlooking the Parque Julio Flórez (named after a locally born poet), the modern **Iglesia de la Renovación** sits on the site where the miracle of the Virgen de Chiquinquirá occurred. Next door is the **Museo Mariano Nacional**, a museum of religious art.

Getting There & Away

All buses operate from the bus terminal, a 10-minute walk from Parque Julio Flórez, south along Carrera 9. There are six buses a day between Villa de Leyva and Chiquinquira (COP$7000, one hour). Buses to Bogotá depart every 15 minutes (COP$14,000, three hours).

SIERRA NEVADA DEL COCUY

Relatively unknown outside of Colombia, the Sierra Nevada del Cocuy is one of the most spectacular mountain ranges in South America. This gorgeous slice of heaven on Earth has some of Colombia's most dramatic landscapes, from snowcapped mountains and raging waterfalls to icy glaciers and crystal-clear blue lakes.

It is the highest part of the Cordillera Oriental, the eastern part of the Colombian Andes formed by two parallel ranges. A chain of beautiful valleys is sandwiched in between. The Sierra Nevada del Cocuy contains 21 peaks, of which 15 are more than 5000m. The tallest peak, Ritacuba Blanco, reaches 5330m (17,483ft).

Because of its climate and topography, the Sierra Nevada del Cocuy ecosystem has a striking abundance of flora, representing some 700 species. It is especially noted for its frailejóns, many which are unique to the region. Fauna include spectacled bears, pumas, white-tailed deer and the famous Andean condor that is a symbol of Colombia. This area is also the ancestral home of the indigenous U'wa people, who still make their home in this harsh terrain.

In 1977, a large swath of this pristine land was set aside for the creation of Parque Nacional Natural (PNN) El Cocuy (p116). With a massive 306,000 hectares, PNN El Cocuy is the fifth-largest national park in Colombia, stretching across the departments of Boyacá, Arauca and Casanare.

The mountains are quite compact, relatively easy to reach and ideal for trekking, though rather more suited to experienced hikers. The starting points for these hikes are the pretty villages of Güicán (p114) and El Cocuy (below). The two rival towns have good food and lodging facilities and scenic beauty that even nonhikers will appreciate.

EL COCUY

☎ 8 / pop 7610 / elev 2750m

Dramatically surrounded by soaring mountains, the pretty colonial village of El Cocuy is the most traveler-friendly entry point to PNN El Cocuy, with at least 10 hotels, several restaurants and a few bars. El Cocuy has preserved its colonial character; every building in town is painted white with sea green trim and topped by red Spanish tiled roofs. The center point of the *pueblo* is the **Iglesia de Nuestra Senora de la Paz**, the salmon-pink church that dominates **Parque Principal**, the town square. After dinner, residents congregate around the square to chat, play basketball and snack on kebabs and *arepas*

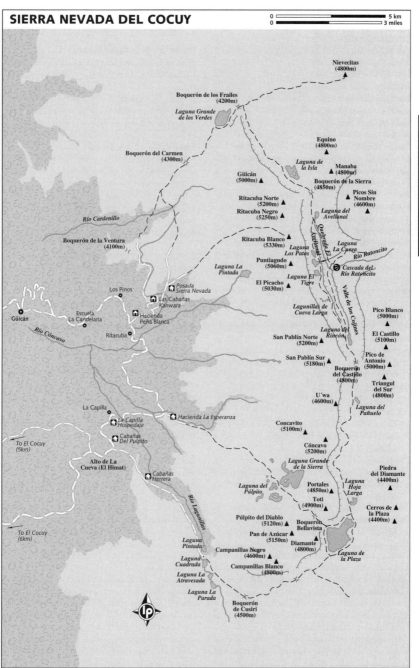

SIERRA NEVADA DEL COCUY

0 ___ 5 km
0 ___ 3 miles

Nievecitas
(4800m)

Boquerón de los Frailes
(4200m)

Laguna Grande
de los Verdes

Equino
(4800m)

Boquerón del Carmen
(4300m)

Laguna de
la Isla

Manaba
(4800m)

Güicán
(5000m)

Boquerón de la Sierra
(4850m)

Picos Sin
Nombre
(4600m)

Ritacuba Norte
(5200m)

Ritacuba Negro
(5250m)

Laguna del
Avellanal

Río Cardenillo

Ritacuba Blanco
(5330m)

Laguna
Los Patos

Laguna
La Cueva

Río Ratoncito

Boquerón de la Ventura
(4100m)

Puntiagudo
(5060m)

Cascada del
Río Ratoncito

Laguna La
Pintada

Laguna El
Tigre

Los Pinos

Posada
Sierra Nevada

El Picacho
(5030m)

Las Cabañas
Kanwara

Lagunillas de
Cueva Larga

Pico Blanco
(5000m)

Güicán

Escuela
La Candelaria

Hacienda
Peña Blanca

Laguna del
Rincón

El Castillo
(5100m)

Río Cóncavo

Ritacuba

San Pablín Norte
(5200m)

San Pablín Sur
(5180m)

Pico de
Antonio
(5000m)

Boquerón
del Castillo
(4800m)

Triangul
del Sur
(4800m)

La Capilla

U'wa
(4600m)

Laguna del
Pañuelo

La Capilla
Hospedaje

Hacienda La Esperanza

Concavito
(5100m)

Cabañas
Del Pulpito

To El Cocuy
(5km)

Cóncavo
(5200m)

Alto de La
Cueva (El Himat)

Laguna Grande
de la Sierra

Piedra
del Diamante
(4400m)

Cabañas
Herrera

Laguna del
Púlpito

Portales
(4850m)

Laguna
Hoja
Larga

Río Lagunillas

Totí
(4900m)

Cerros de
la Plaza
(4400m)

To El Cocuy
(6km)

Púlpito del Diablo
(5120m)

Boquerón
Bellavista

Laguna
Pintada

Pan de Azúcar
(5150m)

Diamante
(4800m)

Campanillas Negro
(4600m)

Laguna
Cuadrada

Laguna de
la Plaza

Campanillas Blanco
(4800m)

Laguna La
Atravesada

Laguna La
Parada

Boquerón
de Cusiri
(4500m)

from street vendors. The plaza also contains a **diorama** of the surrounding mountain range, but in terms of tourist attractions, there is little else to do apart from enjoy the surrounding natural beauty.

Information

Banco Agrario de Colombia (cnr Carrera 4 & Calle 8) The only ATM in town.

Internet cafe (Carrera 6 No 6-42; per hr COP$1500; ☺ 8am-8pm).

Parque Nacional Natural (PNN) El Cocuy Headquarters (☎ 789 0359; cocuy@parquesnacionales.gov.co; Calle 8 No 4-74, ☺ 6am-noon & 1-5pm) All park visitors must report here to register their itineraries and pay the admission fee.

Sleeping & Eating

There is a good selection of hotels in El Cocuy, all located within three blocks of the town square. Most restaurants are located inside hotels. In the evening, street vendors sell *comida corriente* (fast food) in the square.

Casa Vieja (☎ 789 0074, 313 876 8783; Carrera 6 No 7-78; r per person COP$8000) As the name suggests, this cheapie is located in an old colonial house. Owner and artist Roberto Arango has decorated the courtyard garden with his original paintings. The character of the building makes up for the barren rooms, all with shared baths.

Hotel Villa Real (☎ 789 0038; Calle 7 No 4-50; r per person COP$10,000) A pleasant hotel around the corner from the main square has basic rooms with shared baths and hot water. Its popular lunchtime restaurant serves set meals for COP$4000.

Hotel Casa Muñoz (☎ 313 829 1073, 789 0328; Carrera 5 No 7-28; r per person COP$15,000) Located on the main plaza, this new hotel has clean, comfy rooms with cable TV, firm beds and private baths with hot water, all surrounding a pretty courtyard filled with geraniums. The 2nd-floor rooms have hidden lofts that can sleep larger groups.

** our pick La Posada Del Molino** (☎ 310 494 5076, 312 352 9121; laposadadelmolinoelcocuy@yahoo.es; Carrera 3 No 7-51; r per person high/low season COP$30,000/15,000) This 220-year-old renovated colonial mansion is hands-down the best hotel in the region. The building has quite a colorful history – and is reputedly haunted! The six rooms are decorated with fine colonial furnishings and have funky private baths. The gorgeous fossil-strewn courtyard has a babbling brook that will lull you to sleep. The hotel's restaurant (mains COP$4000 to COP$6000) is also the best in town, serving up great local trout and other traditional dishes.

Drinking & Entertainment

Most drinking in town takes place in the many billiards halls or at the cafes on the plaza that transform into bars at night. The only real nightclub, **Fogata** (Carrera 5 No 7-60; ☺ 7pm-midnight Fri), has a rooftop dance floor and covered seating areas but is only open on Friday night.

Getting There & Away

All buses arrive and depart from their respective offices on the plaza along Carrera 5.

Luxurious Concorde buses to Bogotá depart from the plaza, at Carrera 5 No 7-16, at 4am and 6pm daily (COP$35,000, 11 hours); in Bogotá, buses depart from the capital's main terminal to El Cocuy at 7am and 7:30pm daily (COP$40,000, 11 hours). Less comfortable Libertadores and Gacela buses to Bogotá operate on alternate days, departing from Carrera 5 No 7-34, at 5am and 7pm daily (COP$35,000, 11 hours); they depart Bogotá to El Cocuy at 6:30am and 8pm daily.

To Güicán, Cootradatil buses depart at noon and 4pm (COP$2500, 30 minutes).

To Bucaramanga, take the Concorde bus to Capitanejo and then change buses. The total trip takes about 14 hours along mostly unpaved roads that are prone to landslides and delays. You might be better off returning to Tunja and catching the frequent northbound buses to Buca and beyond.

See p117 for information on getting to and from the park.

GÜICÁN

☎ 8 / pop 7869 / elev 2963m

Though not as photogenic or traveler friendly as El Cocuy, the chilly village of Güicán has nevertheless become the main starting point for trekkers heading up to the mountains, mainly because it provides a closer and easier hike to PNN El Cocuy. And for nonhikers, Güicán offers plenty of sights and tourist attractions that don't necessarily involve walking uphill. Most of the city's colonial architecture was destroyed in fires and civil wars. It was replaced with modern, new buildings painted in bold, bright colors. Güicán is the heart of the indigenous U'wa community. Religious tourism is also a major source of revenue, associated with the miracle of the Virgen Morenita de Güicán.

VIRGEN MORENITA DE GÜICÁN

Güicán is known throughout Colombia for the miracle of the Virgen Morenita de Güicán – an apparition of the dark-skinned Virgin Mary that appeared to the indigenous U'Wa people. The story begins in the late 17th century when Spanish conquistadores arrived in the area and set about converting the U'wa to Christianity. Rather than bow to Spanish rule, U'wa chief Güicány, for whom the town is named, led his tribe to their deaths by leaping off the cliff now called El Peñol de Los Muertos. Güicány's wife Cuchumba was spared because she was pregnant. Cuchumba and a handful of survivors fled to the mountains and hid in a cave. On February 26, 1756, an apparition of the Virgin Mary mysteriously appeared on a cloth. The image of Mary had a dark complexion and indigenous features, just like the U'wa, who quickly converted to Christianity.

A small chapel was built in Güicán to house the Virgen Morenita. During one of the many civil wars between the rival towns of Güicán and El Cocuy, the Virgen was stolen and hidden in El Cocuy, supposedly behind a wall in what is now La Posada del Molino hotel. The family residing there was haunted until they returned the Virgen to Güicán, where it resides today under lock and key.

The grand Festival of the Virgen Morenita is celebrated every year on February 2 to 4, attracting faithful religious pilgrims from far and wide.

Sights & Activities

Güicán's most famous attraction is the **Virgen Morenita de Güicán**, an image of a dark-skinned Virgin Mary that appeared to the indigenous U'wa people in 1756 (see the boxed text, above). The shrine to the Morenita is located inside the **Nuestra Senora de la Candelaria** church on Parque Principal (town square). The brown brick and faux marble church isn't much to look at outside, but inside it's richly decorated and painted in pastel pinks, greens and blues.

East of town is a 300m high cliff known as **El Peñol de los Muertos**, where U'wa people jumped to their deaths upon the arrival of the conquistadores rather than live under Spanish rule. The trail to the cliff begins at the end of Carrera 4. A hike to the top of the cliff takes about two hours. The **Monumento a la Dignidad de la Raza U'wa** depicting this mass act of suicide is located at the entrance of town. U'wa artisans are famous for their handmade bags and woolen goods that can be found in many shops around town.

A short, muddy hike along an old stone-paved road called **Camino Deshecho** leads to a boulder covered in ancient **petroglyphs**. Continue down another 20 minutes to reach some *aguas termales*, or **hot spring water pools**. The trail begins at the bottom of Calle 5.

Information

The nearest ATM is in El Cocuy.
Moviestar Internet Cafe (Calle 6 No 5-66; per hr COP$2000; 🕙 9am-1pm & 2:30pm-8pm)

Parque Nacional Natural El Cocuy (Carrera 4 No 3-30; 🕙 8am-noon & 2-6pm) All park visitors must pay the park admission fee here and register their itinerary.

Sleeping & Eating

Hotel El Fraileón (☎ 312 586 0619; Carrera 5, plaza; r per person COP$5000) This is the cheapest place in town, for good reason. The rooms are dark, bare and cramped with worn beds, but at least they're clean. Ask for a room overlooking the town square.

our pick **Hotel El Eden** (☎ 789 7093, 311 808 8334; luishernandonc@hotmail.com; Transversal 2 No 9-58; campsites/dm/r per person COP$5000/11,000/15,000) More Noah's Ark than El Eden, this family-run guesthouse is a favorite with foreigners. The garden is filled with turkeys, ducks, rabbits, gerbils and a trout pond. Rooms are covered floor to ceiling in wood, giving off a wonderful aroma. Most have private baths and some have lofts. There's also a little bar and restaurant. Eden is a 12-minute walk north of the plaza. To get here, walk north up Carrera 4, turn right onto the dirt road leading up past the basketball court, make your first right then second left to the hotel.

Brisas del Nevado (☎ 789 7028, 310 629 9001; Carrera 5 No 4-57; r per person COP$15,000) The comfiest hotel in town also houses Güicán's best restaurant. Most rooms have private baths and TVs. The best rooms are the two private cabañas located in the garden behind the main building.

Getting There & Away

All buses arrive and depart from their respective offices on the main plaza.

Luxurious Concorde buses to Bogotá depart from the plaza at 3am and 5pm daily (COP$35,000, 12 hours); buses from Bogotá to Güicán depart Bogotá's main bus terminal at 7am and 7:30pm daily (COP$40,000, 12 hours). Less comfortable Libertadores and Gacela buses to Bogotá operate on alternate days at 4:30am and 6pm daily (COP$35,000, 12 hours); they depart Bogotá to El Cocuy at 6:30am and 8pm daily.

To El Cocuy, local Cootradatil buses depart at 7am, 11am and 2pm (COP$2500, 40 minutes). Alternatively, take one of the Bogotá-bound buses, which all pass through El Cocuy on their way to the capital. To go to Bucaramanga, Cúcuta, Santa Marta or other points northwest, take a Bogotá-bound bus to Capitanejo and change buses there.

See opposite for information on getting to and from the park.

PARQUE NACIONAL NATURAL (PNN) EL COCUY

PNN El Cocuy is the main attraction of Sierra Nevada Del Cocuy region. Established in 1977, the park covers a massive 306,000 hectares, or about 1181 sq miles. The western boundary of the park begins at the 4000m elevation line; the eastern half drops to just 600m elevation to the Colombian *llanos* (plains).

Most of PNN El Cocuy is made up of a diverse ecosystem known as the *páramo*. This glacially formed, neotropical system of valleys, plains and mountain lakes includes the largest glacier zone in South America north of the equator. Sadly, the park's glacier fields are rapidly melting due to climate change. At the present rate, park officials believe the glaciers will be gone within 20 to 30 years.

Despite the harsh environment, PNN El Cocuy is home to diverse species of flora and fauna. Animals you might encounter include the spectacled bear, also called the Andean bear, deer, eagles, condors, mountain tapirs, chinchillas and the beautiful spotted ocelot. The mountaintop plains are covered in a variety of shrubbery, the best known being the yellow flowered frailejón that is native to the area.

The park has 15 peaks that are at least 5000m. The highest is Ritacuba Blanco at 5330m. The park's most famous landmark is an unusual rock formation called the Púlpito del Diablo (5120m), or devil's pulpit. This outdoor playground is popular for hiking, trekking, camping, climbing and paragliding.

From 1985 until early this century, PNN El Cocuy was occupied by ruthless ELN guerrillas until the Colombian army moved in and cleaned things up. Today, the park is once again safe for visitors (the little-used eastern plains area of the park in Arauca and Casanare is still questionable). Colombian soldiers have a base in the mountains and regularly patrol the trails. This peace has quickly brought visitors back to the peaks. In 2003 fewer than 100 people climbed PNN Cocuy; that figure jumped to 6000 in 2007, according to park officials.

Climbing Cocuy

The mountains of PNN El Cocuy are relatively compact and easy to reach. The complete Güicán–El Cocuy Trek roundtrip circuit takes six or seven days, but there are many shorter day hikes; the hike to the snow line is only about three hours from the northern park boundary.

There is no special experience required. However, due to the elevation and terrain, park officials recommend hikers have at least some previous trekking experience and be in good health. Park entry is prohibited to children under 12, pregnant women and people with heart or lung ailments.

The starting points for hiking PNN Cocuy are the archrival villages of Güicán and El Cocuy. By far the most popular option is to hike the circuit clockwise from Güicán. The hike from here is considered easier, and if you hire horses they are able to climb further up to the snowline before you must continue on foot.

All visitors to the park must first report to the PNN El Cocuy offices in either Güicán or El Cocuy, register their itineraries and pay the park admission fee (COP$25,000 for foreigners and COP$9000 for Colombians). Don't forget to check back in after your hike; if you don't show up by your return date, park officials will launch search and rescue operations.

Guides, while not required, are highly recommended.

Tours

You can hire guides and horses from any of the cabañas near the mountains or at Coopserguías (opposite) in El Cocuy. Expect to pay about COP$40,000 a day for a guide for up to eight people. Horses and horse handlers will each cost about COP$35,000 per day. Solo hikers and small groups can be paired up with others to keep costs down.

Coopserguías (☎ 313 293 8313; www.elcocuy coopserguias.com; cnr Calle 7 & Carrera 6), located on the main plaza of El Cocuy, is a cooperative of local guides that can provide park information and arrange guides, horses and equipment rentals.

Veteran climber **Rodrigo Arias** (☎ 310 211 4130, 313-293-8313; www.colombiatrek.com) of Coopserguías is an experienced, highly recommended guide. He speaks English and can arrange personalized tours and all-inclusive packages for individuals or groups.

When to Go
The only period of reasonably good weather is from December to February. The rest of the year is rainy and there is snow at high altitudes and on the highest passes. The weather changes frequently. The Sierra Nevada is known for its strong winds.

What to Bring
All park visitors must be completely self-sufficient. There are no residents or services inside the park. That means bringing all your own high-mountain trekking equipment including a good tent, a sleeping bag rated to -10ºC, warm and waterproof clothing, good hiking boots, flashlights, first-aid kit, gas stove and food. You cannot buy outdoor equipment in El Cocuy or Güicán, but you may be able to find camping gear in Bogotá. The circuit traverses a glacier, but you won't need any special equipment.

If you don't have a tent or basic trekking gear, the only way to explore the mountains is in a series of short, one-day walks from a base at one of the cabañas. This, however, will give you just a taste of these magnificent mountains.

Sleeping
After a visit to El Cocuy or Güicán, most hikers chose to acclimate to the altitude by staying overnight at one of several cabañas located just outside the park boundaries. The most comfortable cabañas are located in the north end of the park near Güicán. The best-known is **Cabañas Kanwara** (☎ 311 231 6004; r per person COP$25,000). The three A-frame cabins each have 15 beds, a fireplace, kitchen and bath. Other good choices include **Hacienda**

Peña Blanca (☎ 702 0600, 310 232 4839; r per person COP$25,000) and **Posada Sierra Nevada** (☎ 311 237 8619; www.posadasierranevada.com; r per person COP$25,000), the newest and highest at 3950m.

Halfway between El Cocuy and Güicán you'll find the **Cabañas Del Pulpito** (☎ 314 272 9524, 320 297 1111; r per person COP$22,000), previously known as Cabañas Güicáni, and the rustic working farmhouse of **Hacienda La Esperanza** (☎ 310 200 4214, 1 263 8712; haciendalaesperanza@gmail .com; r per person COP$10,000). In the tiny hamlet of La Capilla, there are a few basic rooms above the storefront of **La Capilla Hospedaje & Restaurant** (☎ 316 337 1507; per person COP$10,000).

At the southern end of the park, **Cabañas Herrera** (☎ 311 885 4263) is a comfy but minuscule hut. During our visit, park officials were constructing their own cabaña nearby.

Getting There & Away
From Güicán, it's a five-hour hike straight up to Cabañas Kanwara, where the northern circuit trails begin. Private car hire to one of the cabañas will set you back about COP$100,000. Some cabañas also offer transportation; prices vary depending on destination and group sizes. A much cheaper alternative is to hop a ride on La Lechero (COP$5000), the morning milk trucks that make the rounds to the mountain farms. The lecheros leave Güicán plaza at 5:30am, reach El Cocuy plaza at 6am and make a counter-clockwise circuit back to Güicán. There are several lecheros, so you must ask around to find the one going to your destination. Most lecheros do not stop directly at the cabañas; you'll be let off at the nearest intersection where you must hike up the rest of the way.

Güicán–El Cocuy Circuit Trek
DAYS ONE & TWO: GÜICÁN TO LAGUNA GRANDE DE LOS VERDES
This section can be done in a single day from Güicán, but it would be a hard, rapid ascent to high altitudes. To acclimate yourself, spend a leisurely first day getting to one of the cabañas and stay overnight there.

On day two, hike from Cabañas Kanwara to the top of the Ritacuba Blanco up its gently sloping back face. The ascent takes five hours, but start very early because the top tends to cloud over by about noon.

The next leg is to Laguna Grande de los Verdes. Walk to the Río Cardenillo creek along either a rough road or a path, about two hours

---

WARNING

The circuit is not easy for those without previous trekking experience. The average altitude is between 4000m and 4600m and there is a glaciated pass on the way. There are no people living along the route, so you must be absolutely self-sufficient. There are no short cuts. Most importantly, the weather is unpredictable so you must be prepared for rain or snow at any time.

---

total. Once you cross the creek, it's a steady two-hour ascent to the Boquerón del Carmen pass (4300m). Keep to the right-hand side of the valley as you descend from the pass. The trail crosses the valley and continues along the left-hand slope just below the cliffs, finally arriving at the Laguna Grande de los Verdes (3900m). There are a lot of good camping sites around the lake, including a fabulous, white sandy beach.

DAY THREE: LAGUNA GRANDE DE LOS VERDES TO LAGUNA DEL AVELLANAL

The average walking time between these two lakes is about seven hours. The trail skirts around the eastern side of the Laguna Grande de los Verdes and heads up to the Boquerón de los Frailes pass (4200m). From here onwards, up to Laguna de la Plaza and even further, you'll be enjoying magnificent views of snowy peaks.

After a short descent the trail divides. Take the right-hand branch which heads south along the foot of rocky cliffs. After about three hours you will arrive at the Laguna de la Isla, passing high above its western side. Continue up to the Boquerón de la Sierra pass (4850m). It's often covered with snow, especially in the rainy season, but the trail is easy to find. From the pass, if the weather is clear, you will see the Laguna del Avellanal below and the long, magnificent Valle de los Cojines beyond, lined on both sides by snowy peaks. The trail drops down to the lake where you can camp, although the lake shore is quite rocky. Alternatively, there is a cave a few hundred meters west of the lake where enormous rocks have formed a tentlike roof.

DAY FOUR: LAGUNA DEL AVELLANAL TO LAGUNA DEL PAÑUELO

This leg will require about seven hours of constant walking, not including stops. From the Laguna del Avellanal the trail descends slowly, following the river into the Valle de los Cojines. You will pass a few small waterfalls on your right before reaching the most spectacular of all, the Cascada del Río Ratoncito. Here the main trail turns eastward and follows the river down into Los Llanos. Use this trail down to see the falls only, but then climb back up again to the point where it turns east.

Cross the creek and continue south along the Valle de los Cojines, keeping close to its right-hand (western) side, just above the wide, plain bed of the valley. The trail here is faint and disappears, but don't worry: just head on to the far end of the valley, sticking all the time to the right-hand slope. Once you reach the end of the valley you begin to ascend. From there you will get to the Laguna del Rincón (4400m) in 30 minutes.

From the lake you climb one hour up to the glacial pass, the Boquerón del Castillo (4800m) with its breathtaking views. There is no trail, so just head up to the lowest point between the ranges. Walk carefully, checking the surface for hidden crevasses in the glacier. It's best to use a rope, especially during bad weather. From the pass, it's a one-hour walk down to the small Laguna del Pañuelo, where you will camp for the night. Descend carefully, as there are crevasses on this slope as well.

The pass is often hidden in clouds and fog, especially during the rainy/snowy season. If this is the case, don't attempt to cross – it's too dangerous. Camp at the Laguna del Rincón and cross over the pass the following morning.

DAY FIVE: LAGUNA DEL PAÑUELO TO LAGUNA DE LA PLAZA

This bit may be quite difficult as there is no trail. The walking time can be six to eight hours, depending on how well you find your way. The best advice is to keep close to the rocky walls on your right at all times and stay at roughly the same altitude. Do not descend. Pay special attention when passing El Cóncavo where there are several rock terraces; you should follow the upper ones. Previous trekkers have left behind piles of stones to mark the right trail and you will probably find these helpful signs on the way.

If all goes well, you should reach the Laguna Hoja Larga within five hours. Another hour further, you will arrive at the marvelous, large Laguna de la Plaza where you can pitch your tent.

DAY SIX: LAGUNA DE LA PLAZA TO LAGUNILLAS

Take the path from the southern end of the Laguna de la Plaza, and you'll soon get to the well-defined trail leading to Alto de la Cueva. It's a three-hour walk to the last pass, the Boquerón de Cusiri (4500m), then an hour's descent to the lovely chain of lakes, Lagunillas, where you will find lots of charming campsites. If you are here early enough, you continue on to the Alto de la Cueva.

DAY SEVEN: LAGUNILLAS TO ALTO DE LA CUEVA

From Lagunillas you have an easy four-hour walk beside the Río Lagunillas to the Alto de la Cueva, where the Himat meteorological station is located. You are back on the road. Hitch (transport is scarce) or walk along the road for another four hours to El Cocuy. There are also footpaths to both El Cocuy and Güicán.

SANTANDER

The north-central department of Santander is a patchwork of steep craggy mountains, deep canyons, plummeting waterfalls, raging rivers, unexplored caves and a temperate, dry climate. Mix them together and it's easy to see why Santander has become a favorite destination for outdoor lovers. Extreme sports nuts can chose from white-water rafting, paragliding, caving, rappelling, hiking and mountain biking. More-sane visitors can enjoy exploring the rustic charms of colonial Barichara, shopping in Girón or the nightclubs in the department capital city of Bucaramanga. Foodies will appreciate Santander's fantastic restaurant offerings. Don't miss trying the regional culinary specialty – *hormigas culonas* (fried ants).

SOCORRO

☎ 7 / pop 30,000 / elev 1230m

Socorro is birthplace of the so-called Revolución Comunera, the first massive revolt against Spanish rule. The 1781 rebellion was organized by a peasant woman, Manuela Beltrán, initially in protest against tax rises levied by the Crown, but it soon spread and took on more pro-independence tones. Socorro was one of the first towns in Nueva Granada to declare independence, on July 10, 1810. Colonial rule was brutally re-established in 1816; three years later Simón Bolívar sealed the country's independence.

This pretty colonial town has a few sites that are worthy of a quick detour. The **Plaza de La Independencia** town square has statues honoring the heroes of the Revolución Comunera. The east side of the square is dominated by the **Catedral del Nuestra Señora de Socorro**, built from 1873 to 1943. It houses an image of the Virgen del Socorro, the city's patron saint. The 300-year-old **Casa de la Cultura** (Calle 14 No 12-31; admission COP$2000; ☺ 8am-noon & 2-6pm) houses documents and objects that lay testimony to the revolution, plus exhibits of Guane indigenous artifacts.

Socorro is 20km south of San Gil. All buses trawling the Tunja–San Gil route stop here.

SAN GIL

☎ 7 / pop 50,000 / elev 1110m

For a small city, San Gil packs a lot of punch. This is the outdoor capital of Colombia and a mecca for extreme sporting enthusiasts. The area is best known for white-water rafting, but other popular pastimes include paragliding, caving, rappelling and trekking. Closer to earth, San Gil has a quaint 300-year-old town square and Parque El Gallineral, a beautiful nature reserve on the banks of the Río Fonce.

San Gil may not be the prettiest town in Colombia, but dig beneath the exterior shell and you'll discover a wonderful city of natural beauty and friendly, welcoming residents. Don't be surprised if you end up extending your stay. San Gil definitely lives up to its motto, *'La Tierra de Aventura'* – the land of adventure.

Orientation

Like most Colombian cities, San Gil is laid out in a grid pattern; Calles run north–south and Carreras run east–west. The heart of San Gil is the town square called Parque La Libertad. Towering over the north end of the square is the Catedral Santa Cruz. Standing on the plaza facing the cathedral, Calle 12 is on your right-hand side. Follow this road uphill (north) to reach many of the town's hotels, restaurants and bars. Two blocks south of the plaza is the Río Fonce river that divides the town into northern and southern halves. The waterfront *malecón* promenade runs parallel along the north bank of the river, beginning near the bridge at Calle 10 and ending east at the front gates of Parque El Gallineral.

The main bus terminal is 3km west of San Gil.

Information

There are several ATMs in and around the plaza. The official tourism website is www .sangil.com.co.

Bancolombia (Calle 12 No 10-44) Has an unusually large COP$400,000 daily withdrawal limit.

CoffeEmail (Calle 13 No 9-78; per hr COP$1500; 7:30am-9pm) One of several internet cafes around the plaza.

Foxnet (☎ 724 6659; Centro Comercial El Edén, Carrera 10 No 12-37; per hr COP$1500; 8:30am-noon & 2-9:30pm)

Post office (Carrera 10 No 10-50; 8-11:30am & 2-4pm Mon-Fri) Next to Cajasan Supermercado.

Tourist office (☎ 724 4617; cnr Carrera 10 & Calle 12; 8am-noon & 2-6pm) The main tourist office is on the southeast corner of the plaza. A smaller, rarely manned kiosk is near the entrance to Parque El Gallineral.

Sights

PARQUE EL GALLINERAL

San Gil's showpiece is the mystical **Parque El Gallineral** (☎ 724 4372; cnr Malecón & Calle 6; admission COP$4000; 8am-6pm), a 4-hectare park set on a triangle-shaped island between two arms of the Quebrada Curití and Río Fonce. Nearly all of the 1876 trees are covered with long silvery tendrils of moss called *barbas de viejo*, or old man's beard, hanging from branches to form translucent curtains of foliage and filtered sunlight. It's like a scene set in JRR Tolkien's Middle Earth. Several paths and covered bridges snake through the urban forest and over the rapids. After your hike, relax with a swim in the large spring-fed pool or sip a *cerveza* at one of the pricey restaurants and cafes.

PARQUE LA LIBERTAD

The tree-lined town square plaza of **Parque La Libertad**, also called Parque Principal, is San Gil's most visible landmark and the heart of its social life. On weekend nights, the plaza is packed with multiple generations of Colombian families enjoying the festive atmosphere while street vendors hawk warm *arepas* and cold *cerveza*. The north end of plaza is dominated by the handsome 18th-century stone **Catedral Santa Cruz** (cnr Carrera 9 & Calle 13).

CASA DE CULTURA

One block downhill from the plaza is the **Casa de Cultura** (☎ 724 6986; Calle 12 No 10-31; admission free; 9am-noon & 2-5pm Mon-Sat), an old colonial man-

sion that has temporary art exhibits and a cafe. It's also home to the new **Museo de Arqueología y Antropológico Guane de San Gil** (3-6pm), a small museum exploring the history and culture of the indigenous Guane peoples of Santander.

CASCADAS DE JUAN CURI

Take a day trip to this spectacular 180m-high **waterfall** where you can swim in the natural pool at its base or relax on the rocks. Adrenalin junkies can rappel the sheer face of the falls; book this activity with one of the tour companies following. Juan Curi is 22km from San Gil on the road to Charalá. Buses to Charalá (COP$2500, 30 minutes) depart twice per hour from the east side of the bridge on Calle 10. Ask the driver to let you out at *las cascadas* (cascades), where two 20-minute trails lead up to the falls. The property owner may charge you COP$3000 or COP$5000.

Other nearby watery attractions are the **Pescadarito** (aka Quebrada Curití), a mountain river 12km northeast of San Gil near the village of Curití with several swimming holes and natural waterslides; and **Pozo Azul**, a freshwater pool 1km north of town where locals gather on Sundays for an afternoon of swimming and hard drinking.

Activities & Tours

Several tour agencies in San Gil run whitewater rafting on local rivers. A 10km run on Río Fonce (Class 1 to 3) costs COP$25,000 per person and takes 1½ hours; experienced rafters can tackle the extreme rapids of the Río Suarez (COP$120,000, up to Class 5). Most operators also offer paragliding, caving, kayaking, horseback riding, rappelling/abseiling, mountain biking, quad biking, paintball, hydrospeeding, bungee jumping and ecowalks.

Aventura Total (☎ 723 8888; www.aventuratotal .com.co)

Colombia Rafting Expeditions (☎ 311 283 8647; www.colombiarafting.com; Carrera 10 No 7-83)

Macondo Adventures (☎ 724 4463, 311 828 2905; www.macondohostel.com; Macondo Guesthouse, Calle 12 No 7-26)

Planeta Azul (☎ 724 0000; planetaazulsg@hotmail .com; Parque El Gallineral)

Ríos y Canoas (☎ 724 7220, 724 7091; riosycanoas@ hotmail.com; Parque El Gallineral)

Sleeping

San Gil has plenty of downtown budget and moderately priced lodging options. In addi-

BOYACÁ, SANTANDER &
NORTE DE SANTANDER

tion to the options here, there are many basic cheapie hotels on Calle 10. Folks looking for a little more pampering should check out the luxury hotel-resorts on the outskirts of town along Via Charalá or Via Mogotes.

our pick Macondo Guesthouse (☎ 724 4463, 311 828 2905; www.macondohostel.com; Calle 12 No 7-26; dm per person COP$13,000, r COP$26,000-30,000; 🖵) This laid-back hostel is a bit like crashing at a friend's place. The colonial house has a courtyard with hammocks, cooking and laundry facilities, internet and wi-fi. Rooms are basic but clean, with shared baths. Australian owner Shaun is a treasure trove of information and can book adventure activities and tours. Sooner or later everyone ends up at Macondo. Book ahead.

Santander Alemán (☎ 724 2535, 317 770 9188; igarnica@hotmail.com; Calle 12 No 7-63; r per person COP$15,000-20,000) Blissfully quiet, this lovely family-run guesthouse has five spotless rooms of various sizes. The shared facilities feature an open-air shower where you can bathe under the stars. As a bonus, the on-site restaurant (mains COP$3500 to COP$4500, open breakfast and lunch) has one of the best breakfasts in town.

Centro Real (☎ 724 0387; Calle 10 No 10-41; s/d COP$14,000/20,000; ✂) A friendly, modern hotel with 20 comfy rooms, all with private bathroom. It's one of the nicest of the many budget hotels along this block.

Hotel El Viajero (☎ 724 4817; hotelviajero2@hotmail .com; Carrera 11 No 11-07; s/d COP$16,000/25,000) This place scores big points for its rustic charm and excellent river views off the back deck, and would be better if the rooms weren't the size of closets.

Hotel Mansión del Parque (☎ 724 5662; Calle 12 No 8-71; s/d COP$46,000/88,000) Set in a colonial mansion on the corner of Parque Central, this hotel has large rooms, the best of which have balconies overlooking the plaza.

Eating

San Gil is not the most gastronomic area of Colombia, but it does have some decent restaurants serving home-cooked local cuisine. There are many fast-food joints on Carrera 10 between Calles 11 and 12. Stock up on groceries at **Cajasan Supermercado** (Carrera 10 No 10-50; ☺ 8am-8pm) or **Autoservice Vera Cruz** (Calle 13 No 9-24; ☺ 7:30-9pm). For a true locals' experience, head to **Plaza de Mercado** (Carrera 11 btwn Calles 13 & 14; ☺ 6am-2pm), a bustling covered market where you can grab plenty of *comida corriente*, tamales and fresh-squeezed juices.

Cafetería Donde Betty (cnr Carrera 9 & Calle 12; ☺ 7am-midnight) This pleasant cafe serves breakfast, sandwiches and thirst-quenching fruit shakes.

our pick El Maná (☎ 300 460 6269; Calle 10 No 9-12; set meals COP$7500; ☺ lunch & dinner) This popular, word-of-mouth favorite is the best restaurant in town. Huge set meals feature traditional dishes like chicken in plum sauce, *carne asada* (grilled steak) and grilled mountain trout.

Restaurante Vegetariano Saludable Delicia (☎ 724 3539; Calle 11 No 8-40; mains COP$5000-22,000; ☺ 7am-7:30pm) Vegetarians and vegans will appreciate that Saludable Delicia lives up to its name, providing all-natural healthy, delicious set meals and à la carte dishes like veggie meats, sandwiches, salads and more.

Carnes y Carnes (☎ 724 6246; Carrera 12 No 8-09; COP$13,000-28,000; ☺ lunch & dinner) Carnivores unite at this posh restaurant that specializes in meat, meat and more meat including beef, chicken, pork and seafood. There is no sign identifying this south bank bistro, so just follow your nose.

Drinking & Entertainment

our pick Café Con Verso (Calle 12 No 7-81; drinks COP$6000-8000; ☺ 4pm-late) The colorful hand-painted murals, Sinatra and Hendrix portraits and art-deco decor provide a welcome change of atmosphere to San Gil. The friendly lounge keeps punters happy with strong drinks and chilled-out sounds. Daily pasta specials will keep your tummy happy.

La Habana (☎ 317 389 3886; Carrera 9 No 11-68; ☺ 6pm-midnight Sun-Thu, 6pm-2am Fri & Sat) Located on the 2nd floor of a shopping mall, this hot nightspot is a hidden local gem. The high-reaching walls are decorated in canvas artwork by local artists. Movies are screened at 6:30pm on Wednesdays and Sundays.

Discoteca El Trapiche (☎ 724 4423; Via Charalá; admission COP$3000; ☺ 10pm-dawn Fri & Sat) One of several discos located on the outskirts of San Gil, El Trapiche is a proper nightclub with smoke, lasers and a kicking sound system and wacky DJ churning out salsa and reggaetón. It's located 2km southeast of San Gil on the road to Charalá.

Getting There & Away

San Gil has three bus stations, but you'll most likely arrive at the intercity bus terminal located 3km west of downtown on the road to Bogotá. Local buses shuttle regularly between the terminal and the center, or take a taxi (COP$2800).

Frequent buses depart to Bogotá (COP$35,000, seven hours), Bucaramanga (COP$15,000, 2½ hours), Santa Marta (COP$60,000, 13 hours), Barranquilla COP$70,000, 15 hours), Medellín (COP$65,000, 11 hours) and Cúcuta (COP$40,000, nine hours).

Buses to Bucaramanga (COP$15,000, two hours) via Parque Nacional del Chicamocha depart from the **Cotrasangil bus terminal** (Carrera 11 No 8-10) every 30 minutes until 7:30pm.

The **local bus terminal** (cnr Calle 15 & Carrera 10) has frequent buses to Barichara (COP$3300, 45 minutes) from 5am to 6:30pm. This station also serves Guane, Charalá and Curití.

BARICHARA

☎ 7 / pop 10,000 / elev 1336m

Barichara is the kind of town that Hollywood filmmakers dream about. A Spanish colonial town of striking beauty, it boasts cobblestone streets and whitewashed buildings with red tiled roofs that look almost as new as the day they were created some 300 years ago. It's no wonder that many Spanish-language films and *telenovelas* are shot here. Granted, the movie-set appearance owes a debt to considerable reconstruction efforts made since the town was declared a national monument in 1978.

Barichara is located 20km northwest of San Gil high above the Río Suárez. According to legend, in 1702 a farmer discovered an apparition of the Virgin Mary on a rock in his field. The locals built a small chapel here to commemorate this miracle. Three years later, Spanish Capt Francisco Pradilla y Ayerbe founded the town of Villa de San Lorenzo de Barichara, after the Guane word *barachalá,* meaning 'a good place to rest.'

The town's natural beauty, temperate climate and bohemian lifestyle has long attracted visitors. In recent years, Barichara has become a magnet for affluent Colombians. Compared to Villa de Leyva, Barichara is more upscale but less touristy. Many boutique hotels, spas and gourmet restaurants have opened here in recent years, but the town retains its traditional atmosphere. It is, without a doubt, one of the most beautiful small colonial towns in Colombia. Don't miss it.

Information

There are two ATMs on the plaza; one is to the right of the cathedral and the other is by

Casa de Cultura. The official tourist website is at www.barichara-santander.gov.co.

Hospital (☎ 726 7133; Carrera 2, btwn Calles 3 & 4)
Police (☎ 726 7173; Calle 5 No 6-39)
Post office (☎ 726 7127; Carrera 6 No 4-90; ⏰ 8am-noon & 2-6pm) Adpostal.
Telecom (☎ Carrera 7, No 4-67) Local and international phone calls.
Tourist office (☎ 726 7052, Calle 5 No 6-39, ⏰ 8am-noon & 2-6pm Mon-Fri) Located in the 2nd floor of the police station. On weekends, there is a tourist kiosk on the plaza.

Sights

The main attraction of Barichara is its architecture. The 18th-century sandstone **Catedral de la Inmaculada Concepción** (Parque Principal) is the most elaborate structure in town, looking somewhat too big for the town's needs. Its golden stonework (which turns deep orange at sunset) contrasts with the whitewashed houses surrounding it. The building has a clerestory (a second row of windows high up in the nave), which is unusual for a Spanish colonial church. The cathedral faces **Parque Principal**, the main town square dotted with palm trees, tropical plants, a water fountain and benches perfect for people-watching.

The **Iglesia de Santa Bárbara** (cnr Carrera 11 & Calle 6) atop a hill at the north end of town has been carefully reconstructed in the 1990s (only the facade survived). Continue up the hill behind the church to reach **Parque para las Artes**, a lovely little park decorated with water features and statues carved by local sculptures, and an outdoor **amphitheater** that occasionally hosts live music concerts. From the park, enjoy the breathtaking views of Barichara and the neighboring valley.

The cemetery chapel, the **Capilla de Jesús Resucitado** (cnr Carrera 7 & Calle 3), unfortunately lost a part of its bell tower when it was damaged by lightning. Do visit the cemetery next to the chapel, noted for interesting tombs elaborated in stone. Also have a look at the **Capilla de San Antonio** (cnr Carrera 4 & Calle 5), the youngest of the town's churches, dating from 1831.

The **Casa de Cultura** (☎ 726 7002; Calle 5 No 6-29; admission COP$500; ⏰ 8am-noon & 2-6pm Mon-Sat, 9am-1pm Sun), a colonial house laid out around a fine patio and situated on the main square, features a mishmash collection of fossils, Guane pottery, paintings, typewriters, tools and other tchotchkes.

The **Casa de Aquileo Parra** (Carrera 2 No 5-60) is a small, humble home of Alquileo Parrera,

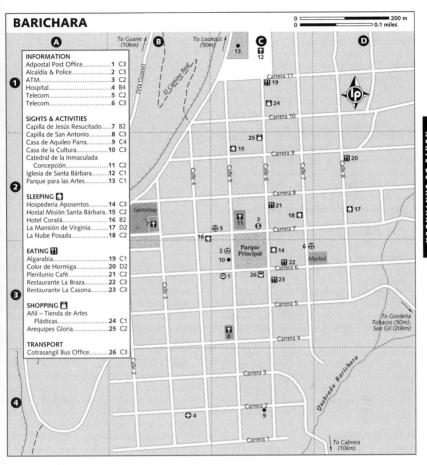

BARICHARA

INFORMATION
Adpostal Post Office...............1 C3
Alcaldía & Police...................2 C3
ATM...................................3 C2
Hospital...............................4 B4
Telecom...............................5 C2
Telecom...............................6 C3

SIGHTS & ACTIVITIES
Capilla de Jesús Resucitado.....7 B2
Capilla de San Antonio...........8 C3
Casa de Aquileo Parra...........9 C4
Casa de la Cultura................10 C3
Catedral de la Inmaculada
    Concepción.....................11 C2
Iglesia de Santa Bárbara........12 C1
Parque para las Artes............13 C1

SLEEPING
Hospedería Aposentos............14 C2
Hostal Misión Santa Bárbara..15 C2
Hotel Coratá......................16 B2
La Mansión de Virginia.........17 D2
La Nube Posada...................18 C2

EATING
Algarabia...........................19 C1
Color de Hormiga.................20 D2
Plenilunio Café....................21 C2
Restaurante La Braza............22 C3
Restaurante La Casona..........23 C3

SHOPPING
Añil – Tienda de Artes
    Plásticas........................24 C1
Arequipes Gloria..................25 C2

TRANSPORT
Cotrasangil Bus Office..........26 C3

who served as Colombia's 11th president (1876–78). There's a small museum but most of the building is now a cooperative for elderly weavers where you can watch them at work. The woman who runs the co-op can give you a tour, though there is little to see.

Activities

Don't miss the spectacular hike to the tiny hamlet of Guane (p125) on the historic **El Camino Real**. This ancient stone-paved road was built by the indigenous Guane people and rebuilt continuously over the centuries. It was declared a national monument in 1988. From Barichara, the 9km easy hike takes about two hours to complete. The trail is mostly downhill, occasionally crossing over the modern highway

to Guane. You'll begin the hike by climbing down the rim of a canyon and then traverse a valley filled with cacti and trees, occasionally encountering grazing goats or cows but rarely other humans. Notice the many fossils embedded in the stone road. El Camino Real begins at the north end of Calle 4, where a sign marks the beginning of the trail. Don't forget your water, sunscreen and proper footwear.

Sleeping

Barichara is not cheap; budget travelers are better off staying in San Gil. Prices listed here can spike 30% or more during *temporada alta* (high season), roughly December 20 to January 15 and Easter week, Semana Santa. During high season, reservations are a must.

Hospedería Aposentos (☎ 726 7294; Calle 6 No 6-40; r per person COP$30,000) On the main plaza, Aposentos is a small, good-value place, with five rooms set around a courtyard. All rooms have private bathroom and TV.

La Mansión de Virginia (☎ 726 7170, 314 233 5907; Calle 8 No 7-26; s/d COP$40,000/70,000) One of the few budget hotels in Barichara, this new friendly establishment has clean, comfy rooms with TV and private baths with hot water.

Hotel Corata (☎ 726 7110, 311 481 3195; Carrera 7 No 4-08; r incl breakfast COP$80,000) Aficionados of historical residences will fall in love Corata, a 300-year-old building decorated with antiques and wood furnishings. The rooms have vaulted ceilings, TV and private bathroom.

Hostal Misión Santa Bárbara (☎ 726 7163, in Bogotá 1 288 4949; www.hostalmisionsantabarbara.info; Calle 5 No 9-12; s/d incl breakfast COP$95,000/150,000; P 🐘) Santa Bárbara, set in a meticulously refurbished colonial mansion, has cozy en suite rooms with period furnishings. The restaurant here gets high marks.

ourpick La Nube Posada (☎ 726 7161, 310 334 8677; www.lanubeposada.com; Calle 7 No 7-39; s/tr COP$99,000/203,000, d COP$132,000-154,000) Hidden behind the unassuming exterior, this old colonial home has been transformed into a gorgeous boutique hotel with sleek, minimalist decor. The eight simply-furnished rooms have queen-sized beds, vaulted ceilings with exposed wood beams and private baths. Spa services are available. The on-site gourmet restaurant/bar is one of the best in town.

Eating & Drinking

Barichara is a foodies' paradise. Many gourmet restaurants have opened in recent years, offering nouveau-Colombian cuisine and traditional regional dishes like *cabrito* (grilled baby goat). The regional specialty is the famous *hormigas culonas* (see the boxed text, right).

There is practically no nightlife. A few corner shops sell aguardiente (anise-flavored liquor), beer and the local specialty, *chicha de maíz*, an alcoholic drink made from maize.

Restaurante La Casona (☎ 726 7251; Calle 6 No 5-68; set mains COP$2000; ✹ noon-6pm) This friendly family restaurant serves cheap set meals and typical regional dishes such as grilled meats.

Plenilunio Café (☎ 726 7485; Calle 6 No 7-74; mains COP$7000-10,000; ✹ 6:30-11pm) This Italian restaurant serves dishes such as crepes and chicken. It's set in a cozy room with just four tables

where you can hang out long after you've eaten, enjoying a game of chess.

Restaurante La Braza (☎ 726 7321; Carrera 6 No 6-31; mains COP$6000-12,000; ✹ noon-6pm) Low-priced Colombian lunches and dinners are served under a thatched roof in this large, open-air restaurant. It specializes in *cabro con pepitoria* (goat meat with blood and organs).

ourpick Color de Hormiga (☎ 726 7156; Calle 8 No 8-44; mains COP$14,000-18,000; ✹ lunch & dinner Wed-Mon) Literally named 'The Color of Ants,' Barichara's best restaurant specializes in dishes made with the region's famous delicacy. The filet mignon drenched in ant sauce and topped with fried ants is a must. There are also many insect-free dishes, like the scrumptious lamb curry and steak with blue cheese. Don't forget to sample the extensive wine and dessert list. The lovely thatched-roof, open-air restaurant faces a lush garden and fishponds.

Algarabia (☎ 726 7414, 313 364 8726; Calle 6 No 10-96; mains COP$15,000-30,000; ✹ lunch & dinner) Set amid a beautiful open-air courtyard garden, this new restaurant is run by friendly Spaniard Francisco and his Colombian wife Sofia. The house specialties include paella and seafood.

Shopping

Barichara is well known for its fine stonework. There are several stone-carving shops along Calle 5 where you can buy sculptures and other stone goods. Barichara is also famous for tobacco. At **Gordelia Tabacos** (☎ 726 7684; www.gordelia.com; Calle 5 No 0-84) you can buy hand-rolled cigars and watch them being made on-site.

Barichara has many boutique shops. **Añil – Tienda de Artes Plásticas** (☎ 311 470 1175; www .anilartesplasticas.com; Calle 6 No 10-46; ☺ 9am-noon & 2-6pm Tue-Sun) is a delightful gallery that sells paintings, sculptures and hand-painted T-shirts by local artists. For sweet tooths, there are a number of shops that sell Colombia's famous caramel-like dessert, *arequipe,* including **Arequipes Gloria** (Calle 6 No 9-29).

Getting There & Away

Buses shuttle between Barichara and San Gil every 45 minutes from 5am to 6:30pm (COP$3300, 45 minutes). They depart from the **Cotrasangil bus office** (☎ 726 7132; Carrera 6 No 5-74) on the main plaza. Buses to Guane (COP$2000, 15 minutes) depart at 6am, 9:30am, 11:30am, 2:30pm and 5:30pm.

GUANE

☎ 7 / pop 1500 / elev 831m

So little happens in the sleepy town of Guane, 10km northwest of Barichara, that everyone stops and stares when a horse cart, or a tourist, trundles past. But the views around the cobblestone town are nice. The handsome main square features a fine rural church, the **Santa Lucía Iglesia**, built in 1720.

Across the square is the unique **Museum of Paleontology & Archaeology** (admission COP$2500; ☺ 8am-noon & 1-5pm), with a collection of more than 10,000 fossils, a 700-year-old mummy, a few conehead skulls, Guane artifacts and religious art. The curator locks the front door and gives a personal tour (in Spanish) whenever someone shows up, so just hang tight.

There are a few basic restaurants but only one hotel in town, the **Hostal Santa Lucia de Mucuruva** (☎ 732 0163, 311 516 6075; r per person incl breakfast COP$35,000). This eclectic colonial estate is one block behind the museum. The funky, simple rooms and courtyard were painted and decorated by the hotel's young manager/artist, Orlando. Guests have free use of the community swimming pool.

Buses to Barichara depart from Guane's plaza at 6:30am, 10am, noon, 3pm and 6pm. Don't make our mistake and miss the last bus; a taxi back to Barichara will set you back at least COP$15,000. During daylight, you can walk back to Barichara along El Camino Real (p123); the uphill, 6km hike will take at least two hours.

PARQUE NACIONAL DEL CHICAMOCHA

Halfway between San Gil and Bucaramanga is the spectacular canyon of Río Chicamocha and Colombia's newest national park, **Parque Nacional del Chicamocha** (www.parquenacionaldelchica mocha.com; Km54 Via Bucaramanga-San Gil; adult/child COP$8000/4000; ☺ 9am-6pm Tue-Thu, 9am-7pm Fri-Sun & holidays). The windy, cliff-hugging road between the two cities is one of the most scenic drives in Santander.

Opened in 2006, the park houses a **Museum of Guane Culture**, several restaurants, a forgettable **ostrich farm** (admission COP$1000) and the **Monumento a la Santandereanidad** commemorating the revolutionary spirit of Santanderians. But the real attraction here is the majestic canyon itself. The best views are from the **mirador**, providing a 360-degree vantage of the area. Or for a real bird's-eye view, adrenalin junkies can zipline (COP$17,000) or paraglide (COP$130,000). By the time you read this, a new cable car will descend to the base of the canyon then ascend to the top of opposite rim.

Any bus between San Gil and Bucaramanga will drop you off at the park. To get back to either city, walk down to the highway and flag a passing bus. For those heading north, a better option is to just go to the parking lot near the park entrance and look for the frequent Copetran minibuses to Bucaramanga (COP$8000, one hour).

BUCARAMANGA

☎ 7 / pop 560,000 / elev 960m

With a greater metropolitan population of about one million people, Bucaramanga, the capital of Santander, is one of the largest cities in Colombia. Surrounded by mountains and packed with uninspiring skyscrapers, this modern city is filled with an air of vibrancy.

Buca, as it's known to locals, was founded in 1622 and developed around what is today the Parque García Rovira, but most of its colonial architecture is long gone. Over the centuries, the city center moved eastwards, and today Parque Santander is the heart of Bucaramanga. Further east are newer, posh neighborhoods peppered with hotels and nightspots.

Dubbed 'The City of Parks,' Buca is filled with lovely green spaces. Unfortunately most of the city is not particularly attractive, and is made even worse by the horrific traffic and

BOYACÁ, SANTANDER & NORTE DE SANTANDER

overpopulation. To ease congestion, Buca is currently constructing a massive public transportation system modeled on Bogotá's TransMilenio, set to open in 2010.

Buca really comes to life at night. Its nightlife is legendary thanks to dozens of clubs, hundreds of bars and 10 universities. Non-party animals may find Buca rather boring. Nevertheless, Buca is worth a stopover on the long road between Bogotá and the coast or as a base to visit nearby colonial town of Girón.

Information

There is no shortage of ATMs; many are clustered near Parque Santander along Calle 35, and in Sotomayor on Carrera 29.

Bancolombia (Carrera 18 No 35-02)

Citibank (Calle 49 No 23-55) Can change traveler's checks.

Click & Play (☎ 642 2882; Calle 34 No 19-46, room 115, Centro Comercial La Triada; per hr COP$1800; ☺ 8am-9pm) Internet and international phone calls.

HSBC (Centro Comercial, Room 121)

Mundo Divisas (Calle 34 No 19-46, room 120, Centro Comercial La Triada; ☺ 8am-noon & 2.30-6pm Mon-Fri, 9am-12:30pm Sat) Money exchange.

Police (☎ 633 9015; Calle 41 No 11-44)

Telenet (☎ 670 5850; Calle 36 No 18-03; per hr COP$1500; ☺ 7:30am-7:30pm) Internet and international phone call office.

Tourist police (☎ 633 8342; Parque Santander; ☺ 24hr) The Tourist Police kiosk has free brochures and maps. For more current information visit www.bucaros.com.

Sights

The **Museo Casa de Bolívar** (☎ 630 4258; Calle 37 No 12-15; admission COP$1000; ☺ 8am-noon & 2-6pm Mon-Fri, 8am-noon Sat) is housed in a colonial mansion where Bolívar stayed for two months in 1828. The museum displays various historic and archeological exhibits, including weapons, documents, paintings, and mummies and artifacts of the Guane people who inhabited the region before the Spaniards arrived.

Diagonally opposite, the **Casa de la Cultura** (☎ 642 0163; Calle 37 No 12-46; admission free; ☺ 8am-noon & 2-6pm Mon-Fri, 8am-noon Sat), in another historic building, features a collection of paintings donated by the local artists.

Museo de Arte Moderno de Bucaramanga (☎ 645 0483; Calle 37 No 26-16; admission COP$2000; ☺ 8am-noon & 2-6pm Mon-Fri, 8am-noon Sat) houses rotating exhibits of modern paintings and sculptures.

Of the city churches, the **Catedral de la Sagrada Familia** (Calle 36 No 19-56), facing Parque Santander, is the most substantial piece of religious architecture. Constructed over nearly a century (1770–1865), it's a massive, eclectic edifice with fine stained-glass windows and a ceramic cupola brought from Mexico. The **Capilla de los Dolores** (cnr Carrera 10 & Calle 35), in the Parque García Rovira, is Bucaramanga's oldest surviving church, erected in stone in 1748–50, but no longer operates as a church.

The verdant **Jardín Botánico Eloy Valenzuela** (☎ 648 0729; admission COP$500; ☺ 8am-5pm) has 7.5 hectares of gardens, a small pond and a Japanese tea garden. The gardens are on the banks of the Río Frío on the old road to Floridablanca, in the suburb of Bucarica. To get there, take the Bucarica bus from Carrera 15 in the city center.

Activities

Bucaramanga's most popular sport is paragliding. The hub for this high-flying activity is atop the Ruitoque mesa. **Colombia Paragliding** (☎ 352 8839, 312 432 6266; www.colombiaparagliding.com; Ruitoque) offers 15-minute tandem rides for COP$50,000, or go all-out and become an internationally licensed paragliding pilot; 10-day courses begin at COP$1,000,000. Owner/instructor Richi speaks English and also runs the KGB and the Nest hostels (below).

Sleeping

Nest (☎ 352 8839, 312 432 6266; www.colombiaparagliding.com; Km2 Via Mesa Ruitoque; dm/r per person COP$10,000/40,000; 🖳) The sister hostel to KGB, this fly-site hostel is located next to Colombia Paragliding's launch pad, 20 minutes from downtown. The majority of guests are paragliding students, but it's also a good choice for anyone seeking peace and quiet. Rooms are basic but comfortable, with shared hot showers, kitchen, hammocks and killer views of the city below.

Our pick Kasa Guane Bucaramanga (☎ 657 6960, 312 432 6266; www.kasaguane.com; Calle 49 No 28-21; dm/s/d per person COP$20,000/35,000/50,000; 🖳 ✗) Better known as KGB, this spiffy new hostel opened in 2008 to rave reviews for its fantastic customer service and amenities. Located in one of the nicest neighborhoods in town, KGB has dorms and private rooms, huge bathrooms with hot water, kitchen and laundry facilities, hammocks, an internet cafe, satellite TV room and pool table. Guests get free access to the local country club's gym, pool and tennis facilities.

BUCARAMANGA

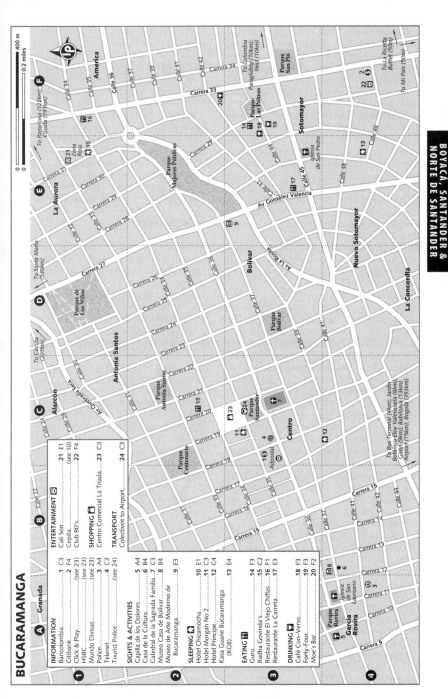

INFORMATION
Bancolombia...............................1 C3
Citibank......................................2 F4
Click & Play...........................(see 23)
HSBC....................................(see 23)
Mundo Divisas........................(see 23)
Police...3 A4
Telenet.......................................4 C3
Tourist Police.........................(see 24)

SIGHTS & ACTIVITIES
Capilla de los Dolores..................5 A4
Casa de la Cultura.......................6 B4
Catedral de la Sagrada Familia...7 C3
Museo Casa de Bolívar.................8 B4
Museo de Arte Moderno de
  Bucaramanga............................9 E3

SLEEPING
Hotel Chicamocha.....................10 E1
Hotel Morgan No 2.....................11 C3
Hotel Príncipe............................12 C4
Kasa Guane Bucaramanga
  (KGB)......................................13 E4

EATING
Guru..14 F3
Radha Govinda's.......................15 C2
Restaurante El Viejo Chiflas.......16 F1
Restaurante La Carreta...............17 E3

DRINKING
Café Con-Verso.........................18 F3
Forty-Four..................................19 F3
Moe's Bar..................................20 F2

ENTERTAINMENT
Cali Son.....................................21 E1
Cepita...................................(see 10)
Club 80's...................................22 F4

SHOPPING
Centro Comercial La Triada......23 C3

TRANSPORT
Colectivos to Airport.................24 C3

Hotel Morgan No 2 (☎ 630 4226; Calle 35 No 18-83; s/d/tr COP$25,000/35,000/45,000; ✗ ✗) Just off Parque Santander, this affordable, central hotel has small rooms, most with fans only. But for COP$2000 extra, you can get a better room with fridge and air-con. Avoid the hot, noisy streetside rooms.

Hotel Principe (☎ 630 4317; www.hotel-principe.net; Carrera 17 No 37-69; s/d COP$59,400/79,200; ✗ ✗) This moderately priced hotel in the heart of downtown is popular with tourists and business guests alike. The large rooms have cable TV, private baths and super-comfy beds. Other amenities include wi-fi, bar and restaurant.

Hotel Chicamocha (☎ 634 3000; Calle 34 No 31-24; s/d COP$189,000/246,000; P ✗ ⌨ 🖥 ✗) For those seeking ultimate comfort, the 10-story, 192-room Hotel Chicamocha is one of the finest in town. Amenities include a swimming pool, gym, sauna, Turkish bath, restaurant, bar and room service.

Eating

Buca is packed with restaurants, from fast-food joints to upscale bistros. Typical regional dishes include *mute* (a thick soup of meat and veggies) and *cabro* or *cabrito* (goat). The legendary *hormiga culona* is a snack you can buy in delis and neighborhood shops.

Guru (☎ 634 7647; Carrera 29 No 42-44; mains COP$3000-17,000; ☽ 5pm-midnight) The lovely patio at this upscale cafe facing Parque La Palmas is a perfect people-watching spot, and the food is great too. Try the scrumptious New York roast beef sandwich or chicken curry.

Radha Govinda's (☎ 643 3382; Carrera 20 No 51-95; set meals COP$5000; ☽ 9:30am-6:30pm Mon-Sat) Vegetarians will delight in this Hare Krishna restaurant serving hot, healthy cuisine in a relaxing environment. The on-site store sells incense, clothing, books, CDs and groceries such as granola and yogurt.

La Ricetta Buffet (Calle 51 No 34-61; all you can eat COP$6000; ☽ lunch) Buffets are relatively unknown in Colombia, so take advantage and pig out at this all-you-can-eat experience serving filling, international comfort food.

Restaurante El Viejo Chiflas (☎ 632 0640; Carrera 33 No 34-10; mains COP$6000-14,000; ☽ 11am-midnight) This is an atmospheric restaurant good for lovers of meat. Try the *parrillada vieto chiflas*, a platter of various meats, designed for two.

Restaurante La Carreta (☎ 643 6680; Carrera 27 No 42-27; mains COP$14,000-30,000; ☽ noon-3:30pm & 6pm-midnight) Housed in a historic mansion, La

Carreta has a 40-year-old tradition and a good address for a fine dinner.

Drinking

Many great bars are located in Sotomayor near Parque Las Palmas. **Café Con-Verso** (Calle 44 No 28-63) is a beautiful chill-out lounge with great music and drinks. Across the street, **Forty-Four** (☎ 643 3681; Calle 44 No 28-56; ☽ 11am-11pm) is a wacky American-diner-themed bar covered in Hollywood memorabilia. Fans of *The Simpsons* will want to check out **Moe's Bar** (☎ 643 1037; Carrera 33 No 44-12; ☽ 6pm-2am), an over-the-top tribute to Homer, Bart and the rest of the Simpson clan (Ay Caramba!).

Entertainment

Bucaramanga comes to life when the sun goes down. *La vida nocturna,* or the nightlife scene, attracts clubbers from around the region. Buca's best bars and clubs are located on the east side of town in the *zona rosa* (nightlife zone) and Sotomayor and on the road to the airport. Some popular venues are **Babilonia** (Km13 Via Aeropuerto), **Mi Pais** (Carrera 34 No 52-07) and **Club 80's** (Carrera 49 No 32-17). For salsa dancing, try **Cepita** (Hotel Chicamocha, Calle 34 No 31-24) and **Cali Son** (cnr Calle 33 & Carrera 31). Most clubs don't get cranking until 11pm and are open until dawn on weekends.

Getting There & Away
AIR

The Palonegro airport is on a *meseta* (plateau) high above the city, off the road to Barrancabermeja. The landing here is quite breathtaking. Local buses marked 'Aeropuerto' link the airport and the city center every hour or so; you catch them on Carrera 15. It's faster to go by *colectivo* (COP$5000), which park in Parque Santander. There are flights to some major Colombian cities, including Bogotá (COP$184,000 to COP$395,000) and Medellín (COP$133,000 to COP$395,000).

BUS

Bucaramanga's bus terminal is situated southwest of the center, midway to Girón; frequent city buses marked 'Terminal' go there from Carrera 15 or take a taxi (COP$6000). Buses depart regularly to Bogotá (COP$70,000, 10 hours), Cartagena (COP$101,000, 12 hours) and Santa Marta (COP$80,000, nine hours), Pamplona (COP$20,000, four hours) and Cúcuta (COP$36,000, six hours).

GIRÓN
☎ 7 / pop 45,000 / elev 780m

The cobbled streets, horse carts and lazy atmosphere of San Juan de Girón are a world away in time, but just 9km from bustling Bucaramanga. The pleasant town was founded in 1631 on the banks of the Río de Oro. In 1963 it was declared a national monument. Today it's a magnet for artists and day-trippers. But if you've already been to Villa de Leyva or Baricharaá, Girón is a bit of a letdown.

Information
Web surfers can get more info from www .giron.gov.co.

AmiNet (Carrera 25 No 30-20; per hr COP$1000; ♥ 9am-10pm)

Banco Popular (Carrera 25) On the eastern side of the Parque Principal. It has an ATM.

el port@l.net (☎ 646 9878; Carrera 25 No 30-86; per hr COP$1500; ♥ 7am-midnight Mon-Fri) Internet facilities plus coffee and snacks.

Tourist office (Secretaría de Cultura y Turismo; ☎ 646 1337; Calle 30 No 26-64; ♥ 8am-noon & 2-6pm) Free guided tours (in Spanish) of the town are available.

Tourist police (☎ 630 2046; cnr Calle 30 & Carrera 27)

Sights
Take the time to stroll about Girón's narrow cobblestone streets, looking at whitewashed old houses, shaded patios, small stone bridges and waterfront *malecón*.

The **Catedral del Señor de los Milagros** on the main plaza was begun in 1646 but not completed until 1876.

Don't miss the pleasant plazas, **Plazuela Peralta** and **Plazuela de las Nieves**, which features a charming village church, the 18th-century **Capilla de las Nieves**.

Sleeping & Eating
Giron Chill Out (☎ 646 1119; www.gironchillout.com; Carrera 25 No 32-02; r COP$30,000) This basic hostel with a bamboo roof has clean rooms with shared baths, kitchen, laundry, TV lounge, terrace and restaurant.

Hotel Las Nieves (☎ 646 8968; www.hotellas nievesgiron.com; Calle 30 No 25-71; s/d COP$35,000/55,000) Circling a courtyard and overlooking the main plaza is this quaint hotel, featuring large but simple rooms with TV, desk and private bathroom. Try for one of the balconied rooms over the plaza.

BOYACÁ, SANTANDER & NORTE DE SANTANDER

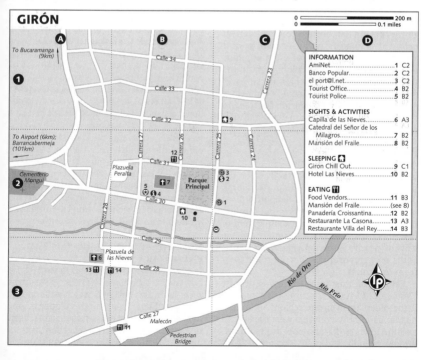

GIRÓN

0 ——— 200 m
0 ——— 0.1 miles

To Bucaramanga (9km)

To Airport (6km); Barrancabermeja (101km)

Cementerio Mongui

Plazuela Peralta

Plazuela de las Nieves

Parque Principal

Río de Oro

Río Frío

Calle 34
Calle 33
Calle 32
Calle 31
Calle 30
Calle 29
Calle 28
Calle 27
Malecón

Carrera 27
Carrera 26
Carrera 25
Carrera 24
Carrera 23
Carrera 28

Pedestrian Bridge

INFORMATION
AmiNet.................................1 C2
Banco Popular......................2 C2
el port@l.net........................3 C2
Tourist Office.......................4 B2
Tourist Police.......................5 B2

SIGHTS & ACTIVITIES
Capilla de las Nieves.............6 A3
Catedral del Señor de los
  Milagros............................7 B2
Mansión del Fraile................8 B2

SLEEPING 🛏
Giron Chill Out.....................9 C1
Hotel Las Nieves.................10 B2

EATING 🍴
Food Vendors.....................11 B3
Mansión del Fraile..........(see 8)
Panadería Croissantina........12 B2
Restaurante La Casona.......13 A3
Restaurante Villa del Rey.....14 B3

For cheap eats, grab a bite at the vendor stalls on the waterfront. Finer restaurants include **Mansión del Fraile** (☎ 646 5408; Calle 30 No 25-27; mains COP$7000-15,000; ☽ noon-6pm), **Restaurante Villa del Rey** (☎ 653 2809; Calle 28 No 27-49; mains COP$7000-15,000; ☽ 8am-6pm) and **Restaurante La Casona** (☎ 646 7195; Calle 28 No 28-09; mains COP$7000-20,000; ☽ noon-6pm). All serve typical hearty food in colonial-style surroundings. The **Panedería Croissantina** (cnr Calle 31 & Carrera 26; ☽ 7am-8pm) bakery is a popular spot for breakfast with fresh coffee, juices, cakes and other baked goodies.

Getting There & Away

Frequent city buses from Bucaramanga deposit you on the corner of Carrera 26 and Calle 32, one block from Parque Principal (the main plaza). Buses back to Buca collect passengers on the corner of Calle 29 and Carrera 26.

NORTE DE SANTANDER

Norte de Santander is where the Cordillera Oriental meets the hot, lowland plains that stretch into neighboring Venezuela. The scenic road from Bucaramanga climbs to 3300m at the provincial border town of Berlin before it begins its rapid descent toward Venezuela. The east side of the mountains offers a cool retreat, and colonial-era towns such as Pamplona make a pleasant stopover on the overland trail. Cúcuta is a dry, hot market town better known for contraband than its sights, though you may need to stop here if you're crossing the border.

PAMPLONA

☎ 7 / pop 45,000 / elev 2290m

Spectacularly set in the deep Valle del Espíritu Santo in the Cordillera Oriental, colonial-era Pamplona is a delightful town of old churches, narrow streets and bustling commerce. With an average temperature of just 16°C, it's a welcome respite from the heat of nearby Bucaramanga and Cúcuta, and a nice stopover if you're en route to or from Venezuela.

Pamplona was founded by Pedro de Orsúa and Ortún Velasco in 1549, making it the oldest town in the region. Soon after its foundation five convents were established and the town swiftly developed into an important religious and political center. A con-

struction boom saw the rise of churches and noble mansions.

Unfortunately, an earthquake occurring in 1875 wiped out a good part of the town. The inviting plaza is now a mix of reconstructed colonial and modern architecture.

Pamplona was a schooling center from its early days, and the traditions have not been lost; today the town is home to the Universidad de Pamplona, and the large student population is very much in evidence. Pamplona has a distinctly cultured air, and boasts more museums than Cúcuta and Bucaramanga combined.

Information

ATM (cnr Calle 6 & Carrera 6)
Banco de Bogotá (Carrera 6) East of Parque Agueda Gallardo. Has an ATM.
Internet cafe (☎ 568 2062; Calle 7 No 5-62; per hr COP$1200; ☽ 8am-8pm)
Post office (☎ 568 2405; Calle 6 No 6-36; ☽ 8am-noon & 2-6pm Mon-Fri) Adpostal.

Sights

Pamplona has quite a collection of museums and almost all are set in restored colonial houses. **Museo Fotográfico** (Carrera 7 No 2-44) is a curiosity rather than a museum, but do go in to see hundreds of old photos. **Museo Arquidiocesano de Arte Religioso** (☎ 568 1814; Carrera 5 No 4-53; admission COP$500; ☽ 10am-noon & 3-5pm Wed-Sat & Mon, 10am-noon Sun) features religious art, comprising paintings, statues and altarpieces, collected from the region. Have a look at **Casa de las Cajas Reales** (cnr Carrera 5 & Calle 4), a great colonial mansion, and at **Casa de Mercado** (cnr Carrera 5 & Calle 6), the 19th-century market building, just off the main square. There are some 10 old churches and chapels in town, reflecting Pamplona's religious status in colonial days, though not many have retained their splendor. The **Iglesia del Humilladero**, at the entrance to the cemetery, boasts the famous Cristo del Humilladero, a realistic sculpture of Christ brought from Spain in the 17th century.

MUSEO DE ARTE MODERNO RAMÍREZ VILLAMIZAR

In a 450-year-old mansion, this **museum** (☎ 568 2999; Calle 5 No 5-75; admission COP$1000; ☽ 9am-noon & 2-6pm Tue-Fri, 9am-6pm Sat & Sun) has about 40 works by Eduardo Ramírez Villamizar, one of Colombia's most outstanding artists, born in Pamplona in 1923. The collection gives an insight into his artistic development from ex-

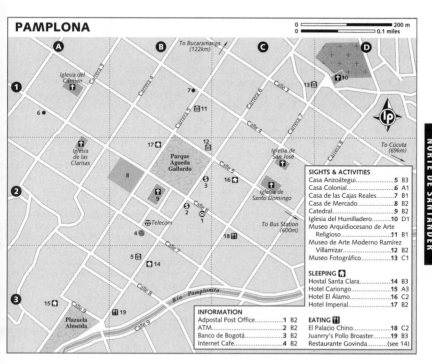

pressionist painting of the 1940s to geometric abstract sculpture in recent decades.

CASA ANZOÁTEGUI

Now housing a museum with a modest collection of exhibits related to the crucial events of the period, **Casa Anzoátegui** (Carrera 6 No 7-48; admission free; 9am-noon & 2-5:30pm Mon-Sat, 9am-noon Sun) was the home of General José Antonio Anzoátegui, the Venezuelan hero of the independence campaign who fought under Bolívar. His strategic abilities largely contributed to the victory in the Battle of Boyacá of 1819. He died here, three months after the battle, at 30.

CASA COLONIAL

One of the oldest buildings in town, **Casa Colonial** (Calle 6 No 2-56; admission by donation; 8am-noon & 2-5pm Mon-Sat) dates from the early Spanish days. The collection includes some pre-Columbian pottery, colonial sacred art, artifacts of several indigenous communities including the Motilones and Tunebos (the two indigenous groups living in Norte de Santander department), plus antiques.

CATEDRAL

The 17th-century Catedral was badly damaged during the earthquake of 1875 and altered in the reconstruction. The five-nave interior (two outer aisles were added at the beginning of the 20th century) is rather austere except for the magnificent main retable that survived the disaster. The central figure of San Pedro was made in Spain in 1618.

Festivals & Events

Semana Santa (Holy Week) The town is known nationwide for its solemn celebrations.
Fiestas del Grito de Independencia (Jun-Jul) This is another important annual event, also called the Fiestas de Pamplona. The feast is celebrated for two weeks preceding July 4, commemorating the day when Pamplona rebels declared their independence from Spain on July 4, 1810. The festival features concerts, bullfights, parades, bands and the must-see beauty pageant.

Sleeping

Hostal Santa Clara (568 4105, 316 835 2338; Carrera 6 No 7-21; s/d with shared bath COP$18,000/22,000, with private bath COP$25,000/30,000) Located in a funky old colonial building, this family-run hotel has comfy basic rooms with TV, hot water and the biggest doors you've ever seen.

Hotel El Álamo (☎ 568 2137; Calle 5 No 6-68; s/d COP$25,000/35,000) Rooms with private bathroom are a bit small but probably the best bet in the budget category. The on-site restaurant serves a decent, cheap breakfast.

Hotel Imperial (☎ 568 2571; Carrera 5 No 5-36; s/d COP$24,000/37,000) Contrary to its name, Imperial is kind of a dive but you can't beat the location. All rooms are clean with comfy beds, TVs and private baths with hot water. Ask for a room facing the plaza.

Hotel Cariongo (☎ 568 1515; www.hotelcariongo.com; cnr Calle 9 & Carrera 5; s/d COP$50,000/80,000; ☐ P) It's clear that the Cariongo has seen better days, but this place still manages to be the best hotel in town. All rooms come with a TV, but not all have hot-water showers. The hotel also houses one of the new nightclubs in town, open on weekends only.

Eating

Juanrry's Pollo Broaster (Carrera 6 No 8B-49; set meals COP$4000; ☼ 11am-10pm) Reasonably priced roasted chicken is what you'll find here. Check out the various caricatures on the walls and see Juanrry the Chicken posing with the likes of Shakira, Michael Jackson and Mick Jagger.

Restaurante Govinda (Hostal Santa Clara, Carrera 6 No 7-21, set meals COP$4000; ☼ lunch) The only vegetarian and vegan option in town, this Hare Krishna–run restaurant has good healthy, cheap and filling set meals.

El Palacio Chino (☎ 568 1666; Calle 6 No 7-32; mains COP$8000-12,000; ☼ 10am-8pm) While not particularly atmospheric, this Colombian attempt at Oriental cooking produces some fresh and hot dishes of soups, noodles and steamed veggies.

Getting There & Away

Pamplona's new bus terminal is just 600m southwest of the main square. You can walk to town in about 10 minutes, or pay COP$2000 for a cab.

Pamplona is on the Bucaramanga–Cúcuta road, and buses pass by regularly to both Cúcuta (COP$13,000, two hours, 72km) and Bucaramanga (COP$25,000, 4½ hours, 124km).

The road from Bucaramanga to Pamplona is in very poor condition, notably near Berlin where most buses stop for a food and toilet break. Passengers prone to motion or altitude sickness should consider taking Dramamine or a similar drug. And bring a sweater.

CÚCUTA

☎ 7 / pop 919,000 / elev 320m

For many visitors, the border town of Cúcuta is either their first or last impression of Colombia, and it isn't a good one. Cúcuta is a hot, muggy, filthy, crime-ridden city; its most well-known attraction is the notoriously dodgy bus station. The only reason to come here is to cross the border to or from Venezuela. If you're catching an early bus out of here, or arriving in the evening, consider staying in nearby Pamplona instead.

For travelers heading to Venezuela, the actual border crossing is at Puente Internacional, 12km south of Cúcuta on the Río Táchira. Be sure to change your Colombian pesos before leaving the country. If possible, stock up on US dollars, which are stronger and more welcomed than bolivares. You'll find several moneychangers on the Colombian side of the bridge.

Information

There are numerous banks with ATMs around Parque Santander.

The Departamento Administrativo de Seguridad (DAS) immigration post (where you have to get an exit/entry stamp in your passport) is just before the border at Puente Internacional, on the left side of the road going toward Venezuela. Remember to move your watch forward one hour when you cross. Once in Venezuela, pick up a tourist card – it's issued directly by the DIEX office in San Antonio del Táchira, on Carrera 9 between Calles 6 and 7.

Bancafé (Calle 10)

Banco de Bogotá (Av 6)

Post office (Calle 8A) Adpostal; north of Parque Nacional.

Tourist office (☎ 571 3395; Calle 10 No 0-30; ☼ 8am-noon & 2-6pm Mon-Fri, 8am-noon Sat) In the offices of Corporación Mixta de Promoción de Norte de Santander.

Venezuelan consulate (☎ 579 1954, 579 1951; Av Camilo Daza, Zona Industrial; ☼ 8am-noon & 1-4pm) Located on the road to the airport, about 3km north of the center. Take any local bus marked 'Consulado' from the bus terminal or from Calle 13 in the center. Get there early to avoid queuing for ages.

Sights

Casa de la Cultura (☎ 571 6689; Calle 13 No 3-67; ☼ 8am-noon & 2-6pm Mon-Fri), has a nice clock tower and temporary art exhibits. **Banco de la**

República (☎ 575 0131; cnr Av Diagonal Santander & Calle 11; ☺ 8am-noon & 2-6pm Mon-Fri) also stages temporary exhibitions in its Area Cultural.

Sleeping

If you must stay overnight, avoid any hotel within six blocks of the bus station, a grimy red-light district unsafe at night.

Hotel Amaruc (☎ 571 7625; Av 5 No 9-73; r COP$50,000-70,000; ☒ ☒) The Amaruc overlooks the central square and all rooms come with TV, desk and phone.

Hotel Bolívar (☎ 576 0764; www.hotel-bolivar.com; Av Demetrio Mendoza; s/d incl breakfast COP$160,000/170,000; ☒ ☐ ☒ ☒) Located outside the city near the airport, this resortlike hotel has 127 luxurious

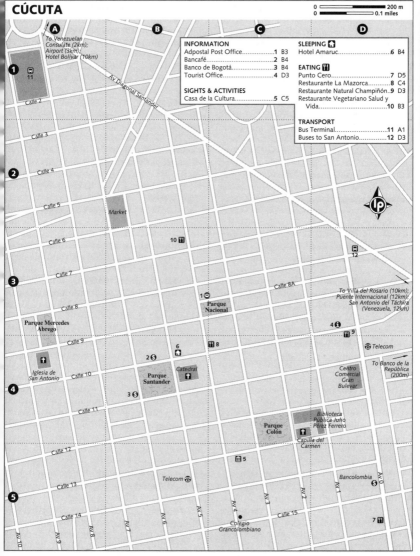

CÚCUTA

```
0 ──────── 200 m
0 ──────── 0.1 miles
```

INFORMATION
Adpostal Post Office................1 B3
Bancafé.....................................2 B4
Banco de Bogotá.....................3 B4
Tourist Office...........................4 D3

SIGHTS & ACTIVITIES
Casa de la Cultura....................5 C5

SLEEPING 🏠
Hotel Amaruc...........................6 B4

EATING 🍽
Punto Cero................................7 D5
Restaurante La Mazorca...........8 C4
Restaurante Natural Champiñón..9 D3
Restaurante Vegetariano Salud y
Vida.....................................10 B3

TRANSPORT
Bus Terminal...........................11 A1
Buses to San Antonio.............12 D3

To Venezuelan Consulate (2km); Airport (3km); Hotel Bolívar (10km)

Av Diagonal Santander

Calle 2

Calle 3

Calle 4

Calle 5

Market

Calle 6

Calle 7

Calle 8

Calle 8A

To Villa del Rosario (10km); Puente Internacional (12km); San Antonio del Táchira (Venezuela, 12km)

Parque Mercedes Abrego

Calle 9

Parque Nacional

Telecom

Calle 10

Iglesia de San Antonio

Parque Santander

Catedral

Centro Comercial Gran Bulevar

To Banco de la República (200m)

Calle 11

Parque Colón

Biblioteca Pública Julio Pérez Ferrero

Capilla del Carmen

Calle 12

Calle 13

Telecom

Bancolombia

Calle 14

Calle 15

Colegio Grancolombiano

AV 10 AV 9 AV 8 AV 7 AV 6 AV 5 AV 4 AV 3 AV 2 AV 1 AV 0

LOS LLANOS

As you head east away from Bogotá, the jagged, mountainous terrain soon drops and flattens out, revealing an endless sea of green grasslands.

This is Los Llanos, or the plains. This mammoth ecosystem is part of the Orinoco River Basin stretching from the foothills of the Colombian Andes to Venezuela, bounded by the Amazon Basin in the south. The Colombian Llanos covers 250,000 sq km, making up nearly a fifth of the country's total area.

Sometimes called the Serengeti of South America, Los Llanos is teeming with wildlife. It harbors more than 100 species of mammals and more than 700 species of birds, about the same number of birds as found in the entire USA. According to the Nature Conservancy, Los Llanos is also home to some of the most endangered species on Earth including the Orinoco crocodile, the Orinoco turtle, giant armadillo, giant otter, black-and-chestnut eagle and several species of catfish.

The flat, grassy plains make this region ideal for cattle grazing. *Llaneros,* or Colombian cowboys, spend long hours herding cattle in grueling conditions on mega ranches, some of which are thousands of acres in size. Their hard, isolated life inspired a unique culture very different from 'mainstream' Colombia. *Llaneros* are associated with their distinctive straw hats, *coleo* rodeos, the *jorop* dance and their bluegrass-like genre of folk music known as *música llanera.*

Los Llanos occupies the Colombian departments of Arauca, Casanare, Guainía, Meta and Vichada. As recently as 2003, much of this area was off-limits to foreigners. Today, many of the bigger cities are safe and open for business including Villavicencio, Puerto López and Puerto Gaitán.

Unfortunately, despite many recent Colombian military victories, FARC rebels and other guerrilla groups still control swaths of Los Llanos. At the time this book went to print, the area south of San José del Guaviare was very dangerous. The road from Puerto López to Puerto Carreño on the Venezuelan border was improving but not yet secure. Stick to the cities and always inquire locally for up-to-date security information before proceeding.

rooms, gym, two swimming pools and a great restaurant.

Eating

Restaurante La Mazorca (Av 4 No 9-67; set meals COP$4000, mains COP$10,000-15,000) Enjoy Creole meals and a choice of wines in this sunny courtyard, decorated with baskets and saddles.

Punto Cero (☎ 573 0153; Av 0 No 15-60; mains COP$8000-12,000; ⏰ 24hr) A welcoming restaurant that offers typical food, such as *bandeja paísa* (a traditional Antioquian platter) and *sancocho* (traditional soup). There are also some more upmarket restaurants further south on Av 0.

Vegetarians can choose between **Restaurante Vegetariano Salud y Vida** (Av 4 No 6-40) and **Restaurante Natural Champiñón** (Calle 10 No 0-05), both of which serve budget set lunches on weekdays.

Getting There & Away
AIR
The airport is 4km north of the city center. Minibuses that are marked 'El Trigal Molinos' (from Av 1 or Av 3 in the center) will drop you 350m from the terminal. A taxi from the airport to the center costs COP$10,000.

The airport handles flights to most major Colombian cities, including Bogotá, Medellín, Cali and Cartagena.

There are no direct flights from Cúcuta to Venezuela. Across the border, San Antonio del Táchira's tiny airport has sporadic flights to Caracas. Better yet, continue 50km further to Aeropuerto Internacional de Santo Domingo south of San Cristobal, which has regular flights to Caracas.

BUS
The notoriously chaotic, disgusting bus terminal is on the corner of Av 7 and Calle 1. Watch your belongings closely. If you are arriving from Venezuela, you might be approached by English-speaking individuals who will kindly offer their help in buying bus tickets and insuring your money. Ignore them – they are con men. Buy tickets directly from bus company offices or drivers.

There are frequent buses heading to Pamplona (COP$12,000, two hours), Bucaramanga (COP$40,000, six hours) and Bogotá (COP$80,000, 16 hours)

To Venezuela, take one of the frequent buses or shared taxis running from Cúcuta's bus terminal to San Antonio del Táchira

Villavicencio, 75km southeast of Bogotá and known as 'La Puerta al Llano' – the gateway to the Llanos – is a bustling, booming town of nearly 400,000 people. The main attractions are its green spaces such as the downtown **Parque de los Fundadores** and **Bioparque Los Ocarros**, a zoo 3km north of town that's home to crocodiles and capybaras. But Villavicencio is most famous for its hopping *discotecas*; **Los Capachos** (Carrera 48 No 17-87; www.loscapachos.com) is one of the largest and most well-known nightclubs in Colombia. The city is a good base for exploring the plains. Many *fincas* (farms) outside the city now offer lodging and horseback-riding tours.

About 100km east of Villavicencio on the Río Meta is the small town of **Puerto López**, the so-called 'belly button of Colombia.' A 30m tall **Alto de Menegua** obelisk marks the geographic center of Colombia.

Parque Nacional Natural (PNN) El Tuparro (www.parquesnacionales.gov.co) is a 548,000-hectare nature reserve on the Venezuelan border, and the only national park in Los Llanos. This biosphere of sandy river beaches and green grasslands is home to some 320 species of birds plus jaguars, tapirs and otters. Getting here won't be easy, but it could be very rewarding. **De Una Tours** (☎ 1 368 1915; www.deunacolombia.com; Carrera 26A No 40-18 Ap 202, La Soledad, Bogotá) in Bogotá organizes guided tours to Tuparro.

Off the beaten path, **Gaviotas** (www.friendsofgaviotas.org), about 100km southeast of Villavicencio, is a 'green' success story. The United Nations called the village a model of sustainable development, and Gabriel García Márquez called founder Paolo Lugari the 'inventor of the world.' The village of 200 people is operated on wind and solar power. Residents farm organically and have planted millions of trees. The town has become a world-class research and development center for green technologies and the commune-like society has no police, no mayor and no weapons. The village was profiled in journalist Alan Weisman's book, *Gaviotas: A Village to Reinvent the World*.

(around COP$1000, in either pesos or bolivares). You can catch *colectivos* and buses headed to San Antonio from the corner of Av Diagonal Santander and Calle 8, in the center. From San Antonio's bus terminal, there are six departures daily to Caracas, all departing late afternoon or early evening for an overnight trip. There are no direct buses to Mérida; go to San Cristóbal and change. *Colectivos* to San Cristóbal leave frequently.

VILLA DEL ROSARIO
☎ 7 / pop 52,000 / elev 280m

About 10km southeast of Cúcuta on the road to the Venezuelan border, is the sedate suburb of Villa del Rosario. Here, Colombia's founding fathers met in 1821 to draw up the constitution of the new country of Gran Colombia, and inaugurate Simón Bolívar as its first president.

Sights

The site of this important event in Colombia's history has been converted into a park, the **Parque de la Gran Colombia**. The park's central feature is the ruin of **Templo del Congreso**, the church (built in 1802) where the sessions of the congress were held. The congress debated in the

sacristy of the church from May to October, before agreeing on the final version of the bill. Then the inauguration ceremony of Bolívar and Santander as president and vice president of Gran Colombia took place in the church. The original church was almost completely destroyed by the 1875 earthquake and only the dome was rebuilt. A marble statue of Bolívar has been placed in the rebuilt part of the church.

The park's other major sight is the **Casa Natal de Santander** (☎ 570 0741; admission COP$1500; ☉ 9-11:30am & 2-5:30pm Mon-Fri), a large country mansion, which was the birthplace of Francisco de Paula Santander and his home for the first 13 years of his life. The house was also damaged by the earthquake of 1875 and restored in a partly altered style. It now houses a modest exhibition of documents and photos relating to Santander's life and to the congress.

Getting There & Away

To get to the Parque de la Gran Colombia from Cúcuta, take the bus to San Antonio del Táchira, which passes next to the park on the way to the border. Don't take buses marked 'Villa del Rosario' – they won't bring you anywhere near the park.

Caribbean Coast

Sun-soaked and stewed in culture, Colombia's 1760km of Caribbean coastline is home to both the country's best beaches and the highest coastal mountain range in the world, the Sierra Nevada de Santa Marta. Together they form the backbone of a diverse, African and pre-Columbian–influenced ethos that permeates everyday life here, giving the *costeños*, as locals are known, a distinct and contagious historical identity different from other Colombians ('lazy' and 'inefficient' are words often used around the rest of Colombia; we'll call it 'carefree' and 'unpredictable').

The area has long been Colombia's tourism bread and butter, drawing more domestic and international visitors than any other part of the country. The crown jewel along the coast is Cartagena, a colonial city with a beauty and romance unrivaled anywhere in Colombia. Under-renovation Santa Marta, the last stop for the legendary liberator Simón Bolívar, also offers a sense of history, but the real reason to visit is nearby Parque Nacional Natural (PNN) Tayrona, a wonderful stretch of preserved beach and virgin rainforest. By contrast, Ciudad Perdida (Lost City) is no picnic to reach, but the exhausting three-day trek has become a rite of passage for many travelers.

The lengthy coast covers a range of ecosystems, from the dense jungles of Darién Gap on the border with Panama in the southwest, to the barren desert of La Guajira near Venezuela in the northeast. Both of these areas are now safe for international tourism, and were both worth the wait. From the northernmost point of the continent at Punta Gallinas in La Guajira – the coast's most stunning landscape by a landslide – and the supremely relaxed beach towns of Capurganá and Sapzurro, these two remarkable areas still feel largely unexplored and poised to lead a tourism renaissance in the country.

HIGHLIGHTS

- Soak up the history as you stroll the colonial streets of sensual old town **Cartagena** (p138)
- Beach-hop from El Zaino to Calabazo through **Parque Nacional Natural Tayrona** (p173)
- Trek through thick Colombian jungle to the mysterious **Ciudad Perdida** (p177), the former pre-Columbian capital of the Tayrona people
- Traverse the feral seaside desertscape at **Punta Gallinas** (p183), South America's stunning northernmost point
- Straddle the Colombian–Panamanian border in the tranquil villages and excellent beaches around **Capurganá & Sapzurro** (p188)

Punta Gallinas
Parque Nacional Natural Tayrona
Cartagena
Ciudad Perdida
Capurganá & Sapzurro

CARIBBEAN COAST

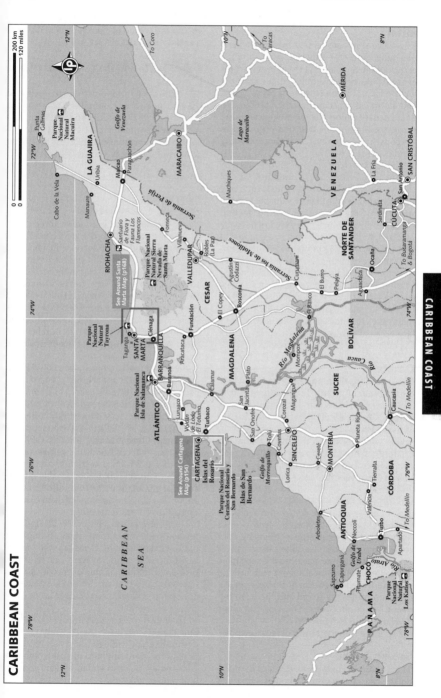

History

The Caribbean coast was inhabited by various indigenous communities long before the arrival of the Spaniards. Two of these groups evolved into highly developed cultures: the Tayrona in the Sierra Nevada de Santa Marta, and the Sinú in what are now the Córdoba and Sucre departments. The technological prowess of these people is best demonstrated in the construction of several villages, including Ciudad Perdida (p177).

The coast was the first region conquered by the Spaniards. Santa Marta (founded in 1525) and Cartagena (1533) are the oldest surviving Colombian cities. Both were valuable Spanish staging posts for missions to the interior and port towns from which plundered riches were sent back to the Old World. Inevitable wealth was accompanied by pirate raids and the entire coast, especially Cartagena, was under siege for most of its early settled existence.

After independence, the Caribbean coast continued to thrive economically, helped by the rise of industrial Barranquilla. Coal remains the current cash cow: Latin America's largest coal-mining operation is the El Cerrejón on the Guajira Peninsula.

Climate

It's so hot here, the homeless often beg not for money but for limeade. Temperatures usually hover around Hades, but the sopping wet humidity is the real killer. To beat the heat, do as the locals do and siesta from noon to 2pm, saving your strength for early morning and evening activities. October brings much rain, while December and January offer cool winds that make travel more pleasant.

Getting There & Away

There are several ways to approach the Caribbean coast. The easiest option is to fly to one of the main cities – there are even some direct flights to Cartagena from North America and Europe, negating the need to fly via Bogotá. You could also approach by land from Venezuela, Medellín or Bucaramanga – the main routes are paved and there are frequent bus connections. You can also come overland from Panama (p187).

For more transportation details, see p310.

Getting Around

The Caribbean coast is well serviced by an extensive coastal bus system, though sometimes you'll need to hop in a boat as well. For more transportation details, see p314.

CARTAGENA & AROUND

The capital of the Bolívar department and the crown jewel of Colombia, Cartagena (in addition to its raw beauty and historical significance) is a major port and the gateway to offshore destinations like the northern section of Parque Nacional Natural (PNN) Corales del Rosario y San Bernardo and sleepy down-shore towns like Mompox.

CARTAGENA

☎ 5 / pop 1 million / elev 2m

Cartagena de Indias is a tale of three cities, all dancing hand in hand in a ménage à trois of Latin juxtaposition. There is the fairy-tale city of romance, legends and sheer beauty, immaculately preserved within the impressive 13km of centuries-old colonial stonewalls. Here in Cartagena's old town, a Unesco World Heritage Site, where a maze of cobbled alleys slither below enormous balconies shrouded in bougainvillea and massive churches cast their shadows across plazas, it's difficult not to get lost in its charms.

But then there is the outer town, full of traffic, working-class bells and whistles, and a chaotic nature that can leave you dazed and confused in mere minutes. It is here where the Cartagena of broken dreams lives on, a workhouse South American city like any other. To the south, the peninsula of Bocagrande – Cartagena's Miami Beach – is where fashionable *cartagenos* sip coffee in trendy cafes, dine in glossy restaurants and live in upscale luxury condos that line the area like guardians to a New World. All three are worth taking in, but none of them could be more different from the other.

Cartagena is a place to drop all sightseeing routines. Instead, just stroll through the old town day and night. Soak up the sensual atmosphere, pausing to ward off the brutal heat and humidity in one of the city's many open-air cafes that sit, not unlike Venice, in enchanting colonial plazas hidden around one corner or another.

Holding its own against Brazil's Ouro Preto and Peru's Cuzco for the continent's most enthralling and righteously preserved colonial destinations, it's hard to walk away from Cartagena – it seizes you in its aged clutches and refuses to let go.

History

Cartagena was founded in 1533 by Pedro de Heredia on the site of the Carib settlement of Calamari. It quickly grew into a rich town, but in 1552 an extensive fire destroyed a large number of its wooden buildings. Since that time, only stone, brick and tile have been permitted as building materials.

Within a short time the town blossomed into the main Spanish port on the Caribbean coast and the major northern gateway to South America. It came to be the storehouse for the treasure plundered from the local population until the galleons could ship it back to Spain. As such, it became a tempting target for all sorts of buccaneers operating on the Caribbean Sea.

In the 16th century alone, Cartagena suffered five sieges by pirates, the most famous (or infamous) of which was that led by Sir Francis Drake. He sacked the port in 1586 and 'mercifully' agreed not to level the town once he was presented with a huge ransom of 10 million pesos, which he shipped back to England.

It was in response to pirate attacks that the Spaniards built up a series of forts around the town, saving it from subsequent sieges, particularly from the biggest attack of all, led by Edward Vernon in 1741. Blas de Lezo, a Spanish officer who had already lost an arm, a leg and an eye in previous battles, commanded the successful defense. With only 2500 poorly trained and ill-equipped men, don Blas managed to fend off 25,000 English soldiers and their fleet of 186 ships. The Spaniard lost his other leg in the fighting and died soon after, but is now regarded as the savior of Cartagena – you can see his statue outside the San Felipe Fortress (p145).

In spite of the high price it had to pay for the pirate attacks, Cartagena continued to flourish. The Canal del Dique, constructed in 1650 to connect Cartagena Bay with the Río Magdalena, made the town the main gateway for ships heading to ports upriver, and a large part of the merchandise shipped inland passed through Cartagena. During the colonial period, Cartagena was the most important bastion of the Spanish overseas empire and influenced much of Colombia's history.

The indomitable spirit of the inhabitants was rekindled again at the time of the independence movement. Cartagena was one of the first towns to proclaim independence from Spain, early in 1810, which prompted Bogotá and other cities to do the same. The declaration was signed on November 11, 1811, but the city paid dearly for it. In 1815, Spanish forces under Pablo Morillo were sent to reconquer and 'pacify' the town and took it after a four-month siege. More than 6000 inhabitants died of starvation and disease.

In August 1819, Simón Bolívar's troops defeated the Spaniards at Boyacá, bringing freedom to Bogotá. However, Cartagena had to wait for liberation until October 1821, when the patriot forces eventually took the city by sea. It was Bolívar who gave Cartagena its well-deserved name of 'La Heroica,' the Heroic City.

Cartagena began to recover and was once again an important trading and shipping center. The city's prosperity attracted foreign immigrants, and many Jews, Italians, French, Turks, Lebanese and Syrians settled here. Today their descendants own many businesses, including hotels and restaurants.

Climate

Cartagena's climate is typically Caribbean; its average annual temperature of 30°C changes very little. Although the days are hot, a fresh breeze blows in the evening, making this a pleasant time to stroll around the city. Theoretically, the driest period is from December to April, while October and November are the wettest months.

Orientation

The heart of the city is the old town, built in two sections, an inner and outer town. Both were surrounded by walls and separated from each other by a channel, the Caño de San Anastasio. The channel was filled in to make way for the construction of the sharp, wedge-shaped, modern district, La Matuna.

The inner walled town consists of El Centro in the west, where traditionally the upper classes lived, and San Diego in the northeast, previously occupied by the middle classes. The outer walled town, Getsemaní, is smaller and poorer, with more modest architecture. Outside the walled town are several monumental fortresses.

Stretching south of the old town is an unusual, L-shaped peninsula, occupied by three districts: Bocagrande, Castillo Grande and El Laguito. This area is packed with top-class hotels, restaurants and nightspots, and is the main destination for moneyed Colombians and international charter tours. Those on smaller budgets, however, prefer to stay in the historic part of town.

Information

BOOKSTORES

Ábaco (☎ 664 8338; cnr Calles de la Iglesia & de la Mantilla No 3-86; ⏰ 9am-8:30pm Mon-Sat, 4-8:30pm Sun) A good selection of books on Cartagena and a few English-language choices. There's also Italian beer and Spanish wine!

INTERNET ACCESS

Most of the listed places are open seven days a week and offer air conditioning – more important than speed in this town.

Contact Internet Café (☎ 664 0681; Calle de la Media Luna No 10-20; per hr COP$1000; ⏰ 8am-9pm)

Micronet (☎ 664 0328; Calle de la Estrella No 4-47; per hr COP$1500; ⏰ 9am-9pm Mon-Fri, to 6pm Sat)

MONEY

There is a wealth of deft street 'moneychangers' fluttering around Cartagena offering fantastic rates to relieve you of your euros or dollars. Don't be fooled. Unless you're the proud owner of a PhD in mathematics and can trick them at their own game, steer clear – *casas de cambio* (currency exchanges) and banks are ubiquitous in the historic center, especially around Plaza de los Coches and Plaza de la Aduana.

Banco de Bogotá (Av Venezuela, Centro Comercial Uno No 105-107; ⏰ 8am-11:30am & 2-4pm Mon-Fri, 8-11:30am & 2-4:30pm Sat)

Citibank (Av Venezuela, Edificio Citibank, piso 1; ⏰ 8am-noon & 2-4:30pm Mon-Fri)

Davivienda (cnr Av Venezuela & Carrera 9) ATM.

Giros y Finanzas (Av Venezuela No 8A-87; ⏰ 8am-5pm Mon-Fri, to 1pm Sat) This *casa de cambio* in the old town represents Western Union.

POST

Deprisa (☎ 664 7822; Av Venezuela, Centro Edificio Citibank, local B1; ⏰ 8am-12:30pm & 2-6pm Mon-Fri, 8am-1pm Sat)

TOURIST INFORMATION

Tourist office (Turismo Cartagena de Indias; ☎ 660 1583; www.turismocartagenadeindias.com; Plaza de la Aduana; ⏰ 9am-1pm & 3-7pm Mon-Sat, 9am-5pm Sun) The main tourist office is situated in Plaza de la Aduana. There are also small booths in Plaza de San Pedro Claver and Plaza de los Coches as well as the administrative offices at Muelle Turístico.

TRAVEL AGENCIES

Aventure Colombia (☎ 314 588 2378; www.aventure colombia.com; Calle del Santíssimo No 8-55; ⏰ 9am-noon & 2-7pm Mon-Thu, 9am-7pm Fri & Sat) This friendly French-Colombian outfit offers excursions throughout Cartagena and the coast, including La Guajira, Tayrona and upscale sailing trips to Panama.

VISA INFORMATION

DAS (☎ 666 0172; Carrera 20B No 29-18, Pie de la Popa; ⏰ 8am-noon & 2-5pm) Immigration and visa extensions; about 1km east of the old town.

Panamanian consulate (☎ 655 1055; Carrera 1 No 10-10, Bocagrande; ⏰ 8am-noon Mon-Sat) Located 2km from the old town.

Venezuelan consulate (☎ 665 0382; Carrera 3 No 8-129, Edificio Centro Executivo, piso 14; ⏰ 9-11:30am & 1:30-4pm Mon-Fri)

Dangers & Annoyances

Cartagena's the safest metropolis in Colombia – some 2000 police officers patrol the old city alone. That said, stay alert at night in less populated areas like Getsemaní, although you are more likely to be irritated by peddlers than become a victim of any crime. Aggressive hassling in the streets by unofficial vendors pushing everything from typical tourist wares to women to cocaine is definitely the No 1 nuisance here. A simple '*No quiero nada*,' or the old Latin American finger shake-off should shoo them off.

Sights

OLD TOWN

Without a doubt, Cartagena's old city is its principal attraction, particularly the inner walled town consisting of the historical districts of El Centro and San Diego. It is a real gem of colonial architecture, packed with churches, monasteries, plazas, palaces and mansions with their overhanging balconies and shady patios.

Getsemaní, the outer walled town, is less impressive but has some charming places and is worth exploring. It is less tourist-oriented, but houses the main concentration of budget accommodations and much of the good nightlife.

The old town is surrounded by **Las Murallas**, the thick walls built to protect it against enemies. Construction began towards the end of the 16th century, after the attack by Francis Drake; until that time Cartagena was almost completely unprotected. The project took two centuries to complete due to repeated damage from both storms and pirate attacks. It was finally finished in 1796, just 25 years before the Spaniards were eventually expelled.

Las Murallas are an outstanding piece of military engineering remarkably well preserved, except for a part of the walls facing La Matuna, which were unfortunately demolished by 'progressive' city authorities in the mid-20th century.

The best approach to experiencing the old town is to wander leisurely, savoring the architectural details, street life and local snacks along the way. Don't just seek out the sights detailed here – there are many other interesting places that you will find while walking around.

The following attractions have been listed in sequence to conveniently connect them in a walking tour.

Muelle Turístico de los Pegasos
This beautiful **walkway** bridges Getsemaní with the old town.

Puerta del Reloj
Originally called the Boca del Puente, this was the main **gateway** to the inner walled town and was linked to Getsemaní by a drawbridge over the moat. The side arches of the gate, which are now open as walkways, were previously used as a chapel and armory. The republican-style tower, complete with a four-sided clock, was added in 1888.

Plaza de los Coches
Previously known as Plaza de la Yerba, the triangular plaza just behind Puerta del Reloj was once used as a slave market. It is lined with old balconied houses with colonial arches at ground level. The arcaded walkway, known as El Portal de los Dulces, is today lined with confectionery stands selling local sweets. The statue of the city's founder, Pedro de Heredia, is in the middle of the plaza.

Plaza de la Aduana
This is the largest and oldest square in the old town and was used as a parade ground. In colonial times, all the important governmental and administrative buildings were here. The old Royal Customs House was restored and is now the City Hall. A statue of Christopher Columbus stands in the center of the square.

Museo de Arte Moderno
The **Museum of Modern Art** (☎ 664 5815; Plaza de San Pedro Claver; adult/child COP$3000/2000; ☺ 9am-noon & 3-6pm Mon-Thu, 9am-noon & 3-7pm Fri, 10am-1pm Sat) is the perfect sized museum (not too huge to overwhelm), housed in a part of the 17th century former Royal Customs House. It presents temporary exhibitions from its own collection, including works by Alejandro Obregón, one of Colombia's most remarkable painters, who was born in Cartagena. There's also sculpture and abstract art – all well worth a look. The second floor houses temporary exhibitions.

Convento & Iglesia de San Pedro Claver
The **convent** was founded by Jesuits in the first half of the 17th century, originally as San Ignacio de Loyola. The name was later changed in honor of Spanish-born monk Pedro Claver (1580–1654), who lived and died in the convent. Called the 'Apostle of the Blacks' or the 'Slave of the Slaves,' he spent all his life ministering to the slaves brought from Africa. He was the first person to be canonized in the New World (in 1888).

The convent is a monumental three-story building surrounding a tree-filled courtyard, and part of it is open as a **museum** (☎ 664 4991; Plaza de San Pedro Claver; adult/child COP$6000/4000; ☺ 8am-5pm Mon-Sat, to 4:30pm Sun). Exhibits include religious art and pre-Columbian ceramics as well as a new section devoted to Afro-Caribbean contemporary pieces like wonderful Haitian paintings and African masks. You can visit the cell where San Pedro Claver lived and died, and also climb a narrow staircase to the choir loft of the adjacent **church** (☎ 664 7256). Guides, should you need one, are waiting by the ticket office and charge COP$10,000/12,000 for a Spanish/English tour for a group of up to seven people. Iglesia de San Pedro Claver was completed in the first half of the 18th century. The church has an imposing stone facade and inside, there are fine stained-glass windows and a high altar made of Italian marble. The remains of San Pedro Claver are kept in a glass coffin in the altar. His skull is visible, making this an alter with a difference.

Museo Naval del Caribe
Opened in 1992 on the 500th anniversary of Columbus' discovery of the New World, the **Naval Museum** (☎ 664 2440; Calle San Juan de

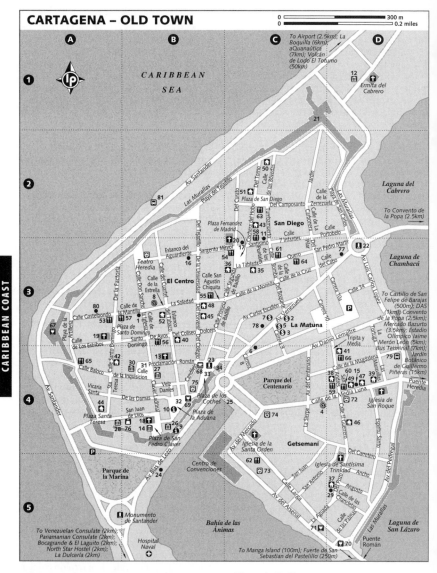

CARTAGENA – OLD TOWN

Dios No 3-62; adult/child COP$6000/3000; 9am-7pm) occupies a great colonial building, once a Jesuit college. It features, for the most part, a grand collection of reconstructed cityscapes and boat models from throughout the centuries, but woefully lacks much in the way of actual artifacts (though there are some nice torpedoes).

Plaza de Bolívar

Formerly the Plaza de Inquisición, this leafy and shaded **plaza**, surrounded by some of the city's most elegant balconied colonial buildings, offers wonderful respite from the Caribbean heat. As expected, a statue of Simón Bolívar stands in the middle of the plaza.

Palacio de la Inquisición

The haunting **Palace of the Inquisition** is one of the finest buildings in town. Although the site was the seat of the Punishment Tribunal of the Holy Office from 1610, the palace wasn't completed until 1776. It is a good example of late-colonial architecture, noted particularly for its magnificent baroque stone gateway topped by the Spanish coat of arms, and the long balconies on the facade.

On the side wall, just around the corner from the entrance, you'll find a small window with a cross on top. Heretics were denounced here, and the Holy Office would then instigate proceedings. The principal 'crimes' were magic, witchcraft and blasphemy. When culprits were found guilty they were sentenced to death in a public auto-da-fé. Five autos-da-fé took place during the Inquisition until independence in 1821. About 800 folk were condemned to death and executed. The Inquisition did not judge the indigenous people.

The palace is today a **museum** (☎ 664 4570; Plaza de Bolívar; adult/child COP$10,000/7000; 9am-6pm Mon-Sat, 10am-4pm Sun), which displays the Inquisitors' gnarly instruments of torture (a scary sight but by far the most fascinating

thing here), pre-Columbian pottery and historical objects dating from both colonial and independence times, including arms, paintings, furniture and church bells. There is also a good model of Cartagena from the beginning of the 19th century and an interesting collection of old maps of the Nuevo Reino de Granada from various periods. There are not, unfortunately, English translations, but guides (COP$15,000/20,000 for Spanish/English) are available should you be so inclined.

Museo del Oro y Arqueología

The **Cartagena Gold Museum** (☎ 660 0778; Plaza de Bolívar; admission free; 10am-1pm & 3-7pm Tue-Fri, 10am-1pm & 2-5pm Sat, 11am-4pm Sun) is like a miniature version of Bogotá's world-class gold museum (p77). Though small, it offers a fascinating collection of gold and pottery of the Sinú (also known as Zenú) people, who inhabited the region of the present-day departments of Bolívar, Córdoba, Sucre and northern Antioquia before the Spanish Conquest. The detail of some pieces are exquisite and should you be heading towards Bogotá, offers just a taste of the bigger and grander museum there.

Catedral

Work on the **Cathedral** (adult/child COP$10,000/7000; 9:30am-6:30pm Tue-Sun) began in 1575, but in 1586, while still under construction, it was partially destroyed by the cannons of Francis Drake, and not completed until 1612. Alterations were made between 1912 and 1923 by the first archbishop of Cartagena, who covered the church with stucco and painted it to look like marble. He commissioned the dome on the tower. Restoration work has uncovered the lovely limestone on the building's exterior. Apart from the tower's top, the church has basically preserved its original form. It has a fortlike appearance and a simply decorated interior with three naves and massive semicircular archways supported on high, stone columns. The main retable, worked in gold leaf, dates from the 18th century.

Like Iglesia de Santo Domingo (below), you can now take a self-guided audio tour that lasts about 25 minutes.

Iglesia de Santo Domingo

The **Santo Domingo Church** (☎ 664 1301; Plaza de Santo Domingo; adult/child COP$10,000/7000; 9am-7pm Tue-Sat, noon-8pm Sun) built toward the end of the 16th century, is reputedly the oldest church in the city. It was originally built in 1539 in Plaza de los Coches, but the original building succumbed to fire and was rebuilt in its present location in 1552. Builders gave it a particularly wide central nave and covered it with a heavy roof, but it seems they were not too good at their calculations and the vault began to crack. Massive buttresses had to be added to the walls to support the structure and prevent it from collapsing. The builders also had problems with the bell tower, which is distinctly crooked.

The interior is spacious and lofty. The legendary figure of Christ carved in wood is set in the baroque altar at the head of the right-hand aisle. The floor in front of the high altar and in the two aisles is paved with old tombstones dating mostly from the 19th century.

The church was previously only open during mass, but you can now take a 20-minute self-guided audio tour.

Iglesia de Santo Toribio de Mangrovejo

Compared with the others, this **church** is relatively small. It was erected between 1666 and 1732 and its ceiling is covered with Mudejar paneling. During Vernon's attack on the city in 1741, a cannon ball went through a window into the church when it was filled with worshipers, but fortunately there were no casualties. The ball is now on display in a glassed niche in the left wall.

Las Bóvedas

These are 23 **dungeons** built between 1792 and 1796 in the city walls, which are more than 15m thick in this part. These dungeons were the last major construction carried out in colonial times and were destined for military purposes. The vaults were used by the Spaniards as storerooms for munitions and provisions. Later, during the republican era, they were turned into a jail. Today they house craft and souvenir shops.

Casa de Rafael Núñez

This **mansion**, just outside the walls of Las Bóvedas, was the home of the former president, lawyer and poet, Rafael Núñez. He wrote the words of Colombia's national anthem and was one of the authors of the constitution of 1886, which was in force (with some later changes) until 1991. The wooden mansion is now a **museum** (☎ 664 5305; adult/child COP$4000/2000; 9am-5:30pm Tue-Fri, 10am-5:30pm Sat, 10am-4pm Sun) featuring some of Núñez' documents and personal possessions. The chapel opposite the house, known as the Ermita del Cabrero, holds his ashes.

Monumento a la India Catalina

The **monument** at the main entrance to the old town from the mainland is a tribute to the Carib people, the group that inhabited this land before the Spanish Conquest. The lovely bronze statue depicts Catalina, a beautiful Carib woman who served as interpreter to Pedro de Heredia upon the arrival of the Spaniards. The statue was forged in 1974 by Eladio Gil, a Spanish sculptor living in Cartagena.

Muelle Turistíco de la Bodeguita

Often incorrectly referred to as Pegasos (given the close location of the two sites), this is the **old port** of Cartagena on the Bahía de las Ánimas. Not much goes on here now other than the departure of tourist boats to Playa Blanca and Isla del Rosario. The new harbor where big ships dock is on Manga Island.

SPANISH FORTS

The old city is a fortress in itself, yet there are more fortifications built at strategic points outside the city. Some of the more important ones are listed here.

Castillo de San Felipe de Barajas

The **castillo** (☎ 666 4790; Av Arévalo; adult/child COP$13,000/7000; ☺ 8am-6pm) is the greatest and strongest fortress ever built by the Spaniards in any of their colonies. The original fort was commissioned in 1630 and was quite small. Construction began in 1657 on top of the 40m-high San Lázaro hill. In 1762, an extensive enlargement was undertaken, which resulted in the entire hill being covered over with this powerful bastion. It was truly impregnable and was never taken, despite numerous attempts to storm it.

A complex system of tunnels connected strategic points of the fortress to distribute provisions and to facilitate evacuation. The tunnels were constructed in such a way that sounds reverberated all the way along them, making it possible to hear the slightest sound of the approaching enemy's feet, and also making it easy for internal communication.

Some of the tunnels are lit and are open to visitors – an eerie walk not to be missed. Take a guide (COP$15,000/25,000 Spanish/English) if you want to learn more about the curious inventions of Antonio de Arévalo, the military engineer who directed the construction of the fortress.

The fortress is a 20-minute walk from the old town, or take a local bus from the Parque del Centenario. A taxi costs COP$5000. Entrance is free the last Sunday of every month between February and November.

Fuerte de San Sebastián del Pastelillo

This **fort**, on the western end of Manga Island, was constructed in the middle of the 16th century as one of the town's first defense posts. It's quite small and not particularly inspiring, but it's quite close to the old town – just across the bridge from Getsemaní. Today the fort is home to the Club de Pesca, which has a marina where local and foreign boats anchor.

CONVENTO DE LA POPA

On a 150m-high hill, the highest point in the city, about 2km beyond Castillo de San Felipe de Barajas is this **convent** (☎ 666 2331; adult/child COP$6000/4000; ☺ 9am-5pm). Its name literally means the Convent of the Stern, after the hill's apparent similarity to a ship's back end, but it's actually the Convento de Nuestra Señora de la Candelaria, founded by the Augustine fathers in 1607. Initially it was just a small wooden chapel, which was replaced by a stouter construction when the hill was fortified two centuries later, just before Pablo Morillo's siege.

A beautiful image of La Virgen de la Candelaria, the patroness of the city, is in the convent's chapel, and there's a charming flower-filled patio. There is also a chilling statue of a speared Padre Alonso García de Paredas straight out of *The Omen*. The priest was murdered along with five Spanish soldiers for trying to spread the good word.

The views from here are outstanding and stretch all over the city. The patron saint's day is February 2 (see p146).

There is a zigzagging access road leading up to the convent (no public transport) and paths cutting the bends of the road. It takes 30 minutes to walk to the top, but it's not recommended for safety reasons and climatic reasons – walking up would be equivalent to a trek in the Mojave! Instead go by taxi, though rates vary wildly (COP$12,000 at one end of the spectrum and as high as COP$40,000!).

MERCADO BAZURTO

For adventurous souls only, Cartagena's labyrinthine central **market** (Av Pedro de Heredia; ☺ 24hr) is both dirty and enthralling, an all-out assault on your senses. If it's marketable, it's for sale here: endless stalls of fruits and vegetables, meat, fish and plenty of options to grab a quick bite or juice up on a chilled beverage. If you can find it, look for Cecilia's restaurant, which sometimes serves up river turtle, shark and cow's tongue (it's located in the area known as Pescado Frito – ask and people can direct you). You won't likely buy anything here, but it's a fascinating glimpse into the daily lives of real *cartagenos*. Don't wear flashy jewelry and pay attention to your camera and wallet, but otherwise grab a taxi (COP$5000 from the old town) and explore away.

Activities

Cartagena has grown into an important scuba-diving center, taking advantage of the extensive coral reefs along its coast. La Boquilla, just outside town, is also popular for kitesurfing.

CARIBBEAN COAST

aQuanáutica (☎ 656 8243; www.kitesurfcolombia
.com; Hotel Las Americas, Cielo Mar) Kitesurfing school.

Cultura del Mar (☎ 664 9312; www.culturadelmar
.com; Calle de la Media Luna No 10-43, Getsemaní) Offers
scuba, snorkeling and an interesting overnight ecotourism
option to Isla del Rosario (p153)

Diving Planet (☎ 664 2171; www.divingplanet.org;
Calle Estanco del Aguardiente No 5-94) Offers PADI-
certification course (COP$770,000).

Dolphin Dive School (☎ 660 0814; www.dolphin
diveschool.com; cnr Parque Fernández Madrid & Calle
Curato, San Diego; 7:30am-7pm Mon-Sat, 2-7pm Sun)
Offers a PADI-certification course (COP$790,000).

Courses

Amaury Martelo (☎ 313 526 3910; www.oceanfamily
.net/Spanish; per hr COP$23,000; 9am-9pm Mon-Fri,
to 6pm Sat) A recommended tutor for private Spanish
lessons.

Nueva Lengua (☎ 660 1736; www.nuevalengua.com;
Calle del Pozo No 25-95, Getsemaní) Five-day minimum
language courses at this casual school start at COP$413,379.

Tours

City tours in a *chiva* (a colorful, traditional
bus) depart daily at 2pm from various hotels
in upscale Bocagrande. The four-hour tour
includes rides around Bocagrande, Castillo
Grande and a walking tour of the walled
city, plus visits to the Convento de la Popa
(p145) and Castillo de San Felipe de Barajas
(p145). Any travel agency can book this for
you, but you'll need to find your own way to
Bocagrande for the pickup point. By taxi, it's
COP$5000 from the old town.

You can also take a city tour in a horse-drawn
carriage, which gives a glance of Bocagrande
and the walled city. The carriages start gathering at the corner of Av San Martín and Calle 4
in Bocagrande around 4pm to 5pm and depart
from there up until midnight. A one-hour tour
that takes in the waterfront to the old town
costs from COP$40,000 to COP$45,000. After
a run around the main streets of the walled city
they return via either Av San Martín or the
waterfront, whichever you prefer. There are
also nighttime tours (p150), which are more a
party parade than a sightseeing tour.

For tours to Isla del Rosario, see p152; for
Volcán de Lodo El Totumo, see p155.

Festivals & Events

Feria Taurina (Jan) The bullfighting season takes place
at the bullring on Av Pedro de Heredia during the first
week of the year.

Fiesta de Nuestra Señora de la Candelaria (Feb 2)
The day of Cartagena's patron saint. A solemn procession is
held on that day at the Convento de la Popa (p145), during
which the faithful carry lit candles. Celebrations begin nine
days earlier, the so-called Novenas, when pilgrims flock to
the convent.

Reinado Nacional de Belleza (Nov) The national
beauty pageant celebrates Cartagena's independence day.
Miss Colombia, the beauty queen, is elected on November
11, the high point of the event. The fiesta, which includes
street dancing, music and fancy-dress parades, strikes up
several days before the pageant and the city goes wild.
The event, also known as the Carnaval de Cartagena or
Fiestas del 11 de Noviembre, is the city's most important
annual bash.

Sleeping

Cartagena has a reasonable choice of accommodations and, despite its touristy status, the
prices of its hotels remain reasonable compared to other large cities. The tourist peak is
from late December to late January but, even
then, it's relatively easy to find a room.

Most travelers stay within the walled
city. In this area, Getsemaní is the principal area of budget accommodations, while El
Centro and San Diego shelter the old city's
top-end hotels.

BUDGET

Budget travelers will find several choices in
the Getsemaní area, especially on Calle de
la Media Luna. Many are dives but there are
a few clean and safe options. The area has
cleaned up its act of late (we said its *act*, not
its streets, mind you) and is generally safe to
walk around at night.

Hotel Holiday (☎ 664 0948; www.holidayhostelcaribe
.com; Calle de la Media Luna No 10-47, Getsemaní; dm/s/d
COP$15,000/20,000/30,000) The long, narrow court-
yard here is the gathering place for a sociable
crowd that surely must mind the incredibly
unmemorable rooms, but digs the lesser dent
a stay makes to their bank accounts.

North Star Hostel (☎ 655 0241; Carrera 3 No 8-96,
Bocagrande; dm COP$15,000-20,000;) As cheap as
it gets in Bocagrande, this newer hostel offers
hotel-level kitchens and bathrooms and nice
air-conditioned dorms on a bustling street on
the peninsula. It's near plenty of great restaurants, just two blocks from the beach, and a
quick COP$1000 bus ride to the old town.

Casa Viena (☎ 664 6242; www.casaviena.com; Calle
San Andrés No 30-53, Getsemaní; dm with air-con COP$15,000,
d with/without bathroom COP$40,000/32,000;) This

longtime Austrian-run staple is on a rowdy street in Getsemaní. There's a helpful staff of Colombians who don't speak English, but charm their point across. The dorm is cramped but wonderfully cold, and the freebies here are considerable (internet, coffee – even local calls), but it must be said you are sacrificing somewhat here on comfort and price in exchange for camaraderie and information. The reluctance to accept reservations is highly irritating.

Hotel Familiar (☎ 664 2464; Calle El Guerrero No 29-66, Getsemaní; s COP$17,000, d from COP$32,000) Another no-frills Getsemaní option that offers a little more peace and quiet than other budget joints. The mazelike second floor is interesting and some of the rooms have massive bathrooms.

Hotel Marlin (☎ 664 3507; www.hotelmarlincartagena col.com; Calle de la Media Luna No 10-35, Getsemaní; s/d with fan COP$25,000/35,000, with air-con COP$40,000/50,000; 🖳 🗷) Tall folks won't be happy here (nor will interior designers with those faux brick walls), but this basic haunt has nice common areas, a laundry and kitchen facilities. Some travelers have reported it's damp.

Hostal La Casona (☎ 664 1301; Calle Tripita y Media No 31-32, Getsemaní; s/d without air-con COP$28,000/42,000, with air-con COP$33,000/49,000; 🗷) This good-value hotel has a wonderful lush courtyard to compensate for its basic but perfectly decent rooms. Very gaudy art, though.

Hotel Las Vegas (☎ 664 5619; Calle San Agustín No 6-08, El Centro; s/d without air-con COP$40,000/50,000, r with air-con COP$60,000; 🗷) Cramped but clean, this totally unremarkable hotel offers a good location-to-value ratio. The doubles with balconies are best, but also the noisiest.

Hotel El Viajero (☎ 664 3289; Calle del Porvenir No 35-68, El Centro; s/d without air-con COP$40,000/60,000, with air-con COP$50,000/70,000; 🖳 🗷) The beds are noticeably stiff, but this is otherwise a perfectly decent place with a nice courtyard and a kitchen for guest use.

MIDRANGE

Casa Villa Colonial (☎ 664 5421; Calle de la Media Luna No 10-89, Getsemaní; s/d with air-con COP$60,000/80,000; 🗷 🖳) Run by the same family that runs the cheaper Hotel Villa Colonial around the corner, this newer and nicer option offers small touches – like colorful bedspreads and plenty of exposed brick –not often seen in Cartagena hotels under COP$100,000. There is a small kitchen for guest use.

Hostal Santo Domingo (☎ 664 2268; Calle Santo Domingo No 33-46, El Centro; r without/with air-con COP$76,700/96,700; 🗷) On a lovely street in El Centro, this place offers slightly more color and pizzazz over some of the ubiquitous basic choices (and we do mean slightly).

Centro Hotel (☎ 664 0461; www.centrohotelcartagena .com; Calle del Arzobispado No 34-80, El Centro; s/d incl breakfast from COP$107,000/134,000; 🖳 🗷) The simple but clean Centro Hotel is perfectly located just steps from Plaza de Bolívar. Well-maintained rooms are arranged around an open courtyard and some offer balcony-type windows that open out onto a narrow ledge over the street.

Casa Relax (☎ 664 1117; Calle del Pozo No 29B-119, Getsemaní; r incl breakfast from COP$130,000; 🖳 🗷 🖳) A good spot to soak up some restored colonial atmosphere without taking out a second mortgage. Run by a pipe-smoking French gentleman, this is Getsemaní's best, with a large pool and colorful rooms with arched bathrooms. Breakfast is excellent. There are charming parrots as well, one of which likes to take a dip in the pool!

Hostal Tres Banderas (☎ 660 0160; www.hotel3 banderas.com; Calle Cochera del Hobo No 38-66, San Diego; r incl breakfast from COP$139,000; 🗷 🖳) This French-Canadian hotel offers pleasant common areas with a relaxing faux waterfall and scattered coconut trees. For an extra COP$10,000, higher floor rooms offer nice balconies but smaller bathrooms; rooms on the ground floor have larger bathrooms but obviously no balcony.

TOP END

Casa La Fe (☎ 664 0306; www.casalafe.com; Calle Segunda de Badillo No 36-125, San Diego; r incl breakfast from COP$200,000; 🖳 🗷) A British-Colombian tag team run this discerning boutique B&B decorated with (tasteful) religious art. Breakfast can be taken in the jungly interior courtyard and the rooftop Jacuzzi is quaint. Higher price rooms offer balconies overlooking Plaza Fernandez de Madrid.

Bantú (☎ 664 3362; www.bantuhotel.com; Calle de la Tablada No 7-62, San Diego; s/d incl breakfast from COP$220,000/265,000; 🗷 🖳 🖳) Two wonderfully restored 15th-century homes make up this lovely 22-room, open-air boutique hotel, rife with exposed brick archways, original stone walls and lush vegetation. Smartly-appointed rooms are full of local artistic touches and were built with *mucho* respect for the historical structure at large. There's a rooftop pool, shower and Jacuzzi as well.

CARIBBEAN COAST

Hotel Sofitel Santa Clara (☎ 664 6070; www
.hotelsantaclara.com; Plaza de San Diego, San Diego; r from
COP$420,000; P ⊠ 🖳 🕿) The original details
preserved in this 17th-century gem are exquisite. The entire hotel was built within the
walls of a convent and the former cloister
now forms massive hallways that surround
the gorgeous interior walls and open-air
courtyard. There is a crypt you can descend
into in the middle of the trendy bar, and little things like original cannonballs (used as
doorstops) and oratories throughout elevate
this choice to a level not reached elsewhere
in the old town.

ourpick La Passion (☎ 664 8605; www.lapassion
hotel.com; Calle Estanco del Tabaco No 35-81, El Centro;
s/d from COP$390,000/540,000; ⊠ 🖳 🕿) Perhaps
what is the most discreet hotel entrance
in town leads to this hidden gem, run by a
French movie producer and his Colombian
partner. The republican-style home dating to the early 17th century features eight
uniquely decorated rooms and a potpourri
of international design touches (Fez, Greece,
Tlaquepaque) offset by modern indigenous
photographs. Some rooms feature Roman
baths and outdoor showers, but the true gem
here is the Santorini-reminiscent pool and
rooftop terrace with front row views of the
Cathedral.

Hotel Charleston Cartagena (☎ 664 9494; www
.hotelescharleston.com; Plaza Santa Teresa, El Centro; r from
COP$720,000; ⊠ 🖳 🕿) The rooms at this former
Convento de Santa Teresa rise up from two
historic courtyards draped in bougainvillea.
Colorful rooms are large and some offer sea
views. In addition to the rooftop pool, fitness
center and restaurants, it's recently added a
new spa.

Eating
Plenty of snack bars all across the old town
serve typical local snacks such as *arepas de
huevo* (fried maize dough with an egg inside),
dedos de queso (deep-fried cheese sticks), empanadas (meat and/or cheese pastries) and
buñuelos (deep-fried maize and cheese balls).

Try typical local sweets at confectionery
stands lining El Portal de los Dulces on the
Plaza de los Coches (p141).

In restaurants, you'll often see the ubiquitous *arroz con coco* (rice sweetened with
coconut) as an accompaniment to most
fish and meat dishes. It's addictive – you'll
miss it when you're gone. Fruit stalls are

also everywhere (often with tropical fruit
looking so ripe and colorful, you'd swear it
was photoshopped).

Part of the charm of eating in Cartagena
is just wandering the various plazas and seeing what strikes your fancy. Plaza Santo de
Domingo and Plaza de San Diego are both
popular options for atmospheric plaza dining
and people-watching, though the former is
way more touristy – the waitresses practically beg you to chose their cafe over the one
next door, promising, *'Es diferente!'* when you
know it probably isn't.

BUDGET
Bocaditos Madrid (☎ 664 6021; Calle Segundo de Badillo
No 36-171, San Diego; set meal COP$4500; 🕑 breakfast &
lunch Mon-Sat) This working-class lunch counter
is a great place to try homey local food at
rock bottom prices. There's no menu, just a
few daily changing options like chicken with
maracuyá (passion fruit).

Gato Negro (☎ 660 0958; Calle San Andrés No
30-39, Getsemaní; mains COP$5000-6000; 🕑 breakfast
& lunch) This new German-run option con-
centrates on breakfast – omelettes, Nutella
crepes, muesli – and offers a set COP$5000
lunch as well. There's also wi-fi, a rarity for
whatever reason.

La Mulata Cartagena (☎ 664 6222; Calle Quero No 9-
58, El Centro; set meal COP$6000-7000; 🕑 lunch) This styl-
ish *comida corriente* (set lunch) option is both
outstanding and cheap. A daily set menu offers
a handful of excellent choices and *aguas fres-
cas* (fresh juices) in an atmosphere entirely too
hip for the price. It's arguably the best value
in Cartagena. There's no sign outside – it's
under the Defensoría del Pueblo.

Several simple restaurants in Getsemaní
serve set meals for around COP$6000 to
COP$12,000. They include **Restaurante
Coroncoro** (☎ 664 2648; Calle Tripita y Media No 31-28,
Getsemaní; 🕑 breakfast, lunch & dinner) and **Getsemaní
Café** (☎ 317 781 5694; Calle San Andrés No 30-34, Getsemaní;
🕑 breakfast, lunch & dinner). In San Diego, **Girasoles**
(☎ 664 5239; Calle de los Puntales 37-01, San Diego; set meals
COP$5000; 🕑 breakfast & lunch), a veggie restaurant
and health food store, does a set menu of
PETA-friendly options that changes daily.

MIDRANGE & TOP END
El Bistro (☎ 664 1799; Calle de Ayos No 4-46, El Centro;
sandwiches from COP$9000, mains COP$10,500-19,500;
🕑 lunch & dinner Mon-Sat) This casual, German-
run restaurant serves up a daily-changing

chalkboard menu of Euro bistro fare accompanied by German bread prepared in-house and Erdinger served in proper ½L glassware. It's hip without trying too hard, and the food is quite good.

BrianZola (☎ 664 2564; cnr Calle San Agustín Chiquita & Calle de la Universidad, El Centro; pizza COP$10,000-19,000, ice cream from COP$4500; ⏰ breakfast, lunch & dinner) This is the spot to cool off with Italian gelato in a plethora of exotic Colombian flavors like *mora* (blackberry), *arequipe* (milk caramel), *zapote* (a type of red avocado) and *guanábara* (soursop). It also does recommendable pizzas. It's attached to Juan Valdéz cafe.

El Rincón de la Mantilla (☎ 660 1436; Calle de la Mantilla No 3-32, El Centro; mains COP$14,000-18,000; ⏰ 8am-midnight Mon-Sat) Decorated with baskets and seashells that gently wave from the rafters, this atmospheric Colombian place specializes in typical coastal fare. Service can be a bit rough.

La Dulceria (☎ 655 0281; Carrera 2 No 6-53, Bocagrande; sandwiches COP$16,000-19,000; ⏰ lunch & dinner) If you're escaping more chaotic El Centro for the plush suburbs of Bocagrande, this is a good option for an excellent selection of salads, sandwiches and Arab sweets such as *baklava*.

La Casa de Socorro (☎ 664 4658; Calle Larga No 8B-12, Getsemaní; mains COP$16,000-40,000; ⏰ lunch & dinner) This is a good little spot to try *comida costeña*, the typical food of the coast. It's a casual spot with nice design touches like paintings on recycled walking planks, and the menu features staples like *robalo* (sea bass) smothered in cheese and garlic, along with more adventurous fare such as snail or turtle soup.

La Cevicheria (☎ 664 5255; Calle Stuart No 7-14, San Diego; mains COP$25,000-52,000, ceviche COP$16,000-42,500; ⏰ lunch & dinner) Celebrity chef Anthony Bourdain dined at this tiny seafooder for his television show and for good reason: unconventional ceviches (shrimp with mango, passion fruit, garlic butter, mozzarella cheese and white wine, for example) offer a culinary quest into the exotic ingredients of Colombia's coast.

La Vitriola (☎ 664 8243; Calle Balocco No 2-01, El Centro; mains COP$20,000-57,000; ⏰ lunch & dinner) This foodie find inside a 400-year-old colonial home is revered the country over. Seafood is the main attraction, specifically *mero* (grouper). The *Don Román* version, with a tamarind and chili sauce, is superb. There's an extensive Chilean and Argentinian wine list to go with the menu as well as live Cuban music nightly.

our pick **El Santíssimo** (☎ 664 7099; Calle Santíssimo 8-19, San Diego; mains COP$25,000-50,000; ⏰ lunch & dinner) This upscale casual spot is doing some very interesting things with the flavors and food of Colombia, and each dish is paired with a suggested wine. The *obatala*, a traditional *costeña* beef stew, is divine. Don't miss it.

8-18 (☎ 664 2632; Calle Gastelbondo No 2-124, El Centro; mains COP$28,000-42,000; ⏰ lunch & dinner Mon-Sat) Very innovative takes on modern *costeña* cuisine is immerging from the glassed-in kitchen at this intimate and trendy boutique restaurant decked out in lime-vegetation decor. The creamy calamari rice with blue cheese is thoroughly satisfying and the bull's tail stewed in red wine is the best seller. One of Cartagena's best.

Drinking

Cartagena's bar scene is centered on the Plaza de los Coches in El Centro and along Calle del Arsenal in Getsemaní, though most of the latter are of the Spring Break variety. Weekends are best and the action doesn't really heat up until after midnight.

Ceiba (El Portal de los Dulces No 32-83, El Centro; juices from COP$2000; ⏰ 8:30am-8:30pm Mon-Fri, 9am-6:30pm Sun) If the street juice-stands scare you, this is a lovely sanitized version on Plaza de los Coches. All the yummy fruits are represented in a much cleaner, hipper environment.

Donde Fidel (☎ 664 3127; El Portal de los Dulces No 32-09, El Centro; ⏰ 11am-2am) Salsa all day, every day is the calling at this hotspot under the city's old walls. Inside, a mixed crowd shimmies and shakes to salsa in cramped quarters while the outside terrace – full of younger revelers waiting for Tu Candela (p150) to open – grooves to the reverberations.

Leon de Baviera (☎ 664 4450; Av del Arsenal No 10B-65, Getsemaní; ⏰ 4pm-4am Tue-Sun) Run by an expat German named Stefan, this is one of the city's few true watering holes. The intimate space fills quickly with locals swilling back 3L tubes of European and local brews. The waitresses are dressed in their St Pauli Girl's best.

La Casa de la Cerveza (☎ 664 9261; Baluarte San Lorenzo del Reducto, Getsemaní; ⏰ 4pm-4am) Another chic spot set high atop the city's walls, similar to Café del Mar, but with stupendous views out toward Castillo de San Felipe. DJs spin tracks nightly and, in case you get hungry, there's also a *parrillada* (restaurant serving grilled meat) with meals priced from COP$20,000 to COP$42,000).

our pick Café del Mar (☎ 664 0506; Baluarte de Santo Domingo, El Centro; cocktails COP$16,000-20,000; ⏲ 5pm-late) Ocean breezes swoop in off the coast and blow on the Beautiful People at this sexy outdoor lounge high atop the western ramparts of the old city. Spectacular views to Bocagrande recall Tel Aviv at night, while the restrooms are practically in Panama. DJs spin nightly from in front of an old lookout tower. A must-see.

Entertainment

A number of bars and discos stay open late. Plenty of them are on Av del Arsenal in Getsemaní, Cartagena's *zona rosa* (nightlife zone). There is definitely an element of sex tourism in the air in Cartagena's nightclubs (don't get too cocky, Don Juan, the girl paying you that extra special attention may be a prostitute).

NIGHTCLUBS

Café Havana (☎ 664 7568; cnr Calle del Guerrero y Calle de la Media Luna, Getsemaní; cover COP$5000; ⏲ 8pm-4am Thu-Sat, 5pm-2am Sun) If you're not into discos but still want to shake your rump, this Cuban hotspot – good for an early evening mojito as well – turns into an all-out salsa throwdown after 11pm that carries out into the street. The musicians aren't Cuban, but you'd never know.

Mister Babilla (☎ 664 7005; Av del Arsenal No 8B-137, Getsemaní; cover COP$10,000; ⏲ 9pm-4am) This massive, multi-space club is the city's best, filled wall-to-ceiling with everything from bird cages to oak barrels to Aerosmith records: there's enough bric-a-brac here to host the world's largest garage sale. The floor is packed, too, with warm-blooded *colombianos* hell bent on a modeling contract.

Quiebra-Canto (☎ 664 1372; Camellon de los Martines, Edificio Puente del Sol, Getsemaní; ⏲ 7pm-4am Tue-Sat) It gets tight with an eclectic crowd of all shapes and sizes at this excellent Getsemaní spot for salsa, Cuban and reggae. It's on the second floor overlooking Pegasos and the clock tower. Beers for COP$6000 mean you pay for the privilege.

Tu Candela (☎ 664 8787; El Portal de los Dulces No 32-25, El Centro; cover COP$10,000; ⏲ 8pm-4am) The narrow, shotgun-style layout of this bar/club makes liberal use of exposed brick – it feels a bit like partying in a wine cave – and is decorated with tribal masks, old transistor radios and brass instruments. The cover charge is recoupable in drinks.

You can also go on a night trip aboard a *chiva* (a typical Colombian bus) with a band playing vallenato and all-you-can-drink aguardiente (be careful!). *Chivas* depart from hotels in Bocagrande around 8pm for a three- to four-hour trip, and leave you at the end of the tour in a discotheque – a good point to continue your party for the rest of the night. Most agencies and hostels can book this for you.

SPORTS

Cartagena's local soccer team, Real Cartagena, plays games at Estadio Olímpico Jaime Merón León, located 5km south of the city in Villa Olímpico. Games run throughout the year. Buy tickets at the stadium. A taxi there will cost around COP$8000 to COP$10,000.

Shopping

Cartagena has a wide range of shops selling crafts and souvenirs, and the quality of the goods is usually high. The biggest tourist shopping center in the walled city is Las Bóvedas (p144), offering handicrafts, clothes, souvenirs and the like. The best wares here are at Artesanías India Catalina II (No 6) for classic homewares and art; D'Yndias (No 15) for high-quality hammocks, Juan Valdéz coffee, and handbags; and La Garita (No 23) for colorful kitchenware, T-shirts and better quality general merchandise.

For something a little more unique, the exclusive artisan homewares and handicrafts at **Upalema** (☎ 664 5032; Calle San Juan de Dios, Edificio Rincon No 3-99, El Centro; ⏲ 9:30am-10pm Mon-Sat, 10am-10pm Sun) aren't reproduced anywhere on the street. It's pricey, but it's top quality stuff, unrivaled elsewhere.

Getting There & Away

AIR

The airport is in Crespo, 3km northeast of the old city, and is serviced by frequent local buses. There are also *colectivos* to Crespo (COP$1000), as well as nicer air-conditioned shuttles called Metrocar (COP$1700), both of which depart from Monumento a la India Catalina (for Metrocar, look for the green-signed buses). By taxi, there's a surcharge of COP$4000 on airport trips. It's COP$10,000 to COP$13,000 from the center to the airport, but should be COP$4000 less if you ask the driver to leave you on the corner of Av 4 and Calle 70, 100m before the airport. The terminal has four ATMs and a *casa de cambio* (in domestic arrivals), which changes cash and traveler's checks.

All major Colombian carriers operate flights to and from Cartagena. There are flights to Bogotá (from COP$280,700, one way), Cali (from COP$314,000, one way), Cúcuta via Bogotá (from COP$375,200), Medellín (from COP$300,000, one way), San Andrés (from COP$273,000, return) and other major cities.

Avianca (☎ 664 7822; www.avianca.com; Av Venezuela, Centro Edificio Citibank, local B1; ☒ 8am-12:30pm & 2-6pm Mon-Fri, 8am-1pm Sat) flies to Miami via Bogotá, major domestic destinations and San Andrés (Thursday, Saturday and Sunday at 10:15am).

Copa (☎ 664 1018; Calle Gastelbondo No 2-107; ☒ 8am-noon & 2-6pm Mon-Fri, 9am-12:30pm Sat) has daily flights to Panama City for from COP$859,000.

AeroRepública (☎ 664 1388; Calle del Cabo, Centro Comercial Invercredito No 18; ☒ 8am-noon & 2-6pm Mon-Fri, 9am-12:30pm Sat) has flights to Bogotá and from there, connections to Cali, Medellín and San Andrés (Monday, Wednesday, Thursday and Friday at 1pm).

At the airport, regional carrier **Ada** (☎ 656 9200) flies direct to Montería (from COP$198,000).

BOAT

A pleasant way of getting to Panama is by sailboat. There are various boats, mostly foreign yachts, which take travelers from Cartagena to Colón via San Blas Archipelago (Panama) and vice versa, but there is no set schedule. The trip takes four to six days and normally includes a couple of days at San Blas for snorkeling and spear fishing. Trips hover around the COP$700,000 mark and often include food. Boats with semi-regular departures include the German-helmed **Papillon** (☎ 314 540 5411; sailwithtom@gmail.com), the French-Brazilian **Atoll** (☎ 301 422 2662; federico_layolle@yahoo.com.br) and **Seeadler** (☎ 507 448 2426; www.sailseeadler.com), run by a bearded German named Guido.

Beware of any con men attempting to lure you into 'amazing' Caribbean boat trips. Inquire at Casa Viena (p146), which posts departing boats and sailing dates as they become available. They also sort out the riffraff, working with trusted yachts and experienced captains (and do not take commissions). It's also a good idea to head down to the yacht club and inspect the boats beforehand and meet the captain – travelers have reported everything from crack-smoking crazies to incompetent sailors at the helm of some of these boats.

BUS

The bus terminal is on the eastern outskirts of the city, far away from the center. The upside is once you arrive, it's nicer than expected. Still, allow yourself 30 to 45 minutes to get there in all but the darkest hours.

Large green and red-signed Metrocar buses shuttle between the city and the terminal every 15 to 30 minutes (COP$1700, 40 minutes). In the center, you can catch them on Av Santander. A taxi from the bus station to El Centro is COP$10,000 plus an additional COP$500 after 8pm.

Several bus companies serve Bogotá and Medellín throughout the day. Among them, **Expreso Brasilia** (☎ 663 2119; www.expresobrasilia .com) heads to Bogotá five times daily (COP$100,000, 18 hours, at 7:30am, 12:30pm, 3:30pm, 5:30pm and 7:30pm) and Medellín six times (COP$85,000, 13 hours, at 7am, 12:30pm, 3:30pm, 5:30pm, 7:30pm and 9:30pm). **Unitransco** (☎ 663 2067) serves Barranquilla (COP$12,000, 2½ hours) with continuing services to Santa Marta (COP$23,000, four hours, at 6:30am, 7:30am, 8:30pm and 10:30am), Mompox once daily (7:30am, COP$35,000, six hours), and Tolú once daily at 6:30am (COP$23,000, three hours). There are additional buses to Barranquilla throughout the day, where you can switch to a bus to Santa Marta if they don't continue on. For Montería, Expreso Brasilia leaves hourly from 6:30am to 3:30pm (COP$35,000, 4½ hours).

If you can't get a seat on the daily bus to Mompox and want to go the alternative route via Mangangue, **Torcoroma** (☎ 663 2119) leaves at 6am and 10am (COP$35,000, three hours) and Expreso Brasilia goes at 6:30am, 7:30am and 10:30am (COP$28,000). For Riohacha on La Guajira Peninsula, **Rapido Ochoa** (☎ 663 2119) leaves at 9:30pm daily (COP$30,000, eight hours).

Expreso Brasilia and **Expreso Amerlujo** (☎ 663 2119) operate buses to Caracas, Venezuela (COP$200,000, 20 hours) via Maracaibo (COP$115,000, 12 hours). Unitransco is a bit cheaper than the other two, but you have to change buses on the border in Paraguachón. Each company has one departure daily. All buses go via Barranquilla, Santa Marta and Maicao. While the service is fast and comfortable, it's not that cheap. You'll save quite a bit if you do the trip to Caracas in stages by local transport, with a change in Maicao and Maracaibo.

On overland trips to Panama, Unitransco/Expreso Brasilia head to Montería (COP$35,000, 4½ hours) where you can switch for buses to Turbo (from COP$25,000, five hours). It's worth noting that if you do not leave Cartagena before 11am, you risk missing the last bus for Turbo and will have to sleep in Montería.

FUERTE DE SAN FERNANDO & BATERÍA DE SAN JOSÉ

On the southern tip of the Isla de Tierrabomba, at the entrance to the Bahía de Cartagena through the Bocachica strait, is **Fuerte de San Fernando**. On the opposite side of the strait is another fort, **Batería de San José**, and together they once guarded access to the bay. A heavy chain was strung between them to prevent surprise attacks in the 1700s.

Originally, there were two gateways to Cartagena Bay, Bocachica and Bocagrande. Bocagrande was partially blocked by a sandbank and two ships that sank there. An undersea wall was constructed after Vernon's attack in order to strengthen the natural barrage and to make the channel impassable to ships. It is still impassable today and all ships and boats have to go through Bocachica.

The fort of San Fernando was built between 1753 and 1760 and was designed to withstand any siege. It had its own docks, barracks, sanitary services, kitchen, infirmary, storerooms for provisions and arms, two wells, a chapel and even a jail, much of which can still be seen today.

The fortress can be reached only by water. Water taxis departing from Muelle Turístico de la Bodeguita in Cartagena do the journey for COP$5000. Admission to the fort is COP$7000. If you require a guide, plan on an additional COP$10,000.

ISLAS DEL ROSARIO

This archipelago, about 35km southwest of Cartagena, consists of 27 small coral islands, including some tiny islets only big enough for a single house. The archipelago is surrounded by coral reefs, where the color of the sea ranges from turquoise to purple. The whole area has been decreed a national park, the Parque Nacional Natural (PNN) Corales del Rosario y San Bernardo.

Sadly, warm water currents have eroded the reefs around Islas del Rosario, and the diving is not as good as it once was. But water sports are still popular and the two largest islands, Isla Grande and Isla del Rosario, have inland lagoons and some tourist facilities. An **oceanario** (aquarium, see below) has been established on the tiny Isla de San Martín de Pajarales.

Tours

The usual way to visit the park is on a one-day tour, and the cruise through the islands has become an established business. Tours depart year-round from the Muelle Turístico de la Bodeguita (p144) in Cartagena. Boats leave between 8am and 9am daily and return about 4pm to 6pm. The cruise office at the muelle sells tours in big boats (COP$40,000 per person) as well as smaller launches, which can be booked privately for COP$65,000, or COP$50,000 for a nonprivate launch. There are also independent operators hanging around offering tours in smaller vessels and often undercutting the above prices. Popular budget hotels in Cartagena (p146) sell these tours too, and may offer lower prices (COP$35,000 is common). Tours usually include lunch, but not the entrance fee to the aquarium (COP$15,000), the port tax (COP$4700), and the national park entrance fee (COP$5300).

The route is roughly similar with most operators, though it may differ a little between small and large boats. They all go through the Bahía de Cartagena and into the open sea through the Bocachica strait, passing between Batería de San José and, directly opposite, the Fuerte de San Fernando.

The boats then cruise among the islands (there is mumbled Spanish narration along the way) and get as far as the aquarium. As the admission fee is not included in the tour, you may decide to pay and visit it or just hang around waiting for the trip to continue. There is a shady wooded area to chill, or you can take a refreshing dip in the sea. The **aquarium** (admission COP$15,000) has various marine species, including sharks, turtles and rays, and runs a dolphin show for tourists. It's kind of fun, but wouldn't hold its own in a more competitive environment. The boats then take you to Playa Blanca on the Isla de Barú for lunch and two hours or so of free time, most of which is spent warding off a consistent barrage of peddlers.

There are two choices at play here – whether or not you want to travel by the bigger, slower boats or the smaller, faster boats; and whether you should go on a tour here at all. There are advantages and disadvantages to the former. The most popular large boat, the *Alcatraz*, can accommodate 160 people. There is food on board, music and room to move around. On the small boats, you are confined to your seat, but you get around quicker and can see more. Reviews are mixed but overall, travelers prefer the big boats for their quality of service. Readers report that pilots of small boats rush around too quickly and safety may be an issue – some small boats have sunk. Travel companies will try to sway you one way or the other, so the best bet is to talk with other travelers or ask at Casa Viena. That said, when you tally the total price including a visit to the aquarium (COP$60,000), you are more or less paying for a visit to an aquarium, a totally mediocre lunch, a hour or so on the beach fending off peddlers, and a whole lot of sailing time. See (p154) for information on how to go independently.

To visit the far superior Islas de San Bernardo, considerably south of the Islas del Rosario section of the park near Cartagena, see p186.

Sleeping & Eating

The islands have some tourist infrastructure so you can stay longer, go sunbathing, swimming, diving, snorkeling or just take it easy in a hammock.

Eco Hotel Las Palmeras (☎ 664 9312; www.cultura delmar.com; Isla Grande; 2-day all-inclusive packages from per person COP$160,000) This Isla Grande ecotourism option, run in concurrence with Cultura del Mar, employs only local women and offers hammocks in a thatched-roof dorm as well as singles and doubles. Rates include three meals and transport from Cartagena. There are only 14 people sharing this personal stretch of beach per day. Extra days are COP$110,000.

Hotel San Pedro de Majagua (☎ 664 6070, ext 4008; www.hotelmajagua.com; Calle del Torno, San Diego in Cartagena; r from COP$264,000) This higher-end option affiliated with Hotel Sofitel Santa Clara (p148) in Cartagena offers both day trips to Isla Grande from a private pier in Cartagena, which include transport and lunch for COP$135,000; and overnight stays on the island in chic stone bungalows with

fiber-woven roofs and minimalist decor. There are two beaches and a restaurant. Hotel guests pay COP$82,000 per person extra for transport.

PLAYA BLANCA

Playa Blanca lives up to its name – it is indeed a lovely stretch of sugary sand and one of the finest beaches around Cartagena. The government has wised up to this, however, and the whole area is under consideration to be zoned a massive resort complex (many homes have already been torn down and the road is being paved). Playa Blanca may be Playa Sayonara in the next few years.

The beach is located about 20km southwest of Cartagena, on the Isla de Barú. It's the usual stop for boat tours to the Islas del Rosario. Peddlers of every ilk descend upon tourists, turning an otherwise idyllic beach into a two-hour nightmare (the only thing worth buying is *cocada*, a sweet coconut treat that comes in a variety of flavors). To be fair, though, this is how folks here earn their living, as invasive as their hawking of wares may sometimes seem. There are also ladies at the ready to perform instant beach massages. Prices range between COP$20,000 to COP$30,000. At other times, it's pretty quiet, and is best appreciated when the tourist machine has left the building. It's also good for snorkeling as the coral reef begins just off the beach. You can rent gear for COP$5000 from peddlers on the beach.

Sleeping & Eating

The beach has some rustic places to stay and a few restaurants all serving more or less the same thing – fresh fish and rice – for around COP$10,000 to COP$15,000.

Campamento Wittenberg (☎ 311 436 6215; witten berg2000@hotmail.com; hammocks COP$9000, dm COP$18,000) This rustic spot, located on the far north side of the beach and tucked away 50m or so from shore, is the most popular with travelers. It's run by a Frenchman, Gilbert, who offers hammocks (with mosquito net) under a thatched roof and two dorms with private showers (hammock sleepers pay COP$1000 for a shower). Gilbert also does a decent breakfast for an extra COP$4500. He is one of the last men standing after various demolitions for the possible resorts, but plans to move on to Sapzurro when the reaper comes. So definitely call ahead. Gilbert also

CARIBBEAN COAST

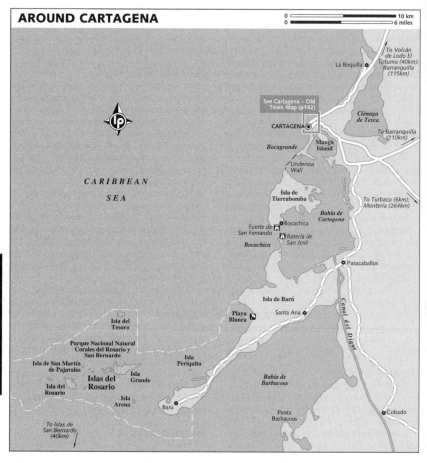

AROUND CARTAGENA

offers sailing lessons and runs snorkeling trips that take in a nearby bird sanctuary.

La Estrella (☎ 312 602 9987; hammock COP$7000, r from COP$15,000, tents COP$25,000) If you want to stay closer to the water, Jose, a friendly local, offers nice tents under thatched roofs that sleep three to four people, typical hammocks (with mosquito net), and a sand-floored hut or two. It's a decent alternative to Gilbert's spot but without the handy English.

Getting There & Away

As these things go in Cartagena, the easiest way of getting to the beach is on a tour, but you'll find it far more peaceful at other times. Head to Av El Lago, behind Cartagena's main market, Mercado Bazurto, in a taxi

(COP$5000), and ask the driver to let you off at the boats to Playa Blanca. Boats depart on a first-come, first-served basis between 7:30am and 9:30am daily except Sunday. The trip takes one hour. Expect to pay COP$20,000 to COP$25,000, but never pay anyone (ie the captain) until you reach the beach. If you do, you will be paying a middleman who will take a cut. If they argue, walk away. Doing it this way is technically against the rules, so forget about it in high season (December to February) when police clamp down.

Alternatively, buses (COP$1200) marked Pasocaballos leave throughout the day from the corner of Av Luis Carlos Lopez and Calle del Concolon in La Matuna. Ask the driver to let you off at the ferry across Canal del Dique

(COP$1000). Once on the other side, take a moto-taxi (COP$8000 to COP$10,000) to Playa Blanca. This route takes about three hours and is a mess after recent rainfall.

LA BOQUILLA

A small fishing village and kitesurfing haven, La Boquilla is 7km north of Cartagena and sits at the northern tip of a narrow peninsula, bordered by the sea on one side and the Ciénaga de Tesca on the other. If you get up at 4am, you can catch locals at the *ciénaga* (lake/lagoon) working with their famous *atarrayas* (round fishing nets) that are common in Colombia, particularly on the Caribbean coast.

There's a pleasant place known as El Paraíso, a five-minute walk from the bus terminus, where you can enjoy a day on the beach. You can also arrange a boat trip with the locals along the narrow water channels cutting through the mangrove woods to the north of the village. Negotiate the price, and pay upon return.

There is a collection of palm-thatched shack restaurants on the beach, which attract people from Cartagena on weekends; most are closed at other times. Fish is usually accompanied by *arroz con coco* (coconut rice) and *patacones* (fried plantains).

Frequent city buses run to La Boquilla from India Catalina in Cartagena (COP$1100, 30 minutes).

VOLCÁN DE LODO EL TOTUMO

No, it's not the world's largest termite mound. About 50km northeast of Cartagena, a few kilometers off the coast, is an intriguing 15m mound, looking like a miniature volcano. It is indeed a volcano, but instead of lava and ashes it spews forth mud.

Legend has it that the volcano once belched fire but the local priest, seeing it as the work of the devil, frequently sprinkled it with holy water. He not only succeeded in extinguishing the fire, but also in turning the insides into mud to drown the devil.

The crater is filled with lukewarm mud with the consistency of cream. You can climb down into the crater and frolic around in a refreshing mud bath. It certainly is a unique experience. The mud contains minerals acclaimed for their therapeutic properties. Most folks spend the time laughing as they try their darndest to sink further than buoyancy will allow. Once you've finished your session,

go and wash the mud off in the lagoon, just 50m away.

The volcano is open from dawn to dusk and you pay a COP$5000 fee to have a bath. Bring plenty of small bills to tip the various locals pampering you during your time here, who will massage you (though they certainly aren't carrying degrees from a massage course), rinse you off (yes, your bathing suit comes off) and hold your camera and take photos (they didn't go to photography school, either). All in all, it's loads of fun.

Getting There & Away

El Totumo is on the border of the Atlántico and Bolívar departments, roughly equidistant between Barranquilla and Cartagena, but Cartagena is a far more popular jumping-off point for the volcano and has better public transport and numerous tours.

The volcano is about 50km northeast of Cartagena by the highway, plus 1km by a dirt side road branching off inland. To get to the volcano, grab a taxi to the main bus terminal (COP$1100), and take an hourly bus bound for Galerazamba. Get off before Galerazamba at Lomita Arena (COP$2500, 1½ hours). Ask the driver to let you off by the petrol station and walk along the highway 2.5km toward Barranquilla (30 minutes), then to the right 1km to the volcano (another 15 minutes). Alternatively, you can grab a moto-taxi for COP$3000. The last direct bus from Lomita Arena back to Cartagena departs at around 3pm.

A tour is a far more convenient and faster way of visiting El Totumo, and not much more expensive than doing it on your own. Several tour operators in Cartagena organize minibus trips to the volcano (COP$25,000 transport only, COP$33,300 with lunch included in Manzanilla del Mar, a small fishing village with an average beach). Tours can easily be purchased through hotels, including Casa Viena (p146) and Hotel Holiday (p146).

MOMPOX

☎ 5 / pop 62,000 / elev 33m

You'll feel you've gone over the river and through the woods before you arrive here, but sleepy Mompox, hugging the banks of the mighty Río Magdalena like a newborn to its maker, will soon have you telling folks it's not about the journey, it's the destination.

Declared a Unesco World Heritage Site in 1995, the atmosphere evoked in the Mompox environs is certainly unique in Colombia (this is Bayou living, South America–style), and is well worth experiencing, despite the hardships of getting here. Surrounded by muddy rivers and thick vegetation, Mompox is 200km southeast of Cartagena, and reached by a combination of bus, boat and car.

Mompox has a long tradition in handworked filigree gold and silver jewelry, which is of outstanding quality. The town's other specialty is its *muebles momposinos* (Mompox-style furniture). Despite the scarcity of timber in the region, several workshops still continue the tradition, making locally crafted items, particularly rocking chairs,

which are renowned nationwide. In the evenings, *momposinos* rock calmly in their rocking chairs, which are as ubiquitous around town as flood protection. The whole thing feels a little Huckleberry Finn (or, should we say, Huck Finnito?).

Mompox also has a tradition in literature and was the setting for *Chronicle of a Death Foretold* by Gabriel García Márquez. Tourism hasn't yet consumed the area, so you might get the town to yourself most days, feeding the romantic notion that you are very much down in the Delta.

History

Traditionally known as Santa Cruz de Mompox, the town was founded in 1540 by

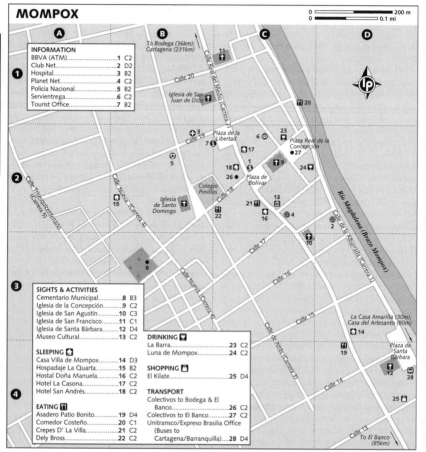

Alonso de Heredia (brother of Cartagena's founder, Pedro de Heredia) on the eastern branch of the Río Magdalena, which in this part has two arms – Brazo Mompox and Brazo de Loba. The town's name comes from Mompoj, the name of the last cacique (tribal head) of the Kimbay people, who inhabited the region before the Spanish Conquest.

Mompox soon became an important trading center and active port through which all merchandise from Cartagena passed via the Canal del Dique and the Río Magdalena to the interior of the colony. When Cartagena was attacked by pirates, Mompox served as a refuge for the families of the city's defenders.

The town flourished and several fair-sized churches and luxurious mansions were built. In 1810 Mompox proclaimed its independence from the Virreynato de la Nueva Granada; it was the first town to do so. Simón Bolívar, who stayed here for a short time during his liberation campaign, said: 'While to Caracas I owe my life, to Mompox I owe my glory.'

Towards the end of the 19th century, shipping on the Río Magdalena was diverted to the other branch of the river, the Brazo de Loba, bringing the town's prosperity to an end. Mompox has been left in isolation, living on memories of times gone by. Little has changed since. The town's colonial character is very much in evidence, as are the airs of a bygone era. It's fun to wander aimlessly about this tranquil town, discovering its rich architectural legacy and absorbing the old-time atmosphere.

Information

ATM (BBVA) (Plaza de Bolívar)

Club Net (☎ 685 5915; Carrera 1 No 16-53; per hr COP$1500; ☽ 7am-9pm) Internet services.

Hospital (☎ 685 6484; Calle 19)

Planet Net (☎ 685 5632; Carerra 2 No 14A-46; per hr COP$2000; ☽ 8am-9pm Mon-Sat) Internet services.

Policia Nacional (☎ 689 0891; cnr Calle 19 & Calle de Atras)

Servientrega (☎ 685 5141; Carrera 1 No 18-15; 7am-noon & 2-5pm Mon-Fri, 7am-noon Sat) Post office.

Tourist office (☎ 311 413 0005; Plaza de la Libertad; ☽ 7am-noon & 2-5pm Mon-Fri) Located on the 2nd floor of the alcaldía building.

Sights & Activities

Frankly, there's not a lot to see or do in Mompox. Its charm lies in simply strolling along the tranquil waterfront and along its quiet residential streets, taking in the town's distinctive and remarkably preserved colonial architecture, known as *arquitectura momposina*. Central streets, and particularly the main thoroughfare, Calle Real del Medio, are lined with fine whitewashed colonial houses. Their characteristic feature is the elaborate wrought-iron grilles based on pedestals and topped with narrow, tiled roofs that cover the windows. Some of the houses boast imposing carved doorways – a mark of the town's former glory and the wealth of its dwellers. The best way to get a feel for the local architecture and atmosphere is to wander through the streets.

The best museum in town is **Museo Cultural** (Calle 2 No 14-15; adult/child COP$3000/2000; ☽ 8am-noon & 2-4pm Mon-Fri, 9am-noon Sat), which is situated in the house where Simón Bolívar once stayed and features a small collection of elaborate religious art.

Mompox has six churches, all dating from colonial days and fairly similar in style and construction. They are open only for mass, which may be just once or twice a week. The tourist office may be able to tell you about the churches' current opening hours. The most interesting and unusual is the **Iglesia de Santa Bárbara**, facing the square of the same name and next to the river. Built in 1630, the church has an octagonal baroque-style bell tower circled by a balcony, unique in Colombian religious architecture.

Iglesia de San Agustín houses the famous, richly gilded Santo Sepulcro, which is one of the most prominent objects carried around the streets during the Semana Santa (Holy Week) processions. The statues of the saints in this church are paraded as well.

Iglesia de San Francisco is one of the oldest churches in town, built in 1580, and has the most interesting interior, particularly the lateral retables. **Iglesia de la Concepción** is the largest local church and is open more frequently than the others.

Mompox is also home to a fascinating **Cementerio Municipal** (Calle 18; ☽ 8am-noon & 2-5pm), which – call it macabre – is the most interesting spot in town to visit. Whitewashed graves and slots for remains are stacked high atop each other, sometimes six together, forming a wall of tombstones around a central chapel. It's well worth a stroll.

In the evening, when the baking heat of day has cooled slightly, you'll see many locals relaxing in front of their homes, sitting in (of course) Mompox-made rocking chairs.

Festivals & Events

Semana Santa (Holy Week) is taken very seriously in Mompox. The celebrations are elaborate, comparable only to those in Popayán (p252). The solemn processions circle the streets for several hours on the evenings of Maundy Thursday and Good Friday. Many images of the saints from the town's churches are involved.

Sleeping

Except during Holy Week, you won't have problems finding accommodations.

La Casa Amarilla (☎ 685 6326; www.lacasaamarilla mompos.blogspot.com; Carerra 1 No 13-59; dm COP$15,000, s/d without bathroom COP$20,000/30,000, with bathroom COP$30,000/40,000) This new hostel is run by a British travel journalist (so he has no excuse). It sits on a little plaza next to the river (and a loud outdoor watering hole) and offers a few four-bed dorms with clean bathrooms, some private options, laundry service, a kitchen, a big communal dining table and a living room. Handy for many travelers, the staff speak English, and you can also rent bikes.

Hospadaje La Quarta (☎ 684 0127; Carrera 4 No 18-57; r with fan per person COP$15,000, with air-con per person COP$25,000; 🏕) Located just out of the historic district behind Iglesia de Santo Domingo, this rustic spot is actually a step up in quality and a step down in price. Simple but colorful, it's the best air-con value for money.

Casa Villa de Mompox (☎ 685 5208; Calle Real del Medio No 14-108; s/d with fan COP$25,000/35,000, with air-con COP$35,000/55,000; 🏕) A quieter spot also offering lower-priced air-con than most. The beds are nice and soft too – a refreshing change of pace in this price range.

Hotel La Casona (☎ 685 5307; Calle Real del Medio 18-58; s/d with fan COP$30,000/50,000, with air-con COP$40,000/70,000; 🏕) This throwback *residencia* divided among two 18th-century homes is a comfortable option with interesting touches like tile-roofed bathrooms in some rooms. Laundry service is available.

Hotel San Andrés (☎ 685 5886; www.hotelsan andresmompox.com; Calle Real del Medio No 18-23; s/d with fan COP$30,000/50,000, with air-con COP$40,000/70,000; 🏕) It feels a bit like sleeping in a pet shop (the place is livened up by parakeets and parrots that inhabit the courtyard), but this is another solid midrange choice, similar to La Casona.

But someone should do something about those gaudy pink bedspreads.

Hostal Doña Manuela (☎ 685 5621; Calle Real del Medio No 17-41; s/d with fan COP$76,000/103,000, with air-con COP$90,000/121,000; 🏕 🏊) Inside a restored colonial mansion in slight disrepair, long arched hallways and two ample courtyards plus a swimming pool and a restaurant help propel this to top digs in town, but it's nothing remarkable. The pool can be used by nonguests (COP$6000).

Eating & Drinking

For a town of its size and isolation, there are some decent spots to eat and drink here. In the evenings, the makeshift food court that commences on the plaza outside the Iglesia de Santo Domingo is a good spot for fresh juices, cheap food and a chance to mingle with locals. You'll also see *butifarras* (small smoked meatballs), sold only on the street by *butifarreros*, who walk along with big pots, striking them with a knife to get your attention.

Comedor Costeño (☎ 685 5263; Calle de la Albarrada No 18-45; set meal COP$3000-7000; 🕗 7am-5pm) This rustic riverfront restaurant in the market area serves wonderful seat meals, including *bocachico* fish numerous ways. Owner Doña Mery is a real gem, but she shows no mercy in her fiery housemade *ají picante* (hot pepper sauce). Lunch plates come with excellent soup, salad, three starches (god bless her) and your chosen fish or meat preparation. You can eat it all right on the river or within the graffitied walls of the tiny dining room.

Asadero Patio Bonito (Calle Real del Medio No 14-25; set meal COP$5000; 🕗 dinner) A super rustic spot – it's basically a few tables on someone's front patio – that offers set meals of grilled meats served on small wooden tablets. The meat is a little tough, but it ain't bad at all.

Crepes D' La Villa (Calle Real del Medio, No 17-56; crepes COP$7000-8000; 🕗 breakfast, lunch & dinner Mon-Sat, breakfast & lunch Sun) This ice-cream parlor, creperie and bakery is a tasty change of pace. The crepes here aren't likely to pass muster in France, but the *momposinos* aren't complaining. Finish off with a sweet treat like *tornillos*, a pastry stuffed with *arequipe* (Colombian milk caramel). It's also a good spot to try *jugo de corozo*, a refreshing juice typical of the coast.

Dely Bross (☎ 685 5644; Calle 18 No 2-37; mains COP$7000-16,000; 🕗 breakfast, lunch & dinner) The nicest restaurant in town features actual tablecloths over local artisan tables and chairs. It does rotisserie chicken and *carne asados* (grilled meats) The specialty is *sobrebarriga momposino*, a thinly-cut flank of beef covered in a tasty stewed-onion-and-tomato sauce.

Luna de Mompox (☎ 311 412 2843; Calle de la Albarrada; ☼ 6pm-1am Mon-Thu, to 3am Fri-Sun) A decent little staple for a drink with tables right on the river's edge.

La Barra (☎ 685 5284; Plaza de la Concepción; ☼ 7pm-1am Tue-Thu, to 3:30am Fri-Sun) This new spot is actually the nicest bar in town, but lacks the longstanding reputation and waterfront location of Luna de Mompox. Still, it seems too stylish for Mompox.

Shopping

Casa del Artesanto (Calle de la Albarrada No 12-155; ☼ 9am-noon & 2-5pm Mon-Sat) It's very difficult to hang around Mompox watching the residents sway away the days in their distinctive rocking chairs and not want one for yourself. This small shop represents a few furniture makers around town – one can be yours for somewhere in the COP$60,000 to COP$100,000 price range. They'll even ship it for you!

El Kilate (☎ 685 5151; Calle 13 No 1-47; ☼ 7am-8pm) Here you'll find a small selection of artisan silver jewelry, including earrings, bracelets and rings, at reasonable prices. Pop your head in next door to watch the artisans at work.

Getting There & Away

Mompox is well off the main routes, but can be reached somewhat adventurously from different directions by road and river. Whichever way you come, however, the journey is time consuming. As Mompox lies between two unbridged rivers, any trip involves a ferry or boat crossing.

Most travelers come to Mompox from Cartagena. Unitransco has a direct bus daily, leaving Cartagena at 7:30am (COP$35,000, eight hours), but service is sporadic. A faster way is to take a bus to Magangué (COP$28,000, four hours); there are six departures per day with Brasilia. When it arrives in Mangangué, continue walking down the road and around to the right at the river and buy a ticket for a *chalupa* (boat) to Bodega (COP$6000, 20 minutes); there are frequent departures until about 3pm. The ticket booth is located across from El Punto del Sabor (locals will guide you for a tip – COP$1000 is sufficient). Once in Bodega, hop in a *colectivo* (shared taxi or minivan) to Mompox (COP$7000, 45 minutes). There

may also be direct *chalupas* from Magangué to Mompox.

In Mompox, **Unitransco/Expreso Brasilia** (☎ 685 5973) buses to Cartagena or Barranquilla (COP$35,000) depart at 6am from near Iglesia de Santa Bárbara (but don't count on it in low season) and there is at list one direct *colectivo* per day direct to Barranquilla driven by **Ivan Vanegas** (☎ 311 417 0150). He even provides pillows and breakfast! Inquire at Casa Amarilla (opposite). *Colectivos* to Bodega and El Banco park on Calle 18 just off the Plaza de Bolívar.

Getting Around

The best way to see Mompox is on foot or by bike. Inquire at Casa Amarilla (opposite) for bike rentals.

NORTHEAST OF CARTAGENA

The departments of Atlántico and Magdalena sit northeast of Cartagena, where the highest coastal mountain range in the world, the Sierra Nevada de Santa Marta, begins to rise from the sea just after Barranquilla. The increasingly more charming Santa Marta, the coast's other colonial city, and the beautiful coastal and mountainous attractions around it (namely Parque Nacional Natural Tayrona and Ciudad Perdida) are some of Colombia's most visited attractions.

BARRANQUILLA

☎ 5 / pop 1.1 million / elev 10m

'*Mira en Barranquilla se baila asi!*' Oh yes, if Barranquilla was only as sexy as Latin pop princess Shakira made it sound on her worldwide smash, 'Hips Don't Lie.' But it isn't. A maze of concrete blocks and dusty streets, Barranquilla is an industrial port that ranks as Colombia's fourth biggest city. There are few tourist attractions and little reason to visit, unless you happen to be around during Barranquilla's explosive four-day Carnaval, one of the most *loco* (crazy) festivals in Colombia. At any other time of the year, you'll likely only visit the bus station on your way to much more agreeable Santa Marta or the tranquil village of Taganga, both just a few more kilometers north and far more appealing to tourists.

That said, this city is legendary for its nightlife, a scene gringos report enjoying even more

CARIBBEAN COAST

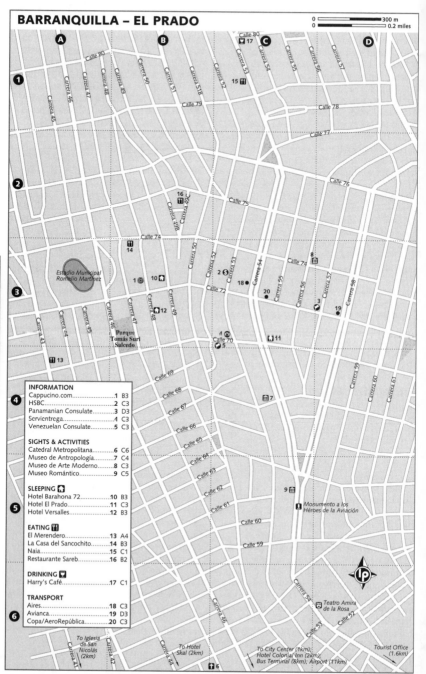

BARRANQUILLA – EL PRADO

0 — 300 m
0 — 0.2 miles

INFORMATION
Cappucino.com......................**1** B3
HSBC......................................**2** C3
Panamanian Consulate..........**3** D3
Servientrega..........................**4** C3
Venezuelan Consulate...........**5** C3

SIGHTS & ACTIVITIES
Catedral Metropolitana..........**6** C6
Museo de Antropología..........**7** C4
Museo de Arte Moderno........**8** C3
Museo Romántico...................**9** C5

SLEEPING
Hotel Barahona 72................**10** B3
Hotel El Prado.....................**11** C3
Hotel Versalles....................**12** B3

EATING
El Merendero.......................**13** A4
La Casa del Sancochito........**14** B3
Naia....................................**15** C1
Restaurante Sareb................**16** B2

DRINKING
Harry's Café........................**17** C1

TRANSPORT
Aires...................................**18** C3
Avianca...............................**19** D3
Copa/AeroRepública............**20** C3

Estadio Municipal
Romelio Martínez

Parque
Tomás Suri
Salcedo

Monumento a los
Héroes de la Aviación

Teatro Amira
de la Rosa

To Iglesia
de San
Nicolás
(2km)

To Hotel
Skal (2km)

To City Center (1km);
Hotel Colonial Inn (2km);
Bus Terminal (8km); Airport (11km)

Tourist Office
(1.6km)

in that they don't have to share it with quite so many fellow travelers.

History

The town was founded in 1629, but did not gain importance until the middle of the 19th century. Despite its potential as a port on the country's main fluvial artery, navigation problems at the mouth of the Río Magdalena hindered development. Most of the merchandise moving up and down the Magdalena passed through Cartagena, using Canal del Dique, which joins the river about 100km upstream from its mouth.

Only at the end of the 19th century did progress really begin. The opening of Puerto Colombia, Barranquilla's port built on the coastline 15km west of the town, boosted the development of the city, both as a fluvial and sea port.

By the early 20th century, Barranquilla was one of the major ports from which local goods, primarily coffee, were shipped overseas.

Progress attracted both Colombians from other regions and foreigners, mainly from the US, Germany, Italy and the Middle East. This, in turn, gave the city an injection of foreign capital and accelerated its growth. It also brought about the city's cosmopolitan character.

Orientation

Barranquilla's limits are marked by a ring road, Via Circunvalación. The city center (where the town was originally settled) is along the Paseo Bolívar, close to the river. Most of this sector, especially the area between the Paseo and the river, is inhabited by wild street commerce – it's actually one vast market stretching to the water like a flattened hillside shantytown.

About 3km to the northwest is El Prado, Barranquilla's new center, and the most pleasant district of the city.

The bus terminal is about 1km off the southern edge of the city, beyond Vía Circunvalación. The airport is still further south.

Information

Cappucino.com (☎ 358 4465; Carrera 48 No 72-65; per hr COP$1500; ⏰ 7:30am-7:30pm Mon-Sat) Internet cafe.
HSBC (Carrera 52 No 72-131; ⏰ 8-11:30am & 2-4pm Mon-Fri) ATM.

Panamanian consulate (☎ 360 1870; Carrera 57 No 72-25, Edificio Fincar 207-208; ⏰ 9:30am-noon & 2-4pm Mon-Fri)
Servientrega (☎ 356 0527; Calle 70 No 52-63; ⏰ 8am-11:30am & 2-6:30pm Mon-Fri, 8am-12:30pm Sat) Post office.
Tourist office (Comité Mixto de Promoción Mixta del Atlántico; ☎ 330 3864; Vía 40 No 36-135; ⏰ 8am-noon & 2-5pm Mon-Fri) The tourist office is in the Antiguo Edificio de Aduana, a healthy hike southeast of El Prado. It has lots of info, but staff aren't champing at the bit to help.
Venezuelan consulate (☎ 360 6285; Carrera 52 No 69-96; ⏰ 8am-noon Mon-Fri)

Sights

The two areas you might want to visit are the city center and El Prado. They are just a few kilometers apart, but a world away from each other.

The city center is cut in two by Paseo Bolívar. Halfway along is the mock-Gothic **Iglesia de San Nicolás** (cnr Paseo Bolívar & Carrera 42), worth entering for its main altarpiece and pulpit.

El Prado is cleaner, greener and safer than the center. Calle 72 is the district's principal shopping street, lined with restaurants, shops and supermarkets. Strolling around, you'll find some architectural relics from the late 19th and early 20th centuries, the time when El Prado began to develop. Note the buildings in the Islamic-influenced Moorish style – you'll find some of them on and just off Carrera 54. Include a visit to the following attractions, most of which are in El Prado or its vicinity.

The modern **Catedral Metropolitana** (cnr Calle 53 & Carrera 46) was completed in 1982. Don't be put off by its squat, heavy, somewhat bunker-like exterior – go inside. The interior features a number of large stained-glass windows spanning all spectrums of the kaleidoscope in the sidewalls and over the main entrance. It's beautiful.

Barranquilla is home to a few worthwhile museums if you need to kill a day here. The confusingly named **Museo Romantico** (☎ 344 4591; Carrera 54 No 59-199; adult/child COP$5000/free; ⏰ 8:30-11:30am & 2-5:30pm Mon-Fri) is actually a museum of the city's history, featuring exhibits relating to Barranquilla's past. Just down the road is the tiny **Museo de Antropología** (☎ 358 8488; Calle 68 No 53-45; admission free; ⏰ 8am-noon & 2:30-5pm Mon-Fri), on the 1st floor of the building of the Universidad del Atlántico, which displays

---

EL GRAN CARNAVAL

Every year, bustling Barranquilla takes off four days to fire up its famous Carnaval, one of the biggest and best that Colombia offers. With a century-long official history (but with traditions dating back much further), the festival preceding Ash Wednesday (February or March) paralyzes all normal city activities, such as urban transport and commerce, as the streets are taken over by dancers, musicians, parades and masquerades.

The Carnaval begins on Saturday with La Batalla de Flores (the Battle of Flowers), a float parade. It continues on Sunday with La Gran Parada, when thousands of party-goers put on costumes and file through the streets. On Monday there is El Festival de Orquestas, a marathon concert of Caribbean music groups. The Carnaval concludes on Tuesday with a symbolic burial of Joselito Carnaval.

Apart from the official program, it is a round-the-clock party, fueled by large quantities of alcohol. An estimated 100,000 cases of rum and aguardiente (anise-flavored liquor) are sold. Although it is getting more commercialized and lacks some of the spontaneity of years ago, it is still the most colorful and maddest of all of Colombia's festivals.

Unfortunately, as at all such crowded events, it's a focus for all sorts of local and visiting thieves and robbers. Be on guard, especially if you plan to photograph or film the event. Think twice before accepting drinks or cigarettes from strangers or new 'friends.'

The last factor to consider is accommodations. Unless you have booked a room well in advance, you can just about forget about finding a place to stay. Furthermore, room rates tend to rise by at least 20%.

---

a small collection of pre-Columbian pottery from different regions, including pieces from the Calima, Tumaco and Nariño cultures. The **Museo de Arte Moderno** (☎ 360 9952; Carrera 56 No 74-22; admission COP$5000; ⏲ 3-7pm Mon, 9am-1pm & 3-7pm Tue-Fri, 9am-1pm Sat) fills its space with rotating exhibitions from its larger permanent collection, which includes nationally renowned painters like Fernando Botero.

Sleeping

The center of budget accommodations is on and around Paseo Bolívar (Calle 34), but this area is seedier than a watermelon in June – just check the number of army personnel present even during the day. You can find rooms here for as little as COP$10,000, but there's little telling what went down in them before you checked in. If you would like to be safer and in a more pleasant environment, stay in El Prado; it's a rather upper-class district so you will pay for the privilege. You'll also find the best food and nightlife, around Carrera 53 and between Calles 79 and 80.

Hotel Skal (☎ 351 2069; Calle 44 No 41-35; s/d with fan COP$20,000/25,000, with air-con COP$28,000/35,000; ▨ ⛺) In the event that backpackers do find their way into downtown Barranquilla, they often stay at this musty option, somewhat made up for by the bonus pool. It's on a safe street next to a police station.

Hotel Colonial Inn (☎ 379 0241; Calle 42 No 43-131; s/d with air-con COP$30,000/40,000, with COP$40,000/50,000; ▨ 🖳) A far more comfortable city center option, with an air of faded glory about the lobby.

Hotel Barahona 72 (☎ 358 4600; www.hotel esbarahona.com; Carrera 49 No 72-19; s/d incl breakfast COP$69,000/94,000; ▨ 🖳) Some of the large rooms in the cheapest El Prado option were recently renovated and a number of them have private saunas. Overall, it's pretty good value for money when you consider the location.

Hotel Versalles (☎ 368 2183; www.hotelversalles inn.com; Carrera 48 No 70-188; s/d incl breakfast COP$105,000/149,000; ℗ ▨ 🖳 ⛺) This modern hotel is an excellent choice, within walking distance from El Prado museums and nightlife, and home to a friendly staff and a uniquely generous 3pm check-out time. There's a pool, wi-fi, spa and some serious, fire hose–strength showers.

Hotel El Prado (☎ 369 7777; www.hotelelprado .com, in Spanish; Carrera 54 No 70-10; s/d incl breakfast from COP$175,000/210,500; ℗ ▨ 🖳 ⛺) One of the coast's grand dames, this 1920s republican-style mansion is Barranquilla's most historic and posh hotel. Rooms are nice but basic, so it's more about soaking up the historical atmosphere within its walls and the large, tropical, pool area.

Eating & Drinking

One of Barranquilla's saving graces is food. You'll find most of the good restaurants in El Prado. In Centro around Paseo Bolivar, you can find cheap eats under COP$2000.

La Casa del Sancochito (☎ 310 770 8185; Calle 74 No 47-48; set meal COP$5000; ☺ lunch) A great little spot serving set meals of Colombian specialties like its namesake, a traditional meat stew, and a yummy curried *carne asada* (grilled meat). The outdoor wooden tables are always full.

Restaurante Sareb (☎ 368 7407; Carrera 49C No 76-139; mains COP$9000-18,000; ☺ lunch & dinner) Barranquilla is home to a healthy Middle Eastern population, so you'll find its Arab food is plentiful and good. This El Prado restaurant does it all – felafel, shawarma and kebabs – relatively cheaply.

El Merendero (☎ 356 5638; Carrera 43 No 70-42; mains COP$9500-19,500; ☺ lunch & dinner) This steakhouse serves up perfectly-seasoned slabs of beef – go for the *punta gorda*, a thin cut – in atmospheric thatched huts. Servings are substantial. The only downside is the lack of air-con – the meat isn't the only thing sizzling!

Harry's Café (☎ 345 6431; Calle 80 No 53-18; mains COP$10,000-28,000; ☺ dinner) Like a TGI Friday drunk on Latin fever, this bar and grill perpetuating itself as 'All-American' is a true scene: gringos mingling with locals. Will they or won't they? Will they or won't they? Let's sit back and watch over another Aguila draft! Everything from REM to Motley Crue provides the soundtrack.

Naia (☎ 368 1316; Carrera 53 No 79-127; mains COP$23,000-39,000; ☺ lunch & dinner Mon-Sat) Come here for *corozo* martinis, Colombia's addictive entrant into the World's Best Cocktail contest. Otherwise, soft earth tones set the mood at this trendy restaurant serving Barranquilla's beautiful. Excellent fusion cuisine (*mero* in guava sauce, *langostino* with *corozo* and pistachio) and a hip front patio make this one-stop shopping for a night on the town.

Entertainment

Barranquilla is home to the most raucous nightlife on the coast. What's hot is always changing; check out La Checa (www.lacheca.com).

Barranquilla's local soccer team is called Junior and they throw down at **Estadio Olympico Metropolitano Roberto Meléndez** (Vía Circunvalación & Av Murillo), south of Centro. You can buy tickets at the gates.

Getting There & Away

AIR

The airport is about 10km south of the city center and is accessible by urban buses that say 'Aeropuerto' (COP$1300). Almost all main Colombian carriers service Barranquilla. El Prado has airline ticketing offices for most major airlines. **Aires** (☎ 368 8845; www.aires.aero; Carrera 54 No 72-27; ☺ 8am-noon & 2-6pm Mon-Fri, 9am-noon Sat) flies to Medellín (from COP$278,000, one way), Montería (from COP$214,000, one way), Panama City (from COP$320,000, one way) and Maracaibo, Venezuela (from COP$700,00, one way). **Copa/AeroRepública** (☎ 360 8239; www.aerorepublica.com; Calle 72 No 54-49; ☺ 8am-6pm Mon-Fri, 9am-1pm Sat) goes to Bogotá (from COP$383,000, one way), Medellín (from COP$316,000, one way), Panama City (COP$670,000, one way) and San Andrés (from COP$912,100, return; at 1pm on Tuesday, Saturday and Sunday), returning the same days at 11am. **Avianca** (☎ 353 4691; www.avianca.com; Calle 72 No 57-79; ☺ 8am-6pm Mon-Fri, 9am-1pm Sat) flies to Bogotá (from COP$280,650, one way), Medellín (from COP$339,100, one way), Cali (from COP$317,060, one way) and Miami (from COP$1,125,740, one way).

BUS

The bus terminal is located 7km from the city center. It's not convenient, and it may take up to an hour to get to the terminal by urban bus. It's much faster to go by taxi (COP$1500, 30 minutes).

Expreso Brasilia (☎ 323 0111; www.expreso brasilia.com) heads several times daily to Bogotá from 5:30am (COP$95,000, two hours) and Medellín from 6am (COP$85,000, 12 hours), as well as Santa Marta every 30 minutes from 2:30am to 11:30pm (COP$10,000, two hours) with continuing services to Riohacha on the Guajira Peninsula (COP$34,000, four hours); and Cartagena every 15 to 30 minutes from 4am to 11pm (COP$10,000, two hours). **Unitransco** (☎ 323 0030) services Tolú hourly every morning (COP$35,000, five hours) and Mompox once daily at 7:30am (COP$40,000, six hours). **La Costeña** (☎ 323 1360) also heads to Santa Marta every 10 minutes from 5am to 8:30pm for slightly less than the competition (COP$7000, two hours).

Expreso Brasilia operates one daily bus at 11pm direct to Maracaibo, Venezuela (COP$85,000, nine hours) and on to Caracas, Venezuela.

CARIBBEAN COAST

SANTA MARTA

☎ 5 / pop 410,000 / elev 2m

Santa Marta is South America's oldest surviving city and the second most important colonial city on Colombia's Caribbean coast. Though the city's glory days are long past, faded away under newer concrete buildings and a somewhat seedy reputation (think more Getsemaní than old town). That said, Santa Marta is not without its charms. Its long waterfront beach attracts throngs of Colombians on holiday and for good reason: it offers liberal amounts of sun, rum and long stretches of sandy beachfront property. It's packed with revelers on weekends, sucking down snow cones, burying themselves in sand, and gathering along the rocky piers for glistening sunsets. And there is something endlessly intriguing about the city's crumbling colonial architecture – a glimpse into a more prosperous past.

Most international travelers simply use Santa Marta as a jumping-off point for nearby attractions, including Ciudad Perdida (p177) and Parque Nacional Natural Tayrona (p173), though that may soon change as all sorts of plans are in place to restore central Santa Marta to its former colonial splendor. The waterfront, Parque Santander and Plaza de Bolívar had already received appealing makeovers at the time of research, and an upscale international marina is in the works in addition to a major pedestrianizing of a healthy chunk of *centro*. El Rodadero, just to the south, remains a fashionable beach resort for well-to-do Colombians, and Playa Brava, a short boat ride from here, is the area's closest decent beach.

The climate is hot, but the sea breeze, especially in the evening, cools the city and makes it pleasant to wander about, or to sit over a beer or juice in one of the numerous open-air waterfront cafes.

History

Rodrigo de Bastidas planted a Spanish flag here in 1525, deliberately choosing a site at the foot of the Sierra Nevada de Santa Marta to serve as a convenient base for the reputedly incalculable gold treasures of the Tayronas. Bastidas had previously briefly explored the area and was aware of the possible riches to be found.

As soon as the plundering of the Sierra began, so did the resistance of the *indígenas*, and clashes followed. By the end of the 16th century the Tayronas had been wiped out and many of their extraordinary gold objects (melted down for rough material by the Spaniards) were in the Crown's coffers.

Santa Marta was also one of the early gateways to the interior of the colony. It was from here that Jiménez de Quesada set off in 1536 for his strenuous march up the Magdalena Valley, to found Bogotá two years later.

Engaged in the war with the Tayronas and repeatedly ransacked by pirates, Santa Marta didn't have many glorious moments in its colonial history and was soon overshadowed by its younger, more progressive neighbor, Cartagena (p138). An important date remembered nationwide in Santa Marta's history is December 17, 1830, when Simón Bolívar died here, after bringing independence to six Latin American countries.

Orientation

In Santa Marta's center, Av Rodrigo de Bastidas (Carrera 1C), which lines the beach, is the principal tourist boulevard, alive until late at night. It provides a nice view over the bay with a small, rocky island, El Morro, in the background.

Most tourist activity occurs between the waterfront and Av Campo Serrano (Carrera 5), the main commercial street.

Another hub of tourist activity, principally for Colombian holidaymakers, is the beach resort of El Rodadero, 5km south of the center. Buses shuttle frequently between the center and El Rodadero; the trip takes 15 minutes.

Information

INTERNET ACCESS

Tamá Café (☎ 431 2289; Carrera 2 No 16-06; per hr COP$1500; ⏰ 8:30am-6:30pm Mon-Fri, 9am-1pm Sat) Organic coffeehouse and internet cafe.

Villa Café.Bar (☎ 431 0431; Calle 17 No 2-43; per hr COP$1500; ⏰ 7am-7pm Mon-Sat)

LAUNDRY

Lavandería Santa Marta (☎ 431 5040; Calle 11 No 2-60; per kg COP$3000; ⏰ 6am-7:30pm)

MEDICAL SERVICES

Hospital Centro Julío Mendez Barreneche (☎ 421 2226; Carrera 14 No 23-42)

MONEY

Banco de Bogotá (cnr Calle 14 & Carrera 4) ATM.

Bancolombia (☎ 421 0185; Carrera 3 No 14-10; ⊗ 8-11:30am & 2-4pm Mon-Thu, 8-11:30am & 2-4:30pm Fri) Changes traveler's checks and US dollars only.

POLICE
Policía Nacional (☎ 421 4264; Calle 22 No 1C-74)

POST
Deprisa (☎ 421 3274; Carrera 3 No 17-26; ⊗ 8am-noon & 2-6pm Mon-Fri, 8am-noon Sat)

TOURIST INFORMATION
Aviatur (☎ 421 3848; Calle 15 No 3-20; ⊗ 8am-noon & 2-4pm Mon-Fri) Make reservations here for the concession's camping and higher-end options (Ecohabs) at Parque Nacional Natural Tayrona (p173).

Fondo de Promoción Turística de Santa Marta (☎ 422 7548; Calle 10 No 3-10, El Rodadero; ⊗ 8am-noon & 2-6pm Mon-Fri, 8am-noon Sat) Santa Marta's member-based tourism office can provide loads more info than its government counterpart.

Parques Nacionales Naturales de Colombia (☎ 423 0758; www.parquesnacionales.gov.co; Calle 17 No 4-06) Limited national park info.

Tourist office (☎ 438 2587; Calle 17 No 3-120; ⊗ 8am-noon & 2-6pm Mon-Fri) The city tourist office.

Sights
MUSEO DEL ORO
The **Gold Museum** (☎ 421 0953; Calle 14 No 2-07; admission free; ⊗ 8-11:45am & 2-5:45pm Mon-Fri) is in the fine colonial mansion known as the Casa de la Aduana (Customs House), but was getting a facelift at the time of research. It has an interesting collection of Tayrona objects, mainly pottery and gold, as well as artifacts of the Kogi and Arhuaco people. Don't miss the impressive model of Ciudad Perdida (p177), especially if you plan on visiting the real thing.

CATEDRAL
This massive whitewashed **cathedral** (cnr Carrera 4 & Calle 17) claims to be Colombia's oldest church, but work wasn't actually completed until the end of the 18th century, and thus reflects the influences of various architectural styles. It holds the ashes of the town's founder, Rodrigo de Bastidas (just to the left as you enter the church). Simón Bolívar was buried here in 1830, but in 1842 his remains were taken to Caracas, his birthplace.

QUINTA DE SAN PEDRO ALEJANDRINO
This **hacienda** (☎ 433 2995; Av Libertador; adult/child COP$10,000/6000; ⊗ 9:30am-4:30pm) on the outskirts of town is where Simón Bolívar spent his last days and died. The hacienda was established at the beginning of the 17th century and was engaged in cultivating and processing sugarcane. It had its own *trapiche* (sugarcane mill) and a *destilería* (distillery).

During the Bolívar era, the hacienda was owned by a Spaniard, Joaquín de Mier, a devoted supporter of Colombia's independence cause. He invited Bolívar to stay and take a rest at his home before his intended journey to Europe. Since it's inauguration, ownership has changed over 15 times. Highlights among the wares in the hacienda include an absolutely decadent marble bathtub.

Several monuments have been built on the grounds in remembrance of Bolívar, the most imposing of which is a massive central structure called the **Altar de la Patria**. Just to the right of this is the **Museo Bolivariano**, which features works of art donated by Latin American artists, including those from Colombia, Venezuela, Panama, Ecuador, Peru and Bolivia, the countries liberated by Bolívar.

The outstanding grounds, home to Santa Marta's 22-hectare **Jardín Botánico**, are also worth a stroll. Some of the property's trees are worth the trip out here alone. A new convention center and concert hall were under construction at time of research.

The *quinta* is in the far eastern suburb of Mamatoco, about 4km from the city center. To get here, take the Mamatoco bus from the waterfront (Carrera 1C); it's a 20-minute trip (COP$1000) to the hacienda.

EL RODADERO
The quiet resort town of El Rodadero has sun, sand, sea and little else. Popular with Colombian tourists, the town has a wide beach lined with high-rise apartment blocks and up-market hotels, plus a collection of restaurants, bars and discos. It gets very crowded during Colombian holiday periods, when prices can skyrocket. El Rodadero is 5km south of Santa Marta's center and is linked by frequent bus services.

Activities
Santa Marta is an important center of scuba diving. Most dive schools have settled in nearby Taganga (p170), but there are also some operators in the city center, including **Atlantic Divers** (☎ 421 4883; Carrera 2 No 10A-38;

CARIBBEAN COAST

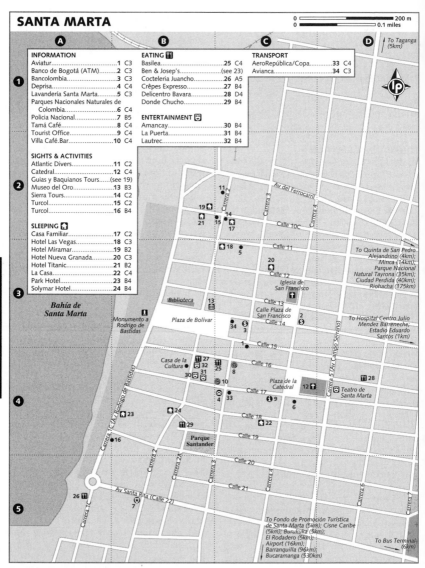

SANTA MARTA

0	200 m
0	0.1 miles

INFORMATION
Aviatur.................................**1** C3
Banco de Bogotá (ATM).........**2** C3
Bancolombia.........................**3** C3
Deprisa.................................**4** C4
Lavandería Santa Marta.........**5** C3
Parques Nacionales Naturales de
  Colombia...........................**6** C4
Policía Nacional....................**7** B5
Tamá Café............................**8** C4
Tourist Office........................**9** C4
Villa Café.Bar.....................**10** C4

SIGHTS & ACTIVITIES
Atlantic Divers.....................**11** C2
Catedral..............................**12** C4
Guías y Baquianos Tours......(see 19)
Museo del Oro.....................**13** B3
Sierra Tours.........................**14** C2
Turcol................................**15** C2
Turcol................................**16** B4

SLEEPING
Casa Familiar.......................**17** C2
Hotel Las Vegas...................**18** C3
Hotel Miramar......................**19** B2
Hotel Nueva Granada............**20** C3
Hotel Titanic........................**21** B2
La Casa...............................**22** C4
Park Hotel...........................**23** B4
Solymar Hotel......................**24** B4

EATING
Basilea................................**25** C4
Ben & Josep's.................(see 23)
Cocteleria Juancho...............**26** A5
Crêpes Expresso...................**27** B4
Delicentro Bavara.................**28** D4
Donde Chucho.....................**29** B4

ENTERTAINMENT
Amancay.............................**30** B4
La Puerta.............................**31** B4
Lautrec...............................**32** B4

TRANSPORT
AeroRepública/Copa.............**33** C4
Avianca...............................**34** C3

To Taganga
(5km)

*Bahía de
Santa Marta*

Av del Ferrocarril

Carrera 2

Carrera 3

Carrera 4

Calle 10C

To Quinta de San Pedro
Alejandrino (4km);
Minca (14km);
Parque Nacional
Natural Tayrona (35km);
Ciudad Perdida (40km);
Riohacha (175km)

Calle 11

Calle 12

Iglesia de
San Francisco

Biblioteca

Calle 13

Calle Plaza de
San Francisco

Monumento a
Rodrigo de
Bastidas

Plaza de Bolívar

Calle 14

To Hospital Centro Julio
Mendez Barreneche;
Estadio Eduardo
Santos (1km)

Calle 15

*Casa de la
Cultura*

Calle 16

Plaza de la
Catedral

Teatro de
Santa Marta

Calle 17

Calle 18

Calle 19

*Parque
Santander*

Calle 20

Carrera 2

Carrera 2a

Carrera 3

Carrera 4

Carrera 5/Av Campo Serrano

Carrera 6

Carrera 7

Calle 21

Av Santa Rita (Calle 22)

To Fondo de Promoción Turística
de Santa Marta (5km); Cisne Caribe
(5km); Burukuka (5km);
El Rodadero (5km);
Airport (16km);
Barranquilla (96km);
Bucaramanga (530km)

To Bus Terminal
(6km)

Carrera 1C

Carrera 1C (Av Rodrigo de Bastidas)

CARIBBEAN COAST

⏰ 8am-8pm). A four-day PADI-certification
course costs COP$550,000.

There's some good **hiking** around Santa
Marta, including walks in the Parque Nacional
Natural Tayrona (p173), though if you're after
some longer and more adventurous trekking,
the hike to Ciudad Perdida (p177) is the
region's showpiece.

Tours

For the most part, Santa Marta's tour market revolves around Ciudad Perdida (p177).
There are now four main outfitters authorized
to escort tourists on the six-day trek, two of
which are based in Santa Marta (see p178
for full details). You'll also find other hiking
options available.

THE SIERRA THINKING MAN'S BUZZ

As you travel up and down the Caribbean coast, you might see Kogi, Arhuaco or Wayuu people hopping on local buses with bags full of seashells. No, they aren't avid collectors. These people, all mountain-dwelling indigenous groups living all over the Sierra Nevadas around Santa Marta, are collecting the shells for a sacred ritual known as the *poporo*. The Kogi, for one, believe shells exist as a sort of spiritual middleman between the light of the sun and the dark of the sea, and they can tell the history of an area by interpreting the shell's color and markings.

For the *poporo*, lighter seashells called *caracucha* are collected in great numbers and heated over a fire before being pounded into a very fine powder. While this is going on, the women collect coca leaves, called *ayo*, and place them in bags full of heated stones to dry them out (the aroma is said to smell like heaven). They take the dried *ayo* to the men, who place it in their mouths and put the fine powder of the shell inside a small vessel called a *totuma* (symbolizing the female being), which men receive as a symbol of reaching manhood. The men then collect small bits of powder on a small stick and place it in their mouths with the leaves and suck on the secretions for 20 to 30 minutes. The mixture causes the coca leaves to release eight amino acids and create a sort of thinking man's buzz, a slow and meditative high.

It is believed the *poporo* instills knowledge, just as others would read a book or go to college. Over time, the leftover spittle from the stick is dabbled on the outside of the *totuma*, causing it to grow and symbolizing wisdom.

Sleeping

Santa Marta's *centro* is jam packed with small hotels and family-run residencies, most of them cheap and fairly laid-back. If the following are full, there are more options just a few steps away, though be warned this area is teeming with prostitutes and all that the world's oldest profession attracts. It's very seedy! Also, the streets around here flood like the Armageddon when it rains – bring your mask and snorkel!

CENTRO

Hotel Miramar (☎ 423 3276; elmiramar_santamarta@ yahoo.com; Calle 10C No 1C-59; dm COP$8000, s/d without bathroom COP$8000/16,000, with bathroom COP$10,000/20,000; 💻) This is the quintessential gringo hangout, though that doesn't make it the Hippie Dippy Ritz-Carlton. It's well-equipped with an in-house tourism agency and its own restaurant serving substantial meals, but some rooms are barely above prison level and flies are rampant around the cafe. Guests are charged for the internet as well. It's in bad need of a makeover.

Hotel Titanic (☎ 421 1947; Calle 10 No 1C-68; dm COP$10,000, r with fan per person COP$12,000) The rival hostel to Miramar, this is a step up in tranquility and cleanliness. You totally lose the good time vibe of the Miramar, but you'll get a lot more sleep.

Casa Familiar (☎ 421 1697; www.hospederiacasafamiliar .freeservers.com; Calle 10C No 2-14; dm/s/d COP$13,000/

18,000/28,000) A friendly, popular hotel, mainly due to its panoramic rooftop. There are private rooms and dorms as well as a high-speed laundry service on the premises.

Hotel Las Vegas (☎ 421 5094; Calle 11 No 2-08; s/d with fan COP$15,000/27,000, with air-con COP$20,000/32,000; 🔀 💻) Rooms are small and simple, but with air-con, cable TV and an independent internet cafe in the lobby it's hard to complain at these prices. Remember though, cockroaches like air-con too.

Solymar Hostal (☎ 431 0208; Carerra 2 No 19-06; s/d with fan COP$40,000/50,000, with air-con COP$50,000/60,000; 🔀 💻) This brand new option is in the best shape of the midrangers, though it's a 33-room hotel not a hostel. It's in a good location for beach action and features a lobby shower so you don't muck up your room with sand.

Hotel Nueva Granada (☎ 421 1337; www.hotelnueva granada.com; Calle 12 No 3-17; s/d with fan COP$50,000/70,000, with air-con COP$65,000/90,000; 🔀 💻 🏊) Though the showers are a joke, the internet wasn't working when we were in, and the rooms are tiny, there's a decent courtyard, free coffee, a very small swimming pool (you won't be shattering any world records in here), and you're three blocks from the waterfront.

Park Hotel (☎ 421 4939; www.parkhotelsantamarta .com; Paseo Bastidas No 18-67; s/d with fan COP$60,000/85,000, with air-con COP$75,000/91,000; 🔀 💻 🏊) None of the hotels along the waterfront are trying too hard, but this one puts in a little more effort with pleasant touches like indigenous wood carvings, colorful bedspreads and a charming central staircase under a candlelike chandelier. The attached bar/restaurant also carries a lot of weight – it's one of the best in town.

ourpick La Casa (☎ 421 2483; www.lacasa santamarta.com; Calle 18 No 3-53; s/d incl breakfast from COP$165,000/195,000; ☒ ☐ ☒) Far and away the best and most interesting place to stay in the area, this three-room boutique hotel, full of socially conscious local art, occupies a restored 18th-century home run by a lovely young woman who has worked with Afro-Caribbean and Sierra indigenous communities for the past decade. Each room in the house is a tribute to those communities and features gorgeous original tile flooring and doors. Breakfast includes organic products

from the Sierra and will be one of the best meals you eat in Colombia. Bird-watching trips to Minca (p170) and yoga workshops can also be arranged.

EL RODADERO

El Rodadero is home to somewhat swanky beach resorts, mostly catering to Colombians flexing their financial might. You will also find several all-inclusive options in the area, where you can eat, drink and sleep your heart out from about COP$229,000 per person per day, depending on the season.

Cisne Caribe (☎ 422 9418; Carrera 3A No 5-74; s/d COP$50,000/70,000; ☐ ☒ ☐) There is no true budget accommodations in El Rodadero, but this cheapish option has a good personality

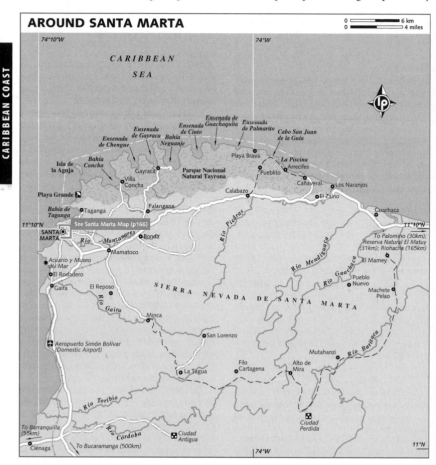

AROUND SANTA MARTA

and a friendly front desk. Big beds dominate the smallish rooms, but all is clean and punctuated by cheesy knickknacks. It's two blocks from the beach.

Hotel La Sierra (☎ 422 7960; www.german moralesehijos.com; Carrera 1 No 9-47; s/d incl breakfast COP$110,000/140,000; ❁ ▣ ▣) A kitschy mix of modern, indigenous and beachfront bygone, this is a great midrange choice in El Rodadero. Floors 6 to 10 have sweeping beach views and romantic balconies fit for two.

Eating

Santa Marta's dining scene has improved in recent years – you can actually gnaw on a few things here that don't make you wish you were somewhere else.

CENTRO

Cocteleria Juancho (Carrera 1 btwn Calle 22 & 23 No 18-67; ceviche COP$4000-12,000; ❁ breakfast, lunch & dinner) This ceviche street stall has been packing in loyal locals of all ilk for 33 years. Here it is all about the shrimp ceviche, which comes in four sizes. It's located next door to the Gino Passcalli store.

Delicentro Bavara (☎ 421 4984; Calle 16 No 5-73; sandwiches COP$7000-12,000; ❁ dinner Mon, Wed-Sun) In a country where a good sandwich is scarce, this hole-in-the-wall counter serves up ones worth writing home about. The excellent toasted Cubans and chicken sandwiches are meticulously prepared (20 minutes) and are worth the wait. There's no sign – look for the brick facade with iron gates.

Crêpes Expresso (☎ 317 280 5039; Carrera 1 No 18-67; crepes COP$5000-15,000; ❁ lunch & dinner Mon-Sat) Artsy French-owned *crepería* that does excellent crepes (though some with canned ingredients) and cocktails as well. The fan turns on with the bathroom light – nice touch in this heat.

Ben & Josep's (☎ 317 280 5039; Carrera 1 No 18-67; mains COP$13,500-22,000; ❁ dinner Mon-Sat) Filets the size of Volkswagens are the specialty at this expat-owned bar/restaurant attached to the Park Hotel (though independent). It's the best of the waterfront options. Drinks commence at 3:30pm (call ahead to reserve an outdoor table on weekends). The only pity is it closes too early and some of the cocktails are very weak, especially ones that call for nothing but alcohol – very hard to do.

Basilea (☎ 431 4138; Calle 16 No 2-58; mains COP$14,000; ❁ lunch & dinner Mon-Sat) If you tire

of coastal cuisine, this intimate Med-French place offers a nice change of pace, serving interesting dishes like the fiery red pepper steak (but where are the steak knives?) in Santa Marta's most refined atmosphere. Save room for the excellent flan.

our pick Donde Chucho (☎ 421 4663; Calle 19 No 2-17; mains COP$23,000-55,000; ❁ lunch & dinner Mon-Sat) Serving the best seafood on the coast, and sitting on prime real estate on the newly renovated Parque Santander. Start with the signature salad (shrimp, octopus, calamari and manta smoked in olive oil) and move on to *robalo au gratin* (mozzarella and parmesan). Divine. If this place doesn't fit your budget, go Monday to Thursday between 6pm to 9pm and enjoy cocktails at 2-for-the-price-of-1. Don't miss it.

EL RODADERO

Burukuka (☎ 438 0388; Detrás del Edificio Cascadas; ❁ lunch & dinner Tue-Sun) Perched on a cliffside high above El Rodadero, this chic spot specializing in steaks turns into an all-night party Thursday to Saturday. Plant yourself on the expansive outdoor patio for a sunset drink, or make a night of it – it's worth the taxi up here.

Entertainment

Santa Marta's nightlife really heats up on weekends and you'll have no trouble finding a place to dance. Previously, hot spots were in El Rodadero (La Escollera is still good in high season if you're out that way), but the party has moved back to Santa Marta for the most part.

BARS

Amancay (Carrera 2A No 16-47; ❁ 4pm-midnight Mon-Wed, to 2am Thu-Sat) This funky bar features Frank Miller strips lining the exposed brick walls and other abstract decor.

La Puerta (☎ 317 384 8839; Calle 17 No 2-29; ❁ 6pm-1am Tue-Wed, to 3am Thu-Sat) This artsy, multi-room space without a sign outside can get a little wild with gringos and students, especially on weekends. It's not known as Oh La La La La Puerta for nothing.

Lautrec (☎ 421 4039; Carrera 2 No 16-08; ❁ 6:30pm-late) This spot has a personality disorder: is it a dark and mysterious haunt for creative types, or a dance club? It's too dark and too noisy, but still a good time. Good on Sunday when most of Santa Marta is cooped up.

SPORTS
El Union Magdalena is Santa Marta's local soccer team. Games are played at Estadio Eduardo Santos, located at Av Liberatador and Carrera 19 less than 2km from Centro. Games run throughout the year. Buy tickets at the stadium. A taxi there costs COP$6000.

Getting There & Away
AIR
The airport is 16km south of the city on the Barranquilla–Bogotá road. City buses marked 'El Rodadero Aeropuerto' will take you there in 45 minutes from Carrera 1C. Flights include Bogotá (from COP$329,00 one way) and Medellín (from COP$298,000, one way).

AeroRepública/Copa (☎ 421 0120; www.aerorepublica .com; Carrera 3 No 17-27; ☺ 8am-6pm Mon-Fri, 9am-1pm Sat).

Avianca (☎ 421 4018; www.avianca.com; Carrera 2A No 14-47; ☺ 8am-6pm Mon-Fri, 9am-1pm Sat)

BUS
The bus terminal is on the southeastern outskirts of the city. Frequent minibuses go there from Carrera 1C in the center.

Expreso Brasilia/Unitransco (☎ 430 6244) offers four buses daily to Bogotá (COP$120,000, 18 hours) and Medellín (COP$122,000, 15 hours). It has departures every 30 minutes until 7:30pm to Barranquilla (COP$10,000, two hours); and hourly departures until 6:30pm to Cartagena (COP$23,000, four hours). It also heads north to Riohacha (COP$21,000, 2½ hours) every 30 minutes until 5pm, with a continuing service to Maicao (COP$28,000, four hours), the last Colombian town before the border with Venezuela. Here you can change for buses to Maracaibo (Venezuela), but don't linger much beyond the bus station – safety has improved dramatically in Maicao, but it remains the distribution center for all sorts of contraband from Venezuela. There are also two direct buses to Tolú (COP$43,000, seven hours) and three to Bucaramanga (COP$83,000, nine hours).

Rapido Ochoa (☎ 430 1040) offers similar services with expanded operations to Tolú via Sincelejo (COP$40,000) four times daily (only the 1:30pm service is direct) and Riohacha (COP$15,000) hourly.

For Venezuela, you are better off catching a direct bus from Santa Marta to Maracaibo (COP$75,000, seven hours) with **Expreso**

Amerlujo (☎ 430 4144) departing daily at noon, with a continuing service to Caracas (COP$165,000, 18 hours). Alternatively, if the times don't work for you, **Cootragua** (☎ 430 1650) goes to Paraguachón (COP$25,000, 4½ hours) on the border at 10am daily, where you can change for Maracaibo. All passport formalities are done in Paraguachón. Change money here, expect a bag search and wind your clock forward one hour when crossing from Colombia to Venezuela.

MINCA
Perched 600m high up in the Sierra Nevada above Santa Marta sits Minca, a small mountain village famous for organic coffee and, perhaps more importantly, much cooler temperatures. There's not much in town itself, but there are a couple of scenic places to hide away in the fresh mountain air for a few days, and the whole place is a haven for bird-watching. There are over 300 species in the vicinity.

Sans Souci (☎ 310 590 9213; sanssouciminca@yahoo .com; camping s/d with tent COP$8000/15,000, without tent COP$10,000/20,000, r per person without bathroom COP$15,000, r per person COP$25,000; 🖳) is a simple, German run *finca* (farm) tucked away above town and offers spectacular views across the Sierra to Santa Marta. You can get a small discount by working on the farm.

With its prime location practically on top of the Rio Gaira and its well-appointed rooms full of the Italian-Colombian owners' art, **Sierra's Sound** (☎ 421 9993; sierrasound.es.tl; Calle Principal; r with/without bathroom COP$40,000/30,000) is a stylish little mountain getaway. The restaurant serves Colombian and Italian meals.

For a good bird-watching guide to the area, try **Francisco Trancoso** (☎ 316 815 9378; francisco_tron coso@hotmail.com).

Minca is reached by taxi (COP$40,000) or moto-taxi (COP$6000), the latter departing from La Y (pronounced *Jay*), an intersection in the suburb of El Yucol 8km west of Santa Marta's *centro* on the way to Riohacha.

TAGANGA
☎ 5 / pop 5000
Taganga is one of those places where the word got out too fast – Gringo Paradise! – and before you could say, 'Ah carajo!' there were more foreigners in this tranquil fishing village than Colombians. Still, with its location set in a beautiful, deep, horseshoe-shaped bay 5km northeast of Santa Marta, and its laid-back

vibe, Taganga remains one of the Caribbean coast's most visited destinations.

Love it or hate it, Taganga has officially arrived on the global tourism map and has a reputation as a party zone. It's become a popular destination for Israeli travelers to unwind after completing their military service. The beach here isn't particularly nice, but with heaps of fishing boats dotting the bay and the imposing Sierras hovering over from behind, Taganga is one of the coast's most picturesque spots.

Most travelers use Taganga as their base for treks to Ciudad Perdida (p177) and visits to Parque Nacional Natural Tayrona (p173), but closer still are better beaches like Playa Grande, a pretty bay northwest of the village.

Walk there on the cliff-hugging path in front of Hotel Bahia Taganga (20 minutes) or take a boat from Taganga (COP$5000).

Information

There are no banks or post offices in Taganga, so load up on cash in Santa Marta before arrival, especially if you are heading to Ciudad Perdida.

Centro de Salud (☎ 421 9067; Calle 14 No 3-05) Medical services, but really, get yourself to Santa Marta.

Litera-Te (☎ 317 273 2862; Calle 20 No 3B-24) Foreign book exchange featuring books in 18 different languages.

Mojito Net (☎ 421 9149; Calle 14 1B-61; per hr COP$1000-2000; ☯ 9am-2am) Air-con internet and a nice spot for a cocktail.

Policia Nacional (☎ 421 9561; Carrera 2 No 17A-38)

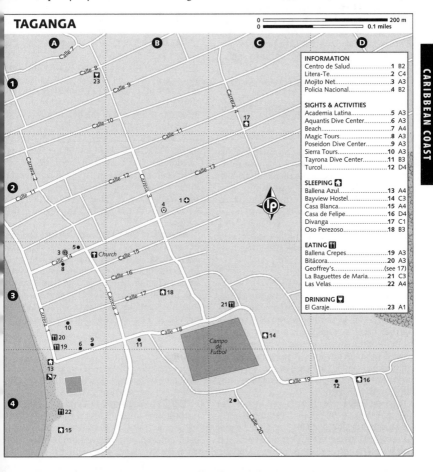

TAGANGA

0 — 200 m
0 — 0.1 miles

CARIBBEAN COAST

INFORMATION	
Centro de Salud	1 B2
Litera-Te	2 C4
Mojito Net	3 A3
Policia Nacional	4 B2

SIGHTS & ACTIVITIES	
Academia Latina	5 A3
Aquantis Dive Center	6 A3
Beach	7 A4
Magic Tours	8 A3
Poseidon Dive Center	9 A3
Sierra Tours	10 A3
Tayrona Dive Center	11 B3
Turcol	12 D4

SLEEPING	
Ballena Azul	13 A4
Bayview Hostel	14 C3
Casa Blanca	15 A4
Casa de Felipe	16 D4
Divanga	17 C1
Oso Perezoso	18 B3

EATING	
Ballena Crepes	19 A3
Bitácora	20 A3
Geoffrey's	(see 17)
La Baguettes de Maria	21 C3
Las Velas	22 A4

DRINKING	
El Garaje	23 A1

Dangers & Annoyances

Being a backpacker hub, Taganga sees its fair share of petty theft. The two biggest problem areas are the beach – keep an eye on your things there and don't leave them unattended – and crimes of opportunity involving your gear and an open window – do not leave valuables within reach of anyone.

Activities

Taganga is a popular **scuba-diving** center, with six dive schools offering dives and courses. Local services here are among the cheapest you'll find anywhere. Four-day open-water PADI courses range in price from COP$540,000 to COP$580,000. The best local schools:

Aquantis Dive Center (☎ 421 9344; www.aquantis divecenter.com; Calle 18 No 1-39; ☺ 6:30am-9pm) Very friendly and very professional, this Belgian-run company offers a bed and diving PADI-certification package for COP$580,000 (with breakfast) in very comfortable rooms at the dive center.

Poseidon Dive Center (☎ 421 9224; www.poseidon divecenter.com; Calle 18 No 1-69; ☺ 7am-7pm)

Tayrona Dive Center (☎ 421 9195; Calle 18 No 1-39) Offers PADI-certification for COP$540,000 in low season.

Courses

Those wanting to brush up on their Spanish skills while also contributing to a local cause should check out **Academia Latina** (☎ 421 9390; www.academia-latina.com; Calle 14 No 1B-75). This Dutch-run Spanish school offers classes starting from COP$150,000 (minimum 10 hours per week), with 25% of your fee going to a foundation to help local children. It's located inside the new Casa Holanda, a 10-room hostel opened post-research for this book.

Sleeping

Oso Perezoso (www.myspace.com/hotelosoperezoso; Calle 17 No 2-36; hammock COP$10,000, r per person incl breakfast from COP$15,000; ☐) Hotel Miramar's (p167) partner hotel in Taganga is a major step up from its Santa Marta partner in crime. Partly owned by an American, it features a lovely rooftop bar – home to rare hammock accommodations – and perfectly presentable rooms, all with private bath.

Casa de Felipe (☎ 421 9120; www.lacasadefelipe .com; Carrera 5A No 19-13; dm COP$12,000-15,000, s incl breakfast COP$30,000, d COP$35,000, apt 2/4 people COP$60,000/100,000; ☐) This lovely hostel run by a friendly Frenchman is one of the better-equipped budget options you'll stumble across. In a beautiful house on lush grounds above the bay, it's all here: pleasant rooms, bar, kitchen, cable TV, storage, numerous hammocks, excellent breakfast, and friendly folk from around the world to get drunk with. The dorms, especially No 5, are particularly great. It's located a few blocks uphill from the beach, past the soccer pitch.

our pick **Divanga** (☎ 421 9092; www.divanga.com, Calle 12 No 4-07; dm COP$20,000, r per person incl breakfast COP$25,000; ☐ ☒) Another French-run place not short on atmosphere – colorful local arts don the walls and doors of the rooms, most of which surround a small but oh-so-inviting swimming pool. There's a rooftop deck and bar that catches a nice sea breeze and the restaurant is above and beyond for a hostel. It's more tranquil than Casa de Felipe, so opt for here if that's a priority.

Casa Blanca (☎ 421 9232; barbus85@latinmail.com; Carrera 1 No 14-61; r per person incl breakfast COP$25,000; ☐) Though the beach isn't exactly the kind you'd give your life savings to invest in, this is beachfront property at its finest. Rooms are simple but clean and offer nice bathrooms. It's at the far south end of the beach.

Bayview Hostel (☎ 421 9128; www.bayviewhostel .com; Carrera 4 No 17B-57; dm incl breakfast COP$20,000, s/d COP$30,000/50,000; ☐ ☒) One of the few good Colombian-run hostels in town, this is another colorful place with a big communal kitchen and simple rooms. The swimming pool is the icing. If you get tired of that, grab a movie from the DVD library and call it a night.

Ballena Azul (☎ 421 9090; www.hotelballenaazul.com; cnr Carerra 1 & Calle 18; r with/without air-con COP$100,000/ 60,000; ☐ ☒ ☐) Its ads would have you think this is South Beach – not quite – but it is the most stylish place to stay. The whitewashed colonial-like home evokes a Santorini feel and it's right on the beach, with an annex next door. The restaurant is the classiest spot in town.

Eating

There are a slew of open-air budget restaurants along the waterfront, where *comida corriente* with fresh fish starts at COP$$8000.

our pick **La Baguettes de Maria** (Calle 18 No 3-47; mains COP$5000-10,000; ☺ lunch & dinner Sun-Fri, dinner Sat) A true traveler's paradise – scrumptious beef, chicken and veggie fillings piled high on baguettes and served in brown paper bags, run by a friendly South African and his Colombian wife. Don't miss the amazing peach iced tea, either. It also does french fries eight ways – perfect to nurse your hangover.

Geoffrey's (☎ 421 9092; Calle 12 No 4-07; mains COP$5000-14,000; ☽ dinner) Not many hostels can boast a French chef, but this restaurant at Divanga (opposite) can do just that. Chicken coconut curry, steak with creamy pepper sauce – this stuff is too good. It draws both guests and visitors alike, both for the prices and the excellent fare.

Bitácora (☎ 421 9121; Carrera 1 No 17-13; mains COP$7000-18,000; ☽ breakfast, lunch & dinner) Semi-stylish spot serving everything from filet mignon smothered in bacon and mushrooms to veggie lasagna. The sundaes are quite a hit as well. At night, it's good for a drink before El Garaje gets going.

Ballena Crepes (☎ 421 9090; cnr Carerra 1 & Calle 18; mains COP$7900-39,000; ☽ breakfast, lunch & dinner) The Ballena Azul hotel's more casual (and some say better) restaurant, across the street from the hotel, is the most varied in town. A healthy list of cheaper options like crepes, burgers and sandwiches sit alongside more expensive seafood choices, all served under a thatched roof by the bay.

Las Velas (☎ 421 9072; Carrera 1 No 18-95; mains COP$12,000-47,000; ☽ breakfast & lunch to 7:30pm) Right on the beach next door to Casa Blanca, Las Velas is known for it's seafood *cazuela* (stew) and lobster in coconut sauce. If you don't like it, you don't pay!

Drinking
El Garaje (☎ 421 9003; Calle 8 No 2-127; ☽ 8:30pm-late Wed-Sat) This is *the* spot in Taganga, well worth the trek from Santa Marta on Wednesday as well, when Santa Marta is dead. It's a sprawling bar under thatched roofs, full of picnic tables and the occasional live tree growing up from the floor. Good fun.

Getting There & Away
Taganga is easily accessible; there are frequent minibuses (COP$1000, 15 minutes) from Carrera 1C and Carrera 5 in Santa Marta. A taxi costs COP$7000. You can also arrive by boat directly from Cabo San Juan de la Guía in Parque Nacional Natural Tayrona for COP$35,000 – much smarter than doing the reverse, see (p176).

PARQUE NACIONAL NATURAL (PNN) TAYRONA
One of Colombia's most popular national parks, Tayrona grips the Caribbean coast like a jungly bear hug at the foot of the Sierra Nevada de Santa Marta. The park stretches along the coast from the Bahía de Taganga near Santa Marta to the mouth of the Río Piedras, 35km to the east, and covers some 12,000 hectares of land and 3000 hectares of sea.

The scenery varies from sandy beaches along the coast in the north to rainforest at an altitude of 900m on the southern limits of the park. The extreme western part is arid, with light-brown hills and xerophytic plant

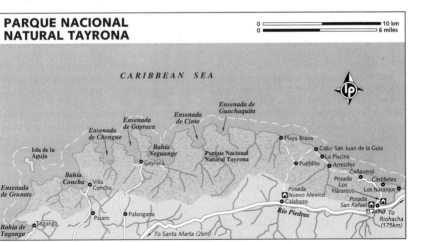

PARQUE NACIONAL NATURAL TAYRONA

0 — 10 km
0 — 6 miles

CARIBBEAN SEA

species, such as cacti. The central and eastern parts of the park are wetter and more verdant, largely covered by rainforest. May and June and September to November are the wettest periods. At least 56 endangered species call the park home, but most stay out of sight, deep in the forest.

The region was once the territory of the Tayrona people, and some archeological remains have been found in the park. The most important of these are the ruins of the pre-Hispanic town of Pueblito (called Chairama in the indigenous language), considered to have been one of Tayrona's major settlements. Here the remains of over 500 dwellings were discovered, estimated to have been home to 4000 people at one point in history.

For many travelers (too many in high season), the park's biggest attraction is its beaches, set in deep bays and shaded with coconut palms. Vicious currents ensure most are not suitable for swimming, though you can swim at a select few, where snorkeling is also popular. Tayrona beaches are among the most picturesque on Colombia's coast. Some of the beaches are bordered by coral reefs providing reasonable snorkeling and scuba-diving opportunities. Snorkeling gear is available for rental in the park if you don't bring your own from Santa Marta. Mosquito repellent is essential and be wary of snakes in the area – if you are bitten, Ecohabs (opposite) keeps antivenin on hand, though most folks don't know it. Do not let them take you to Santa Marta!

Around 95% of Tayrona is privately owned and the park is managed by a concession, Aviatur (p165), who seem to do a very good job of building luxury accommodations, but a poor job of maintaining trails.

One important thing to keep in mind: high season 2009 saw such an influx of tourists that park visitor capacities began to be ignored, leading to overcrowding, poor maintenance of trails, poor conditions of bathroom facilities, and exhausting waits for food and services. Do consider limiting your visit here to the low season (February to November), or be prepared for the possibility that much of Tayrona's charms may be lost in the crowds.

Sights

Tayrona's eastern part features most of the park's attractions and tourist facilities, and

---

FAMILIAS GUARDABOSQUES: CONVERTING COKE TO HOPE

Colombia has made tremendous strides in finding peace within itself while shedding its 'drugs and guns' reputation. One of President Álvaro Uribe's most interesting and rewarding initiatives for travelers is Posadas Ecoturísticas de Colombia (www.posadasecoturisticas.blogspot.com), a program that began In 2006 and helps local folk all over the country to get out of the cocaine industry and into ecotourism and/or sustainable farming of agricultural products like coffee and cacao. This is especially interesting around Parque Nacional Natural (PNN) Tayrona, where families living in the Sierra Nevada have formed government-sponsored forest watch groups called **Familias Guardabosques de la Sierra Nevada de Santa Marta** (☎ 317 730 7404; posasierraneva@yahoo.es; s/d/tr/q COP$80,000/129,000/169,000/199,000) and turned over their coca plantations in exchange for very nice cabaña accommodations around the outskirts of the park.

This is a wonderful accommodations option for those who want to stay near the park but would also like to get more involved with the culture of those that live around it. There are 20 *posadas ecoturísticas* in the six villages in the Tayrona area, all more or less offering the same accommodations (excellent pinewood cabins with nice mattresses, mosquito nets and bathrooms) for the same price. Additionally, a wealth of ecotourism options from bird-watching to rafting are run by the children and neighbors of the cabin owners and can be booked through any of the *posadas*.

Three of the *posadas* nearest PNN Tayrona are **Posada San Rafael,** the largest and most famous of the *posadas* in the area, just 400m from the entrance at park entrance El Zaino. Here they grow their own organic coffee and offer spectacular views to the Sierra Nevadas. It has also developed a relationship with Kogi people in the nearby mountains and offer an excursion to their village – a rare treat; **Posada Los Naranjos**, 800m from the park entrance, offers a more remote setting on the beautiful Rio Piedras, just near where it meets Playa Los Naranjos; and **Posada Nuevo México**, 13km from the park entrance, where you can trek though various types of forest to Cinto Bay, one of the park's most beautiful spots.

is by far the most popular and visited area of the park. Its main gateway is **El Zaíno**, 34km east of Santa Marta on the coastal road to Riohacha, where you pay the COP$31,000 park admission fee (Colombians pay COP$12,000). A COP$3000 insurance supplement is in the works to become mandatory in 2009. And leave the drugs at home, Cheech – the military does a very thorough search at the main gate of all who enter. Unofficial guides gather here, whom you can hire for considerably less than Aviatur's official guides (COP$80,000 vs COP$122,000 for Pueblito, for instance), though guides really aren't necessary if you plan on keeping to the main tourist routes.

From El Zaíno, a 4km paved side road goes northwest to **Castilletes**, the longest beach in the park and the first place you can turn in for the night. A few more kilometers down the road is **Cañaveral**, also on the seaside. Here there is a campground, upscale cabañas (cabins), and a restaurant. The beaches in Cañaveral are good, but there is no shade, and swimming can be dangerous because of treacherous offshore currents. Each year, four to five tourists drown in the waters here. If you don't want to continue walking from here, horses are available to Arrecifes (COP$16,000 one way) and Pueblito (COP$112,000 return).

From Cañaveral, most visitors take a 45-minute walk west along a trail to **Arrecifes**, where there are budget lodging and eating facilities. Bear in mind that sea currents here are just as dangerous as those in Cañaveral.

From Arrecifes, a 20-minute walk northwest along the beach will bring you to **La Piscina**, a deep bay with quiet waters, making it reasonably safe for swimming and snorkeling.

Another 20-minute walk by path will take you to **Cabo San Juan de la Guía**, a beautiful cape with a great beach, and by far the most crowded area of the park.

From the cape, a scenic path goes inland uphill to **Pueblito**, providing some splendid tropical forest scenery. It will get you to Pueblito in a bit more than an hour, but this path is definitely more challenging than others in the park – the majority of the uphill climb is over stones, some of them massive. It is not an easy trail and you can forget about it when it rains or if you have a large pack.

Not much of Pueblito's urban tissue has survived, apart from small fragments of the stone paths and foundations of houses, but it's worth seeing, especially if you aren't planning a trip to Ciudad Perdida (p177).

From Pueblito, a path continues southwest to Calabazo on the main road. After five minutes, the path splits to the right down to **Playa Brava**. Don't listen to the folks working at Cabo, who will tell you there is nothing in Playa Brava. It's a good idea to call ahead to Teyumakke (p176) if you are heading this way; the path is not well-marked and a bit more jungly than others in the park, and you definitely do not want to trek all the way down here to a completely full hotel. You'll reach Playa Brava in about an hour.

Sleeping & Eating

The park is unofficially divided into sections according to the type of traveler you are. In general, Castilletes is for nature lovers and green-minded travelers; Cañaveral is for the well-to-do; Arrecifes is for families; and Cabo San Juan de la Guía is for party people.

In Castilletes, the ecofriendly **Camping Tayrona** (☎ 317 798 2723; www.campingtayrona.com; campsite per person COP$10,000, tents COP$18,000, r per person with/without bath COP$40,000/30,000) are the newest accommodations in the park, housed within a former narco estate. Here you'll find 25 campsites and excellent Quechua tents with mattresses and sheets, in addition to private rooms. A Dutch-Colombian couple heavily involved in the conservation and environmental protection of the park run things here. It sits on 1.5km of beach that is also the park's most popular spot for sea turtle nesting and is swimmable in September and October (other months are only safe for advanced swimmers). Environmentally driven workshops are given on the park, its flora and fauna and astronomy. You can also rent snorkeling equipment. The restaurant (mains COP$7000 to COP$15,000) serves a variety of food, including an excellent *sierra* fish in coconut sauce. At press time, due to problems with the park unit, there was talk that Camping Tayrona could be moved outside park boundaries, likely near Posadas Ecoturísticas (opposite). Please check before heading out.

In Cañaveral, the park's concession operates **Ecohabs** (☎ 344 2748; www.aviatur.com/concesion esparquesnaturales.com; 2-/4-bed cabins COP$440,000; 🖳) – a colony of cabañas featuring small LCD televisions with DIRECTV, L'Occitane bath products and some spectacular views. They are made in the style of Tayrona huts and

CARIBBEAN COAST

are peppered about a coastal hill. Rates rise in the tourist season by about 20%. Another larger cabin at the foot of the hill houses a restaurant. It's by far the nicest spot to stay, but not COP$500,000 nice.

The concession also runs a **campsite** (per person COP$11,000) here but it's right next door to the horse stables, so you won't be taking in any tropical sea breezes. Sites here can be booked at Aviatur's offices in Santa Marta (p165). You can also book through the office in Bogotá (p68).

In Arrecifes, there are three places to stay and eat. The most rustic is **Finca Don Pedro** (☎ 315 656 6195; fincadonpedro@yahoo.es; hammocks COP$10,000, campsite per person COP$12,000), reached via 300m split off the main trail just before Arrecifes. The showers here are oddly non-private, however, kind of like in prison. Meals cost COP$9000. Aviatur also runs **Yuluka** (☎ 344 2748; www.aviatur.com/concesionesparques naturales.com; hammocks COP$16,500, campsite per person COP$11,000, cabañas incl breakfast from COP$308,000), by far the best option for campers. The bathrooms here are five-star, right out of a boutique hotel. The cabins, which hold up to five people, are similar in quality to Ecohabs but without the sea views. The restaurant serves gourmet meals (mains COP$9000) like shrimp brochettes grilled with onions and paprika. Also here is **Finca El Paraíso** (☎ 317 312 1945; www.paraisotayrona.com; campsites COP$8000, hammocks COP$10,000, tents 2-/4-/6-people COP$25,300/30,500/50,000, cabins from COP$40,000), the closest to the beach. It's nicely done, with a fresh juice stand, lockers for personal belongings and a restaurant (mains COP$15,000 to COP$30,000) with a nice beach view.

A 10-minute walk further west along the beach is **Bucarú**, an offspring of El Paraíso. It offers similar facilities for marginally less money (and comfort).

Both Finca El Paraíso and Bucarú can be booked through their **Santa Marta office** (☎ 431 3130; Carrera 7B No 28A-103), or you could just turn up. Most backpackers end up at **Camping Cabo San Juan de la Guía** (campsite COP$10,000, hammocks COP$12,000, tents per person COP$25,000), a campground that rivals those of European festivals in high season. There is a decent beach here as well as a restaurant (mains COP$6000 to COP$20,000). For COP$15,000, you can sleep in the hammocks high atop the *mirador* on the rocks above the beach. There are also cabañas (COP$80,000), but you have to walk

a long way back down to the bathroom. You can rent snorkeling gear here (ask around for Leonard).

Down the mountain from Pueblito through jungly terrain is Playa Brava, a much more primitive beach. **Teyumakke** (☎ 315 480 0241; playabrava@gmail.com; hammocks/campsite per person COP$20,000, cabañas per person COP$60,000; 🖥) is a wonderful ecohab and camping accommodations right on the beach. It's a great place to get away from everyone else and is full of animals – turkeys, peacocks and overfriendly pigs among them (it's like Noah's Ark washed ashore). Most of the food (mains COP$15,000 to COP$20,000) is sourced on premises and the owner, Jorge Dib, can fill you on fascinating Kogi culture. He also makes *guarapo*, the Kogi firewater. You can walk here from Cabo or they will pick you up with horses in Calabazo.

The single most beautiful spot to hang your hat in the area – perhaps in all of Colombia – is just outside the park at Playa Los Naranjos. Here sits the architecturally unique **Barlovento** (r per person incl meals COP$140,000), a private home featuring open-air beds that jut out on a deck over the sea in a spectacular setting where the gorgeous Rio Piedras bursts out of the Sierra Nevadas and empties into the Caribbean. The waves crash right under your mattress. You can book through Aventure Colombia (p140) in Cartagena.

Getting There & Away

Cañaveral is easy to get to on your own from Santa Marta. Take a minibus headed to Palomino and get off in El Zaíno (COP$4000, one hour); Palomino minibuses depart every 20 to 30 minutes from Santa Marta's market (at the corner of Carrera 11 and Calle 11). From El Zaíno, walk for 50 minutes to Cañaveral or catch a ride with locals who regularly shuttle between the two (COP$2000, 10 minutes). Alternatively, a tourist bus departs daily from outside the Santa Marta's Hotel Miramar (p167) at 10am, driving direct to Cañaveral, and returning at 1pm (COP$10,000 one way, COP$16,000 return).

Another option is a boat from Taganga directly to Cabo San Juan de la Guía. Boats with a capacity for 12 people depart the bay at 10am and return to Taganga at 3pm (COP$35,000), though keep in mind that this is illegal, as you're not entering the park through the appropriate gate and therefore not paying admission. This can cause you problems on several fronts. If a ranger sees you and asks for your proof of payment, you won't have it and you'll be fined. The boats have been known to sell the tour round-trip and never return for you; you'll also have to think about what you will say to the police or park rangers when they catch you walking through the park without an entrance bracelet.

CIUDAD PERDIDA

There is rarely anything more mysterious than the discovery of an ancient abandoned town, and Ciudad Perdida (literally 'Lost City') has lived up to its name for four centuries. Known by its indigenous name of Teyuna and the archeological designation Buritaca 200, it was built by the Tayrona people on the northern slopes of the Sierra Nevada de Santa Marta, and was most probably their biggest urban center. Today, it's one of the largest pre-Columbian towns discovered in the Americas.

The city was built between the 11th and 14th centuries, though its origins are much older, going back to perhaps the 7th century. Spread over an area of about 2 sq km, it is the largest Tayrona city found so far, and it appears it was their major political and economic center. Some 2000 to 4000 people are believed to have lived here.

During the Conquest, the Spaniards wiped out the Tayronas, and their settlements disappeared without a trace under lush tropical vegetation. So did Ciudad Perdida, until its discovery by *guaqueros* (grave robbers) in the early 1970s. It was a local man, Florentino Sepúlveda, and his two sons Julio César and Jacobo, who stumbled upon this city on one of their grave robbing expeditions.

Word spread like wildfire and soon other *guaqueros* came to Ciudad Perdida. Fighting broke out between rival gangs, and Julio César was one of the casualties. In 1976 the government sent in troops and archeologists to protect the site and learn its secrets, but sporadic fighting and looting continued for several years. During this time, the *guaqueros* dubbed the site the *Infierno Verde* (Green Hell).

Ciudad Perdida lies on the steep slopes of the upper Río Buritaca valley at an altitude of between 950m and 1300m. The central part of the city is set on a ridge from which various stone paths lead down to other sectors on the slopes. Although the wooden houses of the Tayrona are long gone, the stone structures, including terraces and stairways, remain in remarkably good shape.

There are around 170 terraces, most of which once served as foundations for the houses. The largest terraces are set on the central ridge and these were used for

CARIBBEAN COAST

THE LOST CIVILIZATION

In pre-Columbian times, the Sierra Nevada de Santa Marta on the Caribbean coast was home to various indigenous communities, of which the Tayrona, belonging to the Chibcha linguistic family, were the dominant and most developed group. The Tayrona (also spelt Tairona) are believed to have evolved into a distinctive culture since about the 5th century AD. A millennium later, shortly before the Spaniards came, the Tayrona had developed into an outstanding civilization, based on a complex social and political organization and advanced engineering.

The Tayronas lived on the northern slopes of the Sierra Nevada where they constructed hundreds of settlements, all of a similar pattern. Due to the rugged topography, a large number of stone terraces supported by high walls had to be built as bases for their thatched wooden houses. Groups of terraces were linked by a network of stone-slab paths and stairways.

Recent surveys have pinpointed the location of about 300 Tayrona settlements scattered over the slopes, once linked by stone-paved roads. Of all these, Ciudad Perdida (Lost City), discovered in 1975, is the largest and is thought to have been the Tayrona 'capital.'

Tayrona was the first advanced indigenous culture encountered by the Spaniards in the New World, in 1499. It was here in the Sierra Nevada that the conquerors were for the first time astonished by the local gold, and the myth of El Dorado was born.

The Spaniards crisscrossed the Sierra Nevada, but met with brave resistance from the indigenous people. The Tayronas defended themselves fiercely, but were almost totally decimated in the course of 75 years of uninterrupted war. A handful of survivors abandoned their homes and fled into the upper reaches of the Sierra. Their traces have been lost forever.

ritual ceremonies. Today, the city is quite overgrown, which gives it a somewhat mysterious air.

Archeological digs have uncovered Tayrona objects (fortunately, the *guaqueros* didn't manage to take everything), mainly various kinds of pottery (both ceremonial and utilitarian), goldwork, and unique necklaces made of semiprecious stones. Some of these objects are on display in the Museo del Oro in Santa Marta (p165) and in Bogotá (p77). It's a good idea to visit the museum in Santa Marta before going to Ciudad Perdida.

Tours

Previously one agency, Turcol, had sole access to Ciudad Perdida. However in 2008 the Colombian military has cleared out the paramilitaries in the area, which has effectively opened up the route to Ciudad Perdida to healthy competition – there are now four main agencies guiding groups of travelers on the six-day hike to the ancient ruins, all of which are based in Santa Marta (p164) or Taganga (p170). There are also several other smaller operations, many of which are just middlemen for Turcol. You cannot do the trip on your own or hire an independent guide.

The 'official' price of the tour is about COP$480,000, but nobody is paying this since competition was opened up. All of the agencies are well versed in a little hardcore bargaining and, at the time of research, were all dropping to around COP$325,000 for the all-inclusive six-day tour (though official prices are said to soon be jumping to COP$550,000). Though new competition has forced the agencies to operate at these very low profit margins, the 36 guides who lead the trek are talking about forming a union and driving the prices back up to normal, and refusing to work otherwise. Expect prices to have fluctuated a bit by the time you read this, and to continue to do so until it all shakes out. But whatever you do, do not purchase this trip from agencies in Bogotá, where prices upward of COP$600,000 have been reported.

The price for the tour includes transport, food, accommodations (hammocks with mosquito nets and mattresses on some nights), porters, non-English speaking guides and all necessary permits. Take a flashlight, water container, insect repellent, sunscreen, long pants, two pairs of shoes (strap sandals work best for river crossings) and water purifying pills (depending on which agency you go with). Be wary of snakes, stinging caterpillars, wasps and other things that go bump in the night.

Tours are in groups of four to 12 people, and depart year-round as soon as a group is assembled. In the high season, expect a tour to set off every day. In the low season, every few days between the four agencies (the three new ones will consolidate together depending on group sizes). Helicopter tours, a very expensive option in the past, have been discontinued.

The trip takes three days uphill to Ciudad Perdida, 1½ days at the site and two days back down, covering some 40km return. It is a challenging hike (each day covers five to eight kilometers), but not mercilessly so. There are significant climbs on days one, three and five, all of which can be brutal in the scorching jungle heat. When the sun isn't blazing, it's likely to be muddy, trading a forehead of beading sweat for loose traction and a mud-soaked mess (the driest period is from late December to February or early March). On day three, you will cross the Río Buritaca up to waist-deep nine times; after the last crossing you will encounter Ciudad Perdida's mystical, moss-strewn rock steps – 1260 in total – that lead to the site. Along the way, the food is surprisingly good and the accommodations, often riverside where you can cool off in natural swimming pools, are better than expected. The scenery is nothing short of astonishing.

Worth it? Most definitely. But keep in mind that this is a trek that is more about the journey than the destination – don't expect the world's greatest archeological ruins or to wind up in the 'Machu Picchu of Colombia' as Ciudad Perdida is often called, though the site itself is quite fascinating and you will likely only be sharing it with your group for least half a day in the low season. You will also encounter and interact with Kogi people along the way and the Colombian Army at the site – bring along some things you think 18-year-old boys might miss being stuck in the jungle for six months, and some may let you trade them for their army gear! Best try not to get caught with your army souvenirs by authorities further down the track though.

Guias y Baquianos Tours (Map p166; ☎ 5 431 9667 in Santa Marta; guiasbaquianostour@yahoo.es; Calle 10C No 1C-59, Santa Marta; ☺ 8am-noon & 2-6pm Mon-Sat), located inside Hotel Miramar, was the original agency to offer treks to Ciudad Perdida, but was shut out from 1997 by paramilitaries.

For what it's worth, **Magic Tours** (Map p171; ☎ 5 421 9429 in Santa Marta; magictour186@yahoo.com; Calle 14 No 1B-50, Taganga; ☺ 8am-6pm) was the only agency that answered our emails, and is generally considered be the most professional and respectful of the environment. It's a family-run business that works closely with the Kogi along the route (an interview and photos with a chief, known as the *mamá*, are not uncommon). The food is excellent, coffee is served with Starbucks-like frequency, and many of the guides are *from* the mountains (not Santa Marta).

The German-owned **Sierra Tours** (Map p171; ☎ 5 421 9401 in Santa Marta; www.sierratours-trekking.com; Calle 17 No 1-18, Taganga) is also more professional than most and has come to be a favorite with Israelis. It also offers additional treks in the Sierra Nevadas (Don Diego, for instance). In high season, it also has an office in Santa Marta at Calle 10C No 2-04 (Map p166).

Turcol (Map p166; ☎ 5 421 2256 in Santa Marta; www.buritaca2000.com; Carrera 1C No 20-15, Santa Marta) has the most experience and the most money, due to its monopoly on the route since the late '90s. It offers new mosquito nets, decent grub, purified water and its own housing on some nights of the trek. But judging from its office and employees, professionalism is not the No 1 priority. It has a second office at Calle 10C No C1-83 (Map p166) as well as a satellite office in front of La Casa de Felipe in Taganga (Map p171).

Getting There & Away
Ciudad Perdida lies about 40km southeast of Santa Marta as the crow flies. It's hidden deep in the thick forest amid rugged mountains, far away from any human settlement, and without access roads. The only way to get there is by foot and the return trip takes six days, covering 40 km. The trail begins in El Mamey, which is reached by vehicle.

RESERVA NATURAL EL MATUY
This small **bird sanctuary** (☎ 315 751 8456; reservas@ agroecotur.org; cabañas per person full board COP$120,000) and lodging near Palomino is a nice spot to escape the crowds of PNN Tayrona and lose yourself for a few days on another fine piece of sand. The reserve is tucked away on a private *finca* (farm) boasting 5km of beach banked by the San Salvador and Palomino Rivers. There are six rustic but very well decorated cabañas here, with embroidered bedspreads, outdoor bathrooms and showers, and porches with hammocks. The beach is peppered with coconut trees providing lots of shade as well as plenty of picturesque photo ops. There is no electricity but rustic farm chandeliers are scattered about some of the common areas. The whole vibe instills instant relaxation on initial approach.

Lodging is by reservation only and includes three meals. Mosquito nets are provided as well. Service is friendly and totally unobtrusive. To get here, take a minibus to Palomino (COP$7000, two hours) and the reserve will pick you up when its vehicle is available, or ask a taxi (COP$10,000) or moto-taxi (COP$2000) to drop you at Playa de Tuchi, a five-minute drive from Palomino.

LA GUAJIRA PENINSULA
Everyone from English pirates to Spanish pearl hunters have tried to conquer the Guajira Peninsula – a vast swath of barren sea and sand that ranks as Colombia's northernmost point – but none have succeeded, unable to tame the indomitable Wayuu people, who call this region home. The peninsula is split into three sections: Southern Guajira, home to its capital, Riohacha; Middle Guajira on the border with Venezuela; and Upper Guajira, where you'll find end-of-the-world paradises like Cabo de la Vela and Punta Gallinas, the latter an immaculate collision of desert and sea that is the coast's most remarkable setting.

RIOHACHA
☎ 5 / pop 170,000
Riohacha, 175km northeast of Santa Marta, the gateway to the semi-arid desert that dominates the tip of Colombia, has traditionally been the end of the line. Beyond here something wicked this way comes: Colombia's Wild, Wild Northwest, a diesel and dust landscape dominated by two traditionally feared populations: contraband smugglers, piling everything from refrigerators to cameras to humans onto buses and trucks from Maicao,

near the border with Venezuela, to ship to the rest of Colombia and beyond; and the fiercely independent Guajira people, known as Wayuu, thought of around Colombia as a people not to be crossed, living by their own rule of law on the edge of the continent.

While both factions are still here, much has changed around Riohacha. Those 'dreaded' Wayuu have been tamed by ecotourism – it is now possible to sleep in traditional Wayuu homes all over the peninsula, an emerging tourism sector in Colombia that is ripe for upsurge over the next few years. The town isn't teeming with things to do, so there's no reason to linger, but the picturesque palm-strewn beach that stretches 5km is surprisingly nice and the 1.2km pier, constructed in 1937 and standing today as a symbol of the city, makes for a lovely evening stroll while overnighting here on your way to Cabo de la Vela and beyond.

Orientation

From the highway from Santa Marta, Carrera 15 is the main commercial thoroughfare through town, turning into the beachfront Carrera 1 as it turns east and parallels the beach across the center of the city. Riohacha's main plaza, Parque José Prudencio Padilla, sits two blocks inland between Carreras 7 and 9.

Information

Bancolombia (Parque José Prudencio Padilla) ATM.
Command.com (☎ 727 0600; Calle 6 No 7-07; per hr COP$1500; ☺ 7am-8pm Mon-Sat) Internet services, two blocks east of Parque José Prudencio Padilla.
Deprisa (☎ 727 0462; Calle 7 No 7-04; ☺ 8am-noon & 2-6pm Mon-Fri, 8am-noon Sat) Postal services.
Hospital (☎ 727 3312; Av de los Estudiantes)
Kaí Ecotravel (☎ 311 436 2830; www.kaiecotravel .com) This excellent agency is pioneering ecotourism in the Guajira and has spent years fostering relationships with the Wayuu, allowing access to Punta Gallinas (p183) and Parque Nacional Natural (PNN) Macuira, both Wayuu-controlled. They are the go-to source for tours on the peninsula as well as homestays with indigenous families.
Policía de la Guajira (☎ 727 3879; cnr Calle 15 & Carrera 7)
Tourist office (☎ 727 1015; Carrera 1 No 4-42; ☺ 8am-noon & 2-6pm Mon-Fri) Located on the waterfront, this extraordinarily nice tourism office can help you with lodging, restaurants and information on trips deeper into the Guajira. Beautiful Wayuu handbags and hammocks are also for sale.

Sights & Activities

Riohacha is not wrought with things to see and do. In town, the 1.2km-long **walking pier**, built in 1937, is an impressive piece of maritime architecture and makes for a lovely stroll out to sea. On weekend evenings, the **malecón** (boardwalk) and its parallel street, Carrera 1, fill with revelers taking in the waterfront restaurants and bars. Unless it's raining, you'll find Wayuu women dressed in traditional garb, hawking wonderful handbags and other weaved wares here.

The town's main square, **Parque José Prudencio Padilla**, set two blocks back from the beach, is also a nice surprise, full of verdant trees; it makes for a welcome escape from the blistering sun. The **Cathedral de Nuestra Señora de los Remedios**, with a venerated image of the Virgin on its high alter since colonial times, is also here.

The main attraction around Riohacha itself is a trip out to the **Santuario de Flora y Fauna Los Flamencos**, a 700-hectare nature preserve 25km from town in Camarones. Pink flamingos inhabit this tranquil area in great numbers; up to 10,000 or so call the area home in the wet season (September through to December), and bunches of up to 2000 can usually be seen in one of the four lagoons within the park – quite a dramatic and colorful site.

Admission to the park is free, but if you want to see the flamingos, you'll need to take a canoe (one to three people COP$30,000, per person extra COP$10,000) out on the water. The skippers usually know where the birds are hanging out, but will not take you if they are beyond a reasonable distance. There is also a new **accommodation complex** (☎ 310 369 7763; cabaña/hammock per person incl dinner COP$50,000/40,000) built by the park, where you can spend the night right on the lagoon. The whole area is quite picturesque and tranquil (except on weekends, when the nearby restaurant swarms with drunken locals and pounding reggaetón).

Sleeping & Eating

Fundamentally not a tourist town, Riohacha is only beginning to embrace travelers. For this reason, cheap and plentiful accommodations are slim and none. There is virtually no budget range here, and the midrange is overpriced…dramatically. Still, as you are likely only to stop over here on your way north, don't sweat it. Enjoy the excellent food and don't focus on your lodging.

El Castillo del Mar (☎ 727 5043; hotelcastillodelmar@gmail.com; Calle 9A No 15-352; cabañas with fan per person COP$20,000, s/d with air-con COP$60,000/80,000; 🍴 🖵) It doesn't look like much from the outside but inside, this German-owned hotel is a colorful and homely spot. It's on the beach just five minutes walk from *centro* (though it's barricaded by a prisonlike barrier). Whitewashed castle-style cabañas are large and comfortable, and there's bougainvillea scattered about the property to shake up the color scheme. You can walk into town along the beach. This is pretty much the main option for budget travellers.

Mi Casona (☎ 728 5680 Calle 2 No 10-16; s/d with air-con COP$50,000/60,000; 🍴) This is the cheapest livable option near the beach in *centro*, just two blocks away. It's a small *residenciales* with well-maintained rooms and nice bathrooms. One upside is it is across the street from La Cascada, a great budget restaurant. The downside is it's double the price it should be.

La Cascada (☎ 727 4446; Calle 2 No 9-93; mains COP$10,000-29,000; 🍴 breakfast, lunch & dinner) A great little local's spot serving homestyle *comida corriente* for COP$7000 and fancier dishes like chicken with mandarin sauce. In fact, they love mandarin here – cool off with a refreshing mandarin frappé, a liquid orgasm in this heat.

La Tinaja (☎ 727 3929; Calle 1 No 4-59; mains COP$21,000-55,000; 🍴 breakfast, lunch & dinner) This waterfront restaurant is known for *mariscos* (seafood), especially lobster and seafood crepes. The most popular dish is the platter, smothered across the board *au gratin*.

There are two good local spots to try goat – one of the Wayuu's most popular dishes. Both are owned by the same family. The legendary choice is **Asadero Don Pepe** (☎ 727 4446; Calle 2 No 9-93; mains COP$6000-12,000; 🍴 dinner) – neighboring businesses want it shut down, but this technically 'illegal' restaurant on the waterfront has been here so long, it's invincible; and **El Rancho de Toñe'** (☎ 728 7131; Calle 2 No 9-93; mains COP$6000-12,000; 🍴 dinner Mon-Sat, lunch & dinner Sun). See if they have *friche* – goat cooked in its own fat, traditionally with innards and all (you can hold the innards), and chopped into small chunks. Or *chivo asado*, a more straight-up slab of grilled goat meat. It also does steaks, chicken and *chorizo*.

Getting There & Away

AIR

The airport is 3km southwest of town. A taxi costs COP$5000 from town. **Avianca** (☎ 727 3627; www.avianca.com; Calle 7 No 7-04; 🕑 8am-6pm Mon-Fri, 9am-1pm Sat) operates one flight in and out per day to Bogotá, departing at 12:20pm (from COP$373,000, one way). From Bogotá, the flight leaves for Riohacha at 10:15am.

BUS

The bus terminal is at the corner of Av El Progreso and Carrera 11, about 1km from the center. A taxi to the bus station is COP$3000. **Expreso Brasilia/Unitransco** (☎ 727 2240) services Santa Marta (COP$15,000, 2½ hours) and Barranquilla (COP$20,000, five hours) every 30 minutes; Cartagena (COP$35,000, seven hours) and Maicao (COP$5000, one hour), on the border with Venezuela, hourly; and Bogotá (COP$80,000, 18 hours) once daily at 3pm. A bus bound for Bucaramanga (COP$60,000, 12 hours) also departs once daily at 3pm.

To reach Cabo de la Vela (below), **Cootrauri** (☎ 728 0976; Calle 15 No 5-39) runs *colectivos* as they fill up every day from 5am to 6pm to Uribia (COP$12,000, one hour), where you must switch for the final leg to Cabo (COP$10,000 to COP$15,000, 2½ hours). Just let the driver know you are heading to Cabo and he will drop you off at the switch point. The last car for Cabo leaves Urribia at 1pm. You can also arrange rides from Riohacha direct to Cabo de la Vela from anywhere between COP$150,000 return for one person to as low as COP$75,000 per person with four, but often these are day trips that are not worth the time commitment. Many of these guys hang around the waterfront in Riohacha.

To visit Santuario de Fauna y Flora Los Flamencos, you must catch a *colectivo* from the Francisco El Hombre traffic circle, next to Almacen 16 de Julio, bound for the town of Camerones. The driver will drop you at the entrance to the park.

Buses bound for Caracas (COP$155,000, 18 hours) also depart daily from Riohacha with Expreso Brasilia at 4pm.

CABO DE LA VELA
☎ 5 / pop 1500
The remote Wayuu fishing village of Cabo de la Vela, 180km northwest of Riohacha, juts out from the Guajira Peninsula like the hump of a long lost camel, wandering in the desert

---

LOCAL VOICES: FRANCISCO HUÈRFANO PÁEZ

Age: 41
Occupation: General Director, Kaí Ecotravel
Residence: Uribia
Favorite Colombian Singer: Jonny Buenaventura

'The **Guajira Peninsula** (p179) is a spectacular area with a very special culture. The Wayuu are neither Colombian nor Venezuelan, they are a culturally, socially and historically independent people. It's a border of culture. There is a myth that the Wayuu are dangerous, but really they're very generous and curious. They appear tough and are definitely strong-willed, but are very exotic and full of passion.

'The Guajira is a place to relax and just feel the heat and the Wayuu magic. No itineraries. No hours. No days of the week. Just experience the culture, live and direct.

'**Punta Gallinas** (opposite) is my favorite place in the Guajira for its essence – it is pure nature, totally virgin and infinite.'

---

between the cape and Uribia for days without catching sight of a fellow mammal. The village itself is little more than a dusty rural community of strong-willed Wayuu, living in traditional huts made from cactus that ride right up against the sea. But the surrounding area is a highlight of the Upper Guajira and one of the most beautiful spots in Colombia. The cape for which it's named is full of rocky cliffs above and sandy beaches below, all set against a backdrop of stunning desert colors.

The rustic village has electricity by generator only and there are no fixed phone lines, internet or any of life's numerous other distractions. In the last couple of years, Cabo has become a hotbed of ecotourism and now boasts a wealth of indigenous-style accommodations. It's not as clean as you might want it to be, nor is the beach as nice as you might want it to be, and there's definitely too many flies, but there is something to be said for hanging out in a village on the tip of the continent without a care in the world.

Cabo de la Vela is not for everyone – you are definitely off the grid here. It's not uncommon to see Wayuu men toting large rifles or a goat-slaughtering in someone's living room. But for a certain kind of traveler – you know who you are – Cabo is the sort of place you can lose yourself indefinitely.

The village is best avoided during Semanta Santa (Holy Week) and December and January, when Colombians descend on the area, turning its tranquil atmosphere into a rowdy fiesta.

Sights & Activities
The main activity in Cabo de la Vela is no activity at all, just lazily passing the time in a hammock in this far-flung corner of the continent. If you're too anxious for this sort of thing, this is probably not the place for you, but there are a few options to satiate your wayward needs. Wayuu and tourists alike head to **El Faro**, a small light-tower on the edge of a rocky promontory, for those postcard-perfect sunsets. The view is indeed stunning – just watch out for *langosta*, massive flying beasts the size of model airplanes, named for their keen resemblance to lobster and considered the Guajira's most annoying pest. It's a 45-minute walk from town, or you can wrangle a ride with a local for COP$30,000 or so return. If you set out on your own in summer, the heat can be stifling. Take plenty of water, insect repellent and a hat.

Just beyond El Faro is a far more appealing beach than in the village itself. **Ojo del Agua** is a nicely sized crescent-shaped dark-sand beach bound by 5m-high cliffs. The beach gets its name from a small freshwater pool that was discovered here, a true rarity in the Upper Guajira.

But the jewel of the area is **Playa del Pilón**, far and away the most beautiful beach in Cabo. Here you'll find a startling rust-orange collection of sand backed by craggy cliffs that glow a spectacular greenish-blue color, especially at sunrise and sunset. In wet season, add in lush desert flora and fauna to the mix and the whole scene is rather cinematic (though in high season, you must add in 1000 tourists on the small beach and a few kitesurfers). **Pilón de Azucar**, a 100m hillside, looms over the beach and provides the area's most picturesque viewpoint, the whole of Alta Guajira displayed before you with the Serranía del

Carpintero mountain range in the distance. Picture a tropical beach on the rocky coast of Ireland and you have an idea of the scene here. A statue of **La Virgen de Fátima**, erected here in 1938 by Spanish pearl hunters, stands at the top of the viewpoint as the patron saint of Cabo.

Sleeping & Eating

There are over 60 rustic Posadas Turísticas de Colombia (www.posadasturisticas.com.co) in Cabo de la Vela, part of a government-sponsored ecotourism project that has helped the Wayuu into the hospitality business. Lodging is generally in Wayuu huts fashioned from *yotojoro*, the inner core of the *cardon* cactus that grows rampantly in the desert here. You can choose between smaller hammocks, larger and warmer traditional Wayuu *chinchorros* (locally crafted hammocks) or beds with private bathrooms (though running water is scarce). You will also need to bring your own towel. Nearly all posadas here double as restaurants, more or less serving the same thing – fish or goat in the COP$10,000 to COP$15,000 range and market-price lobster.

Pujuru Hostal-Restaurant (☎ 310 659 4189; www.pujuru.com; hammocks COP$10,000, chinchorros COP$15,000, s/d with bathroom COP$25,000/50,000) Run by an attentive Wayuu woman named Nena, this *posada ecoturística* offers well-constructed huts for private rooms, and luggage lockers for those in hammocks. The generators run from 6pm to 10pm and the restaurant (mains COP$10,000 to COP$15,000) serves up a tasty *pargo rojo* (red snapper), though the shrimp and rice is best avoided. Showers are bucket style.

Hostería Jarrinapi (☎ 311 683 4281; hammocks COP$10,000, r per person COP$30,000) A little fancier

on the infrastructure hierarchy, these huts, complete with a front desk and running water, feel almost like an actual hotel. The generators pump all night, from 5:30pm to 6am. The restaurant (mains COP$5000 to COP$35,000) does the usual suspects, but also cheaper fast food like burgers and hot dogs.

Refugio Pantu (☎ 313 581 0858; chinchorro per person COP$20,000, r per person COP$30,000) If you want to trade solitude for beach, this posada sits north of town, the last one in a long line that extends toward El Faro. Its restaurant and cabañas are *yorotoro chic*, a step-up in construction with liberal use of stone, and hotel-grade bathrooms. President Uribe even slept here in 2005. It's a hike to town and the beach here isn't pretty or sandy.

Getting There & Away

Arriving in Cabo de la Vela is not the easiest trip you'll make in Colombia, so most folks come on an organized tour. That said, it's possible to come on your own, and all the more rewarding. From Riohacha, you must catch a *colectivo* at **Cootrauri** (☎ 728 0976; Calle 15 No 5-39) to Uribia; it will depart as it fills up every day from 5am to 6pm (COP$12,000, one hour). The driver will let you out in front of Panaderia Peter-Pan, from where trucks and 4WDs leave for Cabo (COP$10,000 to COP$15,000, 2½ hours). Non-4WD vehicles are a definite no-go.

PUNTA GALLINAS

Punta Gallinas is the kind of mystical place you read about in books (like the Thai beach in Alex Garland's novel *The Beach*) or see in movies (like Playa Boca del Cielo in the 2001 film, *Y Tu Mamá También*), but rarely stumble upon in real life. Reaching this stunning wildscape, South America's northernmost

---

THE WAYUU CANDY BANDITS

There are only two roads that lead to Cabo de la Vela, neither of which is paved. Depending on weather conditions in the wet season (April, October and November), drivers will take the more direct road northwest out of Uribia, or head east and take the coastal road through Carizal. When weather is not an issue, ask your driver to take the coastal route. Besides the obvious reasons, an amazing thing happens in a small Wayuu village between El Cardón and Carizal. Teams of Wayuu children have set up checkpoint barricades – not unlike the military and police ones throughout the country – and will not let you pass through without a handout. Your driver will buy cookies and candy for this purpose. It is the kind of travel experience money can't buy – one after another you pass through some 10 or so child-manned roadblocks, full of screaming Wayuu offspring trading passage for sweets!

tip, isn't exactly a skip down to the corner store, either. But those that make the effort will be rewarded with one of the most dazzling landscapes in South America, a sanctuary of solitude that equals travel Nirvana.

Located approximately 75km north of Cabo de la Vela, Punta Gallinas is accessed via Bahía Hondita, where burnt-orange cliffs surround an opaque emerald bay with a dazzling wide and wild beach, and translucent waters that stretch kilometers out to sea. There is absolutely nothing here except a large colony of pink flamingos. The bay is home to a mere eight Wayuu families and about 60 people. The land they call home is indeed spectacular: a feral desertscape peppered with vibrant green vegetation (in winter) and buzzing with herds of goat and swarms of *langostas* (lobsters). As the continent gives way to the Caribbean, massive sand dunes toppling 60m in height push right up against the shimmering turquoise sea like a five-story tsunami in reverse. The otherworldly scene here is only trumped by **Taroa Beach**, Colombia's most beautiful and least trampled upon, accessed by sliding down a towering sand dune right into the water. It is here that you will have that treasured travel moment, a flash of discovery so rare in this globalized world, your photos will never do it justice, and nobody will ever believe you.

The only place to stay is in hammocks with a very sweet Wayuu family, who cook wonderful meals (succulent grilled lobster, for instance) and can help show you around the desert. The fact that Punta Gallinas is not a national park is a shame from a preservation standpoint, but it should tell you something about the place: be it a novel or a film, it's almost impossible to believe it's not fiction.

There is virtually no way to reach Punta Gallinas without the help of an organized tour, though don't be put off by the sound of that. We are talking about you and your mates and a couple of Wayuu handling the travel logistics. From September to November, access is by three-hour boat ride from Puerto Bolívar, a short drive from Cabo de la Vela near the El Cerrejón coal mine. The rest of the year, vehicles can reach Bahía Honda, the first of the three side-by-side bays in the area, where a one-hour boat ride lands you in Punta Gallinas. Contact Aventure Colombia (p140) in Cartagena or Kaí Ecotravel (p180) in Riohacha to make the trip; the latter is an ecotourism pioneer in the area.

SOUTHWEST OF CARTAGENA

Unspoiled beaches and the road less traveled characterize the Caribbean coast southwest of Cartagena, an area that, due to security concerns, has seen little international tourism in the last two decades. Secure and at the ready these days, areas like Tolú and Islas de San Bernardo, which previously catered to Colombians, only are now wide open for foreign exploration.

There is quite a notable change in the landscape here from the northern coast through the departments of Sucre, Córdoba, Antioquia and Chocó. Swampy pasturelands dotted with billowing tropical Ceiba trees, ground-strangling mangrove trees and crystalline lagoons flank the seaside around the Golfo de Morrosquillo, while the jungle near the Darién Gap rides right up against cerulean waters and beaches where the Golfo de Urabá gives way to Panama near the serene villages of Capurganá and Sapzurro.

TOLÚ
☎ 5 / pop 36,000

You'd never know it, but the tranquil pueblo of Tolú, the capital of the Golfo de Morrosquillo, is one of Colombia's most visited tourist destinations. Colombians flock here throughout the high season for its small-town feel, wild nightclubs and surrounding beaches and natural playground, but there's rarely a foreigner in sight. The rest of the year, it's a peaceful spot to get off the gringo trail and holiday like the locals. Tolú is a small town where residents choose bicycles over vehicles, and bicycle taxis, known as *bicitaxis*, are an art form: each one decked out with individual personality and flair.

Tolú's lengthy *malecón*, full of seaside bars, restaurants and small artisan stalls makes for a fun stroll, but the main draw for foreign tourists is its proximity to Islas de San Bernardo, part of Parque Nacional Natural (PNN) Corales del Rosario y San Bernardo (p152), the Bernardo section of which is more conveniently accessed from Tolú. Here the picturesque beaches on Isla Múcura, wrought with mangroves and postcard-perfect palm trees, are some of the coast's most idyllic.

Information

Bancolombia (☎ 288 5711; Calle 14 No 2-88; 🕑 8am-4pm Mon-Thu, to 4:30pm Fri) ATM; on the southside of Plaza Pedro de Heredia.

Hospital de Tolú (☎ 288 5256; Calle 16 No 9-61; 🕑 24hr)

iC@fe (☎ 286 0118; Calle 17 No 2-20; per hr COP$1400; 🕑 9am-10:30pm) Internet access.

Mundo Marina (☎ 288 4431; www.clubnauticomundomarina.com; Carrera 1 No 14-40; 🕑 6:30am-8pm) This recommended agency does daily tours departing at 8:30am to Islas de San Bernardo for COP$35,000.

Policia Nacional (☎ 288 5030; cnr Carrera 5 & Calle 16)

Servientrega (☎ 286 0630; Carrera 4 No 15-40; 🕑 8am-noon & 2-5pm Mon-Fri, 8am-noon Sat) Postal services.

Tourist office (☎ 286 0599; Carrera 2 No 15-40; 🕑 8am-noon & 2-6pm) Located in the *alcadía* on the west side of Plaza Pedro Heredia.

Sights & Activities

Tolú is the main jumping-off point for day tours to Islas de San Bernardo (p186). In high season, the town swells with Colombian tourists who come to eat and drink their days away up and down the coast of the Golfo de Morrosquillo from here to Coveñas, where you'll find less infrastructure but better beaches (read *better* but still not great), many of which are dotted with thatched-roof tables fit for drinking an afternoon away.

For a bit of nature, the wonderful **La Ciénega de Caimanera** sits halfway between Tolú and Coveñas. This 1800-hectare nature preserve is part freshwater, part saltwater bog that is home to five varieties of mangroves, the most notable of which, the red mangrove, has roots that twist and tangle in and out of the water like hyperactive strands of spaghetti. The canoe trip here is a pleasant and beautiful way to live an hour and a half of your life, meandering through man-made mangrove tunnels and sampling oysters right off the roots.

To reach the Ciénega, grab any bus heading toward Coveñas and ask to be let off at La Boca de la Ciénega. Canoe guides wait for tourists on the bridge, and charge COP$20,000 for one to two people and as little as COP$8000 per person for larger groups.

Tolú's beaches aren't up to snuff – head 20km south to Coveñas for more agreeable patches of sand. The best is **Playa Blanca**, accessed via moto-taxi from Coveñas. *Colectivos* depart every 10 minutes daily (COP$2500) from near Supermercado Popular at the corner of Carrera 2 and Calle 17 in Tolú.

Sleeping

Villa Babilla (☎ 288 6124; www.villababillahostel.com; Calle 20 No 3-40; s from COP$18,000, d from COP$23,000, r with balcony COP$25,000; 💻) Three blocks from the waterfront, this German-run hostel/hotel offers a gringo-friendly space highlighted by its thatched-roof outdoor TV lounge. There's a kitchen, laundry service and free coffee all day. It's also the only hostel we saw in the entirety of the Colombian coast that had installed showerheads. At time of research, a new three-story structure with apartments and rooms with balconies was nearly finished.

Two decent midrange options on the waterfront are **Hotel Caribe** (☎ 288 5115; hotelcaribe1@yahoo.com; Carrera 1 No 18-82; s/d with fan COP$25,000/40,000, with air-con COP$40,000/65,000), notable for its well-maintained exterior and cozy open-air restaurant; and **Ibatama del Mar** (☎ 288 5110; Carrera 1 No 19-45; s/d with fan COP$15,000/30,000, with air-con COP$30,000/50,000), which offers an interesting courtyard full of old canons, statues and various mini-gardens.

Eating & Drinking

Terraza La 15 (☎ 288 6226; cnr Carrera 1 & Calle 15; mains COP$7000-25,000; 🕑 breakfast, lunch & dinner) This simple waterfront spot serves up bubbling, hot seafood *cazuela*, cheaper chicken dishes and several breakfast choices. It has also thrown down a few tables on the water for an atmospheric tipple.

La Red (☎ 286 0782; Carrera 1 No 19-100; mains COP$7000-25,000; 🕑 breakfast, lunch & dinner) It doesn't look like much, but this waterfront option knows its way around seafood – the *pargo rojo* (red snapper), lightly fried in butter and topped with a creamy seafood sauce, is one of the tastiest small-town dishes on the coast.

There are a series of food stalls known as the **Casino de Comida** at Calle 20 and Carrera 1 on the waterfront, where set meals of fish or meat are served up by eager *cocineras* for around COP$6000.

Getting There & Away

Expreso Brasilia/Unitransco (☎ 288 5223), **Rapido Ochoa** (☎ 288 5226) and **Caribe Express** (☎ 288 5223) share a small bus station on the south west side of Plaza Pedro de Heredia. Buses depart for Cartagena (COP$20,000, three hours) and Montería (COP$15,000, two hours) hourly.

Other sample destinations include Bogotá (COP$100,000, 19 hours) at 8am and 5:30pm; Medellín (COP$70,000, 10 hours, four departures daily); and Santa Marta (COP$45,000, six hours) at 7:30am and 5:30pm.

If you are continuing on to Turbo and the Panamanian border beyond, you must take a bus to Montería and switch there for Turbo. All of the Medellín-bound buses stop in Montería, as does **Transportes Luz** (☎ 288 6069; Calle 16 No 10-79), a good door-to-door option for groups or those that need to make it to Montería beyond standard bus hours. Call ahead for reservations.

ISLAS DE SAN BERNARDO

The 10 archipelagoes that make up the Islas de San Bernardo, set off the coast of Tolú, are a far more spectacular and interesting addition to the Parque Nacional Natural (PNN) Corales del Rosario y San Bernardo than their neighbors to the north (p152).

Carib *indígenas* once called the islands home, but they are more trampled on today by vacationing Colombians, who have done well to keep the islands a secret from foreign tourists. Known for their crystalline waters, mangrove lagoons and white-sand beaches – some of Colombia's best – these picturesque islands stand out on the Caribbean coast as a little oasis of rest and relaxation.

Day tours (COP$35,000) to the archipelago depart daily from the Muelle Turístico in Tolú at around 8:30am. The full day includes fly-bys of one of the world's most densely populated islands, **Santa Cruz del Islote**, where between 850 and 1000 people, mostly fisherman, live on top of each other in what can only be described as a tropical shantytown huddled on 1200 sq meters of cramped space; and Isla Tintípan, the largest of the archipelago's islands. Most of the tourism infrastructure is on **Isla Múcura**, where tours stop for three hours of free time. Here you can rent snorkeling equipment for COP$5000, kick back and have lunch and a beer (not included in the tour), or simply wander the mangrove-heavy landscape. The best beach and snorkeling is on **Isla Palma**, where the tour concludes at the **aquarium** (admission COP$12,000), which is curiously more of a rustic zoo than a waterworld (though there is a foggy window aquarium here). You'll also find monkeys, pink flamingos, loads of birds (including many loose ma-

caws) and even a buffalo! It's strange, but sort of interesting.

Sleeping & Eating
Everything from camping to high-end hideaways are available in San Bernardo, mostly on Isla Múcura and Isla Palma. In high season, you will definitely need to make reservations, and expect considerable price hikes from those listed here.

Estrella de David (☎ 312 893 8220; Isla Múcura; hammocks COP$10,000, campsite per person incl meals COP$40,000) This is the budget option, located at La Punta (where the boats dock) on Isla Múcura. There is a thatched-roof hammock area and very nice bathrooms. Water for a shower is included in the price.

Decameron Isla Palma (☎ 310 657 1994; www .decameron.com; Isla Palma; d from COP$416,000; ☐ ⊠) This Club Med–like all-inclusive resort on Isla Palma offers all the usual suspects with one additional coup: a thin sliver of sand that takes honors for the best beach in the area.

Punta Faro (☎ 1 616 3136 in Bogotá; www.puntafaro .com; Isla Múcura; d 3-night all-inclusive package from COP$1.5 million; ☐ ⊠) This Isla Múcura resort is the chicest in the archipelago, making liberal use of mangrove wood in its beautiful lobby and bedroom furniture, and catering mostly to wealthy Colombians. There is a private beach, three restaurants, two bars and transport from Cartagena. Equipment such as kayaks and snorkel gear is included in the price. Day passes for the beach run a stiff COP$75,000 (including lunch) but are a very handy option for those on a day tour here.

TURBO
☎ 4 / pop 113,000
Previously off limits to foreigners due to *muchos* paramilitaries and guerrillas in the neighborhood, the situation in Turbo at time of research was secure and calm, but ridding yourself of revolutionaries does not a destination make. Part of the department of Antioquia 373km northwest of Medellín, Turbo is a loud and brass workhorse port surrounded by banana plantations and of little interest to travelers. It's a get in, get out town whose one claim to tourism fame is the boat to Capurganá, which is nearly impossible to do without spending the night here. Don't let the door hit you on the ass on the way out – Turbo is best seen through a rearview mirror.

(NEARLY) OVERLAND TO PANAMA

First of all, it is not possible to drive a vehicle from Colombia to Panama – the Pan-American Hwy does not extend through Colombia's jungly Darién Gap, though that doesn't seem to stop some folks from trying. And though daredevils have crossed the 87km stretch in all-terrain vehicles, on foot, and loads of other ways, it is not safe and not recommended.

It is possible and fairly safe, however, to cross the border to Panama (mostly) overland, as opposed to taking a plane or a boat from Cartagena. At the time of research, the following route was secure and calm, but do check ahead for security updates before setting out, and stick to the coastal areas.

1. Make your way to Turbo (opposite). Due to guerrilla activity in the area, the Medellín–Turbo route should be traversed during the day only – leave before noon (COP$51,000, eight hours). From Cartagena, you have to go to Montería (COP$35,000, 4½ hours) and change there for Turbo (COP$25,000, five hours). Buses run regularly from 7am to 5pm (leave Cartagena before 11am or you will be stuck for the night in Montería). In almost all scenarios, you will need to spend the night in Turbo.

2. Catch a boat to Capurganá. One boat departs daily from the Turbo docks (La Wuafa) at 8:30am in low season, and several throughout the day (when full) from 6am in high season (COP$49,000, 2½ hours). Arrive at least an hour early to secure a ticket. Hang on to your hat – this can be a bumpy ride. There is a 10kg baggage limit – COP$500 per kilo over charge applies.

3. Get your Colombian exit stamp at **DAS** (☎ 311 746 6234; ☺ 8am-5pm Mon-Fri, 9am-4pm Sat), near Carpuganá's harbor, one day before departure to Puerto Obaldia (the office will not be open by the time you leave on the morning of your departure). For accommodations in Capurganá, see p189. It's a lovely little town to kill a few days in.

4. Take a *lancha* (small boat) over the border to Puerto Obaldia (COP$20,000, 45 minutes) in Panama. Boats depart Capurganá at 7:30am on Sunday, Monday, Wednesday, and Friday – the same days that flights run from Puerto Obaldia to Panama City. Be at the docks by 7am and ask around for Marcelino or Justino. This is another dicey sea journey depending on sea conditions.

5. Obtain your Panama entry stamp at Panamanian immigration upon disembarking in Puerto Olbaldía. From here, you can fly onward to Panama City on **Aeroperlas** (☎ in Panama 507 315 7500; www.aeroperlas.com) on Sunday, Monday, Wednesday and Friday at 10am (US$80).

For information on shipping a motorcycle or vehicle around the Darién Gap, check out shipping company **Horn Linie** (www.hornlinie.com).

Information
Banco de Bogotá(Calle101 No 12-131) ATM.
Turbo Internet.com (☎ 827 5100; Carrera 13 No 00-00; per hr COP$2000; ☺ 10am-8pm Mon-Fri, to 9pm Sat-Sun) Internet cafe.

Sleeping & Eating
Residencias Florida (☎ 827 3531; Carrera 13 No 99A-56; s/d with fan COP$15,000/25,000; ▣) It doesn't look like much (and it's not), but this simple spot on Turbo's loud Parque Principal is the best choice available for foreigners. The extremely friendly and helpful owner can fill you in on everything you need to know about organizing a boat to Capurganá. It's walking distance from the bus terminals and the docks.

Hotel Saussa (☎ 827 2022; Calle 13 No 99A-28; s/d/tr COP$20,000/30,000/50,000) A small step up from Florida and a good second option. It's right next door to Florida and there's a Chinese restaurant attached.

Mana (Carrera 13; set meals COP$5000; ☺ breakfast, lunch & dinner to 8pm) No street number, no sign, and, in all reality, no name (we had to pry Mana out of them, but it also goes by Inezita) – just homey *comida corriente*. It has a red awning and is across the street from Hotel Saussa.

An *interesting* spot for a drink is the new outdoor bar built in the shape of a boat in Parque Principal. Here you'll find 7-year-olds leading 5-year-olds on donkey rides, a mechanical bull, 9-year-olds driving mini-ATVs and *moto* raffles – you know, the usual.

Getting There & Away
From Cartagena, you must catch a bus to Montería (COP$35,000, 4½ hours) and switch at the shiny new central bus station for the bus to Turbo (COP$25,000 to COP$35,000, five hours). Three companies make the trip with trucks, 4WDs or *busetas* (you know, the ones where they honk and yell the entire journey in

an effort to pick up passengers), as the road is largely unpaved in long stretches and very bumpy. **Sotracor** (☎ 784 9023), **Gomez Hernandez** (☎ 784 9010) and **Coointur** (☎ 784 9008) depart more or less every half hour to hour from 7am to 5pm between the three companies. In Turbo, there is no central bus station but most of the companies of concern are located on Calle 101. Returns to Montería run from 4:30am to 4pm. **Sotrauraba** (☎ 827 2039) heads to Medellín hourly from 5am to 10pm (COP$51,000, eight hours) from Turbo.

Boats to Capurganá (COP$49,000, 2½ hours) leave daily from the port from 6am in high season and once at 8:30am in low season. Boats can fill up quickly with locals – arrive at least an hour early. It can be a wet and bumpy journey, so throw your luggage in a trash bag (vendors sell them for COP$1000), and try not to get stuck in the Gringo Seat – locals will try and force you to sit in the front, where the ride is the most miserable.

For continuing on to Panama, see the boxed text (p187).

CAPURGANÁ & SAPZURRO
☎ 4 / pop 2000

The somewhat isolated resort towns of Capurganá and Sapzurro, minutes from the Panamanian border, have done well to stay off the gringo grid. These two idyllic, laid-back villages and the surrounding beaches are the only ones between here and Punta Gallinas (p183) on the Guajira Peninsula that truly live up to their Caribbean bloodline. But much like Punta Gallinas, access has been both their savior and crutch. Being that these two paradisiacal destinations are only accessible by those willing to put up with the lengthy boat trip from Turbo, or those that can afford to fly, Capurganá and Sapzurro have remained Colombia's least overrun Caribbean jewels. Not to mention that 90% of the tourism here has been homegrown, due to access and security issues in the past (it is on the border, after all). That's all changing now, too; there is at least one foreign-owned hostel and a few more on the way.

Capurganá sits at the northwest edge of Colombia's Chocó department at the entrance to the Golfo de Urabá and offers the most tourism infrastructure – there is no shortage of accommodations and the town remains supremely relaxed, except during Semana Santa (Holy Week) and in November and

December. Sapzurro lies around the corner in a picturesque bay, the last settlement before Panama. It's smaller and offers even more peace and quiet (except for that *one* radio). Neither village is home to any cars.

For those making the overland trek to Panama and vice-versa, these two lax towns make for an ideal spot to break your journey, with swimming, swimming pool–pure beaches and a wealth of nature-related activities in the vicinity. Keep in mind these are border towns, and no ordinary border at that – it's the gateway between South and Central America. There are many soldiers about town.

Information
There are no banks in either town, so it's best to load up on cash before arrival.
Capurganá Tours (☎ 824 3173; www.capurganatours .com; ☽ 8am-noon & 2-6pm Mon-Sat) Friendly English-speaking agency that can book your flights in Panama as well as excursions in the area.
DAS (☎ 311 746 6234; ☽ 8am-5pm Mon-Fri, 9am-4pm Sat) Immigration services for those heading to Panama.
Internet (per hr COP$3000; ☽ 9am-9pm Mon-Sat) In the Jasepca building.
Panamanian consulate (☎ 314 653 4081; ☽ 8am-4pm Mon-Fri) Near the soccer field.

Sights
Both Capurganá and Sapzurro feel different than the rest of the coast; the ramshackle architecture and tranquil vibe feel somehow more Caribbean. Both towns are good for doing not much of anything. Those who do get out and about are rewarded with supreme beaches and wonderful nature opportunities. **El Cielo**, a primitive one-hour jungle hike into the mountains from Capurganá, offers several natural swimming pools and waterfalls along a trail that is also home to howler and squirrel monkeys, toucans and parrots. A pleasant coastal hike to **Aguacate** (one hour) also makes for a nice afternoon, stopping at beaches along the way (empty in low season) and taking in the even less crowded coastal village.

The two best beaches in the area are **La Miel**, just across the Panamanian border from Sapzurro (bring your ID – there is a co-Colombian/Panamanian military checkpoint). It's a quick walk up a series of steep stairs across the border and back down the other side (turn right at the phone booths and follow the sidewalk). The small beach here offers scrumptious white sand and cerulean waters, as does **Playa Soledad**, accessed by a three-hour walk or on a tour. It's better than La Miel as it's longer and cleaner.

Activities

Capurganá is reportedly home to better diving than Taganga (p170). At **Dive and Green** (☎ 316 781 6255; www.diveandgreen.com; ☽ 8:30am-12:30pm & 2-5:30pm) two tank dives cost COP$170,000 and PADI certification costs COP$790,000.

Sleeping & Eating

Restaurants are scarce in Capurganá, so most of the hotels offer all-inclusive packages, though there are a few budget options around the soccer field. Hotel owners often hang around the dock, waiting for passengers.

Camping El Chileno (Sapzurro; hammock COP$7000, campsite per person with/without tent COP$9000/7500, dm COP$20,000) Very rustic camping and hammock accommodations on the nicest end of Sapzurro's beach. Ask anyone in town for 'El Chileno' and they will point you in the right direction.

Hostal Los Delfines (☎ 316 866 3739; Capurganá; r per person with/without meals COP$28,000/12,000) This is a remarkably nice spot for the price – rooms include TVs, private bathrooms and patio hammocks. The owner, Anibal Palacio, always meets the boat from Turbo. It's in Capurganá proper.

Cabaña Darius (☎ 314 622 5638; www.darius capurgana.es.tl; Capurganá; dm COP$15,000, r per person COP$20,000; ☀) Run by a helpful American, this cozy Capurganá cabin offers very well appointed rooms and bathrooms with freshly tiled floors and a nice outdoor kitchen. It's on Playa Roca – a more natural setting than some (the various frogs on property sound like a video game!). Meals start at COP$6000 for breakfast and COP$12,000 for lunch/dinner.

Hostal Playas de Capurganá (☎ 316 482 5783; www .jardinbotanicodarien.com; Capurganá; r per person with/without meals COP$65,000/35,000; ☀) Even more lush than next door at Cabaña Darius (there's a botanical gardens on property), this is another friendly option closer to the beach, though

a collapsed third floor in early 2009 brings maintenance into question. Yoga and tai chi are offered as well. The pool here is shared by Darius.

Hotel Almar (☎ 824 4550; www.hotelalmar.com.co; Capurganá; r per person all-inclusive COP$220,000; ☐ ☒ ☀) This is the most upscale spot in Capurganá on the nicest stretch of sand in town, Playa Blanca. The log cabin–like structure offers roomy accommodations, a large sun deck and there's a dive center on the property. The price includes alcoholic beverages.

Hernán Patacón (mains COP$4000-12,000; ☽ 11:30am-7:30pm) If you have come from any direction other than Panama, you are no doubt sick of smashed fried plantains, known as *patacones*. Here your faith is restored. This beach hut (there is another location in town) on Playa Blanca does larger, thinner versions topped with everything from chicken and mushrooms to *arequipe* (milk caramel) and cheese – a very nice change of pace.

Josefina's (☎ 310 627 1578; mains COP$15,000-35,000; ☽ lunch & dinner) On Playa Blanca, Josefina's does wonderful seafood dishes in large portions with a friendly smile – a rare combo. The *pulpo* (octopus) in salsa *rosada* is excellent. The beachfront tree-stump tables are also good for a sundown beer. In low season, it may not appear to be open, but they will fire up with a few hours notice.

For a good time, all the nightlife action takes place in the various bars circling the soccer field.

Getting There & Away

There are only two ways to reach Capurganá and Sapzurro. The most economical route is to catch a boat from Turbo (COP$49,000, 2½ hours), which departs daily from 6am in high season and once at 8:30am the rest of the year . In low season, the boats depart for Turbo at 7:30am.

ADA (☎ 682 8817; www.ada.aero.com) also operates flights from Medellín (COP$363,000, one way) on Monday, Tuesday, Thursday, Friday and Saturday at noon in low season, and up to three flights daily in high season.

San Andrés & Providencia

The archipelago of San Andrés & Providencia is a case study in tropical multiple personality disorder. Geographically near Nicaragua, historically tied to England and politically part of Colombia, these pristine islands may lack an untainted pedigree, but their diverse history and picture-postcard setting are exactly what make them Colombia's most interesting paradise.

Here you'll find isolated beaches, unspoiled coral reefs and an alluring island flavor that on the surface seem conspicuously Colombian, but in time, the 300-year-old English/Creole-speaking Raizal culture, often pushed aside by Spanish influence, offers an even deeper cultural experience. Caught between two battling cultures, these islands offer a unique experience in South America.

San Andrés, the largest island in the archipelago and its commercial and administrative hub, offers the most tourism infrastructure and has been attracting tourists and mainland Colombians for several decades, most of whom flock to the island on duty-free shopping sprees bookended by a little sun and sand. The crowds, however, are not difficult to escape, and you could easily take up a Robinson Crusoe lifestyle on any of the isolated beaches.

Providencia, by contrast, offers the same turquoise sea, extensive coral reefs and rich underwater life that has made the entire archipelago a paradise for snorkelers and scuba divers – the second-largest barrier reef in the northern hemisphere is here – but none of the commercialism or crowds of its bigger brother to the south. Much of Providencia's colonial heritage is still alive and thriving in small hamlets of multihued wooden homes peppered about the island.

HIGHLIGHTS

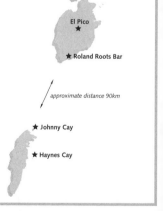

- Groove to reggae rhythms over Old Milwaukees at **Roland Roots Bar** (p202)

- Dig your toes into the pristine sands of beautiful **Johnny Cay** (p193), part of the four-hectare Johnny Cay Natural Regional Park

- Trek through iguana country to **El Pico** (p200) for stunning views of Providencia

- Go into the blue on a **scuba dive** (p194) or in a **semisubmarino** (p194) and gawk at Colombia's prettiest coral reefs and marine life

- Swim with the sting rays at sunset off **Haynes Cay** (p194)

El Pico
★

★ Roland Roots Bar

/ approximate distance 90km

★ Johnny Cay

★ Haynes Cay

History

The first inhabitants of the islands were probably a group of Dutch colonists who made their home on Providencia toward the end of the 16th century. In 1631 they were expelled by the English who effectively colonized the islands, home to the Raizal people, an Afro-Caribbean ethnic group. The English brought in black slaves from Jamaica and began to cultivate tobacco and cotton. The Spanish, irate at the English success on the islands, unsuccessfully invaded the archipelago in 1635.

Because of their strategic location, the islands provided convenient shelter for pirates waiting to sack Spanish galleons bound for home laden with gold and riches. In 1670 legendary pirate Henry Morgan established his base on Providencia and from here he raided both Panama and Santa Marta. Legend has it that his treasures are still hidden on the island.

Shortly after Colombia achieved independence, it laid claim to the islands, although Nicaragua fiercely disputed its right to do so. The issue was eventually settled by a treaty in 1928, which confirmed Colombia's sovereignty over the islands.

Geographic isolation kept the islands' unique English character virtually intact, though things started to change when a flight service connected the islands to the mainland in the 1950s. In 1954 a government plan to make the islands a duty-free zone brought with it tourism, commerce, entrepreneurs and Colombian culture, which slowly began to upend the 300-year-old Raizal identity, pushing it aside in favor of big tourism bucks. Unprepared and unqualified to make a living on tourism, locals were caught off guard.

In the early 1990s, the local government introduced restrictions on migration to the islands in order to slow the rampant influx of people and preserve the local culture and identity. Yet, Colombian mainlanders account for two-thirds of San Andrés' population. English and Spanish have been the two official languages since 1991.

The tourist and commercial boom caused San Andrés to lose much of its original character; it's now a blend of Latin American and English-Caribbean culture, though there is a movement to restore Raizal roots in San Andrés. Providencia has preserved much more of its colonial culture, even though tourism is making inroads into the local lifestyle.

Although the political status of San Andrés and Providencia is unlikely to change, Nicaragua continues to press the issue of its sovereignty over the islands at the International Court of Justice in the Hague. The court reaffirmed Colombia's sovereignty over the main islands in 2007, but said it would rule on the maritime boundary and secondary islands at a later date undetermined at the time of research.

Climate

The climate is typical of the Caribbean islands, with average temperatures of 26°C to 29°C, but humidity can be uncomfortably high. The rainy period is September to December and (a less wet period) May to June. Tourist season peaks are from late December to late January, during the Easter week and from mid-June to mid-July.

Parks & Reserves

In 2005 the Seaflower Marine Protected Area (MPA) was established to strengthen protection of key ecosystems in the marine area of the Seaflower Biosphere Reserve. The MPA includes 65,000 sq km of crystalline waters that are zoned for a variety of uses ranging from complete protection to controlled fishing. The objective of this multiple-use MPA is to foster sustainable development in the archipelago by strengthening conservation of marine biodiversity and also promoting sustainable use. The Seaflower is Colombia's first MPA and is the largest in the Caribbean.

There are one national and three regional parks in the archipelago. These are Parque Nacional Old Providence McBean Lagoon (p198); Johnny Cay Natural Regional Park (p193), a small cay in San Andrés Bay that is the archipelago's most visited tourist site; Old Point Mangrove Regional Park, the largest mangrove forest in San Andrés; and El Pico Natural Regional Park (p200) in Providencia, the archipelago's highest point, known locally as the Peak.

SAN ANDRÉS

☎ 8 / pop 66,000

Just 150km east of Nicaragua and some 800km northwest of Colombia, the seahorse-shaped island of San Andrés counts 27 sq km of cultural tug-of-war as both its asset and its handicap. Covered in coconut palms, San

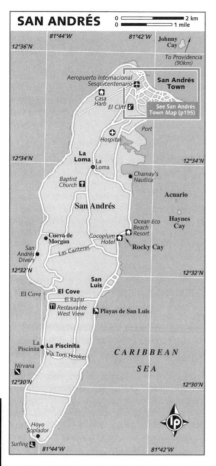

SAN ANDRÉS

0 — 2 km
0 — 1 mile

81°44'W   81°42'W   Johnny
12°36'N   Cay
                                   To Providencia
                                      (90km)
Aeropuerto Internacional   **San Andrés**
Sesquicentenario   **Town**
       Casa
       Harb   El Cliff   See San Andrés
                               Town Map (p195)
                        Port
       Hospital
    La
    Loma La
12°34'N Loma   12°34'N
                       Chamay's
  Baptist   Nautica
  Church
                           Acuario
   San Andrés
                    Ocean Eco   **Haynes**
                    Beach   **Cay**
 Cueva de   Resort
 Morgan Cocoplum
 San   Hotel   **Rocky Cay**
 Andrés   Las Canteras
 Divers
12°32'N   12°32'N
              San
              Luis
 El Cove   **El Cove**
            El Radar
         Restaurante
         West View   Playas de San Luis
   La   **La Piscinita**
 Piscinita Via Tom Hooker   C A R I B B E A N
 Nirvana   S E A
12°30'N   12°30'N

       Hoyo
       Soplador
  Surfing   81°42'W
              81°44'W

Andrés, the largest island in the archipelago, is indeed paradisiacal Caribbean, but not everything here is quite so crystal clear.

Take the downtown area, for instance, at the northern end of the island. Colombians call it El Centro, but the island's English-speaking Raizal people refer to it as North End. The cultural elbowing escalates from there. What's not up for debate, however, is that the commercialized area of town won't be splashed across any postcards anytime soon – it's a monstrosity of ferro-concrete blocks housing one duty-free shop after another, only broken up by the occasional hotel or restaurant.

All is not lost on San Andrés, however. A perfectly charming brick promenade lines

the waterfront here, hugging the floury sands and pristine waters of the coast and making for a lovely spot to enjoy a drink or take an evening stroll. And paradise is just slightly more than a canoe paddle away: the endlessly idyllic Johnny Cay sits off in the distance, just 1.5km from shore. In high season, it can feel as crowded as the Mediterranean, but otherwise Johnny Cay is the archipelago's finest moment.

San Andrés is best appreciated outside of the downtown hubbub. A 30km scenic paved road circles the island, and several minor roads cross inland, providing sufficient infrastructure to get around. There are two other small towns: La Loma (The Hill) in the central hilly region and San Luis on the eastern coast, both far less tourist-oriented than San Andrés Town and boasting some fine English-Caribbean wooden architecture. Excellent scuba diving and snorkeling opportunities abound all around the island – visibility and temperature here are nearly unrivaled in the Caribbean.

It only takes a day or two to suss out the Raizal from the Colombians. At just one third of the island's population, Raizals are now an ethnic minority, but their fading Creole culture – descended from English settlers, African slaves and West Indians from other islands – is what gives San Andrés its unique character, different from that of mainland Colombia.

Information

Banco de Bogotá (Map p195; ☎ 512 4195; Av Colón No 2-86, San Andrés Town) ATM.

Bistronet (Map p195; ☎ 512 6627; Centro Comercial San Andrés, San Andrés Town; per hr COP$3000; ⏱ 8:30am-9pm) Internet.

Costa Rican consulate (☎ 512 6684; Av Juan 23, San Andrés Town; ⏱ 8am-noon & 2-5pm)

Deprisa (Map p195; ☎ 512 3307; Av Colón, San Andrés Town; ⏱ 8am-noon & 2-6pm Mon-Fri, ⏱ 8am-noon Sat) Post office.

Honduran consulate (☎ 512 8481; Oficina Pesquera King Crab, 2nd fl, Zona Portuara; ⏱ 8am-noon & 2-5pm)

Metro Style (Map p195; ☎ 513 1279; Hotel Hernando Henry, Av Américas; per hr COP$2000; ⏱ 8am-9pm Mon-Sat) Internet.

Tourist office (Secretaría de Turismo; Map p195; ☎ 512 5058; www.sanandres.gov.co; Av Newball, San Andrés Town; ⏱ 8am-noon & 2-6pm Mon-Fri) Across from Restaurante La Regatta. It has a tourist information booth at the corner of Avs Colombia and 20 de Julio.

Sights

CUEVA DE MORGAN

This is the cave where Welsh pirate Henry Morgan is said to have buried some of his treasure. The **cave** (Map p192; admission COP$5000) is 120m long, but it's filled with water, so you see only its mouth. You can't enter the cave and there's not much to see here anyway, yet the magic of alleged riches draws in plenty of tourists. Additional distractions here include traditional *mento* dancers shaking it to calypso and *Schottische*, a sort of island polka.

LA PISCINITA

Also known as West View, just south of El Cove, **La Piscinita** (Map p192; admission COP$1000) is a good site for snorkeling, usually with calm water, plenty of fish (which will eat out of your hand) and some facilities, including a restaurant with traditional local food and snorkel rental. When the sea is rough, you can only feed the fish from land.

HOYO SOPLADOR

At the southern tip of the island, the **Hoyo Soplador** (Map p192) is a small geyser where sea water spouts into the air (up to 20m at times) through a natural hole in the coral rock. This phenomenon occurs only at certain times, when the winds and tide are right. An international surf contest is held nearby in January.

LA LOMA

This small town (Map p192) in the inner part of the island, also known as The Hill, is one of the most traditional places here. It is noted for its Baptist church, the first established on the island (in 1847). In 1896 the church was largely rebuilt in pine brought from Alabama. Definitely take a stroll through here – it's the least Colombian-influenced part of the island.

SAN LUIS

Located on the island's east coast, **San Luis** (Map p192) still boasts white-sand beaches and some fine traditional wooden houses. The sea here is good for snorkeling, though conditions can be a little rough. San Luis has no center as such, and is really just a 3km string of mostly ramshackle houses along the coast, but it's a tranquil alternative to San Andrés Town.

JOHNNY CAY NATURAL REGIONAL PARK

This protected 4-hectare coral islet (Map p192) sits about 1.5km north of San Andrés Town. It's covered with coconut groves and surrounded by a lovely, white-sand beach. The sunbathing is good, but be careful swimming here as there are dangerous currents. The cay can fill up far beyond capacity, as tourists fight for space with an estimated 500 iguanas that call it home. Food is available. Boats to Johnny Cay leave from the main San Andrés Town beach (return trip COP$10,000). The last boat back is at 5pm.

ACUARIO

Next to Haynes Cay, off the east coast of San Andrés, **Acuario** (Map p192) is another place frequently visited by tourists by boat (return trip COP$10,000). The surrounding sea is shallow and calm and good for snorkeling. If you forget to bring your snorkeling gear you can rent some on the beach in Acuario.

Activities

Due to the beautiful coral reefs all around, San Andrés has become an important diving center, with more than 35 dive spots.

Banda Dive Shop (Map p195; ☎ 512 2507; www .bandadiveshop.com; Hotel Lord Pierre, Av Colombia, San Andrés Town; ☼ 8am-noon & 2-6pm Mon-Sat) Extra-friendly dive shop offering two-tank dives for COP$150,000 and PADI open-water certification for COP$730,000.

Buzos del Caribe (Map p195; ☎ 512 8931; www .buzosdelcaribe.com; Av Colombia No 1-212, San Andrés Town; ☼ 8am-7:30pm Mon-Sat, 8am-2pm Sat) The oldest and largest facility. It has good equipment and a fine reputation. Two-tank dives cost COP$130,000.

Chamay's Nautica (Map p192; ☎ 513 2077; Via San Luis Km4, San Luis) The go-to shop for watersports. DIY rental possibilities per hour here include kayaks (COP$25,000), windsurfing (COP$70,000) and kitesurfing (COP$100,000).

Karibik Diver (Map p195; ☎ 512 0101; www.karibik diver.com; Av Newball No 1-248, San Andrés Town; ☼ 8am-4pm) This small school provides quality equipment, personalized service and long dives.

San Andrés Divers (Map p192; ☎ 512 0347; www .sanandresdivers.com; Av Circunvalar Km8.5, West Coast) Though not as centrally located as the others, this large shop and school has a great reputation and offers PADI certification for a little less (COP$680,000).

Tours

Coonative Brothers (Map p195; ☎ 512 1923) On the town's beach, this boating co-op provides trips to Johnny Cay

DIVING ON SAN ANDRÉS & PROVIDENCIA

Divers will delight in the underwater viewing opportunities off both San Andrés and Providencia. While the courses may be cheaper at Taganga (p172), the richness of the corals and variety of the marine life rivals almost any place in the Caribbean.

Both San Andrés and Providencia have extensive coral reefs – 15km and 35km respectively. The reefs on both islands are notable for their sponges, which appear in an amazing variety of forms, sizes and colors. Other aquatic inhabitants include barracudas, turtles, lobsters, rays, groupers and red snappers. Wreck divers will want to check out the two sunken ships, the *Blue Diamond* and *Nicaraguense,* off the coast of San Andrés.

The top five dive spots are:

■ **Palacio de la Cherna** A wall dive southeast of San Andrés that begins at 12m and drops off some 300m more. Midnight parrot fish, tiger fish, king crab, lobster, and even nurse and reef sharks are common sightings.

■ **Cantil de Villa Erika** Southwest of San Andrés. Depths range from 12m to 45m along this colorful reef full of sponges, soft and hard corals, sea turtles, manta and eagle rays and sea horses.

■ **Piramide** A shallow dive inside the reef on San Andrés' north side, this is a haven for sting rays. The quantity of fish, octopus and moray eels make it one of the most active spots on the island.

■ **Tete's Place** Large schools of midsized goat fish, grunt fish, schoolmasters and squirrel fish frequent this aquarium-like site 1km offshore at Bahía Suroeste in Providencia.

■ **Manta's Place** Despite its name, there are no manta rays at this Providencia site but rather southern sting rays with wingspans of up to 5m. As you survey the sands between coral mounds, you pass over fields of ghost feather dusters, where brown garden eels withdraw into the sand for protection as you pass.

(COP$10,000) and Acuario (COP$10,000), plus a combined tour to both cays (COP$15,000). It's run by Raizal people and is also a good spot for an excellent local morning pick-me-up, *panela* (raw sugarcane juice) and crab patties.

Mundo Marino (Map p195; ☎ 512 1749; www .mundomarino.com; Centro Comercial New Point Plaza, local 234, San Andrés Town; ☽ 8am-noon & 2:30-6:30pm Mon-Sat, 8:30am-noon Sun) Operates the Captain Morgan party boat, a two-hour evening boat ride (departing at 8:30pm Tue, Thu & Sat) with live music and all-you-can-drink national spirits (per person COP$58,000) as well as the Semisubmarino Nautilus.

Semisubmarino Nautilus (Map p195; 2hr tour COP$43,000) If you are not planning on scuba diving or snorkeling, this trip is probably the next best option for viewing the rich marine wildlife. The Nautilus is a specially designed boat with large windows in its hull, roomy enough for everyone to comfortably sit while it plies the coral beds northeast of the island. Tickets are sold at Mundo Marino.

Snorkeling, Sting Rays, Sunset & Beer (Map p195; ☎ 316 240 2182; 3hr tour COP$55,000) The name says it all, really. Jaime Restrepo runs a slightly flexible tour to swim with the sting rays at Haynes Cay, and throws in some deep-water snorkeling and brews on top of the package. It's somewhat casual and limited to groups of 10. The tour leaves at 3pm from Tonino's Marina.

Sleeping

The overwhelming majority of the island's accommodations can be found in San Andrés Town. There are some hotels in San Luis, but elsewhere there are few places to stay. For the most part, accommodation on the island is more expensive than on the mainland. Rates rise during high season.

SAN ANDRÉS TOWN

Cli's Place (Map p195; ☎ 512 6957; luciamhj@hotmail.com; Av 20 de Julio, San Andrés Town; r per person from COP$30,000) This Raizal-run lodging is part of the island's *posada nativa* program, where you bed down with locals. Cli has four homey rooms, some with kitchenettes. It's reached via the alley next to the park across from Pollo Kikiriki.

Hotel Mary May Inn (Map p195; ☎ 512 5669; gallardo@gmail.com; Av 20 de Julio No 3-74, San Andrés Town; s/d COP$40,000/60,000; ▨) This small and friendly place offers nine simple but cozy rooms in a nice location two blocks from the beach.

Hotel Hernando Henry (Map p195; ☎ 512 3416; Av Las Américas No 4-84, San Andrés Town; s/d with fan COP$40,000/60,000, with air-con COP$45,000/85,000; ▨) You won't send postcards home about this

SAN ANDRES TOWN

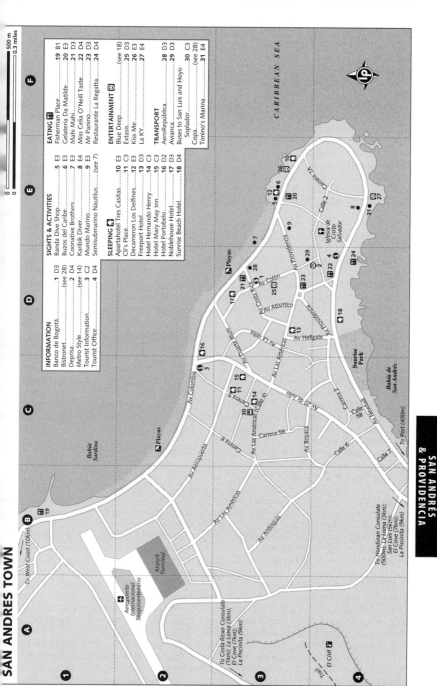

INFORMATION
Banco de Bogotá........................	1 D3
Bistronet..................................	(see 28)
Deprisa...................................	2 D4
Metro Style..............................	(see 14)
Tourist Information...................	3 C2
Tourist Office...........................	4 D4

SIGHTS & ACTIVITIES
Banda Dive Shop.......................	5 E3
Buzos del Caribe........................	6 E3
Coonative Brothers....................	7 E3
Karibik Diver............................	8 E4
Mundo Marino...........................	9 E3
Semisubmarino Nautilus.............	(see 7)

SLEEPING
Apartahotel Tres Casitas............	10 E3
Cili's Place................................	11 C3
Decameron Los Delfines.............	12 E3
Freeport Hotel...........................	13 D3
Hotel Hernando Henry...............	14 C3
Hotel Mary May Inn...................	15 C3
Hotel Portobelo.........................	16 D2
Noblehouse Hotel......................	17 D3
Sunrise Beach Hotel...................	18 D4

EATING
Fisherman Place........................	19 B1
Gelateria Da Matilde..................	20 E3
Mahi Mahi................................	21 D3
Miss Celia O'Neill Taste..............	22 D4
Mr Panino................................	23 D3
Restaurante La Regatta..............	24 D4

ENTERTAINMENT
Blue Deep.................................	(see 18)
Éxtasis.....................................	25 D3
Kiss Me....................................	26 E3
La KY......................................	27 E4

TRANSPORT
AeroRepública..........................	28 D3
Avianca....................................	29 D3
Buses to San Luis and Hoyo	
Soplador..............................	30 C3
Copa..	(see 28)
Tonino's Marina........................	31 E4

place, but with its own water and electrical system, this low budget option offers a leg up on those dependent on the local government for both. Most rooms have a balcony and all come with private bath. There's an internet cafe attached.

Freeport Hotel (Map p195; ☎ 513 1212; Av Las Américas No 2A-101, San Andrés Town; s/d COP$50,000/80,000; 🕸) Gloomy from the outside but nice and bright inside, this functional option offers good value in a clean and friendly environment. Prices include breakfast and dinner.

Apartahotel Tres Casitas (Map p195; ☎ 512 5813; www.apartahoteltrescasitas.com; Av Colombia No 1-60, San Andrés Town; r per person COP$90,000; 🕸 🖭 🖳) A cute yellow and blue clapboard hotel with extra large rooms, all with kitchenettes and separate living areas. Rates include breakfast and dinner.

Hotel Portobelo (Map p195; ☎ 512 7008; www .portobelohotel.com; Av Colombia No 5A-69, San Andrés Town; s/d with breakfast COP$92,500/113,000; 🕸 🖳) This unassuming beachside property is nothing fancy, but offers simple rooms, some with sea views, a small book exchange, cable TV and new air conditioners.

Noblehouse Hotel (Map p195; ☎ 512 8264; www .sanandresnoblehouse.com; Av Colón No 3-80, San Andrés Town; s/d with breakfast COP$95,000/114,000; 🕸 🖳) This Italian-run operation likes to mix its decors: New England Leaf Peeping one moment, Moorish Seaside the next. The 15 large and kitschy rooms here are a comfortable option in town and the staff is super helpful. It's one block from the beach.

Sunrise Beach Hotel (Map p195; ☎ 512 3977; www .sunrisehotel.com; Av Newball, San Andrés Town; s/d from COP$154,000/222,000; 🕸 🖳 🖳) Depending on your viewpoint, the largest hotel on the island either embodies all that is evil about holiday destinations or is vacation hog heaven. It's a modern place, with two restaurants, three bars, a disco, gym, sauna and tennis court. The larger rooms are on the 4th floor and above due to the architectural style of the hotel. Rates include the cheesy lobby singer.

our pick Decameron Los Delfines (Map p195; ☎ 512 4083; www.decameron.com; Av Colombia No 16-86, San Andrés Town; s/d from COP$289,000/444,000; 🅿 🖳 🕸) The first boutique hotel on the island as well as within the Decameron chain, this stylish, 36-room hotel is quiet and discreet. It features an over-water restaurant, a small pool and smart furniture, housed in a design-forward hotel that wouldn't be out of place in Los Angeles.

Casa Harb (Map p192; ☎ 512 6348; www.cas harb.com; Calle 11 No 10-83, San Andrés Town; d from COP$780,000; 🕸 🖳 🖳) Located in an impressiv Republican-style mansion behind the airport this small design B&B is a step above anythin in the archipelago. The five exquisite suites ar individually designed with Asian aesthetic and feature deep soaking tubs. It caters to a exclusive market.

SAN LUIS

This hamlet is a 10-minute drive south of Sa Andrés Town; bus connections are frequent It offers a little more peace and quiet tha El Centro.

Cocoplum Hotel (Map p192; ☎ 513 2121; ww .cocoplumhotel.com; Carretera a San Luis No 43-39; s/ COP$125,000/171,200; 🕸 🖳 🖳) On a private beac shaded with palm trees, this recently reno vated low-key beach resort sports Caribbea architecture and its 44 rooms offer a goo midrange alternative to the higher-end op tions in San Andrés Town. There's a restau rant that serves fresh meals all day, and i open to nonguests. Rocky Cay, a good spo for snorkeling, is nearby.

Ocean Eco Beach Resort (Map p192; ☎ 513 2066; Sa Luis; per person COP$100,000; 🕸 🖳 🖳) This festiv oceanfront hotel with Gaudí-inspired mo saics is another good San Luis option jus five minutes up the road from Cocoplum It boasts a small (private) beach and a larg communal Jacuzzi. Three meals are include in the price.

Eating

You will encounter a change of culinary pac on the islands due to the Creole-Caribbea influence. Staples include breadfruit, whic takes the place of *patacones* (fried plan tains) as the starch of choice, and ubiquitou Caribbean conch.

Be sure to try the most traditional dish rundown (often phonetically spelled 'rondor due to islander accents), a soupy dish of lightl battered fish, plantains, yucca and other gooe starches, all slow cooked in a healthy dose c coconut milk.

Gelateria Da Matilde (Map p195; ☎ 522 2117; A Colombia, San Andrés Town; 🕒 11am-10pm) Damn goo Italian ice cream.

Mr Panino (Map p195; ☎ 512 0549; Av Providencia N 2-47, San Andrés Town; mains COP$11,000-35,000; 🕒 lunc & dinner) An Italian specialty deli with numer ous sandwiches, pasta, risotto and a beautifu octopus *carpaccio*. It's nicer than most others in town, though not pricier.

Fisherman Place (Map p195; ☎ 512 2774; Av Colombia, San Andrés Town; mains COP$12,000-23,000; ☯ noon-4pm) This open-air, beachside restaurant is a great spot to support local fishers and eat well. Rundown and fried fish are the most popular dishes.

Miss Celia O'Neill Taste (Map p195; ☎ 316 690 0074; Av Colombia, San Andrés Town; mains COP$15,000-20,000; ☯ lunch & dinner) A good spot for native food like rundown, stewed crab and stewed fish, served within a colorful home with a large garden and patio. It's across from the Club Nautico.

Restaurante West View (Map p192; ☎ 513 0341; Circunvalar Km11, West View; mains COP$15,000-59,000; ☯ breakfast, lunch & dinner) This West View option looks ordinary but the food stands out. Try the filet of fish. The owner is planning some nifty coconut bungalows.

Mahi Mahi (Map p195; ☎ 512 4115; Hotel Casablanca, Av Colombia, San Andrés Town; mains COP$20,000-38,000; ☯ lunch & dinner) After lengthy travel in Colombia, this chic Thai spot on the waterfront, part of Hotel Casablanca, will send your palate dancing with its curries and island-tinged dishes.

our pick **Restaurante La Regatta** (Map p195; ☎ 512 0437; Av Newball, San Andrés Town; mains COP$18,999-71,580; ☯ lunch & dinner Mon-Sat) One of the islands' best restaurants: the coconut-curry *marinera* is nothing short of perfection. The sweeping Caribbean views and an extraordinarily friendly staff seal the deal.

Entertainment

There are several nightspots in San Andrés Town along the eastern end of Av Colombia. Head here and see what's hot.

Blue Deep (Map p195; Sunrise Beach Hotel, Av Newball, San Andrés Town; cover after 11pm COP$10,000; ☯ 9:30pm-3am Thu-Sat) The biggest disco in town holds 700 sweaty bodies. There is live music (salsa and reggaetón), which provides the soundtrack for a decent mix of locals and tourists, stumbling about after too many frothy rum punches.

Éxtasis (Map p195; ☎ 512 3043; Hotel Sol Caribe San Andrés, Av Colón, San Andrés Town; cover COP$20,000; ☯ 9:30pm-3am Mon-Thu, 9:30pm-4am Fri-Sat) Another good disco, this one with TV screens (soccer, of course) and three rows of lounge chairs for those that prefer voyeurism. You can recoup COP$12,000 of the cover in cocktails.

Kiss Me (Map p195; ☎ 512 9551; Av Colombia, San Andrés Town; ☯ 4pm-4am Tue-Sun) Unfortunately named blue-lit bar/disco with a small dance floor and over-water back patio. It seems to draw a vaguely more metrosexual crowd than others in its vicinity, as well as more locals.

La KY (Map p195; ☎ 512 7779; Av Colombia No 1-30, San Andrés Town; ☯ 4pm-midnight Mon-Thu, 4pm-3am Fri-Sat) This Miami-esque open-air lounge draws a sophisticated and attractive crowd, hopped up on bottle service and donning camera-ready smirks.

Getting There & Away

AIR

The airport is in San Andrés Town, a 10-minute walk northwest of the center, or COP$9500 by taxi. You must buy a tourist card (COP$29,000) on the mainland before checking in for your San Andrés–bound flight. Airlines that service San Andrés include **Avianca** (Map p195; ☎ 512 3349; Av Colón, edificio Onaissi, San Andrés Town; ☯ 8am-noon & 2-6pm Mon-Fri, 8am-1pm Sat) and **AeroRepública** (Map p195; ☎ 512 7619; Sucursal Centro Comercial San Andrés, San Andrés Town; ☯ 8am-noon & 2-6pm Mon-Fri, 9am-1pm Sat). There are direct connections to Bogotá (from COP$312,151), Cali (from COP$369,700), Cartagena (from COP$386,700), Medellín (from COP$369,700) and Barranquilla (from COP$369,700). **Copa** (☎ 512 6248) flies direct to Panama City (from COP$843,600).

Satena Airways (☎ 512 3139; Aeropuerto Internacional Sesquicentenario) operates two flights per day between San Andrés and Providencia in low season (return from COP$376,043) and up to six in high season. Decameron's affiliated airline **Searca** (☎ 512 4045) also flies the route.

BOAT

Cargo boats travel to Providencia from San Andrés and often take passengers, but prepare to stomach a rough, five-hour sea journey. The cost runs from COP$35,000 to COP$40,000.

Getting Around

Local buses circle a large part of the island; they also ply the inland road to El Cove. They are the cheapest way to get around (per ride COP$1100) unless you want to walk. They can drop you off close to all the major attractions.

A bus marked 'San Luis' travels along the east-coast road to the southern tip of the island; take this bus to San Luis and the Hoyo

Soplador. The bus marked 'El Cove' runs along the inner road to El Cove, passing through La Loma. It'll drop you in front of the Baptist church, within easy walking distance of Cueva de Morgan and La Piscinita. You can catch both buses near the Hotel Hernando Henry.

You can travel more comfortably by taxi, which can take you for a trip around the island (COP$50,000). Otherwise, hire a bicycle (COP$10,000/COP$20,000 per half-day/full day). Cycling around San Andrés is a great way to get a feel for the island. Roads are paved and there is little traffic to contend with. You can also hire scooters (COP$40,000 per day) and golf carts (COP$80,000 per day) in addition to the usual suspects – many of the rental businesses are on Av Newball. Shop around as prices and conditions vary.

PROVIDENCIA

☎ 8 / pop 5000

Around 90km north of San Andrés, the much smaller and quainter island of Providencia feels not only like a world away, but like a different country entirely. Tourism has not been bred into the population here, so the quiet, laid-back hamlets that nestle here against white-sand beaches feel much more authentic than San Andrés'. And without a direct connection to the Colombian mainland, the island hasn't seen nearly the same levels of cultural invasion, leaving the original traditions and customs more-or-less intact. All this combined with gorgeous topography standing sentinel over swaths of turquoise-blue sea gives Providencia no small claim to paradise.

Traditionally known as Old Providence, the island covers an area of 17 sq km. It is the second-largest island of the archipelago. A mountainous island of volcanic origin, it is much older than San Andrés and is home to the second-largest barrier reef in the Americas.

Santa Isabel, a village at the island's northern tip, is the local administrative headquarters. Santa Catalina, a small island facing Santa Isabel, is separated from Providencia by the shallow Canal Aury, spanned by a pedestrian bridge.

Strict zoning laws have held large-scale development at bay, and, unlike in San Andrés, English is still widely spoken.

There's much English-Caribbean–style architecture, with each homeowner trying to outdo their neighbor by the stroke of a paintbrush.

What tourist industry does exist can be found in the tiny hamlets of Aguadulce and Bahía Suroeste on the west coast, a 15-minute ride by colectivo (shared minibus or taxi) from the airport. Here you'll find small cottages, hotels and cabañas strung along the road, and a handful of restaurants. While you can see virtually the whole island in a day, travelers end up staying longer than they expected, scuba diving, hiking or just lying in a hammock with a Club Colombia in hand.

Friendly locals, warm seas and impressive mountainous topography all help make Providencia Colombia's Eden.

Information

Banco de Bogotá (Santa Isabel; ☷ 8-11:30am & 2-4pm Mon-Thu, 8am-11:30am & 2-4:30pm Fri) ATM.
Communication Center (☎ 514 8871; Santa Isabel; per hour COP$2500; ☷ 9am-12:30pm & 4-9pm Mon-Sat & 2:30-9pm Sun) Aside from the exorbitant hotel option, this is the island's only internet.
Tourist office (☎ 312 315 6492; Santa Isabel) Located in the Hotel Aury building next to the pier.

Sights & Activities

Providencia's beaches are pleasant, but relatively small and narrow. The main ones are at Bahía Aguadulce, Bahía Suroeste and (the best) at Bahía Manzanillo at the southern end of the island.

PARQUE NACIONAL NATURAL (PNN) OLD PROVIDENCE MCBEAN LAGOON

To protect the habitat, a 10-sq-km area in the island's northeast was declared **Parque Nacional Natural (PNN) Old Providence McBean Lagoon** (foreigner/Colombian COP$9000/6000) in 1995. About 10% of the park's area covers a coastal mangrove system east of the airport; the remaining 905 hectares cover an offshore belt including the islets of Cayo Cangrejo and Cayo Tres Hermanos. An 800m-long ecopath helps you identify different species of mangroves and the fauna that inhabit them.

SANTA CATALINA

Some tiny, deserted beaches exist on the island of Santa Catalina, worth a look if only to see Morgan's Head, a rocky cliff in the shape of a human face, best seen from the water. An

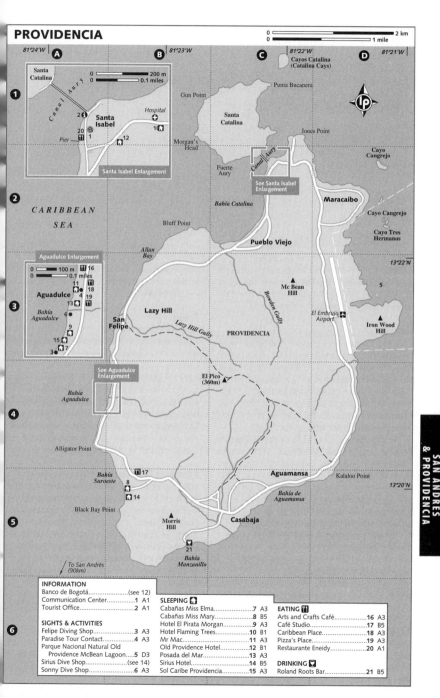

PROVIDENCIA

INFORMATION
Banco de Bogotá.....................(see 12)
Communication Center...............1 A1
Tourist Office.............................2 A1

SIGHTS & ACTIVITIES
Felipe Diving Shop.......................3 A3
Paradise Tour Contact.................4 A3
Parque Nacional Natural Old
 Providence McBean Lagoon.....5 D3
Sirius Dive Shop.................(see 14)
Sonny Dive Shop.........................6 A3

SLEEPING
Cabañas Miss Elma.......................7 A3
Cabañas Miss Mary.......................8 B5
Hotel El Pirata Morgan.................9 A3
Hotel Flaming Trees....................10 B1
Mr Mac.......................................11 A3
Old Providence Hotel.................12 B1
Posada del Mar..........................13 A3
Sirius Hotel................................14 B5
Sol Caribe Providencia...............15 A3

EATING
Arts and Crafts Café...................16 A3
Café Studio.................................17 B5
Caribbean Place.........................18 A3
Pizza's Place...............................19 A3
Restaurante Eneidy.....................20 A1

DRINKING
Roland Roots Bar........................21 B5

SAN ANDRÉS & PROVIDENCIA

LOCAL VOICE: ELIZABETH TAYLOR

Age: 42
Occupation: General Director, Coralina (Corporation for the Sustainable Development of the Archipelago of San Andrés, Old Providence & Santa Catalina)
Residence: San Andrés
Favorite Caribbean Author: Derek Walcott

'The culture of the San Andrés & Providencia (p190) is distinct from the rest of Colombia. Native islanders are still defined by their Anglo-African roots, English mother tongue, and Protestant religious background. Their language, folklore and cultural history have been conserved through oral tradition for more than 300 years.

'My favorite spot in the islands is the top of **Cayo Cangrejo** (Crab Cay, p198) in Old Providence [to] view the multicolored sea. This is one of the most beautiful, peaceful places in the islands.

'Don't miss hiking to the top of **El Pico** (The Peak, below) – a one-hour walk through the best-preserved tropical transitional forest on the islands culminates in a spectacular view of the hills of Old Providence spread out below, the island of Santa Catalina to the north, and the barrier reef stretching for miles to the east and north.'

---

underwater cave is at the base of the cliff. The shoreline changes considerably with the tides; during high tide beaches get very narrow and some totally disappear.

HIKING

The mountainous interior of the island, with its vegetation and small animal life, is attractive and provides pleasant walks. Probably nowhere else in Colombia can you see so many colorful lizards scampering through bushes. Beware of a common shrub with spectacular hornlike thorns; ants living inside have a painful bite. Mosquitoes also abound on the island.

Don't miss a trip to **El Pico Natural Regional Park** for outstanding 360-degree views of the Caribbean. The most popular trail begins in Casabaja. Ask for directions as several paths crisscross on the lower part (further up there are no problems), or ask in Casabaja for a guide. Some locals will take you up for a small charge. It is a steady 1½-hour walk to the top. Carry drinking water because there is none along the way.

SNORKELING & DIVING

Snorkeling and diving are the island's other big attractions. You can rent snorkeling gear in Aguadulce (COP$10,000). Diving trips and courses can be arranged with recommended local operators **Felipe Diving Shop** (☎ 514 8775; www.felipediving.com), run by a native Raizal, and **Sonny's Dive Shop** (☎ 514 8231; www.buceo providencia.com), both in Aguadulce; and **Sirius Dive Shop** (☎ 514 8213; www.siriusdivecenter.com) in

Bahía Suroeste. Each offers an open-water or advanced course for about COP$650,000 to COP$700,000.

Tours

Paradise Tour Contact (☎ 514 8283; www.oldprovidence .com.co; Aguadulce; ☼ 8am-noon & 2-6pm Mon-Sat) This small agency offers tours and a range of other services including bicycle rental (per day COP$10,000) and tours to El Pico (per person COP$40,000 to COP$65,000), horseback rides (COP$40,000), kayak trips (COP$40,000) and boat excursions around the island (per person COP$40,000 to COP$65,000). Boats normally call at the Canal Aury, Morgan's Head, Cayo Cangrejo and Roland Roots Bar.

Festivals & Events

Crab migration (May to June) This annual event lasts for a week or two. There may be many crabs on the move then, particularly in Aguadulce and Bahía Suroeste, and roads can be closed to provide safe crossing for them. They aren't absent the rest of the year, either. Keep a look out!
Cultural Festival (June) Providencia's major event is in the last week of June. It includes music and dance, a parade of motorcycles and, just for kicks, an iguana beauty pageant.

Sleeping & Eating

Generally speaking, accommodations and food are expensive on Providencia, even more so than on San Andrés. Most travelers stay in Aguadulce, but there are also some lodging and eating facilities in other areas of the island, including Santa Isabel and Bahía Suroeste.

AGUADULCE

This 20-house hamlet offers peace, quiet and little else. There are more than a dozen places to stay; some have their own restaurants and offer a bed-and-board package. For better or worse, the Decameron chain has taken over most of the best places to stay, so independent travelers can be shut out in high season.

Mr Mac (☎ 514 8168; s/d COP$30,000/50,000) Mr Mac is the cheapest option in town, and considering ol' Mac is getting pretty old and frail to maintain the pace, it's still not a bad option at all. Rooms are large, with kitchenettes, and are right on the water.

Hotel El Pirata Morgan (☎ 514 8067; www.hotel piratamorgan.com; s/d incl breakfast COP$90,000/150,000; ❄ ☐ ☎) A solid option in the center of town, with a handy minimarket downstairs. It lacks of the Caribbean flair of the others, but is also a little cheaper, and offers more lush surroundings than elsewhere on the beach. It's the only hotel, though, without English-speaking front-desk staff.

Posada del Mar (☎ 514 8168; pousadelmar@latinmail com; s/d incl breakfast COP$110,000/150,000; ❄) Well-maintained Barbie-colored midrange option featuring large rooms, all with balconies housing hammocks facing the beach.

Sol Caribe Providencia (☎ 514 8036; www solarhoteles.com; r per person COP$175,000; ❄ ☐ ☎) Following the island's kaleidoscopic color scheme, this bright yellow hotel is the most upmarket in Aguadulce. There's a pleasant seaside restaurant, rooms with nice hardwood furniture and colorful Caribbean art, and very expensive internet (COP$10,000 per hour). Rates include breakfast and dinner (without them, knock off COP$35,000).

Cabañas Miss Elma (☎ 315 303 4208; philhuffington@ yahoo.es; r per person COP$180,000; ❄) The colorful common areas and wonderfully casual seaside restaurant here are pretty idyllic, but the disappointing interiors are more country house than Caribbean and rather plain at that. Rates include three meals.

Arts & Crafts Café (☎ 514 8297; �---1:30-9pm) This French-run shop/cafe is a good place for espresso and its famous *paleta* popsicles made from island fruits. It's also a great spot for artisanal products like honey, marmalade and tamarind wine. There's a book exchange as well.

Pizza's Place (☎ 514 8224; mains COP$6000-55,000; ☐ dinner) A cheaper option, doing sandwiches (COP$6000) and pizza (from COP$13,000) in addition to a handful of island staples.

Caribbean Place (☎ 514 8698; mains COP$18,000-53,000; ☐ lunch & dinner) Though this wonderful island seafooder isn't cheap, Bogotá-trained chef Martin Quintero is doing serious food in a casual atmosphere. Highlights include mountainous black crab, unique to the archipelago in Colombia.

SANTA ISABEL

Strangely, Santa Isabel, despite its gorgeous location in a picturesque bay attached to Santa Catalina, doesn't see much tourism. A touch of work making it over and this place would be much more appealing to travelers.

Old Providence Hotel (☎ 514 8691; s/d COP$45,000/80,000; ❄) This hotel offers bland but big rooms, with cable TV and air-con, in the center of town.

Hotel Flaming Trees (☎ 514 8049; s/d COP$50,000/80,000; ❄) The best choice in this part of the island; offers nine spacious air-con rooms with fridge, TV and local art.

Restaurante Eneidy (☎ 514 8758; mains COP$8000-40,000; ☐ noon-3pm & 6-10pm) This open-air restaurant is certainly the best place to eat in town, though don't expect any James Beard–nominated dishes.

BAHÍA SUROESTE

This is the second tourist destination after Aguadulce, but there aren't as many facilities. Still, it's the nicest beach and more convenient for hiking, horseback riding and beach drinking.

Cabañas Miss Mary (☎ 514 8454; www.missmary hotel.com; s/d incl breakfast COP$96,000/132,000; ❄ ☐) Miss Mary provides nicely dressed up rooms right on the beach, each with large patios and hammocks. There's cable TV and ever-elusive hot water.

Sirius Hotel (☎ 514 8213; www.siriushotel .net; s/d cabañas from COP$85,000/137,000, s/d from COP$103,000/168,000; ❄ ☐) You'll find a little more character than in most spots on the island, as well as a dive shop on premises. The suites are large and comfortable (the cabañas less so) but both are on the beach.

ourpick Café Studio (☎ 514 9076; mains COP$15,000-40,000; ☐ 11am-10pm Mon-Sat) The island's best restaurant is run by a Canadian woman and her Raizal husband, Wellington, who cooks the island dishes 'she can't get right.' The results are both memorable and reasonably priced. Try Wellington's conch, cooked in his own Creole sauce made with wild basil from their garden, or anything in garlic sauce. Save room for the cappuccino pie!

Entertainment

ourpick Roland Roots Bar (☎ 514 8417; Bahía Manzanillo) This travelers' icon encapsulates island life in one ridiculously atmospheric beach bar – booths fashioned from bamboo under ramshackle thatched roofs spread among the sands, all set to a booming reggae soundtrack. Roland is an island legend for his late-night parties and his *coco locos* – jazzed up piña coladas served in coconuts.

Getting There & Away

Satena and Searca fly between San Andrés and Providencia (from COP$376,043 return) twice per day each in low season, several more in high. You are most likely to buy a return in San Andrés before arriving, but buy your ticket in advance in the high season and be sure to reconfirm the return trip at Providencia's airport.

Getting Around

Getting around the island isn't the easiest thing to do without your own transportation.

Colectivos and pickup trucks run along the road in both directions; it's COP$2500 for a ride of any distance. There may be only one or two per hour, but locals will often stop and offer you a ride.

Pickup trucks congregate at the airport waiting for incoming flights and ask as much as COP$18,000 for any distance. To avoid overpaying, walk a bit further from the airport and wave down a *colectivo* or pickup truck passing along the road for the usual COP$2500 fare, though this might not be the best solution if you are carrying lots of bags.

Taxis are hard to come by and quite expensive compared to on the mainland. From the airport, count on COP$15,000 to Santa Isabel and COP$18,000 to Aguadulce. The bottom line is that if you call, you'll pay for it; if you can spare the time to wait for a ride, you'll get off much cheaper.

A pleasant way to get around is by bicycle, which can be rented from Paradise Tour Contact (see Tours, p200). You can also rent a scooter (per day COP$40,000 to COP$50,000) from a few small operators in Aguadulce and Santa Isabel.

Medellín &
Zona Cafetera

Welcome to *país paisa – paisa* country. Settled by Europeans attracted by the fertile soil and moderate mountain climate, it is a region of coffee plantations and flower farms, lush cloud forest and vibrant student towns, and the busy metropolis of Medellín. It is a jewel in the crown of Colombia, and not to be missed.

In Medellín, the country's second city, towers soar skyward, with ambition matched only by its inferiority complex – Chicago to Bogotá's New York. It is an attractive city that seduces most travelers instantly, with its just-perfect climate, green spaces, great restaurants, museums and public art work, and thumping discos.

The three main towns of the Zona Cafetera are Manizales, Pereira and Armenia. The principal business interests here are coffee, manufacturing and university students – there are a dozen universities between the three towns. It is a region of fantastic biodiversity, and the nature reserves are stunning. The *paisas* (people from the department of Antioquia) are sharp-eyed entrepreneurs, descendants of self-sufficient small farmers, not slave-owning plantation owners. They work hard and are proud of what they've achieved.

Parque Nacional Natural Los Nevados is a highlight of any visit here, a high-mountain refuge of mostly extinct volcanoes whose peaks soar above 5000m. You can visit the snow line from Manizales or spend the night on the *páramo* (high-mountain plains) in a tent or in the comfortable cabins of El Cisne. You can take a mountain-biking tour through the park, and there are mountaineering opportunities on the peaks for those suitably equipped.

HIGHLIGHTS

- Explore the nature parks around Manizales – **Los Yarumos, Reserva Ecológica Río Blanco & Recinto del Pensamiento** (p223) – brimming with local orchids, hummingbirds and butterflies

- Bathe in the thermals springs at **Termales de Santa Rosa** (p230) as waterfalls crash nearby

- Sample the many fine restaurants and bars in **Medellín** (p210), and stroll along the bustling city's **Milla de Oro** (p205)

- Spend the night in **Río Claro** (p219), your hotel room open to the jungle, the river roaring below

- Crane your neck to see the tops of the majestic wax palms in the cloud forest of the **Valle de Cocora** (p237)

★ Medellín
Río Claro ★

★ Manizales
★ Termales de Santa Rosa

★ Valle de Cocora

Climate

The climate in the region is a pleasant, permanent springtime. The altitude of the region varies from a low of 1410m in hot Pereira to a chillier 2150m in Manizales, with Medellín somewhere in the middle at 1494m. You will want to pack shorts and a hat for daytime, and trousers and a sweater for nighttime. And be sure to bring along an umbrella – when it rains here, it pours.

National, State & Regional Parks

The big daddy of national parks here is Parque Nacional Natural (PNN) Los Nevados, which soars above 5000m. Recinto de Pensamiento, Los Yarumos and Reserva Ecológica Río Blanco, outside of Manizales, boast beauti-

ful species of orchids and butterflies. East of Pereira are Santuario Otún Quimbaya and Parque Ucumarí. Armenia's botanical gardens are well worth a visit, as is the stunning Valle de Cocora, and its majestic wax palms outside Salento.

Getting There & Away

Medellín and Pereira airports both receive international flights. The region is well serviced by buses to Bogotá, Cali and the Caribbean coast.

Getting Around

You should have no problem getting around using the region's frequent, cheap bus services.

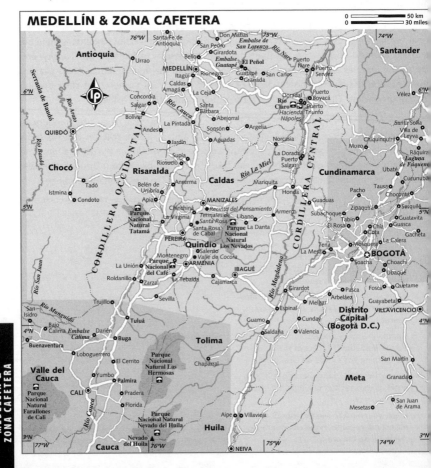

MEDELLÍN & ZONA CAFETERA

MEDELLÍN

☎ 4 / pop 2.5 million / elev 1494m

Quickly becoming the third most popular city with tourists in Colombia (after Cartagena and Bogotá), Medellín packs the punch of a city twice its size. Situated in a narrow valley, the city's skyline reaches for the heavens, setting high-rise apartment and office buildings against a backdrop of jagged peaks in every direction. Its pleasant climate gives the city its nickname – the City of Eternal Spring – and the moderate temperatures put a spring in the locals' step, at work and at play. It's a bustling city of industry and commerce, especially textile manufacturing and exported cut flowers. On the weekends Medellín lets its hair down, and the city's many discos attract the beautiful people.

True to its *paísa* roots, Medellín affects an indifference to the rest of Colombia, and puts on metropolitan airs – the traffic officers wear Italian-style round boxy hats, many discos prefer techno to salsa or vallenato, and the city looks overseas for inspiration for its next great public works project. The popularity of mullet haircuts among the young male inhabitants, however, reveals the city's true nature – an ambitious country town whose ambition masks a great anxiety about its place in the world.

History

Spaniards first arrived in the Aburrá Valley in the 1540s, but Medellín was not founded until 1616; early development started in El Poblado. Historians believe that many early settlers were Spanish Jews fleeing the Inquisition. They divided the land into small haciendas, which they farmed themselves – very different from the slave-based plantation culture that dominated much of Colombia. With their focus on self-reliance, these early *paísas* had little interest in commercial contact with neighboring regions. For these reasons, they came to be known as hard workers with a fierce independent streak – traits they've exported throughout the Zona Cafetera and, increasingly, the rest of Colombia.

Medellín became departmental capital in 1826 but long remained a provincial backwater, which explains why its colonial buildings are neither sumptuous nor particularly numerous. The city's rapid growth began only at the start of the 20th century, when the ar-rival of the railroad, together with a highly profitable boom in coffee production, quickly transformed the city. Mine owners and coffee barons invested their profits in a nascent textile industry, and their gamble paid off. Within a few decades, Medellín had become a large metropolitan city.

By the 1980s the city's entrepreneurial spirit was showing its dark side. Under the violent but ingenious leadership of Pablo Escobar (see p30), Medellín became the capital of the world's cocaine business. Gun battles were common, and the city's homicide rate was among the highest on the planet. The beginning of the end of the violence came with Escobar's death in 1993, and today Medellín is among the safest cities in Latin America.

Orientation

The city sprawls north and south along the valley floor. Slums hug the upper reaches of the hills. The city center is a compact grid around Parque de Bolívar, but the de facto center has shifted 4km south to El Poblado and the so-called *Milla de Oro* (Golden Mile), which stretches along Av Poblado, an area crammed with upscale shopping malls, exclusive hotels, casinos, high-rise condominiums, and many of Medellín's best restaurants and bars.

For a less-sanitized taste of the city, walk down Pasaje Junín in Central Medellín, the long pedestrian mall full of bakeries and bars, clothing stores and spruikers touting their wares, flower stalls and CD stores, juice bars, girlie bars and dens of gambling and vice.

Medellín's modern metro system runs the length of the valley and can take you to most tourist sites.

Information

INTERNET ACCESS

There are plenty of internet cafes in El Poblado and the center. Most charge around COP$2000 per hour.

Comunicaciones La 9 (Map p211; ☎ 266 2105, Calle 9 No 41-64) You can also make phone calls.

gamespot (Map p211; ☎ 266 7723; www.gamespot .com.co; Calle 7 No 47-10) Attracts the online gamer crowd. Fast connection, loud music.

Llámame (Map p211; ☎ 352 4783; tecnimovil@gmail .com; Carrera 43A No 70-36) Right near Parque Linear.

PC Genius (Map p211; ☎ 311 5296, 300 353 5831; pecegenius@gmail.com; Carrera 36 No 8A-33) Four computers in this secondhand computer store.

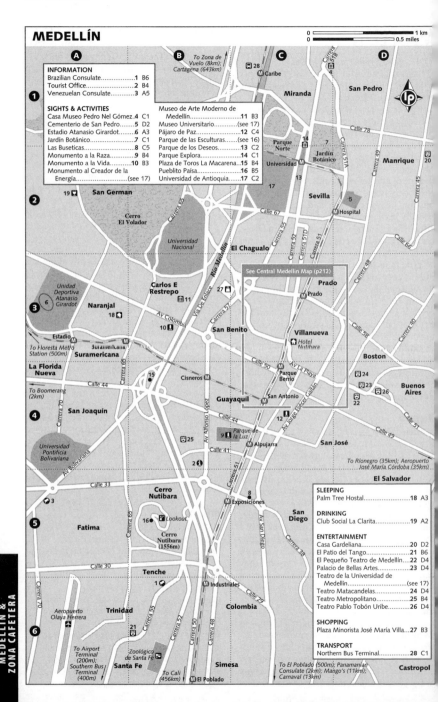

MEDELLÍN

0 — 1 km
0 — 0.5 miles

INFORMATION
Brazilian Consulate...................1 B6
Tourist Office..........................2 B4
Venezuelan Consulate............3 A5

SIGHTS & ACTIVITIES
Casa Museo Pedro Nel Gómez.4 C1
Cementerio de San Pedro........5 D2
Estadio Atanasio Girardot.......6 A3
Jardín Botánico.......................7 C1
Las Buseticas..........................8 C5
Monumento a la Raza..............9 B4
Monumento a la Vida...........10 B3
Monumento al Creador de la
    Energía.........................(see 17)

Museo de Arte Moderno de
    Medellín..........................11 B3
Museo Universitario...........(see 17)
Pájaro de Paz........................12 C4
Parque de las Esculturas......(see 16)
Parque de los Deseos............13 C2
Parque Explora.....................14 C1
Plaza de Toros La Macarena...15 B4
Pueblito Paisa.......................16 B5
Universidad de Antioquia......17 C2

SLEEPING
Palm Tree Hostal........................18 A3

DRINKING
Club Social La Clarita.................19 A2

ENTERTAINMENT
Casa Gardeliana.........................20 D2
El Patio del Tango......................21 B6
El Pequeño Teatro de Medellín...22 D4
Palacio de Bellas Artes...............23 D4
Teatro de la Universidad de
    Medellín.............................(see 17)
Teatro Matacandelas..................24 D4
Teatro Metropolitano.................25 B4
Teatro Pablo Tobón Uribe..........26 D4

SHOPPING
Plaza Minorista José María Villa...27 B3

TRANSPORT
Northern Bus Terminal................28 C1

MEDICAL SERVICES
Staff at both clinics speak some English.
Clínica Las Vegas (Map p211; ☎ 315 9000; www
.clinicalasvegas.com; Calle 2 Sur No 46-55)
Clínica Medellín (Map p211; ☎ 311 2800; www
.clinicamedellin.com; Calle 7 No 39-290)

MONEY
Banco Santander (Map p212; Carrera 49 No 50-10)
Bancolombia (Map p211; CC Oviedo) Good for cash
advances on Visa cards.
CC Oviedo (Map p211; Carrera 43A No 6 Sur-15) There are
lots of moneychangers, ATMs and bank branches in Centro
Comercial (CC) Oviedo.
Citibank (Map p211; Carrera 43A No 1A Sur-49, El Poblado)
Davivienda (Map p211; Poblado Exito) Inside the Exito
supermarket.

TOURIST INFORMATION
Tourist office (Subsecretaría de Turismo; Map p206;
☎ 444 4144, 232 4022; www.culturayturismomedellin
.com; Av Alfonso López) In the Palacio de Exposiciones.

VISA INFORMATION
DAS (☎ 238 9252; Calle 19 No 80A-40, Barrio Belén;
☼ 8am-noon & 2-5pm Mon-Fri) For visa extensions. From
El Poblado take the Circular Sur 302/303 bus heading south
along Av Las Vegas, or take a taxi (COP$6000).

Sights
MUSEUMS & ART GALLERIES
In the grand art-deco Palacio Municipal, the
Museo de Antioquia (Map p212; ☎ 251 3636; www
.museodeantioquia.org; Carrera 52 No 52-43; adult/student
COP$8000/4000; ☼ 10am-5:30pm Mon-Sat, to 4pm Sun)
is Colombia's second-oldest museum and
one of its finest. The collection includes pre-
Columbian, colonial and modern art collections, as well as many works donated by
native son Fernando Botero. For more Botero,
head across the street to the **Plazoleta de las
Esculturas** (Map p212), home to more than 20
of Botero's sculptures.

Botero's massive bronze woman's torso, **La
Gorda** (Map p212) reclines in front of the Banco
de la República in Parque Berrío. There are
three more Botero sculptures in Parque San
Antonio, including the **Pájaro de Paz** (Bird of
Peace; Map p206).

The **Casa Museo Pedro Nel Gómez** (Map p206;
☎ 233 2633; Carrera 51B No 85-24; admission free; ☼ 9am-
noon & 2-5pm Mon-Fri, 9am-noon Sat) has an extensive
collection of the works of prolific Medellín
artist Pedro Nel Gómez (1899–1984), set in
the house where the artist lived and worked.

Palacio de la Cultura Rafael Uribe Uribe (Map p212;
☎ 251 1444; www.seduca.gov.co; Carrera 51 No 52-03; admission free; ☼ 8am-4:30pm Mon-Fri, to 2pm Sat), adjacent
to the Berrío metro station in an ornate black-
and-white building, hosts concerts and events,
art expositions, conferences and workshops.
Check its website for what's on.

Rodrigo Arenas Betancur (1919–95),
Colombia's favorite designer of monuments,
is also well-represented in Medellín. His sinu-
ous, 14m-high **Monumento a la Vida** (Map p206;
Centro Suramericana, cnr Av Colombia & Carrera 64B) was
unveiled in 1974. Even more impressive is
Monumento a la Raza (Map p206; Centro Administrativo
La Alpujarra, Calle 44), which tells the story of
Antioquia in dramatically twisting metal.
It's set in the grounds of the **Parque de la Luz**
(previously known as Plaza de Cisneros) amid
a small forest of 24m-tall spiral lamps.

On the campus of the Universidad de
Antioquia be sure to check out the **Museo
Universitario** (Map p206; ☎ 219 5180; http://museo
.udea.edu.co; Calle 67 No 53-108; admission free; ☼ 8am-
5:45pm Mon-Thu, 8am-3:45pm Fri, 9am-12:45pm Sat). It has
an interesting collection of pre-Columbian
pottery, as well as galleries devoted to art
and the natural sciences. Out the front is
the **Monumento al Creador de la Energía** (Map
p206), another trippy, grandiose sculpture
by Rodrigo Arenas Betancur.

Located in what looks like an unassuming
apartment building in a leafy suburb west of
the city center, the **Museo de Arte Moderno de
Medellín** (Map p206; ☎ 230 2622; www.educame.gob.co;
Carrera 64B No 51-64; admission free; ☼ 10am-1pm & 2-6pm
Mon-Fri, 10am-5pm Sat) stages changing exhibitions
of contemporary Colombian art.

Occupying a mock-Gothic castle built in
1930 in El Poblado, the **Museo El Castillo** (☎ 266
0900; Calle 9 Sur No 32-269; admission COP$7000; ☼ 9-11am
& 2-5pm Mon-Fri, 9-11:30am Sat) was once home to a
wealthy Antioquian landowner. Inside are the
family's belongings, including furniture and
artwork from around the world. Outside there
are pleasant, French-style formal gardens.

Parque Explora (Map p206; ☎ 516 8300; www.parque
explora.org; Carrera 52 No 73-75; admission COP$7000-25,000;
☼ 8:30am-6pm Tue-Fri, 10am-6pm Sat & Sun) is a science
museum kids will love, and may tickle the
adult's inner child as well. Loosely modeled
on San Francisco's famous Exploratorium, the
Parque Explora offers a series of interactive
exhibits on physics, biology and nanotechnol-
ogy. There's also a radio/television workshop,
a 3D cinema and an aquarium.

MEDELLÍN &
ZONA CAFETERA

CHURCHES

Standing guard over Parque Berrío is **Basílica de la Candelaria** (Map p212; cnr Carrera 50 & Calle 51). Built in the 1770s, it's Medellín's most important church.

Overlooking Parque de Bolívar, the vast **Catedral Metropolitana** (Map p212; cnr Calle & Carrera 48) boasts a neo-Romanesque design. Construction began in 1875 and was completed in 1931. Its spacious but dim interior has Spanish stained-glass windows and a German-made pipe organ.

Ermita de la Veracruz (Map p212; cnr Calle 51 & Carrera 52) is the city's oldest church. Its construction was reputedly begun in 1682, but it wasn't inaugurated until 1803. It has a stone facade and a white-and-gold interior.

The **Cementerio de San Pedro** (Map p206; ☎ 212 0951; Carrera 51 No 68-68; ☟ 7:30am-5:30pm), established in 1842, has a collection of ornate tombstones, sepulchral chapels and mausoleums. Many recent graves are decked out with paraphernalia related to passions of the deceased, from cars to football to tango music. Take the metro to Estación Hospital.

PARKS

Newly refurbished and fabulous, the **Jardín Botánico** (Map p206; ☎ 444 5500; Carrera 52 No 73-182; admission free; ☟ 9am-5pm) boasts 600 species of trees and plants, a lake, herbarium, auditorium and the Orquideorama, where an orchid display is held in March and April. The gardens are easily accessed from the nearby metro stop Universidad. Just across the street is the sleek, all-concrete **Parque de los Deseos** (Map p206), which has been known to host free concerts.

On top of the 80m-tall hill **Cerro Nutibara** (Map p206), 2km southwest of the city center, sits the kitschy **Pueblito Paísa**, a miniature version of a typical Antioquian township. Views from an adjacent platform across the city are stunning. There's also an art gallery at the top and an open-air theater. Take the metro to Industriales and walk 10 minutes to the base of the hill, then 10 more to the top. It's the green hill on your left as you exit the station.

On the slopes of Cerro Nutibara is the **Parque de las Esculturas** (Sculpture Park; Map p206), which contains modern abstract sculptures by South American artists, including such prominent names as Edgar Negret, Carlos Rojas and John Castles.

Activities
PARAGLIDING

There are good thermal winds around Medellín, making it a good paragliding spot. **Zona de Vuelo** (☎ 388 1556, 312 832 5891; www.zonadevueloparapentemedellin.com; Km5.6 Via San Pedro de los Milagros) offers tandem flights (Colombians/foreigners COP$70,000/80,000) and 10-day long courses (COP$1.1 million). It can also organize trips to the surrounding region.

SOCCER

Medellín has two teams, **Independiente Medellín** (DIM, www.dim.com.co) and **Atlético Nacional** (www.atlnacional.com.co). Both play at **Estadio Atanasio Giradot** (Map p206) near the aptly named Estadio metro station.

Tours

Las Buseticas (Map p206; ☎ 262 7444; www.lasbuseticas.com; Carrera 43A No 34-95) For a good guided, three-hour city tour (COP$40,000-50,000).

Turibus (Map p212; ☎ 371 5054; www.seditrans.com; tours COP$15,000; ☟ 9am-5pm Tue-Sat) Offers get-on, get-off tours of the city's most iconic attractions. Pick it up in Parque Poblado or Parque de Bolívar.

Courses
SPANISH COURSES

Universidad EAFIT (Map p211; ☎ 261 9541; www.eafit.edu.co; Carrera 49 No 7 Sur-50) offers intensive short-term and longer-term Spanish study in a group setting. See its website for the latest schedule and prices.

DANCE COURSES

Academía Dance As (Map p211; ☎ 266 1522, 300 602 0683; www.danceas.com; Carrera 46 No 7-9, Patio Bonito) A good spot for one-on-one salsa or tango lessons (COP$25,000 per hour).

Festivals & Events

Feria Taurina de La Macarena (Jan & Feb; cnr Autopista Sur & Calle 44) The bullfighting season takes place at the Plaza de Toros La Macarena (Map p206), the 11,000-seat, Moorish-style bullring built between 1927 and 1944.

Feria Nacional de Artesanías (late Jul or early Aug) A huge craft fair held at the sports complex Estadio Atanasio Girardot (Map p206). It attracts artisans from around the country and is a good opportunity to buy crafts at bargain prices.

Feria de las Flores (early Aug) Medellín's most spectacular event is this weeklong feria. The highlight is the Desfile de Silleteros, when up to 400 *campesinos* (peasants) come down from the mountains and parade along the streets carrying flowers on their backs.

Alumbrado Navideño (Dec & Jan) A colorful Christmas illumination of the city, with thousands of lights strung across the streets and parks. The lights stay on from December 7 to January 7.

Festival de Poesía de Medellín (July; www.festival depoesiademedellin.org) This international festival attracts poets from five continents.

Festival Internacional de Jazz (Sep; www.medejazz .com) Many North American bands come for this festival. There are usually a couple of free concerts.

Sleeping

El Poblado has quickly become the place to stay for most travelers. It is close to the bars and restaurants, and is safe, even late at night. Those not interested in partying, or who want a less-sanitized experience of Medellín, may like to stay in the more rough-and-tumble center.

BUDGET

Palm Tree Hostal (Map p206; ☎ 260 2805; www.palm treemedellin.com; Carrera 67 No 48D-63; dm/s/d COP$17,000/25,000/34,000; 🖳) The oldest backpacker hostel in Medellín has fallen on hard times. The *zona rosa* (nightlife zone) has shifted to El Poblado, and the backpacker traffic with it. Still, if you want to avoid the party crowd and actually see some sights, the enthusiastic new management will happily assist you. There's free internet, cable TV, DVDs, book exchange, and you can rent bikes. It's near the Suramericana metro station.

Black Sheep (Map p211; ☎ 311 1589, 311 341 3048; www.blacksheepmedellin.com; Transversal 5A No 45-133; dm/tw/tr/q COP$18,000/45,000/60,000/80,000, s COP$35,000-45,000, d COP$45,000-55,000; 🖳) This popular Kiwi-owned hostel has long been a Medellín favorite. There's a pleasant common room, big screen TV with cable and DVDs, four desktop computers plus free wi-fi for guests. Most Sundays the owner does a hangover-busting barbecue for COP$10,000. At the time of research, plans were underway to build a second story consisting entirely of private double rooms. Construction should be finished by the time you read this.

Casa Kiwi (Map p211; ☎ 268 2668; www.casakiwi hostel.com; Carrera 36 No 7-10, El Poblado; dm COP$18,000, d COP$36,000-80,000; 🖳) This American-owned hostel is the oldest backpackers in El Poblado, and is situated right in the heart of the *zona rosa*. A recent expansion has added many new double rooms, making it attractive for singles and couples alike. There's free wi-fi, plus a pool table, kitchen, bike rental and a big DVD library.

Pit Stop Hostel (Map p211; ☎ 574 352 1176; www .pitstophostel.com; Carrera 43E No 5-110; dm COP$18,000-22,000, s COP$40,000-50,000, d COP$60,000-70,000, tr COP$90,000; 🖳 🗻) Party hearty, me hearties! This backpackers' mini-resort boasts a swimming pool and an Irish-themed sports bar with a monster flat screen TV. Bring your bikini and lie poolside, just don't bring in any liquor or beer – it's preferred you buy it on-site. There's even a small basketball court, a pool table and a steam room.

Hotel Conquistadores (Map p212; ☎ 512 3232; www.webteam.com.co/hconquist; Carrera 54 No 49-31; s/d COP$20,000/28,000) Not a hostel, but a small family-owned hotel for those wanting to avoid the backpacker crowd. Catering principally to budget business travelers, staff swear up and down it never takes couples *por rato* (by the hour). All rooms have private bath, hot water and cable TV. A small restaurant serves budget meals.

Tiger Paw Hostel (Map p211; ☎ 311 6079, www .tigerpawhostel.com; Carrera 36N 10-49; dm COP$20,000, d with/without bath COP$70,000/60,000; 🖳) This new American-owned hostel is right in the heart of the action. A bar area greets you as you come in the door, and there's a large flat screen TV where you can play video games. The street-side rooms are noisy. Check a few rooms before deciding. The three six-bed dorms are the nicest in Medellín, and there's also a small kitchen you can use.

MIDRANGE

Provenza Hostal (Map p211; ☎ 326 5600; www .provenzahostal.com; Carrera 35 No 7-2; s/d/tr/q COP$90,000/120,000/150,000/180,000; 🖳) This stylish, simply-decorated and well-managed small hotel offers clean rooms with private bath. There's free desktop internet, and rates includes breakfast on the sunny patio. Right in the heart of the *zona rosa*.

Hotel La Habana Vieja (☎ 312 2557; www.hotel lahabanavieja.com; Calle 10 Sur No 43A-7, El Poblado; s/d COP$100,000/117,000; 🖳) This Colombian-style B&B is popular with domestic business travelers. Built on the side of a hill just off Av Poblado (Carrera 43A), the reception area has red plush furniture and lots of hanging pot plants, although suffers from some road noise. The downstairs rooms, which are still above ground, face away from the street and are quiet. Paisley furniture decorates the downstairs lounge. Amenities include gas hot water, cable TV and fans.

TOP END

Estelar Poblado Plaza (Map p211; ☎ 268 5555; www .hotelpobladoplaza.com; Carrera 43A No 4 Sur-75; s/d/tr/ste COP$273,000/351,000/432,000/405,000; P ✗ ☐) Right on the *Milla de Oro*, this fine hotel has a fountain out front, fresh-cut heliconias in the lobby, and a gym and sauna on the premises. There's a desktop computer on every floor as well as free wi-fi. The service is not world-class but the location and accommodations are both superb.

Hotel Dann Carlton (Map p211; ☎ 1 800 094 5525; www.danncarlton.com; Carrera 43A No 7-50; s/d COP$420,000/450,000, ste COP$530,000-770,000) Expect rose petals strewn about your room when you arrive, and a fresh bunch of same on the bed. Service is attentive at this top-notch hotel, and a few staff members speak English. The suites in particular are huge, with attached sitting room, walk-in closet and massive bathroom. There's a revolving restaurant on the 19th floor with great views of the city. Ask for a room with a view over the adjacent Parque Linear.

Eating

El Poblado is full of upscale restaurants. The Las Palmas district, up in the foothills overlooking the city, has several top eateries with superb views. For something more authentic, stroll down Pasaje Junín, in central Medellín, during the day.

EL POBLADO

Carulla (Map p211; ☎ 361 7777; ⌚ 24hr) This supermarket is right next to CC Oviedo. It has a great salad bar (including fruit salad) with selections sold by weight. A good place to sample Colombia's many wonderful tropical fruits. Sandwiches and hot food too.

Flor de Canela (Map p211; ☎ 311 5877; Carrera 43B No 8-65; mains COP$7000-12,000; ⌚ breakfast, lunch & dinner Mon-Fri, breakfast & lunch Sat) Lots of local office workers eat here. It does a good set meal, with specials like pumpkin soup, spaghetti bolognese and sometimes traditional dishes like *ajiaco* (a typical Bogotá stew).

Café Le Bon (Map p211; ☎ 266 8872; lebon@epm.net .co; Calle 9 No 39-09; ⌚ 9am-1am Mon-Sat, to 11pm Sun) One of Medellín's few real coffee shops, Le

Bon would not be out of place in a funky arts neighborhood in any North American city. Choose from 14 types of espresso and 10 of cappuccino. It's also a good spot for breakfast (COP$7000 to COP$15,000), and serves lunch and snacks throughout the day, including soup, salads, and both sweet and savory crepes. In the evening the stereo stays leashed, making it a quiet spot for a cocktail or a beer.

Il Forno (Map p211; ☎ 266 9402; Carrera 37A No 8-9, mains COP$7000-18,000) Set in the middle of the *zona rosa*, this open-air Italian restaurant doesn't do gimmicks or discounts, just good, solid food at a fair price. It serves pizza and sandwiches, lasagna and ravioli, and even steak. There's a good range of salads for the herbivores. Desserts are a mere COP$6000. It may not be gourmet, but at this price, who cares?

Alex Carne de Res (Map p211; ☎ 352 3740; Carrera 48 No 10-70; mains COP$7500-14,500; ⌚ lunch & dinner) For a decent budget steak, Alex can't be beat. The building is roofed in palm thatch and there's salsa on the stereo. On Sunday it offers many typical regional platters. You'll find it below the highway overpass near the El Poblado metro station, opposite CC Monterrey.

Pasilú (Map p211; ☎ 311 2527; Carrera 47 No 7-49; mains COP$8000-15,000; ⌚ 10am-8pm Mon-Wed, to midnight Thu-Sat) This gourmet budget option is right next to the footbridge by the metro station. It does a great set meal, and also sandwiches any time of day. Serves wine and beer.

Il Castello (Map p211; ☎ 312 8287; Carrera 40 No 10A-14; mains COP$19,000-36,000) For authentic, top-quality Italian food, look no further than Il Castello. Try the *fettucine trento* (lobster served with a brandy and cream sauce), or the many pastas, raviolis and pizzas. It has an exceptional wine list; you'll imbibe your drop of red in large balloon glasses. Tucked just off Calle 10, you'll spot the place by the many expensive cars parked out front.

Thaico (Map p211; ☎ 311 5639, 352 2166; Calle 9A No 37-40; mains COP$20,000-30,000; ⌚ noon-1am Mon-Sat, to 9pm Sun) Don't expect chopsticks or even spicy food here, at what is one of the very few Thai joints in Colombia. Still, the food's not bad, especially before 7pm, when all meals are half-price and cocktails are three-for-one (normally COP$12,000 to COP$15,000 each). Great subdued, relaxed atmosphere, and a prime spot for a long, liquid lunch.

Bahía Mar (Map p211; ☎ 352 0938, 312 758 7796, Calle 9 No 43B-127; mains COP$20,000-50,000; ⌚ lunch

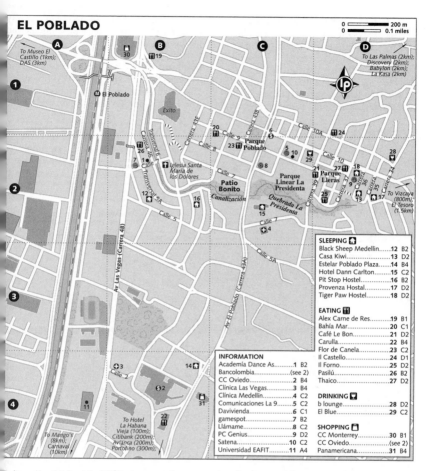

EL POBLADO

0 — 200 m
0 — 0.1 miles

To Museo El
Castillo (1km);
DAS (3km)

El Poblado

Exito

To Las Palmas (2km);
Discovery (2km);
Babylon (2km);
La Kasa (2km)

Iglesia Santa
María de
los Dolores

Parque
Poblado

Calle 10A

Patio
Bonito

Parque
Linear La
Presidenta

Parque
Lleras

Canalización

Quebrada La
Presidenta

To Vizcaya
(800m);
El Tesoro
(1.5km)

Av Las Vegas (Carrera 48)

Av El Poblado (Carrera 43A)

Universidad EAFIT

To Hotel
La Habana
Vieja (100m);
Citibank (200m);
Avianca (200m);
Portofino (300m);

To Mango's
(8km);
Carnaval
(10km)

INFORMATION
Academía Dance As............**1** B2
Bancolombia....................(see 2)
CC Oviedo........................**2** B4
Clínica Las Vegas...............**3** B4
Clínica Medellín.................**4** C1
Comunicaciones La 9..........**5** C2
Davivienda......................**6** C1
gamespot........................**7** B2
Llámame...........................**8** D2
PC Genius.........................**9** D2
Satena.............................**10** C2
Universidad EAFIT.............**11** A4

SLEEPING
Black Sheep Medellin.......**12** B2
Casa Kiwi........................**13** D2
Estelar Poblado Plaza.......**14** B4
Hotel Dann Carlton..........**15** C2
Pit Stop Hostel.................**16** B2
Provenza Hostal...............**17** D2
Tiger Paw Hostel..............**18** D2

EATING
Alex Carne de Res...........**19** B1
Bahía Mar......................**20** C1
Café Le Bon...................**21** D2
Carulla..........................**22** B4
Flor de Canela................**23** C2
Il Castello......................**24** D1
Il Forno.........................**25** D2
Pasilú...........................**26** B2
Thaico..........................**27** D2

DRINKING
b lounge.......................**28** D2
El Blue..........................**29** C2

SHOPPING
CC Monterrey.................**30** B1
CC Oviedo....................(see 2)
Panamericana................**31** B4

& dinner Mon-Sat, lunch Sun) This top notch seafood place offers *mariscos* in a Caribbean setting. Merengue plays on the stereo, and the signature dish is *langostino Providencia* (Providencia-style king prawns). The tables are laid out simply with blue tablecloths on top of white. They also do enormous shrimp cocktails and light platters of seafood crepes. A top choice for seafood in Medellín.

LAS PALMAS

Discovery (☎ 232 9518, 232 9608; Km1, Las Palmas; mains COP$17,000-60,000; ☷ lunch & dinner) Perched on the edge of the northern foothills in the Las Palmas district, Discovery has amazing views, and even better food. The specialty is seafood – try the *cazuela de mariscos al coco*

(seafood stew with coconut, COP$35,000), or the *parrilla mixta* (mixed grill, COP$36,000). There's live music on Friday and Saturday night.

CENTRAL MEDELLÍN

Café Colombo (Map p212; ☎ 513 4444, ext 183; Carrera 45 No 53-24; cafecolombo@colomboworld.com; mains COP$11,000-23,000; ☷ lunch & dinner Mon-Sat) On the top floor of the building also housing the Centro Colombo Americano, this minimalist spot serves up light meals along with stunning views of the city and mountains. Go for the set meal (COP$15,500), which changes weekly, or try the crepes, pasta, steak or trout. Its 10th-floor outdoor terrace is a great spot for cocktails early in the evening.

MEDELLÍN &
ZONA CAFETERA

Los Toldos (Map p212; ☎ 512 3675; Calle 54 No 47-11; mains COP$15,000-18,000; ☼ lunch & dinner) Elderly waiters wear traditional *paísa* costumes at this typical *paísa* place. Old-style Colombian folk music plays on the stereo. Go for the daily special, around COP$15,000, or indulge in a hearty *bandeja paísa* (platter). It prepares typical desserts like *arequipe*, *breva* and *quesito* (sample all three sweet and creamy treats for COP$5000). It's a bit camp but the food is excellent.

Drinking

The city's *zona rosa* is in El Poblado, a Disneyland of upscale restaurants and bars. The Las Palmas district sits perched on the

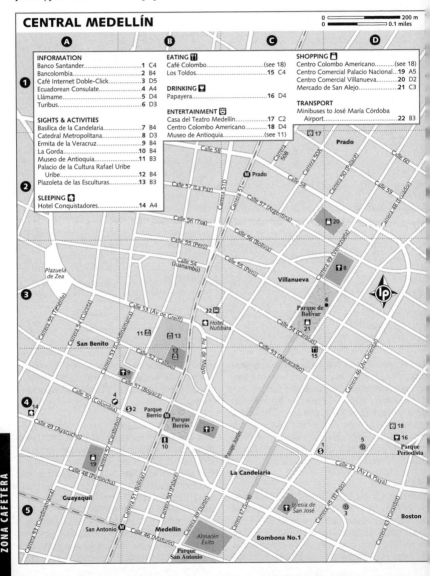

CENTRAL MEDELLÍN

0	200 m
0	0.1 miles

INFORMATION
Banco Santander...............................1 C4
Bancolombia..2 B4
Café Internet Doble-Click................3 D5
Ecuadorean Consulate.....................4 A4
Llámame...5 D4
Turibus...6 D3

SIGHTS & ACTIVITIES
Basílica de la Candelaria..................7 B4
Catedral Metropolitana....................8 D3
Ermita de la Veracruz.......................9 B4
La Gorda..10 B4
Museo de Antioquia........................11 B3
Palacio de la Cultura Rafael Uribe
Uribe..12 B4
Plazoleta de las Esculturas............13 B3

SLEEPING
Hotel Conquistadores......................14 A4

EATING
Café Colombo...............................(see 18)
Los Toldos...15 C4

DRINKING
Papayera...16 D4

ENTERTAINMENT
Casa del Teatro Medellín.................17 C2
Centro Colombo Americano...........18 D4
Museo de Antioquia......................(see 11)

SHOPPING
Centro Colombo Americano.........(see 18)
Centro Comercial Palacio Nacional...19 A5
Centro Comercial Villanueva..........20 D2
Mercado de San Alejo.....................21 C3

TRANSPORT
Minibuses to José María Córdoba
Airport..22 B3

northern foothills of Medellín, and its numerous thumping discos boast spectacular views of the city. Several large discos also cluster on the highway out of town. For a more grunge experience, check out the bars around Parque del Periodista.

b lounge (Map p211; ☎ 311 5048; cnr Calle 10A & Carrera 34; ☾ 9pm-3am Wed-Sat) This small, groovy bar attracts a relatively young crowd. Feather boas hang from the ceiling, and the Wednesday night karaoke is very popular. There's a wooden terrace outside facing the car dealership across the street. On the edge of the ever-expanding *zona rosa* at the time of our research.

Babylon (☎ 381 8169; Km1, Las Palmas; cover COP$10,000; ☾ 9pm-3am Thu-Sat) Decked out in Wonder Woman and Superman memorabilia (plus stacks and stacks of old televisions), this dimly lit disco offers the best value drinks in Las Palmas. Seating is at heavy wood picnic tables, and projector screens show cartoons all night long. On Thursday it does an all-you-can-drink-night for COP$30,000 (women free).

Carnaval (☎ 309 6229; Calle 80 Sur No 50-61, Entrada La Estrella; cover COP$15,000-20,000; ☾ 10pm-6am Thu-Sat) A five-minute taxi ride past Mango's on the highway is this massive disco. It attracts DJs from around the world. This is your late night option – no one shows up until 3am. The retractable roof opens and closes to let in a breath of fresh night air.

Club Social La Clarita (Map p206; ☎ 257 1223; Carrera 69 No 71-21, Robledo; cover COP$10,000; ☾ 11pm-6am Fri & Sat) This late-night disco doesn't get going until around 2am on the weekend, and then goes till dawn. A fair whack north of the center, this is where locals come to drink and dance to Colombian crossover. Sometimes has live music and dancers.

El Blue (Map p211; ☎ 266 3047; Calle 10 No 40-20; cover COP$10,000) Just off Parque Lleras, this place is devoted to rock, often hosting live bands. It has a large outdoor patio and caters to a mostly laid-back crowd. Thursday is big because there's no cover charge. One of the very few pick-up joints in Colombia, this is the place *paísa* girls go to meet gringo boys.

La Kasa (☎ 381 2663; Km1 Las Palmas; cover COP$10,000, women free) This popular split-level disco plays techno, accompanied by half a dozen electronic disco balls. Three bars will keep you well lubricated, and the fish

WHAT'S ON IN MEDELLÍN

www.guiaturisticademedellin.com
A bilingual guide to the city. Bookstores sell hard copies for COP$9000.
www.medellin.gov.co The government website is a good source of local information.
medellin.vive.in For galleries, cinema, theater and concerts.
El Colombiano (www.elcolombiano.com.co) The broadsheet's Thursday supplement is worth a look.
Opción Hoy (www.opcionhoy.com) Monthly publication.

in the two tanks built into the walls guarantee you a captive audience for your latest dance moves. One of the very best places for techno in Medellín; best for a visit on Thursday and Saturday.

Mango's (☎ 277 6123; Carrera 42 No 67A-151; cover COP$16,000) This upscale disco is tricked out in a western theme – all the waiters are dressed like cowboys. Scantily clad models and dwarfs dance for the crowds. The city's rich and beautiful come here to show off – it's among the most expensive nightclubs in Medellín.

Papayera (Map p212; ☎ 239 3400; Calle 53 No 42-55) Also known as Eslabon Perdido (the missing link), Eslabon Prendido (the tipsy link) or just 'Es La Bon,' this punnily-named bar is famous for its Tuesday night live salsa jams. It's a few blocks from Parque Periodista, a seedy area where a number of edgy bars cluster.

Entertainment
CINEMA
In addition to Medellín's many mainstream cinemas, check out the **Museo de Antioquia** (Map p212; ☎ 251 3636; www.museodeantioquia.org; Carrera 52 No 52-43), which shows free films most Tuesdays at 4pm. For classic English-language films, check out the **Centro Colombo Americano** (Map p212; ☎ 513 4444; www.colomboworld.com; Carrera 45 No 53-24; admission COP$5000).

THEATER
Medellín has the liveliest theater scene outside of Bogotá. There are a dozen or so theaters doing work that ranges from classical to the experimental. For event listings see www.medellinenescena.org.

Teatro Pablo Tobón Uribe (Map p206; ☎ 239 7500; Carrera 40 No 51-24) This is Medellín's major mainstream theater.

Casa del Teatro Medellín (Map p212; ☎ 254 0397; www.casadelteatrodemedellin.com; Calle 59 No 50A-25) Hosts different local theater groups year-round. The theater library has a large collection specializing in Colombian theater.

Teatro Metropolitano (Map p206; ☎ 232 4597; www.teatrometropolitano.com; Calle 41 No 57-30) Inaugurated in 1987, Medellín's largest and most modern theater hosts concerts, opera and ballet and is home to Medellín's Philharmonic Orchestra.

CLASSICAL MUSIC

Both Teatro Metropolitano and **Teatro de la Universidad de Medellín** (Map p206; www.udem.edu.co/UDEM/Servicios/Teatro) present concerts of classical and contemporary music. Another regular stage for concerts and recitals is the 300-seat Sala Beethoven in the **Palacio de Bellas Artes** (Map p206; ☎ 229 1400; Carrera 42 No 52-33).

TANGO

Once the preferred dance of the we're-not-really-Colombian *paisas*, it now lingers on in the memories on the older generation, and those with a taste for nostalgia.

Casa Gardeliana (Map p206; ☎ 212 0968; casagardeliana medellin@hotmail.com; Carrera 45 No 76-50; admission free; ⏰ 9am-5pm) Located in Barrio Manrique, the Casa Gardeliana was the main tango venue for years, hosting tango bands and dance shows. It still has them from time to time, though now it's basically a small tango museum, featuring memorabilia related to tango and Carlos Gardel.

Compañía de Baile A Puro Tango (☎ 279 5576, 282 8310; www.espectaculosapurotango.com) This dance company puts on tango shows in different venues every month. Check the website for upcoming events.

El Patio del Tango (Map p206; ☎ 351 2856; Calle 23 No 58-38; mains COP$18,000-30,000; ⏰ dinner Wed-Sun) Now the tango's major stage in Medellín, this steak restaurant is decorated like a typical Buenos Aires tango dive. There are often shows on Friday and Saturday nights.

Shopping

Medellín is Colombia's major textile producer so there are plenty of clothes to choose from, and sometimes you can get good deals on surplus goods.

Centro Comercial Palacio Nacional (Map p212; cnr Carrera 52 & Calle 48) A palatial building from 1925 in the center, it has been transformed into a shopping mall with more than 200 budget shops (most selling clothing and footwear). The area around the Palacio, nicknamed El Hueco (The Hole) by the locals, features plenty of bargain stores.

Plaza Minorista José María Villa (Map p206; cnr Carrera 57 & Calle 55) Home to a huge, bustling undercover market with more than 2500 stalls, selling mostly food. It was established in 1984 to remove hawkers from the streets. Open daily.

Mercado de San Alejo (Map p212; Parque de Bolívar; ⏰ 1st Sun each month) A colorful craft market great for cheap buys or simply to stroll around.

For some finer shopping, head to the upscale malls of El Poblado, including **El Tesoro** (Carrera 25A No 1AS-45), **Vizcaya** (Calle 9 No 30-382) and **CC Oviedo** (Map p211; Carrera 43A No 6S-15). All have a variety of European and American fashion stores.

BOOKSTORES

Centro Colombo Americano Central Medellín (Map p212; ☎ 513 4444, Plaza San Fernando, Carrera 45 No 53-24); El Poblado (Map p211; ☎ 326 4444; Carrera 43A No 1-50; www.colomboworld.com) The two locations both sell English-language books, including Lonely Planet titles. The downtown site also has a large lending library you can join, and the El Poblado location shows free English-language movies Monday at 7pm in the adjacent food court.

Panamericana (Map p211, ☎ 448 0999; up127@pan americana.com.co; Carrera 43A No 6S-150; ⏰ 9:30am-9pm Mon-Sat, 11am-7:30pm Sun) This huge bookstore sells some English titles. It also sells maps of Medellín, plus laptops and accessories.

COMPUTER STORES

CC Monterrey (Map p211; ☎ 268 0100; Carrera 48 No 10-45) Scores of small computer shops sell digital equipment at budget prices.

Getting There & Away

AIR

Medellín has two airports. All international flights depart from Aeropuerto José María Córdoba, 35km southeast of the city near the town of Ríonegro. Avianca domestic flights depart from here, including its frequent shuttle service to Bogotá. Buses shuttle between the city center (behind the Hotel

Nutibara) and the airport every 15 minutes (COP$6000, one hour, 4am to 10pm), or take a taxi (COP$48,000).

The smaller Aeropuerto Olaya Herrera is situated next door to the southern bus terminal. Many domestic flights leave from here, including Satena's service from Medellín to the Pacific coast.

BUS

Medellín has two bus terminals. The Northern Bus Terminal (Terminal de Norte), 3km north of the city center, handles buses to the north, east and southeast, including Santa Fe de Antioquia (COP$9000, 1¾ hours), Cartagena (COP$65,000, 13 hours), Barranquilla (COP$65,000, 14 hours), Santa Marta (COP$75,000, 16 hours) and Bogotá (COP$50,000, nine hours). It is easily reached from the center by metro in seven minutes (alight at Estación Caribe) or by taxi (COP$10,000).

The Southern Bus Terminal (Terminal de Sur), 4km southwest of the center, handles all traffic to the west and south, including Manizales (COP$8500, five hours), Pereira (COP$14,000, five hours), Armenia (COP$18,000, six hours) and Cali (COP$45,000, nine hours). From El Poblado it's a quick taxi ride (COP$3500).

Getting Around

METRO

Medellín's **Metro** (www.metrodemedellin.org.co; single ticket COP$1400; ⏱ 4:30am-11pm Mon-Sat, 5am-10pm Sun) is Colombia's only commuter rail line. It opened in 1995 and consists of a 23km north–south line and a 6km east–west line. Trains run at ground level except for 5km through the central area where they go on elevated tracks. The metro company also operates two cable car lines, called Metrocable, built to service the slum-dwelling residents on the surrounding hills, and a third line (to Santa Elena) is planned. The rides themselves afford magnificent views and make for a lovely way to check out the town.

BUS

Medellín is well-serviced by buses, although most travelers will find the metro and taxis sufficient for their needs. The majority of routes originate on Av Oriental and Parque Berrío. Buses stop running around 10 or 11pm.

AROUND MEDELLÍN

Long off-limits to Colombian tourists, who remained trapped in their cities by La Violencia, the countryside around Medellín is now secure and bustling with crowds. To the east lies the man-made reservoir Embalse Guatapé, a popular weekend getaway spot. Nearby is El Peñol, a 200m-high granite monolith you can climb. From the top you'll find great views over the lake.

To the north of the city lies Santa Fe de Antioquia, a sleepy colonial town that was once the capital of the department. These days it attracts weekenders from Medellín looking to warm up – set at a mere 550m, many hotels and restaurants have pools you can splash around in. The Puente de Occidente, an unusual local bridge, is also worth a visit.

Three hours east of Medellín is Río Claro. This nature reserve lies along a peaceful river where you can go rafting, kayaking or just paddle around. There are also canopy lines that zigzag back and forth across the river, and several cathedral-sized caves you can visit.

GUATAPÉ

☎ 4 / pop 2000 / elev 1925m

A two-hour bus ride from Medellín takes you to the pleasant holiday town of Guatapé. A ghost town for many years, tourism has returned to Guatapé with a vengeance. There's a good selection of hotels catering to weekend visitors – prices almost halve during the week – and restaurants serving hearty *paísa* food. It makes a great day trip, especially on the weekend, when the town is packed with Colombian tourists, and a festival atmosphere reigns. There are boats that can take you out onto the lake – including several with bars and dance floors – and a canopy line that zooms along the shorefront.

Guatapé is also well known for the fresco-like adornment of the traditional houses. Brightly painted bas-relief depictions of people, animals and shapes cover the bottom half of many houses.

Information

The **tourist office** (☎ 861 0555) in the *alcaldía* (town hall) on the main square was closed temporarily at the time of our visit. On the weekend a small shack on the waterfront dispenses advice and offers free tours of the town.

Sights

A block up from the main square is **Calle de los Recuerdos**, a cobblestone street that angles uphill and boasts the best example of the local frescoes.

The small **Museo Turístico** has an array of pottery shards, old typewriters, and odds and sods. It is open on the weekend and local guides will show you around at no cost. The youthful enthusiasm of the guides makes up for the rather mediocre quality of the exhibits. During the week contact the curator **Alvaro Idarraga** (☎ 320 632 5199) and he'll open the museum for you.

La Casa Familiar Garcia, the oldest and biggest house in Guatapé, is still occupied by descendents of the Garcia family, but they leave their front door open so you can wander into the central courtyard. Take note of the ornate, painted folding doors as you enter. Very typical of Guatapé.

The **Iglesia del Calma** boasts a Greco-Roman exterior and a polished wood interior. It was built in 1811 as a form of penance, or so the story goes, by a man who killed an orange thief.

Activities

BOATING

Three boating companies can take you out onto the water. The standard tours include a trip to La Cruz (the submerged tip of the church the lake now covers), a trip to La Piedra (an impressive sight from the water) and to the Isla de las Fantasias. A luxury resort was under construction on the island when we visited, and you can go for a walk around the perimeter.

The larger boats serve beer and have a dance floor. All the tours take around two hours return. The larger boats charge around COP$10,000 per person, with beer costing a mere COP$2000; smaller boats cost COP$80,000 (maximum 8 people). You can also charter a boat for the same price. Pablo Escobar's old holiday home sits out on the lake, abandoned for more than 15 years; some people like to visit it.

CANOPYING

A **canopy ride** (☎ 861 1083; per ride COP$10,000; ☺ 9am-6pm) at the shore of the lake runs tourists in a bucket seat across to a large hill on the opposite side. This exhilarating activity is known as *cable vuelo* in this area.

Sleeping

There are plenty of good accommodations options in town. Prices halve during the week.

El Descanso del Arriero (☎ 861 0878, 312 257 6953; Calle 30 No 28-82; s/d COP$35,000/57,000) The best budget option in Guatapé is just one block from the main plaza. It's an old colonial building with shutters opening onto an interior courtyard; all rooms are on the second floor. A restaurant on-site has a good view of a park.

Guatatur (☎ 861 1212, 312 295 3199; www.hotel guatatur.fincasagroturisticas.com; hotelguatatur@hotmail.com; Calle 31-04; s/d COP$65,000/76,000; Ⓟ) This modestly priced resort specializes in weekend package deals for Medellín couples. Several of the rooms have views of the lake, and the suites have Jacuzzis and even better views. Staff can organize boat trips, horseback riding, jet skis and visits to the nearby monastery. The best hotel in the center of town.

Eating

There's no shortage of good eats in Guatapé, centered mainly around or near the plaza.

La Fogata (☎ 861 1040, 310 822 0241; www.geocities.com/lafogataguatape; Av El Malecón; mains COP$5500-8500) Right opposite the lake with a view of the water and the boats, this place does amazing *paísa* food, including breakfast (COP$4500) if you stay the night. Go for the *trucha* (trout), or if you're really hungry, a *bandeja paísa*. It also rents rooms upstairs.

Getting There & Away

If you're coming on a day trip, it makes sense to climb El Peñol before venturing onward to Guatapé, as it can get cloudy and rain in the afternoon. Buses to and from Medellín run about once an hour. There are both buses (COP$10,000, two hours) and shared taxis (COP$14,500, 1½ hours).

On weekends and holidays jeeps shuttle frequently between El Peñol and Guatapé (COP$3000, 10 minutes), but are rare during the week. Returning from Guatapé on the weekend be sure to buy your return ticket immediately upon arrival, as buses fill up fast. The ticket office is on the uphill side of the main plaza.

EL PEÑOL
elev 2100m

El Peñol (aka La Piedra, 'The Rock'; per climb COP$5000) is a 200m-high granite monolith set near the edge of a lake. A brick-and-mortar staircase of 649 steps rises up through a broad fissure in the side of the rock. From the top there are magnificent views of the region, the fingers of the lake sprawling amid a vast expanse of green mountain.

The bus from Medellín will drop you off at a gas station. Take the cobblestone road that curves up and past the gas station (1km) to reach the parking lot at the base of the rock. Here there are a host of restaurants, tourist shacks selling knickknacks, and a bronze statue of the first man to climb the rock. Numerous restaurants serve lunch (COP$7000-12,000). There are bathrooms just after you pass through the turnstile. Two shops sell religious trinkets halfway up. At the top, shops sells fruit juice, ice cream and *salpicón* (fruit salad punch in watermelon juice), but no beer.

SANTA FE DE ANTIOQUIA
☎ 4 / pop 12,500 / elev 550m

This sleepy colonial town is the region's oldest settlement and was once the capital of Antioquia. Founded in 1541 by Jorge Robledo, the clock stands still at 1826, the year the government moved to Medellín. Set on the low-lying banks of the Río Cauca, these days it attracts tourists from Medellín looking to warm up in its steamy climate.

Because it was eclipsed for so long by its neighbor 80km to the southwest, its colonial center never fell to the wrecking ball and today it looks very much like it did in the 19th century. The narrow streets are lined with whitewashed houses, all single-story construction and many ranged around beautiful courtyards. You'll also see elaborately carved – and typically Antioquian – woodwork around windows and doorways.

Santa Fe de Antioquia makes a great day trip from Medellín, especially on the weekend, when *país* come to splash around in the many swimming pools at hotels and restaurants in town. The Puente de Occidente (p219) is also worth a look. There are lots of artisans and jewelry makers in town whose workshops are worth exploring, and don't miss sampling *pulpa de tamarindo*, the beloved sour-sweet candy made with tamarind from the surrounding valley. Pick up a pack from one of the vendors on Plaza Mayor, the town's sleepy main square. During the week you'll find steep discounts on accom-

modations, when you'll likely have the whole town to yourself.

Information
Copidrogas (☎ 853 1274, 853 1637; Plaza Mayor) This fully stocked pharmacy also delivers.
Listo Comunicaciones (☎ 853 3357; ☺ 6:30am-10pm; per hr COP$1000) Internet open seven days. On the main square; also has telephone cabins. Sign outside says 'Telecom.'
Tourist office (Oficina de Fomento y Turismo; ☎ 853 4139; Plaza Mayor; ☺ 8am-noon & 2-6pm) The tourist office is in the Palacio Municipal on the main plaza, and has useful information on where to stay, and on local craftsman and jewelry makers.

Sights
Of the town's four churches, the **Iglesia de Santa Bárbara** (cnr Calle 11 & Carrera 8; ☺ 5-6:30pm, plus Sun morning mass) is the most interesting. Built by Jesuits in the second half of the 18th century, the church has a fine, baroque facade. The interior has an interesting, if time-worn, retable over the high altar. The **Museo de Arte Religioso** (☎ 853 2345; Calle 11 No 8-12; admission COP$1000; ☺ 10am-5pm), next door to Santa Bárbara church, has a collection of religious objects, including paintings by Gregorio Vásquez de Arce y Ceballos.

The **Catedral** (Plaza Mayor; ☺ morning & evening mass, plus 11am Sun service) is sometimes referred to as the Catedral Madre, as it was the first church built in the region. However, the original church was destroyed by fire, and the large building you see today was not completed until 1837. Until that year, Iglesia de Santa Bárbara did the honors as the cathedral. Once inside, have a look at the *Last Supper* in the right transept, and at an image of San Francisco de Borja with a skull in the transept opposite.

The two remaining churches, the mid-17th-century **Iglesia de Chiquinquirá** (cnr Carrera 13 & Calle 10), also known as La Chinca, and the 1828 **Iglesia de Jesús Nazareno** (cnr Carrera 5 & Calle 10), are generally open only for evening mass at 7pm daily. Admirers of funerary art may want to visit the local **cemetery** at the southeastern end of Calle 10, which has historic tombstones and a 150-year-old cemetery chapel.

Festivals & Events
Semana Santa (Holy Week) Like most traditional towns dating from the early days of the Spanish Conquest, Santa Fe celebrates this with pomp and solemnity. Book accommodations in advance.

Fiesta de los Diablitos (Dec) The town's most popular festival is held annually over the last four days of the year. It includes music, dance, craft fair, and – like almost every feast in the country – a beauty contest and bullfights.

Sleeping

Most people come to Santa Fe as a day trip, but the town has about a dozen hotels catering to all budgets. Prices during the week are much lower than on the weekend.

Hostal Plaza Mayor (☎ 853 3448; Plaza Mayor; r per person COP$25,000, with 3 meals COP$50,000; P) Set in an old colonial building on the main square, this perfectly adequate option will do when everything else is full. There's a pool out back, but was it closed when we visited, and some of the newer rooms are built of bessa brick. Be sure to check a few before deciding.

our pick Hotel Caserón Plaza (☎ 853 2040; halcaraz@edatel.net.co; Plaza Mayor; s/d/tr/q COP$67,000/127,000/180,000/233,000; P ✕ ⊠) On the town's main square, this inn was once home to a member of the local gentry. Rooms are ranged around an attractive courtyard, and there is a nice pool and garden in the back, plus a decent restaurant. Meals are extra.

Eating & Drinking

There are plenty of decent budget restaurants on the main plaza.

Buffalo Bill (☎ 853 1072, 314 784 5072; Plazoleta de la Chinca; mains COP$18,000-28,000; ⊠ noon-midnight Sun-Thu, to 3am Fri & Sat; ⊠) During the day this vaguely cowboy themed restaurant pumps out grilled meat and fish. At night they push the tables aside and it turns into one of Santa Fe's only discos. For day-trippers, consider its Día de Sol promotion – COP$35,000 gets you a main meal of your choice and all-day access to its large swimming pool.

Restaurante Portón del Parque (☎ 853 3207; Calle 10 No 11-03; mains COP$18,000-30,000; ⊠ lunch & dinner) Occupying an elegant colonial house with high ceilings and a flowery courtyard, this restaurant is widely considered the best in town. The kitchen prepares top-quality traditional food, including *ajiaco* (local stew of Bogotá) and *arequipe con leche* (supersweet dessert of milk and sugar).

Getting There & Away

There are at least six buses daily (COP$9000, 1¾ hours) to/from Medellín's Northern Bus

PUENTE DE OCCIDENTE

The white peaked towers of this 19th-century bridge jut skyward against a backdrop of green hills. The **Puente de Occidente** (Western Bridge), a 291m-long bridge over the Río Cauca, was designed by José María Villa and constructed between 1887 and 1895. When built, it was one of the first suspension bridges in the Americas. It carried general traffic until 1978, when it was declared a national monument. Buses are now banned, though cars can still use it.

The bridge is 5km east of Santa Fe on the road to Sopetrán. A small fleet of Chinese-made tricycle moto-taxis now usher tourists to and from the bridge (COP$12,000 return). These open-air taxis seat three and, as there is often a queue to cross the bridge, will offer to let you off on the near side, so you can walk across, and then pick you up on the other side.

On the far side of the bridge you'll find **Camping Occidente** (☎ 855 0088, 385 8210; dm COP$30,000). There isn't any camping, but there are six-person dorm rooms that include access to the enormous pool. There is also a restaurant and bar, plus ice-cream stands and *tiendas de artesanías* (handicraft stores). If you just want to use the pool it's COP$6000. The place is packed on the weekends and empties during the week.

Terminal. There are also shared taxis that leave when full (COP$13,000, 1½ hours) from the second floor of the bus terminal in Medellín.

RÍO CLARO
elev 350m

Three hours east of Medellín and five hours west of Bogotá is the **Reserva Natural Cañon de Río Claro** (☎ 265 8855; www.rioclaroelrefugio.com; Autopista Medellín–Bogotá Km132; campsite per person COP$5000, r per person incl 3 meals COP$55,000–80,000). A river has carved a stunning canyon from its marble bed. Here you can visit a spectacular cave, go kayaking, white-water rafting, canopying, or just swim and hike along its banks. It's also a favorite spot for bird-watchers, who come to see everything from hummingbirds to herons to vultures.

Set 2km south of the Medellín–Bogotá highway, the reserve offers a variety of accommodation options. The most impressive are a 15-minute walk upriver from the restaurant – the rooms face the open jungle, and you fall asleep to the roar of the river beside you and the loud thrum of crickets in the night. You'll wake to see mist rising up through the jungle-clad canyon. There are also bunk beds, twin rooms and double rooms above the restaurant/visitors center. It also manages a motel-style property at the edge of the highway, but it suffers from the constant highway road noise.

Be sure to visit the **Caverna de los Guácharos** (COP$8000), a spectacular nearby cave. Cavern after cavern soar high and hollow like great cathedrals. A stream runs through the cave, about 1km long. The entrances are guarded by shrill, shrieking flocks of *guácharos*, a batlike nocturnal bird. You'll be given a life vest and be expected to swim part of the way.

The river is a fine place to paddle a kayak (COP$20,000) or go rafting (COP$20,000). The rapids are Class I – hard-core rafters may be disappointed. Five canopy cables crisscross the river, and make for a diverting afternoon zipping across the river (COP$20,000).

You must bring your own swimsuit, towel and flashlight. On weekends the reserve is often full of Colombian high school students – you may prefer to come during the week. The food served is second-rate, with fruit and vegetables making only cameo appearances. Cooking is only permitted in the camping area. Beer is for sale in the restaurant but hard liquor is forbidden. It is requested you book with at least a week's notice.

Orientation & Information
The reserve is 24km west of Doradal. There are two ATMs in town on the main square and an internet cafe, @**nberdi.com** (☎ 834 2057; ⏱ 8am-10pm; per hr COP$2000), half a block from the park above the Comcel sign.

Getting There & Away
Most Medellín–Bogotá buses will drop you at the entrance. From any other direction, look for transport to Doradal. From here it's COP$4500 to Río Claro in a shared taxi, or hail any passing intercity bus.

LA DANTA
This small town makes an interesting day trip from Río Claro. There are several caves

---

HACIENDA NÁPOLES

Once the site of Pablo Escobar's country retreat and private zoo, this new **theme park** (☎ 834 2129, 317 330 4918; www.haciendanapoles.com; admission COP$20,000) is refurbishing the ruins. There's a large *mariposario* (butterfly enclosure) – the stereo plays Vivaldi's 'Four Seasons' on continuous loop. Escobar's 18 pet hippopotamuses somehow survived decades of neglect; there are zebras, *dantas* (tapirs) and ostriches too. Loudspeakers blast 'dinosaur noises' as you rock up at the main gate – there are numerous life-sized replicas of dinosaurs, constructed by the artist Escobar employed. The main house has been left in ruins as a reminder of the mayhem Escobar once caused the country; his collection of burned 1920s automobiles is still here too.

Nápoles is an ambitious project that has a long way to go. Dozens of workers were busy when we visited, but we were the only tourists there. A four-star African-themed hotel is being built, and an aquarium, canopy cables, reptile park and horseback-riding facilities are all in the works.

The turnoff to the hacienda is 1km from Doradal. From here it's 2km more to the entrance, and 2km further still to the center of the action. There's no public transport here. Taxis and moto-taxis leave from the main park in Doradal. Be cautioned: drivers might try to rip you off. Average price for the trip should be COP$15,000 to COP$20,000 each way.

---

and a marble mine you can visit, but the real draw are the two *artesanía* workshops run by former paramilitaries, most of whom retired after losing a leg or two in combat. There is a *guadua* (bamboo) workshop (☎ 311 714 6333, 320 621 0818) where men make sofas, lamps, cups and smaller knickknacks. More interesting is the marble workshop, where you'll find marble sculptures of animals, football-team shields, and even detailed renderings of earthmovers. It's best to call before visiting as they are not always open. If you ask politely they may tell you about their experiences as paramilitaries.

A recommended guide is **Blanca Luz** (☎ 313 852 1912). If you decide to spend the night, try the **Hotel Campestre La Caverna** (☎ 314 687 6092; s COP$20,000, d & tr COP$30,000; P 🚻).

There is infrequent bus service between La Danta and Doradal, which you can pick up at *la partida de La Danta* (the highway turnoff to La Danta). The last bus back leaves between 4:30 and 5pm (COP$2000, 30 minutes). Or take a moto-taxi direct to Río Claro (COP$15,000, 30 minutes). From *la partida* you can hail any passing Medellín-bound bus back to Río Claro.

ZONA CAFETERA

The Zona Cafetera, also called the Eje Cafetero (Coffee Axle), generally refers to the triangle formed by Bogotá, Medellín and Cali, although in practice this means the three small cities of Manizales, Pereira

and Armenia. The region continues to produce a sizable portion of Colombia's coffee crop, and there are numerous coffee farms you can visit.

The area boasts spectacular natural beauty. There are stunning vistas everywhere – Salento, in particular, and the adjacent Valle de Cocora, are jaw-dropping. Parque Nacional Natural (PNN) Los Nevados soars above 5000m and offers trekking opportunities through the striking *páramo* (high-mountain plains). The nightclubs of the region also has spectacular natural beauty.

The region was colonized by *paísas* in the 19th century during the *colonización antioqueña*, and to this day remains culturally closer to Medellín than either Cali or Bogotá, in everything from its traditional architecture to its cuisine.

MANIZALES
☎ 6 / pop 370,000 / elev 2150m
The northern wheel of the Coffee Axle, Manizales is a pleasantly cool, midsized university town, surrounded on all sides by green mountain scenery. There is a strong student vibe, and many excellent restaurants and nightclubs cater to their tastes and budgetary requirements. Manizales is also the gateway to PNN Los Nevados and the three nearby nature reserves – Recinto del Pensamiento, Río Blanco and Los Yarumos. Several coffee farms offer popular tours.

Manizales is the capital of the Caldas department, and was founded in 1849 by a group of Antioquian colonists looking to escape the civil wars of that time. According to local legend, the original settlement consisted of 20 families, including the family of Manuel Grisales, after whom the new city was named. Manizales' early development was hindered by two earthquakes in 1875 and 1878, and a fire in 1925. For this reason there's not a lot of historical interest left – the real attractions are the surrounding nature activities and the town's popping nightlife.

Orientation

Manizales is built on a ridgeline. The entire city stretches along one main thoroughfare – Av Santander (Carrera 23) – and houses and businesses slope down either side.

The de facto city center has shifted from around Plaza de Bolívar to Cable Plaza (Av Santander near Calle 65), the former cable-car station east of the center that now hosts a large shopping mall. The churches and museums remain in the old center but the best eating and accommodations options cluster near Cable Plaza.

Information

Banco de Crédito (Casa Luker, next door to Cable Plaza) Recommended for changing money.

Bancolombia (cnr Calle 21 & Carrera 22)

Cambiamos SA (☎ 889 7270; Cable Plaza; ☷ 9am-7pm Mon-Sat) Inside the Corulla supermarket. Also an agent for Moneygram.

Citibank (Carrera 23 No 53B-20) Thieves know about Citibank's high withdrawal limits too. Take a taxi back to your hotel.

Internet Cable (☎ 897 5949; Av Santander No 63-82; ☷ 8am-10pm; per hr COP$2000) Ten computers, plus phone cabins. Open seven days. Two blocks west of Cable Plaza.

MAC (☎ 890 1016; Calle 65 No 24-109; ☷ 7:30am-7:30pm Mon-Fri, to noon Sat) Three computers for internet.

Tourist office (Centro de Información Turística de Caldas; ☎ 884 2400; www.caldasturistico.gov.co, www.ict .gov.co; Calle 19N No 21-44) On the ground floor of the Gobernación de Caldas.

Dangers & Annoyances

Mind the unpainted sidewalk traffic pylons. You are likely to bang your shins at least once.

Sights

The Plaza de Bolívar is the city's main square, with the mandatory statue of Bolívar by Rodrigo Arenas Betancur. It is known as Bolívar-Cóndor, since the sculptor endows Colombia's founder with distinctly birdlike features. The **Palacio de Gobierno**, a pretty neo-classical confection built in 1927, stands on the northern side of the plaza.

The square's south side is dominated by the odd but impressive **Catedral de Manizales** (☎ 882 2600; COP$5000; ☷ 9am-6pm Thu-Sun). Begun in 1929 and built of reinforced concrete, it is among the first churches of its kind in Latin America, and its main tower is 106m high, making it the highest church tower in the country. You can climb to the top for great views of the city.

The **Museo del Oro** (☎ 884 3851; Carrera 23 No 23-6, Piso 2; admission free) is located a block south of the Plaza de Bolívar in the Banco de la República building. It has a small collection of Quimbaya gold, and ceramic artifacts.

A short walk east of Plaza de Bolívar is the **Iglesia de la Inmaculada Concepción**. Built at the beginning of the 20th century, it has a beautiful, carved-wood interior reminiscent of a ship's hull.

At Chipre, 2km north and uphill of the center there's a new **mirador** (lookout tower) that was nearing completion when we visited. There are stunning views even from the base. Buses run along Av Santander from Cable Plaza to Chipre every 30 seconds (yes, that frequently!) or so (COP$1100, 15 minutes).

Tours

The most popular tour is a full-day trip up the slope of Nevado del Ruiz (see p225).

Kumanday Adventures (☎ 885 4980, 315 590 7294; kumandaycolombia@gmail.com; Av Santander No 60-13) This full-service adventure tour company, next door to the Universidad Católica, offers mountaineering and mountain-biking tours nationwide. It also rents a few dorm beds on-site. Staff can organize visits to **Ecoturismo Termales La Quinta** (2600m; r per person incl 3 meals COP$150,000-200,000), an exclusive mountain resort on the edge of Los Nevados. It's possible but difficult to get there on your own. Contact Kumanday for details. Also rents tents and sleeping bags.

Festivals & Events

Feria de Manizales (Jan) The highlight of Manizales' annual festival are the bullfights – the feria attracts some of the world's best bullfighters, and Colombia's feistiest bulls. You'll also find the usual assortment of parades and craft fairs, and of course a beauty pageant.

Festival Internacional de Teatro (Sep & Oct) Held annually since 1968, this is one of two important theater festivals in Colombia (the other is in Bogotá). The festival lasts about a week and includes free concerts in Plaza de Bolívar.

Sleeping

High season is January for the feria, when prices more than double.

Mountain House (☎ 887 4736; www.mountainhouse manizales.com; Calle 66 No 23B-137; dm/r incl breakfast COP$17,000/36,000; 🖳) It may be the only hostel in town, but that hasn't let it stop being a fine hostel anyway. A short walk from the *zona rosa*, this is one of the few hostels where backpackers and Colombian travelers mix. The Colombian management is a great source of information about the region. Some of the dorms don't have windows, so look before you leap. Will also loan jackets and gloves for trips to Los Nevados. A second, nearby hostel with a tour agency was in the works at time of research.

Regine's Hotel (☎ 096 887 5360; Calle 65A No 23B-113; regineshotel@hotmail.com; s/d COP$109,000/133,000; 🖳) This B&B-style family-run hotel offers boutique accommodations close to Cable Plaza. The upstairs rooms are much better than those downstairs, and cost the same. Breakfast and wi-fi are included in the price, and the outdoor garden patio is a great place to watch the sunrise.

Estelar Las Colinas (☎ 884 2009, 1 800 051 4000; www.hotelesestelar.com; Carrera 22 No 20-20; s/d COP$140,000/185,000; 🅿 🖳) The poshest place in the center, this modern glass-and-concrete hotel isn't pretty to look at but it has large, comfortable rooms, plus a good restaurant. Prices include a generous buffet breakfast. It was building a sister hotel adjacent to Cable Plaza at time of our visit.

Varuna Hotel (☎ 881 1122; Calle 62 No 23C-18; www .varunahotel.com; s/d COP$248,000/296,000, ste COP$303,000-391,000; 🅿 🖳) A popular business traveler option, this shiny new hotel offers minimalist-style rooms with polished wood floors right on Av Santander, a short walk from Cable Plaza. It has cable TV, free wi-fi and a restaurant serving breakfast, lunch and dinner. Ask for an upstairs room with a view.

Eating

Carulla (🕑 8am-10pm) Full-service supermarket in Cable Plaza for those who want to cook.

La Suiza (☎ 885 0545; Carrera 23B No 64-06; mains COP$8000-12,000; 🕑 9:30am-8:30pm Mon-Sat, 10am-7:30pm Sun) This scrumptious bakery does great pastries and even homemade chocolate. It also does good budget breakfasts, plus light lunches, such as mushroom crepes and chicken sandwiches. One block from Cable Plaza.

Valentino's Gourmet (☎ 885 9471; Carrera 23 No 63-128; 🕑 10am-10pm) This small cafe, popular with students, does the best hot chocolate in town. Choose from 20 different espresso and cappuccino styles, and gourmet chocolates too.

Los Geranios (☎ 886 8738; Carrera 23 No 71-67, Milan; mains COP$14,400-16,900) Famous for its large portions of traditional Colombian food, this place is great if you're hungry or just fueling up for a late night. The menu includes *bandeja paísa*, five kinds of *sancocho*, *ajiaco*, steak, chicken and even a few fish dishes. Meals come with five different kinds of sauce. For dessert try a yummy ice-cream sundae. The place is decorated with miniature models of Colombian churches and a loud TV accompanies your meal.

Don Juaco (☎ 885 0610; Calle 65 No 23A-44; 🕑 10:30am-9:30pm) Right in the heart of the *zona rosa*, this popular restaurant faces the main drag and is always full. The sign says 'snaks' but we can't figure out why. It does great burgers, and the lunch special is excellent value – *cazuela de pollo* (think chicken pot pie without the pastry), with bread, salad, dessert and coffee for COP$14,000.

Club Manizales (☎ 884 1611; Carrera 23 No 25-60C; mains COP$18,000-33,000; 🕑 lunch & dinner Mon-Sat) The public dining room of this private club is one of the best places to eat in the city. The specialty is seafood – try the *langostinos al whisky* (king prawns in whiskey, COP$33,000), *jaibas thermidor* (crab thermidor, COP$18,000) or the *trucha mediterraneo* (trout with mushroom and shrimp sauce, COP$20,000). It has a decent wine list, and cocktails are a mere COP$7500.

Drinking & Entertainment

The main *zona rosa* is along Av Santander near Cable Plaza. There are several *viejotecas* (nightclubs for patrons 30 and over) near the bullring, 1km southwest of the center. For a drink with a view there are a few *estancos* (small liquor shop with outdoor tables) in Chipre near the *mirador*.

Thursday is a big night in Manizales, when many of the students party hearty before heading home for the weekend to visit their families. Note that many nightclubs do not serve beer, only bottles of liquor.

Bar C (☎ 886 7103, barcmanizales@hotmail.com, Via Acueducto Niza, ☾ 10pm-3am Thu, to 4:30am Fri & Sat) When all the bars in Manizales close at 2am, anyone left standing comes here. Set up on a mountaintop about 3km east of Cable Plaza, there are great views of the city and the stars. A neighboring restaurant serves food until late. DJs play mostly Colombian crossover to please the late-night student crowd. Good selection of top-shelf liquor.

Bar La Plaza (☎ 885 2515; Carrera 23B No 64-80; ☾ 11am-11pm Mon-Wed, to 2am Thu-Sat) This is the place to start your evening. A delicatessen by day, at night it fills up fast, and by 9pm you'll have to wait for a table. The music isn't too loud, so you can converse. There's a young student vibe, and it also offers gourmet sandwiches (COP$10,000) and snack platters of quality salami and cheese to help line your stomach. Does good cocktails.

our pick **Puerto Rico Salsateca** (☎ 883 7935; Av Centenario No 24-132; cover COP$10,000; ☾ 8pm-1am Wed & Thu, to 2am Fri & Sat) This swish salsa joint is one of the grooviest we've ever seen. The hollow dance floor fills up with water, the numbered tables have buttons that light up a board on the wall (to call the waiter over), the back window has great views of the city lights, and the English-speaking ex-cruise-ship bartender mixes a mean manhattan. There are even drums and maracas you can borrow to play along with the music.

VIP (☎ 886 3578; Carrera 23 No 63-122; cover COP$5000) The biggest nightclub in town, when VIP packs them in, it seems like half the population of Manizales is here. Two large bars will keep you well lubricated until late. Plays classic dance tunes and remixes, and some techno. On night's when it's popping, this is the place to see and be seen. Huge dance floor.

There's also a couple of old-style tango bars on the so-called Calle de Tango (Calle 24). Check out **Los Nuevos Faroles** (☎ 884 6912; Calle 24 No 22-46; ☾ 8pm-2am Thu-Sat) and **Reminiscencias** (☎ 320 326 3924; Calle 24 No 22-42; ☾ 7pm-2am Thu-Sat), just next door.

The **Teatro Los Fundadores** (☎ 878 2530; cnr Carrera 22 & Calle 27) is Manizales' leading theater; it also has a cinema.

Getting There & Away
AIR
Aeropuerto La Nubia (☎ 874 5451) is 8km southeast of the city center, off the road to Bogotá. Take the urban bus to La Enea, then walk for five minutes to the terminal, or grab a cab (COP$8000). Avianca, ADA and Aires offer frequent service to Bogotá, Medellín and Armenia.

A new international airport near Palestina, an hour west of Manizales, is in the works, but won't be opening until at least 2012.

BUS
A new bus terminal was under construction outside Manizales on the highway when we visited, and should be finished by the time you read this. Two cable car lines are in the works to shuttle travelers from the new terminal to Cable Plaza and the city center, but we saw no signs of construction as yet.

Buses depart regularly to Bogotá (COP$25,000, eight hours), Medellín (COP$8500, five hours) and Cali (COP$11,000, five hours). Minibuses to Pereira (COP$4000, 1¼ hours) and Armenia (COP$7000, 2¼ hours) run every 15 minutes or so.

The old **bus terminal** (Av 19 No 15-04), if it's still open, is a short walk northwest of Plaza de Bolívar.

AROUND MANIZALES
Recinto del Pensamiento
elev 2100m

Set in the cloud forest 11km from Manizales, this **nature park** (☎ 887 4913, 874 4157; www.recintodelpensamiento.com; Km11 Via al Magdalena; admission COP$8000; ☾ 9am-4pm Tue-Sun) boasts a fine *mariposario* (butterfly enclosure), several short walks you can do through an impressive orchid-populated forest, a medicinal herb garden and a mature bonsai garden, plus there is good bird-watching in the morning. You'll also see big plantations of *guadua* and *chusqué* (two kinds of Colombian bamboo); note the enormous convention center in the shape of a shitake mushroom built of *guadua*. Several pens showcase deer, ostrich, zebras, llamas and sheep, and the fish pond contains some medium-sized local species *tilapia* and *mojarra*, which you can feed (fish food COP$1000). There's even a *telesilla* – a ski-lift-style cable car that can take you to the top of the mountain slope on which the park sits.

Admission includes 2½ hours of mandatory guide service; a couple of the guides speak some English. The *telesilla* costs COP$10,000, but it's a pleasant half-hour walk to the top of the hill if you prefer.

Come on sunny days, when you'll see more butterfly activity. Bird-watchers should request their bird list brochure.

To get here, take the bus marked Sera Maltería from Cable Plaza in Manizales (COP$1100, 30 minutes, every 10 minutes), or take a taxi (COP$5000, 10 minutes).

Reserva Ecológica Río Blanco
elev 2100-3800m

Three kilometers northeast of Manizales lies this undeveloped nature reserve. It is a protected area of high biodiversity and protects numerous endangered species, including the *oso andino* (spectacled bear). There are 362 species of bird present in the park, including 13 of Colombia's 80 endemics. It attracts bird-watchers from around the world, but even the amateur will be delighted by the quantities of hummingbirds, butterflies and orchids you'll see in the peaceful calm of this cloud forest. It makes a great half-day excursion – best in the morning, as it often rains in the afternoon.

There are four trails. The most popular is a pleasant 3.5km stroll uphill through cloud forest. At 2550m you'll arrive at **Viveros** (Colombians/foreigners incl 3 meals per night COP$34,500/COP$53,600), a group of cabins that accommodates 35. Only groups of credentialed bird-watchers or orchid-hunters may stay here; it's not open to the general public. At Viveros you'll see many different kinds of hummingbirds feeding. There are also several deer and two endangered *osos andinos* in a nearby enclosure.

Before you can visit you must request permission (free) from the offices of **Fundación Ecológica Gabriel Arango Restrepo** (☎ 886 7777, ext 1164; www.fundegar.com; Av Kevin Ángel No 59-181). You can walk to the office from Cable Plaza (one hour) or take a cab (COP$2600, five minutes). You must employ the services of a local guide (COP$20,000 per day, COP$15,000 per half-day, up to 15 people). They will organize a *taxista amigo* (tourist taxi) to take you to the main gate (COP$10,000, 20 minutes). The guide will meet you at the gate and take you into the reserve. Ask at the office for a copy of the bird list. To get back to Manizales, ask at Viveros to call a *taxista amigo*. From here it's

a 40 minute walk downhill to the gate, where the taxi will pick you up.

There are longer walks you can do in the reserve, but they are long and little-used, and camping is not permitted. Inquire at the office if you're interested.

Los Yarumos

Set on a hill overlooking Manizales, this 53-hectare municipal **nature park** (☎ 875 5621; ecoparquelosyarumos@epm.net.co; Calle 61B No 15A-01; base admission COP$3200; ☽ 9am-5pm Tue-Sun) has panoramic views of the city. A museum has an impressive collection of preserved butterflies, insects and birds, and a food court offers budget meals and serves beer. A half-dome concert shell hosts free concerts and cultural events on weekend afternoons. Tour guides can show you around for free, and several speak some English.

There are numerous short walks you can do through mature secondary forest, plus five canopy cables can zip you around the park (COP$19,000). There's rock-climbing, horseback riding, *barranquismo* (rappelling through a waterfall), and sometimes an ice-skating rink. The full-day do-everything package costs COP$33,000.

Yarumos is a great place to come on a clear afternoon, when you can see the three peaks of El Ruiz, Santa Isabel and El Cisne. Sunsets here are likewise spectacular.

Yarumos is a 40-minute walk from Cable Plaza in Manizales, or take a taxi (COP$3000).

Coffee Farms (Fincas)

Hacienda Guayabal (☎ 6 850 7831, 314 772 4856; www.haciendaguayabal.com; Km3 Via Peaje Tarapacá, Chinchiná; P ✿), a working coffee farm (1400m) near Chinchiná, offers 1½ hour tours (COP$15,000) of the estate, including the coffee fields and on-site processing plant, plus you can use the swimming pool afterward. Guides are Spanish-speaking only. The main harvest is from October to December; the secondary harvest is May and June.

To get here, take any bus from Manizales to Chinchiná (COP$5000, 30 minutes), then from Chinchiná take the bus marked 'Guayabal Peaje' (COP$1000, 10 minutes, every 15 to 30 minutes). Ask the driver to let you off before the toll booth at the small village of Guayabal; from here it's a 2km walk. Take the first left going north. Walk two minutes and take the first right. From here you'll be able to see the sign that says 'Hacienda Guayabal' hanging from the power lines. Walk three minutes more until you come to a crossroads. Turn left. Four minutes' walk more and you're there. There's sometimes a bus outside the church in the group of houses at the turnoff that can take you to the hacienda (COP$800, five minutes).

Hacienda Venecia (☎ 885 0771, 884 4459, 312 850 9270; www.haciendavenecia.com; P R), single-origin coffee farm (1300m), has won numerous awards for its coffee. The well-preserved *paísa* farmhouse has, until recently, been used to entertain international coffee buyers, but at the time of our research was about to open as a boutique hotel (call for prices). The gardens are well-kept, and there's a pond with lily pads and a round blue pool. The rooms are full of books and old photographs, and the wraparound verandah has hammocks and rocking chairs to rock away the evening. The house is decorated with saddles, chaps and bridles, and there's a real no-hole billiard table in the small bar area.

You can also visit the coffee operation with advance notice (COP$20,000 including transport, COP$15,000 without). To get here, take the jeep to Hacienda Venecia from the terminal in Manizales (COP$3200, 30 minutes, 7am, noon, 5pm).

PARQUE NACIONAL NATURAL (PNN) LOS NEVADOS

Following a spine of snow-covered volcanic peaks, this 583-sq-km national park provides access to some of the most stunning stretches of the Colombian Andes. With altitudes ranging from 2600m to 5325m, it encompasses everything from humid cloud forests and *páramo* to the perpetual snows of the highest peaks. The main peaks, from north to south, are El Ruiz (5325m), El Cisne (4750m), Santa Isabel (4950m), El Quindío (4750m) and El Tolima (5215m).

Thirty-seven rivers are born here, and provide water to 3.5 million people in four departments. The glaciers in the park are receding, and research is underway to measure the impact on the environment.

The best months to see snow in Los Nevados are October and November and from March to May. Outside of those times you're more likely to get the dry windy conditions favorable to trekking and good views.

Nevado del Ruiz

This is the highest volcano of the chain. Its eruption on November 13, 1985, killed more than 20,000 people and swept away the town of Armero, a town on the Río Lagunillas. El Ruiz had previously erupted in 1845, but the results were far less catastrophic; today, the volcano has returned to its slumber. It's nicknamed the 'sleeping lion of Manizales.'

Most people who visit the park will climb the upper slopes of Nevado del Ruiz as part of an organized tour from Manizales. The principal access road into the park is from the north. It branches off from the Manizales–Bogotá road in La Esperanza, 31km from Manizales, and winds its way 33km up to the snowline at about 4800m at the foot of Nevado del Ruiz. You'll pass through the unique landscape of the *páramo*, stopping at Laguna Negra (3760m) for breakfast along the way.

The volcano actually has three craters: Arenas, Olleta and Piraña. It's possible to summit the main one, Arenas (5325m), but you must request permission from **Parques Nacionales** (☎ 886 4703, 885 4581) in Manizales at least a week in advance. It is a technical climb but is not considered difficult mountaineering.

The entrance to the park is at Las Brisas (4050m). **Concesión Nevados** (☎ 881 2065; mercadeo nevados@gmail.com; Calle 64A No 24-30 in Manizales) will charge you admission (Colombians/foreigners COP$26,000/COP$40,000; ☼ 7:30am-2:30pm). About 7km uphill from Las Brisas is Chalet Arenales (4150m), where you can camp (COP$7000 per person), and 10km further up the road is a shelter known as El Refugio (4800m), which sells coffee, snacks and rolls of film. From here it's a half-hour walk to the flag pole (4900m); if conditions permit you can walk 1½ hours further to 5100m, then 30 minutes back down. The snow glare can be ferocious; wear sunglasses and sunscreen.

The extinct Olleta crater (4850m), on the opposite side of the road, is covered with multi-colored layers of sandy soil and normally has no snow. The walk to the top will take about 1¼ hours from the road, and it's possible to descend into the crater.

Centro de Visitantes El Cisne

our pick Twenty-four teeth-shattering kilometers from Las Brisas is this **hotel** (campsite per person COP$7000; r per person incl 2 meals COP$98,000). Set at a gasping 4180m, the rustic cabins at El Cisne were refurbished in 2006 and now

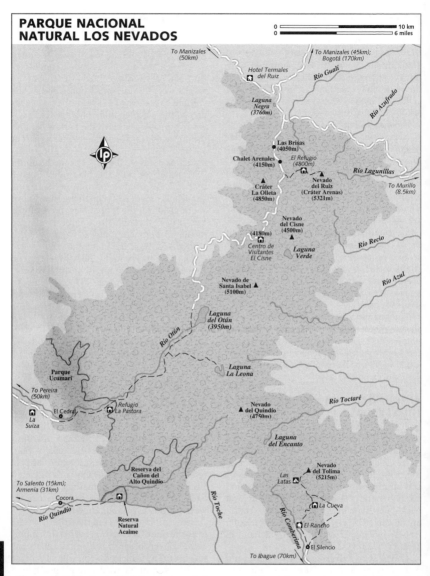

PARQUE NACIONAL
NATURAL LOS NEVADOS

offer comfortable, heated lodging surrounded by the striking landscapes of high mountain *páramo*. There are a mixture of accommodations for 30 people, plus a camping area. It's a romantic getaway that will leave you breathless (literally). It's also a good base from which to explore the peaks, valleys and lakes of Los Nevados, although if you intend to summit any of them be sure to request permission from the Manizales National Parks office well in advance.

Comfamiliares (see Tours, opposite), which administers the Los Nevados park concession, provides early morning transport from Manizales to El Cisne (Colombians/foreigners COP$64,000/81,000).

Nevado del Tolima

The Nevado del Tolima (5215m), the second-highest volcano in the chain, is the most handsome of all with its classic symmetrical cone. On a clear day it can be seen from as far away as Bogotá. Its last eruption took place in 1943.

It is best reached via Ibagué, the ugly capital of the Tolima department. The southern reaches of Los Nevados still harbor a guerrilla presence, so be sure to check conditions before attempting this climb. A recommended guide is **'Truman' David Bejarano** (☎ 273 4433, 315 292 7395).

It's a challenging climb, requiring ice axe and crampons, though if you make your base camp you can rejuvenate afterwards in the natural hot springs at El Rancho (2650m).

The southern part of the park is accessible only by foot. From Refugio La Pastora in the Parque Ucumarí (p231) a 15km trail goes uphill to the Laguna del Otún. Another access route begins from Cocora, from where a path heads uphill to the *páramo* and on to the extinct Nevado del Quindío (4750m). Neither of these routes is popular with hikers and in the past there have been occasional instances of guerrilla activity on both trails. Be sure to check current conditions.

Tours

Most tourists visit Los Nevados as part of an all-day group excursion to Nevado del Ruiz from Manizales. **Ecosistemas** (☎ 880 8300; ecosistemas2000@yahoo.com; Carrera 21 No 23-41) and **Comfamiliares** (☎ 886 0737, 316 472 8545; cnr Carrera 25 & Calle 50) offer similar services. Ecosistemas includes a visit to Hotel Termales del Ruiz (see above); Comfamiliares uses Termales del Otoño (see below). The standard one-day tour costs COP$95,000 for foreigners, including transport, breakfast and lunch, and admission to the national park and the thermal baths. They can both organize longer, multiday tours of the park as well.

If you want to spend a night or two in Los Nevados, Ecosistemas is recommended, as they will let you use the return leg of your tour on a different day.

Comfamiliares includes a stop at **Termales El Otoño** (☎ 874 1412; www.termaleselotono.com; Km5 Antigua Via al Nevado; ☼ 10am-10pm Mon-Thu, 8am-midnight Fri-Sun; admission COP$17,000) outside Manizales on the way back to town, which helps alleviate the cracking headache and nausea you will experience on the trip down the mountain. It sells beer, liquor and snacks. On weekends the place turns into a party zone, and there are 15 luxury cabins nearby (COP$155,000 to COP$294,000). To get here on your own take the bus marked 'Termales El Otoño' from the Manizales terminal (COP$1200, 40 minutes).

Tour company Ecosistemas (see left) runs the spectacular **Hotel Termales del Ruiz** (r per person COP$45,000) at the edge of the national park, and their tours all include a stop here on the way down the mountain. It has a restaurant and thermal springs, and price includes breakfast and access to the thermal springs. Ecosistemas offers transport here (COP$100,000 per group), or take the 2pm bus to Murillo (COP$10,000, 1½ hours) and get off at the crossroads, from where it's a 1½-hour walk downhill to the hotel. Returning to Manizales, you can generally hitch a lift with other guests on the weekend, or walk back uphill (minimum two hours) to the crossroads and take the Murillo bus, which passes around 8:30am.

PEREIRA

☎ 6 / pop 455,000 / elev 1410m

A throbbing lust pulsates through this city, the hum of desire and greed. By day, sharp-nosed *paísas* pursue profit, too busy, too avaricious for too long to beautify their otherwise ordinary-looking town. In the hot afternoons, juice vendors line the city streets, selling *jugo de borojó* (a local fruit, reputedly an aphrodisiac). Twenty-four hour restaurants serve ready-made meals to a city too busy to linger over its food. At night, on weekends, in Pereira's throbbing *discotecas*, concupiscent locals gyrate to their carnal desires.

Nowhere is a city's statue to Bolívar more emblematic of its people than here. Set in the middle of the main square, presiding over the city's commerce and interaction, sits Arenas Betancur's **Bolívar Desnudo**, an 8.5m-high, 11ton bronze statue of the Liberator, naked on horseback, urging his stallion forward with a manic passion, buttocks clenched to his plunging steed.

Founded in 1863, Pereira is the capital of Risaralda and the Zona Cafetera's largest city. The Dosquebradas district outside the city is a major manufacturing center, and business travelers easily outnumber tourists. The town itself is a bit thin on attractions, perhaps because earthquakes have repeatedly damaged the town center, most recently in 1995 and 1999.

The biggest drawcard here is the nightlife; work hard, party hard is the motto here. The town is also a good base for visiting the nearby thermal springs (p230), and venturing up into Parque Ucumarí (p231) and Santuario Otún Quimbaya (p231).

Information

There are numerous ATMs across the street from the Pereira bus station in the LA14 shopping center.

Bancolombia (Carrera 8 No 17-56)

Ciber Matrix (☎ 335 5705; www.cibermatrix.com; Carrera 8 No 20-58; ☼ 8am-9pm Mon-Sat, to 7pm Sun)

Cybernet (☎ 339 8898; Calle 19 No 7-49; ☼ 8am-9:30pm Mon-Sat, 10am-8pm Sun) On Plaza de Bolívar.

Giros & Finanzas (Centro del Comercio, Carrera 7 No 16-50) Agent for Western Union.

Hospital San Jorge (☎ 335 6333; Carrera 4 No 24-88)

Tourist office (Oficina de Fomento y Turismo; ☎ 335 1676, 334 0706; www.risaralda.com.co; fomentoalturismo@pereira.gov.co; cnr Carrera 10 & Calle 17) In the Palacio Municipal.

Festivals & Events

Fiestas de Pereira (Aug) The town switches into super-party-mode to celebrate the city's founding, with live music, dance shows, art exhibits and the obligatory beauty pageant.

Sleeping

Hotel Cumanday (☎ 324 0416; Carrera 5A No 22-54; s/d COP$35,000/40,000) A step up from the rest, this small hotel caters to tourists, and offers discounts during the week. Facilities include hot water, cable TV and laundry service; there's also an exercise machine in the lobby you can use. Rooms at the back are quieter.

ourpick Hotel Mi Casita (☎ 333 9995; www.hotelmicasita.com; Calle 25 No 6-20; s COP$45,000-50,000, d COP$59,000-69,000; 🖳) One of the few hotels that specifically caters to tourists, this pleasant midrange option offers some of the best value in Pereira. Not far from the Parque El Lago, the 18 private rooms have hot water, cable TV and free wi-fi, and there's a small restaurant area with a sunny glass roof.

Hotel Abadia Plaza (☎ 335 8398; www.hotelabadiaplaza.com; Carrera 8 No 21-67; s/d COP$144,000/180,000; 🅿 🖳) This stylish new place is as close as Pereira comes to a boutique hotel, with original art on the walls, plush rooms with marble

bathrooms and noise-resistant windows. Price includes breakfast, free wi-fi, and there's a gym and sauna you can use.

Hotel Castilla Real (☎ 333 2192; www.hotelcastillareal.com; Calle 15 No 12B-15; 🅿 🗶 🖳) This fine small hotel caters principally to business travelers. The 24 rooms have air-con, cable TV and minibar, and the restaurant serves breakfast and dinner. The service is excellent.

Hotel de Pereira (☎ 335 0770; www.hoteldepereira.com; Carrera 13 No 15-73; s/d/tr COP$199,000/259,000/318,000; 🗶 🖳) It may not be the poshest, but it's certainly the largest hotel in town. Its 10 floors range around a large interior atrium, with leather furniture in the lobby below. Prices halve during the week.

Eating

Grajales Autoservicios (Carrera 8 No 21-60; mains COP$8000-14,000; ☼ 24hr) At this large, self-service 24-hour restaurant-cum-bakery you can put together your own lunch or dinner. It's also good for breakfast.

Mama Flor (☎ 335 4793; Calle 11 No 15-12, Los Alpes; mains COP$17,000-26,000; ☼ noon-11pm Mon-Sat, to 5pm Sun) Set up on a hill in a quiet residential neighborhood, this old-time restaurant is famous for its down-home Colombian food. Eat out on the large covered verandah with a decent bottle of wine. Grill is a specialty here; try the *parrilla de carnes* (mixed grill, COP$43,000), which is big enough for two. If you fancy fish, go for the *robalo* (sea bass)

ourpick El Mirador (☎ 331 2141, 331 5747; elmiradorparrillashow@yahoo.com.ar; Entrada Avenida Circunvalar Calle 4; mains COP$24,000-38,000; ☼ noon-2am Mon-Sat) Outside the city on top of a mountain with fantastic views of the twinkling lights of Pereira is this gem. The real highlight is the live tango shows on Friday and Saturday night – be sure to book in advance. The shows start at 10pm, and no one shows up much before 9pm. The food follows the Argentine theme – order the *churrasco Argentina* (grilled meat, COP$24,000) and wash it down with a bottle of Malbec (COP$65,000). Taxis add a COP$2000 surcharge for the trip.

Drinking

There are many lively bars in Sector Circunvalar, but the official *zona rosa* is a little ways outside of the city in Sector La Badea, where all the nightclubs are located.

Bar Celona (☎ 324 4721; Av Circunvalar No 8-136; ☼ 6pm-3am) Owned by an unashamed

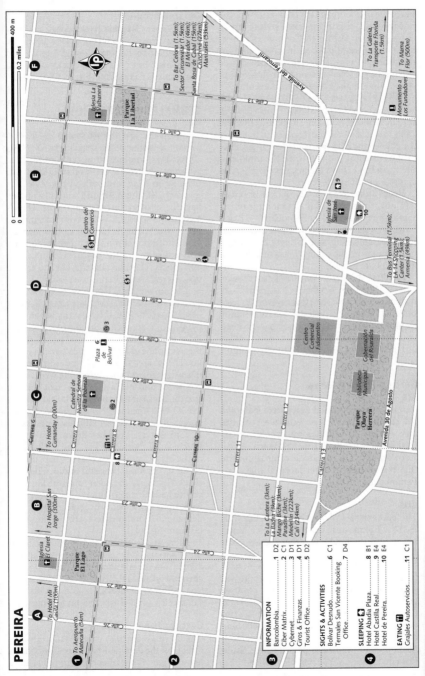

PEREIRA

INFORMATION
Bancolombia	1 D2
Ciber Matrix	2 C1
Cybernet	3 D1
Giros & Finanzas	4 D1
Tourist Office	5 D2

SIGHTS & ACTIVITIES
Bolívar Desnudo	6 C1
Termales San Vicente Booking Office	7 D4

SLEEPING
Hotel Abadía Plaza	8 B1
Hotel Castilla Real	9 E4
Hotel de Pereira	10 E4

EATING
Grajales Autoservicios	11 C1

FC Barcelona football fan (club posters decorate the walls) this down-home style drinkery plays good ol' fashioned Colombian music; don't be surprised if the entire crowd joins in the chorus to a favorite song. It's spread over two floors; the smaller second level has view of street. A good place to start your evening.

our pick **La Cantera** (☎ 330 5593, 317 456 9345, 300 600 2247; La Badea; cover COP$10,000; ☾ 9pm-3am Fri & Sat) The first club you come to as you enter the *zona rosa* is also the most spectacular. Set on the edge of the cliff, one wall is open-air to let in the twinkling city lights. In the middle of the twinkling, 2m in the air, sits the DJ, who spins Colombian crossover.

Mango Biche (☎ 343 7520, 330 8072; La Badea; cover COP$10,000; ☾ 8pm-6am) This salsa joint is of the same genre as Mango's of Medellín – a large, barnlike structure with waiters dressed as *paisa* peasants. Huge quantities of flea market junk hang from the ceiling. Plays mostly salsa and some merengue.

Paradise (☎ 322 8840, Transversal 7 Deturas de Makro; cover COP$10,000; ☾ 9pm-4am Fri & Sat) Set apart from the main *zona rosa*, this cavernous space puts the DJ up on a pedestal, where he spins techno till late. There are three bars to keep you well-lubricated, and an equal number of fish tanks for you to talk to if you don't speak Spanish.

Getting There & Away

AIR
Pereira's international **Aeropuerto Matecaña** (☎ 326 0021, 314 2765) is 5km west of the city center, 20 minutes by urban bus, or COP$8000 by taxi. Airlines Avianca, Aires, AeroRepública and Satena offer domestic flights and budget international flights to Panama and Miami.

BUS
The **bus terminal** (☎ 321 5834, 335 4437; Calle 17 No 23-157) is 1.5km south of the city center. Many urban buses will take you there in less than 10 minutes.

There are regular departures to Bogotá (COP$44,000, nine hours); all buses go via Armenia, not Manizales. A number of buses go to Medellín (COP$28,000, five hours) and Cali (COP$22,000, four hours). Minibuses run every 15 minutes to Armenia (COP$5000, one hour) and Manizales (COP$5000, 1¼ hours). Minibuses to Manizales pass through Santa Rosa de Cabal (COP$2500, 45 minutes).

Getting Around
Pereira's new **Megabus** (www.megabus.gov.co) system runs crosstown and out to Dosquebradas. It's similar to Bogotá's TransMilenio and Cali's Mio, but on a smaller scale. The taxi minimum is COP$3200 with a COP$700 surcharge after 7pm.

TERMALES DE SANTA ROSA
☎ 6 / elev 1950m
These spectacular **thermal springs** (☎ 363 4959; www.termalessantarosadecabal.com; admission COP$24,000; ☾ 9am-11pm) are located at the foot of three adjacent waterfalls, the largest 170m high. Opened in 1945 and built in the style of a Swiss chalet, the hotel and tourist complex have the air of another place and time. There's a complete spa service for those wanting the luxury treatment, including exfoliation, massage and thermal mud treatments. You can also just come for the day to laze around in 40°C pools. There's a cafeteria, bar and a more upscale restaurant in the hotel lobby.

The on-site **Hotel Termales** (☎ 363 4966; r per person COP$120,000-180,000, campsite per person COP$95,000, with own tent COP$75,000) offers luxury accommodations in a sprawling three-story mansion. Price includes three meals and access to the thermals. The older Casa Finca portion of the hotel has shared showers. There are discounts in the low season and during the week.

Owned and managed by the neighboring spa, the adjacent **Balneario de Santa Rosa thermals** (☎ 363 4948; admission COP$20,000; ☾ 9am-midnight) are cheaper but only slightly less impressive. A 25m-waterfall crashes down next to the four nearby thermal pools, and Colombian music blasts from the speakers. A bar and cafeteria serves food, beer and liquor. There's a shaded lounge with wicker furniture for when you've had too much sun. From the entrance, walk up a stone path through a lovely garden about 10 minutes to reach the *balneario* (swimming hole)

There are no accommodations on-site for these springs, but small three hotels cluster 500m from the entrance to the *balneario*. The cheapest is **Cabaña el Portal** (☎ 315 582 5001, 314 888 9958; r per person COP$20,000). It has hot water and satellite TV, and also serves budget meals.

Getting There & Away
The thermals are 9km east of Santa Rosa de Cabal, off the Pereira–Manizales road. *Chivas* leave *la galería* (market area) in Santa Rosa

at 7am, noon and 3:30pm (COP$2700, 45 minutes), returning to Santa Rosa de Cabal at 8am, 1pm and 4pm. Jeeps can take you out here for around COP$20,000. The *chivas* turn around and go back to Santa Rosa soon after their arrival at the springs. There are sometimes additional departures on weekends.

There is frequent daytime service Santa Rosa–Pereira (COP$1700, 40 minutes). Buses to Chinchiná pass the old railway station on the edge of town every 15 minutes (COP$3000, 30 minutes). From there you can grab a bus uphill to Manizales (COP$5000, 30 minutes) or northbound to Medellín (COP$24,000, five hours, hourly).

TERMALES SAN VICENTE
☎ 6 / elev 2250m

Set at the head of a steep 200m-wide valley and straddling a cold creek, these newer **thermals** (☎ 333 6157; www.sanvicente.com.co; admission COP$18,000, r per person COP$80,000-145,000, campsite per person COP$44,000) are 18km east of Santa Rosa de Cabal but feel a world away. There are five thermals pools (37°C) – the water is sold for its reputed medicinal properties – and the spa offers the full range of spa treatment, including mud therapy, algae facials, peels and massage. Numerous thermal springs bubble up from the earth nearby, in one spot emerging to mix with an adjacent creek, allowing you to bathe in a warm stream. There are three natural saunas, built over 80°C to 90°C hot springs below. A 300m-canopy line zips across the narrow valley to a 30m-waterfall you can rappel down. Several muddy trails lead upward to other waterfalls; there's also a paintball court, and you can rent mountain bikes to explore the valley further. The only TV is in the common room.

Cabins range from split-log rustic to modern minimalist with working fireplace and private thermal pool. Most have electric shower heads. Rates includes admission and breakfast; the VIP plan also includes lunch and dinner. Those on a budget should ask about the COP$50,000 rooms, which have low attic ceiling and shared bathrooms. They aren't advertised, but are good value.

San Vicente lies near the edge of Parque Nacional Natural Los Nevados. A 19km pitted road leads upward toward Laguna del Otún (3950m). The paving of this road was underway at our visit, and it may be possible to visit the national park from San Vicente in the future.

The baths are operated from the Pereira **booking office** (Map p229; ☎ 333 6157; Carrera 13 No 15-62), where you can make inquiries and bookings. It offers one daily bus service to the thermals at 9am (8am weekends), returning at 5pm (COP$18,000 return, 1¼hr). You can also take a jeep from *la galería* in Santa Rosa de Cabal (COP$50,000). Be sure to book a day or two in advance, especially for weekends and holidays. Don't go on Monday when the pools are drained for cleaning.

SANTUARIO OTÚN QUIMBAYA

This nature reserve 18km southeast of Pereira protects a 489-hectare area of high biodiversity between 1800m and 2400m. Set on the Río Otún, it boasts more than 200 species of birds and butterflies and two rare species of monkey, among other wildlife. The reserve has a visitor center in La Suiza (Map p226), and several short hiking trails. Two guides who speak some English are available (COP$29,000 per day). The best time to come is August and September, and December and January, when the persistent drizzle eases somewhat.

The visitors center at **La Suiza** (Map p226; ☎ 315 5600, 314 880 3828; concesionotunquimbaya@hotmail.com; admission foreigners/Colombians, COP$25,000/COP$9000) provides accommodations (dorm with/without bath COP$31,000/25,000) and budget meals. There are electric shower heads (24-hour electricity) but no central heating, and fires are not allowed. Ask for a room on the second floor, which have small balconies facing the forest and birdsong. A large satellite TV blares in the lobby. It is considering offering double beds in the future.

The visitors center is located in Vereda La Suiza, a small municipality. **Transporte Florida** (☎ 334 2721, Calle 12 No 9-40; La Galeria) in Pereira offers daily *chiva* service (COP$3100, 1½ hours) at 7am, 9am and 3pm, with extra service at noon on weekends. The *chiva* continues past the visitors center to El Cedral, where it immediately turns around and heads back. The *chiva* terminal is in a dangerous part of town; ask your taxi driver to take you all the way into the parking area.

PARQUE UCUMARÍ

Established in 1984 just outside the western boundaries of the Parque Nacional Natural (PNN) Los Nevados, this 42-sq-km reserve protects a rugged, forested land around the middle course of the Río Otún, about 30km southeast of Pereira. More than 185 species of bird have been recorded here.

From here you can hike up Río Otún, leading through a gorge to PNN Los Nevados. You can even get to Laguna del Otún (3950m) but it's a steady, six- to eight-hour walk uphill. It's possible to do the return trip within a day, though it's a strenuous hike. If you have camping gear, it's better to split the trek and do some side excursions up in the *páramo*.

The cabins at **La Pastora** (Map p226; ☎ 313 749 8354; dm/campsite per person COP$14,500/6000), at an elevation of 2500m, offer accommodations and budget meals. It has ecological paths traced through verdant hills and you can see the lush vegetation and spot some of the park's rich wildlife. The guy who runs the place will build a bonfire and play his guitar at night.

To get here from Pereira, take the *chiva* to El Cedral (1950m). From here it's a 5km, 2½-hour walk, or rent a horse (COP$15,000 to COP$20,000). The nature reserve is run by **Grupos Ecológicos de Risaralda** (GER; ☎ 331 865 5548) in Pereira.

ARMENIA
☎ 6 / pop 245,000 / elev 1640

Armenia is the third wheel on the Coffee Axle, and feels that way. Devastated by an earthquake in 1999 that flattened much of the city center, Armenia has never fully recovered. The center of the city is makeshift – check out the hastily-reconstructed cathedral, made of prefab concrete slabs – and the de facto center has moved north of downtown, along Av Bolivar to Portal del Quindío, a large upscale mall.

Most travelers will pass through Armenia only long enough to change buses for Salento. Still, the city is good for a day trip – the new pedestrian mall that stretches along Carrera 14 makes for a pleasant stroll, and Parque de la Vida is worth a visit.

Armenia was founded in 1889, and in 1966 became the capital of the newly created Quindío department. Like its two larger neighbors, the city trades principally in coffee and students.

Information
Bancolombia (at the bus station) Handy if you run short in Salento.
Hospital San Juan de Diós (☎ 749 3500; cnr Av Bolivar & Calle 17N)

JH Sistema (☎ 741 2695; Calle 21 No 14-29 piso 2; ☺ 8am-9pm Mon-Sat, 10:30am-7pm Sun) This enormous internet cafe is just off Plaza de Bolívar. Also has numerous telephone cabins.
Portal del Quindío (Av Bolivar No 19N-46) This big mall has numerous ATMs. Several nearby banks change US dollars.
Red Central (☎ 741 4702; Calle 21 No 16-26; ☺ 8am-9pm Mon-Sat) Internet per hour COP$1400.
Tourist office (Corporación de Cultura y Turismo; ☎ 741 2991; www.quindioturistico.com; Plaza de Bolívar) On the ground floor of the Gobernación del Quindío building. Very helpful staff; lots of information.

Festivals & Events
Desfile de Yipao (Oct) An important part of Armenia's annual birthday party celebration is this fantastic parade, when the local working jeeps are loaded down with literally tons of *plátano* (plantain), coffee etc and paraded through town.

Sights
Museo del Oro Quimbaya (☎ 749 8433; museo quimbaya@banrep.gov.co; Av Bolívar No 40N-80; admission free; ☺ 10am-5pm Tue-Sun) This is one of Colombia's best gold museums, featuring an excellent collection of ceramics and gold artifacts of Quimbaya culture. It's in the Centro Cultural, 5km northeast of the center. Grab bus 18, 36 or 27 northbound on Av Bolívar (COP$1100), or take a taxi (COP$5000).

Parque de la Vida (☎ 746 2302; cnr Av Bolivar & Calle 7N; admission COP$1000) This large city park is north of town on Av Bolívar. There are waterfalls, several small lakes, forest areas and gardens, and kiosks selling food and drink.

Plaza de Bolívar is home to the **Catedral de la Inmaculada Concepción**, the city's new concrete cathedral.

Tours
Millenium Turs (☎ 301 288 0910, 313 658 2123; millenium turs@hotmail.com) Experts in Quindío and Armenia, this small tour agency, which is run out of a private home, specializes in mid-range and top-end tour packages. It employs bilingual guides.

Sleeping
Hotel Casa Real (☎ 741 4550; Carrera 18 No 18-36; s/d COP$24,000/35,000) Among Armenia's cheap hotels, this is the best of a bad lot. The rooms are small and quite basic, and many don't have windows.

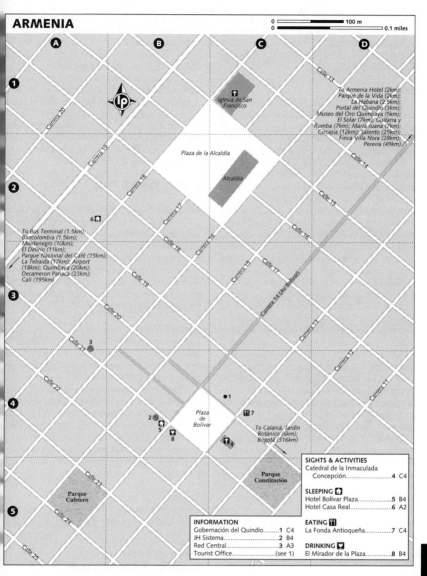

ARMENIA

Hotel Bolívar Plaza (☎ 741 0083; www.bolivarplaza .com; Calle 21 No 14-17; s/d/tr COP$113,000/145,000/180,000; P 🖥) This new boutique hotel has a sleek, almost nautical facade that rises just across from Plaza de Bolívar. Rooms are smallish but shiny new, and many have small balconies that look out onto the Cordillera Central, making this place Armenia's most economical splurge. There's also an upper-floor restaurant that has good food and great views.

our pick Armenia Hotel (☎ 746 0099, 1 800 097 8080; www.armeniahotelsa.com; Av Bolívar No 8N-67; s/d/tr COP$198,000/241,000/343,000; P 🖥) The best hotel in town, the Armenia has nine floors built around a vaulted interior atrium with a glass ceiling. The rooms have carpet and *guadua* furniture, and of course cable TV and minibar. The lobby restaurant has live music everyday at lunch and dinner. Price includes breakfast. Ask for a room with a view of the neighboring Parque de la Vida.

Eating

There are plenty of cheap eats in the center during the day. At night and weekends, head north to the Portal del Quindío – there are budget eats in the food court and numerous good midrange options clustered nearby.

La Fonda Antioqueña (☎ 744 1927; Carrera 13 No 18-59, piso 2; mains COP$10,000-15,000; ☼ 8am-6pm) A block from Plaza de Bolívar is this fine *paísa* restaurant. It serves traditional fare, including *bandeja paísa*, and on weekends, *sancocho*. There are good views of the countryside from the 2nd-floor perch. Be sure to try *mazamorra*, a typical Zona Cafetera drink made of cooked corn with a guava *bocadillo* (sweet), served with a splash of milk.

ourpick La Fogata (☎ 749 5501; Carrera 13 No 14N-47; mains $15,000-35,000; ☼ restaurant noon-1am Mon-Sat, noon-6pm Sun) This fine restaurant is one of the best in town. It does good steaks and seafood, and the menu offers a few twists, like *bistec de caballo* (horse steak) and *vuelve a la vida*, a fish soup rumored to be an aphrodisiac. The restaurant sits on a triangular property not far from CC Portal del Quindío – look for the manicured bushes outside. The point of the triangle is an attached cafe-bar, open Monday to Saturday from 5pm to midnight, that serves gourmet cocktails (COP$15,000).

El Solar (☎ 749 3990; restaurante-elsolar@hotmail.com; Km2 Via Circasia; mains COP$17,000-26,000; ☼ noon-midnight Mon-Sat, to 5pm Sun) Just a few hundred meters from the *zona rosa* is this top-notch grill restaurant with the funky decor. Kids' bikes, umbrellas and empty wine bottles dangle from the ceiling, and bamboo shoots creep in from the outside. Friday night is a big night here, when there's live music and beer prices double after 8pm. Afterward walk 200m downhill and take your pick of half-a-dozen discos.

Drinking

Armenia has a lively bar scene, although not as good as Manizales or Pereira. Your best options are in the *zona rosa*.

ourpick Maria Juana (☎ 749 5185; Km2 Via Circasia; ☼ 8pm-3am Fri & Sat) A groovy bar with a downstairs lounge space, outdoor patio and live music shows from 11pm. At closing time

there are plenty of taxis to take you back to Armenia (COP$12,000 to COP$15,000).

Guitarra y Rumba (☎ 749 3422, 749 5179; Km2 Via Circasia; ☼ 8:30pm-3am Thu-Sat) Has a big disco space and cover band every night.

For a drink with a rowdy student crowd, try **La Habana** (☎ 745 0054; Calle 12N No 14-39; ☼ 10am-2am Mon-Thu, to 3am Fri & Sat), just outside the gates of the Universidad de Quindío. For a quiet beer on the main plaza, the **Mirador de la Plaza Taberna** (☎ 744 9183; ☼ 7am-3am Mon-Sat, to 10pm Sun) also serves espresso and has photos of Armenia before the earthquake.

Getting There & Away

AIR

Aeropuerto El Edén (☎ 747 9400, 747 5707) is 18km (COP$15,000 by taxi) southwest of Armenia, near the town of La Tebaida on the road to Cali. Avianca, EasyFlight and Aires offer service to Bogotá. Easyflight and ADA fly to Medellín. A new runway was under construction at the time of writing, and international airport status applied for – flights from Miami are expected in the future.

BUS

The **bus terminal** (☎ 747 3355, 747 5705; Calle 35 No 20-68) is 1.5km southwest of the center and can be reached by frequent city buses that run along Carrera 19 (COP$1100).

There are plenty of buses to Bogotá (COP$37,000, eight hours) and to Cali (COP$20,000, 3½ hours). There are regular minibuses to Pereira (COP$5000, one hour), Manizales (COP$16,000, three hours) and Salento (COP$3000, 30 minutes). There are also direct buses to Popayán (COP$30,000, six hours).

TRAIN

There is infrequent passenger train service from La Tebaida (near Armenia) to Cali (see p242).

AROUND ARMENIA
Jardín Botánico del Quindío

Armenia's 15-hectare **botanical garden** (☎ 742 7254; Km3 Via al Valle, Calarcá; admission COP$12,000; ☼ 9am-4:30pm) has the best *mariposario* in the Zona Cafetera. The 680-sq-meter butterfly house is in the shape of a giant butterfly and houses up to 1500 butterflies (up to 50 different species). There's a 22m-tall lookout tower amid the secondary forest with views of the gardens and butterfly house. There's also a small museum with a collection of dead butterflies, a geology exhibit, and a new interactive show for kids is planned – 2m-tall robotic insects will discuss their importance to the environment.

The gardens have an extensive collection of palms, ferns and orchids, and more than 110 birds have been recorded here. A guide is mandatory (tipping is optional). Two speak some English. The best time to see birds is before dawn – call a day or two in advance to organize a guide. Give yourself at least two hours to leisurely stroll through the gardens.

To get here, take a bus to Calarcá (COP$1000, 20 minutes) from the bus station, and ask the driver to let you off at the gardens. You can also pick it up at Parque Fundadores.

Coffee Farms (Fincas)

Coffee-farm tourism began here in Quindío, and there are hundreds of *fincas* catering to a variety of tastes, mostly Colombian. Numerous publications catalog and rate them. The Armenia tourist office has a lengthy list of options. Also check out Haciendas del Café (www.clubhaciendasdelcafe.com) and Hoteles con Encanto (www.loshotelesconencanto.com).

Finca Villa Nora (☎ 741 5472, 310 422 6335; finca illanora@hotmail.com; r per person COP$140,000; P), about halfway between Armenia and Pereira, is a working coffee, avocado, macadamia and guava farm offering accommodations in its traditional white-and-red-trimmed house with a wide wraparound verandah. It's simpler in style than many, and the owner runs both the lodging and the farm. There's a small pool and a barbecue. Many rooms have shared baths, and there's only one TV. Staff can pick you up from Armenia airport (COP$40,000) or from Quimbaya (free).

The exclusive, quiet country retreat **Bambusa** (☎ 676 2645, 311 506 9915; www.hacienda bambusa.com; r COP$235,000-250,000; P) is ideal if you want an English-speaking host and guide. The owner's son is an artist and former traveler who speaks excellent English. More than 200 species of birds have been recorded here, and you may also spot foxes, armadillos, or maybe even a jaguar. It used to be a coffee farm, but now they grow *plátano* and run some cattle. It's a long way off the main road and cannot be reached by public transport. Staff can pick you up from Armenia (COP$55,000).

El Delirio (☎ 741 5106; casadelirio@hotmail.com; Km1 Via Montenegro; s/d/tr COP$120,000/140,000/200,000; P), just outside Montenegro, is an old-fashioned farmhouse that feels like grandma's house, with decorative lacy pillows, flowers, antiques and B&W photographs of long-dead matadors. The house is surrounded by a small coffee plantation, and there's a pretty pool. There are hammocks you can laze around in, accompanied by the sounds of birds.

Panaca

This **farm-themed park** (☎ 1 800 012 3999, 310 404 2238; www.panaca.com.co; admission COP$27,000-41,000; 9am-6pm Tue-Sun) caters to city Colombians nostalgic for their rural past. Located just outside Quimbaya, a short bus ride from Armenia, it has more than 4500 domestic animals, including many rare domestic breeds. The real highlight of any visit are the animal shows, especially pig races in the *cerdódromo* (pig-o-drome!).

Immediately adjacent to Panaca across a footbridge is the four-star all-inclusive resort **Decameron Panaca** (☎ 758 2204, 1 800 051 0765; r per person COP$216,000). It feels just like a Caribbean resort – king-sized beds, big swimming pools, evening shows, themed restaurants – except there's no beach. Staff can organize tours throughout the region and can arrange English-speaking tour guides.

To get here, take any bus from Armenia to Quimbaya (COP$2000, 45 minutes). Shared taxis leave from Quimbaya's main square when full (COP$3000, 10 minutes).

Parque Nacional Del Café
☎ 6 / elev 1300m

This **theme park** (☎ 741 7417; www.parquenacionaldel cafe.com; Km6 Via Montenegro; admission COP$17,000-45,000; 9am-4pm Wed-Sun) has surprisingly little to do with coffee, but does have a rollercoaster and a waterslide. There's a small coffee museum, bumper cars and a horse-riding trail. At the entrance is an 18m-lookout tower that has great views over Armenia. There's also a short nature trail that zigzags downhill to the river and loops though a number of attractions, including a traditional coffee plantation, a cemetery for the local Quimbaya people, and a big stand of bamboo. A cable car offers bird's-eye views of the park, and links the museum with a re-creation of a typical Quindian town. Don't bother to come if it's raining, as most attractions are outdoors.

Buses depart Armenia bus terminal every 15 minutes (COP$1400, 30 minutes, 7am to 7:10pm). Not all buses return to the terminal; they may just drop you in town.

SALENTO
☎ 6 / pop 3500 / elev 1900m

Set amid gorgeous green mountains 24km east of Armenia, this small town survives on coffee production, trout farming and, increasingly, tourists, who are drawn by its quaint streets, typical *paisa* architecture, and proximity to the spectacular Valle de Cocora. It was founded in 1850, and is one of the oldest (and possibly the smallest) town in Quindío.

The main drag is Calle Real (Carrera 6), full of *artesanías*, restaurants and internet cafes. At the end of the street are stairs leading up to Alto de la Cruz, a hill topped with a cross. From here you'll see the verdant Valle de Cocora and the mountains that surround it. If the skies are clear (usually only early in the morning), you can spot the snowcapped tops of the volcanoes on the horizon.

For even better views, walk 200m past the **El Portal de Cocora** (see opposite) and look for the blue gate on your left to **Chalet Mundo Nuevo** (☎ 759 3394). This small hotel, built on a spit of land that juts out into the adjacent valley, gives you amazing views in both directions. Ask nicely and you'll be allowed to linger amid the flowers and views.

Information
Banco Agrario de Colombia (in the main square) The only ATM in town. Sketchy reliability.
Nef-sistem.net (☎ 312 212 6153; cnr Carrera 1 & Calle 6; per hr COP$1800) Internet; near the fire station.
Real.net (☎ 759 3458; Calle Real No 4-24; per hr COP$2000)

Activities
TEJO
There's a small *cancha de tejo* (Carrera 4 Calle 3-32). Go throw rocks at gunpowder (see p90). You know you want to.

HORSEBACK RIDING
Álvaro Gomez (☎ 096 759 3343, 311 375 8293) gets good reviews. He offers trips to several nearby waterfalls, along an old, unfinished railway track, plus a longer day trip up into Cocora. He charges COP$25,000 to COP$30,000 per person for a half-day trip, more for night tours or trips to Valle de Cocora.

COFFEE FARMS (FINCAS)
There are three nearby coffee farms (*fincas* you can visit. Plantation House owns a small *finca* a short walk from the hostel, and is one of the few places that does tours (COP$4000 in English. Nearby traditional growers **Don Elías** and **Don Gustavo** also offer similar tour in Spanish (COP$5000). Ask at your hote for details on how to tee up a tour with either of them.

Sleeping
our pick **Plantation House** (☎ 316 285 2603, 315 40 7039; Calle 7 No 1-04; www.theplantationhousesalento.com dm COP$15,000-16,000, s COP$27,000, d COP$32,000-60,000 [P] [🖳]) The English owner of this hostel ha single-handedly put Salento on the gringo trail. Two buildings accommodate travelers one with doubles and another, across the road with dorms. There's no TV, but the dorm building does have a working fireplace you can use. The owner is an avid reader and ha one of the best English-language book swaps bookstores in Colombia. To get here, get of the bus at the fire station, turn right and walk uphill 100m. Turn right again, another 100m or so and it will be on your left.

Hosteria Calle Real (☎ 759 3784; hosteriacallereal@ho mail.com; Carrera 6 No 2-20; r per person COP$30,000) Housed in a typical *paisa* home with a pleasant, plant filled courtyard, this place has small and rathe basic rooms, but there are rocking chairs to linger in, and it does breakfast (COP$5000). It' in the middle of things on Calle Real.

Camping Monteroca (☎ 315 413 6862, 310 422 3720 www.campingmonteroca.com; Boquía; campsite per perso COP$45,000) Four kilometers downhill from Salento on the road to Armenia is this camp ground. It offers 'exotic lodgings' such as a trailer and walk-in tents decorated in psych edelic and African safari themes. Two have waterbeds. There's a full kitchen with stove and fridge, and an open-air shower with ho water. Set right on the Río Quindío next to a nature reserve, it's a good spot for bird-watch ing. There's a barbecue area, plus hammock. to lounge around in. It also rents two-perso tents (COP$20,000).

Eating & Drinking
On weekends the plaza explodes with food stalls and cheap, set meals disappear from every restaurant menu.
Rincón del Lucy (☎ 313 471 5497; Carrera 6 No 4-02 mains COP$5000; ☼ breakfast & lunch) The best se

meal in town, it also does the only set meal on the weekends. Sit on great tree trunk slabs of tables to eat your rice, beans, trout, beef or chicken, with a banana and soup. Also serves breakfast (COP$3500).

Sueño de Fresas (☎ 759 3395; www.salento.com.co; Plaza Principal; ☺ 2pm-7pm Mon-Fri, 9am-10pm Sat & Sun) Strawberries and cream. Exotic tropical fruit and ice cream combos. What more can we say? Next to the church.

Café Jesús Martín (☎ 316 620 7760; cafejesusmartin bedoya@yahoo.com; Carrera 6A No 6-14; ☺ 8am-midnight) Open a mere two weeks when we passed through, this groovy cafe serves top-quality espresso coffee roasted and prepared in the owner's Salento factory. It's got a distinctly upper-crust feel to it; if swilling the dregs with farmers in the nearby pool hall isn't your thing, come here. Also serves wine, beer, and light salads and sandwiches.

El Portal de Cocora (☎ 759 3075; mains COP$17,000-24,500; ☺ 11am-6pm Fri-Sun) Located on the road toward Valle de Cocora, about 500m from the main square, this restaurant has views of a storybook green valley. Come for a juice or a beer, or linger over trout, chicken or beef. It also has two self-contained cabins (small/large COP$120,000/240,000) with great views. The smaller cabins accommodates a couple, the larger has two twin rooms, and so sleeps six.

Getting There & Away

Minibuses run to/from Armenia every 20 minutes (COP$3000, 30 minutes, 6am to 8pm). If you miss the last bus to Salento, take a bus to Circasia (COP$1400, 25 minutes) until 10pm, and take a taxi from there (COP$15,000, 15 minutes). You can also take a taxi direct from Armenia (30 minutes). The official price is COP$50,000 but you can usually haggle the driver down to COP$30,000 to COP$35,000.

There is also direct service to/from Pereira (COP$4700, 1½ hours) three times daily during the week, more on the weekend. You can also take an Armenia-bound bus to Los Flores (two flower shops just south of the Salento junction, COP$1000, 20 minutes)

and grab any northbound Pereira bus (30 minutes, COP$5000).

VALLE DE COCORA

In a country full of beautiful landscapes, Cocora is one of the most striking. The valley stretches east of Salento into the lower reaches of Los Nevados, with a broad, green valley framed by sharp peaks. Everywhere you'll see *palma de cera* (wax palm), the largest palm in the world (up to 60m tall). It's Colombia's national tree. Set amid the misty green hills, they are breathtaking to behold.

The most popular walk is the 2½ hour walk to the **Reserva Natural Acaime** (Map p226; admission COP$2000). As you arrive in Cocora the trail is on the right-hand side as you walk into the valley and away from Salento. The well-signposted trail starts in Cocora by a blue gate and a shop and goes down past the trout farm. The first part of the trail is through grassland and wax palm. The second part of the trail is through cloud forest. At Acaime there are basic accommodations, and you can usually get a hot chocolate (with cheese) here. You'll also see plenty of hummingbirds feeding.

About 1km before you reach Acaime there's a turnoff to the La Montaña ranger post. A more difficult path leads directly from Acaime to La Montaña (one hour), if you want to do the loop, and the views from here and the trail back down to Cocora are spectacular. From La Montaña to Cocora is 1½ hours downhill.

Longer walks are possible in the national park, staying with local farmers. Inquire at Plantation House (p236) for more information. It is possible to go to Acaime on horseback, though a guide is recommended – horses without a guide have been known to refuse to cross the rivers!

Jeeps leave Salento's main square for the small hamlet of Cocora (COP$3000, one hour), where there is a trout farm and a few *tiendas* (shops) selling snacks and drinks. There are four departures during the week, more on the weekend. You can also contract a jeep privately (COP$24,000). Go early.

Cali & Southwest Colombia

The southwestern corner of Colombia is a diverse region. Sweaty Cali, famous for its salsa nightclubs, is a bustling metropolis, and well worth a visit. Colonial Popayán boasts some of the finest architecture in the country. Eastward lie the archaeological ruins of Tierradentro and San Agustín, set amid jaw-dropping scenery, and the anomalous Desierto de la Tatacoa. Southward there's Pasto, a surprisingly hip town a few hours from the border, and Santuario de Las Lajas, a cathedral built across a breathtaking gorge just a short taxi ride from Ecuador.

Cali is the biggest city here. While it's nearly the same size as Medellín, it is often overlooked by travelers. It's a city eager to make friends – in addition to its many nightclubs, it also has funky cafes in the old colonial neighborhood of San Antonio, and the dining district of Granada is not to be missed. Cali is also a great base for hikes into the surrounding area.

Archaeological buffs should be sure to check out San Agustín and Tierradentro, Colombia's two most important archaeological sites. While the ruins themselves may not be King Tut's tomb, they are set amid stunning panoramas of Andean beauty. Halfway between San Agustín and Bogotá, outside the sleepy river port of Neiva, you'll find the Desierto de la Tatacoa, a small cactus-clad region with an observatory – come for the stargazing and sleep in the desert.

On the march to Ecuador you'll come to frequently ignored Pasto, the source of many Colombian jokes. While it does have a noticeable Ecuadorean influence, there are still good restaurants and bars, and every January the town goes crazy with its Festival de Blanco y Negro – a must if you're passing through. Finally, don't miss the Santuario de Las Lajas when you cross the border – it really is as spectacular as the photos look.

HIGHLIGHTS

- Learn to swivel your hips and boogie in the sweaty salsa joints of **Cali** (p246)

- Soar above the waves amid green mountain scenery while kitesurfing **Lago Calima** (p248)

- Spend the night stargazing in Colombia's tiniest desert, the **Desierto de la Tatacoa** (p267)

- Take a boat ride on **Laguna de la Cocha** (p264) and visit cloud-forest-clad Isla Carota in the middle

- Hike the hills of **Tierradentro** (p258) to visit ancient tombs and gawk at the stunning scenery

CALI & SOUTHWEST COLOMBIA

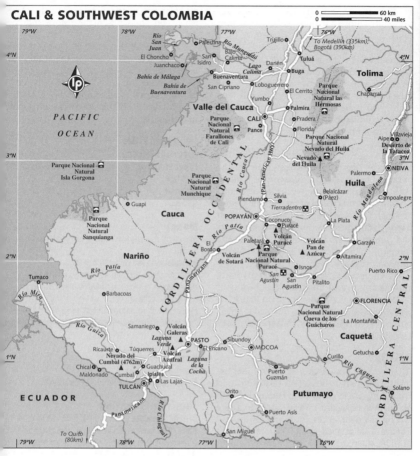

Climate

The climate varies dramatically by region and altitude. Cali is hot and humid, the border reaches with Ecuador are cooler and drier. In the Desierto de la Tatacoa the mercury sometimes hits 50°C.

National, State & Regional Parks

The archaeological sites of San Agustín (p255) and Tierradentro (p258) are both protected areas, whose topography is even more stunning than the archaeological stuff. Laguna de la Cocha (p264) and Laguna Verde (p264) outside Pasto are worth a visit, and the Parque Nacional Natural Farallones de Cali (p247), outside of Cali, offers numerous hiking opportunities.

Getting There & Away

Cali's airport receives flights from North and South America and Europe. Efficient buses connect the area to the rest of the country. See p310 for more on travel to/from Colombia.

Getting Around

Buses can take you everywhere you want to go in Southwest Colombia. See p314 for more details on domestic travel.

CALI

☎ 2 / pop 3.5 million / elev 969m

Cali is not an immediately likable city. For one thing, it is muggy and hot. For another, it's an industrial and transportation hub whose business is business, not tourism. *Caleños* shrug off criticism of their city with the saying, '*Cali es Cali y lo demás es loma, ¿oís?*' (Cali is Cali, and the rest [of Colombia] is just mountain, ya hear?).

Those who dig deeper and spend some time here will find a welcoming, friendly city with great nightlife, good restaurants, and plenty to do, especially in the evening, when a cool mountain breeze dissipates the heat of the day.

Go to San Antonio, the old colonial center, and linger over a beer or ice cream in the park, or better still, a *champú* or *lulada*, both fruit drinks made with *lulo*, a unique Colombian fruit typical of the Valle de Cauca, of which Cali is the capital. Wander through Barrio Granada's many upscale restaurants and boutiques, or hang out at Chipichape shopping mall and marvel at the local plastic surgeons' prowess.

Nowhere are Colombia's racial diversity and harmony, and the incredible beauty of Colombian women, more apparent than here. Cali women are nationally renowned for their sense of style and beauty, and the way they carry themselves .

HISTORY

After helping Francisco Pizarro conquer the Incas, Sebastián de Belalcázar (also known in Latin America as Benalcázar) quarreled with his former boss and moved north to strike out on his own. After founding Quito and Popayán, he arrived in the Valle del Cauca in 1536, where he dubbed his new settlement Santiago de Cali.

Over the centuries Spaniards shipped in thousands of African slaves to work the valley's sugarcane and cotton plantations. The Valle remains a major agricultural producer, and in higher regions also produces grapes and coffee.

Cali was a small town in orbit to departmental capital Popayán well into the 20th century, when railroads, and later highways, overtook the rivers as the dominant form of transport. To this day more than half of Colombia's exports pass through Cali on their way to Buenaventura (p279).

ORIENTATION

Cali is built along the western edge of the wide Valle de Cauca. The city center is laid out in a grid plan around the Plaza de Caycedo. This is where you'll find most of the historic churches and museums.

Southwest of the center lies San Antonio, the colonial heart of Cali. North lies the bustling, upscale Av Sexta (Av 6N), and nearby Av 9, where you'll find Granada, the city's dining district. Further north along Sexta is Chipichape, one of the largest shopping malls in Colombia.

INFORMATION
Internet Access
Paper Store (☎ 660 3616; Calle 15N No 6N-40; per hr COP$1800)
Sc@nner (☎ 660 2014; Av Sexta No 15N-37; per hr COP$2000)

Money
Most of the major banks have offices on Av Sexta.
Bancolombia (cnr Calle 15N & Av 8N)
Citibank (Av 5N No 23AN-49, Parque Versalles)
Davivienda Versalles (cnr Av 6AN & Calle 22N); Granada (cnr Av 8N & Calle 18N)
Financiera Cambiamos SA (☎ 660 3706; ☽ 9am-7pm Mon-Sat) In the Carulla supermarket. Agents for MoneyGram.

Post
Deprisa (Calle 12 No 2AN-37)
Servientrega (Av 4NA No 10-123, local 2)

Tourist Information
British consulate (☎ 660 1031; Calle 22N No 6-42, Office 401) Organizes outings several times a year for Commonwealth expats and English-speaking passersby.
DAS (☎ 664 3808; Av 3N 50N-20, La Flora)
Tourist office (Secretaría de Cultura y Turismo; ☎ 886 0000, ext 2400; Carrera 7 btwn Calle 9 & Calle 10) On the 1st floor of the Gobernación building.

Travel Agencies
Comfenalco Valle (☎ 886 2727; Calle 5 No 6-63, torre C) Comfenalco's travel agency is one of the best in town. Organizes trips nationwide.

DANGERS & ANNOYANCES
During the day, the city center is alive with street vendors and crowds. After dark and on Sunday it can get dodgy. Take extra care with your belongings.

The area between Sexta and the Guest House Iguana (p243) and nearby hostels is the main hangout spot for *putos* – transexual

CALI

0 ————— 400 m
0 ————— 0.2 miles

SIGHTS & ACTIVITIES
ADN	13	B2
Iglesia de la Ermita	14	C3
Iglesia de la Merced	15	C5
Iglesia de San Antonio	16	B6
Iglesia de San Francisco	17	D4
Museo Arqueológico La Merced	18	C5
Museo de Arte Moderno La Tertulia	19	A6
Museo del Oro	20	C5
Torre Mudéjar	21	D4

SLEEPING
Café Tostaky	22	C6
Calidad House	23	A2
Casa de Alféraz	24	B4
Guest House Iguana	25	A1
Hotel Intercontinental	26	B5
Hotel Pensión Stein	27	B5
La Casa Café	28	C6
Posada San Antonio	29	C5

INFORMATION
Bancolombia	1	B2
British Consulate	2	B1
Comfenalco Valle	3	C5
Davivienda	4	B1
Davivienda	5	B2
Deprisa	6	B3
Ecuadorean Consulate	7	B1
Panamanian Consulate	8	C4
Paper Store	9	B2
Sc@nner	10	B2
Servientrega	11	B3
Tourist Office	12	D4

EATING
Baharoque	30	C6
Barra de Mayolo	31	B3
El Solar	32	B2
Paladar	33	A1
Restaurante Vegetariano Salud Vibrante	34	B3

DRINKING
Café y Chocolate	35	C6
La Casa Café1	(see 28)	
Macondo	36	C6
Saloon	37	B3

ENTERTAINMENT
Cinemateca La Tertulia	(see 19)	
Lugar a Dudas	38	B2
Teatro Municipal	39	C5

prostitutes sporting astonishing surgical alterations. Be warned: late at night, when tricks dry up, they have been known to rob travelers at knifepoint. After 11pm, take a taxi home, even if it's just a few blocks.

SIGHTS

The **Zoológico de Cali** (☎ 892 7474; www.zoologico decali.com.co; cnr Carrera 2A Oeste & Calle 14 Oeste; admission COP$8000; ☻ 9am-5pm) has a good collection of species indigenous to Colombia, including *chiguiros* (capybaras), *oso hormigueros* (anteaters), condors, monkeys and a *mariposario* (butterfly enclosure). It's 2km southwest of the center in Barrio Santa Teresita and is most easily accessed by taxi.

The **Museo Arqueológico la Merced** (☎ 889 3434; Carrera 4 No 6-59; admission COP$4000; ☻ 9am-1pm & 2-6pm Mon-Sat) is housed in the former La Merced convent, Cali's oldest building. Its five rooms contain a small collection of pre-Columbian pottery left behind by the major cultures from central and southern Colombia.

In the same complex you'll find the **Iglesia de la Merced** (cnr Carrera 4 & Calle 7; ☻ 6:30-10am & 4-7pm). Begun around 1545, it remains the city's oldest church. It's a lovely whitewashed building in the Spanish colonial style, with a long, narrow nave, and humble wood and stucco construction. Inside, a heavily gilded baroque high altar is topped by the Virgen de las Mercedes, the patron saint of the city.

The **Museo del Oro** (☎ 684 7754; Calle 7 No 4-69; admission free; ☻ 10am-5pm Mon-Sat), one block away from La Merced, has a small but fine collection of gold and pottery of the Calima culture.

Iglesia de San Francisco (cnr Carrera 6 & Calle 10) is a neoclassical construction dating from the 18th century. Next to the church are the Convento de San Francisco and the Capilla de la Inmaculada with the adjacent **Torre Mudéjar** (cnr Carrera 6 & Calle 9), an unusual brick belltower, one of the best examples of Mudejar art in Colombia.

Overlooking the Río Cali, the neo-Gothic **Iglesia de la Ermita** (cnr Av Colombia & Calle 13), constructed between 1930 and 1948, houses the 18th-century painting of *El Señor de la Caña* (Lord of the Sugarcane); many miracles are attributed to the image.

The small 1747 **Iglesia de San Antonio** is set atop a hill, the Colina de San Antonio, west of the old center. It shelters valuable *tallas quiteñas*, 17th-century carved-wood statues of the saints, representing the style known as the Quito School. The church also affords a good view of the city.

Museo de Arte Moderno La Tertulia (☎ 893 2441; Av Colombia No 5 Oeste-105; admission COP$4000; ☻ 10am-6pm) presents temporary exhibitions of contemporary painting, sculpture and photography. It's a 15-minute walk from the city center along the Río Cali.

If you're into contemporary art, try Cali's leading contemporary art gallery, **ADN** (☎ 661 2847; www.adn-colombia.org; Calle 16N No 9N-44; admission free; ☻ 11:30am-8pm Mon-Sat). There's a small café and bookstore on-site.

ACTIVITIES
Tejo
A small, working-class bar, **Club Social Los Amigos** (☎ 442 1258; Calle 49 No 8A-23) has two *canchas de tejo* where you can play a round of this unique Colombian game where you throw a heavy metal disc onto gunpowder, which then lets off a satisfying bang! A taxi here will cost around COP$6000.

Soccer
Cali has two *fútbol* teams. Deportivo Cali (www.deporcali.com) plays in the new Estadio Deportivo Cali near the airport in Palmira. America de Cali (www.america.com.co) plays in the city at **Estadio Pascual Guerrero** (cnr Calle 5 & Calle 24). Any Palmira-bound bus can take you to the former; the Mio passes right outside the latter.

Tren Turístico Café y Azucar
Colombia's long-neglected rail network now offers scenic excursions from Cali to El Cumbre, on the road to Buenaventura, and La Tebaida, near Armenia. All trips include live music, cafeteria and bar service, and include several hours at a mountain *finca* (farm) with a pool (COP$45,000). There's also a nighttime party train (COP$25,000), *chiva*-style (see p318).

Plans are afoot to extend service to Buenaventura (p279), Pereira and Manizales. Trains run here from the Cali **train station** (Av Vásquez Cobo No 23N-47) near the bus terminal, a few kilometers from the city center.

Hiking
CERRO DE LAS TRES CRUCES
No trip to Cali is complete without visiting the Three Crosses that tower over the city. The views of the city are spectacular. It's a

hefty two- to three-hour walk return, or take a taxi (COP$35,000).

KM18–DAPA
Eighteen kilometers west of the city lies mile-marker **Kilometro 18**. There are numerous bars and restaurants here. At 1800m it's pleasantly cool, and the nearby cloud forest is an Important Bird Area (see www.mapalina.com, in Spanish) with high biodiversity. The walk from here to Dapa (four hours) is a pleasant stroll. There are numerous crossroads – always take the left-hand fork.

Dapa (www.vivedapa.com), with a population of 2500, is a spread-out holiday area off the Cali–Yumbo road. There are hotels (and motels) and restaurants here, open principally on the weekend. There are other little-trafficked roads you can walk along, including to a tea plantation in El Chicoral.

There are regular bus services to Km18 (COP$1000, one hour). Look for the bus labeled 'Dagua.' Buses and jeeps service Dapa every half hour (COP$3000, 30 minutes).

COURSES
Dance Courses
For a complete guide to salsa schools and discos in Cali, see www.salsapower.com.

Recommended schools include **Compañía Artística Rucafé** (☎ 557 8833; Carrera 36 No 8-49, El Templete) and **Escuela de Baile Acrosalsa Latina** (☎ 437 3145; Carrera 33A No 45-38, El Vergel). You'll pay around COP$20,000 per hour for private instruction in your hotel, less in a studio or in a group.

Spanish Courses
The well-regarded **Universidad Santiago de Cali** (☎ 518 3000, ext 421; http://virtual.usc.edu.co/espaextranjeros; cnr Calle 5 & Carrera 62) is a Cali institution and runs a Spanish-language program for foreigners. See the website for latest prices and schedules.

FESTIVALS & EVENTS
Cali's big bash is the **Feria de Cali** (www.feriadecali .com) from Christmas to New Year, with parades, music, theater, a beauty pageant and general citywide revelry. The bull-fighting season runs for two weeks from mid-December to mid-January, and attracts top bullfighters and some feisty bulls.

Calle del Arte (Sep) San Antonio hosts this street-closing festival with live music, *artesanías* (local craft stalls), theater, dance and food.

Festival Internacional de Blues (May) Organized by the Centro Cultural Colombo Americano (www.colombo americano.edu.co). Attracts an international crowd of Latino blues musicians.

Festival de Música del Pacífico Petronio Álvarez (Aug) A festival of Pacific music, heavily influenced by the African rhythms brought by the many slaves that originally populated the Pacific coast.

Festival Mundial de Salsa (Sep; www.festivalsalsacali .com) Don't miss this one. Amazing dancers.

SLEEPING
For a taste of Cali's colonial past, lay your head in San Antonio.

Budget
La Casa Café (☎ 893 7011; lacasacafecali.blogspot.com; Carrera 6 No 2-13, San Antonio; r per person COP$15,000; 🖳) This groovy cafe-bar (p245) with internet also rents pleasant private rooms on the 2nd floor of this colonial building. Two have quiet street views of San Antonio. The four rooms share one bathroom. Sometimes hosts art exhibitions and live music downstairs.

Guest House Iguana (☎ 660 8937; www.iguana.com .co; Av 9N No 22N-46; dm COP$16,000, s/d without bathroom COP$26,000/34,000, s/d COP$32,000/40,000; 🖳) The largest hostel in Cali, the Swiss-owned Iguana has moved from its decade-long digs into two nearby houses. Both stretch down the side of a hill, offering good views of the city. One houses private rooms, the other dorms; both have kitchens. Walking distance to the restaurants in Granada and Chipichape.

Calidad House (☎ 661 2338; www.calidadhouse.com; Calle 17N No 9AN-39; dm/s/d COP$17,000/21,000/35,000; 🖳) This otherwise fine hostel has a reputation with travelers for somewhat unfriendly service. But it's been around many years and will most likely be around many more. A handy last resort if everything else is full.

Café Tostaky (☎ 893 0651; www.cafetostaky.blogspot .com; Carrera 10 No 1-76; dm/s/d without bathroom COP$18, 000/22,000/30,000; 🖳) This French-owned hostel is right in the heart of San Antonio. All the rooms have shared bathroom. There's a kitchen you can use, plus there's free internet and cable TV. Downstairs it runs a groovy cafe (open 5pm to 11pm) that serves crepes and good coffee. Worth visiting even if you're not staying here.

Midrange
our pick **Posada San Antonio** (☎ 893 7413; www.posada desanantonio.com; Carrera 5 No 3-37; s/d/tr/q COP$55,000/

70,000/105,000/140,000; 🖳) Right in the heart of San Antonio, this old colonial building surrounds a pleasant courtyard. All have private bath and cable TV, and breakfast is included in the price. There's no air-con, but the upper third of the doors open separately, letting the air circulate while you sleep.

Hotel Pensión Stein (☎ 661 4927; www.hotelstein .com.co; Av 4N No 3-33; s with fan/air-con COP$110,000/140,000, d with fan COP$125,000-138,000, d with air-con COP$152,000-175,000; 🅿 💥 🖳 🕭) This castlelike stone mansion is a bit of Bavaria in the tropics. Think heavy wood beams and doors, decorative collector plates on the walls, and old-world upholstery in the sitting room. There's a small pool serenaded by a muzak-playing stereo. Breakfast is included.

Top End

Casa de Alférez (☎ 661 8111; www.sofitel.com.br; Av 9N No 9-24; s incl breakfast COP$433,000-540,000, d incl breakfast COP$454,000-561,000; 🅿 💥 🖳) This ultra-luxurious five-star hotel offers rooms with king-sized feather beds. Huge French windows open onto small balconies on a lovely, tree-lined street. The excellent restaurant downstairs is open to the public. Rates include a buffet breakfast.

Hotel Intercontinental (☎ 882 3225; www.inter continental.com; Av Colombia No 2-72; s/d COP$450,000/550,000, ste COP$520,000-1,300,000; 🅿 💥 🖳 🕭) This landmark hotel sits right on the Río Cali, on the border of San Antonio. Its nine floors offer all the creature comforts, including a swimming pool, spa and gymnasium. It offers big weekend discounts, and there's a casino next door.

EATING

The best cheap eats in town are in the **LA 14 supermarket** (cnr Av 6AN & Calle 28) and **Chipichape** (www.chipichape.com; Calle 38N No 6N-35) shopping mall. LA 14 has half-a-dozen small eateries, including its own bakery, which does excellent meat pies (*pastel de carne*), pizza by the slice, *buñuelos* (deep-fried doughy balls of curd cheese and flour), *pan de bono* (bagel-shaped bun with a tart flavor), etc. The restaurants in Chipichape offer sincere attempts at Chinese and Mexican food, as well as more upscale choices such as grill restaurant Leños y Carbon.

Restaurante Vegetariano Salud Vibrante (☎ 660 5454; Av Sexta 13N-17; mains COP$5000; 🕑 8am-7pm Mon-Fri, to 3pm Sat) Your best bet for a cheap veggie meal in Cali. Staff makes its own soy

milk and wholemeal bread. Also sells good veggie empanadas.

Baharoque (☎ 893 5318; baharoque@hotmail.com; Calle 2 No 4-23; mains COP$6000-18,000; 🕑 lunch daily, dinner Thu-Sun) This new San Antonio restaurant serves a great set meal for COP$6000. Sample amazing salads garnished with tropical fruit, plus good steaks and chicken for you carnivores. Sundays see old-fashioned Cali dishes served, such as *arroz atollado*, a kind of risotto, and of course *sancocho* and *ajiaco*, both types of Colombian stew.

Crêpes y Waffles (☎ 667 5475; Av 6AN No 24A-70; mains COP$10,000-22,000; 🕑 noon-10pm Mon-Sat, to 11pm Sun) What's Cali without an afternoon sitting on the outdoor patio at Crêpes with a monster ice-cream sundae and some friends? It does excellent salads, and the salad bar is good value. Also serves sweet and savory crepes and, wait for it, waffles.

Barra de Mayolo (☎ 667 4239, 661 0166; Av 9AN No 10-10; tapas COP$12,000-15,000; 🕑 lunch daily, dinner Mon-Sat) This Spanish tapas bar has some of the best food in Granada. Tapas selection includes fried calamari, Spanish ham and chorizo, as well as sample platters big enough for groups to share. Try the *paella* (COP$26,500 to COP$35,000), or whole suckling pig (COP$210,000), prepared specially if you give advance notice.

San Antonio Pizza (☎ 893 6726; Carrera 10 Oeste No 1-93; pizzas COP$14,000-36,000; 🕑 4-11pm Mon-Wed, noon-11pm Thu-Sun) At the top of the park on your left as you walk uphill, it serves pizza by the slice (COP$4400 to COP$6600) and also delivers. The menu boasts a vegetarian pizza, and other creative variations, including pesto pizza and fruit pizza with pineapple, peach and cherry.

Paladar (☎ 668 6803; Av 6AN No 23-27; mains COP$15,000-20,000; 🕑 9:30am-8:30pm Mon-Sat) It looks like a cafeteria, but wait till you see what it serves – homemade lasagna, casseroles of every sort, even the occasional stewed rabbit. The dessert selection is divine – cakes, pies, mousses; it makes us drool just thinking about it. The *pastel Paladar* (the house specialty, a multilayered chocolate and mocha cake) is orgasmic, and if you like lemon meringue pie, get in before noon – it goes quickly.

our pick Cali Viejo (☎ 893 4927; restaurantecaliviejo@ starmedia.com; Bosque Municipal; mains COP$16,000-58,000; 🕑 noon-11pm Mon-Sat, to 5pm Sun; 🅿) Set in the lush grounds of the Bosque Municipal, the city park adjoining the zoo, Cali Viejo shows off Cali's Pacific roots. Seafood is the star here –

try the *cazuela de mariscos* (seafood stew, COP$41,000) or lobster (COP$58,000) – but it also does a great *sancocho* (COP$20,000). Wash it down with a *champú* or *lulada*, or a shot of the homemade aguardiente. The dining room has no walls, letting a breeze blow through. If you're coming here from the zoo, take a taxi or flag down a passing bus; the area is a bit isolated and, hence, a bit sketchy.

El Solar (☎ 653 4628; Calle 15N No 9N-62; mains COP$18,000-34,000; ☽ lunch & dinner) The waiters can be forgiven for being pretentious; the food really is that good. On the menu you'll find top quality Italian food – risottos, pastas, seafood and steak. Also worth trying is the authentic Peruvian ceviche (raw fish marinated in lime) and lobster (COP$45,000).

Kaiserhaus (☎ 653 0288; kaiserhaus.cali@yahoo.com; Calle 29N No 6BN-51; mains COP$25,000-28,000; ☽ lunch & dinner Tue-Sat) This German restaurant prepares its own authentic sausage and sauerkraut. The breezy 2nd-floor balcony is a great spot for a bratwurst and imported German beer. Also does *picadas* (COP$37,000 to COP$67,000) – mounds of toothpickable sliced sausage, enough for four to six. The pretzels (COP$500) with mustard make a great snack.

DRINKING
Cafes
Café y Chocolate (☎ 300 789 4961, 315 427 8457; cafe chocolate05@yahoo.com; Carrera 9 No 2-09; ☽ 4-11pm Tue-Sat) This groovy little cafe at the foot of Parque San Antonio is a hopelessly romantic place to take a date. The mellow lounge atmosphere is perfect for an early evening drink, and you can order nibbles, but no real food. Some weekends it hosts live music.

La Casa Cafe (☎ 893 7011; lacasacafecali@yahoo .com; Carrera 6 No 2-13; ☽ 4-10pm Tue-Sun) This funky cafe has Jenga sets, card games and dominoes you can borrow, while lingering over coffee, juice, desserts and beer. The internet cafe (open 9am to 9:30pm, COP$2000 per hour) is right next door, and you can even sleep here (see p243).

ourpick Macondo (☎ 893 1570; http://macondocafe .blogspot.com; Carrera 6 No 3-03; ☽ noon-midnight Mon-Sat, 4:30pm-midnight Sun) This San Antonio institution does great coffee, a wide range of desserts, light sandwiches and salads, and serves beer and wine till late. Jazz plays on the stereo and the smell of coffee is in the air. Try the scrumptious cocktails, like the Melquiades (mango, chocolate, coffee, Baileys, whiskey and black-

berry sauce) or the Macondo de Lulo (coffee ice cream with fresh *lulo* and whiskey).

Bars
Narguila (☎ 683 1845; www.narguila.com; Calle 25N No 5AN-23; cover COP$5000; ☽ 7pm-2am Thu-Sat) This popular hookah bar has no tables, just cushions on the floor, where you sit and smoke flavored tobacco from a water pipe. No dancing, just relaxing. Also serves Middle Eastern food and snacks.

Bar Oz (☎ 690 5163; Calle 8 No 38-90, Menga, Callejón Inducon; ☽ 7pm-6am) Located about a kilometer from the main strip in Menga, down a country road past several small farms, this disco boasts large replicas of the Sphinx, a small pond, bonfires in good weather, and a restaurant (mains COP$16,000 to COP$27,000) specializing in grilled meat. Don't come if it's raining.

Blues Brothers (☎ 661 3412; Av 6AN No 21-40; cover COP$5000 Thu; ☽ 8pm-2am Tue-Thu, 8pm-3am Fri & Sat) This loud bar is an obligatory stop on Thursday nights, when a live salsa band raises the roof (11:30pm to 1:30am). Staff mix great (if expensive) cocktails, and some nights the bartenders dance on top of the bar and pour shots of liquor down your throat.

Saloon (☎ 660 4116; elsaloon@yahoo.com; Av 9N No 13N-01; ☽ 4pm-2am Mon-Thu, to 3am Fri & Sat) This edgy, arty bar has a student vibe. Foreign DJs sometimes spin here, and every other Friday there's live music. You can get sandwiches and light salads (COP$10,000 to COP$12,000). It also sometimes host art installations. It's on the second floor of a white building in the heart of Granada.

ENTERTAINMENT
Cali is famous for its bar-hopping weekend *chiva* tours. Board the bus and dance your way through gridlock as you visit six or so discos. All tours begin at the Hotel Intercontinental and end in Juanchito, late at night. The two best-known operators are **Cali Chivas** (☎ 882 4550) and **Viajes Organesoff** (☎ 667 3131; www.viajesoganesoff.com). Expect to pay around COP$15,000 to COP$20,000 per person, or

COP$300,000 to COP$400,000 per bus. You'll enjoy yourself more if you put together your own group and contract the *chiva* privately.

For the latest on what's on around town, check the entertainment columns of Cali's broadsheet, *El País* (www.elpais.com.co). Also check out www.calicultura.com, which publishes a free paper at the beginning of most months, and the indispensable www.caliescali .com. For complete listings of restaurants, bars and nightclubs, plus theater, live music, festivals and other seasonal events, pick up a copy of *Entoncesq* (www.entoncesq.com).

Nightclubs

Av Sexta is full of bars and clubs. They all suck. The best nightclubs are a taxi-ride away. The hippest new spot in town is Parque del Perro, where bars and restaurants surround the park. There are also bars near El Gato, and just outside the Cali municipal boundary is Menga, where numerous discos (not constrained by the *ley zanahoria*, see boxed text, p245) are open till dawn. Further afield is Juanchito, where several big *salsatecas* (salsa dance clubs) cluster.

Cali is more socially conservative than Medellín or Bogotá – *caleños* go out to dance, not to meet new people. If your goal is to meet new people, try Chipichape's many tiny bars in the early evening, or the slopes of Parque San Antonio on the weekend.

Changó (☎ 662 9701; Via Cavasa, Juanchito; ⌚ 2pm-6am) The most famous *salsateca* in Juanchito, this huge, sophisticated club has candlelit plush booths and a big, smoking-hot dance floor. Most of the week there's no cover charge (Sunday costs COP$5000), but it's a COP$10,000, 20-minute taxi ride from town. Sometimes there are dance shows.

Kukaramakara (☎ 653 5389; Calle 28N No 2bis-97; cover COP$10,000; ⌚ 9pm-2am Thu-Sat) This big disco is famous for its live music, usually salsa. Come early if you want a table, or hang out on the 2nd-floor interior balcony, looking down at the band below.

Praga (☎ 691 4646; www.clubpraga.net; Km1 Antigua Via a Yumbo; cover COP$8000-10,000; ⌚ 9pm-6am Thu-Sat) The biggest, most expensive nightclub in Cali, Praga attracts the richest and most beautiful people – if you've got it, this is where you come to flaunt it. On Thursday there's no cover charge, plus domestic liquor is 2-for-1 till midnight.

Tienda Vieja (☎ 513 4444; www.tiendavieja.com; cnr Autopista Sur & Carrera 43; ⌚ 4pm-1am Thu, 4pm-3am Fri & Sat, 2pm-2am Sun) This happy, well-worn but well-loved Cali institution plays salsa and Colombian crossover. Seating is in small, colorful wooden chairs – they're not comfortable, but then you came here to dance, right? In the same complex there's also a good grill restaurant, Rancho de Jonas.

ourpick Tin Tin Deo (☎ 514 1537; www.tintindeocali .com; Calle 5 No 38-71, San Fernando; cover COP$10,000-15,000; ⌚ 7pm-2am Thu, to 3am Fri & Sat) This exciting salsa joint attracts some of the best dancers in Cali. Posters of famous salsa singers look down on you from the wall, and industrial fans keep the room from overheating. Drinks are moderately priced, and the cover charge is *consumible,* that is, you get it back in drinks at the bar. Also sometimes plays *música del pacífico* (music from the Pacific coast).

Cinemas

Cali's many shopping malls all have cinemas, including **Chipichape** (www.chipichape.com; Av Sexta No 39N-25), **Cosmocentro** (Calle 5 No 50-00), **Palmetto Plaza** (www.palmettoplaza.com; Calle 9 No 48-51), and **Unicentro** (www.unicentro.com; Carrera 100 No 5-169).

For more thought-provoking fare, check the program of the **Cinemateca La Tertulia** (☎ 893 2939; Museo de Arte Moderno La Tertulia, Av Colombia No 5 Oeste-105), which generally has two shows daily from Tuesday to Sunday. Attracting large crowds for its weekend art-house screenings is **Lugar a Dudas** (☎ 668 2335; www.lugaradudas.org; Calle 15N No 8N-41; admission free; ⌚ 11am-1pm & 2-7pm Tue-Sat). It serves coffee and snacks.

Theater

The city's oldest existing theater, **Teatro Municipal** (☎ 684 0593; Carrera 5 No 6-64), was completed in 1918. Today it's used for various artistic forms, including musical concerts, theater and ballet. Frequent free concerts are held at **Teatro al Aire Libre Los Cristales** (☎ 558 2009; Carrera 14A No 6-00), an open-air amphitheater.

SHOPPING

ourpick Parque Artesanía(⌚ 10am-8pm) On Loma de la Cruz, this is one of Colombia's best *artesanía* markets. You'll find authentic, hand-made goods from the Amazon, Pacific coast, southern Andes, and even Los Llanos.

CC La Pasarela (www.lapasarela.net; Av 5AN No 23DN-68) is a two-story shopping center that's elbow-to-elbow computers and parts. You'll find great prices on laptops and repairs; highly recommended is **La Bodeguita** (☎ 667 6637).

GETTING THERE & AWAY

Aeropuerto Palmaseca (☎ 666 3200) is 16km northeast of the city, off the road to Palmira. Minibuses between the airport and the bus terminal run every 10 minutes until about 8pm (COP$3000, 30 minutes), or take a taxi (around COP$50,000).

Avianca offer frequent shuttle services to Bogotá. Satena flies to Ipiales on the border, and to Guapi on the coast. LAN Peru flies non-stop to Lima, and Tame flies to Esmeraldas, Ecuador. There are also international flights to Miami and Madrid.

GETTING AROUND

Cali's new air-conditioned electric bus network, the **Mio** (www.metrocali.gov.co), will remind many of Bogotá's TransMilenio. It was still being rolled out when we visited but is largely operational. The main route will run from north of the bus terminal along the river, through the center and down the entire length of Av Quinta (Av 5). Other routes will spread out across the city over the coming years. Ticket price at time of research was COP$1500 per ride.

The **bus terminal** (☎ 668 3655) is 2km north of the center. It's a sweaty walk in Cali's heat – take the Mio, or a taxi (COP$3000 to COP$5000).

Buses run regularly to Bogotá (COP$65,000, 12 hours), Medellín (COP$42,000, nine hours) and Pasto (COP$60,000, nine hours). Pasto buses will drop you off in Popayán (COP$17,000, three hours) and there are also hourly minibuses to Popayán (COP$20,000, 2½ hours). There are regular departures to Armenia (COP$15,000, four hours), Pereira (COP$18,000, four hours) and Manizales (COP$24,000, five hours).

AROUND CALI

PARQUE NACIONAL NATURAL (PNN) FARALLONES DE CALI

This 150,000-hectare **national park** (www.farallones decali.com) protects the headlands around Cali. There are numerous one-day and multiday hikes in the park you can do, including Pico Pance and Pico de Loro. The gateway to the park is the small holiday town of Pance.

Closed for many years due to La Violencia (p27), the national park was tendering for a concession-holder at time of our research, and should be open again by the time you read this.

PANCE

☎ 2 / pop 2000 / elev 1550m

This small holiday town in the mountains is full of holiday *fincas* (farms). The weather is a pleasantly cool change from the heat of Cali. On the weekend its one street opens and all the bars and restaurants are in full flower. During the week it's empty and you can't even get a meal.

Come on the weekend, preferably Sunday, to eat and drink your way down the hill. You can also do a day hike to some nearby water-falls, or organize the longer treks to Pico de Loro or Pico Pance.

Activities

Pico de Loro is a seven-hour hike return from Pance. Pico Pance is three to four days; from the top it is said you can see Pasto and the Ecuadorean frontier.

Some opportunistic guides in Pance may try to rip you off. It's best to avoid using them if possible. Your best bet is to join a group tour organized by **Ecoaventura** (☎ 893 7403; www .farallonesdecali.com/ecoaventura.htm), which owns a small campground with tents on the slopes of Pico Pance.

For Pico de Loro expect to pay COP$10,000 to COP$20,000 per person; for Pico Pance, COP$15,000 per person per day.

To visit the nearby waterfalls, walk 1km downhill from town to the bridge and turn right. Walk 3km uphill to El Topacio, the ruins of an old resort. The watchman will let you pass unofficially for COP$2000. It's a 20-minute walk to the waterfalls. You don't need a guide.

Sleeping & Eating

our pick **Anahuac** (☎ 331 4828, 315 407 2724; www .resevanaturalanahuac.com; campsite per person COP$6000-12,000, r per person COP$15,000) This small, well-developed private nature reserve sits next to Río Pance amid secondary forest and a small farm growing fruit and flowers. There's a four-room brick cabin and a four-room wood cabin, but the small two-story *bohíos* – tiny huts with mattresses lofted above with win-dows facing birdsong and forest – will appeal most to travelers. There's a wood-fired stove in a basic kitchen where you can cook. You can camp with your tent or theirs, or just come out for the day (COP$3000). Serves budget meals all week long.

Getting There & Away

A dozen buses per day leave from the bus terminal in Cali heading to Pance roughly every hour (COP$2000, 1½ hours). They run the length of Av Quinta.

LAGO CALIMA

This manmade reservoir attracts kitesurfers and windsurfers from around the world for its year-round winds. The lake covers the flooded Darién valley of Río Calima, and was built in 1965. Some 86km from Cali, its temperate climate also attracts *caleños* looking to cool off on weekends. The green hills that surround that lake are populated with holiday *fincas*.

Every afternoon, around lunchtime, a brisk mountain thermal picks up, bringing wisps of cloud and a steady 18-knot wind down from the mountains. From July to September this can increase to 25 knots. Kitesurfing and windsurfing competitions are held in these months, when world champions in the two sports come to compete. Water temperature is a steady 18°C.

Most tourist activity stretches along the northern bank of the lake, from the small town of Darién (below) at the eastern end to the dam to the west. There are three kitesurf/windsurf schools outside the town along the shore. There's no beach; launching points are from grassy slopes that lead down to the water.

Because transport is infrequent – most Colombian tourists come in their own cars – Lago Calima makes a difficult day trip. You're better off coming for a day or two, especially on the weekend, when the many holidaymakers give the place a party atmosphere. Many kitesurfers end up spending weeks or even months here.

DARIÉN

☎ 2 / pop 20,000 / elev 1800m

This small town has a few budget hotels, a couple of supermarkets, two ATMs, an internet cafe, and on the weekends, several lively discos. Most everything clusters within two or three blocks of Parque Los Fundadores, the main plaza. It's a perfectly pleasant little town but is nothing special: a trip to Lago Calima is the drawcard.

Information

Compu Calima (☎ 317 752 6758; Carrera 7 No 7-50; 🕑 8:30am-noon & 2-8pm; per hr COP$2000) Internet access; next to the gas station.

Tourist office (Secretaría de Cultura y Turismo; ☎ 253 3117; turismodarien@yahoo.com; Calle 11 No 6-25, Parque Principal)

Sights

You'll find a small collection of old pottery at the **Museo Arqueológico Calima** (☎ 253 3121; Calle 10 No 12-50; admission COP$2500; 🕑 9am-5pm Mon-Fri, 10am-6pm Sat & Sun).

Activities

KITESURFING & WINDSURFING

Three schools offer classes and rentals. Expect to pay roughly COP$40,000 per hour for windsurfing instruction and COP$50,000 to COP$80,000 per hour for kitesurf instruction. Rentals go for around COP$40,000 to COP$50,000 per hour. If you've got your own gear, you'll pay COP$20,000 to COP$30,000 for each water entrance.

Located in a big warehouse, **Escuela Pescao Windsurf y Kitesurf** (☎ 311 352 3293, 316 401 6373; www .pescaowindsurfing.com; campsite s/d COP$20,000/30,000, cabins for 6-10 people COP$150,000) sits right on the edge of the lake. The wheelchair-bound former champion kitesurfer will shout instruction through a megaphone. It offers accommodations in the warehouse in tents with mattresses and sleeping bags.

Considered by many to have the best water entrance on the lake is the private club **Velas y Vientos** (☎ 668 7642; www.velasyvientos.com). It rents an adjacent steep-peaked chalet-style cabin (COP$120,000 up to four people), and there are four-man tents available (COP$30,000 per tent). Sometimes there are bonfires on the shore at night. A restaurant serves food. Also rents kayaks (COP$25,000 per hour) and offers instruction (COP$20,000 per hour).

On the grounds of the resort complex **Calima Windsurf Club** (☎ 683 1068, 889 8048; www .calimawindsurfclub.com) is **Viento Extremo** (☎ 315 554 2131; www.vientoxtremo.com), which rents jet skis and boats. This ambitious hotel complex has big plans for future expansion. A small eatery serves budget meals.

BOATING

Numerous captains offer excursions on the lake. Try **El Arriero Paísa** (☎ 253 3597; restaurante arrieropaisa@yahoo.es; entrada 5), a small resort that also organizes boat trips. Also try the **M/N Bonba** (☎ 315 555 4745), which leaves from the Muelle Lago Marina next to the Comfandi complex. Expect to pay around COP$12,000 to COP$15,000 per person, minimum six people.

Sleeping

Cogua (☎ 317 513 7332; cogua.colombiakite.com; dm/d without bathroom COP$20,000/30,000) The closest thing to a hostel in Darién, the Colombian owner of Cogua has four rooms with shared bath and hot water and a kitchen you can use. There are two patios, one facing the lake and another facing the mountains. The owner also runs a small kiteboard factory, where he makes custom boards from coconut fiber and *guadua* (a type of bamboo). He'll even let you design and custom-make your own board. Cogua is a short walk west of town in a private condo complex.

Hostería Los Veleros (☎ 684 1000; www.comfandi .com.co; s/tw/d/tr/q incl full board COP$156,000/190,000/ 200,000/227,000/256,000; 😰) The best hotel on the lake, Los Veleros is part of the Comfandi complex, and prices include three meals and admission to the recreation center, with three pools, Jacuzzi and sauna, and activities for the kids. Some of the rooms have balconies with spectacular views of the lake. Packed on the weekend, during the week you'll have the place to yourself. An on-site disco on Saturday night sometimes goes till dawn.

Eating

El Fogón de la Abuela (☎ 316 298 2928; Carrera 6A No 8-61; mains COP$5000-10,000) This cheap restaurant does the best set meals in town – which is to say, pretty average. It's on a noisy street two blocks from the main square.

Meson llama (☎ 667 9703, 315 488 5599; www.meson ilama.com; mains COP$18,000-22,000) About 10km from Darién is this large, exposed-timber restaurant with huge windows and views of the lake. It does all the basics very well – *sancocho* (a typical Colombian stew), *churrasco* (grilled meat) baby beef and trout. Worth it just for the views.

Getting There & Away

There is a direct bus service every hour to/ from Cali (COP$10,000 to COP$12,000, 2½ hours) during the day. You can also take any bus to Media Canoa (a large roundabout on the road to Buga, COP$5000 to COP$6500, one hour) and grab a passing Buga–Darién bus (COP$4600, 1½ hours). Coming from the north, get off in Buga and grab the half-hourly service to Darién (COP$6500, 1½hours).

Note that there are two bus routes that come out here to Lago Calima and Darién. They cost the same. If you're going direct to Darién, ask for the bus to Jiguales; for the kitesurf/windsurf schools, ask for the bus that goes along the lakeshore.

Getting Around

There are no taxis in Darién. Jeeps sometimes hang out on the main square, and can take you around town and along the lakeshore, but these are expensive (around COP$20,000).

Buses shuttle between Darién and the dam (COP$1500), past the kite schools, from 9am to 9pm on the hour, except for noon to 2pm, when they run on the half-hour.

CAUCA & HUILA

These two departments are home to Popayán, one of Colombia's loveliest colonial cities, plus the country's two most important archaeological sites – San Agustín and Tierradentro. Here you'll also find the peculiar Desierto de la Tatacoa, a striking anomaly outside Neiva, halfway between Bogotá and San Agustín.

In the days of river travel in Colombia, both Cauca and Huila were major hubs of commerce. The introduction of the railroad and highways in the early 20th century stunted their growth, and these days a sleepy languor envelops the region.

POPAYÁN

☎ 2 / pop 240,000 / elev 1760m
This small colonial town is famous for its chalk-white facades (its nickname is La Ciudad Blanca, or 'the White City'), and is second only to Cartagena as Colombia's most impressive colonial settlement. It sits at the southern end of the Valle de Cauca, and for hundreds of years was the capital of southern Colombia, before Cali overtook it.

The town was founded in 1537 by Sebastián de Belalcázar, and Popayán became the most important stopping point on the road between Cartagena and Quito. Its mild climate attracted wealthy families from the sugar haciendas of the hot Cali region. In the 17th century they began building mansions, schools and several imposing churches and monasteries.

The city is famous for its elaborate Semana Santa (Holy Week) celebration, when tourists from around the world come to see the religious pageantry. Popayán is also famous for its food, and plays host every September to a food festival that attracts chefs (and eaters) from around the world. The city has numerous universities, and there's a lively cafe and bar culture catering to local students.

In March 1983, moments before the much-celebrated Maundy Thursday religious procession was set to depart, a violent earthquake shook the town, caving in the cathedral's roof and killing hundreds. Little damage is visible today.

Information

Bancolombia (Parque Caldas) Bank.

Cambiamos SA (☎ 820 5288; cnr Carrera 7 & Calle 6) Agents for MoneyGram.

Davivienda (Parque Caldas) Bank.

Hospital San José (☎ 820 0975; Carrera 6 No 10N-142)

Internet ADSL (☎ 822 5801; Carrera 11 No 4-36; per hr COP$1000; ☉ 8am-10pm) Internet access; next to Hosteltrail.

National Park Office (Parques Nacionales Naturales de Colombia; ☎ 823 1212, 823 1279; www.parques nacionales.gov.co; Carrera 9 No 25N-6)

Tourist office (Oficina de Turismo de Popayán; ☎ 824 2251; Carrera 5 No 4-68)

Tourist police (☎ 822 0916; turismodecau@hotmail .com; Carrera 7 No 4-36) More helpful than the regular tourist office. In the *gobernación* building.

Sights & Activities

The **Iglesia de San Francisco** (cnr Carrera 9 & Calle 4) is the city's largest colonial church and arguably the most beautiful. Inside are a fine high altar and a collection of seven unique side altars. The 1983 earthquake cracked open the ossary, revealing six unidentified mummies. Two are left, and you can visit them on a one-hour **guided tour** (admission COP$1000; ☉ 8am-noon & 4-6pm) of the church that includes the five-story bell tower and the outdoor cupolas. Look for the tourist policeman outside the church doors who conducts the tours.

Other colonial churches in town include the **Iglesia de Santo Domingo** (cnr Carrera 5 & Calle 4), **Iglesia de San José** (cnr Calle 5 & Carrera 8) and the **Iglesia de San Agustín** (cnr Calle 7 & Carrera 6). Built in 1546, **Iglesia La Ermita** (cnr Calle 5 & Carrera 2) is Popayán's oldest church and worth seeing for its fine main retable and the fragments of old frescoes, which were only discovered after the earthquake.

Casa Museo Mosquera (☎ 824 0683; Calle 3 No 5-38; admission COP$2000; ☉ 8am-noon & 2-5pm) is housed in an 18th-century mansion that was once home

to General Tomás Cipriano de Mosquera, a politician and historian who was Colombia's president on four occasions between 1845 and 1867. Note the urn in the wall; it contains Mosquera's heart.

Museo Arquidiocesano de Arte Religioso (☎ 824 2759; Calle 4 No 4-56; admission COP$2000; ☉ 9am-12:30pm & 2-5pm Mon-Fri, 9am-2pm Sat) has a good collection of religious art, including paintings, statues, altar pieces, silverware and liturgical vessels, most of which date from the 17th to 19th centuries.

The neoclassical **cathedral** (Parque Caldas) is the youngest church in the center, built between 1859 and 1906 on the site of a previous cathedral, which had been completely destroyed by an earthquake.

Museo Guillermo Valencia (☎ 820 6160; Carrera 6 No 2-69; admission COP$2000) is dedicated to the Popayán-born poet who once lived here. The late-18th-century building is full of period furniture, paintings, old photos and documents related to the poet and his son, Guillermo León Valencia, who was Colombia's president from 1962 to 1966.

It is worth strolling past the early-20th-century **Teatro Guillermo Valencia** (cnr Calle 3 & Carrera 7). Ask nicely at the box office and they may give you an ad-hoc tour.

Located just next door to the theater is the neoclassical **Panteón de los Próceres** (Carrera 7), which shelters the remains of Popayán's most illustrious sons, including General Tomás Cipriano de Mosquera and botanist Francisco José de Caldas (1770–1816).

Just north of the historic center, two unusual bridges cross the small Río Molino. The small one, **Puente de la Custodia**, also frequently called Puente Chiquita (Little Bridge), was constructed in 1713 to allow priests to cross the river to bring the holy orders to the sick of this poor northern suburb. About 160 years later, the solid 240m-long 11-arch **Puente del Humilladero** was built alongside the old bridge, and is still in use.

Just east of the historic center you'll find the **Museo de Historia Natural** (☎ 820 9861; Carrera 2 No 1A-25; admission COP$3000; ☉ 8am-noon & 2-5pm Tue-Sun). One of the best of its kind in the country, it's noted for its extensive collection of insects, butterflies and, in particular, stuffed birds.

The **Capilla de Belén**, a chapel set on a hill just east of the city center, offers good views over the town. **El Morro de Tulcán**, a hill topped with

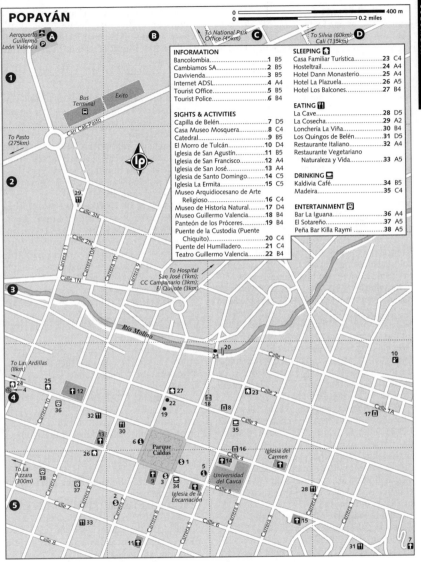

POPAYÁN

an equestrian statue of the town's founder, provides even better vistas. It's said to be the site of a pre-Columbian pyramid and is a good place to watch the sunset.

The 10-hectare private nature reserve **Las Ardillas** (☎ 830 5555, 310 829 7188; www.canopylasardillas .com; admission COP$20,000-25,000; ⏰ 9am-6pm Sat & Sun) has six canopy lines totaling 1200m that you

can ride. There's a swimming pool and sauna, and a restaurant serves drinks and snacks. There are also several nearby waterfalls along the Río Honda you can visit. The reserve is 8km south of Popayán. Take any bus bound for Timbío (COP$1000, 20 minutes) and get off at the Mi Bohío gas station. From here's it's a 2.4km walk to the actual site.

Festivals & Events

Popayán's **Semana Santa** (Holy Week) celebrations are world-famous, especially the nighttime processions on Maundy Thursday and Good Friday. Thousands of believers and tourists from all over come to take part in this religious ceremony and the accompanying festival of religious music. Hotel prices quadruple at this time; book well in advance.

In the first week of September the city plays host to the **Congreso Nacional Gastronómico** (www.corporaciongastronomicapopayan.com). Every year top chefs from a different country are invited to come and cook up a storm. Admission to all of the week's events costs COP$260,000.

Sleeping

Casa Familiar Turística (☎ 824 4853; Carrera 5 No 2-07; dm/s/d COP$12,000/14,000/28,000) The main hostel in town before Hosteltrail arrived, the Colombian owners offer budget beds in their colonial building. There's hot water and laundry facilities, and two big, friendly dogs.

Hosteltrail (☎ 831 7871, 314 696 0805; www.hosteltrail.com; Carrera 11 No 4-16; dm COP$15,000, s/d with bathroom COP$35,000/40,000, s/d without bathroom COP$25,000/30,000; 🖳) This new Scottish-owned hostel is the budget traveler's choice in Popayán. In a concrete building on the edge of the colonial center, the owners have gone out of their way to make the it comfortable, and are an excellent source of local information. Wi-fi, TV/DVD, luggage storage and kitchen facilities are available.

ourpick Hotel Los Balcones (☎ 824 2030; hotellosbalcones@emtel.net.com; Carrera 7 No 2-75; s/d/apt COP$53,000/75,000/111,100; 🖳) Climb 200-year-old stone stairs to your room in this 18th-century abode. In the lobby, MC Escher sketches hang next a case of ancient pottery and plush leather furniture. Rooms are spacious and have a TV, plus free wi-fi. It also has an apartment with a small kitchen for rent.

Hotel La Plazuela (☎ 824 1084; hotellaplazuela@hotmail.com; Calle 5 No 8-13; s/d/tr/q incl breakfast COP$165,000/230,000/294,000/359,000) In a beautiful, white-washed mansion complete with a lovely arcaded courtyard, this small but classy hotel was fully refurbished after the 1983 quake, and still has much of the original, antique furniture. Ask for a room facing one of the interior courtyards, they are quieter.

Hotel Dann Monasterio (☎ 824 2191; www.hotelesdann.com; Calle 4 No 10-14; s/d/tr incl breakfast COP$230,000/290,000/385,000, ste incl breakfast COP$340,000-780,000; Ⓟ 🍴 🖳 🐾) This Franciscan monastery-turned-hotel offers large, elegantly appointed rooms around a vast, arcaded courtyard. There's a pool in the back garden. Prices include a free round of golf at the local *club campestre*.

Eating

A local specialty is *empanada de pipián*, empanadas served with a spicy satay-style peanut sauce. Be sure to try a *champú* or *lulada* on the main square.

Restaurante Vegetariano Naturaleza y Vida (☎ 822 1118; Carrera 8 No 7-19; mains COP$2800; 🕓 7am-8pm Mon-Sat) This nothing-special veggie restaurant will do if you're in a bind. Sometimes serves veggie burgers.

La Cave (☎ 316 753 7670; Calle 4 No 2-07; mains COP$7000-18,000; 🕓 breakfast, lunch & dinner Mon-Fri, breakfast & lunch Sat & Sun) This French restaurant has French food and service to match (that is, the food is good, the service can be a little snooty). It does awesome sandwiches, such as chicken *cordon bleu* or pork with raisins, and also serves pasta, steak and savory crepes.

La Pizzarra (☎ 831 1313; Carrera 13 No 6-17B, Valencia; pizza COP$15,000-20,000; 🕓 3pm-11pm) Cartoons with pizza punchlines adorn the walls of this top-notch pizza parlor. Located just outside the colonial center, the low prices represent great value. Try gourmet options such as chicken, olives and sun-dried tomatoes. Delivery is an extra COP$1000.

La Cosecha (☎ 821 5628; cnr Carrera 11 & Calle 3N; mains COP$15,000-23,000; 🕓 noon-11pm) This reliable grill restaurant does great beef and chicken dishes on an open-air grill, and has Club Colombia on tap.

Lonchería La Viña (☎ 824 0602; Calle 4 No 7-79; 🕓 9am-midnight) The sister restaurant to La Cosecha. Serves the same menu but with far less atmosphere.

Restaurante Italiano (☎ 824 0607; Calle 4 No 8-83; mains COP$7500-35,000; 🕓 breakfast, lunch & dinner) Swing open the saloon doors of this Swiss-owned Italian joint and you'll find great pizza and pasta, and a decent wine list. If the prices put you off, go for the set meal (COP$7500), one of the best we've had in Colombia.

ourpick El Quijote (☎ 823 4104; Calle 10N No 8-14; mains COP$12,000-25,000; 🕓 lunch & dinner) On the highway outside of town is the best restaurant in Popayán. Quijote does great grilled meat, fantastic salads and has live guitar music on the weekend. The huge outdoor patio faces a small park. Well worth the short taxi ride.

Los Quingos de Belén (☎ 822 1256; www.losquingos .com; Calle 5 No 0-13; mains COP$15,000-22,000) This is the place to come for typical regional special- ties, including *bandeja paísa* (platter of sau- sage, beans, egg, rice and *arepa*) and, on the weekends, *sancocho* and *ajiaco*. There's salsa on the stereo, a breezy outdoor dining area to relax on, and cocktails and pizza.

Drinking

CAFES

There are numerous cafes in the center popu- lar with local students. Check out **Kaldivia Café** (☎ 820 5334; Calle 5 No 5-63; ⏰ 8:30am-8:30pm Mon-Sat), which roasts its own coffee and does great iced coffee drinks. **Madeira** (☎ 839 4192; cnr Calle 3 & Carrera 5; ⏰ 9am-8:30pm Mon-Fri, 2-8:30pm Sat) hosts live music on Saturday and serves coffee in tiny earthenware cups.

BARS

Most of Popayán's nightlife clusters outside of town on the highway. Be sure to check out **CC Campanario** (www.campanariopopayan.com; Carrera 9 No 24AN-21; ⏰ 9am-1am). This monster new shop- ping mall has a huge drinking hall and is a cas- ual place to meet people in the early evening. There's also a gourmet food court nearby.

Entertainment

In the center, **El Sotareño** (☎ 824 1564; Carrera 6 No 8-05; ⏰ 4pm-3am Mon-Sat) is a 40-year-old classic, and plays tango, bolero and *ranchera* (trad- itional music of Mexico) on scratched old vinyls. For salsa, try **Bar La Iguana** (☎ 316 281 0576; Calle 4 No 9-67; ⏰ 4pm-3am Mon-Sat), which cranks the volume on weekends and shows videos on a large projection screen. For a taste of Ecuador, **Peña Bar Killa Raymi** (☎ 822 0603; Calle 6 No 9-51; ⏰ 5pm-3am Wed-Sat) hosts live, amplified panpipe musicians, and has a great atmosphere.

Late night, your discos of choice are **Millenio** (☎ 829 6734; www.millenio.com.co; Autopista Norte; cover COP$10,000; ⏰ 9pm-3am Fri & Sat), which plays techno in a warehouselike space, and **Palo Santo** (☎ 314 623 3690; Autopista Norte; cover $10,000 consumible; ⏰ 7pm-3am Thu-Sat), where the crowd dances on table tops to Colombian crossover. Both are COP$7000, 15-minute taxi rides from the center.

Getting There & Away

AIR

Aeropuerto Guillermo León Valencia is right behind the bus terminal, 1km north of the city center. Avianca, Satena and Aires fly to Bogotá. Satena also flies to Guapí.

BUS

The bus terminal is 1km north of the city center. There are frequent services to Cali by both bus (COP$12,000, three hours) and minibus (COP$20,000, two hours). There are several daily buses direct to Armenia (COP$42,000, seven hours).

There are three morning buses to San Agustín (COP$18,000, five hours). The road is being paved, so expect this travel time to shorten. There are also a couple of buses to Tierradentro (COP$18,000, five hours).

There are hourly buses to Pasto (COP$30,000, six hours). The road from Popayán to the Ecuadorean border is one of the few major routes in Colombia you should not travel after dark, not because of guerrilla activity but rather late-night bandits.

COCONUCO

There are two thermal springs near the town of Coconuco, south of Popayán on the road to San Agustín. On weekends they are elbow- to-elbow kids and rum-soaked parents; during the week they are empty, and you'll likely be the only guest.

On weekends and evenings people come to party while loud music blares at 24-hour **Agua Hirviendo** (☎ 314 618 4178; admission COP$4000; ⏰ 24hr). You read that right, a 24-hour ther- mal springs. Several cabins rent rooms nearby (ahem, both by the hour and over- night), and adjacent restaurants serve meals until late, including breakfast. There are two large thermal pools and waterslides for the kids, all set amid rolling green hills, at an altitude of 1800m.

The water is not nearly as piping hot as Agua Hirviendo, but **Termales Aguatibia** (☎ 824 1161, 315 578 6111; termaguatibia@yahoo.es; admission COP$5000; ⏰ 8am-7pm) is a more family-oriented spa and has a lot less concrete. Set at an altitude of 2560m amid spectacular green scenery, the restaurant has great views of the countryside and serves budget meals (under COP$10,000). There are three thermal pools, a thermal mud springs and a small thermal lake – you can rent inflatable rafts (COP$4000 per hour). There are several short walks nearby, and you can also rent horses (COP$4000 per hour). A fourth pool was under construction at the time of our visit.

PARQUE NACIONAL NATURAL (PNN) PURACÉ

Forty-five kilometers east of Popayán along the unpaved road to La Plata lies this 83,000-hectare **national park** (☎ 823 1279, in Popayán 823 1212; admission Colombians/foreigners COP$6000/15,000; 🕑 8am-6pm). It's the only place in Colombia you can see condors. Three of the great vultures have been reintroduced to the park, and the park wardens will tempt them down with food so you can see them up close.

The visitors center (3350m) rents unheated **cabins** (campsite per person COP$6000, r per person Colombian/foreigner COP$20,000/26,000) and serves budget meals; there's no hot water, but some cabins have working fireplaces.

In good weather you can summit **Volcán Puracé** (4750m). It's about five hours up and three hours down along a well-signposted trail, although because of the difficulty of the climb a guide is recommended – ask at the visitors center. The best time to climb is December and January; the weather from June to August can be foul. Consider spending the night before in a cabin to get an early start to the day.

To get here, take any La Plata–bound bus to the **Cruce de la Mina** (COP$8000, 1¼ hours). The schedule changes frequently, but there is usually a bus at 4:30am and at 10am. From here it's a 1.5km walk uphill to the **Cruce de Pilimbalá**. Turn left for the visitors center (1km) or go straight to visit the **sulfur mine** (1.5km) – its purples and greens are like something out of a science-fiction novel, with the volcanic crater towering above. You can go 200m into the mine tunnel to a shrine to the Virgin Mary.

About 8km past the Cruce de la Mina are the **Termales de San Juan** (3200m), which bubble up amid an otherworldly *páramo* setting – spectacular. Unlike Coconuco (p253), these thermals aren't for bathing. It's a 1.1km-walk from the highway along a well-marked path. There you'll find a ranger station (often unoccupied) with bathrooms and a small shack selling hot drinks and meals.

The last bus back to Popayán passes the Cruce de la Mina at 5pm. As public transport is sketchy, this can be a difficult day trip. If you've got the cash, consider hiring a taxi for the day (COP$140,000). Be sure to bring a copy of your passport for the military checkpoint in the town of Puracé.

There is hourly transport from Popayán to Coconuco (COP$3000, one hour, 31km) during the week, more on the weekends. From here jeeps depart for Agua Hirviendo (COP$1000) or Termales Aguatibia (COP$3000) when full (eight people), or take a moto-taxi (COP$3000).

SILVIA
☎ 2 / pop 5000 / elev 2647m

A picturesque mountain town 53km northeast of Popayán, Silvia is the center of the Guambiano region. The Guambiano people don't live in Silvia itself, but in the small mountain villages of Pueblito, La Campana, Guambia and Caciques. The whole community numbers about 12,000.

The Guambiano are considered one of the most traditional indigenous groups in Colombia. They speak their own language, dress traditionally and still use rudimentary farming techniques. They're also excellent weavers.

On Tuesday, market day, they come to Silvia to sell their fruit, vegetables and handicrafts. This is the best time to visit the town. Almost all the Guambiano come in traditional dress; men in blue skirts with a pink fringe and bowler hats, the women in hand-woven garments and beaded necklaces, busily spinning wool. They come in *chivas* and tend to congregate around the main plaza. They don't like cameras, and will get aggressive if you take their picture.

The market begins at dawn and goes until the early afternoon. It is not a tourist market – fruit and vegetables, raw meat, discount clothing and shoes dominate – but you may find a poncho or sweater that takes your fancy.

From the main plaza, walk uphill to the church for 360-degree views of the surrounding countryside (also handy for getting great shots of the market if you have a telephoto lens).

Silvia attracts weekend tourists from Cali looking to cool off, and there are numerous hotels in town if you decide to stay, plus one disco.

Buses depart Popayán roughly every hour (COP$5000, 1½ hours), with extra early morning services on Tuesdays.

SAN AGUSTÍN
☎ 8 / pop 30,000 / elev 1695m

Five thousand years ago, two primitive cultures lived in the adjacent river valleys of the Magdalena and the Cauca. Divided by uncrossable peaks, the rivers were their highways, and here, near San Agustín, within several days march of each other, lie the headwaters of both rivers. It is here that those two civilizations met to trade, to worship, and to bury their dead.

The volcanic rocks thrown great distances by the now-extinct nearby volcanoes proved irresistible to the local sculptors, who made up for their lack of skill with great enthusiasm – more than 500 life-sized statues scatter the green hills surrounding San Agustín. Many of them are anthropomorphic figures, some realistic, others resemble masked monsters. Others depict sacred animals such as the eagle, jaguar and frog. The largest is 7m high. Archeologists have also uncovered a great deal of pottery, but very little in the way of gold – unlike the Tayrona on the Caribbean coast, there was no gold here to mine.

Little else is known about the peoples of San Agustín. They didn't have a written language and had disappeared many centuries before the Europeans arrived on the scene.

Only keen archaeology buffs will derive much delight from the statues themselves. The ancient sculptors never achieved a high level of sophistication; don't expect King Tut's tomb. Nor is the town of San Agustín particularly interesting – it is small and ugly and full of opportunists trying to rip you off.

The real reason to come to San Agustín is the spectacular scenery that surrounds the town, and to enjoy hiking and horseback riding in the region, with the archaeology as a side dish, not the main course. Two tour operators also offer white-water rafting on the nearby Río Magdalena. Connected by a good road to Bogotá and served by fast overnight buses, San Agustín attracts the Colombian dreadlocked crowd from Bogotá, attracted by the, err, ubiquitous local weed.

Orientation
The statues and tombs are scattered in groups over a wide area on both sides of the gorge formed by the upper Río Magdalena. The most important sight is the Parque Arqueológico, which boasts the largest number of statues and a museum. The second most important is the Alto de los Ídolos, 4km southwest of San José de Isnos on the other side of Río Magdalena from San Agustín town. You buy one admission ticket (COP$7000), which is valid for two consecutive days for entry to both parks. There's no admission fee to other archeological sites.

The town of San Agustín centers around two main plazas, Plaza de Bolívar near the church and Plaza Civica near the police station.

Information
There are numerous tour agencies masquerading as the 'official tourist office.' The real **tourist office** (☎ 837 3062, ext 15; adarmesirma@hotmail.com; cnr Calle 3 & Carrera 12; ☯ 8am-noon & 2-5pm Mon-Fri) is in the *alcaldía* (town hall) building and is staffed by a member of the tourist police; look for the sign, in English, that says 'Government Tourist Office.' The government sets the official prices for all tours in town. Drop by and ask for a copy of the current list.
Banagrario (cnr Carrera 13 & Calle 4) Bank.
Enter.net (☎ 837 3832, 314 451 5261; Carrera 10 No 3-46; per hr COP$1500; ☯ 7am-11pm) A dozen computers.
Hospital Arsenio Repizo Vanegas (☎ 837 3565; Calle 3 No 2-51)
Internet Galería Cafe (☎ 311 885 7589; Calle 3 No 12-16; per hr COP$1300; ☯ 8am-10pm) Internet access right across from the government tourist office. Sometimes hosts live music events, and sells beer.
MegaRed (Calle 3 No 12-73) Internet cafe.
Tourist police (☎ 837 3606; Carrera 3 No 11-56)

Sights
You'll need three days to see all the archaeological sights – one day for the archaeological park; one day on horseback to El Tablón, La Chaquira, La Pelota and El Purutal (four hours); and one day for a jeep tour to El Estrecho, Alto de los Ídolos, Alto de las Piedras, Salto de Bordones and Salto de Mortiño (six hours).

The going rate for a guide is around COP$30,000 per day, and COP$40,000 for an English-speaking guide. Horses rent for around COP$20,000 per half-day, plus you'll be expected to pay for the guide's horse (thus making it cheaper to go in a group). Jeep tours go for around COP$150,000 per day (maximum five people).

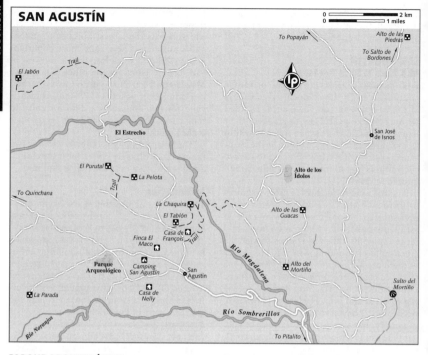

SAN AGUSTÍN

0 _____ 2 km
0 _____ 1 miles

PARQUE ARQUEOLÓGICO

The 78-hectare **archeological park** (admission COP$7000; ⏰ 8am-4pm) is 2.5km west of the town of San Agustín. There are in total about 130 statues in the park, either found *in situ* or collected from other areas, including some of the best examples of San Agustín statuary. Plan on spending around three hours in the park. Guides congregate in the museum's outdoor cafe, but you don't really need one.

At the entrance to the park is the **Museo Arqueológico** (⏰ 8am-5pm Tue-Sun), which features smaller statues, pottery, utensils, jewelry and other objects, along with interesting background information about the San Agustín culture.

Besides the various clusters of statues (called *mesitas*) is the **Fuente de Lavapatas**. Carved in the rocky bed of the stream, it is a complex labyrinth of ducts and small, terraced pools decorated with images of serpents, lizards and human figures. Archeologists believe the baths were used for ritual ablutions and the worship of aquatic deities.

From here, the path winds uphill to the **Alto de Lavapatas**, the oldest archeological site in

San Agustín. You'll find a few tombs guarded by statues, and get a panoramic view over the surrounding countryside.

ALTO DE LOS ÍDOLOS

Located across the Río Magdalena 4km southwest of San José de Isnos (a clutch of houses 26km from the town of San Agustín), this is the second-most important **archeological park** (admission COP$7000; ⏰ 8am-4pm) in the region. It's home to the largest statue (7m) in the San Agustín area.

ALTO DE LAS PIEDRAS

This site is 7km north of Isnos and has tombs lined with stone slabs painted red, black and yellow. One of the most famous statues, known as Doble Yo, is here; look carefully as there are actually four figures carved in this statue. You'll also find an intriguing statue of a female figure in an advanced state of pregnancy.

EL TABLÓN, LA CHAQUIRA, LA PELOTA & EL PURUTAL

These four sites are relatively close to each other, so they can be seen in one trip. Most people visit as part of a horseback-riding tour. Don't miss La Chaquira with divinities carved into the mountain face and overlooking the stunning gorge of the Río Magdalena.

LAGUNA DEL MAGDALENA

You can trek on horseback to the birthplace of the Río Magdalena (3327m), 60km from San Agustín. The region was historically infested by guerrillas but is now considered safe. It's not a common trip. Tatacoa Aventura (right) and Finca El Maco (right) may be able to organize it for you. Expect to pay around COP$150,000 per person for the trek. The driest times of the year to visit are August and September, and January and February.

OTHER ATTRACTIONS

There are several more archeological sites to see if you are not in a hurry, including **La Parada**, **Quinchana**, **El Jabón**, **Naranjos** and **Quebradillas**.

Apart from its archeological wealth, the region is also noted for its natural beauty, and features two spectacular waterfalls, **Salto de Bordones** and **Salto de Mortiño**. It's also worth a walk or ride to **El Estrecho**, where the Río Magdalena passes through 2.2m narrows. All these sights are accessible by road.

Nearby farmers come to buy and sell at San Agustín's **market**, held on Monday. It's a raucous scene with few tourists. Besides fruit, vegetables and *panela* (dried sugarcane juice) you'll find clothing, shoes and bags at budget prices. If you miss the Monday market, head for **La Galería** (cnr Calle 3 & Carrera 11; ⏱ 5am-4pm). It's open the rest of the week, but is more subdued.

Activities

Many tour operators offer horseback-riding activities in the region. Your accommodations venue will most likely also have great information. Ask at the operators and hotels listed for further details.

WHITE-WATER RAFTING

Two companies offer rafting on the Río Magdalena. They offer similar trips at similar prices. There are half-day tours (COP$40,000 per person) with rapids Class II to IV for novices, and full-day, Class V tours (COP$100,000 to COP$120,000) for experienced pros. Minimum four people per group.

The French owner of **Magdalena Rafting** (☎ 311 271 5333; www.magdalenarafting.com) has 20 years experience guiding in Europe. He offers guide services in English, French and Spanish, and prices include wetsuit rental. He can also organize two- to three-day rafting and kayaking tours for the hard-core types.

Colombian-owned **Tatacoa Aventura** (☎ 877 9422, 311 492 6571; www.tatacoaventura.com) offers a similar service. Guides speak Spanish only, and it doesn't have wetsuits. It can also organize horseback-riding trips in the region, and other activities.

Sleeping

Try to make decisions about where to stay and eat independent of bus and taxi drivers, tour operators and locals, who are frequently known to make suggestions to travelers in return for kickbacks with some local owners. Travelers are then charged inflated prices. You'll enjoy your time in San Agustín more if you stay outside the center of town.

ourpick **Finca El Maco** (☎ 837 3437, 311 271 4802; www.elmaco.ch; campsite per person COP$7000, hammock COP$10,000, dm COP$14,000, r per person COP$18,000-20,000; P 🖥) Set 1km outside of town in the countryside, this Swiss-owned hostel is the budget choice in San Agustín. There are a variety of cabins set amid a pretty garden. The on-site restaurant serves homemade organic yoghurt and cheese, wholemeal bread, green salads, and an excellent curry. The owner runs a small tour company, and can organize trips in the region. Take the road to the Parque Archaeológico and turn right at the Hotel Yalconia. From here it's a 400m-walk uphill, past the public swimming pool.

Casa de François (☎ 314 358 2930; www.lacasade francois.com; dm/s/d COP$14,000/16,000/32,000) Set in a garden on a hill just above town and with views of the hills, this funky *hostal* is built principally of glass bottles embedded in concrete. Accommodations are basic but clean, and you can use the kitchen.

Finca El Cielo (☎ 313 493 7446; www.fincaelcielo.com; Via al Estrecho; r per person COP$40,000) A few hundred meters after the Anacaona is this pretty posada. Built of *guadua* and with tremendous views out over the surrounding, misty green hills, it gets far few visitors than it deserves. The friendly owner and his wife live on the ground floor and prepare good home-cooked meals with advance notice.

Hacienda Anacaona (☎ 837 9390; www.anacaona -colombia.com; Via al Estrecho; r per person COP$130,000-180,000) This long-established colonial-style hotel caters principally to Colombians. During the week prices drop to as low as COP$25,000 per person. Frequent *colectivos* from town can drop you here (COP$1200). The hotel is set amid a well-maintained garden and has good views.

There are numerous budget hotels in the center of town. Your best bet is **Residencias El Jardín** (☎ 837 3455; www.hosteltrail.com/eljardin; Carrera 11 No 4-10; r per person COP$15,000-18,000), or try the **Hotel Colonial** (☎ 837 3159; Calle 3 No 11-25; r per person $10,000-15,000).

Eating

Surabhi (☎ 837 3336; Calle 5 No 1409; set meal COP$4000; ☺ 8am-8pm) Run by a former hotel chef, this small restaurant produces a very good Colombian set meal. The juices are excellent, and there's actually something resembling a salad on your plate. Great value.

Restaurante Brahama (☎ 301 417 1077; Calle 5 No 15-11; set meal COP$4000; ☺ 8am-9pm) The place to come if you're in dire need of a vegetarian meal. The thick chocolate pancakes are reportedly excellent, too.

our pick Donde Richard (☎ 312 432 6399; Via al Parque Arqueológico; mains COP$14,000-16,000; ☺ noon-6pm Mon-Fri, to 8pm Sat & Sun) This grill restaurant on the road to the Parque Arqueológico does the best food in town. The *asado huilense*, the local specialty of slow-cooked, marinated pork, is not to be missed. A great spot for lunch on the way back from the park.

Pizza Manía (☎ 311 271 4788; Carrera 13 No 3-43; pizzas COP$14,000-24,000, lasagna COP$6500; ☺ 5-10pm Wed-Mon) Owned by an expat German woman, this small shopfront sells great, freshly made pizza. She even makes her own chorizo, and on weekends, lasagna from scratch.

El Fogón (☎ 837 3431; Calle 5 No 14-30; ☺ lunch & dinner) The set menu at lunch time is good value (COP$4000) but dinner (COP$14,000) is overpriced. El Fogón also serves as a central landmark in the town.

Drinking

Bars are clustered in town near the police station. Also worth a look are **El Faro** (☎ 320 247 2051, 311 424 7711; Carrera 13 No 6-50; ☺ 4pm-late Wed-Mon), a groovy small bar four blocks up the hill from the plaza that sometimes hosts live music, and **Territorio Libre** (☎ 314 324 1853; Calle 5 No 14-27 ☺ 8pm-2:30am Fri & Sat), a rocking disco opposite El Fogón – in the chilly wee hours it lights a small bonfire out back.

The small cultural center **Fundación Kafka** (☎ 837 3925, 320 330 8923; glenamasabel@yahoo.es; Calle 3 No 12-22; ☺ 9am-10pm) is dedicated to all things San Agustín, and on weekends often hosts live music or shows classic cinema. Sells coffee, beer and books about the region's history.

Getting There & Away

Bus offices are on the corner of Calle 3 and Carrera 11 (known as Cuatro Vientos). There are regular minibuses to Neiva (COP$20,000, four hours) and several buses day and night to Bogotá (COP$45,000, 12 hours). Not all Pitalito–Popayán buses (COP$20,000, five hours) stop in San Agustín. If you're in a hurry or want to save a few pesos, take a shared taxi 5km to the crossroads, or *cruce* in Spanish (COP$2000, 10 minutes). Arriving from Popayán, buses with few passengers will drop you here and pay your taxi fare to San Agustín. Be aware that some hotel owners may bribe taxi drivers to bring you directly to their hotel.

For Tierradentro, go to Pitalito (COP$5000, 45 minutes) and change for La Plata (COP$20,000, 2½ hours), where you can get a bus to San Andrés (COP$15,000, 2½ hours). Alternately, from Pitalito take any Neiva-bound bus to Garzón (COP$10,000, one hour) and take any of the more frequent shared taxis to La Plata (COP$10,000, 1½ hours). From La Plata there are services several times a day to Tierradentro (COP$10,000, 2½ hours). Some buses may drop you at the crossroads. From here it's a 20-minute walk uphill to the Tierradentro museums and hotels.

Getting Around

Half a dozen new taxis now service San Agustín. They can take you around town and, more importantly, to your lodging outside of town. The fixed rates are posted inside the cab, but after dark the cabbies have been known to try to overcharge foreigners.

A bus runs the 2km to the park every 15 minutes (COP$800) from the corner of Calle 5 and Carrera 14. *Chivas* and vans ply the nearby country roads, especially from Saturday to Monday. They can take you to and from your hotel for around COP$1000.

TIERRADENTRO

☎ 2 / elev 1750m

Tierradentro is the second most important archaeological site in Colombia. Like San Agustín, the real attraction here is the astonishing beauty of the surrounding hills. Where San Agustín is noted for its statuary, Tierradentro is remarkable for its elaborate underground tombs. So far, archeologists have discovered about 100 of these unusual funeral temples, the only examples of their kind in the Americas. There is a fabulous half-day walk you can do that takes in all the major tomb sites amid gorgeous mountain scenery.

Orientation & Information

Scattered across the hills around the town of San Andrés de Pisimbalá, Tierradentro consists of five separate sites, four with tombs and one with above-ground statuary, plus two adjacent museums. The hotels are adjacent to the museums, a 25-minute walk from San Andrés. Some of the tombs have electric lighting, but it isn't always functioning; bring a flashlight (torch).

There is no tourist office, bank or internet service near Tierradentro. Several of the hotels offer Comcel cell-phone minutes.

Sights

Measuring 2m to 7m in diameter, the tombs are scooped out of the soft volcanic rock that forms the region's undulating hillsides. They vary widely in depth; some are just below ground level, while others are as deep as 9m. The domed ceilings of the largest tombs are supported by massive pillars. Many are painted with red and black geometric motifs on white backgrounds. In addition, figures are carved into the columns and walls of many chambers.

Little is known about the people who built the tombs and the statues. Most likely they were of different cultures, and the people who scooped out the tombs preceded those who carved the statues. Some researchers place the 'tomb' civilization somewhere between the 7th and 9th centuries AD, while the 'statue' culture appears to be related to the later phase of San Agustín development, which is estimated to have taken place some 500 years later.

Admission to the **archaeological park** (8am-4pm), museums and the tombs costs COP$7000 and is valid for two days.

BURIAL SITES & STATUES

You can visit all the burial sites in Tierradentro on a four-hour, 14km walk. The walk takes you through some spectacular scenery, and it's well worth doing the entire loop. You can go either clockwise or counterclockwise. If you do it clockwise, you can't start until 8am, when the guards arrive to unlock the tomb sites, but you get to walk downhill from Aguacate. On the other hand, you can start earlier by walking it in reverse, because the tombs aren't locked at Aguacate, but you have a stiffer uphill climb at the beginning of the hike.

Going counterclockwise, a 20-minute walk uphill from the museums lies **Segovia**, the most important burial site. There are 28 tombs here, some with well-preserved decorations. Twelve of the tombs have electric lighting, which works only sporadically. The tombs are open 8am to 4pm.

A 15-minute walk uphill from Segovia brings you to **El Duende**, where there are four tombs, though their decoration hasn't been preserved. From here it's a 25-minute walk along the highway to **El Tablón**, which has nine crude, weather-worn stone statues, similar to those of San Agustín (p255), excavated in the area and now thrown together under a single roof. The better preserved statues can be seen in the Museo Arqueológico. If you're walking, be aware the site is poorly signposted; look up and to the left until you see the faded blue sign. You can also get to El Tablón from the main San Andrés road, which is well-signposted but muddy.

Continue into town. Next to the restaurant La Portada you'll find the path to **Alto de San Andrés**, with four tombs; two have remarkably well-preserved paintings. Another tomb is closed to due damage from a 1994 earthquake. Another has caved in completely.

El Aguacate is the most remote burial site, but has the best views. From Alto de San Andres it's a 1½-hour walk, then downhill another 1½ hours to the museum. There are a few dozen tombs, but most have been destroyed by *guaqueros* (tomb raiders). Only a few vaults still bear the remains of the original decoration.

MUSEUMS

It makes sense to visit the tombs in the morning, before the heat of the day unfolds. Finish your day at the two museums in the afternoon.

The **Museo Arqueológico** contains pottery urns used to keep the ashes of the tribal elders. Some of the urns are decorated with dotted patterns and, in some cases, with representations of

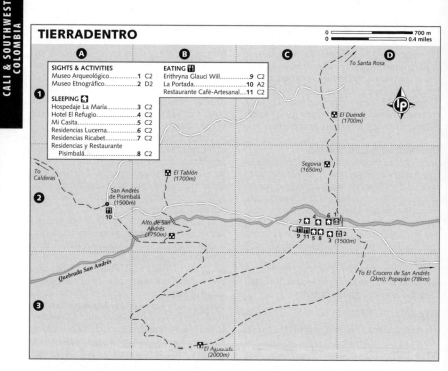

TIERRADENTRO

SIGHTS & ACTIVITIES
Museo Arqueológico...............1 C2
Museo Etnográfico.................2 D2

SLEEPING
Hospedaje La María................3 C2
Hotel El Refugio......................4 C2
Mi Casita...............................5 C2
Residencias Lucerna................6 C2
Residencias Ricabet................7 C2
Residencias y Restaurante
  Pisimbalá............................8 C2

EATING
Erithryna Glauci Will................9 C2
La Portada............................10 A2
Restaurante Café-Artesanal....11 C2

animals. There are also miniature models of
what the tombs may have looked like when
they were freshly painted.

The **Museo Etnográfico** has utensils and artifacts of the Páez people, and exhibits from
colonial times, including a *trapiche* (sugarcane
grinder), *bodoqueras* (blow-dart guns) and
traditional indigenous clothing.

SAN ANDRÉS DE PISIMBALÁ
A 25-minute walk uphill from the museums
is this little town. There's one good restaurant and a couple of *tiendas* (shops) selling
snacks and drinks. The town is mildly famous
for its thatched, white adobe **church**, which is
often locked. A small *artesanías* shop sells
miniature replicas of the church. There's no
internet or ATM.

Sleeping
Half-a-dozen basic lodgings are clustered
within the 500m stretch uphill of the museum. All charge COP$8000 to COP$15,000
for a room. One of the best budget options
is **Residencias y Restaurante Pisimbalá** (☎ 311 612
4145), which has five rooms and also serves

meals. The on-site *tienda* sells a locally made
coca-flavored wine.

Other options include **Hospedaje La María**
(☎ 312 803 8947), **Residencias Lucerna**, which has a
kitchen you can use, **Residencias Ricabet** (☎ 312
279 9751, 312 795 4636), further uphill with a park
bench outside where you can wait for the
morning bus, and **Mi Casita** (☎ 312 764 1333).

The motel-like **Hotel El Refugio** has long been
closed, but you can use the swimming pool for
COP$3000. Ask around for the *vigilante* who
guards the place.

There are no hotels in San Andrés de
Pisimbalá.

Eating & Drinking
Most of the hotels listed above serve budget
meals. Also worth noting are **Erithryna Glauci
Will** (☎ 312 450 2895), the bar opposite Ricabet.
The second-floor deck has great views, and
if there are five or more of you, you can do a
barbecue. The *tienda* downstairs sells snacks
and drinks.

A couple of doors down is **Restaurante Café-
Artesanal** (☎ 311 337 0573; www.tierradentro-pisimbala
.blogspot.com) where you can get good budget

meals. It also sells hand-crocheted necklaces and earrings, and *chicha de caña* (fermented sugarcane juice), a tasty beverage. Look for the orange flowering vine that creeps around the verandah, or ask around town for the cafe run by the two dwarfs. Locals will point you in the right direction.

The only restaurant in San Andrés, **La Portada** (☎ 825 2927, 311 601 7884; set meal COP$4500) can have lunch ready if you call in advance. Be sure to try the owner's homemade ice cream. You can buy them here or at Erithryna Glauci Will. They are excellent. Also rents horses for COP$4000 per hour.

Getting There & Away

Most buses pass the museums and hotels on a side trip to San Andrés, although some stop only at El Crucero de San Andrés, a 20-minute walk downhill from the museums. There are three to four services a day to Popayán (COP$17,000, four hours), and to La Plata (COP$10,000, 2½ hours), where you can change for San Agustín or Bogotá. For either destination it's a good idea to get an early start on the day, as both are long journeys on rough roads.

NARIÑO

Welcome to Ecuador – almost. Nariño is Colombia's most southwesterly department, and the Ecuadorean influence here is strong.

The Andes here loom high and forbidding on their southerly march. The 'volcano alley' that runs the length of Ecuador begins here – pleasant Pasto, the departmental capital, sits a mere 8km from an active volcano covered in patchwork farmland.

Most people visit the region only to cross the border, but it's worth spending a few days here. Pasto is good for a weekend, Laguna de la Cocha is unmissable, and the towering Santuario de Las Lajas near Ipiales is an astonishing sight to behold.

PASTO

☎ 2 / pop 385,000 / elev 2551m

Just two hours from Ecuador, Pasto is the capital of the department and the logical jumping-off point for the border. It's also a good base for visiting Laguna de la Cocha, Laguna Verde and Volcán Galeras.

The rest of Colombia makes fun of Pasto – *pastuso* jokes are like old-time Polack jokes.

The local fondness for *cuy* (guinea pig) is also mocked. While it's true the town doesn't feel very Colombian, it doesn't feel very Ecuadorean either, and is worth a visit if only to experience this unique mélange.

The town is built at the foot of Volcán Galeras in the fertile Atriz valley. It has several fine colonial buildings as well as a bustling downtown area. The weather here is cool – so cool, in fact, you'll see *helado de paila* advertised, which is ice cream made fresh in a copper tub sitting on a platform of ice.

The town was founded by Lorenzo de Aldana in 1537 and was an important cultural and religious center in colonial and republican times. Earthquakes have unfortunately destroyed much of its historic character; a handful of churches and palaces have been rebuilt in the original style. The city is also known for *barniz de Pasto,* a processed vegetable resin used to decorate wooden objects in colorful patterns.

Information

Most of the major banks are around Plaza de Nariño.

Cambios Colombia (☎ 723 8044; CC Belalcázar) On the 2nd floor. Irregular hours.

Ciber C@fe PC Rent (☎ 723 8298; Calle 18A No 25-36; per hr COP$1600; ☽ 8am-9pm Mon-Fri, 9am-8pm Sat, 2-6pm Sun) Internet access.

Shirakaba Money Exchange (☎ 723 9890; Calle 18 No 24-73) Yellow building on Plaza de Nariño.

Tourist office (Oficina Departamental de Turismo de Nariño; ☎ 723 4962; www.emprendecaminoconocea narino.com; Calle 18 No 25-25) Just off Plaza de Nariño. Run by knowledgeable staff during the week and tourist police on the weekend.

Sights & Activities

On Pasto's main square, **Iglesia de San Juan Bautista** dates from the city's first days; it was rebuilt in the mid-17th century. Grand outside and gold-encrusted inside, it is a fine example of colonial baroque architecture.

For insight into the pre-Columbian cultures of Nariño, check out the **Museo del Oro** (☎ 721 9108; Calle 19 No 21-27; admission free; ☽ 8:30am-noon & 2-6pm Mon-Fri), which has a small but interesting collection of indigenous gold and pottery.

The **Museo Taminango de Artes y Tradiciones** (☎ 723 5539; Calle 13 No 27-67; admission COP$1000; ☽ 8am-noon & 2-6pm Mon-Fri, 9am-1pm Sat) has a hodgepodge of antiques but is worth seeing

CALI & SOUTHWEST
COLOMBIA

since it's housed in a meticulously restored *casona* (large house) from 1623, reputedly the oldest surviving house in town.

Sleeping

Koala Inn (☎ 722 1101; Calle 18 No 22-37; s/d COP$20,000/30,000, without bathroom COP$14,000/25,000) Founded in 1992 by an Australian, this basic cheapie has been in Colombian hands for many years. The hot water (a necessity in chilly Pasto) is intermittent, the toilets have no seats, the streetside rooms are noisy, the staff can't be relied on for tourist advice, and the hotel uses a floor wax that smells like a chemical factory.

Hotel San Sebastian (☎ 721 8851; Carrera 22 No 15-78; s/d/tr COP$30,000/47,000/64,000) Of the many cheap hotels that cluster in the center, this is the best value. Rooms have hot water and cable TV, and are clean. The hotel is on the third and fourth floor of the building. There's lots of budget competition nearby if it's full.

Hotel El Dorado (☎ 723 3260; hoteleldoradopasto@ hotmail.com; Calle 16A No 23-42, Pasaje Dorado; s COP$85,000-115,000, d COP$110,000-140,000; ⓟ 🖳) Midway down a small, narrow market alley is this quiet midrange option – look for the glass double doors. The lobby vaults high to a glass ceiling, and the four floors have rooms without exterior windows, which makes for a restful slumber. A breezy rooftop lounge has great views of the surrounding hills.

Loft Hotel (☎ 722 6733; www.lofthotelpasto.com; Calle 18 No 22-33; d incl breakfast COP$140,000-195,000, ste incl breakfast COP$168,000-270,000; ⓟ 🖳) This luxurious, minimalist spot has everything you could possibly want, except for a window or a view. Expect plush leather furniture, shiny new wooden floors, and king-size beds. There's even a sauna and day spa to beat the Pasto chill.

Eating

Salón Guadalquivir (☎ 723 9604; Plaza de Nariño; snacks COP$3000-10,000; ⏱ 8am-12:30pm & 2:30-7:30pm Mon-Sat) This cozy cafe serves classic *pastuso* treats, including *quimbilito* (a sweet pastry of raisin, vanilla and sweet corn) and *tamales de añejo* (the Pasto version of *tamales*). The walls are lined with posters from the annual Carnaval de Blancos y Negros (below).

La Merced (☎ 723 8830; Carrera 22 No 17-37; mains COP$6000-50,000; ⏱ 7am-10pm) This big bustling cafeteria is hugely popular, and does everything from hamburgers to lobster. It offers an everchanging roster of daily specials (COP$12,500 to COP$14,000). The streetside bakery sells the obligatory strawberries 'n' cream, plus pizzas from COP$15,000.

Caffeto (☎ 729 2720; www.krkcaffeto.com; Calle 19 No 25-62; mains COP$8000-18,000; ⏱ 8am-9pm Mon-Sat) This fancy-schmancy bakery does gourmet sandwiches, omelettes and salads served on unusual crockery. The cakes are stupendous, and it does enormous ice-cream sundaes and serves real espresso coffee. Enough to satisfy even the most jaded traveler's inner yuppie.

Asadero de Cuyes Pinzon (☎ 731 3228; Carrera 40 No 19B-76, Palermo; cuy COP$25,000; ⏱ 9am-10pm Mon-Sat, 9:30am-3pm Sun) *Pastusos* get dressed up to eat at this place about 1.5km from the center of town. There's only one thing on the menu: *asado de cuy* (grilled guinea pig). You'll be given plastic gloves so you can rip the grilled rodents apart and share them. One *cuy* is big enough for two. Pasto is the only place in Colombia where *cuy* is mainstream and popular.

Drinking

Pasto has some cozy bars and a couple of decent discos. Numerous drinkeries are located a few blocks north of Plaza de Nariño. Av de Estudiantes has a number of budget restaurants and bars. **Centro Comercial Valle de**

CARNAVAL DE BLANCOS Y NEGROS

Pasto's major event is **Carnaval de Blancos y Negros** (www.carnavaldepasto.org) held on January 5 and 6. Its origins go back to the times of Spanish rule, when slaves were allowed to celebrate on January 5 and their masters showed approval by painting their faces black. On the following day, the slaves painted their faces white.

On these two days the city goes wild, with everybody painting or dusting one another with grease, chalk, talc, flour and any other available substance even vaguely black or white in tone. It's a serious affair – wear the worst clothes you have and buy an *antifaz*, a sort of mask to protect the face, widely sold for this occasion. Asthmatics should not attend – you'll be coughing up talcum powder for days afterwards.

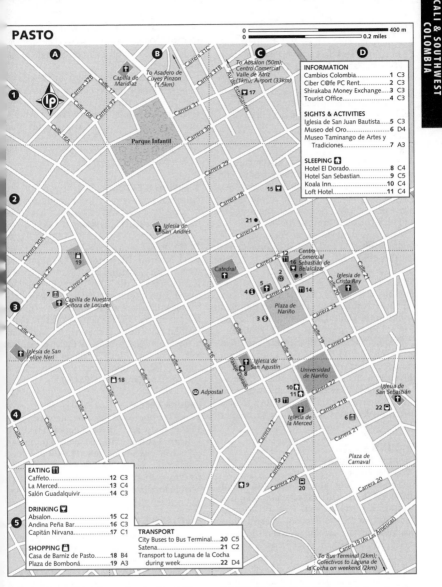

PASTO

INFORMATION
Cambios Colombia....................1 C3
Ciber C@fe PC Rent..............2 C3
Shirakaba Money Exchange.....3 C3
Tourist Office.........................4 C3

SIGHTS & ACTIVITIES
Iglesia de San Juan Bautista.....5 C3
Museo del Oro.......................6 D4
Museo Taminango de Artes y
    Tradiciones.........................7 A3

SLEEPING
Hotel El Dorado.....................8 C4
Hotel San Sebastian...............9 C5
Koala Inn..............................10 C4
Loft Hotel.............................11 C4

EATING
Caffeto................................12 C3
La Merced...........................13 C4
Salón Guadalquivir...............14 C3

DRINKING
Absalon................................15 C2
Andina Peña Bar..................16 C3
Capitán Nirvana...................17 C1

SHOPPING
Casa de Barniz de Pasto........18 B4
Plaza de Bombóná................19 A3

TRANSPORT
City Buses to Bus Terminal.....20 C5
Satena................................21 C2
Transport to Laguna de la Cocha
    during week......................22 D4

Atriz (cnr Carrera 42 & Av Panamericana), about 1km from town, has a number of discos (plus a movie theater).

Two good bars on Calle 20 (along the stretch known as Av de Estudiantes) are **Absalon** (☎ 731 0695; Calle 20 No 31C-23; ☽ 6pm-1am Mon-Sat), a mellow spot that plays Colombian music, and **Capitán Nirvana** (☎ 317 668 3038, 316 865 9699; Calle 20 No 30-56; ☽ 4pm-2am), the place for rock 'n' roll in Pasto (the name is a reference to Metallica).

On the weekends, don't miss the live, amplified Andean panpipe music at **Andina Peña Bar** (☎ 316 690 6933; CC Sebastián de Belalcázar; ☽ 6pm-2am Wed-Sat) . Get here before 10pm if you want a seat.

Shopping

A wide range of *barniz de Pasto* artifacts can be bought at **Casa del Barniz de Pasto** (cnr Carrera 25 & Calle 13). **Plaza de Bombóna** (Calle 14 btwn Carreras 28 & 30; ◷ 7am-7pm Mon-Sat, to 1pm Sun) is a covered market with craft shops that sell bargain leathergoods, plus *lechona* (stuffed pig) if you get the munchies for some roast pork.

Getting There & Away

AIR

The airport is 33km north of the city on the road to Cali. *Colectivos* go there from Calle 18 at Carrera 25 (COP$5000, 45 minutes). Pay the day before your flight at the airline office or at a travel agency, and the *colectivo* will pick you up from your hotel.

Avianca and Satena service Pasto, with daily flights to Bogotá and Cali and connections to other cities.

BUS

The bus terminal is 2km south of the city center. Urban buses go there from different points in the central area, including Carrera 20A at Calle 17, or take a taxi (COP$4000).

Frequent buses, minibuses and *colectivos* go to Ipiales (COP$8000, two hours); sit on the left for better views. Plenty of buses ply the spectacular road to Cali (COP$38,000, nine hours). These buses will drop you off in Popayán in six hours. More than a dozen direct buses depart daily to Bogotá (COP$90,000, 22 hours).

AROUND PASTO

Laguna de la Cocha

☎ 2 / elev 2760m

Set amid rolling green hills, and often shrouded in mist, this spectacular lake is a must-do day trip on your visit to Pasto. At the mouth of the Río Encano, where it empties into the lake, are numerous restaurants serving roast chicken, grilled *cuy*, *sancocho* and of course trout, which is farmed along the shores of the lake.

You can take a boat ride around the lake, stopping at **Isla Corota** (admission COP$1000; ◷ 8am-5pm) along the way. The island is a national park, and at an altitude of 2830m offers a rare glimpse of a well-preserved, evergreen cloud forest. There's a small chapel and a biological research station on the island; a 550m-long boardwalk takes you the length of the island to a *mirador* (lookout) with good views of

the surrounding lake. Boats to the island cost COP$20,000 for 10 to 15 people. The boat will wait for you and take you on a circle of the island on the way back.

Shared taxis to the lake (COP$3500, 45 minutes) leave from the corner of Carrera 21 and Calle 20 (Map p263) in Pasto during the week, and opposite the Al Kosto hardware store (cnr Calle 21 and Carrera 7; off Map p263) on weekends and holidays. Shared taxis seat four people; if you're in a hurry, pay for all four seats (COP$14,000).

SLEEPING & EATING

Numerous hotels cater to romantic couples looking for a weekend away. The most spectacular is the **Hotel Sindamanoy** (☎ 721 8222; www .hotelsindamanoy.com; s/d/tr/ste COP90,000/105,000/115,000/ 125,000; 🅿 ⌨), whose faux–Swiss chalet facade you'll see from Isla Corota. It has impressive views of the island and lake. The overall decor is a flashback to the '70s – rooms have yellow carpet, stucco walls, and fake wood paneling, but many also have working fireplaces. The restaurant (mains COP$14,000 to COP$21,500) is the best place to eat in the area. By boat from the restaurants at the edge of the lake near the Río Encano, it's COP$20,000 return if you're coming just for lunch; from Pasto direct in a taxi you'll pay around COP$15,000.

Laguna Verde

You'll see photos of this emerald green lake all over Pasto. It sits in the crater of the extinct Volcán Azufral (3800m), near Túquerres (3700m), a two-hour journey west of Pasto. Contact the tourist office in Pasto for the latest information on how to get here. You may be able to join an existing tour. Pasto-based

---

VOLCÁN GALERAS

Just 8km from the center of Pasto, Volcán Galeras (4267m) continues to grumble and threaten. Its lower slopes are a patchwork of farms and bright green pastureland. There's a lookout tower at the top, and on a clear day you can see as far as Tumaco (p281) and the Pacific coast.

The trail was officially closed to the public in 2006 due to seismic activity, although you may still be able to climb. Contact the helpful tourist office (p261) in Pasto for the latest update.

guide **Orfa Marina** (☎ 730 4287, 315 511 7464; camino delvientoTE@hotmail.com) sometimes organizes group outings (COP$50,000, minimum 20 people).

IPIALES
☎ 2 / pop 75,000 / elev 2900m

Only 7km from the border with Ecuador, Ipiales is an uninspiring commercial town driven by trade across the frontier. There is little to see or do here, except for the colorful Saturday market, where the campesinos (peasants) from surrounding villages come to buy and sell goods. A short side trip to the Santuario de Las Lajas is the real draw, though the Panamerican from Pasto is also thrilling.

Buses and shared taxis offer regular service from the Ipiales bus station to Rumichaca (COP$1400, 10 minutes).

Information
Comcel (☎ 725 4392; Plaza la Pola; per hr COP$2000; 7am-10pm) Internet access and phone calls; on the main square.
Ecuadorean consulate (☎ 773 2292; Carrera 7 No 14-10; 8:30am-noon Mon-Fri)
HAEV Comunicaciones (☎ 773 3088; Carrera 7 No 15-27; per hr COP$1500; 7am-10pm) Internet access.

Sleeping
There are few good reasons to spend the night in Ipiales. Pasto (p261) is a far nicer city, and those wanting to visit Las Lajas will

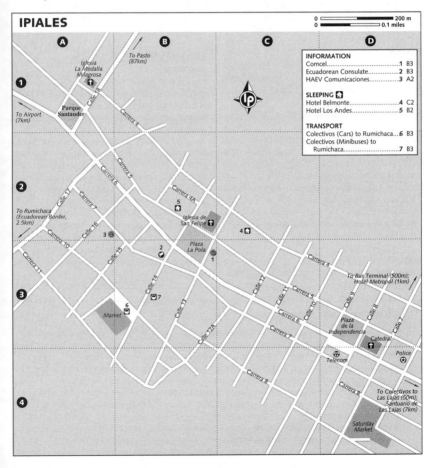

CALI & SOUTHWEST
COLOMBIA

find cheap, decent accommodations right next to the sanctuary (see opposite).

Hotel Belmonte (773 2771; Carrera 4 No 12-111; s/d COP$11,000/18,000) For a long time the backpackers' choice in Ipiales, but we can't figure out why. Think genteel, grandmotherly poverty but with electric shower heads and cable TV.

Hotel Metropól (773 7976; Carrera 2A No 6-10; s/d/tw COP$15,000/20,000/25,000) Just across the street from the main bus station, this concrete-block hotel has musty-smelling rooms with private bathroom. Also used by the hour by amorous local couples. Look for the green sign; it's about 1km from the center of town.

Hotel Los Andes (773 4338; Carrera 5 No 14-44; s/d/tr COP$48,000/68,000/98,000;) The top place in town, Los Andes has 33 rooms around an interior courtyard. A loud TV in the lobby echoes up to all the rooms. Some of the rooms have street views – not necessarily an improvement.

Eating
Budget restaurants cluster around Plaza de la Independencia. Vendors sell Colombian and Ecuadorean favorites at Las Lajas.

Getting There & Away
AIR
The airport is 7km northwest of Ipiales, on the road to Cumbal, and is accessible by taxi (COP$10,000). Satena has flights to Cali, with onward connections to other cities.

There are no direct flights from Ipiales to Ecuador, but you can easily get to Tulcán, from where Tame has daily flights to Quito. Heading to Tulcán from the border, you pass the airport 2km before reaching town.

BUS
Ipiales has a new, large bus terminal, about 1km northeast of the center. Urban buses can take you into the center of town (COP$900), or grab a taxi (COP$3000).

There are frequent buses to Bogotá (COP$100,000, 25 hours). Several companies run regular buses to Cali (COP$68,000, 10 hours). All these buses will drop you in Popayán in eight hours. Don't travel at night on this route; see p253 for more information.

There are plenty of buses, minibuses and *colectivos* to Pasto (COP$5000 to COP$8000, 1½ to two hours). They all depart from the bus terminal. Sit on the right for better views.

Frequent *colectivos* travel the 2.5km to the border at Rumichaca (COP$1300), leaving from the bus terminal and the market area near the corner of Calle 14 and Carrera 10. After crossing the border on foot, take another *colectivo* to Tulcán (6km). On both routes, Colombian and Ecuadorean currency is accepted.

SANTUARIO DE LAS LAJAS
elev 2600m
Built on a stone bridge spanning a deep gorge, the neo-Gothic Santuario de Las Lajas is a strange but spectacular sight. It's also a hugely popular destination for pilgrims in need of a miracle. They place their faith in the Virgin Mary, whose image is believed to have emerged from an enormous vertical rock 45m above the river sometime in the mid-18th century. Plaques of thanksgiving line the walls of the canyon, many from prominent Colombian politicians.

The church is directly against the rocky wall of the gorge where the image appeared. A gilded painting of the Virgin, accompanied by Santo Domingo and San Francisco, has been painted directly on the rocks just to be sure there is no confusion. The first chapel was built in 1803; today's church, designed by Nariño architect Lucindo Espinoza, was built between 1926 and 1944.

In the lower floors of the church a **museum** (admission COP$1000; 🕒 8:30am-5pm) has exhibits on the history of the church, plus some religious and pre-Columbian art.

The sanctuary is located 7km southeast of Ipiales. Shared taxis and vans run regularly from the corner of Carrera 6 and Calle 4 in Ipiales (COP$2000, 20 minutes) and from the town's bus station (COP$1800, 15 minutes). You can also pay for all four seats (COP$7200). There are direct shared taxis from Pasto if you prefer the greater creature comforts that city offers.

Sleeping & Eating
Casa Pastoral (☎ 775 4463, 316 740 0601; www .sanctuariodelaslajas.org; s/tr/q COP$10,000/30,000/40,000, d COP$16,000-20,000) Run by nuns for a long time, this large, basic hotel caters to the faithful and heathen alike. Some rooms have views of the cathedral. All rooms have private bath with hot water, and a large cafeteria serves simple budget meals. Take the first set of stairs on your left as you walk downhill toward the cathedral. Bookings are recommended. Two other hotels next door offer a similar style of accommodations.

Restaurante El Santuario (☎ 775 4436; mains COP$3000-7000; 🕒 6am-3pm) Crossing the bridge heading away from the church, walk along the opposite side to get to this small restaurant with great views. It serves breakfast, lunch, snacks and coffee. The waterfalls a bit further along offer the best views of the church.

DESIERTO DE LA TATACOA
Halfway between Bogotá and San Agustín lies the **Tatacoa Desert**. It is a striking landscape of eroded cliffs and gullies, sculpted by the infrequent rain. Because of the dry, clear conditions, lack of light pollution, and location at the equator, Tatacoa is a great spot for stargazing – the skies above both the northern and southern hemispheres are spread out for all to see.

Tatacoa isn't really a desert, although the thermometer says otherwise – it can hit 50°C times. It's technically semi-arid dry tropical forest, averaging 1070mm of rain per year. Surrounded by mountains in every direction, the peaks around Nevado de Huila (5750m) grab most of the incoming precipitation, leaving 330-sq-km Tatacoa arid for most of the

year. The result is an ecosystem unlike anywhere else in Colombia – there are scorpions and weasels, fruit-bearing cacti, and 72 bird species have been recorded here.

To get here, you'll have to pass through Neiva, the hot, sleepy capital of the Huíla department and a port on the Río Magdalena. There's nothing in Neiva of interest. Take a bus to Villavieja, an hour's ride northwest of Neiva. You can spend the night in Villavieja or, better yet, spend the night in the desert.

Be sure to bring sturdy shoes (there are cactus spines on the ground) and a flashlight (torch).

VILLAVIEJA
☎ 8 / pop 7700 / elev 440m
This small desert town was founded in 1550 and has largely been forgotten about since. A few families continue to eke out a living raising cattle, but most have turned to tourism – hordes of *bogotano* tourists come on weekends and holidays to warm up.

Information
At the local **library** (🕒 7:30am-noon & 2-6pm Mon-Fri), out back of the museum, you can use the internet for free. Next door is the office of the single **police officer** (☎ 312 453 2488) who patrols the region. He offers tourist information when not riding his motorcycle around.

There's no ATM in town, but **Banco Agrario** (☎ 879 7503, 879 7513; Calle 4 No 30; 🕒 8am-1pm Mon-Fri) will let you withdraw cash with a cash-card and passport.

Sights & Activities
The region used to be a sea bed and contains numerous important fossils from the Myocene era; paleontologists continue to work in La Venta, a remote region of the desert. You can see some of their findings at the **Museo Paleontológico** (☎ 879 7744; admission COP$1500; 🕒 8:30am-noon & 2-5pm) on the main square.

Be sure to visit **Conservas del Desierto** (☎ 879 7567; conservasdeldesierto@yahoo.es; Carrera 5 No 5-78; 🕒 8am-5pm), which sells various products made from the locally grown Nopal cactus, including cactus sweets, pickled cactus heart, and cactus wine (8.7% alcohol). The cactus is reputed to have medicinal properties, and is quite tasty.

As you leave town you'll pass through **Bosque del Cardón**, a small cactus forest. Four kilometers from Villavieja is **El Cusco**, where

CALI & SOUTHWEST COLOMBIA

you'll find the **Observatorio Astronómico de la Tatacoa** (☎ 879 7584, 310 465 6765; viewings COP$7000). A lookout point across the road has impressive views, and is a fine place to watch the sunset. The observatory is normally open to the public in the evenings, but was closed when we were there.

Every July at the new moon, university groups and Colombian stargazing enthusiasts congregate here for a four-day, three-night **Fiesta de Estrellas** (Star Party).

Below the lookout point are the **Laberintos del Cusco** (Cusco Labyrinths). The most striking landscapes can be seen here. As you stand on the front porch of the visitors center, walk down to the main road and turn left. At the red-roofed bar (100m) look for the trail that heads downhill. Follow the trail and turn left at the green sign. Follow this path out to the main road.

Four kilometers past the observatory is **Ventanas**, so named for its commanding views out over the desert. Another 5km takes you to **Los Hoyos**, where there are cabins (see right), a private swimming hole, and a less-impressive walk.

Javier Fernando Rua Restrepo (☎ 310 465 6765; www.tatacoa-astronomia.com), a local astronomer, can show you around the sky from the rooftop of the visitors center. He uses two tripod telescopes, and is an expert at taking photos through the lens with your digital camera. He also rents two-man tents (COP$10,000).

Sleeping & Eating

There are several basic hotels in town but most travelers prefer to spend the night in the desert itself. Bring earplugs – the roosters crow all night long.

Built in the 1500s, the ancient flagstones of the **Hotel La Casona** (☎ 879 7636; Calle 3 No 3-60; dm/d per person COP$15,000/20,000) have seen better days. Two private rooms are used principally by local amorous couples. Two big dorm rooms cater to large groups. There's also the brightly painted **La Portada** (☎ 311 833 2386; Carrera 2 No 7-07; per person COP$15,000) on the edge of town on the road to the desert.

The best eats in town are **Sol y Sombra** (☎ 879 7582; Carrera 4A No 5-86; meals COP$4000-5000; ☺ breakfast, lunch & dinner) and **Restaurante Monterrey** (☎ 310 315 5063; Carrera 4 No 4-43; meals COP$4000-5000; ☺ breakfast, lunch & dinner).

In the desert, all accommodations are basically four concrete walls with a corrugated tin roof. All serve meals.

Behind the observatory is a large **campground** (campsite per person COP$2000, shower COP$1000, toilet per day COP$500) with room for 40 tents. You can also rent a hammock for COP$7000 and string it up outside on the Greek pillars on the front porch. The building is powered by solar panels.

Doña Elbira (☎ 312 559 8576; s/d COP$15,000/30,000) has five cabins scattered across the desert scrub, about 1km after the observatory. Across the way is **Rincón de Cabrito**, a food stand that opens on the weekend and sells goat's milk, cheese, *arequipe* (a sweet dessert of milk and sugar) and other goat-milk based desserts.

In Los Hoyos **Estadero Los Hoyos** (☎ 311 536 5027; s/d/tr COP$20,000/30,000/40,000) has two rooms in a single cabin. For COP$3000 you can walk down and bathe in the swimming hole; on weekends a small bar nearby serves beer.

Getting There & Away

Vans hop the 37km between Neiva and Villavieja (COP$5000, one hour) from 5am to 7:30pm. They leave with a minimum of five passengers; there are frequent services in the early morning and late afternoon, but during the day you could wait an hour or two.

There are frequent services between Bogotá and Neiva (COP$20,000, five hours). Buses run between Pitalito (near San Agustín) and Neiva every hour or so (COP$20,000, five hours).

Getting Around

There is one **moto-taxi** (☎ 310 301 9756) in town. A true monopolist, he'll charge you COP$15,000 to COP$20,000 to take up to three people to the observatory. You could walk the 4km, but there's no shade, shelter or water between the town and the observatory.

Pacific Coast

This is where the jungle meets the sea. It's a wild, untamed area, drenched in up to 10m of rain per year. The beaches, unlike those of the Caribbean, are fine, gray sand. There is only one road to the interior, from Buenaventura to Cali; all other transport is by light plane and boat.

The Pacific is famous for its whale-watching. Between July and October whales come from as far away as Antarctica to calve and nurse their young. You can see them all along this coast. In places they come so close to the shore you can spot them from the beach.

The incredible marine life here also attracts deep-sea fishers and adventurous scuba divers. Bahía Solano is famous for its fishing – rated among the best the world – and catch-and-release anglers come year-round to try their luck with blue marlin and sailfish. Likewise, Isla Malpelo is famous for some of the most challenging and rewarding diving in the world.

There are a full range of resorts on this coast, though none are typical beach retreats. The beaches near Bahía Solano, El Valle and outside Nuquí, in particular, all host top-notch resorts. Travelers on a budget should check out Ladrilleros, a coastal town near Buenaventura with a fine beach and good surf, and San Cipriano, a tiny hamlet hidden in the jungle accessible only by a motorcycle-driven railway trolley.

The population is mostly descended from African slaves who once toiled here. There remain a few isolated pockets of indigenous peoples; there is some racial tension between the two. The isolation on this coast has allowed the people to preserve much of their culture – the traditional cuisine here is famous. But the area's relative isolation also means there is poor infrastructure and poverty is widespread.

PACIFIC COAST

HIGHLIGHTS

- Scuba dive with whales off **Isla Gorgona** (p284) during whale-watching season or join a whale-watching tour at **El Valle** (p275) or **Ensenada de Utría** (p276)

- Surf the Pacific's 2m-waves at **Ladrilleros** (p281)

- Swim with hundreds of hammerhead sharks at Colombia's most difficult scuba dive destination, **Isla Malpelo** (p283

- Linger amid tropical gardens on the black-sand beaches of **Guachalito** (p278

- Go catch-and-release sportfishing for blue marlin and sailfish near **Bahía Solano** (p272)

Climate

It rains a lot here. Don't come planning to sunbathe. Rain is lightest from January to March, and heaviest from August to November. The average temperature is 28°C up and down the coast, but often feels much cooler because of the rain.

National, State & Regional Parks

Parque Nacional Natural (PNN) Isla Gorgona (p284) and PNN Isla Malpelo (p283) are both protected marine parks boasting excellent diving. PNN Ensenada de Utría (p276), halfway between El Valle and Nuquí, attracts whales in season, which play in a narrow bay, just a few hundred meters offshore.

Dangers & Annoyances

The Pacific coast, especially the Chocó, remains on the front lines of Colombia's civil conflict. The beaches in the Chocó were heavily patrolled by Colombian marines at our visit, with marines outnumbering tourists three-to-one. We felt safe, but conditions here are liable to change, and you may like to confirm things are still safe before planning a visit.

Getting There & Away

Only the Cali–Buenaventura highway links the Pacific coast to the rest of Colombia. Most travelers arrive by light plane from Cali or Medellín. See p274 for details on air travel to the Pacific Coast. It's also possible, but difficult, to arrive from Ecuador or Panama by cargo boat. See p274 for more details.

Getting Around

There are no roads along the Pacific coast. Boat travel is your only option for traveling in the region.

CHOCÓ

The Chocó is one of the wettest places on earth. On average the Chocó coast averages 16m to 18m of rain per year. This fact defines the region, the people and its culture. When the sun shines, it's too hot to move too fast, and when it rains – which is almost every day – no one wants to go out and get wet. No wonder people joke about *hora chocoana* (Chocó time). Life here is slow.

Traveling on the Chocó coast is like wandering through a ghost town. Where did all the people go? Pre-2001 this was a major tourist destination. Then La Violencia (the violence to which Colombia is prone, which comes and goes at various times in various areas) came to the Chocó, substantially destabilizing the area. Consequently dozens of hotels and resorts are empty, begging for guests.

Conditions have recently improved dramatically, and the area is quite safe despite the large military presence in all of the towns along the coast. In some cases the Colombian marines outnumber tourists three-to-one. They are friendly and if you are a foreigner will take particular care that nothing happens to you. All the same, if men with guns unnerve you, you may not enjoy your time here. For a complete listing of Chocó beach resorts, see www.hotelesmarselva.com.

BAHÍA SOLANO
☎ 4 / pop 8000

Bahía Solano is the largest settlement on the Chocó coast. It is famous for its deep-sea sportfishing – some of the best in the world – and as a base to go whale-watching (see p58). The town itself consists of half a dozen muddy, unpaved streets, and holds little of interest. However, there are numerous good beach resorts a short boat ride away, where you can go surfing, scuba-diving, organize whale-watching trips, or go deep-sea fishing.

The town sits at the mouth of the Río Jella and faces north into the ocean. It is surrounded by hills. All the hotels in the town itself are down by the waterfront in Barrio El Carmen. There is no beach in or near town.

Information

There is no tourist information office in town. Pick up a copy of the new quarterly *La Guía de Bahía* for a map, tourist info and tide tables.

EMERGENCY
Police (☎ emergency 112, 682 7082, 682 7057) On the waterfront.

INTERNET ACCESS
Bahia.com (☎ 312 457 6292; per hour COP$2400; ⏲ 7am-9pm) Fastest internet in town. International calls COP$500 per minute via Skype. Owns its own generator. Opposite Hotel Bahía.

MEDICAL SERVICES
Beatriz Argotte (☎ 310 372 2988) The only dentist in town. In the back room of Bahia.com.

PACIFIC COAST

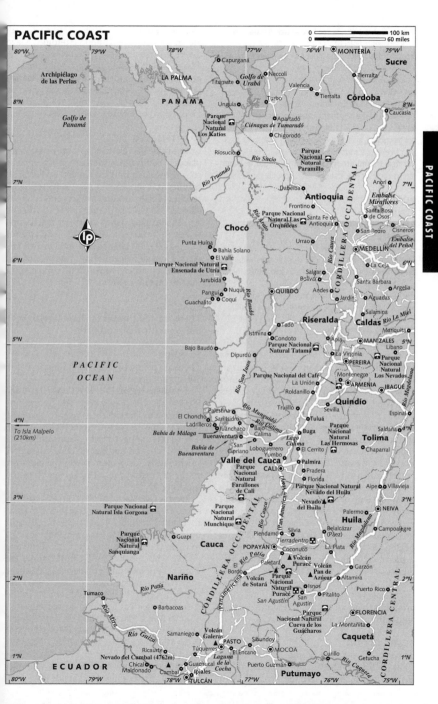

Drogas Bahía (☎ 682 7064) Pharmacy that stocks the basics. Opposite Hotel Bahía.
Hospital Julio Figueroa Villa (☎ emergency 112, 682 7266, 682 7070, 682 7884; ✆ 24hr)

MONEY
Banco Agrario de Colombia (☎ 682 7522; ✆ 8am-2pm Mon-Fri) The only bank in town, with the only ATM on the Chocó coast. ATM dispenses maximum COP$400,000 per transaction, assuming the power grid is working. After long weekends it's sometimes empty.
Servicio Inmediato Nacional (☎ 682 7001) You can receive domestic wire transfers here. Opposite the hospital.

POST
Deprisa (☎ 682 7033)
Servientrega (☎ 682 7835) Opposite Banco Agrario.

VISA INFORMATION
Capitanio de Puerto (☎ 682 7074) Register with the harbormaster if arriving under your own sail. On the waterfront.
DAS (Departamento Administrativo de Seguridad; ☎ 682 6984, 313 745 8611) On the waterfront; opened in 2007.

Sights & Activities
HIKING
Near the south end of town flows the **Quebrada Chocolatal**. You can hike upriver about half an hour to the **Cascada Chocolatal** that empties into an icy-cold swimming hole. The jungle towers over you on both sides of the riverbank, in a cascade of flowers and birdsong. On the same road a narrow, overgrown path leads upward to a small shrine to the Virgin Mary. It's a 15-minute walk each way that offers great views over the town and the beach.

You can also walk to **Playa Mecana**, a 5km-long beach strewn with coconut palms. You must leave at or before low tide (*mareada baja*). It's 1½ hours each way. You can also organize a boat ride up the adjacent Río Mecana in a wooden canoe for around COP$5000 per person. A recommended guide is Antonio, a member of the local Emberá tribe. His guide services go for COP$50,000 per day. The management at Rocas de Cabo Marzo (right) can put you in touch with him. There are mangroves along the river, and a small shop upriver sells drinks and snacks.

SCUBA DIVING
There is good scuba diving in 500m-deep Bahía Solano. The warship *Sebastián de Belalcázar*, which survived the attack on Pearl Harbor, was sunk near Playa Huína to create an artificial reef (Buqué Hundido). Cave divers may like to explore the caves near Cabo Marzo. You'll need experience and your own gear. A recommended dive master is **Rodrigo Fajando** (☎ 682 7416). Expect to pay around COP$100,000 per dive to cover boat and gasoline from Bahía Solano.

SPORTFISHING
Colombia's Pacific coast is one of the only places in South America where you can pull in record-breaking blue marlin and sailfish. The fishing zone stretches north to the southern reaches of Panama, and attracts anglers from all over the world. The best time to come is April to August, when there are catch-and-release tournaments. Expect to pay around COP$1,600,000 per day for four to five anglers. Consider negotiating the price of the gasoline separately, so you don't wind up giving the captain a free tank.

SURFING
There are good waves on **Playa Almejal**. Both beach resorts rent surfboards.

Sleeping
There are plenty of basic flophouses in Bahía Solano not listed here.

Hotel Bahía (☎ 682 7048, 682 7047; s/d/tr COP$40,000/ 55,000/55,000; ✖) This is your best budget option in town. The elderly owner is considered the grandmother of tourism in Bahía Solano. The rooms are paved in linoleum and have a TV and fan, and one has air-con, although it smells musty. Get a room away from the street so the generator doesn't wake you up in the morning. It also serves budget meals.

Rocas de Cabo Marzo (☎ 682 7433; r per person incl full board COP$100,000; ▣) After being forced to leave their hotel at Bahía Tebada (see boxed text, opposite), the managers used their savings to open this simple posada. One of the few people who speaks English in the zone, the Tom Selleck look-alike owner also organizes sportfishing tournaments, owns a scuba tank compressor, and offers guide services in the surrounding area. The food is excellent.

Hotel Balboa Plaza (☎ 682 7075; www.hotelesmar selva.com; Carrera 2A No 6-73; s/tw/tr COP$48,000/45,000/ 45,000, d COP$56,000-90,000, ste COP$60,000-270,000; ✖) Built by Pablo Escobar in 1985, the Balboa remains the largest hotel in town. The outside looks pretty ragged but inside it's a well-

A FISHING LODGE, LOVED AND LOST

The Pacific coast has seen its share of dark times. The owners of **Rocas de Cabo Marzo** (opposite) tell the following story.

In 1991 several prominent Colombian families built a luxury sportfishing camp 32km north of Bahía Solano in Bahía Tebada, surrounded by the jungle and sea. There they fished for marlin, tuna, wahoo, and amber jack, among others. It quickly became famous, and they began hosting international fishing tournaments. American and European fishermen came, and it got write-ups in the fishing magazines.

The owners decided that it would be more profitable to turn the site into a hotel, and in 1992 Enrique and Nancy arrived with their 15-month-old son to run the place. They decorated it and built gardens.

The hotel attracted presidents and senators, mayors and bankers, ambassadors and the world's wealthy. It was the heart of the '90s, times were good, and there was no talk of guerrillas or La Violencia here.

Then, in 2000, the Fuerzas Armadas Revolucionarias de Colombia (FARC) arrived. They came one quiet night asking for food, medicine and gasoline. This frightened the guests. Later came the paramilitaries, hunting FARC, asking also for supplies. One Saturday night in 2001, at a small hotel called La Resaca, near Cupica, 16km north of Bahía Tebada, the paramilitaries came. Within hours the FARC arrived, and there was a shootout. All of the paramilitaries were killed. FARC members took the owner, thinking him a paramilitary collaborator, and killed him with a bullet in the mouth. Enrique and Nancy buried him.

After that they decided it was time to leave. They stripped the hotel of everything – scuba-dive compressor, even the sinks in the bathroom, and left only the shell of the building, which has since collapsed and now sits, decomposing, between the jungle and the sea.

The region is safe now, but no building remains, and they are left with only the land and memories.

appointed lodging, with a pool and bar, and live music when there's enough guests to justify it. Third-floor rooms have a good view of the sea. The back garden has hammocks where you can lounge amid roses, heliconias and a starfruit tree.

Eating

All the hotels listed here have restaurants and all include (or offer) a three-meal plan. If you're after a cheap, local meal, head down to the no-name shacks on the beach, where you can get fried fish and *patacones* (fried plantains) for COP$4000.

Cabalonga Restaurant (☎ 682 7103, 312 302 0109; mains COP$10,000-14,000; ⏰ 8:30am-10pm) One of the few proper restaurants in town, this Venezuelan-owned establishment adjoins a fine tropical garden. On weekends it turns into a bar and may sometimes stay open till midnight.

Jimy's Pizzería (☎ 682 7712; pizzas COP$13,000-38,000) Down by the water with a view of the wharf, this place does pizza by the slice (COP$5000), plus hamburgers and grilled meat too. Beers are cheap.

Drinking

One block from the waterfront is **Discoteca Bartolo** (☎ 314 438 4815), where locals come to party on the weekend. One kilometer south of town at the wharf sits a no-name bar. It used to be the tourist information center before tourism bottomed out in the early 2000s. On weekends you can hear the reggaetón all the way from town.

Shopping

You'll find a good variety of locally made *artesanías* (handicrafts) at rock-bottom prices, some made by the local indigenous peoples. Worth a look are the carvings of *tagua*, a hard resin sometimes called 'vegetable ivory.' The resemblance is striking, and you'll find necklaces and small carved animals of *tagua* for COP$5000 to COP$10,000. There are two good no-name *artesanía* shops at the airport, and two more in town.

Also be sure to try the *pescado ahumado* (smoked fish) at one of the airport stalls. **Patricia Cujar** (☎ 314 625 8806, 094 682 7511) is famous for her smoked tuna, and will ship anywhere in Colombia.

> ## WARDING OFF THE EVIL EYE
>
> *Cabalonga*, a hard nut grown in the Chocó, is worn on a necklace by indigenous children to ward off the *mal de ojo* (evil eye) that some elderly women are thought to possess.

Getting There & Away

There are no roads to Bahía Solano. Most people fly in. There are also cargo boats to/from Buenaventura.

AIR

Aeropuerto José Celestino Mutis is serviced by Satena, Aexpa and ADA. If you're coming from Bogota buy a ticket Bogotá–Bahía Solano – the flight touches down in Medellín but is almost the same price as Medellín to Bahía Solano.

The airport's nickname is *'Sal Si Puedes'* (get out if you can). Because of the heavy rainfall, planes are sometimes unable to leave. It would be unwise to book international connections for the same day you leave Bahía Solano.

A moto-taxi to/from the airport costs around COP$5000.

BOAT

To/From Buenaventura

For a brief period in 2006-2007, there was a speedboat running tourists up from Buenaventura; then FARC kidnapped someone and the service got cancelled. You can still travel up the coast on the many cargo boats that bring supplies each weekend. The journey takes around 20 hours, generally leaving in the afternoon and arriving midmorning (both ways), depending on the tides. One recommended supply boat is the **Renacer El Pacífico** (☎ 2 242 4785, 314 883 4021; Muelle El Piñal, Km4, Bodega Aldemar Montes, Buenaventura). It charges COP$120,000 for a *camarote* (bunk bed). Be sure to call several days in advance, as service is infrequent. You may like to bring a hammock with you, as it may be more comfortable to sleep on deck. Most of the boats return southward on Sunday or Monday.

To/From Panama

It is possible to travel onward to Panama from here (six to 10 hours). Boats run infrequently north to Jaqué, Panama, when full (per person COP$150,0000, six to 10 passengers). A captain recommended to us in Bahía Solano is **'Profesor' Justino**. Ask around town or at your hotel to seek him out. If he's in town, and is willing and able and feeling so inclined, he may take you up the coast.

Be sure to stamp out of Colombia at the DAS office in Bahía Solano before leaving town. To enter Panama you'll need a yellow fever vaccination and enough cash to prove you can travel onwards (a minimum of US$500). Once you reach Jaqué and stamp in to Panama, there are flights for around US$85 to Panama City, usually Tuesday and Thursday. Copa and Air Panama offer the route, but were flying out of the nearby Piñas private airfield as the Jaqué airfield was under renovation.

The boat trip is long, rough journey but sailors tell us the voyage – which passes through the Archipélago Las Perlas in Panama – is beautiful, especially during whale season.

To/from El Valle

Jeeps leave opposite the school when full, usually late morning (COP$10,000, 15km), or take a motorcycle (COP$20,000). The road is slowly being paved from both ends, but the middle is a cesspool of monster-sized craters. The jeeps jolt over and through; motorcycles go around them.

AROUND BAHÍA SOLANO
Punta Huína

A 15-minute (COP$50,000) boat ride takes you to this pretty beach with a mixture of gold and black sand. It's lined with coconut palms and several modest resorts. A small indigenous community lives here, along with descendants of African slaves. All the following hotels offer package deals, including the flights from Medellín, boat transfers from Bahía Solano, three meals per day, and usually some activities. There was no cell-phone signal here when we visited, but a small **Compartel** (☎ 8 522 4621) office offers satellite phone calls.

There are several short jungle walks you can do in the vicinity, including **Playa de los Deseos**, **Cascada El Tigre** and **Playa Cocalito**. It's possible to walk here from Bahía Solano (four hours). A guide (COP$50,000) is recommended.

SLEEPING

Cabañas Brisas Del Mar (☎ in Medellín 269 5150; r per person COP$50,000) Your best budget option on Punta Huína. There are five rooms with meter-high gaps between the walls and the ceiling (expect to hear your neighbor snoring at night, or worse). There are great views of the ocean from the top floor. The owner has his own boat and scuba tanks and can take you out whale-watching or scuba diving. It's next door to Playa Oro.

Posada Los Delfines (☎ 320 626 3174, 314 728 4498; piedaddelfines@hotmail.com; r per person all-inclusive COP$70,000) This small posada is also the only bakery on Playa Huína. The baker and posada owner produces yummy guava donuts, empanadas and pastries. The rooms are basic, and there's no sea view, but a front and back balcony face a heliconia-filled garden.

Playa de Oro Lodge (☎ in Medellín 682 7481, toll free 1 800 091 4151; www.hotelesdecostaacosta.com; r per person COP$70,000, r per person all-inclusive COP$100,000) This family-oriented resort is right on the beach, and surrounds a small garden and playground for the kids. The rooms are simple and have black-and-white linoleum floors. Each has a small wooden patio with its own hammock, and 2nd floor rooms have good views of the sea. A games room has a ping-pong table and board games. A big bar area boasts a view of the sea and a loud satellite TV.

El Refugio de Mr Jerry Ecolodge (☎ in Cali 2 330 9562, in Bahía Solano 4 682 7233; www.mrjerrybahiasolano .com; s/d/tr per person COP$115,000/110,000/110,000, cabin per person COP$120,000) Mr Jerry is a chain-smoking, bearded Dutchman who's spent decades on this coast. His colorfully painted hotel sits at the north end of the beach, and offers 30 basic rooms decorated throughout with bookshelves stacked with hundreds of English-language paperbacks. Out back a tropical garden grows much of the food the restaurant serves. There's free snorkeling gear you can borrow.

To the north of Bahía Solano are several beaches with hotels.

Playa Potés

Marlin Azul (☎ in Medellín 310 461 0917, 316 742 1040; r per person all-inclusive COP$150,000) The 'Blue Marlin' caters principally to sport fishermen. Rooms are basic – mattresses are of thin, sagging foam – and there's no mosquito nets. There's several triples and two doubles with private bath. Set a little way back from the beach, there are good views of the ocean and during whale season you may catch sight of one. Fishing trips can also be organized. A few native huts next door also rent cheap rooms. It will cost COP$200,000 minimum for boat rental here.

Playa de Paridera

Mapara Crab Beach Hotel (☎ 682 7525, 313 681 4001; www.maparacrab.com; cabaña per person all-inclusive COP$104,000) The cabañas of this secluded resort line the beach, just 5m from the water. There are good box-spring mattresses and mosquito screens (but no nets). The patios all have hammocks facing the sea. A new bar-restaurant was being built when we were there. The beach is often covered in the tiny crabs, typical of this area. The hotel is managed by the owners of Rocas de Cabo Marzo (p272) in Bahía Solano. Price includes three meals and transport by boat.

EL VALLE

☎ 4 / pop 3500

On the southern side of the peninsula from Bahía Solano sits its smaller neighbor, El Valle. At the west end of town is the pleasant Playa Almejal, with two good resorts. El Valle is a more pleasant spot than Bahía Solano, and is a good jumping off point to visit Ensenada de Utría. It's also a good place to spot turtles during nesting season (September to December) on Playa Almejal or at Estación Septiembre.

Orientation

El Valle is a one-street town. The road from Bahía Solano runs through the center, becomes Calle Valle and dead-ends at the beach. At Tío Tigre a footbridge crosses the Río Valle and a path wends through cabins to the shore. There are no taxis or public transport in El Valle.

Information

El Valle businesses offer tourist information through the **Tío Tigre Asociación** (☎ 682 7907; www .tiotigre-ecoturismo.com). The association can help you with information about the region, organize tours, and also rent bikes (COP$12,000 per day) plus a five-man tent (COP$20,000) near a shower block. The owners of the Bahía Solano branch of internet cafe **Bahía.com** were planning to open an internet cafe in El Valle at the time of research.

Apuestos Unidades del Chocó (☎ 094 682 7960; ☼ 8am-noon & 2-8pm) Receive domestic wire transfers here.

Hospital El Valle (☼ 24hr) There's one doctor and one nurse in this rudimentary facility.

National parks office (Parques Nacionales de Colombia; ☎ 422 0883, in Medellín 422 0884; parqueutria@yahoo .com) The national parks office is devoid of information.

PACIFIC COAST

Police (☎ 682 7952)
Servientrega (☎ 682 7835)
Telecom (☎ 682 7902; ☹ 7:30am-9pm Mon-Sat, 8am-noon & 4-9pm Sun) One computer with dial-up internet (per hr COP$2400).

Sights & Activities
TURTLE WATCHING
On Playa Cuevita, 4.8km south of El Valle along the coast, is the turtle-nesting sanctuary of **Estación Septiembre** (☎ in Bogotá 1 245 5700; Colombians/foreigners COP$16,000/COP$20,000). From September to December sea turtles arrive to lay eggs. The best time to see them is at night. There are cabins here you can stay in (hammock COP$20,000, rooms per person COP$40,000).

The beach here is too steep to land a boat. You can walk here from El Valle (two hours) or ride a bike (30 minutes). If you have a lot of luggage you'll need to organize horses or mules Contact Estación de Septiembre in advance to organize this. You can also organize a night-time guided walk from El Valle (COP$20,000 per person) to see the turtles. Ask at your hotel to find a guide; many guides freelance.

CASCADA DEL TIGRE
A two-hour walk north through the jungle past gigantic trees and along the shore takes you to this waterfall. There's a swimming hole where you can bathe. Local guides charge COP$20,000 per person (negotiable) including lunch. It's a full-day excursion.

PARQUE NACIONAL NATURAL (PNN) ENSENADA DE UTRÍA
This narrow inlet of water is one of the best places to see whales close-up from land. During the calving season they enter the *ensenada* (inlet) and play just a few hundred meters from shore. Long closed due to security concerns, the **Centro de Visitantes Jaibaná** (Colombians/foreigners COP$9000/COP$25,000), on the eastern shore of the *ensenada*, was reopening at the time of research, including newly refurbished cabins for up to 30 people. There's good snorkeling and diving nearby, but you'll have to bring your own equipment. The visitors center has rudimentary grade school exhibits on flora and fauna, and several whale and dolphin skeletons are on display outside. There are a number of short walks you can do in the nearby mangroves, and at night you may see glow-in-the-dark mushrooms.

Mano Cambiada in Nuquí (see p277) has the concession to run the park. It runs the **cabins** (r per person all-inclusive COP$96,000) and offers boat transport to/from El Valle and Nuquí (COP$50,000 per person, 1½ hours), or Bahía Solano (COP$500,000 per boat). It can also organize a guide (COP$30,000, four hours) from El Valle to take you on foot to Lachunga at the mouth of the Río Tundo at the northwestern corner of the *ensenada*. From here you can be picked up in a launch (free) and taken to the visitors center.

Sleeping
Hotel Valle (☎ 682 7907, 314 617 8970; hotelvalle@gmail.com; r without bathroom COP$20,000, r COP$30,000, apt COP$40,000) This budget home-style posada is your best cheap option in El Valle. The smaller rooms share an interior shower block, and there's a breezy terrace with hammocks and ocean glimpses upstairs. There's a TV in the homey downstairs living room, and food is served. A cabin near the beach (Cabaña Arrecifes) can also be rented for COP$35,000 per person.

Hotel Playa Alegre (☎ 451 1229, 315 571 5142; www.playaalegre.com; cabañas per person COP$140,00) Next to El Almejal is this cheaper but still excellent choice. Cabins surround a small pond full of blue freshwater shrimp. A palm-thatched restaurant faces the ocean. One cabin uphill has spectacular views. Look for the two-story watchtower and the peeling white picket fence.

El Almejal (☎ in Medellín 230 6060; www.almejal.com.co; cabañas per person COP$170,000) The most luxurious and expensive resort in the Bahía Solano area, El Almejal also has the most ingenious cabin design – opposite walls of the sitting room area open completely, allowing a breeze to pass through. A small creek spills into a man-made swimming hole near the back of the cabins; select a nearby cabin for the soothing sound. A turtle-breeding facility collects and hatches turtle eggs before returning them to the sea (September to December). Concrete stairs behind the hotel lead uphill to a lookout point – in whale-watching season you can sometimes spot them playing just off the coast. Nonguests may use the spot; just swing by reception first to ask permission.

Eating
Residencia La Coti (☎ 682 7948; mains COP$6000-7000; ☹ lunch & dinner) A grandmotherly local cooks

'interior food' for Colombian visitors wanting more than fish and rice, but if you give her notice she can prepare you local specialties, such as *jaíba con coco* (mollusc in coconut milk). Sit at her kitchen table and eat surrounded by her collection of knick-knacks.

Drinking

El Valle has one of the most picturesque bars in the world. About 200m past El Alemejal on the main beach, built on top of a rocky outcropping, is **El Mirador** (Fri & Sat). You can sit at the makeshift tables and suck down rum while the stereo blasts reggaetón at the crashing waves.

Less spectacular, at the opposite end of El Valle on the road to Bahía Solano, is **Claro de Luna** (Wed-Sun).

GETTING THERE & AWAY

There's no port in El Valle. If you're departing by boat be sure to do so only at high tide; boats have been known to run aground trying to leave at low tide.

For boat transport to Panama, the services of **Santos 'El Bebé' Reyes** (☎ 682 7977) come recommended.

NUQUÍ

☎ 4 / pop 6500 / temp 27°C

Further south along the coast is the small town of Nuquí. It boasts a fine beach, free of flotsam and driftwood, and the secluded nearby beach of Guachalito has some of the best resorts along this coast.

Arriving or departing by boat (which most travelers will) is like something out of a Vietnam war movie, with swift boats with machine guns, sandbag bunkers with camouflage tarps and marines patrolling the beach. Despite this, it feels quite safe here; in any event, men with grenades dangling from their chest add spice to the adventure!

The town itself is paved in a mixture of concrete and gravel, unlike the mucky streets of Bahía Solano, but has no car traffic, except for the solitary moto-taxi, and the occasional policeman on bicycle.

Information

Apuestas Unidades (☎ 683 6067) Receive domestic wire transfers here.
Banco Agrario (☎ 683 6496) No ATM.
Droguería Nuquí (☎ 683 6105; 24hr) Pharmacy.
Hospital San Pedro Claver (☎ 683 6003)

Mano Cambiada (☎ 314 618 8900, 311 872 7887; www.nuquipacifico.com) Tourist information center across from the airport.
Police (☎ 112) On the waterfront.
Satena (☎ 683 6031, 311 876 8957)
Telechoco (☎ 683 6207; per hr COP$2000; 7am-9:30pm Mon-Sat) Internet access and telephone *cabinas*.

Sights

An Olympic-sized beach, **Playa Olímpica** (5km-long), sits just south of the mouth of the Río Nuquí, and stretches as far as the eye can see. A local named Señor Pastrana can paddle you across the river in his dugout canoe (COP$5000). To find him, walk south along the main beach road, past the church; he lives a block from the river.

Tours

A man with a boat and an office near the hotels, **Ecce Homo**, offers tours to Playa Olímpica and then up the Río Nuquí into the jungle (COP$10,000 to COP$30,000 per person), also to Guachalito, including Cascada de Amor and Las Termales (COP$45,000 to COP$50,000 per person, minimum five), and into PNN Ensenada de Utría (opposite; COP$1,350,000 per boat). His prices vary depending on group size and the cost of gasoline.

Sleeping

Hotels cluster at the northern end of town, near the beach. A big chunk of beachfront property was for sale at our visit, causing much chatter among the locals – a mega-development may be in the works.

Iraka del Mar (☎ 683 6016, 313 767 3780; Carrera 58 No 9-46; r per person COP$40,000) Known for many years as the Rocío del Mar, this hotel sits facing the beach, across the street from Palmas de Pacífico (another budget hotel). A rock pool water feature greets you in the lobby; a long-unused dining area perches on the 2nd floor. There are two bodyboards you can borrow.

Vientos de Yubarta (☎ 312 217 8080, 312 776 7849; ameli_06@hotmail.com; r per person incl 2 meals COP$80,000) This new hotel sits a kilometer north of town along the beach. The attractive bamboo-and-wood construction houses good box-spring mattresses, and some rooms have windows facing both the jungle and sea. Nuquí's big, clean beach is 100m from the front door. Given its current lack of guests wanting its accommodation facilities, the place has turned into something of a bar for locals, who come to drink heavily and play loud music. The moto-taxi can take you here along the inner beach road.

Eating
Unless you're a group, hotels in Nuquí do not serve food. A number of local women cook for tourists in their home. The best is **Doña Pola** (☎ 683 6254; meals COP$8000), down a side street near the hotels. Be sure to order a few hours before you want to eat. Her meals are big enough for two people.

Shopping
Artesanías Margot (☎ 683 6058) Next to the airport, this small *artesanías* shop has a great selection of wooden carvings and other local arts and crafts. It even sells authentic blow-dart guns.

Getting There & Away
AIR
Aeropuerto Reyes Murillo (☎ 683 6001) is serviced by Satena, with flights to Medellín and Quibdó. Aexpa offers charter flights.

At the airport local women sell *mecocadas* (COP$1000), a tasty confection of coconut and guava paste.

BOAT
To/From El Valle
Transporte Maritimo (☎ 683 6145) offers Tuesday and Saturday services to El Valle (COP$40,000, 1½ hours). Boats leave Nuquí around dawn and depart El Valle around 4pm.

To/From Buenaventura
Three cargo boats service Nuquí from Buenaventura. The *Nuquí Mar* comes recommended. She departs Nuquí every eight days or so. Go down to the port in Nuquí and look for the sign that says 'Peligro Prohibido Fumar.' Ask for **Gigo** (☎ 312 747 8374), the owner. It's a 20-hour trip (bunk below deck COP$80,000) and the price includes food.

GUACHALITO
A half-hour boat ride west of Nuquí is Guachalito. It's a long beach, clear of flotsam and debris. This is the most idyllic beach on the entire Chocó coast – there are orchids and heliconias everywhere, the jungle encroaches on the beach, platter-sized mushrooms grow on the beach-side trees and coconut palms sway over the gray-sand beach.

Orientation
The Gonzalez family inhabits the east end of the beach. Several hotels scatter along 8km of the beach to Las Termales. On the way you'll pass El Terquito and El Terco, two almost-islands that serve as landmarks. You can walk the length of the beach (1½ hours).

Sights & Activities
CASCADA DE AMOR
A 1km (20 minutes) walk from the Gonzalez settlement, 200m inland from the beach, is a natural, 2m-deep swimming hole; a pretty waterfalls empties into a natural rock pool. Another 15-minute walk uphill takes you to an even bigger and more beautiful waterfall.

LAS TERMALES
A gravel path leads 500m inland from the *caserío* of Las Termales to the thermals themselves (admission COP$4000). The concrete pool has tepid water and spills into a cool adjacent river. A small path leads 30 minutes to another river and undeveloped hot springs.

Restaurant **Salomon** (☎ 683 6474, 683 6029) on the beach serves meals (COP$10,000) and beer. Be sure to call a day in advance if you want to eat.

Sleeping
Originally Guachalito referred only to the Gonzalez family settlement at the eastern end of the beach. Four generations live here, and their five posadas – run by competing siblings – all offer a similar level of comfort at a price of COP$100,000 to COP$150,000 per person, all-inclusive with no transport. Discounts for stays of three to four nights are offered. Price varies depending on the size of your group.

At **Mary Rio** (☎ 314 656 9688, 313 695 1599), you'll stay with the family and eat at their kitchen table. **La Joviseña** (☎ 314 683 8847) offers four detached cabins spread throughout a large garden. **Peñas de Guachalito** (Estadero Las Palmas, Restaurante el Cangrejo, ☎ 310 469 7785, 314 786 0458) has one of the most spectacular beach bars you'll ever visit – sit facing the waves, a tropical garden sprawling about you, coconut palms swaying above. A seafood lunch or dinner (COP$10,000 to COP$12,000) can be prepared with advance notice. Luna a Miel and No Te Olvides are older and less attractive but also rent rooms. You can book by calling any of the other posadas.

La Cabaña de Beto y Marta (☎ 311 775 9912; r per person all-inclusive COP$180,000) A 10-minute walk west of the Guachalito settlement is this delightful hotel owned by two *paísas* (Antioquians). Their four secluded cabins have hammocks and chairs on the deck to sit on at dusk and watch the sunset. The whole thing is set amid a spectacular garden, including lots of fruits and vegetables you'll find on your plate come dinnertime. It's located just past the military guardhouse near the Cascada del Amor.

Pijibá Lodge (☎ in Medellín 474 5221; www.pijiba lodge.com; r per person COP$138,000) The three duplex cabins of Pijibá are right next door to El Cantil. The gardens are nice but not the best in Guachalito, and it caters to couples by pushing two single beds together. Still, there are hammocks out on the deck, windsurf gear and surfboards can be rented and whale-watching trips can be organized. The food here has an excellent reputation.

our pick El Cantil (☎ 252 0707, in Medellín 352 0729; www.elcantil.com; r per person COP$180,000) The most luxurious hotel on this beach, El Cantil has six duplex cabins, and is surrounded by papaya plants and coconut palms. A small hydroelectric plant produces power for the restaurant and bar; the cabins are entirely without electricity. Candles are provided, or bring your flashlight (torch). The restaurant (which is famous for its food) sits a short walk up the hill, giving good views to spot whales in season. Diving expeditions can be organized and surfing guides can show you where the best spots are. The hotel runs the 'Surfing the Jungle' (www.nuquilatin procolombia.com) surfing competition in November.

Cabañas Ixtlán (☎ 683 6045; r without bathroom per person COP$150,000) A short climb uphill after El Cantil is this small posada. It's built of free stone walls and doors of *damagua* (a tree bark that when dried appears like leather) with concrete and wood floors. There are four rooms with one shared bathroom; the shower juts out into the open air, allowing you to shower in the rain. There are new box-spring mattresses, and great views from the top deck through ripe coconuts palms of the sea, where you may spot whales in season.

Piedra Piedra (☎ 315 596 3386; www.piedrapiedra .com r per person COP$140,000) A little bit past Ixtlán is Piedra Piedra. Set up the hill above a rocky outcrop into the sea (hence the name) amid a fruit and vegetable garden, the rooms consist of saggy mattresses and *damagua* privacy screens. The 1st-floor room has a little more privacy. Kayaks can be rented.

Getting There & Away
There are regular boat services from Nuquí to Guachalito. On Mondays, Wednesdays and Fridays the fast boat (COP$18,000, 30 minutes) leaves Arocia (west of Guachalito) at 6am, passing by the hotels around 6:30am to 7am, returning from Nuquí around 1pm to 2pm. On Tuesdays, Thursdays and Saturdays a slower boat services the same route (COP$16,000, one hour).

SOUTH COAST

BUENAVENTURA
☎ 2 / pop 200,000
The largest (and only) city on this coast, Buenaventura is Colombia's busiest port. More than 60% of Colombia's legal exports pass through these docks; much of her illegal exports pass through here too. The city has two parts. The main docks and city center are on an island in the bay, with slums stretching east on the continental side. A bridge connects the two.

The only reason to come here is transport. Most tourist traffic runs through the *muelle turístico* (tourist wharf). This part of town is quite safe, and there are many restaurants and hotels that cluster nearby. Cargo boats depart from El Piñal, just under the bridge.

Information
BanCafé Bank; just outside tourist wharf.
Ciber P@cífico (☎ 240 1409; per hr COP$2000); 8am-8:30pm Mon-Sat, 1-8pm Sun) Internet and phone calls, just outside the tourist wharf.

Sleeping
Hotel Titanic (☎ 241 2046; Calle 1A No 2A-55; s COP$45,000-50,000, d/ste COP$60,000/85,000; ❄ 💻) One block from the entrance to the tourist wharf is this five-story hotel. All rooms have cable TV, air-con and ethernet wall outlets. The rooftop bar-restaurant has good views over the water. Many rooms lack windows; suites accommodate up to five people.
Hotel Estelar Estación (☎ 243 4070; www.hotel esestelar.com; Calle 2 No 1A-08; s/d COP$259,000/294,000, ste COP$319,000-354,000; ℗ 💻 🐾) The best hotel

QUIBDÓ & ISTMINA

The Chocó has long aroused our curiosity, and we were looking forward to visiting Quibdó and Istmina for this guidebook. There is a speedboat on the Río Atrato that takes mostly Colombian travelers downriver to Turbo (p186) on the Caribbean coast. It is also possible, but far more dangerous, to take a cargo boat from neighboring Istmina down the Río San Juan to the Pacific coast, not far from Buenaventura.

At the time of our research, however, we were specifically warned by the Colombian military not to visit the region, as they could not guarantee the safety of foreign travelers. French-Colombian politician Ingrid Betancourt had just been rescued (see p31), and FARC were on the warpath; the region around Quibdó and Istmina has long been a lawless region, with the paramilitaries and FARC sharing de facto power.

This may change. We hope it does. If you decide to go you should check current conditions and exercise great caution. While the two towns remain nominally in control of the Colombian military, the badly pitted roads and both rivers are plagued by (whatever their overt political persuasion) thugs and bandits. Malaria is also endemic in the region; but while repellent and a mosquito net can guard against malaria, there is no good antidote to a gun pointed at your head.

in town is a flashback to Colombia's flapper days. Built in the roaring '20s and since refurbished, this white neoclassical confection boasts deluxe rooms and verandahs all the way around. It offers whale-watching packages in season (COP$339,000 per person), and the pool (open 9am to 6pm) is open to the public for COP$14,000.

Eating

Buenaventura's market, La Galería, is famous for its food. A dozen stalls surround the 2nd floor of the market. Many are owned by *costeña* grandmothers, preparing *sancocho de pescado* (fish in coconut milk) as their foremothers have for centuries. The market is a bustling, crowded chaos of butchers, fishmongers, greengrocers and vendors selling *pescado ahumado* (smoked fish). The usual assortment of cutpurses haunt the market, so take care with your belongings.

A taxi here from the tourist wharf will cost around COP$3000. Specify that you want to go to La Galería in Pueblo Nuevo.

Getting There & Away

BUS

There are frequent services between Cali and Buenaventura (COP$18,000, three to four hours). From Cali sit on the left side of the bus for the best views.

BOAT

Tourist speedboat services heading north and south depart from the tourist wharf. Cargo boats leave from El Piñal.

AROUND BUENAVENTURA
Juanchaco & Ladrilleros
☎ 2 / pop 3500

An hour's boat ride north of Buenaventura are Juanchaco and neighboring Ladrilleros. Juanchaco faces Bahía Malaga and accumulates a fine collection of Buenaventura's garbage on its beaches. Ladrilleros, on the other side of the peninsula, faces the roaring open waves of the Pacific Ocean. Its 6km of gray sand are clean as far as the eye can see. The waves aren't bad either – during the rainy season (or rather, rainier season, August to November) the ocean comes crashing in 2m-to 3m-high waves.

Ladrilleros is a popular weekend getaway spot for people from Cali; during the week you will likely have the place to yourself.

Two large military bases nearby guard both the shipping channels and the tourist areas. The region was considered safe when we were there.

INFORMATION

There are information booths in both towns, sometimes staffed by student volunteers from Buenaventura. Several work for local hotels so take their advice with a grain of salt.

There are no ATMs here, and few people accept credit cards. You'll find the nearest ATM is just outside the *muelle turístico* in Buenaventura.

MiFono (☎ 521 5201; per hr COP$2500; ☽ noon-9pm Mon-Sat) At the edge of Juanchaco on the road to Ladrilleros. Only internet in the area. You can also make phone calls here.

ACTIVITIES

Surfing

The best time for surfing is the wet(ter) season (August to November). **Pedro Romero** (☎ 320 666 2491; Cabaña Villa Malaty, Sector Villa Paz, hacia La Barra) rents surfboards (COP$15,000 per hour), bodyboards (COP$5000 per hour) and kayaks (COP$30,000 per hour). On weekends and holidays you'll find him on the beach (from 6:30am to sunset). Otherwise find him at the address above.

SLEEPING

There are a dozen or more hotels in Ladrilleros. Most are pretty basic. There's nothing top end.

El Morro (☎ 334 2998, 310 386 8100; r per person incl two meals COP$45,000) At the far end of the beach, this small hotel is the undisputed champion of sea views in Ladrilleros. The rooms are basic, but have private bathrooms and fans. Their bar is open to the public, and a great spot for a beer and a sunset.

Aguamarina Cabañas (☎ 246 0285, 311 728 3213; www.reservaaguamarina.com; cabañas per person COP$40,000) Formerly known as Cabañas Carvajal, these attractive two-story cabins sit perched on the ocean bluff. There's a dirt volleyball court, and picnic benches where you can sit and admire the views. The new owner also offers guide services in the surrounding region, including budget whale-watching tours.

Hotel Palma Real (☎ 246 0335; www.hotelpalma realcolombia.com; r per person COP$60,000-70,000; ❷ ❷) This upscale hotel is popular with *caleños* on romantic getaways. There's a Jacuzzi and a pretty pool, and a poolside bar serves drinks and plays loud music. There are only

ocean glimpses through the dense jungle. The entrance is on the beach next to that of El Morro.

EATING & DRINKING

Half a dozen basic eateries serve budget meals of fish and rice. La Zarca and Doña Francia are considered the two best in town. Order early in the day and they can prepare lobster or shrimp ceviche (seafood cooked and served with mayonnaise and ketchup).

On a bluff overlooking the sea, the **Templo del Ritmo** (☎ 246 0104; ❷ Thu-Sat) cranks up the volume on weekends, when *caleños* come to party.

Getting There & Away

The most reliable boat operator on the *muelle turístico* is **Asturias** (☎ 242 4620, 242 3696, 313 767 2864; barcoasturias@yahoo.com). Its two boats offer daily services to Juanchaco (COP$50,000 return, 1¼ hour) at 10am, 1pm and 4pm, returning at 8am, 1pm and 4pm. The return fare is good for 15 days.

From Juanchaco it's 2.5km to Ladrilleros. The road loops around a naval airbase that divides the two towns. You can walk (30 minutes) or hop on a motorcycle (COP$2000, five minutes). Large groups can haggle with the jeep drivers who hang out at the end of the Juanchaco beach (COP$20,000-ish).

SAN CIPRIANO

☎ 2 / pop 500

This tiny town is as famous for its mode of arrival as for the town itself. Situated on the little-used Cali–Buenaventura railroad and 15km from the nearest road, residents have

---

BORDER CROSSING: TUMACO

This small town is of interest only to those wanting to cross into Ecuador by sea. It's a long, difficult journey with no perceivable pay-off. We've never known or heard of anyone who bothered – we certainly didn't. There continues to be small pockets of guerrilla activity along the Ecuadorean side of the border, although the risk is low.

Cargo boats leave from El Piñal in Buenaventura (see p279) bound for Tumaco (COP$60,000, 20 hours). There are also buses from Popayán (p249) and Pasto (p261), but there is guerrilla activity in this part of Nariño. Stamp out in the **DAS office** (☎ 727 2010) in Tumaco. There are buses from here to Inguli, where you must cross the Río Mira. Then there are *chivas* to Monte Alta (one hour), where small boats can take you to San Lorenzo, Ecuador (1½ hours). Stamp in here. From here it's five hours to Esmeraldas.

There are reports that a cargo boat now offers overnight passage on Fridays from Buenaventura to Esmeraldas. Ask around at the port on Isla El Morro. You'll find budget accommodations on Playa El Morro, 1km from the port.

PLAYA JUAN DE DIOS

Opposite Juanchaco at the mouth of Bahía Malaga are the secluded, rustic cabins of **Hotel Arcoiris** (☎ 314 888 1280; www.ecomun.org/playa.htm; dm/d incl meals COP$60,000/150,000, campsite per person incl meals COP$45,000). The 'Hotel Rainbow' is run by two Colombian hippies. There is no electricity, and therefore no television, music or lights after dark; there are driftwood bonfires at night. The beach is 200m long and receives a fair amount of plastic flotsam from Buenaventura. Large groups aren't hosted so you are assured a peaceful stay. It has two kayaks you can rent, and offers tours in the nearby mangroves (COP$15,000, 1½ hours). Meals are freshly caught fish, and there is also good vegetarian fare. Beer is not always available, so if you want to drink you may want to bring something with you. You must take all your nonorganic waste with you as there is no garbage collection service.

Boat operator Asturias can drop you off on their way to Juanchaco (COP$32,000, one hour).

---

jury-rigged railroad trolley carts to shuttle themselves to and from Córdoba, the nearest town. Some power their journey with long poles they use to push themselves along. Others have bolted motorcycles to their trolleys, the front wheel fixed in the air, the back wheel in contact with one of the rails.

Sights & Activities

The town is in the middle of the jungle on the Pacific side of the mountain range. A nearby river makes for a relaxing swim. You can go inner-tubing along much of its length, and there are several waterfalls you can walk to. On weekends the town fills up with Cali holidaymakers; during the week you'll likely have the place to yourself.

La Fundación San Cipriano charges COP$1500 admission to the area.

Sleeping & Eating

Half a dozen hotels offer extremely basic lodging. Most offer budget meals. On weekends a couple of bars blast out the music for partying *caleños*.

Cabañas Carvajal (☎ 320 644 8241; r per person COP$5000) Quite possibly the cheapest hotel in Colombia, Carvajal is also the backpacker's choice in San Cipriano. It offers tours to a nearby waterfall for COP$5000 per person (2½ hours return); the local guides charge COP$25,000. Inner-tubing trips on the river (COP$5000) can also be organized. It involves a 1½-hour walk upriver and then you float back down to the hotel. The budget meals are reported to be excellent, and vegetarians can be catered for. It's the first building on the right from where the trolley drops you off.

Hotel David (☎ 312 815 4051; r without bathroom per person COP$10,000) Several hundred meters after

you pay your admission fee you'll find the 'best' hotel in town: hard mattresses, shared bathrooms, serves food. Most of the rooms are doubles but there are also a few quads and twins.

Getting There & Away

From Cali, take any bus heading to Buenaventura and get off at the junction to Córdoba (COP$18,000, three hours). From here it's a 1km walk downhill to the railway line. The posted return fare for a rail trolley to San Cipriano is COP$16,000. This is a ridiculous price. We had no trouble haggling a return fare of COP$10,000; sharper bargainers may go lower.

From Buenaventura, take the Ruta 5 bus marked Córdoba from the terminal (COP$2000, one hour). The bus runs every half hour or so. If you don't want to walk back uphill you can grab this bus back to the junction for a few hundred pesos. Buenaventura taxis can also deliver you to Córdoba for COP$25,000 to COP$40,000.

GUAPI

☎ 2 / pop 5000

This small fishing town is the main launching point for Isla Gorgona. It is famous for *ceviche guapense* (cooked seafood with mayonnaise and ketchup), and also for its *artesanías* – you'll find handmade musical instruments and intricately wrought gold jewelry, plus the usual assortment of hand-woven goods.

The town itself holds little of interest. The main drag is Calle Segunda, paved in brick, where the locals go about their business. Those looking for boats headed north or south should go down to the waterfront where the various companies have open-air kiosks that sell tickets.

Sleeping & Eating

Hotel Río Guapi (☎ 840 0983, 840 0196; s/d/tr COP$32,000/48,000/70,000) A block from where the Aviatur boat leaves for Gorgona, the Río Guapi's 40 rooms are the best in town. The floors are tile, the walls concrete, and there's a fan and cable TV. The downstairs restaurant is one of the best places to try *ceviche guapense* (COP$10,000).

Shopping

Several *artesanía* shops at the airport sell handicrafts at inflated prices.

Aquilino Cuero Solis (☎ 311 336 8018; cnr Carrera 3 & Calle 7) makes traditional musical instruments, especially drums, including *marimbas*, *tambores*, *conunos* (all types of drum) and *guasas* (a kind of rainstick). Prices vary greatly. Expect to pay somewhere between COP$80,000 to COP$250,000 for a handmade drum, depending on size.

Eber Mansilla (☎ 313 603 5196; Calle Segunda) has a good reputation for his work in gold, coconut and *tagua*. He didn't have any gold to show us when we were there, but he's worth checking out.

Getting There & Away

AIR

Aeropuerto Juan Casino Solis (☎ 840 0188) is serviced by Satena with flights to Cali and Popayán. Aexpa also offers a charter service. The coconut and guava sweets on sale at the airport are worth trying.

BOAT

Pacífico Express (☎ 840 1212, 241 6507, 313 715 3335, 313 655 9059) offers daily services from Buenaventura in a covered speedboat powered by three 200-horsepower outboard motors (COP$80,000, three to four hours).

There are a number of boats that can take you southbound to the village of Charco (COP$35,000, 50 minutes), and from there to Tumaco (COP$85,000, 3½ hours). Inquire on the waterfront.

PACIFIC COAST

ISLA MALPELO

This tiny, remote Colombian island has some of the best diving in the world. It's a mere 1643m long and 727m wide, and is 506km from the mainland. It is the center of the vast **Santuario de Flora y Fauna Malpelo** (ecoturismo@parquesnacionales.gov.co; admission per day Colombian/foreigner on foreign-flagged boat COP$133,000/75,000, Colombian/foreigner on Colombian-flagged boat COP$75,000/71,000) and is the largest no-fishing zone in the eastern Tropical Pacific, and provides a critical habitat for threatened marine species.

The diversity and, above all, the size of the marine life is said to be eye-popping, including over 200 hammerhead sharks and 1000 silky sharks. It is also one of the few places where sightings of the short-nosed ragged-tooth shark, a deepwater shark, have been confirmed. The volcanic island has steep walls and impressive caves. The best time to see the sharks is January to March, when colder weather drives them to the surface to feed. A small contingent of Colombian soldiers guard Malpelo, and it's forbidden to set foot on the island.

The quality of the diving is matched only by the difficulty of getting there, and the difficulty of the diving itself. The island can only be visited as part of a live-aboard dive cruise, usually lasting eight days. Travel time is 30 to 36 hours each way from Buenaventura, and there is no decompression chamber on the island. There are strong currents that pull you up, down, and sideways – you may well surface kilometers from where you entered the water.

Only advanced divers with experience and confidence should attempt this trip. You'll need your own wet suit (minimum 5mm), with hood, gloves, diving computer, dive horn and decompression buoy.

Boats from three countries offer this trip. Your cheapest options are the Colombian-flagged *Doña Mariela* or *Maria Patricia* (see p284). Both charge around COP$3,500,000 per diver for eight days. The **Inula** (☎ in Germany 49 5130 790326, in Panama 507 6672 9091; www.inula-diving.de), out of Puerto David, Panama, offers the trip for around US$3500 per diver, and the **Undersea Hunter** (☎ 506 2228 6613; www.underseahunter.com) out of Puntarenas, Costa Rica charges roughly US$6500 per diver. The Undersea Hunter may stop offering this trip as of 2009. Check their website for the latest.

Only one dive boat at a time is permitted near Malpelo. There are only a handful of cruises each year, and they fill up fast.

PACIFIC COAST

PARQUE NACIONAL NATURAL (PNN) ISLA GORGONA

Todo está prohibido, goes the joke on this island – everything is forbidden. Somehow this seems rather appropriate; it was the site of a prison from 1960 to 1984. Now it's a **national park** (admission Colombians/foreigners COP$9000/25,000) with a resort on the grounds of the former prison. And everything is forbidden – park guards will search your bags for liquor, fishing gear and aerosol cans, and confiscate them; no liquor, wine or beer may be consumed on the island. Since fishing and gardening are both forbidden, meals consist mainly of defrosted beef, frozen vegetables and canned fruit.

The two main reasons to come here are scuba diving and whale-watching, preferably at the same time. Gorgona is not on any of the main shipping channels, so whales continue to come here every year to calve and raise their young. Several boats offer live-aboard diving trips to Gorgona, if you prefer not to stay on the island. There's also good snorkeling along the adjacent coral reef, and a few short walks you can do around the island, including to the remains of the prison.

The island itself is 38km off the coast, 11km long by 2.3km wide. It is covered in young, secondary rain forest (the convicts chopped down most of the trees for cooking fuel), which harbors an abundance of poisonous snakes. It was Francisco Pizarro who named the island while visiting on the way to conquer Peru – two of his men died from snakebites.

Gorgona is also noted for a large number of endemic species, including monkeys, lizards, bats and birds. This is due to its long separation from the mainland. Two species of freshwater turtles and a colony of *babillas* (spectacled caimans) live at Laguna Ayatuna. Sea turtles come during breeding season and lay eggs on the beaches.

In darker times, Gorgona was one of the few safe places tourists could visit on the Pacific coast. Now that conditions have improved, you'll find there are better beaches and wilder jungle elsewhere.

The concession to the island is owned by **Aviatur** (☎ 840 0871; www.parquegorgona.com.co; per person incl full board COP$253,000; 🖳). No new building is permitted here; accommodation is in the remodeled former prison staff quarters. Most people visit as part of a package tour (around COP$1,000,000 per person) including flights from Guapi via Cali or Popayán. A package tour taken from Medellín or Bogotá will fly you here via Cali. Boat transport and accommodations on the island are also included, but diving and activities cost extra.

Dangers & Annoyances

Gorgona got its Greek mythology–derived name for a reason: it's an island full of poisonous snakes. It's forbidden to go walking on the island without a guide or after dark. You'll be given gumboots to protect against snakebites.

Activities

DIVING TOURS

For divers who don't want to stay on the island, two boats out of Buenaventura offer weekend live-aboard diving trips, departing the *muelle turístico* on Friday night and returning Monday morning. The *Maria Patricia* (owned by Asturias) and the *Doña Mariela* (☎ 681 2724, 514 4699, 311 630 5121) both charge around COP$850,000 to COP$900,000 per diver, including six or seven dives, meals, transport, and a visit to the island. They can also provide transport to the island (bunk below deck COP$120,000, 10 hours), including dinner and breakfast.

Getting There & Away

Aviatur runs a speedboat to the island most days (COP$110,000 return, 1¼ hours), although it's best to book in advance. From Buenaventura, Pacifico Express (see p283) runs a daily speedboat to Guapi. With a minimum of 10 passengers it can take you direct to Gorgona (COP$110,000, four to five hours).

Numerous cargo boats ply this route, including the *Andrés Paula, El Clipper, El Discovery, Juan Diego* and *El Costa Azul*, and can occasionally drop you off directly on the island. There is service most days leaving Buenaventura in the late afternoon and arriving at Guapi in the early morning. In Buenaventura boats depart from Muelle El Piñal. Information and reservations are available from **Bodega Liscano** (☎ 244 6089, 244 6106), near the wharf.

Amazon Basin

mazon. The very word evokes images of pristine jungle, incredible wildlife and one famous ver. The Amazon basin, which Colombians call Amazonia, is unimaginably massive. The 43,000-sq-km region accounts for a third of Colombia's total area – about the size of California and larger than Germany. Visitors can never quite account for the strange exhilaration ney feel when they come face-to-face with the rainforest for the first time.

With transportation mainly limited to the rivers that crisscross the jungle, indigenous locals ave been able to keep their cultures more or less intact. The region remains an ethnic and nguistic mosaic, with more than 50 languages (not counting dialects) belonging to some 0 linguistic families.

Unfortunately, isolation has also made Amazonia a hotbed for cultivation of the coca plant nd cocaine production. The canopied jungle provides a natural hideout for leftist guerrillas. Despite recent Colombian military success stories, rebels still control parts of Guaviare, aquetá and Putumayo departments.

Fortunately, tourist-friendly Amazonas is one of the safest departments in Colombia. It its on a quirky strip of land that penetrates Brazil and Peru, and was not part of Colombia ntil 1922. From Leticia you can venture up and down the river to explore the rainforest, ayak alongside pink dolphins or just chill out in a hammock and sleep to the sounds of he jungle. The allure of the Amazon is an experience you won't soon forget.

AMAZON BASIN

HIGHLIGHTS

- Sample the tender Amazonian fish known as the *pirarucú* at one of the pleasant outdoor restaurants in **Leticia** (p286)
- Be serenaded by parrots in the rainforest of **Parque Nacional Natural Amacayacu** (p292)
- Stroll through the car-free, sustainable remote village of charming **Puerto Nariño** (p293)
- Kayak alongside pink dolphins through the warm waters of the mighty **Lago Tarapoto** (p293)
- Slip silently into the jungle by canoe up the tributaries of the **Río Yavarí** (p294)

LETICIA

☎ 8 / pop 37,000 / elev 95m

As the capital city of the Amazonas province, Leticia is the largest city for hundreds of miles yet still looks and feels very much like a small frontier town. It's located on the Amazon River at the crossroads – or more accurately, the cross river – point where Colombia, Brazil and Peru meet. Leticia is located more than 500 miles from the nearest Colombian highway. Yet despite its isolation, Leticia is a remarkable little border town with brightly painted houses, pleasant outdoor cafes and restaurants and a wide selection of hotels.

Leticia was founded in 1867 as San Antonio. The origin of its current name has been lost to history. In any case, it was part of Peru until 1922 when both countries signed a controversial agreement that ceded the land to Colombia. In 1932 a small war broke out between Colombia and Peru, finally ending in 1933 after the League of Nations negotiated a cease-fire, ultimately awarding Leticia to Colombia. In 1970s Leticia became lawless hub of narcotics trafficking until the Colombian army moved in and cleaned things up.

Today, a long-standing military presence keeps the city and surrounding region safe. The most dangerous part of your trip may be dodging the swarms of motorcyclists who disregard traffic laws and pedestrians. Visitors can freely move between Leticia and its sister city of Tabatinga, in Brazil, plus the Peruvian island of Santa Rosa. Travelers wishing to venture further into either country must meet immigration requirements.

The best time to visit is July and August during the dry season; February to April is the wettest. The Amazon River's water level is at its highest in May and June, then drops by nearly 15m from August to October. Despite the oppressive heat, humidity and man-eating mosquitoes, Leticia makes a pleasant base for exploring the rest of the Amazon basin.

Orientation

Leticia is on the banks of the Amazon on the Colombia–Brazil border. Just across the frontier sits Tabatinga, a Brazilian town much the same size as Leticia, with its own airport and port. Leticia and Tabatinga are virtually merging; there are no border checkpoints between them. Frequent *colectivos* (shared taxis or minibuses) link the towns, or you can just walk.

On the island in the Amazon opposite Leticia/Tabatinga is Santa Rosa, a small Peruvian village. Boats head there from Leticia's Muelle Fluvial (river pier) and the market, and Tabatinga's Porto da Feira.

On the opposite side of the Amazon from Leticia, about 25km downstream, is the Brazilian town of Benjamin Constant, the main port for boats downstream to Manaus. Boats shuttle regularly between Tabatinga and Benjamin Constant.

Information

INTERNET ACCESS

There are several internet cafes in town, all charging about COP$1500 per hour. Connections are generally sluggish. **Papeleri Internacional** (Av Internacional No 6-40; ☯ 8am-11pm) and **Centro de Negocios** (Carrera 10 No 8-96; ☯ 7am-10pm) have a good selection of terminals in air-conditioned premises.

LAUNDRY

Lavandería Aseo Total (☎ 592 6051; Carrera 10 No 9-3; per kg COP$2700; ☯ 7am-9pm Mon-Sat, 8am-1pm Sun)

MEDICAL SERVICES

San Rafael de Leticia Hospital (☎ 592 7075; Av Vásquez Cobo No 13-78). You'll also find many pharmacies along Carrera 10 and elsewhere.

MONEY

There are many ATMs, but it's next to impossible to change traveler's checks here. To exchange currency, look for the *casas de cambio* on Calle 8 between Carrera 11 and the market. They change US dollars, Colombian pesos, Brazilian reais and Peruvian soles. Shop around as rates vary. Businesses in both Tabatinga and Leticia generally accept both reais and pesos.

Banco BBVA (cnr Carrera 10 & Calle 7) ATM.
Banco de Bogotá (cnr Carrera 10 & Calle 7) ATM.
Bancolombia (Calle 8 s/n, btwn Carreras 11 and 10) ATM.
Cambio Amazonas (☎ 592 5134; Carrera 11 No 7-96; ☯ 8am-noon & 2-6pm Mon-Sat) Currency exchange.

TOURIST INFORMATION

Tourist office (Secretaría de Turismo y Fronteras; ☎ 592 7569; Calle 8 No 9-75; ☯ 8am-noon & 2pm-5pm Mon-Fri)

VISA INFORMATION

Locals and foreigners are allowed to come and go between Leticia and Tabatinga without visas or passport control, but if you plan

LETICIA

0 — 300 m
0 — 0.2 miles

INFORMATION
Amazon Jungle Trips	1 C6
Banco BBVA	2 B6
Banco de Bogotá	3 B6
Bancolombia	4 B5
Brazilian Consulate	5 B4
Cambios Amazonas	6 B5
Centro de Negocios	7 B5
DAS (exit & entry passport stamps)	(see 36)
DAS (Visa extensions)	8 B5
Lavandería Aseo Total	9 B5
Papelería Internacional	10 C5
Peruvian Consulate	11 C4
San Rafael de Leticia Hospital	12 A4
Tanimboca	13 B4
Tourist Office	14 B5

SIGHTS & ACTIVITIES
Galería Arte Indigena	15 B5
Museo del Hombre Amazónico	16 A5
Museo Uirapuru	(see 15)
Parque Santander	17 A5

SLEEPING
Decalodge Ticuna	18 B6
Hospedaje Los Delfines	19 A4
Hotel Anaconda	20 B6
Hotel de la Selva	21 B5
Hotel La Frontera	22 C6
Hotel Yurupary	23 B5
Mahatu Jungle Hostel	24 B5

EATING
A Me K Tiar	25 B5
Cozinha de Fazenda	26 B5
La Casa del Pan	27 A4
La Cava Amazonica	28 B5
Local Market	29 A5
Restaurante El Sabor	30 B5
Tierras Amazónicas	31 B5

DRINKING
Mossh Bar	32 B5
Várzea	33 A3

ENTERTAINMENT
Barbacoas	34 B5
Discoteca L'Boom	35 B5
Emociones	(see 35)

TRANSPORT
Aeropuerto Internacional Alfredo Vásquez Cobo	36 A1
AeroRepública	37 B6
Boat Dock	38 A5
Minibuses to Tabatinga	39 B5
Satena	40 B5
Taxi Stand	41 B5
Transportes Fluviales	42 A5

AMAZON BASIN

on heading further into either country, you must get your passport stamped at the DAS office at Leticia's airport or at **Policía Federal** (Av da Amizade 650; ☻ 7am-noon & 2-6pm), near the hospital in Tabatinga.

Citizens of some countries, including the USA, Canada, Australia and New Zealand, need a visa to enter Brazil and it may be costly, especially for US citizens. Bring a passport photo and yellow-fever vaccination certificate to the **Brazilian Consulate** (☎ 592 7530; Carrera 9 No 13-84; ☻ 8am-noon & 2-4pm Mon-Fri).

If you're coming from or going to Iquitos, get your entry or exit stamp at the **Policía Internacional Peruviano (PIP)** office on Isla Santa Rosa, or visit the **Peruvian Consulate** (☎ 592 7204; Calle 11 No 5-32; ☻ 8am-1pm & 3-6pm Mon-Fri).

Travelers coming here from Brazil may need to visit the **Colombian Consulate** (☎ 412 2104; Rua General Sampaio 623, Tabatinga; ☻ 8am-2pm Mon-Fri) to get the necessary visa.

If you need a Colombian visa extension, head to the downtown **DAS office** (Calle 9 No 9-62; ☻ 7:30am-noon & 2-6pm Mon-Sat, 7:30am-noon & 2-4pm Sun). Be aware: there are two DAS offices, and each have different responsibilities. The downtown DAS handles visa extensions and residency issues. Passport stamps, required for entry and exit, are obtained from the DAS office at the airport.

Sights & Activities

Museo del Hombre Amazónico (☎ 592 7729; Carrera 11 No 9-43; admission free; ☻ 8-11:30am & 2-5pm Mon-Fri) This small museum is located inside the dolphin-pink-colored Biblioteca del Banco de la República building, has a small collection of indigenous artifacts including musical instruments, textiles, tools, pottery and weapons, and lots of freaky-looking ceremonial masks.

The **Galería Arte Indígena** (☎ 592 7056; Calle 8 No 10-35; ☻ 9am-noon & 3-7pm Mon-Sat, 9am-noon Sun) is Leticia's largest craft shop selling artifacts from local indigenous groups. At the back of the shop is **Museo Uirapuru** featuring an exhibition of historic crafts (not for sale).

A visit to **Parque Santander** just before sunset makes for an impressive spectacle as you witness thousands of small screeching *pericos* (parrots) arriving for their nightly rest in the park's trees.

Some 11km from downtown, you'll find the **Serpentario Nacional Amero** (☎ 592 6692; www.nativa.org; Km11 Via Tarapacá; admission adult/child COP$7000/5000; ☻ 8am-4pm) where you can get up

close and personal with boas, anacondas an other slithery creatures on show at this snak sanctuary. Take a taxi or the bus (COP$250(from Parque Orellana.

Let's face it! You're never too old to clim a tree. At **Reserva Tanimboca** (☎ 592 7679, 3 774 5919; Km8 Via Tarapacá; ☻ 6am-6pm) visito can monkey around atop 35m high tree then slide 80m along zip lines from on tree to another through the beautiful fore canopy (COP$60,000). Other activities in clude kayaking (COP$20,000) and noctu nal jungle hikes (COP$150,000). Or splurg for an overnight stay in a **treehouse** (s/d COP$150,000/COP$200,000/COP$300,000).

Isla de Los Micos, located 35km north up stream from Leticia, is a 450-hectare islan reserve of birds, giant Victoria Regia wate lilies and thousands of capuchin monkeys. I was founded by American entrepreneur Mik Tsalickis, who built a small tourism empire i Leticia until he was caught in 1989 trying t smuggle 3000kg of cocaine into the US. A fe vendors on the island sell snacks and craft Any of the tour guides (below) can arrange day trip to the island.

Tours

The real jungle begins well off the Amazo proper, along its small tributaries. Th deeper you go, the more chance you hav to observe wildlife in relatively undamage habitats and to visit indigenous settlement This involves time and money, but the expe rience can be rewarding. A three- to four-da tour is perhaps the best way to balance th cost of the trip with the insight it will giv you into the workings of the jungle. Severa companies also organize multiday tours t the small nature reserves along the Río Yava (p294) on the Brazil–Peru border. Alway agree on price, activities and duration befor embarking on your trip. Avoid any unsolic ited tour guides who approach you in th airport or streets.

Two highly experienced guides we recom mend are Enrique 'Kike' Arés of **Omshant** (☎ 311 489 8985; www.omshanty.com) and Felipe Ullo of **Selvaventura** (☎ 311 287 1307; selvaventura@gma .com). Both speak English and Spanish; Felip also speaks Portuguese. They can arrang pretty much whatever your heart desires.

Also recommended:
Amazon Jungle Trips (☎ 592 7377; amazonjungle trips@yahoo.com; Av Internacional No 6-25) With 20 years

of experience, Amazon Jungle is one of the oldest and most reliable tour companies in Leticia. Owner Antonio Cruz Pérez speaks English and can arrange individually tailored tours including trips to their Reserva Natural Zacambú in Río Yavarí.

Tanimboca (☎ 310 827 9412, 321 207 9909; Carrera 10 No 11-69) In addition to the activities at Reserva Tanimboca, the friendly folks here can organize boat or hiking trips into the jungle outside Leticia, including trips to indigenous villages. The owner and several of the guides speak English.

Sleeping

Note that prices can skyrocket during high season, especially around Christmas and Easter.

BUDGET

Mahatu Jungle Hostel (☎ 311 539 1265; www.mahatu.com; Carrera 7 No 9-69; dm per person COP$15,000, d COP$25,000/30,000; 🖳) An urban jungle in the heart of Leticia, this charming hostel is the new favorite in town, with simple but sparkling clean rooms, shared baths and kitchen and free use of internet and bicycles. Owner/philosopher Gustavo Rene speaks English, Spanish, Dutch, French and Portuguese.

Hotel de la Selva (☎ /fax 592 7616; hoteldelaselvaleticia@hotmail.com; Calle 7 No 7-28; s/d COP$40,000/55,000, with air-con COP$70,000/90,000; 🗶) Rooms are small with basic furnishing, but the plant-filled common area makes this friendly place even more welcoming.

MIDRANGE & TOP END

Hospedaje Los Delfines (☎ 592 7388; losdelfinesleticia@hotmail.com; Carrera 11 No 12-81; s/d COP$40,000/60,000) A 10-minute walk from the center, this small, family-run place has nine spacious if basic rooms with beds and hammocks, surrounding a gorgeously landscaped courtyard filled with flowers and fruit.

Hotel La Frontera (☎ 592 5600; fronterahotelet@hotmail.com; Av Internacional No 1-04; s/d/tr incl breakfast COP$55,000/80,000/120,000; 🗶) The modern La Frontera hotel is appropriately named as it's just 4m from the Brazilian border. The 16 rooms have bath, fan, air-con and cable TV.

ourpick Hotel Yurupary (☎ 592 7983; www.hotelyurupary.col.nu, in Spanish; Calle 8 No 7-26; s/d/tr COP$79,000/85,000/95,000; 🗶 🖳) This moderately priced favorite has large, recently refurbished rooms with private baths, TV, air-con and wi-fi. The outside courtyard features a refreshing swimming pool, garden, bar and restaurant.

Hotel Anaconda (☎ 592 7119; www.hotelanaconda.com.co; Carrera 11 No 7-34; s/d per person incl breakfast COP$123,000/114,000; 🗶 🖳) Once the finest hotel in Leticia, Anaconda is looking a bit dated. The 50 well-worn rooms have a distinctly utilitarian feel. The courtyard with pool and outdoor dining is more pleasing to the eye.

Decalodge Ticuna (☎ 592 6948; www.decameron.com; Carrera 11 No 6-11; s incl breakfast & dinner COP$228,000-281,000, d per person incl breakfast & dinner COP$175,000-228,000; 🅿 🗶 🖳 🖳) For those seeking the ultimate in luxury and comfort, Decalodge is hands down the best hotel in Leticia. Its plush, contemporary cabañas have huge, comfy beds, private baths and hammocks, opening up to a lush courtyard and pool. There's also a large open-air bar and a restaurant that serves high-end Amazonian cuisine. The on-site travel agent can book regional tours and activities.

Eating

There's no shortage of good food in Leticia. The local specialty is fish, including the delicious *gamitana* and *pirarucú*. Prices tend to be a bit higher than in 'mainland' Colombia, but most restaurants serve cheap set meals, especially at lunchtime. You can also find cheap food stalls and fresh fruit and veggies at the **local market** (Calle 8 & waterfront; 🕓 6am-4pm).

La Casa del Pan (☎ 592 7660; Calle 11 No 10-20; 🕓 6:30am-11pm Mon-Sat) Facing Parque Santander, this bright, bustling bakery is a great spot for breakfast (eggs, bread, coffee and fruit juice for COP$3500) or a late afternoon coffee.

Cozinha de Fazenda (Carrera 9 No 7-56; mains COP$2000-8000; 🕓 breakfast, lunch & dinner) From the same folks who own Restaurante El Sabor comes this great family-run restaurant with home-cooked meals. House specialties include grilled fish with garlic, onions and yucca. The real winner here is the breakfast menu, with such options as banana pancakes, French toast and omelettes.

Restaurante El Sabor (☎ 592 4774; Calle 8 No 9-25; mains COP$6000-10,000; 🕓 6am-11pm Mon-Sat) This legendary, hole-in-the-wall diner is a Leticia tradition. It serves set meals (COP$6000), vegetarian dishes, fruit salads, plus unlimited free fruit juice with your meal.

A Me K Tiar (☎ 592 6094; Carrera 9 No 8-15; mains COP$5000-13,000; 🕓 lunch & dinner) Serving good *parrilla* (grilled meat) and Mexican favorites at great prices, this place is crowded with locals and tourists alike. The outdoor terrace is a great people-watching spot. Wash your meal down with cold beer or fresh juices.

La Cava Amazonica (☎ 592 4935; Carrera 9 No 8-23; set meals COP$6000, mains COP$10,000-17,000; ☼ lunch & dinner) This open-air restaurant is a locals' lunchtime favorite. The set meals include huge portions of soup, salad, a meat dish and side of veggies, all for just COP$6000. It can get quite crowded during the weekday lunch rush.

Tierras Amazónicas (☎ 592 4748; Calle 8 No 7-50; mains COP$8000-21,000; ☼ 10am-11pm Tue-Sun) At first glance, this looks like an unapologetic tourist trap. The menu is written on a wooden plank; the walls are covered in kitschy Amazonia knickknacks. Nonetheless, it's a fantastic place for a fun dinner. The specialty is fish. The pan-grilled *pirarucú* is heavenly. There's a full bar, and live music most nights. This is the *real* rainforest cafe.

Drinking & Entertainment

Discoteca L' Boom (Calle 9 No 10-40; ☼ 9pm-2am Thu, 9pm-4am Fri & Sat) Also known as Kahlúa, this is the only real nightclub in Leticia, and not a particularly good one. The dimly lit interior looks more like a strip club, complete with mirrored walls and stripper poles. DJs crank out salsa, cumbia, vallenato and reggaetón tunes. The adjoining chill-out bar, Emociones, is much more inviting, with a terrace overlooking the city.

Várzea (☎ 320 316 6083; Carrera 10 No 14-12; ☼ 6pm-2am Tue-Sun) Off the beaten track on the road to the airport, this trendy little neighborhood bar was one of Leticia's best-kept secrets – until now. It has a friendly atmosphere with great music and strong drinks. It also happens to serve the best pizza in town, with a huge selection of toppings. What more do you need?

Mossh Bar (☎ 592 7097; Carrera 10 No 10-08; ☼ 4pm-2am Tue-Thu, 4pm-4am Fri & Sat) This trendy bar facing Parque Santander is a step up from the usual Leticia watering holes. The modish interior is decorated in red, white, black and chrome. The full bar serves strong drinks, with hefty prices to match.

Barbacoas (☎ 592 2005; Carrera 10 8-28; ☼ 6am-2am) Unlike most Colombian billiards clubs that only cater to men, ladies are warmly welcomed at Barbacoas – probably because the pool tables are hidden in a separate back room. The sidewalk cafe is a pleasant place to people-watch over a beer or coffee.

Getting There & Away

There are no overland crossings to Leticia.

AIR

All foreigners must pay COP$15,500 tourist tax upon arrival at Leticia's airport, Aeropuerto Internacional Alfredo Vásquez Cobo, to the north of the town.

AeroRepública (☎ 592 7666; www.aerorepublica .com.co; Calle 7 No 10-36; ☼ 8am-noon & 2-6pm Mon-Fri 8am-noon Sat) has daily flights to Bogotá. The Colombian Air Force–operated airline, **Satena** (☎ 592 5419; www.satena.com; Calle 9 s/n; ☼ 8am-noon & 2-6pm Mon-Fri, 8am-noon Sat), flies to Bogotá on Monday, Wednesday and Friday. Prices vary widely, but expect to pay about COP$300,000 for a one-way flight; Satena is usually cheaper. Book early for the best rates.

Trip (www.voetrip.com.br) flies from Tabatinga International Airport to Manaus daily (COP$600,000). The airport is 4km south of Tabatinga; *colectivos* marked 'Comara' from Leticia will drop you nearby. Don't forget to get your Colombian exit stamp at Leticia's airport and, if needed, a Brazilian visa, before departure.

BOAT
To Manaus (Brazil)

Boats to Manaus leave from Tabatinga's Porto Fluvial on Wednesday and Saturday at 2pm with a stop in Benjamin Constant. The journey to Manaus takes three days and four nights and costs around COP$150,000 if you bring your own hammock, or about COP$555,000 for two people in a double cabin.

Traveling upstream from Manaus to Tabatinga, the trip usually takes six days, and costs about COP$250,000 in your hammock or COP$750,000 for a double cabin. See the boxed text, opposite, for more information.

To Iquitos (Peru)

Transtur (☎ +51 65 221 356; www.transtursa.com; Rua Marechal Mallet 248, Tabatinga) operates high-speed passenger boats between Tabatinga and Iquitos. Boats leave from Tabatinga's Porto da Feira at 5am on Wednesday, Friday and Sunday, arriving in Iquitos about 10 hours later. The boats call in at Santa Rosa's immigration point. Don't forget to get your Colombian exit stamp at the Leticia airport DAS office the day before departure. The journey costs COP$140,000 in either direction, including breakfast and lunch.

THE SLOW BOAT TO BRAZIL

Traveling by boat may not be the fastest way to get around, but it's one of the most rewarding ways to experience real life on the Amazonas. These bare-bone boats are the main mode of transportation on the Amazon River, and are often packed to the gills with humans, cargo and sometimes animals.

Note that these are not luxury cruise ships. Tickets are relatively cheap, and include all on-board meals. You should bring your own snacks, bottled water and spending money; ship stores sell beer and snacks. It's a long journey, so bring a good book and any other little luxuries that will make your trip more comfortable. Note these boats can get very crowded.

To organize your trip, head down to the Porto Fluvial a day or two in advance and ask around to find the next boat to Manaus. Board the boat and inform the crew you want to join them. Boats come to Tabatinga one or two days before their scheduled departure back down the river. You can string up your hammock or occupy the cabin as soon as you've paid the fare, saving on hotels. Food, however, is only served after departure. Beware of theft on board.

Note there are no roads out of Iquitos into Peru. You have to fly or continue by river to Pucallpa (five to seven days), from where you can go overland to Lima.

Getting Around

The main mode of public transport is by moto-taxi, the big red motorcycles that zip around town without a care in the world. The base rate is COP$1000. Hang on tight! Frequent *colectivos* (COP$1000 to COP$5000) link Leticia with Tabatinga and the 'Kilometer' villages north of Leticia's airport. Standard taxis can be quite expensive; a short ride to the airport can set you back COP$15,000.

TABATINGA (BRAZIL)

☎ 97 / pop 45,300 / elev 95m

This gritty, unattractive border town doesn't have much to offer in terms of tourist attractions. Most visitors are only here to catch a boat to Manaus or Iquitos, or on a quick border-hop just to say they've been to Brazil. While distinctly less pleasant than Leticia, you might consider staying here if you're taking an early-morning boat to Iquitos. For visa information see p286 and for information on getting there and away, see opposite. Prices listed below are in Colombian pesos, which are widely accepted in Tabatinga. Brazil's telephone country code is +55.

Sleeping

Avoid the hotels near the border; some of them double as brothels.

International Bagpacker Hostel (☎ 3412 3846, 312 585 8855; amazondiscover@hotmail.com; Rue Pedro Teixeira No 9; dm per person COP$15,000, s/d COP$25,000/35,000)

Calling this place 'basic' would be an overstatement. But it's conveniently located just three blocks from Porta da Feira, perfect if you're catching an early boat.

Eating & Drinking

Restaurante Tres Fronteiras do Amazonas (☎ 3412 2341; Rua Rui Barbosa; mains COP$9000-20,000 ⏰ 9am-11pm) This attractive palm-thatched open-air restaurant offers a wide choice of fish and meat dishes, plus a selection of drinks, including *caipirinhas* (the national cocktail of Brazil made with limes, sugar and cachaça, a Brazilian version of rum). The food is straightforward, but hearty and delicious.

Churrascaria Tia Helena (☎ 3412 2165; Rua Marechal Mallet 12; all you can eat COP$22,000; ⏰ lunch & dinner) At this delicious all-you-can-eat restaurant, waiters bring skewered meats directly from the grill, and carve them up at the table in classic Brazilian fashion. The place is no-frills; think cement floors and fluorescent lights.

Scandalos (☎ 9152 8777; www.portaltabatinga.com.br/scandalos.htm; cnr Avenida da Amizade & Rua Pedro Teixeira; ⏰ 10pm-late Fri & Sat) Located about five blocks from the border, this is the best nightclub in the region, attracting a young, sexy crowd dancing till dawn. Live music most Saturdays.

ISLA SANTA ROSA (PERU)

Five minutes by boat from Leticia, this tiny island village on the Amazon River has a few rustic *hospedajes* (hostels), some thatch-covered bars and restaurants but not much else. It's home to a few hundred people and lots of free-range chickens and turkeys. About the only real tourist attraction here is a giant

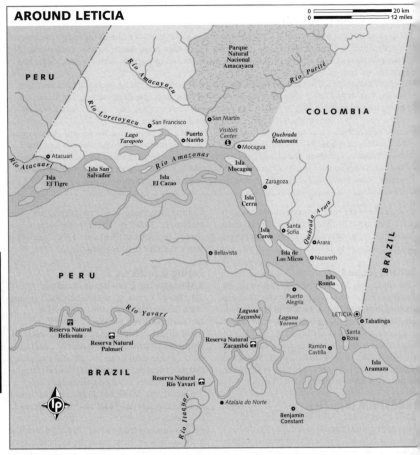

AROUND LETICIA

blue 'Welcome to Peru' sign where you can pose for photos. If you are coming from or going to Iquitos, you'll need to come here and visit the **Policía Internacional Peruviano (PIP)** office to get your exit/entry stamp in your passport. Everything is located along the single paved footpath through town. Water taxis (COP$4000) ply the Leticia–Santa Rosa route from dawn to dusk.

PARQUE NACIONAL NATURAL (PNN) AMACAYACU

Sprawling across almost 300,000 hectares, **PNN Amacayacu** (☎ 522 2890; admission foreigners/Colombians COP$21,000/8000) is an ideal spot from which to observe the Amazonian rainforest up close. About 75km upriver from Leticia, the park is

home to 500 species of birds and 150 mammals and dozens of reptiles including crocs boas and anacondas. And millions of mosquitoes. Activities include bird-watching, kayaking and multiday hikes.

The recently renovated visitor amenities include dorm lodges with shared baths, four luxury cabins with private baths and a restaurant. The luxury hotel chain Decameron now runs the park's tourist facilities, and with them came sky-high prices. A simple dorm bunk will set you back a whopping COP$83,000 per person; rooms start at COP$160,000 per person.

High-speed boats to Puerto Nariño (see p294) will drop you off at the visitors center (COP$22,000, 1½ hours from Leticia). Boats often fill up; buy your tickets in advance. Getting back to Leticia can be a bit trickier. The best option is to flag down a high-speed boat returning from Puerto Nariño; they pass by the visitors center at around 11:30am and 4:30pm, but won't stop if they're full. As a last resort, try flagging down one of slow cargo ships or *peque-peques* (small motorized boats) back to Leticia.

PUERTO NARIÑO

☎ 8 / pop 2000 / elev 110m

The tiny Amazonian village of Puerto Nariño is a world-class model for sustainable living. Here, 75km upriver from Leticia, this ecological community is living proof that man and nature can peacefully coexist.

Puerto Nariño has elevated the concept of green living to an art form. Motorized vehicles are banned. The spotless city is laid out on a grid of landscaped, pedestrian-only sidewalks. Every morning, citizen brigades fan out to tidy up the town.

The little town's ambitious recycling and organic waste management programs would put most world cities to shame. Trash and recycling bins are located on practically every corner. Rainwater is collected in cisterns for washing and gardening. Electricity comes from the town's energy-efficient generator, but only runs until midnight. Fall asleep to the sounds of jungle chit-chat and the pitter-patter of raindrops on tin roofs.

The majority of Puerto Nariño's residents are indigenous Tikuna, Cocoma and Yagua peoples. Their community experiment in ecological living has led to an important source of income: ecotourism. This tranquil town is a great base from which to visit the pink dolphins of Lago Tarapoto by kayak, explore the jungle on foot or simply chill out in a hammock, enjoying the sights and sounds of the Amazon.

Information

There are no banks or ATMs in Puerto Nariño, and credit cards are not accepted anywhere. Bring plenty of cash from Leticia.

Compartel (cnr Carrera 6 & Calle 5; per hr COP$2000; ☻ 8am-9pm Mon-Sat) Provides internet access plus local and international telephone service.

Hospital (cnr Carrera 4 & Calle 5)

Tourist office (☎ 313 235 3687; cnr Carrera 7 & Calle 5; ☻ 8am-noon & 2-5pm Mon-Fri) Located inside the *alcaldía* Municipal town hall building.

Sights & Activities

Fundación Omacha (omacha.org), located on the riverfront just east of the docks is a conservation and research center working to save the Amazon's pink dolphins and manatees. Next door, the **Centro de Interpretación Natütama** (admission by donation; ☻ 8am-noon & 2-5pm Wed-Mon) has a fascinating museum with nearly 100 life-sized wood carvings of Amazonian flora and fauna. There's also a small turtle hatchery outside.

Casa Museo Etnocultural (cnr Carrera 7 & Calle 5; admission free; ☻ 8am-noon & 2-5pm Mon-Fri), located in the *alcaldía* town hall building, has a small display of artifacts exploring the region's indigenous populations.

For a bird's-eye view of the village, climb the **Mirador** (COP$5000; ☻ 5am-5pm) tower, located at the top of Calle 4.

You can **hike** to several nearby indigenous villages including **San Martín** (three hours) and **20 de Julio** (30 minutes) by following the sidewalks leading out of town.

Lago Tarapoto, 10km west of Puerto Nariño, is a beautiful jungle lake that is home to the Amazon's famous pink dolphins (*botos*). You may also spot an Amazonian manatee and varied flora including the Victoria Regia, the world's largest water lily. A half-day trip to the lake in a *peque-peque* can be organized from Puerto Nariño (COP$50,000 for up to four people). Locals can take you on boat excursions to many other places, including the Parque Nacional Natural Amacayacu.

Sleeping

There are about a dozen hotel options in town.

Cabañas del Friar (☎ 311 502 8592, 320 596 6330; altodelaguila@hotmail.com; r per person COP$15,000) About 30 minutes west of town, famous friar Hector José Rivera and his crazy monkey Tata run this hilltop jungle oasis overlooking the Amazon. The complex includes several simple huts, shared facilities and a lookout tower. Friar Hector can arrange kayak trips, jungle walks and visits to indigenous villages. To get there, take Carrera 6 west out of town across the big bridge and just ask around for 'Casa del Fraile.'

Hotel Lomas del Paiyü (☎ 313 237 0840; Carrera 6 No 7-74; elider_10@hotmail.com; r per person without/with private bath COP$20,000/25,000) This tin-roofed, family-run hotel is an old but reliable choice, with 10 basic, clean rooms.

AMAZON BASIN

ourpick Hotel Napü (☎ 310 488 0998; Calle 4 No 5-72; olgabeco@yahoo.com; r per person COP$25,000) Our favorite hotel has the look and feel of a treehouse fort. The rooms are simple but comfortable, with basic furnishings, fan and shared baths. Try for rooms 7 and 8 of the back building, which share a balcony with hammocks overlooking the courtyard garden and jungle.

Hostal Asaí (☎ 592 6656, 311 477 8973; hostalasai@ yahoo.es; Carrera 6 No 6-65; r per person COP$30,000) Run by the Casa Selva folks across the street, the Hostal Asaí is a whimsical A-frame, thatch-covered house with shared baths and common area. There is a kitchen sink, but no fridge or stove.

Casa Selva (☎ 315 333 2796; casaselvahotel@yahoo .es; Carrera 6 No 6-78; s/d/tr COP$100,000/120,000/155,000) A tall, handsome wood building two blocks up from the dock is the most luxurious option in town. The 12 tasteful rooms have private bath, fan and balcony, surrounding a two-story courtyard and restaurant (mains COP$10,000).

Eating & Drinking

Puerto Nariño is sorely lacking worthy restaurant options. There are a few fast-food joints and grocery stores on the main road facing the river. 'Nightlife' involves drinking at one of the hole-in-the-wall bars fronting the basketball courts.

Restaurant Tucanare (Carrera 6 No 5-29; ☽ breakfast, lunch & dinner) A locals' favorite, this popular neighborhood eatery has great set meals of soup, serving of meat and side of veggies, all for just COP$5000.

Las Margaritas (Calle 6 No 6-80; set meals COP$5000-10,000; ☽ breakfast, lunch & dinner) Hidden behind a picket fence under a huge *palapa* (thatched roof), Las Margaritas is the best restaurant in town. The huge set meals of the day include local specialties like *pirarucú* and *carne asada* (grilled steak).

Getting There & Away

High-speed boats to Puerto Nariño depart from Leticia's dock at 8am, 10am and 2pm daily (COP$23,000, two hours); return boats to Leticia depart at 7:30am, 11am and 4pm.

You can purchase tickets at **Transportes Fluviales** (☎ 592 5999, Calle 8 No 11; ☽ 7am-1pm) near the riverfront in Leticia. Boats can get very full, so buy your tickets early or the day before.

RÍO YAVARÍ

Within reach of large stretches of virgin forest, the meandering Río Yavarí offers some of the best opportunities to see the Amazon up close and undisturbed. A few privately owned reserves provide simple accommodations plus guided tours and activities including kayaking, bird-watching, dolphin watching, jungle treks and visits to indigenous settlements. The lodges provide accommodations and food.

Costs take into account the number of people in the party, length of the stay, season and number of guided tours; count on COP$100,000 to COP$200,000 per person per day. There are no regularly scheduled boats, so you will have to arrange transportation with the reserves or hire a private boat in Leticia; expect to pay COP$150,000 one way plus fuel.

Note visitors to Río Yavarí must get a Brazilian entry stamp and, if necessary, a visa in Tabatinga or Leticia (see p286).

Reserva Natural Zacambú

Zacambú is the reserve nearest to Leticia, about 70km by boat. Its lodge is on Lake Zacambú, just off Río Yavarí, on the Peruvian side of the river. The lodge is simple, with small rooms without bathrooms, and a total capacity of about 30 guests.

Zacambú sits on a flooded forest that is a habitat for many species of butterflies. Both the lodge and tours are run from Leticia by **Amazon Jungle Trips** (☎ 592 7377; amazonjungle trips@yahoo.com; Av Internacional No 6-25).

Reserva Natural Palmarí

About 105km by river from Leticia, Palmarí's rambling lodge and research center sits on the high, south (Brazilian) bank of the river, overlooking a wide bend where pink and grey dolphins often gather. It's the only lodge with access to all three Amazonian ecosystems: *terra firme* (dry), *várzea* (semiflooded) and *igapó* (flooded).

The lodge itself features rooms with private bathrooms, a large round *maloca* (communal house) with hammocks and a viewing tower providing sweeping vistas. The lodge has good food and helpful guides, and offers a wide choice of walking trips and boat excursions. The reserve is managed from Bogotá by owner **Axel Antoine-Feill** (☎ 310 786 2770; www.palmari.org; Carrera 10 No 93-72), who can speak several languages including English. His representative in Leticia is **Francisco Avila** (☎ 592 4156, 310 569 0203), though Francisco only speaks Spanish and Portuguese.

Prices include room and board (per day COP$150,000 for a bed or COP$100,000 per hammock). Excursions will cost extra. You'll find the Palmarí reserve offers the best walking options around the region.

Reserva Natural Heliconia

About 110km from Leticia, Heliconia provides room and board in thatch-covered cabins, plus tours via boat or foot of the river, creeks and jungle. There are also organized visits to indigenous villages and special tours devoted to bird-watching and dolphin watching. The reserve is managed from Leticia (☎ 592 5773, 311 508 5666; www.amazonheliconia.com).

Directory

CONTENTS

ACCOMMODATIONS

There are three main kinds of accommodations in Colombia: backpacker hostels, budget hotels (frequented by Colombians), and top-end hotels. The few midrange hotels on offer tend to cater to Colombian business travelers.

Camping

For a long time camping was out of bounds in Colombia. While the civil conflict continues to rage in remote regions of the country, more and more Colombians are strapping on a pack and getting reacquainted with their beautiful country. In many cases sleeping in a tent is considered a novelty, and many campgrounds charge more to pitch a tent than you would spend for a night in a hotel.

Hostels

Backpacker tourism is booming in Colombia, and new hostels are opening every month. All have dorm beds for around COP$15,000 to COP$22,000, and most have a few private rooms for COP$35,000 to COP$80,000. These are great if you want to meet with other foreigners, and most hostel owners are excellent sources of information on local activities and sights.

Many of the most established hostels are members of the **Colombian Hostels Association** (www.colombianhostels.com). The most comprehensive listing of hostels is at www.hosteltrail.com; the owners also run their own hostel in Popayán.

Hotels

Also sometimes called *residencias, hospedajes* or *posadas*, a hotel generally suggests a place of a higher standard, or at least a higher price. Cheaper accommodations are usually clustered around markets, bus terminals and in the backstreets of the city center. If you speak Spanish and wish to avoid the gringo trail, a budget private room with hot water, air-con and cable TV goes between COP$20,000 and COP$25,000 – cheaper than a hostel.

Midrange hotels as such don't really exist in Colombia. Prices tend to jump rapidly from budget cheapies to three- and four-star hotels, with little in between. Nevertheless, there are often a handful of hotels in the COP$50,000 to COP$150,000 range, usually in the city center, which cater primarily to Colombian business travelers.

All the major cities have top-end hotels charging COP$150,000 to COP$1,000,000 per night. Prices vary greatly and don't always reflect quality. Most will accept payment by

---

BOOK YOUR STAY ONLINE

For more accommodation reviews and recommendations by Lonely Planet authors, check out the online booking service at www.lonelyplanet.com/hotels. You'll find the true, insider lowdown on the best places to stay. Reviews are thorough and independent. Best of all, you can book online.

PRACTICALITIES

- Colombians use the metric system for weights and measures, except for petrol, which is measured in US gallons. Food is often sold in *libras* (pounds), which is equivalent to 500g.

- Electrical outlets accept US-type, flat, two-pin plugs. Electricity is 110V, 60 cycles AC.

- All major cities have daily newspapers. Bogotá's leading newspaper, *El Tiempo,* has reasonable coverage of national and international news, culture, sports and economics. The leading newspapers in other large cities include *El Espectador* and *El Colombiano* in Medellín, and *El País* and *El Occidente* in Cali. *Semana* is the biggest national weekly magazine. Another major weekly, *Cambio,* is an important opinion-forming magazine. *Poder* is also worth a read.

- Colombia has plenty of national and local TV stations. Each region has its own TV station; Bogotá TV is dominated by **City TV** (www.citytv.com.co). Nationwide channels include **Caracol TV** (www.canalcaracol.com.co) and **RCN TV** (www.canalrcn.com), Canal Uno and Señal Colombia.

- Cable TV offers a near-complete selection of English-language programming. If it's dubbed, check your remote, there is often a Change Language button.

- Radio stations are likewise plentiful. College radio usually offers the best variety; try Universidad Javeriana (94.9 FM) or Universidad Nacional (106.9 FM).

---

credit card. The best choice of top-end hotels is in Bogotá, Medellín and Cartagena.

Motels

Motel always means 'love motel,' ie rooms rented by the hour. By law and custom these are located on the outskirts of town. Most Colombians live with their families until they are married, making motels a regular part of many people's sex lives.

Many budget and some midrange hotels double as 'love motels,' especially in smaller towns.

Resorts

There are a handful of package-style resorts on the Caribbean coast and on San Andrés. Most are frequented by Colombians, rather than foreign package tourists, and are usually excellent value. The Pacific coast also has several good all-inclusives, but they are definitely for the more adventurous type as the area is quite remote and is heavily patrolled by the army. For a selection of some of the best small resorts, see www.posadasturisticas.com.co.

If you are booking a package resort deal from outside the country, you are exempt from the 10% IVA hotel tax. Some hotels may not know this rule, so be sure to ask for the discount.

BUSINESS HOURS

The office working day is, theoretically at least, eight hours long, usually from 8am to noon and 2pm to 6pm weekdays, but in practice offices tend to open later and close earlier. Many offices in the larger cities have adopted the so-called *jornada continua*, a working day without a lunch break. It's nearly impossible to arrange anything between noon and 2pm though, as most of the staff are off for their lunch. Most tourist offices are closed on Saturday and Sunday, and travel agencies usually only work to noon on Saturday. The many competing post offices are not open for standard hours across the country. For example, in Bogotá most are open from 9am to 5pm from Monday to Friday, with some branches also open on Saturday morning, but on the Caribbean coast most companies close for lunch.

As a rough guide only, usual shopping hours are from 9am to 5pm from Monday to Friday; some shops close for lunch. On Saturdays most shops are open from 9am to noon, or sometimes until 5pm. Large stores and supermarkets usually stay open till 8pm or 9pm Monday to Friday; some also open Sunday. Shopping hours vary considerably from shop to shop and from city to countryside. In remote places, opening hours are shorter and are often taken less seriously.

Restaurants opening for lunch open at noon. Those serving breakfast open by 8am. Most of the better restaurants in larger cities, particularly in Bogotá, tend to stay open until 10pm or longer; restaurants in smaller towns often close by 9pm or earlier. Many don't open at all on Sunday. Most cafes are open from 8am until 10pm, while bars usually open around 6pm

DIRECTORY

and close when the law dictates, usually 3am (although some are open till dawn).

The opening hours of museums and other tourist sights vary greatly. Most museums are closed on Monday but are open on Sunday. The opening hours of churches are even more difficult to pin down. Some are open all day, others for certain hours only, while the rest remain locked except during Mass, which in some villages may be only on Sunday morning.

CLIMATE CHARTS

Colombia's proximity to the equator means its temperature varies little throughout the year. The temperature does change with altitude, creating various climatic zones ranging from hot lowlands to freezing Andean peaks, so you can experience completely different climates within a couple of hours of travel.

As a general rule, the temperature falls about 6°C with every 1000m increase in altitude. If the average temperature at sea level is 30°C, it will be around 24°C at 1000m, 18°C at 2000m and 12°C at 3000m.

The altitude also affects the difference between daytime and nighttime temperatures. The higher the altitude, the greater the difference. Consequently, in the highlands there can be warm days but freezing nights, while in the lowlands days and nights are almost equally hot.

Colombia has two seasons: the dry (la sequía) and the rainy season (época de lluvia). The pattern of seasons varies in different parts of the country, and has been greatly affected over recent years by El Niño and La Niña.

As a rough guide, in the Andean region there are two dry and two rainy seasons per year. The main dry season is from December to March, with a shorter and less dry period between July and August. This general pattern has wide variations throughout the Andean zone.

The weather in Los Llanos has a more definite pattern: there is one dry season, between December and March, while the rest of the year is wet. The Amazon doesn't have a uniform climate but, in general, is quite wet year-round.

COURSES

Spanish-language courses are run by universities and language schools in the larger cities. It is generally cheaper and better value to arrange a private one-on-one tutor. Popular

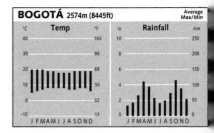

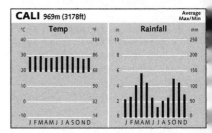

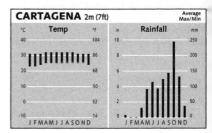

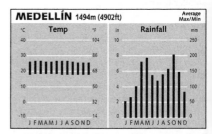

backpacker hotels are the best places to ask about independent teachers. Enrolling in a university course is useful if you want to extend your stay beyond the six months a tourist visa permits you.

Dance classes are also popular, especially salsa. Most hostels and hotels can suggest a teacher; expect to pay around COP$20,000 per hour for private instruction. In Medellín you may also be able to study the tango.

CUSTOMS REGULATIONS

Colombian customs are looking for large sums of cash (inbound) and drugs (outbound). If they have the slightest suspicion you are carrying either you can expect an exhaustive search of your belongings and your person. Customs are much stricter at the airport than at the land and sea crossings. Expect to be questioned in Spanish or English by a well-trained police officer. The latest method is x-raying your intestines: if you look in any way out of the ordinary, or fail to give a convincing response to the officer's questions, they will x-ray your intestines to see if you are a drug mule.

In other respects customs regulations don't differ much from those in other South American countries. You can bring in personal belongings and presents you intend to give to Colombian residents. The quantity, kind and value of these items shouldn't arouse suspicion that they may have been imported for commercial purposes. You can bring in items for personal use such as cameras, camping equipment, sports accessories or a laptop computer without any problems.

Be sure to hang onto your receipts for any big-ticket items. Foreigners may request a refund of the 16% IVA (sales tax) on all goods purchased during their stay in Colombia. Get to the airport with plenty of time to submit your receipts to DIAN (Dirección de Impuestos y Aduanas Nacionales; the customs bureau).

DANGERS & ANNOYANCES

Most travelers will find Colombia safer on average than all of the country's immediate neighbors. Street crime can be a problem,

especially in Bogotá. Use common sense and avoid travel to dodgy parts of town (and the countryside).

Theft & Robbery

Theft is the most common travelers' danger. In general, the problem is more serious in the largest cities. The more rural the area, the quieter and safer it is. The most common methods of theft are snatching your day pack, camera or watch, pickpocketing, or taking advantage of a moment's inattention to pick up your gear and run away.

Distraction can often be part of the thieves' strategy. Thieves tend to work in pairs or groups; one or more will distract you while an accomplice does the deed. There are hundreds, if not thousands, of possible ways to distract you, and new scams are dreamt up every day. Some thieves are even more innovative and will set up an opportune situation to separate you from your belongings. They may begin by making friends with you, or pretend to be the police and demand to check your possessions.

If you can, leave your money and valuables somewhere safe before walking the streets. In practice, it's good to carry a decoy bundle of small notes, maximum COP$50,000 to COP$100,000, ready to hand over in case of an assault; if you really don't have a peso, robbers can become frustrated and, as a consequence, unpredictable.

Armed hold-ups in the cities can occur even in some more upmarket suburbs. If you are accosted by robbers, it is best to give them what they are after, but try to play it cool and don't rush to hand them all your valuables at once – they may well be satisfied with just your decoy wad. Don't try to escape or struggle – your chances are slim, and people have been murdered for pocket change. Don't count on any help from passersby.

Be careful when drawing cash from an ATM as some robberies have been reported. Criminals may watch you drawing money, then assault you either at the ATM or a convenient place nearby. It may be safer to get an advance from the cashier inside the bank, even if this takes a while.

Police

While the Colombian military is highly trustworthy and the federal police have a reputation as untouchables, local cops have more

---

GOVERNMENT TRAVEL ADVICE

Government websites with useful travel advisories:

- **Australian Department of Foreign Affairs** (☎ 300 139 281; www.smarttraveller .gov.au)
- **British Foreign Office** (☎ 0845 850 2829; www.fco.gov.uk)
- **Canadian Department of Foreign Affairs** (☎ 800 267 6788; www.dfait-maeci .gc.ca)
- **US State Department** (☎ 888 407 4747; http://travel.state.gov)

of a mixed reputation. They don't get paid a lot of money, and incidents of bribery and bullying of tourists are commonplace.

Always carry a photocopy of your passport with you, including your entry stamp, and never carry drugs of any kind, either on the street or when traveling. If your papers are in order and they can't squeeze you for a bribe, they have no excuse to bother you.

In tourist areas, there are an increasing number of so-called tourist police; many speak some English. They are uniformed and easily recognizable by the Policía de Turismo labels on their arm bands. Go to them first if you can.

If your passport, valuables or other belongings are stolen, go to the police station and make a *denuncia* (report). The officer on duty will write a statement according to what you tell them. It should include the description of the events and the list of stolen articles. Pay attention to the wording you use, include every stolen item and document, and carefully check the statement before signing it to ensure it contains exactly what you've said. Your copy of the statement serves as a temporary identity document and you'll need to present it to your insurer to make a claim. Don't expect your things to be found; it's unlikely your claim will be followed up much beyond filing the report.

If you happen to get involved with the police, keep calm and be polite, and always use the formal '*usted*.' Keep a sharp eye out when they check your gear.

Be wary of criminals masquerading as plainclothes police. They may stop you on the street, identify themselves with a fake ID, then ask to inspect your passport and money. Under no circumstances should you agree to a search. Call a uniformed police officer, if there happens to be one around, or decent-looking passersby to witness the incident, and insist on phoning a bona fide police station. By that time, the 'officers' will probably have discreetly walked away.

Drugs

Cocaine and marijuana are cheap and widely available in Colombia. Purchasing and consuming drugs, however, is not a good idea. Never travel with drugs (strip searches are not uncommon), and if you insist on purchasing drugs be very careful who you buy from. Most police aren't interested in busting you, but rather in shaking you down for a bribe (although this can't be said of *every* policeman). The standard bribe for possession hovers between COP$500,000 and COP$1,000,000, although people have been known to cut their trip short after forking over US$3500.

Sometimes you may be offered drugs on the street, in a bar or at a disco, but never accept these offers. The vendors may well be setting you up for the police, or their accomplices will follow you and stop you later, show you false police documents and threaten you with jail unless you pay them off.

There have been reports of drugs being planted on travelers, so keep your eyes open. Always refuse if a stranger at an airport asks you to take their luggage on board as part of your luggage allowance. Needless to say, smuggling dope across borders is a crazy idea. Have you ever seen the inside of a Colombian prison?

SPIKED DRINKS

Burundanga is a drug obtained from a species of tree widespread in Colombia and is used by thieves to render a victim unconscious. It can be put into sweets, cigarettes, chewing gum, spirits, beer – virtually any kind of food or drink – and it doesn't have any noticeable taste or odor.

The main effect after a 'normal' dose is the loss of will, even though you remain conscious. The thief can then ask you to hand over your valuables and you will obey without resistance. Cases of rape under the effect of burundanga are known. Other effects are loss of memory and sleepiness, which can last from a few hours to several days. An overdose can be fatal.

Burundanga is not only used to trick foreigners – locals have been on the receiving end too, losing their cars, contents of their homes and sometimes their life. Think twice before accepting a cigarette from a stranger or a drink from a new 'friend.'

Guerrillas & Paramilitaries

There are still isolated pockets of guerrilla activity in remote parts of Colombia, particularly the high mountains and the deep jungle. Parts of the Chocó and the jungle regions east of the Andes (except Leticia and surrounds) may be dangerous. The southern regions of Los Nevados National Park are said to harbor armed gunmen.

If you stick to the gringo trail it is unlikely that you will encounter guerrillas. Going off the beaten track, however, should be done with great caution. Your worst-case scenario is kidnapping, for financial or political ends. If it makes you feel more comfortable, avoid night buses or fly intercity, although this is probably being overcautious.

DISCOUNT CARDS
Unless you are a Colombian high-school student your student card will be of little financial advantage. That said, Colombia is a relatively cheap country to travel in, and students with modest budgets will find the country pleasantly gentle on the wallet.

EMBASSIES & CONSULATES
Most of the countries that maintain diplomatic relations with Colombia have their embassies and consulates in Bogotá. Some countries also have consulates in other Colombian cities.

Argentina (Map p64; ☎ 1 288 0900; Av 40A No 13-09, piso 16, Bogotá)

Australia (Map pp74-5; ☎ 1 236 2828; Carrera 16 No 86A-05, Bogotá)

Bolivia Bogotá (Map p64; ☎ 1 215 3274; Transversal 12 No 119-95); Cali (☎ 2 553 6386; Carrera 40 No 5C-102)

Brazil Bogotá (Map pp74-5; ☎ 1 218 0800; Calle 93 No 14-20, piso 8); Cali (☎ 2 893 0615; Carrera 2 Oeste No 12-44); Leticia (Map p287; ☎ 8 592 7530; Carrera 9 No 13-84); Medellín (Map p206; ☎ 4 265 7565; Calle 29D No 55-91)

Canada (Map p64; ☎ 1 657 9914; Carrera 7 No 115-33, piso 14, Bogotá)

Chile (Map pp74-5; ☎ 1 620 6613; Calle 100 No 11B-44, Bogotá)

Costa Rica Bogotá (Map p64; ☎ 1 636 2681; Calle 103 No 16-60); San Andrés (Map p192; ☎ 8 512 4938; Novedades Regina, Av Colombia)

Cuba (Map pp74-5; ☎ 1 621 7054; Carrera 9 No 92-54, Bogotá)

Ecuador Bogotá (Map p64; ☎ 1 542 7121; Calle 72 No 6-30); Cali (Map p241; ☎ 2 661 2264; Av 5AN No 20N-13, L-103); Ipiales (Map p265; ☎ 2 773 2292; Carrera 7 No 14-10); Medellín (Map p212; ☎ 4 512 1303; Calle 50 No 52-22, oficina 603)

France Bogotá (Map pp74-5; ☎ 1 638 1400; Carrera 11 No 93-12); Bucaramanga (☎ 645 9393; Calle 42 No 37-19)

Germany (Map p64; ☎ 1 423 2600; www.bogota.diplo .de; Carrera 69 No 25B-44, piso 7, Bogotá)

Honduras Bogotá (Map p64; ☎ 1 249 2195; Calle 65 No 8-26, oficina 201); San Andrés (Map p192; ☎ 8 512 3235; Hotel Tiuna, Av Colombia)

Israel (Map p64; ☎ 1 327 7500; Calle 35 No 7-25, piso 14, Bogotá)

Italy (Map pp74-5; ☎ 1 218 7206; Calle 93B No 9-92, Bogotá)

Japan (Map p64; ☎ 1 317 5001; Carrera 7 No 71-21, torre B, piso 11, Bogotá)

Mexico (Map pp74-5; ☎ 1 610 4070; Calle 82 No 9-25, Bogotá)

Netherlands (Map pp74-5; ☎ 1 638 4243, 638 4244; Carrera 13 No 93-40, oficina 201, Bogotá)

Panama Barranquilla (Map p160; ☎ 5 360 1872; Carrera 54 No 64-245); Bogotá (Map pp74-5; ☎ 1 257 4452; Calle 92 No 7-70); Cali (Map p241; ☎ 2 880 9590; Calle 11 No 4-42, oficina 316); Cartagena (Map p142; ☎ 5 664 1433; Plaza de San Pedro Claver No 30-14); Medellín (☎ 4 268 1358; Carrera 43A No 7-50, oficina 1607)

Peru Bogotá (Map pp74-5; ☎ 1 257 0505; Calle 80A No 6-50); Bogotá (Map pp74-5; ☎ 1 257 6846; Calle 90 No 14-26); Cali (☎ 2 660 2052; Av 7N No 24N-57); Leticia (Map p287; ☎ 8 592 7755, 9 592 7204; Calle 11 No 5-32)

Spain (Map pp74-5; ☎ 1 618 1288, 622 0090; Calle 92 No 12-68, Bogotá)

Switzerland (Map pp74-5; ☎ 1 349 7230; Carrera 9A No 74-08, oficina 1101, Bogotá)

UK Bogotá (Map pp74-5; ☎ 1 326 8300; www.britain. gov.co; Carrera 9 No 76-49, piso 9); Cali (Map p241; ☎ 2 660 1031; Calle 22N No 6-42, oficina 401).

USA (Map p64; ☎ 1 315 0811; Calle 22Dbis No 47-51, Bogotá)

Venezuela Barranquilla (Map p160; ☎ 5 358 0048; Carrera 52 No 69-96); Bogotá (Map pp74-5; ☎ 1 640 1213; Carrera 11 No 87-51, piso 5); Bogotá (Map p64; ☎ 1 636 4011; Av 13 No 103-16); Cartagena (☎ 5 665 0382; Carrera 3 No 8-129); Cúcuta (☎ 7 579 1956; Av Camilo Daza); Medellín (Map p206; ☎ 4 351 1614; Calle 32B No 69-59)

FOOD
Colombia offers good, stomach-filling food at great prices (although don't expect much in the way of gourmet). Standards of hygiene in food preparation are high.

There are plenty of budget places serving meals for less than COP$10,000. Lunch is the easiest budget meal to find; a cheap breakfast and dinner can be a little bit harder to track down, as most Colombians eat these meals at home.

Midrange restaurants (COP$10,000 to COP$20,000) tend to be a step up in quality and service. You can get a good steak or chicken dinner in this category.

Top-end restaurants generally cost more than COP$20,000. You can (should) expect superb cooking with creative flair at this price. Don't hesitate to complain – if you don't like it, send it back. COP$25,000 is a lot of money for a meal in Colombia.

GAY & LESBIAN TRAVELERS

Compared to some Latin American countries, homosexuality is well tolerated in Colombia. There is a substantial gay undercurrent in the major cities and as long as you don't broadcast the fact in public (holding hands, kissing, etc) you are unlikely to be harassed.

In a quirk of law, Colombia recognizes same-sex couples. The law regarding de facto couples does not specify gender, and many gay couples have exploited this loophole to register their civil unions with the government.

Bogotá has the largest and most open gay and lesbian community, and therefore is the best place to make contacts and get to find out what's going on. Check the website www.gaycolombia.com for more information.

Gay bars, discos and other venues are limited to the larger cities, and come and go frequently. Again, Bogotá offers the largest choice. See p88 for some gay hangouts.

HOLIDAYS

The following days are observed as public holidays in Colombia.

Año Nuevo (New Year's Day) January 1
Los Reyes Magos (Epiphany) January 6*
San José (St Joseph) March 19*
Jueves Santo & Viernes Santo (Maundy Thursday and Good Friday) March/April (Easter). The following Monday is also a holiday.
Día del Trabajo (Labor Day) May 1
La Ascensión del Señor (Ascension) May*
Corpus Cristi (Corpus Christi) May/June*
Sagrado Corazón de Jesús (Sacred Heart) June*
San Pedro y San Pablo (St Peter and St Paul) June 29*
Día de la Independencia (Independence Day) July 20
Batalla de Boyacá (Battle of Boyacá) August 7
La Asunción de Nuestra Señora (Assumption) August 15*
Día de la Raza (Discovery of America) October 12*
Todos los Santos (All Saints' Day) November 1*
Independencia de Cartagena (Independence of Cartagena) November 11*
Inmaculada Concepción (Immaculate Conception) December 8
Navidad (Christmas Day) December 25

When the dates marked with an asterisk do not fall on a Monday, the holiday is moved to the following Monday to make a three-day long weekend, referred to as the *puente*

(bridge). Any holiday falling on a Tuesday (or Thursday) also turns the preceding Monday (or following Friday) into a holiday as well.

INSURANCE

Ideally, all travelers should have a travel-insurance policy, which will provide some security in the case of a medical emergency, or the loss or theft of money or belongings. It may seem an expensive luxury, but if you can't afford a travel health insurance policy, you also probably can't afford medical emergency charges abroad if something goes wrong.

If you do need to make a claim on your travel insurance, you must produce a police report detailing loss or theft (see p299). You also need proof of the value of any items lost or stolen. Receipts are the best bet, so if you buy a new camera for your trip, for example, hang on to the receipt.

Colombian law stipulates that hospitals must treat you, whether or not you can pay. If you don't have the Spanish to insist on this right, you may have difficulty getting treatment. You will, in any event, get more prompt assistance with a fistful of cash.

INTERNET ACCESS

Colombia is a wired country. There's internet almost everywhere, and it's cheap – rarely more than COP$2000 per hour. In smaller towns and remoter destinations there may not be *banda ancha* (broadband), but rather dial-up or a satellite link. Most internet cafes are open long hours, from 7am to 10pm, but with more limited hours on the weekends. Most cafes provide a range of related services such as printing, scanning and faxing, and some offer cheap international calls.

Most hostels and many midrange to top-end hotels offer wi-fi. Shopping centers often have free wi-fi, and the major airports also have wi-fi, although it isn't free.

As always, you should consider the security implications of using the internet while traveling. Besides the risk of having a laptop stolen, keylogger trojans are a real risk in internet cafes – be very careful in choosing where you access your online banking. You may also like to set up a trip-specific webmail account, or use an account with fastmail.fm, which lets you generate one-time passwords that expire within the hour, making them virtually useless to a digital thief.

For internet resources, see p16. Where the internet icon (🖳) appears in reviews, it indicates that there is internet service available, either wi-fi or desktop, and usually (but not always) both.

LEGAL MATTERS

If arrested you have the right to an attorney. If you don't have one, one will be appointed to you (and paid for by the government). There is a presumption of innocence and you can expect a speedy trial.

The most common situation that most travelers find themselves in involves drugs. It is illegal to buy, sell or consume drugs in any quantity. However, the Ley 30 de 1986 specifies that simple possession of small quantities of drugs is legal. The legal limits are marijuana (20g), hashish (5g) and cocaine (1 g). Be aware that the government is trying to change this law. Further, spouting law to underpaid cops is not likely to improve their moods.

If you do get caught with drugs, the best thing to do is obliquely suggest a bribe. '*En mi país, se puede pagar una multa* (in my country, you can just pay a fine).' The standard bribe for possession of small quantities of drugs is around COP\$500,000 to COP\$1,000,000. The sooner you pay the bribe, the cheaper it will be. If you wind up back at the station,

you'll have to bribe everyone there too, though not all cops can be bribed. You really don't want to see the inside of a Colombian prison. Play it safe; you're better off avoiding drugs in Colombia.

MAPS

It's difficult to find detailed maps of Colombia outside the country itself. Check with good travel bookstores and map shops to see what's

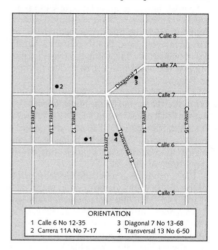

ORIENTATION	
1 Calle 6 No 12-35	3 Diagonal 7 No 13-68
2 Carrera 11A No 7-17	4 Transversal 13 No 6-50

ORIENTATION

Colombian cities, towns and villages have traditionally been laid out on a grid plan. The streets running north–south are called Carreras, often abbreviated on maps to Cra, Cr or K, whereas those running east–west are called Calles, labeled on maps as Cll, Cl or C. This simple pattern may be complicated by diagonal streets, called either Diagonales (more east–west and thus like Calles), or Transversales (more like Carreras).

All streets are numbered and the numerical system of addresses is used. Each address consists of a series of numbers, eg Calle 23 No 5-43 (which means that it's the building on Calle 23, 43m from the corner of Carrera 5 toward Carrera 6), or Carrera 17 No 31-05 (the house on Carrera 17, 5m from the corner of Calle 31 toward Calle 32). Refer to the Orientation map (see p303) for examples.

The system is very practical and you will soon become familiar with it. It is usually easy to find an address. It's actually one of the most precise address systems in the world; if you have an address you can determine the location of the place with pinpoint accuracy.

In the larger cities the main streets are called Avenidas or Autopistas. They each have their own names and numbers, but are commonly known just by their numbers.

Cartagena's old town is the only Colombian city where centuries-old street names have withstood the modern numbering system. Streets in some other cities (eg Medellín) have both names and numbers, but elsewhere only numbers are used.

The Colombian system of designating floors is the same as that used in the USA; there is no 'ground floor' – it is the *primer piso* (1st floor). Thus, the European 1st floor will be the *segundo piso* (2nd floor) in Colombia.

DIRECTORY

available. In the USA, **Maplink** (☎ 805 692 6777; www.maplink.com; 30 S La Patera Lane, No 5 Santa Barbara, CA 93117) has an excellent supply of maps. A similarly extensive selection of maps is available in the UK from **Stanfords** (☎ 020 7836 0189; www .stanfords.co.uk; 12-14 Long Acre, London WC2E 9LP).

Within Colombia, folded road maps of the country are produced by various publishers and are distributed through bookstores. Of special note is the Movistar *Guía de Rutas,* a Spanish-language guidebook to Colombia with excellent maps. You can buy it at any tollbooth (ask the bus driver beforehand to buy it for you), and is also sold in a handful of bookstores, including the *teleférico* gift shop at the bottom of Cerro de Monserrate in Bogotá.

The widest selection of maps of Colombia is produced and sold by the **Instituto Geográfico Agustín Codazzi** (IGAC; Map pp74-5; ☎ 369 4075; www .igac.gov.co; Carrera 30 No 48-51, Bogotá), the government mapping body, which has its head office in Bogotá and branch offices in departmental capitals.

IGAC produces general and specialist maps of the country, plus departmental maps, city maps, and 1:100,000 scale *planchas* (sheets) broken down into more detailed 1:25,000 scale maps. Unfortunately, most maps are long out of date. If the office runs out of color maps (usually the case) it makes a black-and-white copy of the original. Maps cost somewhere between COP$10,000 and COP$40,000 per sheet, depending on the type and size.

MONEY

The Colombian peso (COP$) is the unit of currency in Colombia. It fluctuates freely on the exchange markets, and in recent history has varied between COP$1500 to COP$2500 to the US dollar.

Unlike many of Colombia's neighbors, where the US dollar is the de facto currency or the actual legal tender, Colombians use the peso exclusively. For this reason we have provided all prices in this book in Colombian pesos (COP$).

For exchange rates at the time of publication, see the inside front cover.

ATMs

Almost all major banks have ATMs, and they usually work fine with cards issued outside Colombia. A debit card is usually best and will have the lowest fees. Check with your home

bank and credit-card company before leaving. Ask about fees and inform them of your travel dates (if they suddenly see money extracted from Colombia they may freeze your account, assuming that your card has been stolen).

Most banks have a maximum cash withdrawal limit of COP$400,000 pesos per transaction. Davivienda allows a maximum of COP$500,000 from most branches, and Citibank will let you take a maximum of COP$1,000,000 per withdrawal.

Cash

There are paper notes of COP$1000, $2000, $5000, $10,000, $20,000 and $50,000. The coins you will use are primarily the $100, $200 and $500; the $20 and $50 are rarely seen outside of supermarkets, and some people may refuse to accept them. There used to be a $1000 coin but it was widely counterfeited and has been withdrawn from circulation; Colombians will refuse to accept $1000 coins, and you should do the same.

Small change is scarce on the Caribbean coast, the Pacific coast and in small towns; hoard your change. Forged peso notes do exist; to avoid forgeries change money only with licensed moneychangers and pay taxi drivers with exact change whenever possible.

Credit Cards

Credit cards are common in Colombia and used extensively in the major cities and larger towns. When paying with a credit card, you will be asked, '¿a cuantas cuotas?' (how many payments?). Colombian customers can choose to divide the payment over one to 24 months. Foreign cardholders should just say 'one.'

The most useful card for cash advances is Visa, as it's accepted by most banks. MasterCard is honored by a few banks. Other cards are of limited use.

You can get advance payments on cards from the cashier in the bank or from the bank's ATM. In either case you'll need your PIN number.

Make sure you know the number to call if you lose your credit card, and be quick to cancel it if it's lost or stolen.

Money Changers

You are better off using your ATM card in Colombia, as you will get a much better exchange rate. The US dollar is the only foreign currency worth trying to change in Colombia;

expect dismal rates for euros, pounds sterling, Australian dollars etc.

Many but not all banks change money; in major cities and in border regions there are usually several *casas de cambio*. Avoid changing money on the street. Most unofficial moneychangers are laundering drug money; the ones on the street have fast fingers and often dodgy calculators, making it highly unlikely you'll get a fair deal. Colombia produces more than 25% of the world's counterfeit US notes, which is yet another reason to avoid changing money on the street.

Your passport is required for any banking transaction. You'll also have to provide a thumbprint. There's a fair amount of paperwork involved in changing money (to prevent money laundering). Most *casas de cambio* will see you on your way in five to 10 minutes; banks are often crowded and can take a lot longer.

Shop around for the best rate, as it can vary by several percent in the same city, or even the same block.

International Transfers

If you need money sent to you quickly, **MoneyGram** (www.moneygram.com) and **Western Union** (www.westernunion.com) are your two principal options. MoneyGram is much cheaper, and is what most overseas Colombians use to send remittances home to their families.

Your sender pays the money at their nearest MoneyGram or Western Union branch, along with a fee, and gives the details on who is to receive it and where. You can have the money within 15 minutes. When you pick it up, take along photo identification and the numbered password they'll give the sender.

Both services have offices in all the major cities and most smaller towns.

Tipping & Bargaining

In midrange and top-end restaurants expect to see a 10% service charge added to the bill. In midrange restaurants it's acceptable to decline to pay the service charge with a polite '*sin servicio, por favor.*' In top-end restaurants refusing the pay the service charge is likely to bring a manager to your table to inquire what was wrong with your meal.

Bargaining is limited to informal trade and services, such as markets and street stalls. In areas where taxis are not metered, especially the Caribbean coast, haggling is essential. If you don't like the price make a point of going to the next taxi in the queue. Haggling is also very productive for intercity buses. Outside of holiday periods you can usually get a 30% to 40% deduction on the quoted price simply by shopping around.

Traveler's Checks

Traveler's checks are neither well-known nor understood in Colombia. You're better off bringing your bank card and getting cash from the ATM. If you must travel with traveler's checks, make sure they are in US dollars, as you will get the best exchange rate. Do not bring checks in euros, pounds sterling, etc. Banks in major cities change US dollar traveler's checks at rates 2% to 5% *higher* than the cash rate (though still not as good as just using your ATM card). Exchange rates vary from bank to bank, so shop around. Some banks charge a commission for changing checks.

POST

Postal service in Colombia is expensive and largely inefficient. There is no government-run postal service and there are numerous private companies operating. These include **Avianca** (www.aviancaexpress.com), **Adpostal** (www .adpostal.gov.co), **Deprisa** (www.deprisa.com) and **Servientrega** (www.servientrega.com). Break open the piggy bank if you're planning on sending postcards home: it'll cost you around COP$10,000 per postcard.

If you want to receive a package in Colombia, you have a choice. The sender can ship via a courier like DHL, which guarantees fast, dependable delivery, but also guarantees Colombian customs will open the box and charge you an exorbitant duty (for example, we've heard of someone who got nailed for COP$80,000 for a shipment of used books). If you're not in a hurry, have the package sent via regular, budget airmail (four to eight weeks). We have successfully received many packages in this way that would otherwise have incurred significant import duties.

The poste restante system in Colombia is not reliable. You're better off contacting a hostel or hotel and asking them to hold onto a package for you. If you're desperate you might try Avianca's office in Bogotá (Your Name, c/o Lista de Correos Avianca, Edificio Avianca, Carrera 7 No 16-36, Bogotá). Mail is kept for one month. Courier companies do not accept mail sent to Lista de Correos.

SHOPPING

Colombia is famous for its emeralds, leather goods, woolen ponchos, basket-weaving and, on the Pacific coast, gold jewelry.

Buying emeralds is difficult. Or rather, if you aren't knowledgeable about these gemstones, you are unlikely to strike a good deal. Mined chiefly from the Muzo area, emeralds are sold in the flourishing emerald street market at the southwestern corner of Av Jiménez and Carrera 7 and nearby Plaza Rosario in Bogotá, where dozens of *negociantes* (traders) buy and sell stones – sometimes on the sidewalks.

The emerald industry has done a complete about-face from its 'wild west' days when criminal activity and questionable labor practices (including allegations of child labor) were associated with the mines. In 2005 the government abolished all tariffs and taxes on the mining of emeralds, which effectively ended the black market and its associated elements. Tourists can now safely buy emeralds in good conscience knowing they're not supporting criminal gangs or violence in Colombia. Still, unless you know something about emeralds you are likely to pay too much .

Colombian handicrafts vary from region to region. Some areas and towns are famous for particular local crafts. Boyacá is the largest handicraft manufacturer, with excellent handwoven items, basketry and pottery. The Pacific coast also has an interesting selection of basketwork, plus the occasional blow-dart gun. Guapi is famous for its musical instruments, especially handmade drums. You may also find some good handwrought gold jewelry here. If you don't make it to the Pacific coast, the Parque Artesanías (p246) in Cali is a good place to shop.

Pasto is known for its woodwork – decorative items covered with the *barniz de Pasto,* a kind of vegetable resin. Ceramic miniatures of *chivas* (traditional buses) have become a popular souvenir.

Hammocks are another tempting buy and come in plenty of regional variations, from the simple, practical hammocks made in Los Llanos to the elaborate *chinchorros* of the Guajiro people. Another well-known *indígena* product is the *mola* (rectangular cloth with colored designs) made by the Cuna people, sold in plenty of craft shops.

Ruanas (Colombian woolen ponchos) are found in the colder parts of the Andean zone, where the climate justifies it. In many villages they are still made by hand with simple patterns and natural colors. Bogotá and Villa de Leyva are good places to buy them.

The best and most fashionable *mochilas* (a kind of woven handbag) are those of the Arhuaco from the Sierra Nevada de Santa Marta. They are not cheap, but are beautiful and usually of good quality.

Leather goods (mostly boots and bags) are a better buy. They are relatively cheap and are among the best in South America; the best selection is in Bogotá.

Be sure to keep receipts for any big ticket items like emeralds, electronics, etc. Foreign

---

ONE WORD: PLASTICS

Colombia has some of the most innovative – and prolific – plastic surgeons in the world; just head to a high-end nightclub in Cali or Medellín to see their prodigious results. The boobs may not be real, but they sure are big. Throw in a little rhinoplasty, a dash of liposuction, some light dermal abrasion, and just a hint of dental reconstruction, and suddenly an evening at the mall starts to look like a Miss Universe pageant.

Because procedures in Colombia often cost about a third of what they would in the US or Europe, Colombia's plastic surgeons are attracting a small flood of vanity tourists who come not to admire the Andes or Amazon but their own refurbished beauty. Many clinics even offer package deals, including hotels and airfare, sending visitors home with a fresh outlook on life, especially those who get Lasik (laser-assisted in-situ keratomileusis). Pioneered by Colombian eye surgeon José Barraquer and beginning in the 1940s, Lasik cures poor eyesight by reshaping the cornea with lasers. Colombia is considered a leader in the field.

Business has grown so quickly that the US State Department has issued advice specifically for Americans considering elective surgery in Colombia. They don't discourage the practice, but they do suggest that you thoroughly research who your surgeon will be – sound advice to apply anywhere, of course.

tourists may request a refund of the 16% IVA (sales tax) from the customs authorities when they leave the country.

SOLO TRAVELERS

Travelers on their own are unlikely to have any problems traveling in Colombia. There are hostels in all major cities and many smaller locales, and you'll often find yourself traveling with other foreigners you meet along the way.

If you are going to remote regions unfrequented by or unused to foreign visitors, or if you're concerned about security in general, traveling with a friend will certainly ease your mind, and may lessen the likelihood of street crime.

TELEPHONE & FAX

The telephone system in Colombia is modern and works well for both domestic and international calls. Telecom is the national provider; ETB and Orbitel offer competing services. Public telephones exist in cities and large towns, but they are few and far between, and many are out of order. For directory assistance or information call ☎ 123.

It is possible to call direct to just about anywhere in Colombia. The exception is if you're using a cell phone: you cannot dial a cell phone from a landline (or vice versa). If you don't have a cell, you can use one at a corner store (see right for more info). Landline phone numbers are seven digits countrywide, while cell-phone numbers are 10 digits. Area codes are single digits, and you'll find them included immediately under the headings of the relevant destinations throughout this book.

All calls by default go through Telecom (☎ 09). However, you can specify Orbitel (☎ 05) or ETB (☎ 07) by dialing that prefix immediately before the number. There's no need to worry much about this unless you're in Colombia long enough to own and operate your own landline.

Colombia's country code is ☎ 57. If you are dialing a Colombian number from abroad, drop the prefix of the provider (05, 07 or 09) and dial only the area code and the local number.

Email cafes almost always have a few telephone booths *(cabinas)* where you can make local calls for around a few hundred pesos a minute. Most generally offer a fax service as well.

INTERNATIONAL COLLECT CALLS

Reverse-charge or collect calls *(llamadas de pago revertido)* are possible to most major countries. Here are the international direct-dialing numbers of some countries.

Canada	☎ 01 800 919 0057
France	☎ 01 800 933 0057
Italy	☎ 01 800 939 0057
Spain	☎ 01 800 934 0010
UK	☎ 01 800 944 0057
USA	AT&T ☎ 01 800 911 0010;
	MCI ☎ 01 800 916 0001;
	Sprint ☎ 01 800 913 0010

Cell Phones

Colombians love their cell phones, and in urban areas almost everyone has at least one. The three major providers are Movistar, Comcel and Tigo, with newcomer Ola a distant fourth. Comcel has the best nationwide coverage, and is the most useful to the traveler. Cell phones are cheap, and many travelers end up purchasing one – a basic, no-frills handset will set you back around COP$40,000 to COP$50,000, or you could bring your own cell phone from home and buy a Colombian SIM card. A SIM card costs COP$10,000, which includes COP$10,000 worth of prepaid calling minutes. Because it is expensive to call between networks you could, at least in theory, buy a SIM card for each of the three providers and swap them out to change networks.

Colombian cell-phone companies do not charge you to receive calls, only to make them. Street vendors selling *minutos* (minutes) are seen almost everywhere. Many corner stores also have cell phones you can use. These vendors purchase prepaid minutes in bulk, and it is always cheaper to make calls with them than to use credit on your own handset. For this reason many Colombians use their handsets to receive calls only and use street vendors when they need to make calls.

Vendors generally have at least three cell phones – one for each network. The first three digits of the 10-digit number indicate the cell phone provider, so state the prefix you're calling to and they'll give you the right phone. Expect to pay COP$200 to COP$300 per minute for a call to the same network (more late at night or in smaller towns).

To purchase a phone you'll need to show identification. This is supposedly for security but in fact it's to prevent the street vendors from purchasing phones in bulk and competing with the cell phone provider's own call centers. There have been cases of identity theft (they will photocopy your documents) so only purchase a cell phone from a provider's official retail outlet.

TIME

All of Colombia lies within the same time zone, five hours behind Greenwich Mean Time. There is no daylight-saving time.

TOILETS

There are a handful of public toilets in Colombia. In their absence use a restaurant's toilet. Museums and large shopping malls usually have public toilets, as do bus and airport terminals.

You'll often (but not always) find toilet paper in toilets, so it's wise to carry some with you. Never flush toilet paper. The pipes are narrow and the water pressure is weak, so toilets can't cope with toilet paper. A wastebasket is normally provided.

The most common word for toilet is *baño*. Men's toilets will usually bear a label saying *señores, hombres* or *caballeros,* while the women's toilets will be marked *señoras, mujeres* or *damas*.

Bus-station restrooms will usually charge COP$500 to COP$800 plus COP$200 for toilet paper. If you're a guy wanting to do some stand-up business, ask a bus company employee where the driver's urinal *(orinario)* is, usually outside along a back wall, which they will sometimes let you use for free.

TOURIST INFORMATION

Colombia has a number of good regional and national websites offering information (sometimes in English) about what to do and where to stay. The country's principal portal is www.turismocolombia.com. You'll find the relevant regional websites listed throughout this book.

Municipal and regional tourism offices vary greatly in quality throughout the country. Most cater principally to domestic Colombian tourists, and few speak English. They usually have at least a few brochures on the local region. In some of the more touristed places you'll find specially trained tourist police who offer both information and aid in case you run into troubles.

TRAVELING WITH CHILDREN

As with most Latin Americans, Colombians adore children. Due to a high rate of population growth, children make up a significant proportion of the population, and they are omnipresent. Few foreigners travel with children in Colombia, but if you do plan on taking along your offspring, they will find plenty of local companions.

Basic supplies are usually no problem in the cities. There are quite a few shops devoted to kids' clothes, shoes and toys; **Pepeganga** (www.pepeganga.com) in particular is recommended. You can also buy disposable diapers and baby food in supermarkets and pharmacies. Pick up a copy of Lonely Planet's *Traveling with Children* for general tips.

VISAS

Nationals of some countries, including most of Western Europe, the Americas, Japan, Australia and New Zealand, don't need a visa to enter Colombia.

All visitors get an entry stamp in their passport upon arrival. Most travelers receive 60 days. It's worth asking for 90, but we only know of a handful of people who've had this granted. Double-check your stamp immediately; errors are sometimes made.

If traveling overland, make sure you get an entry stamp or you'll have troubles later. Overstaying your welcome can result in heavy fines, and in some cases can result in being barred entry in the future. Similarly, make sure you get your departure stamp or there will be trouble the next time around.

Visa Extensions

Tourist visas can generally be extended for 30 days up to a total of six months, and every 30 days you have to head back to DAS for a visa extension. The regulation used to be up to six months per twelve-month period (forcing you to leave the country for six months), but at the time of research the regulation had been changed to six months per calendar year, making it theoretically possible to spend twelve months (1 July to 30 June of the following year) in the country without leaving. You should double-check this with **DAS** (Departamento Administrativo de Seguridad; www.das.gov.co) if you are planning a lengthy stay, as what has changed once may change again.

To apply for a 30-day extension, you'll be asked to submit photocopies of all the used pages of your passport, show an onward ticket (or at least an unpaid flight reservation), and pay COP$60,600 into the DAS bank account (which sometimes changes). DAS may also take a full set of fingerprints. DAS can provide you with a photocopied list of the application requirements; expect the process to take an entire morning or afternoon. It can be done at any DAS office in Colombia, which are present in all the main cities and some smaller towns.

You'll usually (but not always) get the extension on the spot – sometimes they'll take your fingerprints, send them to Bogotá for a background check and tell you to come back in a week.

All other visas, including student, work and marriage visas, are processed exclusively in Bogotá through DAS.

VOLUNTEERING

Volunteering is a practice that is still in its infancy in Colombia.

Globalteers (☎ 44-07771502816; www.globalteers .com; 54 Woodchester, Yate, Bristol, BS37 8TX, UK) Offers voluntourism positions of one to 12 weeks in Medellín working with street kids. Expect to pay around US$830 per week.

Fellowship for Reconciliation (☎ 1-510-763-1403; www.forcolombia.org; 369 15th St, Oakland, CA 94612, USA) Employs principally US-citizen volunteers for 12- to 18-month periods of service near combat regions in Urabá and also in Bogotá. Applicants must be proficient in Spanish, be physically fit, committed to nonviolence, and be

at least 23 years old. Volunteers receive living expenses, a stipend, travel costs, training and medical insurance.

WOMEN TRAVELERS

Women traveling in Colombia are unlikely to encounter any problems.

The usual caveats apply: bring your street smarts, don't wander alone in dodgy neighborhoods after dark, and keep an eye on your drink. Female travelers are also more likely to be victims of a bag-snatching or mugging attempt, as you will be perceived as less likely to fight back. You should also be careful taking taxis alone after dark – while rare, there have been reports of taxi drivers raping single female passengers.

Those who wish to avoid attention from local men should dress modestly and consider wearing a cheap wedding band.

WORK

There is a small but growing demand for qualified English-language teachers in Colombia. Some schools may be willing to pay cash-in-hand for a short period of time, but for longer-term employment you will have to find a school willing to organize a work visa. As a general rule, the more popular the city is among travelers, the harder it will be to find employment – for example, Medellín is crammed with English teachers, while Cali goes lacking. Don't expect to get rich teaching English: you're unlikely to make more than a few million pesos a month, and usually much less.

Transportation

CONTENTS

GETTING THERE & AWAY

ENTERING THE COUNTRY

Most travelers will arrive in Colombia by plane, or overland from Ecuador, Venezuela or Brazil. There are also numerous sailboats that bring travelers from Panama via the San Blas Islands.

You'll need a valid passport (with at least six more months of validity) and some nationalities will need a visa. Most travelers will get a 60-day tourist visa, which can be extended up to six months per calendar year. When arriving by plane (but not overland) you'll be given a customs form. You're supposed to keep this and return it at the time of your departure (or face a stiff fine), but no one we know has ever been asked for this form when they left the country. Keep it with your passport just in case, though.

For information on visas, see p308.

Flights and tours can be booked online at www.lonelyplanet.com/travel_services.

AIR
Airports & Airlines

Colombia's biggest international airport is Bogotá's **El Dorado** (BOG; ☎ 1 413 9053, 1 425 1000; www.bogota-dc.com/trans/aviones.htm). Other airports servicing international flights include Cartagena's **Rafael Nuñez airport** (CTG; ☎ 5 359

6273), Barranquilla's **Ernesto Cortissoz airport** (BAQ; ☎ 5 334 8052; www.baq.aero), **San Andrés airport** (ADZ; ☎ 8 512 6110), Medellín's **Jose Maria Codova airport** (MDE; ☎ 4 601 1212), **Pereira airport** (PEI; (☎ 6 326 0021) and Cali's **Alfonso Bonilla Aragón airport** (CLO; ☎ 2 442 2624). Charter airlines also fly package tourists into Cartagena and San Andrés.

Avianca (AV; ☎ 1 404 7862; www.avianca.com), Colombia's flagship airline, connects Bogotá with Europe (Madrid), North America (New York, Los Angeles, Miami and Mexico City), Central America (San José and Panama City) and South America (Caracas, Quito, Guayaquil, Lima, Santiago, Buenos Aires, São Paulo and Rio de Janeiro). It has a well-serviced fleet and a reasonable safety record.

Other airlines flying to and from Colombia include the following. Bogotá addresses for these airlines can be found on p91.
Air France (AF; ☎ Bogotá 1 413 0505; www.airfrance.com) Hub Charles de Gaulle Airport, Paris.
American Airlines (AA; ☎ Bogotá 1 439 7777, 1 744 9955; www.aa.com) Hub Dallas-Fort Worth Airport.
British Airways (BA; ☎ 1 800 934 5700, 1 900 331 2777 toll free; www.britishairways.com) Hub Heathrow Airport, London.
Continental (CO; ☎ 1 800 944 0219 toll free; www.continentalairlines.com) Hub George Bush Airport, Houston.
Copa (CM; ☎ Bogotá 1 623 1566; www.copaair.com) Hub Panama City.
Iberia (IB; ☎ Bogotá 1 610 5066; www.iberia.com) Hub Madrid Barajas Airport.
Spirit Air (SA; ☎ Bogotá 1 800 672 6717, 1 547 8309; www.spiritair.com) Hub Miami.
TACA (TA; ☎ Bogotá 1 637 3900; www.taca.com) Hub San Salvador Airport.

THINGS CHANGE...

The information in this chapter is particularly vulnerable to change. Check directly with the airline or a travel agent to make sure you understand how a fare (and ticket you may buy) works and be aware of the security requirements for international travel. Shop carefully. The details given in this chapter should be regarded as pointers and are not a substitute for your own careful, up-to-date research.

TRANSPORTATION

CLIMATE CHANGE & TRAVEL

Climate change is a serious threat to the ecosystems that humans rely upon, and air travel is the fastest-growing contributor to the problem. Lonely Planet regards travel, overall, as a global benefit, but believes we all have a responsibility to limit our personal impact on global warming.

Flying & Climate Change

Pretty much every form of motor travel generates CO_2 (the main cause of human-induced climate change) but planes are far and away the worst offenders, not just because of the sheer distances they allow us to travel, but because they release greenhouse gases high into the atmosphere. The statistics are frightening: two people taking a return flight between Europe and the US will contribute as much to climate change as an average household's gas and electricity consumption over a whole year.

Carbon Offset Schemes

Climatecare.org and other websites use 'carbon calculators' that allow jetsetters to offset the greenhouse gases they are responsible for with contributions to energy-saving projects and other climate-friendly initiatives in the developing world – including projects in India, Honduras, Kazakhstan and Uganda.

Lonely Planet, together with Rough Guides and other concerned partners in the travel industry, supports the carbon offset scheme run by climatecare.org. Lonely Planet offsets all of its staff and author travel.

For more information check out our website: lonelyplanet.com.

Tickets

Colombia requires, technically at least, that visitors have an onward ticket before they're allowed into the country. This is quite strictly enforced by airlines and travel agents, and none will sell you a one-way ticket unless you already have an onward ticket. Upon arrival in Colombia, however, hardly any immigration officials will ask you to present your onward ticket.

The trick, of course, is to purchase a fully-refundable ticket with your credit card and request a refund upon arrival in Colombia. If arriving overland, a printout of an unpaid reservation may also be sufficient to get past the border guards. Scruffy looking travelers are more likely to be asked to show an onward ticket than those neatly attired.

Australia & New Zealand

Unless you have an around-the-world ticket, the best way to get to Colombia is via Argentina or Chile. Your second best option is to fly via Los Angeles – Avianca now offers nonstop flights from LAX to Bogotá. Some online fare-compare sites will try and route you through New York or Miami – unless you want to spend 48 hours on a plane, avoid this option.

Lan Chile (www.lan.com) flies from Sydney via Auckland to Santiago, and has flights on to Bogotá. Expect to pay between A$3000 and A$3500 for the Sydney–Bogotá return flight. The Auckland–Bogotá fare will be only marginally lower. **Aerolíneas Argentinas** (www.aerolineas.com.ar) flies three times a week between Auckland and Buenos Aires, and has arrangements with other carriers to cover the Auckland–Australia leg. Aerolíneas Argentinas can fly you on to Bogotá for roughly the same price as Lan Chile.

Do compare prices on the airlines' websites and fare-compare sites like www.zuji.com.au. If you prefer a bricks-and-mortar travel agent the following offer the cheapest fares and have branches throughout Australia and New Zealand:

Flight Centre (☎ in Australia 133 133, in New Zealand 0800 243 544; www.flightcentre.com)

STA Travel (☎ in Australia 1300 733 035, in New Zealand 0508 782 872; www.statravel.com)

Canada

Air Canada offers a daily nonstop service between Toronto's Pearson Airport and Bogotá El Dorado for around C$900. You may also find discounts if you're willing to fly via New York or Miami.

A good choice for student, youth and budget airfares is **Travel Cuts** (☎ 866-246 9762; www.travelcuts.com).

Central America

Colombia has regular flight connections with most Central American capitals. Sample round-trip airfares include: Guatemala City–Bogotá US$400 to US$500, San José (Costa Rica)–Bogotá US$380 to US$420 and Panama City–Bogotá US$220 to US$270.

There are no flights to Nicaragua due to the ongoing diplomatic dispute over ownership of San Andrés and Providencia. For other Central American destinations it may work out cheaper to go via San Andrés and then get a domestic flight to the Colombian mainland. See p197 for details.

Continental Europe

A number of airlines, including British Airways, KLM, Air France and Iberia, link Bogotá, Medellín and Cali with European cities. Colombia is one of the cheapest South American destinations to reach from Europe. Expect to pay in the ballpark of €1100 for a 90-day return fare from Madrid, and around €1400 from Paris.

Some recommended agencies:

Anyway (☎ 0892 302 301; www.anyway.fr) French travel agent.

CTS Viaggi (☎ 06 462 0431; www.cts.it) Italian company that specializes in student and youth fares.

NBBS Reizen (☎ 0900 1020 300; www.nbbs.nl, in Dutch) Branches in most Dutch cities.

Nouvelles Frontiéres (☎ 08 25 00 07 47; www.nouvelles-frontieres.fr, in French) Many branches in Paris and throughout France.

STA (☎ in Paris 01 43 59 23 69, Frankfurt 069 430 1910; www.statravel.com) Branch offices across Europe.

South America

Airline tickets in South America are expensive. If you are traveling to Ecuador, Venezuela or Brazil, you will find it cheaper to fly domestically to the land border (Ipiales, Cúcuta or Leticia, respectively), cross the land border and take another domestic flight to your final destination.

That said, there are plenty of intercontinental flights flying out of Bogotá, plus a few out of Cali and Medellín. You can fly Bogotá–Quito (US$400), Cali–Quito (US$350), and Cali–Lima (US$450). Plenty of flights also connect Bogotá and Caracas (U$450).

Further afield, a flight to Santiago, Chile, will set you back around US$700, and to Buenos Aires US$800. Expect to pay around US$1000 for São Paulo or Rio de Janeiro in Brazil.

DEPARTURE TAX

The departure tax in Colombia is one of the highest in South America. Tourists spending more than 60 days in the country pay US$65 (or the peso equivalent, adjusted twice per month). If you spend less than two months in country the tax is US$33, which is often included in your airline ticket price. Payment is accepted in both dollars and pesos.

UK

Compared to other European cities, London has reasonably priced fares to Bogotá. You'll find plenty of deals listed in the travel sections of weekend editions of London newspapers. Advertisements for many travel agents appear in the travel pages of the weekend broadsheets, such as the *Independent* on Saturday and the *Sunday Times*. Look out for free magazines, such as *TNT,* which are widely available in London.

Prices for discounted flights from London to Bogotá start at around UK£350 one way and UK£450 return. Bargain hunters may find lower prices, but make sure you use a travel agent affiliated with the ABTA (Association of British Travel Agents). If you have bought your ticket from an ABTA-registered agent who then goes out of business, ABTA will guarantee a refund or an alternative. Unregistered bucket shops are sometimes cheaper, but can be riskier. Travel agents include:

Flightbookers (☎ 0800 082 3000; www.ebookers.co.uk)
STA (☎ 08701-630 026; www.statravel.co.uk)
Travel Bag (☎ 0800 082 5000; www.travelbag.co.uk)

USA

The major US gateway for Colombia is Miami, from where several carriers, including American Airlines, Avianca and Spirit Air, depart. A 90-day return ticket normally costs US$400 to US$500 depending on the season.

Another important gateway to Colombia is New York, from where American Airlines and Avianca have flights to Bogotá. A 30-day return ticket is around US$550 to US$650 depending on the season.

On the West Coast, the major departure point is Los Angeles, but flights to Bogotá can be expensive. Avianca is the only carrier to offer nonstop flights from LAX. The cheapest 60-day return fares will probably be somewhere between US$700 and US$800. The cheapest flights are with TACA, which makes stops in El Salvador and Costa Rica. TACA is not recommended during the hurricane season (September to November) because almost daily bad weather in San José frequently causes planes to be diverted to other airports, and you'll miss your connection.

Venezuelan carrier **Aeropostal** (www.aeropostal .com) sometimes offers good fares for their Miami–Caracas–Bogotá route.

For discount travel agencies, check the Sunday travel sections in newspapers such as the *Los Angeles Times, San Francisco Examiner, Boston Globe, Chicago Tribune* and *New York Times*.

STA Travel and Council Travel are two of the most reputable discount travel agencies in the USA. Although they both specialize in student travel, they may offer discount tickets to nonstudents of all ages.

Cheap Tickets (www.cheaptickets.com)
Orbitz (☎ 888 656 4546; www.orbitz.com)
STA Travel (☎ 800 781 4040; www.sta-travel.com)

BORDER CROSSINGS

Colombia borders Panama, Venezuela, Brazil, Peru and Ecuador, but has road connections with Venezuela and Ecuador only. These are the easiest and the most popular border crossings.

You can also cross the border to Peru and Brazil at the three corners near Leticia, and there is boat service to and from Panama and Ecuador.

Brazil & Peru

The only viable border crossing from these two countries into Colombia is via Leticia in the far southeastern corner of the Colombian Amazon. Leticia is reached from Iquitos (Peru) and Manaus (Brazil) by riverboat. See p290 for details. The area around Leticia is safe.

Ecuador

Virtually all travelers use the Carretera Panamericana border crossing through Tulcán (Ecuador) and Ipiales (Colombia). See p265 for information. Parts of the Panamericana (particularly the section between Pasto and Popayán) continue to be plagued by late-night bandits; you're advised to travel this leg only during the daytime.

It is possible but difficult to cross the border along the Pacific coast near Tumaco (see p281).

The Putumayo border crossing is not safe at this time.

Panama

Sailboats operate between Colón in Panama and Cartagena in Colombia; see p151. This is a popular form of intercontinental travel, and generally passes through (and stops in) the beautiful San Blas Islands along the way. You can also take small coastal boats from Sapzurro (see p188) across the border to Puerto Olbadia, Panama, from where you can fly to Panama City.

It is possible but more difficult to arrange transport from Bahía Solano (see p270) to Jaqué in Panama. From here you can continue along Panama's Pacific coast to Panama City or fly.

Venezuela

There are four border crossings between Colombia and Venezuela. By far the most popular with travelers (and probably the safest) is the route via San Antonio del Táchira (Venezuela) and Cúcuta (Colombia), on the main Caracas–Bogotá road. See p134 for details.

There is another reasonably popular border crossing at Paraguachón, on the Maracaibo (Venezuela) to Maicao (Colombia) road. Take this if you plan to head from Venezuela straight to Colombia's Caribbean coast. Buses and shared taxis run between Maracaibo and Maicao, and direct buses between Caracas/Maracaibo and Santa Marta/Cartagena. Your passport will be stamped by both Colombian and Venezuelan officials at the border. See p170 and p151 for details.

Not so popular is the border crossing between Colombia's Puerto Carreño and either Puerto Páez or Puerto Ayacucho (both in Venezuela). Still less useful is the crossing from El Amparo de Apure (Venezuela) to Arauca (Colombia), a guerrilla-ridden region.

ORGANIZED TOURS

Some overland South America companies do visit Colombia, but not many. They are often constrained by their insurance coverage, which is void in any area deemed unsafe by the overly-cautious US State Department or UK Foreign Office. You might try:

Dragoman (☎ 1728 861 133; www.dragoman.co.uk)
Exodus Travels (☎ 020 8673 0859; www.exodus.co.uk)

TRANSPORTATION

Intrepid Travel (☎ 1 866 360 1151; www.intrepid travel.com)

Last Frontiers (☎ 01296 653 000; www.lastfrontiers .co.uk)

Wild Frontiers (☎ 44 20 7736 3968; www.wild frontiers.co.uk)

For a comprehensive listing of tour operators in Colombia, see the Latin American Travel Association's website at www.lata.org.

GETTING AROUND

AIR

Colombia's two principal domestic carriers are Avianca and AeroRepública. The government-owned airline, Satena, provides service to many small towns and villages across the country. A number of smaller airlines and charter airlines compete on some of the more popular routes.

Prices are usually fixed between the airlines, but it can be worthwhile checking out their websites just in case. Ticket prices to some destinations drop the last week or two before the date; for some other destinations, they may rise significantly.

While you can reserve domestic airline tickets online you will not be able to pay online with a foreign credit card. You'll have to take the booking reference and go to a licensed travel agent and pay in cash or credit card (plus a few thousand pesos for the in-person booking service.)

Some airlines offer packages to major tourist destinations (for example, Cartagena and San Andrés), which can cost not much more than you'd pay for air tickets only. If purchasing these package deals from overseas you are exempt from the 10% IVA (sales tax) – be sure to ask for this discount, as many Colombians are unaware of it.

Airlines in Colombia

Colombia has more than half a dozen main passenger airlines and another dozen smaller carriers. The on-board service of the major carriers is OK. As flight time is usually not much longer than an hour, don't expect any gastronomic treats; on most flights you get no more than a snack. The following fly a variety of routes:

ADA (☎ 2 444 4232; www.ada-aero.com) This Medellín-based carrier offers regional flights.

AeroRepública (☎ 1 320 9090; www.aerorepublica .com.co) The second-biggest airline covers much the same domestic territory as Avianca.

Aexpa (1 800 011 6288; www.aexpa.com) Offers charter services to the Pacific coast.

Aires (☎ 1 336 6039; www.aires.com.co) This smaller operation uses mostly turbo planes and travels to smaller localities.

Avianca/SAM (☎ 1 404 7862; www.avianca.com) Longtime principal domestic airline, with the widest network of both domestic and international routes. Avianca has merged with the Medellín-based SAM.

EasyFly (☎ 1 800 012 3279; www.easyfly.com.co) A budget carrier offering regional flights.

Satena (☎ 1 281 7071; www.satena.com) This is the commercial carrier of the FAC (Colombian Air Force) and services flights to the vast areas of the Amazon (p285), Los Llanos (p134) and the Pacific coast (p269); it lands at 50 small towns and villages that would be otherwise virtually inaccessible.

BICYCLE

Colombia is not the easiest of countries for cyclists. Road rules favor drivers and you'll end up fighting traffic on main roadways. Never assume that a driver will give you right of way. On the plus side, most roads are paved and security is improving. Even the smallest towns will have a repair shop and you can get your bike fixed cheaply and easily. Bike rentals are uncommon but you can buy a bike almost anywhere. However, if you want something really reliable, bring your own bike and all your own kit.

It is also worth noting that cities are becoming more bike-friendly, with new bike tracks and Ciclovia (the weekend closure of selected streets to cars and buses, making them tracks for bikers and skaters instead).

Some bike shops and hostels rent bikes.

BOAT

Cargo boats ply the Pacific coast, with the port of Buenaventura (p279) as their hub. Travelers with sufficient time can get a bunk bed below deck for the journey northbound to the Chocó (p270) or southbound to Guapi (p282) and Isla Gorgona (p284).

Before railroads and highways were built, river transport was the principal means of transport in mountainous Colombia. The only safe river journey you're likely to take is on the Amazon from Leticia, upriver to Iquitos, Peru or downriver to Manaus, Brazil; see p290 for details.

MAIN DOMESTIC FLIGHTS

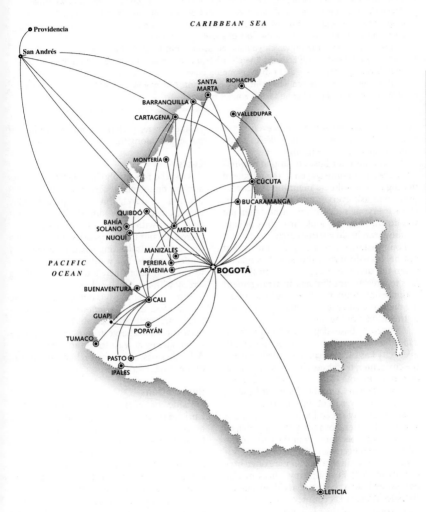

The Río Atrato and Río San Juan in the Chocó should both be avoided at present due to guerrilla activity in the region.

BUS

Buses are the principal means of intercity travel, and go just about everywhere. Most long-distance intercity buses are more comfortable than your average coach-class airplane seat, and the overnight buses sometimes have business class–sized seats. A word of warning: Colombian bus drivers turn the air-con down to arctic temperatures. Wear a sweater, a beanie, and gloves, or better yet, bring a blanket. Bus drivers also tend to crank up the music and/or action movie (dubbed in

---

TO NIGHT BUS, OR NOT TO NIGHT BUS?

There was a time when taking night buses in Colombia was not a good idea. The Fuerzas Armadas Revolucionarias de Colombia (FARC) used to control many of the major highways. This is no longer the case, and night buses to most destinations are a comfortable way to avoid wasting a day in transit, plus saving you the cost of a night's accommodation.

The only major route on which you should avoid night travel is the road from Popayán to Pasto and the border with Ecuador. There is no longer guerrilla activity, but armed thieves have been known to stop buses and rob everyone on board.

This advice could change while this book is in print. You may like to double-check online or at your accommodation before taking a night bus.

Spanish) on the bus's television, even in the middle of the night. You may like to travel with a couple pairs of earplugs.

It is common for buses to stop at *requisas* (military checkpoints), even in the middle of the night. The soldiers manning the checkpoint will ask everyone to get off the bus, check everyone's identification, and then pat you down. They may look through your bags or, more rarely, do a strip search.

Long-distance buses stop for meals, but not necessarily at mealtimes; it depends on when the driver is hungry or when the bus gets to a restaurant that has an arrangement with the bus company. Buses are locked during the stops, and everyone must get off, even in the middle of the night.

All intercity buses depart from and arrive at a *terminal de pasajeros* (passenger terminal). Every city has such a terminal, usually outside the city center, but always linked to it by local transport. Bogotá is the most important bus transport hub in Colombia, handling buses to just about every area of the country.

The highway speed limit in Colombia is 80km per hour, and bus companies are obliged to put a large speedometer at the front of the cabin, so passengers can see how fast the bus is going (although in practice they are often broken or disabled). Bus company offices are also obliged by law to post their accident/fatality statistics at the ticket counter, which can give you a good idea of their safety record.

Classes

Most intercity buses are air-conditioned and have good leg room. On shorter routes (less than four hours), smaller *busetas* ply their trade. There are sometimes also vans, which cost more but are faster. In remote country areas, where the roads are bad, ancient *chivas* (many former US school buses) service

smaller towns, picking up and dropping off passengers along the way.

Costs

Bus travel is reasonably cheap in Colombia. As a rule of thumb, buses cost around COP$4000 per hour of travel. Outside of peak holiday times, bus prices are almost always negotiable. Start with a polite, *'hay discuento?'* (Is there a discount?), then work your way down the counters, indicating what the previously quoted fare was. You want to take the second-to-cheapest offer; there's usually something wrong with the cheapest bus.

When you get on a bus out on the road, you pay the fare to the *ayudante* (driver's sidekick) and rarely get a ticket. *Ayudantes* have been known to charge gringos more than the actual fare or at least to round the price up. Ask other passengers beforehand to be sure of the correct fare.

Reservations

Outside of peak holiday periods (like Christmas and Easter), reservations are not needed. Just rock up to the bus station an hour before you want to leave and grab the first bus going. On some minor routes, where there are only a few departures a day, it's worth considering buying your ticket several hours before the scheduled departure.

A common trick, especially with smaller buses, is to say they only need one passenger to leave, then they lock your bag in the back and you end up waiting an hour for the bus to leave, watching other buses leave before you do. Don't get into the bus or pay until you see the driver start the engine and prepare to leave.

CAR & MOTORCYCLE

Considering how cheap and extensive bus transport is in Colombia, there is little reason to bring your own vehicle. What's more, the security situation remains dodgy in remote and rural parts of the country, substantially increasing the risk of vehicle theft and/or assault in isolated parts of the country. Check government websites for warnings before setting out anywhere remote.

In the cities, on the other hand, traffic is heavy, chaotic and mad. Driving 'manners' are wild and unpredictable. It takes some time to get used to the local style of driving, but even if you master it, the risk of an accident remains high.

Colombians drive on the right-hand side of the road and there are seat belt requirements, so buckle up or risk a fine. The speed limit is 60km per hour in the city and 80km per hour on the highway. The nationwide highway police telephone number is ☎ 767.

If you do plan to drive in Colombia, bring your driver's license. The driver's license from your country will normally do, but if you want to be 100% sure, bring along an International Driving Permit as well.

Bring Your Own Vehicle

There's no way of bringing your vehicle to South America other than by sea or air, involving time, substantial cost and a lot of paperwork. You'll spend less (and be safer) traveling in Colombia by bus.

If you really wish to bring your car from Central America to Colombia, there are cargo boats between Colón (Panama) and Cartagena. There is no set schedule and no set price for shipping a car, so bargain hard. On arrival in Colombia the car is given a one- or two-month permit. You will require international insurance: local insurance policies are not expensive, but you cannot buy them for a car that has foreign plates.

Several of the sailboats that ply the route via the San Blas Islands to Panama can carry motorcycles.

Rental

Several international rental car companies, such as **Avis** (www.avis.com), **Hertz** (www.hertz.com) or **Budget** (www.budget.com), operate in Colombia. But why would you bother? Taxis are a cheap, stress-free way to get around the cities, and intercity bus transport is frequent, cheap and comfortable. Expect to pay around COP$120,000 to COP$150,000 per day, plus gasoline. You'll get better deals, as always, by booking online. Carefully check clauses pertaining to insurance and liability before you sign a rental contract. Pay close attention to any theft clause as it may load a large percentage of any loss on to the hirer.

Motorcycles

Some cities, especially in the north, use motorcycle-taxis, which are a quick way of getting around if you're on your own. These, however, are not the safest method of transport and are even illegal in some places, including Cartagena (though no one seems to stop them). There may be options of renting a motorcycle, especially in resort-type areas such as San Andrés (p191).

Helmet laws are enforced.

Tricycle Moto-Taxi

Chinese-made *tuk-tuks* are becoming increasingly popular in smaller tourist towns. Moto-taxis seat three and have a covered roof, plus a tarp that can be lowered around the sides in case of rain. You'll see these in Santa Fe de Antioquia (p217), the Desierto de la Tatacoa (p267), and many of the small towns on the Pacific coast (p269).

HITCHHIKING

Hitchhiking in Colombia is uncommon and difficult. Given the complex internal situation, drivers don't want to take risks and simply don't stop on the road. As intercity buses are fast, efficient and relatively cheap, it's not worth wasting time on hitching and taking a potentially serious risk.

LOCAL TRANSPORTATION

Taxis are cheap and reliable, and for most travelers will be their principal means of urban transport.

Bus

Almost every urban centre of more than 100,000 inhabitants has a bus service, as do many smaller towns. The standard, speed and efficiency of local buses vary from place to place, but on the whole they are slow and crowded. City buses have a flat fare, so the distance of the ride makes no difference. You get on by the front door and pay the driver or his assistant. You never get a ticket.

In some cities or on some streets there are bus stops (*paraderos* or *paradas*), while in most others you just wave down the bus. To

BUSSING ABOUT, CHIVA-STYLE

The chiva is a Disneyland-style vehicle that was Colombia's principal means of road transport several decades ago. Also called bus de escalera (which roughly translated means 'bus of stairs,' referring to the stairs along the side) in some regions, the chiva is a piece of popular art on wheels. The body is made almost entirely of wood and has wooden benches rather than seats, with each bench accessible from the outside. The body of the bus is painted with colorful decorative patterns, each different, with a main painting on the back. There are homebred artists who specialize in painting chivas. Ceramic miniatures of chivas are found in just about every Colombian handicraft shop.

Today, chivas have almost disappeared from main roads, but they still play an important role on back roads between small towns and villages. There are still a few thousand of them and they are most common in Antioquia, Huila, Nariño and on the Caribbean coast. Chivas take both passengers and any kind of cargo, animals included. If the interior is already completely packed, the roof is used for everything and everybody that doesn't fit inside. Chivas usually gather around markets, from where they depart for their journeys along bumpy roads. They are rare guests at bus terminals.

Night city tours in chivas are organized by travel agents in most large cities and have become a popular form of entertainment. There is normally a band on board playing local music, and a large stock of aguardiente (anise-flavored liquor) to create the proper atmosphere. The tour usually includes some popular nightspots and can be great fun.

let the driver know that you intend to get off you simply say, or shout, 'por aquí, por favor' (here, please), 'en la esquina, por favor' (at the corner, please) or 'el paradero, por favor' (at the coming bus stop, please).

There are lots of different types of local buses, ranging from old wrecks to modern air-conditioned vehicles. One common type is the buseta (small bus), a dominant means of urban transport in cities such as Bogotá and Cartagena. The bus fare is somewhere between COP$600 and COP$1500, depending on the city and type of bus.

A bus or buseta trip, particularly in large cities such as Bogotá or Barranquilla, is not a smooth and silent ride but rather a sort of breathtaking adventure with a taste of local folklore thrown in. You'll have an opportunity to be saturated with loud tropical music, learn about the Colombian meaning of road rules, and observe your driver desperately trying to make his way through an ocean of vehicles.

Colectivo

Colectivo in Colombia can mean a midsized bus, a shared taxi, an overloaded jeep, and everything in between. They are most popular in short intercity hops of less than four hours. Because they are smaller than regular buses, they can travel quicker, and charge around 30% more as a result. They often depart only when full.

In some cities they depart from and arrive at the bus terminal, but in smaller towns they are usually found in the main square. The frequency of service varies largely from place to place. At some places there may be a colectivo every five minutes, but elsewhere you can wait an hour or longer until the necessary number of passengers has been collected. If you're in a hurry you can pay for all the seats and the driver will depart immediately.

Mass Transit

Mass transit is growing increasingly popular in Colombia. Bogotá boasts the TransMilenio, and Cali has just opened a similar project, called the Mio. Medellín has its famous Metro, the only commuter rail line in the country. Pereira, too, has recently built its MegaBús system, another electric bus line. Other cities and even smaller towns are considering following suit.

Taxi

Taxis are cheap, convenient and ubiquitous in the major cities and most midsized towns. In the interior of the country all taxis have meters; on the Caribbean coast, it's haggle or pay extra, and many drivers are eager (especially in Cartagena) to see just how much they can take advantage of your naïveté. That said, a surprising proportion of taxi drivers are honest individuals; the better you speak Spanish, the more bargaining power you'll have, and the less likely you'll pay hyperinflated prices.

There are occasionally deceptive, untrustworthy individuals masquerading in fake taxis. This is rare, but if you are concerned, it is always safer to call for a taxi, which costs a mere few hundred pesos extra. Major bus terminals also offer predictive fares – indicate your destination at the counter and show the printed slip to the driver, who is obliged to charge you no more than whatever the computer spits out. Taxi fares are always per taxi, never per number of passengers. Many taxis have somewhat flimsy doors – be kind, do not slam doors when getting into or out of the vehicle.

Don't use taxis with a driver and somebody else inside. Taxi drivers sometimes have a friend along for company or for security reasons, but such a situation may be unsafe for you; some cases of robbery have been reported.

A taxi may also be chartered for longer distances. This is convenient if you want to visit places near major cities that are outside local transport areas but too near to be covered by long-distance bus networks. You can also rent a taxi by the hour in the major cities – a good way to make your own impromptu tour. Expect to pay around COP$20,000 per hour for this service.

ORGANIZED TOURS

Aviatur (Map pp70-1; ☎ 1 286 5555; www.aviatur.com; Avenida 19 No 4-62, Bogotá) Colombia's largest tourist company owns and operates resorts across Colombia. They principally cater to the domestic market. They have offices in all the major cities.

Colombia 57 (☎ in UK 0800 078 9157, in Colombia 313 401 5691; www.colombia57.com) This British-owned, Manizales-based tour operator specializes in custom-tailored midrange and top-end tours countrywide.

Colombian Journeys (☎ 1 618 0027; www.colombian journeys.com; Calle 81 No 11-68, oficina 208, Bogotá) Bogotá-based company offering multilingual tours countrywide.

De Una Tours (☎ 1 368 1915; Carrera 26A No 40-18 Ap 202, La Soledad, Bogotá; www.deunacolombia.com) This Dutch-owned company offers tours nationwide, including many off-the-beaten-path destinations.

Ecoguías (Map p64; ☎ 347 5736, 212-1423; www .ecoguias.com; Carrera 3 No 55-10, Bogotá; ☼ 9am-5:30pm Mon-Fri) A long-standing British-owned adventure travel company, Ecoguías focuses on ecotourism trips to various regions of the country, such as Ciudad Perdida (p177), the coffee region and the Pacific coast (p269).

Promotora Neptuno (☎ 1 520 5620; www.neptuno .org; Carrera 7bisA No 123-15, Bogotá) A German-owned tour company based in Bogotá.

TRAIN

Colombia has a nationwide network of train track that is largely unused. The Tren Turístico Café y Azucar (coffe and sugar tourist train) out of Cali now offers occasional excursions into the mountains, and can also serve as infrequent transport between La Tebaida, near Armenia, and Cali, and also El Cumbre, on the road to Buenaventura, and Cali. See p242 for more details.

Those visiting San Cipriano (p281), just off the Cali–Buenaventura highway, can enjoy the novel sensation of traveling on a railroad handcart powered by a motorcycle.

TRANSPORTATION

Health David Goldberg MD

CONTENTS

Most visitors travel to Colombia without incident, but there are certain medical conditions to be aware of and several things you can do to prevent sickness. Most illnesses are the result of Colombia's tropical-zone location. If traveling anywhere along the coast or jungle, you can bank on little tropical nuisances – infected bug bites, rashes or heat exhaustion. Other, more dangerous afflictions, including malaria and yellow fever, can strike travelers who get further off the beaten track or spend a lot of time trekking through national parks. Dengue fever is a risk in lowland population centers. Other problems can occur in the mountains, including *soroche* (altitude sickness). The good news is that Colombia has some of the best medical care in South America. Prices for treatment are usually reasonable and the local pharmacy network is developed and extensive: even in small towns there are *droguerías* (pharmacies), and those in the cities are usually well stocked.

BEFORE YOU GO

If you require a particular medication take an adequate supply with you; it may not be available locally. Take the original prescription specifying the generic rather than the brand name; this makes getting replacements easier. It's also wise to have the prescription with you to prove you're using the medication legally. You can register online with the **International Association for Medical Assistance to Travelers** (IAMAT; www.iamat.org).

INSURANCE

Buying a travel insurance policy to cover medical problems is recommended. There is a wide variety of policies and your travel agent will have recommendations.

RECOMMENDED VACCINATIONS

Yellow-fever vaccine is required for visitors to the national parks along the coastal regions. Travelers limiting their visit to the main cities and mountainous regions may not need to be immunized for yellow fever, but be aware that some countries, such as Australia, will not let you into the country if you're flying direct from Colombia without a yellow-fever vaccine. Check your country's government health information for specifics. No other vaccines are legally mandated, but the vaccines on p321 are strongly recommended.

MEDICAL CHECKLIST

Colombian pharmacies stock all kinds of drugs, and medication can be cheaper than in Western countries. There are few restricted drugs; almost everything is sold over the counter. Many drugs are manufactured locally under foreign license. Be sure to check expiry dates.

- adhesive or paper tape
- altitude sickness pills (acetazolamide or dexamethasone)
- antibacterial ointment (eg Bactroban) for cuts and abrasions
- antibiotics
- antidiarrheal drugs (eg loperamide)
- antihistamines (for hay fever and allergic reactions)
- anti-inflammatory drugs (eg ibuprofen)
- bandages, gauze, gauze rolls
- DEET-containing insect repellent for the skin
- iodine tablets (for water purification)
- motion sickness pills (eg Dramamine)
- oral rehydration salts
- permethrin-containing insect spray for clothing, tents and bed nets

VACCINATIONS

Vaccine	Recommended for	Dosage	Side effects
chickenpox	travelers who've never had chickenpox	2 doses 1 month apart	fever; mild case of chickenpox
hepatitis A	all travelers	1 dose before trip; booster 6-12 months later	soreness at injection site; headaches; body aches
hepatitis B	long-term travelers in close contact with the local population	3 doses over 6-month period	soreness at injection site; low-grade fever
measles	travelers born after 1956 who've had only one measles vaccination	1 dose	fever; rash; joint pains; allergic reactions
rabies	travelers who may have contact with animals and may not have access to medical care	3 doses over 3-4 week period	soreness at injection site; headaches; body aches
tetanus-diphtheria	all travelers who haven't had booster within 10 years	1 dose lasts 10 years	soreness at injection site
typhoid	all travelers	4 capsules by mouth, 1 taken every other day	abdominal pain; nausea; rash
yellow fever	all travelers, except those limiting their trip to the major cities and mountainous regions of the country	1 dose lasts 10 years	headaches; body aches; severe reactions are rare

HEALTH

- pocket knife
- scissors, safety pins, tweezers
- steroid cream or cortisone (for poison ivy and other allergic rashes)
- sunblock

INTERNET RESOURCES & BOOKS

A good place to start is the Lonely Planet website (www.lonelyplanet.com). The World Health Organization publishes a superb book, *International Travel and Health,* which is revised annually and is available online at no cost at www.who. int/ith.

If you plan to travel in remote areas, you might consider taking a health guide such as Lonely Planet's *Healthy Travel Central & South America* or *Staying Healthy in Asia, Africa & Latin America* by Dirk Schroeder.

IN TRANSIT

DEEP VEIN THROMBOSIS (DVT)

Blood clots may form in the legs during plane flights. Most are reabsorbed uneventfully, but some may break off and travel through the blood vessels to the lungs, where they could cause complications.

The chief symptom of DVT is swelling or pain of the foot, ankle or calf, usually but not always on just one side. When a blood clot travels to the lungs, it may cause chest pain and difficulty breathing.

To prevent the development of DVT on long flights you should walk about the cabin, perform isometric compressions of the leg muscles (ie contract the leg muscles while sitting), drink plenty of fluids and avoid alcohol.

JET LAG & MOTION SICKNESS

Jet lag is common when crossing more than five time zones, resulting in insomnia, fatigue, malaise or nausea. To avoid jet lag try drinking plenty of fluids (nonalcoholic) and eating light meals. Upon arrival, get exposure to natural sunlight and readjust your schedule (for meals, sleep etc) as soon as possible.

Antihistamines such as dimenhydrinate (Dramamine) and meclizine (Antivert, Bonine) are usually the first choice for treating motion sickness. Their main side-effect is drowsiness. An herbal alternative is ginger, which works like a charm for some people.

IN COLOMBIA

AVAILABILITY & COST OF HEALTH CARE

Adequate medical care is available in major cities, but may be difficult to find in rural areas. For an online guide to physicians, dentists, hospitals and pharmacies in Colombia, go to the US embassy website at http://bogota.usembassy.gov/root/pdfs/medservices.pdf. Most doctors and hospitals will expect payment in cash, even if you have travel health insurance.

If you develop a life-threatening medical problem, you'll probably want to be evacuated to a country with state-of-the-art medical care. For air ambulance service in Colombia, call **Aeromedicos** (☎ 1 413 9160, 413 8915; Ambulancia Aerea, El Dorado International Airport, Bogotá, entrada 2, int 1, oficina 105).

Since this may cost tens of thousands of dollars, be sure you have insurance to cover this before you depart.

FUNGAL INFECTIONS

Fungal infections occur more commonly in hot weather and are most likely to be found between the toes or fingers or around the groin. The infections are spread by infected animals or humans; you may contract them by walking barefoot in damp areas, for example. Moisture encourages these infections.

To prevent fungal infections wear loose, comfortable clothes, avoid artificial fibers, wash frequently and dry thoroughly. Use flip-flops while taking a shower in bathrooms of cheap hotels. If you become infected, wash the infected area daily with a disinfectant or medicated soap, and rinse and dry well. Apply an antifungal cream or powder. Tea-tree based ointments are effective.

INFECTIOUS DISEASES
Cholera

Cholera is an intestinal infection acquired through ingestion of contaminated food or water. The main symptom is profuse, watery diarrhea, which may be so severe that it causes life-threatening dehydration. The key treatment is drinking oral rehydration solution. Antibiotics are also given, usually tetracycline or doxycycline, though quinolone antibiotics such as ciprofloxacin and levofloxacin are also effective. In recent years, only a small number of cholera cases have been identified and a cholera vaccine is no longer required.

Dengue Fever

Dengue fever is a viral infection and the number of cases reported from Colombia has risen sharply in recent years, especially in Santander, Tolima, Valle del Cauca, Norte de Santander, Meta and Huila. Dengue is transmitted by Aedes mosquitoes, which bite preferentially during the daytime and are usually found close to human habitations, often indoors. Dengue is especially common in densely populated, urban environments.

Dengue usually causes flulike symptoms, including fever, muscle aches, joint pains, headaches, nausea and vomiting, which are often followed by a rash. The body aches may be quite uncomfortable, but most cases resolve uneventfully in a few days.

There is no treatment for dengue fever. The only thing to do is take analgesics such as acetaminophen/paracetamol (Tylenol) and drink plenty of fluids, preferably with hydration salts. Avoid aspirin as this may cause hemorrhaging. Severe cases may require hospitalization for intravenous fluids and supportive care. There is no vaccine. The cornerstone of prevention is insect protection measures.

Hepatitis A

Hepatitis A is the second most common travel-related infection (after traveler's diarrhea). It's a viral infection of the liver that is usually acquired by ingestion of contaminated water, food or ice, though it may also be acquired by direct contact with infected persons. The illness occurs throughout the world, but the incidence is higher in developing nations. Symptoms may include fever, malaise, jaundice, nausea, vomiting and abdominal pain. Most cases resolve without complications, though hepatitis A occasionally causes severe liver damage. There is no treatment.

The vaccine for hepatitis A is extremely safe and highly effective. And if you get a booster six to 12 months later, it lasts for at least 10 years. Because the safety of hepatitis A vaccine has not been established for pregnant women or children under age 2, they should instead be given a gammaglobulin injection.

Hepatitis B

Like hepatitis A, hepatitis B is a liver infection that occurs worldwide but is more common in developing nations. Unlike hepatitis A, the disease is usually acquired by sexual contact or by exposure to infected blood, generally through blood transfusions or contaminated needles. The vaccine is recommended only for long-term travelers (on the road more than six months) who expect to live in rural areas or have close physical contact with the local population.

Hepatitis B vaccine is safe and highly effective. However, a total of three injections is necessary to establish full immunity. Several countries added hepatitis B vaccine to the list of routine childhood immunizations in the 1980s, so many young adults are already protected.

HIV & AIDS
Infection with the human immunodeficiency virus (HIV) may lead to acquired immune deficiency syndrome (AIDS), which is a fatal disease. Any exposure to blood, blood products or body fluids may put the individual at risk. The disease is often transmitted through sexual contact, and in Colombia it's primarily through contact between heterosexuals.

HIV and AIDS can also be contracted through infected blood transfusions, and you should be aware that not all hospitals screen blood supplies. The virus may also be picked up through injection with an unsterilized needle. Acupuncture, tattooing and body piercing are other potential dangers.

Intestinal Worms
These parasites are common in humid, tropical areas. They can be present on unwashed vegetables or in undercooked meat, or you can pick them up through your skin by walking barefoot. Infestations may not show up for some time and, although they are generally not serious, can cause further health problems if left untreated. A stool test on your return home is not a bad idea if you think you may have contracted them. Medication is usually available over the counter and treatment is easy and short.

Malaria
Malaria is transmitted by mosquito bites, usually between dusk and dawn. The main symptom is high spiking fevers, which may be accompanied by chills, sweats, headache, body aches, weakness, vomiting or diarrhea. Severe cases of malaria may involve the central nervous system and lead to seizures, confusion, coma and death.

Taking malaria pills is strongly recommended for all rural areas below 800m. Risk is highest in the departments of Amazonas, Chocó, Córdoba, Guainía, Guaviare, Putumayo and Vichada. There is no malaria risk in the major cities.

There is a choice of three malaria pills, all of which work about equally well. Mefloquine (Lariam) is taken once weekly, starting one to two weeks before arrival and continuing through the trip and for four weeks after return. The problem is that a certain percentage of people develop neuropsychiatric side effects, which may range from mild to severe. Atovaquone/proguanil (Malarone) is a newly approved combination pill taken once daily with food starting two days before arrival and continuing through the trip and for seven days after departure. Side effects are typically mild. Doxycycline is a third alternative, but may cause an exaggerated sunburn reaction.

In general, Malarone seems to cause fewer side effects than mefloquine and is becoming more popular. The chief disadvantage is that it has to be taken daily.

Protecting yourself against mosquito bites is just as important as taking malaria pills, since none of the pills are 100% effective. If you have the chance to buy an insecticide-impregnated mosquito net before your trip, do so, as they are not yet available in Colombia.

If you may not have access to medical care while traveling, you should bring along additional pills for emergency self-treatment, which you should take if you can't reach a doctor and you develop symptoms that suggest malaria, such as high spiking fevers. One option is to take four tablets of Malarone once daily for three days. However, Malarone should not be used for treatment if you're already taking it for prevention. Antimalaria drugs are available free of charge at any Colombian hospital as part of the country's antimalaria policy. Ask for the *gota gruesa* (thick smear) test.

If you develop a fever after returning home, see a physician, as malaria symptoms may not occur for months.

Rabies
Rabies is a viral infection of the brain and spinal cord that is almost always fatal. The rabies virus is carried in the saliva of infected animals and is typically transmitted through an animal bite, though contamination of any break in the skin with infected saliva may result in rabies. In Colombia, a rabies outbreak caused by large numbers of bat bites was reported in May–June 2004 from Birrinchao, along the Purricha river in the Chocó region.

HEALTH

Rabies vaccine is safe, but a full series requires three injections and is quite expensive. Those at high risk of rabies, such as animal handlers and spelunkers (cave explorers), should certainly get the vaccine.

All animal bites and scratches must be promptly and thoroughly cleansed with large amounts of soap and water, and local health authorities contacted to determine whether or not further treatment is necessary.

Sexually Transmitted Diseases

Sexual contact with an infected partner can result in you contracting a number of diseases. The use of condoms lessens the risk of infection considerably.

The most common sexually transmitted diseases are gonorrhea and syphilis, which in men first appear as sores, blisters or rashes around the genitals and a discharge or pain when urinating. Symptoms may be less marked or not present at all in women. Syphilis symptoms eventually disappear, but the disease continues and may cause severe problems in later years. Gonorrhea and syphilis are treatable with antibiotics.

Tetanus

This potentially fatal disease is difficult to treat, but is easily prevented by immunization. Tetanus occurs when a wound becomes infected by a germ that lives in soil in the feces of horses and other animals. It enters the body via breaks in the skin, so the best prevention is to clean all wounds promptly and thoroughly and use an antiseptic. Use antibiotics if the wound becomes hot or throbs or pus is seen. The first symptom may be discomfort in swallowing or stiffening of the jaw and neck; this can be followed by painful convulsions of the jaw and whole body.

Typhoid Fever

Typhoid fever is caused by ingestion of food or water contaminated by a species of *Salmonella* known as *Salmonella typhi*. Fever occurs in virtually all cases. Other symptoms may include headache, malaise, muscle aches, dizziness, loss of appetite, nausea and abdominal pain. Either diarrhea or constipation may occur. Possible complications include intestinal perforation, intestinal bleeding, confusion, delirium or (rarely) coma. Unless you expect to take all your meals in major hotels and restaurants, typhoid vaccine is a good idea.

The drug of choice is usually a quinolone antibiotic such as ciprofloxacin (Cipro) or levofloxacin (Levaquin), which many travelers carry for treatment of traveler's diarrhea. However, if you self-treat for typhoid fever you may also need to self-treat for malaria since the symptoms of the two diseases may be indistinguishable.

Typhus

This is spread by ticks, mites and lice. It begins as a severe cold followed by a fever, chills, headaches, muscle pains and a body rash. There is often a large and painful sore at the site of the bite, and nearby lymph nodes become swollen and painful.

Yellow Fever

Yellow fever is a life-threatening viral infection transmitted by mosquitoes in forested areas. The illness begins with flulike symptoms which may include fever, chills, headache, muscle aches, backache, loss of appetite, nausea and vomiting. These symptoms usually subside in a few days, but one person in six enters a second, toxic phase characterized by recurrent fever, vomiting, listlessness, jaundice, kidney failure and hemorrhage, leading to death in up to half of all cases. There is no treatment except for supportive care. The vaccine is highly recommended for visitors to the country's national parks along the coast, specifically Parque Nacional Natural Tayrona and Ciudad Perdida.

The vaccine should be given at least 10 days before any potential exposure to yellow fever and remains effective for approximately 10 years. Reactions to the vaccine are generally mild and may include headaches, muscle aches, low-grade fevers or discomfort at the injection site. Severe, life-threatening reactions have been described but are extremely rare.

TRAVELER'S DIARRHEA

To prevent diarrhea, avoid tap water unless it has been boiled, filtered or chemically disinfected (iodine tablets); only eat fresh fruits or vegetables if cooked or peeled; be wary of dairy products that might contain unpasteurized milk; and be highly selective when eating food from street vendors.

If you develop diarrhea, be sure to drink plenty of fluids, preferably an oral rehydration solution containing lots of salt and sugar.

A few loose stools don't require treatment but if you start having more than four or five stools a day you should start taking an antibiotic (usually a quinolone drug) and an antidiarrheal agent (such as loperamide). If diarrhea is bloody or persists for more than 72 hours or is accompanied by fever, shaking, chills or severe abdominal pain you should seek medical attention.

ENVIRONMENTAL HAZARDS
Altitude Sickness

Altitude sickness may develop in travelers who ascend rapidly to altitudes greater than 2500m, including those flying directly to Bogotá. Being physically fit does not in any way lessen your risk of altitude sickness. Symptoms may include headaches, nausea, vomiting, dizziness, malaise, insomnia and loss of appetite. Severe cases may be complicated by fluid in the lungs (high-altitude pulmonary edema) or swelling of the brain (high-altitude cerebral edema). Most deaths are caused by high-altitude pulmonary edema.

The standard medication to prevent altitude sickness is a mild diuretic called acetazolamide (Diamox), which should be started 24 hours before ascent and continued for 48 hours after arrival at altitude. Possible side effects include numbness, increased urination, tingling, nausea, drowsiness, nearsightedness and temporary impotence. For those who cannot tolerate acetazolamide, most physicians prescribe dexamethasone, which is a type of steroid. A natural alternative is gingko, which some people find quite helpful. The usual dosage is 100mg twice daily.

To lessen the chance of altitude sickness, you should be sure to ascend gradually or by increments to higher altitudes, avoid overexertion, eat light meals and avoid drinking alcohol.

If you or any of your companions show any symptoms of altitude sickness, you should not ascend to a higher altitude until the symptoms have cleared. If the symptoms become worse, immediately descend to a lower altitude. Acetazolamide and dexamethasone may be used to treat altitude sickness as well as prevent it.

Animal & Snake Bites

Do not attempt to pet, handle or feed any animal, with the exception of domestic animals known to be free of any infectious disease. Most animal injuries are directly related to a person's attempt to touch or feed the animal.

Any bite or scratch by a mammal, including bats, should be promptly and thoroughly cleansed with large amounts of soap and water, followed by application of an antiseptic such as iodine or alcohol. The local health authorities should be contacted immediately for possible postexposure rabies treatment, whether or not you've been immunized against rabies. It may also be advisable to start an antibiotic, since wounds caused by animal bites and scratches frequently become infected. One of the newer quinolones, such as levofloxacin (Levaquin), which many travelers carry in case of diarrhea, would be an appropriate choice.

In the event of a venomous snake bite, place the victim at rest, keep the bitten area immobilized, and move the victim immediately to the nearest medical facility. Avoid tourniquets, which are no longer recommended.

Heatstroke

To protect yourself from excessive sun exposure, you should stay out of the midday sun, wear sunglasses and a wide-brimmed sun hat, and apply sunscreen with SPF 15 or higher, with both UVA and UVB protection. Travelers should also drink plenty of fluids and avoid strenuous exercise when the temperature is high.

Mosquito & Tick Bites

Try to prevent mosquito bites by wearing long sleeves, long pants, hats and shoes (rather than sandals). Bring along a good insect repellent, preferably one containing DEET, which should be applied to exposed skin and clothing, but not to eyes, mouth, cuts, wounds or irritated skin. Use sparingly though – neurologic toxicity has been reported from DEET, but is extremely rare.

FOLK REMEDIES	
Problem	**Treatment**
altitude sickness	gingko
jet lag	melatonin
mosquito bite prevention	oil of eucalyptus, soybean oil
motion sickness	ginger

Insect repellents containing certain botanical products, including oil of eucalyptus and soybean oil, are effective but last only 1½ to two hours. DEET-containing repellents are preferable for areas where there is a high risk of malaria or yellow fever. Products based on citronella are not effective. For additional protection, you can apply permethrin to clothing, shoes, tents and bed nets, but not directly to your skin.

Don't sleep with the window open unless there is a screen. Use a bed net when available or at least a mosquito coil. Repellent-impregnated wristbands are not effective.

To protect yourself from tick bites, follow the same precautions as for mosquitoes, except that boots are preferable to shoes, with pants tucked in. Be sure to perform a thorough tick check at the end of each day. Ticks should be removed with tweezers, grasping them firmly by the head. Insect repellents based on botanical products, described above, have not been adequately studied for insects other than mosquitoes and cannot be recommended to prevent tick bites.

Water

Tap water in Bogotá and other big cities is safe to drink, but if you're pregnant or want to be more careful, use bottled water instead. In very remote areas, boil water for one minute to purify. At altitudes greater than 2000m (6500ft), boil for three minutes. Another option is to disinfect water with iodine pills.

Language

CONTENTS

Colombia's official language is Spanish and, apart from some remote indigenous groups, all inhabitants speak it. On San Andrés and, particularly, Providencia, Creole English is widely used. Many indigenous groups use their native languages. There are about 65 indigenous languages and nearly 300 dialects spoken in the country.

English speakers can be found in large urban centers, but it's certainly not a widely spoken or commonly understood language, even though it's taught as a mandatory second language in the public school system. Once you leave urban areas, Spanish will virtually be the only medium of communication. You'll probably manage to travel without knowing a word of Spanish, but you'll miss out on a good part of the pleasure of meeting people, and your experience of the country will be limited.

Spanish is quite an easy language to learn and, as a bonus, it's useful in most other Latin American countries as well. It's well worth making some effort to learn at least the essentials before setting off. Colombians will offer much encouragement, so there's no need to feel self-conscious about vocabulary, grammar or pronunciation. To help you on your way, grab a copy of Lonely Planet's compact *Latin American Spanish*

Phrasebook. Another good resource is the University of Chicago *Spanish-English, English-Spanish Dictionary*. For a thorough glossary of Colombian slang, check out Francisco Celis Albán's *Diccionario de Colombiano Actual*.

COLOMBIAN SPANISH

The Spanish spoken in Colombia is generally clear and easy to understand. There are regional variations, but these won't be noticeable to visitors, apart perhaps from the *costeños* from the Caribbean coast, who tend to speak fast and may be difficult to understand.

The use of the forms *tu* ('you' informal) and *usted* ('you' polite) is flexible in Colombia, unlike Spain, where *tu* is generally only used among friends. Strangers can often use *tu*, while a husband and a wife may use *usted* when speaking to each other and to their children. While either form is OK, the best advice is to answer in the same form that you are addressed in – and always use *usted* when talking to the police. In Cali and the rural parts of the mountain areas the use of *vos* is quite common.

Note that Colombians, like all Latin Americans, do not use *vosotros* (the plural of *tu*); *ustedes* is commonly used.

Latin American Spanish vocabulary has lots of regional variations and differs noticeably from European Spanish. Colombian Spanish has altered the meaning of some words or taken their secondary meaning as the main one. Colombians have also created plenty of *colombianismos* – words or phrases used either nationally or regionally, but almost unknown outside Colombia.

Colombians and other South Americans normally refer to the Spanish language as *castellano* rather than *español*.

PRONUNCIATION

Pronunciation of Spanish is easy as many sounds are similar to English and the relationship between pronunciation and spelling is consistent. Unless otherwise indicated, the following English examples take standard American pronunciation.

LANGUAGE

The most significant pronunciation differences between the Spanish of Colombia and that of Spain are: **ll** – as 'y' in Colombia, as 'ly' in Spain; **z** and **c** before **e** and **i** – as 's' in Colombia, not the lisped 'th' of Spain.

Vowels & Diphthongs

a	as in 'father'
e	as in 'met'
i	as the 'i' in 'police'
o	as in British English 'hot'
u	as the 'u' in 'rude'
ai	as in 'aisle'
au	as the 'ow' in 'how'
ei	as in 'vein'
ia	as the 'ya' in 'yard'
ie	as the 'ye' in 'yes'
oi	as in 'coin'
ua	as the 'wa' in 'wash'
ue	as the 'we' in 'well'

Consonants

Spanish consonants are generally the same as in English, with the exception of those listed below.

The consonants **ch**, **ll** and **ñ** are generally considered distinct letters, but in dictionaries **ch** and **ll** are now often listed alphabetically under **c** and **l** respectively. The letter **ñ** still has a separate entry after **n** in alphabetical listings.

b	similar to English 'b,' but softer; referred to as 'b larga'
c	as in 'celery' before **e** and **i**; elsewhere as the 'k' in 'king'
ch	as in 'choose'
d	as in 'dog'; between vowels and after **l** or **n**, it's closer to the 'th' in 'this'
g	as the 'ch' in the Scottish *loch* before **e** and **i** ('kh' in our pronunciation guides); elsewhere, as in 'go'
h	invariably silent
j	as the 'ch' in the Scottish *loch* ('kh' in our pronunciation guides)
ll	as the 'y' in 'yellow'
ñ	as the 'ni' in 'onion'
r	as in 'run,' but strongly rolled
rr	very strongly rolled
v	similar to English 'b,' but softer; referred to as 'b corta'
x	usually pronounced as **j** above; as in 'taxi' in other instances
z	as the 's' in 'sun'

Word Stress

In general, words ending in vowels or the letters **n** or **s** are stressed on the second-last syllable, while those with other ending have stress on the last syllable. Thus *vace* (cow) and *caballos* (horses) are both stressed on the next-to-last syllable, while *ciudae* (city) and *infeliz* (unhappy) are stressed on the last syllable.

Written accents generally indicate words that don't follow the previous rules, eg *sótano* (basement), *América* and *porción* (portion).

GENDER & PLURALS

In Spanish, nouns are either masculine or feminine, and there are rules to help determine gender (there are, of course, some exceptions). Feminine nouns generally end with **-a** or with the groups **-ción**, **-sión** or **-dad**. Other endings typically signify a masculine noun. Endings for adjectives also change to agree with the gender of the noun they modify (masculine/feminine singular **-o/-a**). Where both masculine and feminine forms are included in this language guide, they are separated by a slash, with the masculine form first, eg *perdido/a* (lost).

If a noun or adjective ends in a vowel, the plural is formed by adding **s** to the end. If it ends in a consonant, the plural is formed by adding **es** to the end.

ACCOMMODATIONS

I'm looking for ...

Estoy buscando ...	e·stoy boos·kan·do ...	
a hotel	*un hotel*	oon o·tel
a boarding house	*una posada*	oo·na po·sa·da
a youth hostel	*un hostal para extranjeros*	oon os·tal pa·ra eks·tran·khe·ros

Are there any rooms available?

¿Hay habitaciones libres?	ai a·bee·ta·syo·nes lee·bres

I'd like a ... room.	*Quiero una habitación ...*	kye·ro oo·na a·bee·ta·syon ...
double	*doble*	do·ble
single	*sencillo*	sen·see·yo
twin	*con dos camas*	kon dos ka·mas

How much is it per ...?	*¿Cuánto cuesta por ...?*	kwan·to kwes·ta por ...
night	*noche*	no·che
person	*persona*	per·so·na

MAKING A RESERVATION

(for phone or written requests)

To ...	A ...
From ...	De ...
Date	Fecha

I'd like to book ...	Quiero reservar ...
in the name of ...	en nombre de ...
for the nights of ...	para las noches del ...
credit card ...	tarjeta de crédito ...
number	número
expiry date	fecha de vencimiento

Please confirm ...	Puede confirmar ...
availability	la disponibilidad
price	el precio

private/shared	baño privado/	ba·nyo pree·va·do/
bathroom	compartido	kom·par·tee·do
full board	pensión	pen·syon
	completa	kom·ple·ta
too expensive	demasiado caro	de·ma·sya·do ka·ro
cheaper	más económico	mas e·ko·no·mee·ko
discount	descuento	des·kwen·to

Does it include breakfast?
¿Incluye el / een·kloo·ye el
desayuno? / de·sa·yoo·no
May I see the room?
¿Puedo ver la / pwe·do ver la
habitación? / a·bee·ta·syon
I don't like it.
No me gusta. / no me goos·ta
It's fine. I'll take it.
OK. La alquilo. / o·kay la al·kee·lo
I'm leaving now.
Me voy ahora. / me voy a·o·ra

CONVERSATION & ESSENTIALS

Greetings in Colombia have become an elaborate ritual; the short Spanish *hola* has given way to an incalculable number of expressions, all of them meaning something between 'Hello' and 'How do you do.' Here are some examples:

¿Qué más? / ke mas
¿Que hubo? / ke oo·bo
¿Cómo le va? / ko·mo le va
¿Cómo le ha ido? / ko·mo le a ee·do
¿Cómo está? / ko·mo es·ta
¿Cómo ha estado? / ko·mo a es·ta·do
¿Qué me cuenta? / ke me kwen·ta

¿Qué más (de nuevo, / ke mas (de nwe·vo,
de su vida)? / de soo vee·da)
¿Qué hay (de cosas, / ke ai (de ko·sas,
de bueno)? / de bwe·no)

This list could be continued for several more pages. When people meet or phone each other, they always begin the conversation with a long exchange of these and similar expressions.

You may find it funny, surprising, irritating, ridiculous, tiring, fascinating – but whatever you say about it, it is typically Colombian and you should learn some of these expressions to keep to the local style.

Hello.	Hola.	o·la
Good morning.	Buenos días.	bwe·nos dee·as
Good afternoon.	Buenas tardes.	bwe·nas tar·des
Good evening/	Buenas noches.	bwe·nas no·ches
night.		
Bye/See you soon.	Hasta luego.	as·ta lwe·go
Goodbye.	Adiós.	a·dyos
Yes.	Sí.	see
No.	No.	no
Please.	Por favor.	por fa·vor
Thank you.	Gracias.	gra·syas
Many thanks.	Muchas gracias.	moo·chas gra·syas
You're welcome.	De nada.	de na·da
Pardon me.	Perdón.	per·don

(used before asking for information)
Excuse me. Permiso. per·mee·so
(used when asking to get past)
Forgive me. Disculpe. dees·kool·pe
(used when apologizing)

How are things?
¿Qué más? / ke mas
What's your name?
¿Cómo se llama? (pol) / ko·mo se ya·ma
¿Cómo te llamas? (inf) / ko·mo te ya·mas
My name is ...
Me llamo ... / me ya·mo ...
It's a pleasure to meet you.
Mucho gusto. / moo·cho goos·to
The pleasure is mine.
El gusto es mío. / el goos·to es mee·o
Where are you from?
¿De dónde es? (pol) / de don·de es
¿De dónde eres? (inf) / de don·de e·res
I'm from ...
Soy de ... / soy de ...
May I take a photo?
¿Puedo sacar / pwe·do sa·kar
una foto? / oo·na fo·to

Where are you staying?

¿Dónde está		*don*-de es-*ta*
alojado/a? (pol m/f)		a-lo-*kha*-do/a
¿Dónde estás		*don*-de es-*tas*
alojado/a? (inf m/f)		a-lo-*kha*-do/a

DIRECTIONS

How do I get to ...?

¿Cómo puedo llegar a ...? ko-mo pwe-do ye-gar a ...

Is it far?

¿Está lejos? es-ta le-khos

Go straight ahead.

Siga derecho. see-ga de-re-cho

Turn left.

Voltée a la izquierda. vol-te-e a la ees-kyer-da

Turn right.

Voltée a la derecha. vol-te-e a la de-re-cha

Can you show me (on the map)?

¿Me lo podría indicar me lo po-dree-a een-dee-kar
(en el mapa)? (en el ma-pa)

SIGNS

Entrada	Entrance
Salida	Exit
Información	Information
Abierto	Open
Cerrado	Closed
Prohibido	Prohibited
Servicios/Baños	Toilets
Hombres/Varones	Men
Mujeres/Damas	Women

---

north	*norte*	*nor*-te
south	*sur*	soor
east	*este*	es-te
west	*oeste*	o-es-te

here	*aquí*	a-kee
there	*allí*	a-yee
avenue	*avenida*	a-ve-nee-da
block	*cuadra*	kwa-dra
street	*calle*	ka-ye

HEALTH

I'm sick.

Estoy enfermo/a. (m/f) es-toy en-fer-mo/a

I need a doctor.

Necesito un médico. ne-se-see-to oon me-dee-ko

Where's the hospital?

¿Dónde está el hospital? don-de es-ta el os-pee-tal

I'm pregnant.

Estoy embarazada. es-toy em-ba-ra-sa-da

I've been vaccinated.

Estoy vacunado/a. (m/f) es-toy va-koo-na-do/a

I'm allergic	*Soy alérgico/a*	soy a-ler-khee-ko/a
to ...	*a ...* (m/f)	a ...
antibiotics	*los antibióticos*	los an-tee-byo-tee-kos
nuts	*nueces*	nwe-ses
penicillin	*la penicilina*	la pe-nee-see-lee-na

I'm ...	*Soy ...*	soy ...
asthmatic	*asmático/a* (m/f)	as-ma-tee-ko/a
diabetic	*diabético/a* (m/f)	dee-ya-be-tee-ko/a
epileptic	*epiléptico/a* (m/f)	e-pee-lep-tee-ko/a

I have ...	*Tengo ...*	ten-go ...
a cough	*tos*	tos
diarrhea	*diarrea*	dya-re-a
a headache	*un dolor de*	oon do-lor de
	cabeza	ka-be-sa
nausea	*náusea*	now-se-a

EMERGENCIES

Help!	*¡Socorro!*	so-ko-ro
Fire!	*¡Incendio!*	een-sen-dyo
I've been robbed.	*Me robaron.*	me ro-ba-ron
Go away!	*¡Déjeme!*	de-khe-me
Get lost!	*¡Váyase!*	va-ya-se

Call ...!	*¡Llame a ...!*	ya-me a ...
an ambulance	*una ambulancia*	oo-na am-boo-lan-sya
a doctor	*un médico*	oon me-dee-ko
the police	*la policía*	la po-lee-see-a

It's an emergency.

Es una emergencia. es oo-na e-mer-khen-sya

Could you help me, please?

¿Me puede ayudar, me pwe-de a-yoo-dar
por favor? por fa-vor

I'm lost.

Estoy perdido/a. (m/f) es-toy per-dee-do/a

Where are the toilets?

¿Dónde están los baños? don-de es-tan los ba-nyos

LANGUAGE DIFFICULTIES

Do you speak (English)?

¿Habla (inglés)? (pol) a-bla (een-gles)
¿Hablas (inglés)? (inf) a-blas (een-gles)

Does anyone here speak English?

¿Hay alguien que hable ai al-gyen ke a-ble
inglés? een-gles

(don't) understand.
(No) Entiendo.   (no) en·*tyen*·do

How do you say ...?
¿Cómo se dice ...?   *ko*·mo se *dee*·se ...

What does ... mean?
¿Qué quiere decir ...?   ke *kye*·re de·*seer* ...

Could you please ...?	*¿Puede ..., por favor?*	*pwe*·de ... por fa·*vor*
repeat that	*repetirlo*	re·pe·*teer*·lo
speak more	*hablar más*	a·*blar* mas
slowly	*despacio*	des·*pa*·syo
write it down	*escribirlo*	es·kree·*beer*·lo

NUMBERS

0	*cero*	*se*·ro
1	*uno/a* (m/f)	*oo*·no/a
2	*dos*	dos
3	*tres*	tres
4	*cuatro*	*kwa*·tro
5	*cinco*	*seen*·ko
6	*seis*	seys
7	*siete*	*sye*·te
8	*ocho*	*o*·cho
9	*nueve*	*nwe*·ve
10	*diez*	dyes
11	*once*	*on*·se
12	*doce*	*do*·se
13	*trece*	*tre*·se
14	*catorce*	ka·*tor*·se
15	*quince*	*keen*·se
16	*dieciséis*	dye·see·*seys*
17	*diecisiete*	dye·see·*sye*·te
18	*dieciocho*	dye·see·*o*·cho
19	*diecinueve*	dye·see·*nwe*·ve
20	*veinte*	*vayn*·te
21	*veintiuno*	vayn·tee·*oo*·no
30	*treinta*	*trayn*·ta
31	*treinta y uno*	*trayn*·tai *oo*·no
40	*cuarenta*	kwa·*ren*·ta
50	*cincuenta*	seen·*kwen*·ta
60	*sesenta*	se·*sen*·ta
70	*setenta*	se·*ten*·ta
80	*ochenta*	o·*chen*·ta
90	*noventa*	no·*ven*·ta
100	*cien*	syen
101	*ciento uno*	*syen*·to *oo*·no
200	*doscientos*	do·*syen*·tos
1000	*mil*	meel

SHOPPING & SERVICES

I'd like to buy ...
Quiero comprar ...   *kye*·ro kom·*prar* ...

I'm just looking.
Sólo estoy mirando.   *so*·lo es·*toy* mee·*ran*·do

May I look at it?
¿Puedo mirarlo?   *pwe*·do mee·*rar*·lo

How much is it?
¿Cuánto cuesta?   *kwan*·to *kwes*·ta

That's too expensive for me.
Es demasiado caro para mí.   es de·ma·*sya*·do *ka*·ro *pa*·ra mee

Could you lower the price?
¿Puede ofrecerme un discuento?   *pwe*·de o·fre·*ser*·me oon dis·*kwen*·to

I don't like it.
No me gusta.   no me *goos*·ta

I'll take it.
Lo llevo.   lo *ye*·vo

Do you accept ...?	*¿Aceptan ...?*	a·*sep*·tan ...
credit cards	*tarjetas de crédito*	tar·*khe*·tas de *kre*·dee·to
traveler's checks	*cheques de viajero*	*che*·kes de vya·*khe*·ro

less/more	*menos/más*	*me*·nos/mas
large/small	*grande/pequeño*	*gran*·de/pe·*ke*·nyo

I'm looking for (the) ...	*Estoy buscando ...*	es·*toy* boos·*kan*·do ...
ATM	*el cajero automático*	el ka·*khe*·ro ow·to·*ma*·tee·ko
bank	*el banco*	el *ban*·ko
bookstore	*la librería*	la lee·bre·*ree*·a
embassy	*la embajada*	la em·ba·*kha*·da
exchange office	*la casa de cambio*	la *ka*·sa de *kam*·byo
general store	*la tienda*	la *tyen*·da
laundry	*la lavandería*	la la·van·de·*ree*·a
market	*el mercado*	el mer·*ka*·do
pharmacy	*la farmacia/ la droguería*	la far·*ma*·sya/ la dro·ge·*ree*·a
post office	*los correos*	los ko·*re*·os
supermarket	*el supermercado*	el soo·per·mer·*ka*·do
tourist office	*la oficina de turismo*	la o·fee·*see*·na de too·*rees*·mo

What time does it open/close?
¿A qué hora abre/cierra?   a ke *o*·ra *a*·bre/*sye*·ra

I want to change some money/traveler's cheques.
Quiero cambiar dinero/ cheques de viajero.   *kye*·ro kam·*byar* dee·*ne*·ro/ *che*·kes de vya·*khe*·ro

What's the exchange rate?
¿Cuál es la taza de cambio?   kwal es la *ta*·za de *kam*·byo

I want to call ...
Quiero llamar a ...   *kye*·ro ya·*mar* a ...

LANGUAGE

airmail	correo aéreo	ko·re·o a·e·re·o
letter	carta	kar·ta
registered mail	certificado	ser·tee·fee·ka·do
stamps	estampillas	es·tam·pee·yas

TIME & DATES

What time is it?	¿Qué hora es?	ke o·ra es
It's (one) o'clock.	Es la (una).	es la (oo·na)
It's (seven) o'clock.	Son las (siete).	son las (sye·te)
midnight	medianoche	me·dya·no·che
noon	mediodía	me·dyo·dee·a
half past two	dos y media	dos ee me·dya

now	ahora	a·o·ra
today	hoy	oy
tonight	esta noche	es·ta no·che
tomorrow	mañana	ma·nya·na
yesterday	ayer	a·yer

Monday	lunes	loo·nes
Tuesday	martes	mar·tes
Wednesday	miércoles	myer·ko·les
Thursday	jueves	khwe·ves
Friday	viernes	vyer·nes
Saturday	sábado	sa·ba·do
Sunday	domingo	do·meen·go

January	enero	e·ne·ro
February	febrero	fe·bre·ro
March	marzo	mar·so
April	abril	a·breel
May	mayo	ma·yo
June	junio	khoo·nyo
July	julio	khoo·lyo
August	agosto	a·gos·to
September	septiembre	sep·tyem·bre
October	octubre	ok·too·bre
November	noviembre	no·vyem·bre
December	diciembre	dee·syem·bre

TRANSPORT
Public Transport

What time does	¿A qué hora ...	a ke o·ra ...
... leave/arrive?	sale/llega?	sa·le/ye·ga
the bus	el autobus	el ow·to·boos
the plane	el avión	el a·vyon
the ship	el barco	el bar·ko

airport	el aeropuerto	el a·e·ro·pwer·to
bus station	la estación de	la es·ta·syon de
	autobuses	ow·to·boo·ses
bus stop	la parada de	la pa·ra·da de
	autobuses	ow·to·boo·ses
luggage check	guardería/	gwar·de·ree·a/
room	equipaje	e·kee·pa·khe
ticket office	la boletería	la bo·le·te·ree·a

I'd like a ticket to ...
Quiero un boleto a ...   kye·ro oon bo·le·to a ...
What's the fare to ...?
¿Cuánto cuesta hasta ...?   kwan·to kwes·ta a·sta ...

student's (fare)	de estudiante	de es·too·dyan·te
1st class	primera clase	pree·me·ra kla·se
2nd class	segunda clase	se·goon·da kla·se
one-way	ida	ee·da
return	ida y vuelta	ee·da ee vwel·ta
taxi	taxi	tak·see

Private Transport

pickup (truck)	camioneta	ka·myo·ne·ta
truck	camión	ka·myon
hitchhike	hacer dedo	a·ser de·do

I'd like to	Quiero	kye·ro
hire a/an ...	alquilar ...	al·kee·lar ...
bicycle	una bicicleta	oo·na bee·see·kle·ta
car	un carro	oon ka·ro
4WD	un quatro por	oon kwat·ro
	quatro	por kwat·ro
motorbike	una moto	oo·na mo·to

Is this the road to ...?
¿Se va a ... por   se va a ... por
esta carretera?   es·ta ka·re·te·ra
Where's a gas/petrol station?
¿Dónde hay una   don·de ai oo·na
gasolinera/bomba?   ga·so·lee·ne·ra/bom·ba
Please fill it up.
Lleno, por favor.   ye·no por fa·vor
I'd like (20) liters.
Quiero (veinte) litros. kye·ro (vayn·te) lee·tros

| diesel | diesel | dee·sel |
| gas/petrol | gasolina | ga·so·lee·na |

leaded (regular)	*gasolina con*	ga·so·*lee*·na kon
	plomo	*plo*·mo
unleaded	*gasolina sin*	ga·so·*lee*·na seen
	plomo	*plo*·mo

(How long) Can I park here?
¿(Por cuánto tiempo) Puedo aparcar aquí?
(por *kwan*·to *tyem*·po) *pwe*·do a·par·*kar* a·*kee*

Where do I pay?
¿Dónde se paga?
don·de se *pa*·ga

I need a mechanic.
Necesito un mecánico.
ne·se·*see*·to oon me·*ka*·nee·ko

The car has broken down in ...
El carro se ha averiado en ...
el *ka*·ro se a a·ve·*rya*·do en ...

The motorbike won't start.
No arranca la moto.
no a·*ran*·ka la *mo*·to

I've run out of gas/petrol.
Me quedé sin gasolina.
me ke·*de* seen ga·so·*lee*·na

I've had an accident.
Tuve un accidente.
too·ve oon ak·see·*den*·te

TRAVEL WITH CHILDREN

| **I need ...** | *Necesito ...* | ne·se·*see*·to ... |
| **Do you have ...?** | *¿Hay ...?* | ai ... |

  a car baby seat
  un asiento de seguridad para bebés
  oon a·*syen*·to de se·goo·ree·*da* pa·ra be·*bes*

  a child-minding service
  un servicio de cuidado de niños
  oon ser·*vee*·syo de kwee·*da*·do de *nee*·nyos

  (disposable) diapers/nappies
  pañales (de usar y tirar)
  pa·*nya*·les (de oo·*sar* ee tee·*rar*)

  an (English-speaking) babysitter
  una niñera (que habla inglés)
  oo·na nee·*nye*·ra (ke *a*·bla een·*gles*)

  infant formula (milk)
  leche en polvo para bebés
  le·che en *pol*·vo *pa*·ra be·*bes*

  a highchair
  una trona
  oo·na *tro*·na

  a potty
  una pelela
  oo·na pe·*le*·la

  a stroller
  un cochecito
  oon ko·che·*see*·to

LANGUAGE

Also available from Lonely Planet:
Latin American Spanish Phrasebook

Glossary

See p48 for useful words and phrases dealing with food and dining. See the Language chapter (p327) for other useful words and phrases. Spanish speakers wanting a complete reference to Colombian slang should pick up a copy of the *Diccionario de Colombiano Actual* (2005) by Francisco Celis Albán.

aguardiente – anise-flavored liquor
asadero – place serving roasted or grilled meats
atarraya – circular fishing net widely used on the coast and rivers
AUC – Autodefensas Unidas de Colombia; a loose alliance of paramilitary squads known as *autodefensas*
auto-da-fé – public execution of heretics, which took place during the Inquisition until Colombia's independence in 1821
autodefensas – right-wing squads created to defend large landowners against guerrillas, also called *paramilitares* or just *paras*
ayudante – driver's assistant on buses

balneario – a swimming hole, often servers liquor and food
bambuco – musical genre of the Andean region
banda ancha – broadband internet
baquiano – person who hires out horses or mules for horseback-riding excursions, and usually accompanies the group as a guide
bomba – gas station; a bomb
burundanga – drug extracted from a plant, used by thieves to render their victim unconscious
buseta – small bus/van that is a popular means of city transport

cabaña – cabin, usually found on beaches or up in the mountains
cable vuelo – the activity of canopying or zip lining
cacique – indigenous tribal head; today the term is applied to provincial leaders from the two traditional political parties, also called *gamonales*
caipirinha – Brazilian cocktail made with *cachaça* (sugarcane rum), lime juice, sugar and ice
caleño/a – person from Cali
campesino/a – rural dweller, usually of modest economic means; peasant
carro – car
casa de cambio – money-exchange office
caserío – hamlet

casona – big, rambling old house
ceiba – common tree of the tropics; can reach a huge size
chalupa – small passenger boat powered by an outboard motor
chiguiro – capybara; the world's large rodent common to Los Llanos
chinchorro – hammock woven of cotton threads or palm fiber like a fishing net; typical of many indigenous groups; the best known are the decorative cotton hammocks of the Guajiros
chiva – traditional bus with its body made of timber and painted with colorful patterns; still widely used in the countryside
ciénaga – shallow lake or lagoon
cinemateca – art-house cinema that screens quality films
climatizado – air-conditioned; term used for air-con buses
colectivo – shared taxi or minibus; a popular means of public transport
comida corriente – fast food; set lunch
corrida – bullfight
costeño/a – inhabitant of the Caribbean coast
criollo/a – Creole, a person of European (especially Spanish) blood, but born in the Americas
cuatro – small, four-stringed guitar, used in the music of Los Llanos
cumbia – one of the most popular musical rhythms (and corresponding dance) of the Caribbean coast; African in origin
currulao – popular dance of the Pacific coast, of mixed African-Spanish origin, usually accompanied by a *marimba*

danta – tapir; large, hoofed mammal of tropical and subtropical forests
DAS – Departamento Administrativo de Seguridad; the security police, responsible for immigration
denuncia – official report/statement to the police
droguería – pharmacy

ELN – Ejército de Liberación Nacional; the second-largest guerrilla group after the FARC
esquina – street corner

FARC – Fuerzas Armadas Revolucionarias de Colombia; the largest guerrilla group in the country
finca – farm; anything from a country house with a small garden to a huge country estate
frailejón – espeletia, a species of plant typical of the *páramo*

gamonales – see *cacique*
giros – wire transfer
gringo/a – any white male/female foreigner; sometimes, (but not always) used in a derogatory sense
guácharo – oilbird; a species of nocturnal bird living in caves
guadua – the largest variety of the bamboo family, common in many regions of moderate climate
guaquero – tomb raider
guayabo – hangover; warranted after an aguardiente session

hacienda – country estate
hospedaje – lodging (in general); sometimes, a cheap hotel

indígena – indigenous; also indigenous person
IVA – *impuesto de valor agregado*, a value-added tax (VAT)

joropo – typical music of Los Llanos, also referred to as *música llanera*

La Violencia – Colombia's main civil war, which began in 1946; also used to refer in general to Colombia's troubles
lancha – launch, motorboat
llanero/a – inhabitant of Los Llanos
(Los) Llanos – literally 'plains'; vast plains between the Andes and the Río Orinoco

malecón – waterfront promenade
maloca – large, communal house of some indigenous groups; usually a wooden structure thatched with palm leaves
maracas – gourd rattles; an accompanying instrument of the *joropo* and other rhythms
marimba – percussion instrument
mecha – small triangular envelope with gunpowder, used in the game of *tejo*
merengue – musical rhythm originating in the Dominican Republic, today widespread throughout the Caribbean and beyond
meseta – plateau
mestizo/a – person of mixed European-indigenous blood
mirador – lookout, viewpoint
mochila – bucket-shaped shoulder bag, traditionally made by *indígenas*, today produced commercially
mola – colorful, hand-stitched applique textile of the Cuna people; a rectangular piece of cloth made of several differently colored, superimposed layers sewn together
muelle – pier, wharf
mulato/a – mulatto; a person of mixed European-African blood
multa – a fine

Navidad – Christmas
nevado – snowcapped mountain peak

orquídea – orchid

país – person from Antioquia
paradero – bus stop; in some areas called *parada*
paramilitares – paramilitaries; see also *autodefensas*
páramo – high-mountain plains, at an elevation of between 3500m and 4500m, typical of Colombia, Venezuela and Ecuador
parapente – paragliding
pasillo – type of music/dance played in the Andean region
pastuso/a – person from Pasto
piso – story, floor
plaza de toros – bullfighting ring
poporo – a vessel made from a small gourd, used by the Arhuacos and other indigenous groups to carry lime; while chewing coca leaves, *indígenas* add lime to help release the alkaloid from the leaves; a sacred ritual of the indigenous people of the Caribbean coast
porro – musical rhythm of the Caribbean coast; also, leek (the vegetable)
propina – tip (eg for the waiter in a restaurant)
pueblo paísa – a typical Antioquian town
puente – literally 'bridge'; also means a three-day-long weekend (including Monday)

refugio – rustic shelter in a remote area, mostly in the mountains
requisa – police document search, sometimes a body search; military checkpoint
ruana – Colombian poncho
rumba – party; popular musical style originating in Cuba

salsa – type of Caribbean dance music of Cuban origin, very popular in Colombia
salsateca – disco playing salsa music
Semana Santa – Holy Week, the week before Easter Sunday
sobrecargo – surcharge
son – one of the main rhythms of Afro-Cuban music, a kind of slow salsa
soroche – altitude sickness

taberna – pub/bar/tavern
tagua – hard ivory-colored nut of a species of palm; used in handicrafts, mainly on the Pacific coast
tejo – traditional game, popular mainly in the Andean region; played with a heavy metal disk, which is thrown to make a *mecha* (a sort of petard) explode
Telecom – state telephone company
teleférico – cable car
telenovela – TV soap opera
terminal de pasajeros – bus terminal
torbellino – music/dance typical of the Andean region

totuma – cup-like vessel made from the hollowed-out dried fruit of a tree cut in half; used in some areas for drinking, washing etc; vessel used in the *poporo*
trapiche – traditional sugarcane mill
tunjo – flat gold figurine, often depicting a warrior; typical artifact of the Muisca people

vallenato – music typical of the Caribbean region, based on the accordion; it's now widespread in Colombia
viejoteca – Colombian disco for those in the 30s or 40s-plus crowd

zambo/a – person of mixed African-indigenous ancestry

The Authors

JENS PORUP
Coordinating Author, Medellín & Zona Cafetera, Cali & Southwest Colombia, Pacific Coast

Jens went to Colombia looking for danger and was greatly surprised when he found none, but decided to stay anyway. He lived in Cali for two years, where he wrote several guidebooks for Lonely Planet. He has lived on three continents, is fond of ancient Greek poetry, worked for several years as a Perl programmer, loves dancing salsa, has written numerous plays for the theater and recently finished a novel about Colombia. He currently divides his time between North America and Colombia. You can follow Jens' doings on his website, www.jensporup.com.

KEVIN RAUB
Caribbean Coast, San Andrés & Providencia

Kevin grew up in Atlanta and started his career as a music journalist in New York City, working for *Men's Journal* and *Rolling Stone*. The rock 'n' roll lifestyle took its toll, so in need of an extended vacation he took up travel writing. In Colombia he has taken to the skies in government helicopters over cartel country, suffered a mild crush on a former mayoress of Santa Fe de Antioquia and toured with DJ Paul Oakenfold – all before it was fashionable. He has previously coauthored a number of Lonely Planet guidebooks. He lives in Brazil.

ROBERT REID
Bogotá

Raised in Oklahoma, Robert studied journalism at the University of Oklahoma and took frequent trips south of border (way past Texas) into Latin America, where he studied Spanish and worked hard at blending in. After many years working in-house at Lonely Planet, he reviewed Bogotá hotels for Lonely Planet's website in 2006 and *may* have written the first-ever 'hey, Bogotá is actually safe' article, which appeared in papers such as the *Miami Herald*. He keeps up his website (www.reidontravel.com) from his home in Brooklyn, NY, and has researched many Lonely Planet guidebooks.

CÉSAR G SORIANO

Boyacá, Santander & Norte de Santander, Amazon Basin

Like many *extranjeros*, César's first introduction to Colombian culture was a certain hip-shaking, belly-dancing songstress named Shakira. Since then, this Mexican-American has been properly educated in all things Colombian including *arepas*, *tintos*, aguardiente, cumbia, capybaras, beauty pageants and the Santanderan delicacy of fried fat ants. A career journalist and former *USA TODAY* foreign correspondent, César has authored many other Lonely Planet guidebooks. He has traveled extensively throughout Latin America. César and his wife, Marsha, live in London.

CONTRIBUTING AUTHOR

Dr David Goldberg MD wrote the Health chapter. He completed his training in internal medicine and infectious diseases at Columbia-Presbyterian Medical Center in New York City, where he has also served as voluntary faculty. At present, he is an infectious diseases specialist in Scarsdale, New York, and the editor-in-chief of the website MDTravelHealth.com.

Behind the Scenes

THIS BOOK

This is the 5th edition of Colombia. Jens Porup served as coordinating author, writing most of the front and back chapters as well as the Medellín & Zona Cafetera, Cali & Southwest Colombia, and Pacific Coast chapters. Kevin Raub covered the Caribbean Coast and San Andrés & Providencia chapters. Robert Reid researched and wrote the History and Bogotá chapters. César Soriano covered the Boyacá, Santander & Norte de Santander and Amazon Basin chapters as well as the Environment chapter. Dr David Goldberg MD contributed the Health chapter. The previous edition of this book was written by Michael Kohn and Robert Landon, and the first three editions were written by Krzysztof Dydyński. This guidebook was commissioned in Lonely Planet's Oakland office, and produced by the following:

Commissioning Editors Jay Cooke, Kathleen Munnelly
Coordinating Editor Martine Power
Coordinating Cartographer Sam Sayer
Coordinating Layout Designer Carlos Solarte
Managing Editor Brigitte Ellemor
Managing Cartographers Shahara Ahmed, Alison Lyall
Managing Layout Designer Laura Jane
Assisting Editors Justin Flynn, Laura Gibb, Carly Hall, Evan Jones, Averil Robertson, Dianne Schallmeiner, Kate Whitfield
Assisting Cartographer Andy Rojas

Cover Designer Kate Slattery
Project Managers Chris Girdler, Debra Herrmann
Language Content Coordinators Quentin Frayne, Branislava Vladisavljevic

Thanks to Lucy Birchley, Andras Bogdanovits, Jessica Boland, David Carroll, Melanie Dankel, Sally Darmody, Brice Gosnell, Martin Heng, John Mazzocchi, Clara Monitto, Raphael Richards, Brendan Streager

THANKS
JENS PORUP

Thanks go first to Jay Cooke for keeping the faith. César, Kevin and Robert made a fine team. The usual suspects: Kelvin in Medellín, German in Bogotá, Tony in Popayán, the boys in Manizales. My biggest thanks go to *mi conejita cresposita*, who waited.

KEVIN RAUB

Special thanks to my wife, Adriana Schmidt, for not hounding me with worrisome emails during research. At Lonely Planet: Jay Cooke, Catherine Craddock, Kathleen Munnelly and Jens Porup. Along the way: Laura Cahnspeyer, Richard McColl, Simon Heyes, Kim MacPhee, Francisco Vergara, Hans Kolland, Mathieu Perrot, Francisco Huérfano, Irma Jurrius, Jorge Dib, Angela Gómez, Francisco

THE LONELY PLANET STORY

Fresh from an epic journey across Europe, Asia and Australia in 1972, Tony and Maureen Wheeler sat at their kitchen table stapling together notes. The first Lonely Planet guidebook, *Across Asia on the Cheap*, was born.

Travelers snapped up the guides. Inspired by their success, the Wheelers began publishing books to Southeast Asia, India and beyond. Demand was prodigious, and the Wheelers expanded the business rapidly to keep up. Over the years, Lonely Planet extended its coverage to every country and into the virtual world via lonelyplanet.com and the Thorn Tree message board.

As Lonely Planet became a globally loved brand, Tony and Maureen received several offers for the company. But it wasn't until 2007 that they found a partner whom they trusted to remain true to the company's principles of traveling widely, treading lightly and giving sustainably. In October of that year, BBC Worldwide acquired a 75% share in the company, pledging to uphold Lonely Planet's commitment to independent travel, trustworthy advice and editorial independence.

Today, Lonely Planet has offices in Melbourne, London and Oakland, with over 500 staff members and 300 authors. Tony and Maureen are still actively involved with Lonely Planet. They're traveling more often than ever, and they're devoting their spare time to charitable projects. And the company is still driven by the philosophy of *Across Asia on the Cheap*: 'All you've got to do is decide to go and the hardest part is over. So go!'

Troncoso, Jean-Philippe Gibelin, Tassiana Ruiz Molina, Janneth Ordoñez, Lola Ryan, Elizabeth Taylor and David Guggenheim.

ROBERT REID

Many people helped a lot on this. Thanks to Jay Cooke of Lonely Planet for offering me the job, Lonely Planet readers who sent in letters, and Jens Porup for many great suggestions for both chapters. In Bogotá, thanks to Ben Schiek and Milena for tips around Macarena; German Escobar at Platypus for endless advice, and Francoise Nieto-Fong for the selfless late-night endurance for clubbing, and many more *bogotanos* for taking time to answer my confusion.

CÉSAR G SORIANO

At Lonely Planet, thanks to Jay Cooke, Kathleen Munnelly and Jens Porup. In Colombia, special thanks to travelmates Deirdre Corrigan and Joana Santos for their help reviewing bars and restaurants; it was a tough job but someone had to do it. Along the way, thanks to Andy Farrington, German Escobar, Oscar Gilède, Shaun Clohesy, Axel Antoine-Feill, Enrique 'Kike' Ares, Friar Hector, Sandra at Casa Muñoz, and KGB's Paola who nursed me back to health. Kudos to shutterbug Laura Pohl for my mugshot. To my favorite travel partner on this lonely planet, my wife, Marsha, thank you for your love and support. *Te Amo.*

OUR READERS

Many thanks to the travelers who used the last edition and wrote to us with helpful hints, useful advice and interesting anecdotes:

A Chris Adam, Jason Anderlite, Adriana Arango, Carolina Araque, Manuela Arigoni, Sally Attenborough **B** Barbara Bansemer, Patrick Bates, Catherine Beckmann, Edward Benedikovics, Oya Berk Demirel, Iain Bisset, Peter Blincowe, Luz Stella Bonilla, David Boutin, Ron Bowman, Michel Braendli, Irene J Brooks, Maria Browne **C** Peter Calingaert, Javier Cartagena, Mauricio Castro Iragorri, Emma Channon, Tony Clark, Larisa Clarke, Doug Colbert, Dan Coplan, Mark Corwin, Danielle Cox, German Coy, Michael Croke, Kenneth Crosby **D** Frederic de Pardieu, Hans de Wit, Georgia Dessain, Giacomo di Como, Alison Dieguez, David Durfee, Paul Duus **E** Richard Elliott, Volker Elstermann, Omar Enciso **F** Graham Farhall, Marcel Feurer, Mario Frasca, Rudy Friederich **G** Gianluca Gaio, Sandra Milena García Blanco, Brett Gardner, Ronald Gardner, Silvia Garre, Larry Gillispie, Paula Gomez, Leonardo Grimaldi Salcedo **H** Samuel Haldemann, Roy Halvorsen,

Daniel Hayek, Karin Henken, Britt Hunt **J** Fiona James **K** Paul Kennedy, Ursula Kirchner, Samir Kiuhan, Erik Klemetti, Gregor Kos, Peter Koz, Sanja Krizan, Peter Kuehleitner **L** Yarden Levy, Pérez Lugo, Mark Lynch **M** René Mally, Brian Mann, Yossi Margoninsky, Doug Mcclelland, Gregor Meise, Lali Michelsen, Maurizio Mina, Devon Mitchell, Ian Morley, Sophia Mueller **N** Erik Norderfeldt **O** Sophia O'Donnell, Katherine O'Kelly, Robineau Ophélie **P** Tom Padding, Juergen Paudtke, Alexandra Paudtke, Oscar Payan, Robert Peacock, Montse Pejuan, Arja Perälä, Anonymous Person, Dominique Pollach, Yvette Proenza **R** Ashley Rhodes, Thomas Rice, Martha Rincon, Raul Rodriguez, Frauke Roeser **S** Kris Schillemans, Steve Scott-Robson, Keith Sergeant, Rotem Shefy, Rosita Sherrard, Angelina Skowronski, Luke Smith, Anne Sol, Sally Squires, SJ Srinivas, Rachel Stenner, Mike Stevens, Joy Stollings, Jordan Strauss, Natalie Sutton, Johan Svensson **T** Nicole Thorpe, Mitch Tyndal **U** Kathy Utigard **V** Sjef Van Hoof **W** Kyle Walker, Kathleen Weigelt, Adam Weisman, Tony Wheeler, Elke Wiese, Michael Wilson, Jonathan Wright.

ACKNOWLEDGMENTS

Many thanks to the following for the use of their content:

Globe on title page ©Mountain High Maps 1993 Digital Wisdom, Inc.

Index

D
dance 42
dance courses 208, 243, 298
dangers 13-14, 299-301
 Bogotá 68
 Cali 240, 242
 Cartagena 140
 Chocó 270, 280
 drink spiking 300
 drugs 300
 guerrillas & paramilitaries 300-1
 Istmina 280
 PNN Isla Gorgona 284
 police 299-300
 Quibdó 280
 Taganga 172
 theft 299
Dapa 243
Darién 248-9
deforestation 55-6
departure tax 312
Desierto de la Tatacoa 267
discount cards 301
diving, see scuba diving
dolphin-watching
 botos 52, 293
 Río Yavarí 294-5
Drake, Francis 139
drinks 43-5
 aguardiente 45
 coffee 28, 43-4, 86
 water 44-5
drink spiking 300
driving, see car travel
drugs 32, 300

E
ecolodges 15, 174, 181
economy 35-6
ecotourism
 Puerto Nariño 293
 Punta Gallinas 183-4
ecowalks 120
Ejército de Liberación Nacional (ELN) 29, 31
El Bogotazo 27-8, 63
El Cocuy 112-14
El Fósil 110
El Peñol 216-17
El Pico Natural Regional Park 200
El Purutal 257

000 Map pages
000 Photograph pages

El Tablón 257
El Valle 275-7
El Zaíno 175
electricity 297
email services 302-3
embassies 301
emeralds 53, 91, 306
emergencies, see inside front cover
endangered species 52
environment 51-6
 books 51, 58, 135
environmental issues 55-6
 books 54
Escobar, Pablo 30-1, 220
Estación Astronómica Muisca (El Infiernito) 110
ethnicity 37, see also indigenous cultures
events, see festivals
exchange rates, see inside front cover

F
farms, see haciendas & farms
fax services 307-8
Feria de Cali 18, 243, 6
Feria de Manizales 221-2
festivals 17 18
 Alumbrado Navideño 18, 209, 8
 Carnaval de Barranquilla 17, 162
 Carnaval de Blancos y Negros 17, 262
 Congreso Nacional Gastronómico 18, 252
 Feria de Cali 18, 243, 6
 Feria de las Flores 17, 208-9
 Feria de Manizales 17, 221-2
 Festival de Cine de Bogotá 18, 80
 Festival de Música del Pacífico Petronio Álvarez 17, 243
 Festival Iberoamericano de Teatro 17, 80
 Festival Internacional de Jazz 18, 209
 Festival Internacional de Teatro 18, 222
 Festival Mundial de Salsa 17, 243
 Fiesta de Nuestra Señora de la Candelaria 17, 146
 Reinado Nacional de Belleza 18, 146
 Rock al Parque 18, 80
 Semana Santa (Mompox) 17, 158
 Semana Santa (Popayán) 17, 252
food 43, 301-2
 arepas 47
 bakeries 46

books 43, 46
 customs 47
 fried ants 47, 124
 hormigas culonas 47, 124
 language 48-50
 set meals 46
 supermarkets 46
 vegetarian travelers 47
forts
 Batería de San José 152
 Castillo de San Felipe de Barajas 145
 Fuerte de San Fernando 152
 Fuerte de San Sebastián del Pastelillo 145
Fuerzas Armadas Revolucionarias de Colombia (FARC) 29-30, 31-2, 134-5, 273, see also guerrillas & paramilitaries

G
Gaitán, Jorge Eliécer 27-8
galleries, see museums
García Márquez, Gabriel 40
gardens, see parks & gardens
Gaviria, César 31
gay travelers 302
geography 51
Gilède, Oscar 107
Girón 129-30, **129**
gold 25, 91, 97
gold museums
 Armenia 232
 Bogotá 77
 Cali 242
 Cartagena 143
 Manizales 221
 Pasto 261
 Santa Marta 165
Guachalito 278-9
Guane 125
Guapi 282-3
Guatapé 215-16
guerrillas & paramilitaries 28-30, 300-1, see also FARC
Güicán 114-16

H
Hacienda Nápoles 220
haciendas & farms
 coffee farms 224-5, 235, 236
 Hacienda Nápoles 220
 Quinta de San Pedro Alejandrino 165
handicrafts 306

paragliding 57
  Bucaramanga 126
  Medellín 208
  Parque Nacional del Chicamocha 125
  San Gil 120
paramilitaries 28-30, 300-1
parks & gardens
  Jardín Botánico del Quindío 234-5
  Jardín Botánico Eloy Valenzuela 126
  Jardín Botánico José Celestino Mutis 79
  Jardín Botánico (Medellín) 208
  Jardín Botánico (Santa Marta) 165
  Las Ardillas 251
  Los Yarumos 224
  Panaca 235
  Parque de la Gran Colombia 135
  Parque de la Luz 207
  Parque de la Vida 232
  Parque de las Esculturas 208
  Parque de los Deseos 208
  Parque El Gallineral 120
  Parque La Libertad 120
  Parque Santander 288
  Parque Simón Bolívar 79
  Parque Ucumarí 231-2
  Recinto del Pensamiento 223
Parque Arqueológico 256
Parque Nacional del Café 235-6
Parque Nacional del Chicamocha 125
PNN Amacayacu 292-3
PNN El Cocuy 116-19
PNN Ensenada de Utría 276
PNN Farallones de Cali 247
PNN Isla Gorgona 284
PNN Los Nevados 225-7, **226**
PNN Old Providence McBean Lagoon 198
PNN Puracé 254
PNN Tayrona 173-7, **173**
Parque Natural Chicaque 98
Parque Ucumarí 231-2
passports 310
Pasto 261-4, **263**
Pereira 227-30, **299**
Pinilla, Gustavo Rojas 28
Plan Colombia 32
planning 13-16, 301, 302
plants 52-3
plastic surgery 306
Playa Blanca 153-5, 7
Playa Brava 175
Playa de Paridera 275

Playa del Pilón 182
Playa Juan de Dios 282
Playa Potés 275
plazas
  Plaza de Bolívar (Bogotá) 69-72
  Plaza de Bolívar (Cartagena) 142
  Plaza de la Aduana 141
  Plaza de los Coches 141
  Plazoleta de las Esculturas 207
police 299-300
Popayán 249-53, **251**
population 36
postal services 305
practicalities 297
Providencia 190, 198-202, **199**
Pueblito 175
Puente de Boyacá 104-5
Puente de Occidente 7, 219, 7
Puerto Nariño 293-4
Punta Gallinas 183-4

Q
Quibdó 280

R
radio 297
rafting, see white-water rafting
Ramírez Villamizar, Eduardo 42, 130-1
rappelling
  San Gil 120
  Villa de Leyva 107
Ráquira 111
Recinto del Pensamiento 223-4
religion 38
Reserva Ecológica Río Blanco 224
Reserva Natural Acaime 237
Reserva Natural El Matuy 179
Reserva Natural Heliconia 295
Reserva Natural Palmarí 294-5
Reserva Natural Zacambú 294-5
resorts 297
Reyes, Rafael 27
Río Claro 219
Riohacha 179-81
robbery 299, see also safe travel

S
Salento 236
Salmona, Rogelio 78
salsa 39, 208, 243, 298
San Agustín 255-9, **256**, 6
San Andrés 190, 191-8, **192**, **195**
San Andrés de Pisimbalá 260
San Cipriano 281-2
San Gil 119-22, 6

Santa Cruz del Islote 186
Santa Fe de Antioquia 217-19, **218**
Santa Marta 164-70, **166**
Santander 119-30
Santuario de Flora y Fauna de Iguaque 110-11
Santuario de Flora y Fauna Los Flamencos 180
Santuario de Las Lajas 267
Santuario Otún Quimbaya 231
Sapzurro 188-9
scuba diving 57-9
  Bahía Solano 272
  Capurganá 189
  Cartagena 145-6
  itineraries 23
  PNN Ensenada de Utría 276
  PNN Isla Gorgona 284
  Providencia 194, 200
  San Andrés 194
  Santa Marta 165-6
  Santuario de Flora y Fauna Malpelo 283
  Taganga 172
sculpture 41-2, see also monuments & sculptures
  Fernando Botero 41-2, 72, 162, 207
shopping 306-7
Sierra Nevada del Cocuy 112, **113**
Silvia 254-5
snorkeling 57-9
  Acuario 193
  Cartagena 145-6
  Islas de San Bernardo 186
  PNN Ensenada de Utría 276
  Playa Blanca 153
  Providencia 200
soccer 36
  Medellín 208
Socorro 119
solo travelers 307
Southwest Colombia 238, 249-68, **239**
sportfishing
  Bahía Solano 272
sports 36-7, see also tejo
stargazing
  Desierto de la Tatacoa 267
  Observatorio Astronómico de la Tatacoa 268
Suesca 95-7
surfing
  Bahía Solano 272
  Juanchaco 281
  Ladrilleros 281

INDEX

GreenDex

Sustainable tourism is still finding its feet in Colombia. In most cases ecolodges use solar panels or grow their own vegetables not because they are trying to be trendy, but because they are in remote places and it's cheaper to do it that way. Like most of Latin America, the concept of 'green' is like vegetarianism – a weird foreign concept that few practice. That said, Colombia still manages to boast several world-class ecolodges, and the country's many nature reserves and national parks are among the most beautiful in Latin America.

We want to keep developing our sustainable-tourism content. If you think we've omitted someone who should be listed here, or if you disagree with our choices, email us at www.lonelyplanet .com/contact. For more information about sustainable tourism and Lonely Planet, see www .lonelyplanet.com/responsibletravel.

MAP LEGEND
ROUTES

Tollway	One-Way Street
Freeway	Street Mall/Steps
Primary Road	Tunnel
Secondary Road	Track
Tertiary Road	Unsealed Road
Lane	Walking Trail
Pedestrian Overpass	Walking Path

TRANSPORT

Ferry	Rail (Underground)
Metro	Tram
Bus Route	Cable Car, Funicular
Rail	

HYDROGRAPHY

River, Creek	Canal
Intermittent River	Water
Swamp	Lake (Dry)
Reef	Lake (Salt)

BOUNDARIES

International	Regional, Suburb
State, Provincial	Ancient Wall
Disputed	Cliff
Marine Park	

AREA FEATURES

Airport	Forest
Area of Interest	Land
Beach, Desert	Market
Building	Park
Campus	Sports
Cemetery, Christian	

POPULATION

CAPITAL (NATIONAL)	CAPITAL (STATE)
Large City	Medium City
Small City	Town, Village

SYMBOLS

Sights/Activities
Beach
Castle, Fortress
Christian
Diving, Snorkeling
Islamic
Monument
Museum, Gallery
Point of Interest
Ruin
Surfing, Surf Beach
Zoo, Bird Sanctuary

Eating
Eating

Drinking
Drinking
Café

Entertainment
Entertainment

Shopping
Shopping

Sleeping
Sleeping
Camping

Transport
Airport, Airfield
Bus Station
General Transport
Parking Area
Taxi Rank

Information
Bank, ATM
Embassy/Consulate
Hospital, Medical
Information
Internet Facilities
Police Station
Post Office, GPO
Telephone
Toilets

Geographic
Lookout
Mountain, Volcano
National Park
Waterfall

LONELY PLANET OFFICES

Australia
Head Office
Locked Bag 1, Footscray, Victoria 3011
☎ 03 8379 8000, fax 03 8379 8111
talk2us@lonelyplanet.com.au

USA
150 Linden St, Oakland, CA 94607
☎ 510 250 6400, toll free 800 275 8555
fax 510 893 8572
info@lonelyplanet.com

UK
2nd fl, 186 City Rd,
London EC1V 2NT
☎ 020 7106 2100, fax 020 7106 2101
go@lonelyplanet.co.uk

Published by Lonely Planet Publications Pty Ltd
ABN 36 005 607 983

© Lonely Planet Publications Pty Ltd 2009

© photographers as indicated 2009

Cover photograph: Providencia island, INC Superstock, Photolibrary.
Many of the images in this guide are available for licensing from
Lonely Planet Images: www.lonelyplanetimages.com.

MIX
Paper from responsible sources
www.fsc.org   FSC™ C021741